Uniform Investment Adviser Law Exam

Series 65
9th Edition

Securities License Exam Manual

Financial Education   **KAPLAN UNIVERSITY** SCHOOL OF PROFESSIONAL AND CONTINUING EDUCATION

At press time, this edition contains the most complete and accurate information currently available. Owing to the nature of license examinations, however, information may have been added recently to the actual test that does not appear in this edition. Please contact the publisher to verify that you have the most current edition.

This publication is designed to provide accurate and authoritative information in regard to the subject matter covered. It is sold with the understanding that the publisher is not engaged in rendering legal, accounting, or other professional services. If legal advice or other expert assistance is required, the services of a competent professional should be sought.

SERIES 65 UNIFORM INVESTMENT ADVISER LAW EXAM, 9TH EDITION
©2015 Kaplan, Inc.

If you find imperfections or incorrect information in this product, please visit www.kaplanfinancial.com and submit an errata report.

Published in September 2015 by Kaplan Financial Education.

Printed in the United States of America.

ISBN: 978-1-4754-3212-1

PPN: 3200-6323

Contents

Introduction

INTRODUCTION

Thank you for choosing Kaplan for your educational needs and welcome to the Series 65 License Exam Manual (LEM). This manual applies adult learning principles to give you the tools you'll need to pass your exam on the first attempt.

Why do I need to pass the Series 65 exam?

Most states require passing a qualification examination by those who give investment advice, or perform certain related functions. The North American Securities Administrators Association (NASAA) has created the Series 65 Uniform Investment Adviser Law Exam as one of the options that may be used to meet that requirement.

Are there any prerequisites?

There are no prerequisites to sit for the Series 65 exam. However, the test assumes that the applicant has a broad range of knowledge or experience with investments. Because a significant percentage of our students come to us without that background, this manual attempts to cover all of the basics as well as the more advanced material tested. Those of you with a Series 6 or Series 7 registration will find these basics a good review that will help set the stage for learning the intricate topics you will need to know.

Examination Waivers

Passing the Series 65 or Series 66 (in conjunction with the Series 7) normally is a prerequisite to getting licensed as an investment adviser representative. However, most states will allow an individual to substitute one of the following certifications for passing the exam:

- CFP®—CERTIFIED FINANCIAL PLANNER™ (granted by the CFP Board of Standards);
- CIC—Chartered Investment Counselor (granted by the Investment Adviser Association);
- ChFC®—Chartered Financial Consultant® (granted by the The American College of Financial Services);
- PFS—Personal Financial Specialist (granted by the American Institute of Certified Public Accountants); and
- CFA®—Chartered Financial Analyst® (granted by the Chartered Financial Analyst Institute).

The individual applicant still has to go through other state licensing requirements, such as filing a Form U-4 or Form U-10 and payment of fees.

What is the Series 65 exam like?

The Series 65 is a 3-hour, 140-question exam (130 questions scored) prepared by the North American Securities Administrators Association (NASAA) and administered by FINRA. It is offered as a computer-based exam at Prometric testing centers around the country.

What score must I achieve to pass?

You need a score of at least 72% (94 questions correct of the 130 scored) on the Series 65 exam to pass and become eligible for registration as a **Registered Investment Adviser Representative**.

What topics will I see on the exam?

The questions you will see on the Series 65 exam do not appear in any particular order. The computer is programmed to select a new, random set of questions for each exam taker according to the preset topic weighting of the exam. Each Series 65 candidate will see the same number of questions on each topic but will see a different mix of questions. The Series 65 exam is divided into 4 critical function areas.

	Number of Questions	Percentage of Exam
1. Economic Factors and Business Information	19	14
2. Investment Vehicle Characteristics	31	24
3. Client Investment Recommendations and Strategies	40	31
4. Laws, Regulations, and Guidelines, including Prohibitions on Unethical Business Practices	40	31

When you complete your exam, you will receive a printout that identifies your performance in each area.

PREPARING FOR THE EXAM

How Is the License Exam Manual organized?

The License Exam Manual consists of four units (chapters). Each of these units corresponds to one of the function areas tested. Furthermore, each of the units is divided into sessions covering specific areas within the unit. The introduction to each session indicates the number of questions you can expect the exam to ask about that session's material. For students attending one of our classes, live or online, the class lecture will follow the sequence of these sessions.

There will be a test at the end of each unit. These questions have been selected to repeat and reinforce the information presented in the reading.

In order that the material being presented is properly explained, it sometimes happens that a term or phrase is used prior to its formal introduction in the course. In almost all cases, you can consult the glossary for the definition or the index to locate a more complete discussion.

In addition to the regular text, the LEM also has some unique features designed to help with quick understanding of the material. When additional emphasis is valuable to your comprehension, the following distinctions are made:

TAKE NOTE   Each Take Note provides special information designed to amplify important points.

TEST TOPIC ALERT   Each Test Topic Alert reviews content that is especially likely to appear on the exam.

EXAMPLE   Examples provide practical applications that convert theory into understanding.

QUICK QUIZ   Quick Quizzes are a quick interactive review of what you just read. These ensure you understand and retain the material.

Additional Study Resources

To accompany and supplement your License Exam Manual, your study package may contain additional study resources. Be sure to spend some time on your homepage, view the best practices video, and understand all that is available to help you study.

SecuritiesPro™ Qbank

Coordinating with the LEM, the SecuritiesPro QBank includes a large number of questions that are similar in style and content to those you will encounter on the exam. You may use it to generate tests by a specific unit or combination of units. The QBank also allows you to create weighted mock exams that mimic your test. There is no limit on the number of QBank exams you can create.

Another important point is that the online questions are "live." That is, unlike this manual, which, once printed, can't be changed, our questions can be updated with a moment's notice. This enables us to keep current with rule changes and, to the extent possible, with new topics as they are added to the Series 65 exam. When we author questions covering new material that is not in this manual, there will be an asterisk (*) placed after the reference number, indicating the general area where this topic belongs and that there is no specific information dealing with it other than this (or similar) questions and the exam tips and content updates link.

Practice and Mastery Exams

Depending on the study package purchased, you may also have a fixed practice exam or a fixed practice and mastery exam. These exams are designed to closely replicate the true exam experience, both in terms of the degree of difficulty and topical coverage. They provide scores and diagnostic feedback, but you will not be given access to, or be able to obtain from Kaplan, correct answers or question explanations. The practice and mastery exams are sound indicators of potential actual exam scores—the better you do on these exams, the more likely you are to pass your actual exam. These may only be taken once each.

Video Library

You may also have access to various topics from our video library. These short, engaging videos cover key topics from your manual. If your package includes access to our video library, please review the topics as you complete your reading assignments in the study manual.

Of particular importance, especially if you don't have a securities license (Series 6 or Series 7), are the four classroom videos—Equity Securities, Debt Securities, Investment Company Securities, and Economic Factors and Business Information. These four are unique to the Series 65 and, for optimal results, should be viewed prior to attending class (live or OnDemand).

Because the other videos are not exam specific, you may encounter material that is not covered in your License Exam Manual. Just skip ahead until the slide shows something familiar.

Exam Tips & Content Updates Link

Don't forget to monitor your Exam Tips & Content Updates (located on your homepage)—when rules and regulations change, or we want to share new information regarding your exam, it is posted there.

And one more thing. In addition, try as we may, in a text this large, errors are difficult to avoid. When we become aware of them, we acknowledge them in the **Corrections** tab, also located on your homepage.

What topics are covered in the course?

The License Exam Manual consists of four units, each devoted to a particular area of study that you will need to know to pass the Series 65. Each unit is divided into study sessions devoted to more specific areas with which you need to become familiar.

The Series 65 License Exam Manual addresses the following topics:

Unit	Topic
1	Laws, Regulations, and Guidelines, including Prohibitions on Unethical Business Practices
2	Investment Vehicle Characteristics
3	Economic Factors and Business Information
4	Client Investment Recommendations and Strategies

How much time should I spend studying?

Plan to spend approximately 60–120 hours reading the material and carefully answering the questions. Spread your study time over the 4–5 weeks before the date on which you are scheduled to take the Series 65 exam. Your actual time may vary depending on your reading rate, comprehension, professional background(those with a securities background will generally require less time and that is the reason for the wide range in recommended study hours), and study environment.

What is the best way to structure my study time?

The following schedule is suggested to help you obtain maximum retention from your study efforts. Remember, this is a guideline only, because each individual may require more or less time to complete the steps included.

Step 1. Read a unit, session by session, and complete all exercises. Review rationales for all questions whether you got them right or wrong (time will vary based on the size of the unit).

Step 2. In the SecuritiesPro QBank, create a minimum of two 40 question exams for each unit as you go. Carefully review all rationales. Use the reference number to locate additional or related information on the test topic in your LEM if needed (3–4 hours per unit).

- Do not become too overwhelmed or bogged down in any one unit. You don't want to lose sight of the finish line because you're having trouble with one hurdle. Keep moving forward. It's a steady pace that wins the race.

- View rationales after each question initially and spend time studying each rationale in order to learn the concepts. Later, you will want to create exam scenarios in which scores and rationales are viewed at the end of each exam.

- Perfection is not the goal during the reading phase; a score in the high-60s to low 70's is good initially.

Step 3. When you have completed all the units in the License Exam Manual and their unit tests, using the SecuritiesPro QBank, concentrate on comprehensive exams covering all the material. With your comprehensive testing it is best to view correct answers and rationales only after the test is completed. Plan to spend at least one week testing prior to a scheduled class (4 hours for every 130 questions).

- You should complete at least five weighted mock exams prior to class. Review all of your answers and rationales. Also, review your LEM and video library as needed.

- Your goal is to consistently score in the 80s.

Step 4. Complete online practice and mastery exams. You should complete each exam while observing the time limits for the actual exam. Upon completing the exam, you will receive a diagnostic report that identifies topics for further review (3 hours per exam). We recommend taking the practice exam prior to a scheduled class and the mastery exam afterward.

How well can I expect to do?

The exams prepared by NASAA are not easy. You must display considerable understanding and knowledge of the topics presented in this course to pass the exam and qualify for registration.

If you study diligently, complete all sections of the course, and consistently score in the 80s on the tests, you should be well prepared to pass the exam. However, it is important for you to realize that merely knowing the materials will not enable you to pass unless you can apply your knowledge to the questions you are given and understand the essence of the information behind the question.

TEST-TAKING TIPS

Passing the exam depends not only on how well you learn the subject matter, but also on how well you take exams. You can develop your test-taking skills, and improve your score, by learning a few test-taking techniques.

- Read the full question.
- Avoid jumping to conclusions—watch for hedge clauses.
- Interpret the unfamiliar question.
- Look for key words and phrases.
- Identify the intent of the question.
- Memorize key points.
- Use a calculator.
- Beware of changing answers.
- Pace yourself.

Each of these pointers is explained below, including examples that show how to use them to improve your performance on the exam.

Read the full question

You cannot expect to answer a question correctly if you do not know what it is asking. If you see a question that seems familiar and easy, you might anticipate the answer, mark it, and move on before you finish reading it. This is a serious mistake. Be sure to read the full question before answering it. Mistakes are often made when assuming too much (or too little).

Avoid jumping to conclusions—watch for hedge clauses

The questions on NASAA exams are embellished with distractors as choices. To avoid being misled by seemingly obvious answers, make it a practice to read each question and each answer twice before selecting your choice. Doing so will provide you with a much better chance of doing well on the exam.

Watch out for hedge clauses embedded in the question. Examples of hedge clauses include the terms *if, not, all, none,* and *except.* In the case of *if* statements, the question can be answered correctly only by taking into account the qualifier. If you ignore the qualifier, you will not answer correctly.

Qualifiers are sometimes combined in a question. Some that you will frequently see together are *all* with *except* and *none* with *except.* In general, when a question starts with *all* or *none* and ends with *except,* you are looking for an answer that is opposite to what the question appears to be asking.

Interpret the unfamiliar question

Do not be surprised if some questions on the exam seem unfamiliar at first. If you have studied your material, you will have the information to answer all the questions correctly. The challenge may be a matter of understanding what the question is asking.

Very often, questions present information indirectly. You may have to interpret the meaning of certain elements before you can answer the question. Be aware that the exam will approach a concept from different angles.

Look for key words and phrases

Look for words that are tip-offs to the situation presented. For example, if you see the word *prospectus* in the question, you know the question is about a new issue. Sometimes a question will even supply you with the answer if you can recognize the key words it contains. Few questions provide blatant clues, but many do offer key words that can guide you to selecting the correct answer if you pay attention. Be sure to read all instructional phrases carefully. Take time to identify the key words to answer this type of question correctly.

Identify the intent of the question

Many questions on NASAA exams supply so much information that you lose track of what is being asked. This is often the case in story problems. Learn to separate the story from the question.

Take the time to identify what the question is asking. Of course, your ability to do so assumes you have studied sufficiently. There is no method for correctly answering questions if you don't know the material.

Memorize key points

Reasoning and logic will help you answer many questions, but you will have to memorize a good deal of information. Some memorization will be automatic as you go over the material and answer questions; some you will simply have to do systematically.

Use of a calculator

For the most part, there are only a few questions that will require the use of a calculator. Any math will be simple math; add, subtract, multiply, and divide. We recommend using a calculator for math. A calculator will be supplied upon request.

Avoid changing answers

If you are unsure of an answer, your first hunch is the one most likely to be correct. Do not change answers on the exam without good reason. In general, change an answer only if you:

■ discover that you did not read the question correctly; or

■ find new or additional helpful information in another question.

Pace yourself

Some people will finish the exam early and some do not have time to finish all the questions. Watch the time carefully (your time remaining will be displayed on your computer screen) and pace yourself through the exam.

Do not waste time by dwelling on a question if you simply do not know the answer. Make the best guess you can, mark the question for *Record for Review*, and return to the question if time allows. The easiest questions are generally at the beginning and the end of the test; make sure that you have time to read all the questions so that you can record the answers you do know.

THE EXAM

How do I enroll in the exam?

To obtain an admission ticket to a NASAA exam, you or your firm must file an application form and processing fees with FINRA. To take the exam, you should make an appointment with a Prometric Testing Center as far in advance as possible of the date on which you would like to take the exam.

You may schedule your appointment at Prometric 24 hours a day, 7 days a week, on the Prometric secure website at **www.prometric.com**. You may also use **www.prometric.com** to reschedule or cancel your exam, locate a test center, and get a printed confirmation of your appointment. To speak with a Prometric representative by phone, please contact the Prometric Contact Center at **1-800-578-6273.**

What should I take to the exam?

Take one form of personal identification with your signature and photograph as issued by a government agency. No personal items, food, or drink, including coffee and water, are permitted inside the testing room. Personal items include, but are not limited to, pens, pagers, cellular phones, watches, hats, non-medical electronic devices, outerwear, purses, and wallets. Personal items must be kept in your assigned locker or returned to your car prior to the start of your exam. As the testing vendor is not responsible for any personal items, they encourage you to bring only your identification into the center.

Erasable note boards and pens will be provided to you upon admittance to the testing room. If you need additional note boards or pens, please alert your proctor. The note boards and pens must be returned at the end of your exam.

If you need a calculator for your testing session, please see the test center administrator. You will be provided with a non-programmable, non-printing calculator.

Additional trial questions

During your exam, you will see 10 extra trial questions (that is why the test is 140 questions long). These are potential exam-bank questions being tested during the course of the exam. These questions are not identified as such and are not included in your final score.

Exam results and reports

At the end of the exam, your score will be displayed, indicating whether you passed. The testing center will print your results and affix their stamp as physical evidence of your passing.

The next business day after your exam, your results will be mailed to your firm and to the self-regulatory organization and state securities commission specified on your application.

Unit 1

Laws, Regulations and Guidelines, Including Prohibitions on Unethical Business Practices

This unit consists of three sessions:

Session 1   Federal Securities Regulations

Session 2   State Regulation Under the Uniform Securities Act (USA)

Session 3   Federal and State Regulation of Investment Advisers and Their Representatives

In total there will be 40 questions on this material, representing 31% of the Series 65 Exam.

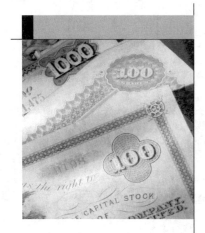

1

Federal Securities Regulations

This session discusses federal laws that govern the issuance of corporate securities to the public and the regulation of exchanges on which they trade. The major federal legislation addressed are the Securities Act of 1933, the Securities Exchange Act of 1934, the Investment Company Act of 1940, and the Insider Trading and Securities Fraud Enforcement Act of 1988.

The Series 65 exam will include approximately six questions on the federal regulatory structure as it pertains to the issuance of securities and the registration of exchanges and broker-dealers who trade on these exchanges.

When you have completed this session, you should be able to:

- **compare** and contrast the significant registration provisions and exemptions from the Securities Act of 1933;

- **describe** the registration requirements of the Securities Exchange Act of 1934 regarding exchanges, broker-dealers, and agents;

- **describe** the principal provisions of the Investment Company Act of 1940;

- **discuss** the disclosure requirements, antifraud provisions, and prohibitions against market manipulation under the Securities Exchange Act of 1934;

- **list** prohibitions against market manipulation; and

- **recognize** the application of the Insider Trading and Securities Fraud Enforcement Act of 1988.

1. 1   THE SECURITIES ACT OF 1933

The **Securities Act of 1933** (also called the **Paper Act**, the **Truth in Securities Act**, and the **Prospectus Act**) regulates the issuing of corporate securities sold to the public (**initial public offerings** or **IPOs**) and through **subsequent public offerings (SPOs)**, sometimes referred to as "**SEOs,**" seasoned (i.e., secondary) equity offerings of U.S. equity securities. The act requires securities issuers to make full disclosure of all material information in their registration materials in order for investors to make fully informed investment decisions.

Issuer information must be disclosed to the Securities and Exchange Commission (SEC) in a registration statement and published in a **prospectus**. In addition, the act prohibits fraudulent activity in connection with the sale, underwriting, and distribution of securities. The act provides for both civil and criminal penalties for violations of its provisions.

Even though registration under the Uniform Securities Act (the law that deals with regulation by the states) will be covered in detail in the next session, where appropriate, mention will be of the similarities and differences between certain federal and state definitions.

1. 1. 1   DEFINITIONS

Definitions under the Securities Act of 1933 are similar to those you will see under state securities law under the Uniform Securities Act (described in Session 2), and, for exam purposes, those are the ones to concentrate on learning. The most important definitions under the Securities Act of 1933 are those that follow.

1. 1. 1. 1   Security

The definition of a *security* is very broad, but here are the terms most likely to be used on your exam.

The fundamental definition of a security was determined in a case heard before the U.S. Supreme Court. That case, known as the Howey Case, defined an **investment contract** as a security if it met four conditions:

- the investment of money;
- in a common enterprise (pooling);
- with an expectation of profits; and
- that results solely from the efforts of others.

On the basis of Howey, a **security** is any of the following:

- Stock
- Bond
- Debenture
- Right or warrant
- Note
- Put, call, or other option
- Limited partnership interests
- Certificate of interest in a profit-sharing arrangement

1. 1. 1. 2   Issuer

Any person who issues or proposes to issue any security is an **issuer**. Most issuers are businesses, and the term *issuer* would also apply to a government entity.

1. 1. 1. 3   Underwriter

Any person who has purchased from an issuer with a view to selling is an **underwriter**. This term does not include a brokerage firm earning a commission on a retail sale to the public.

1. 1. 1. 4   Person

The term *person* is very broad and includes an individual, a corporation, a partnership, an association, a joint stock company, a trust, any unincorporated organization, or a governmental or political subdivision thereof. We will explain this in further detail when covering the Uniform Securities Act in the next session.

1. 1. 1. 5   Prospectus

A **prospectus** is any notice, circular, letter, or communication, written or broadcast by radio or television, that offers any security for sale or confirms the sale of a security. A **tombstone** advertisement (one that simply identifies the security, the price, and the underwriters) is not considered a prospectus nor an offering of the subject security. The term *prospectus* does not include oral communications.

1. 1. 1. 6   Sale

The term *sale* or *sell* includes a contract for sale or the disposition of a security for value. An **offer to sell** refers to any attempt or offer to dispose of a security or an interest in a security for value or a solicitation of an offer to buy a security for value.

TAKE NOTE

The sale of a security does not include:

- preliminary negotiations or agreements between the issuer and underwriter; or

- a gift of securities.

Any security given or delivered with, or as a bonus on account of, any purchase of securities is presumed to constitute a part of that purchase and to have been offered and sold for value.

QUICK QUIZ 1.A

1. The term *issuer*, as defined in the Securities Act of 1933, would include:
   I. a government entity issuing exempt securities.
   II. a corporation issuing securities in an exempt transaction.
   III. an antique dealer selling items from a collection of rare books.
   A. I and II
   B. II and III
   C. III only
   D. I, II, and III

2. Under the Securities Act of 1933, which of the following is NOT a security?
   A. A convertible bond.
   B. A stock warrant.
   C. A stock right.
   D. A term life insurance policy

Quick Quiz answers can be found at the end of the unit.

The SEC does not approve securities registered with it, does not pass on the investment merit of any security, and never guarantees the accuracy of statements in the registration statement and prospectus.

In its review process, the SEC merely attempts to make certain that all pertinent information is fully disclosed in the registration statement and prospectus by requiring that:

■ the issuer file a registration statement with the SEC before securities are offered or sold in interstate commerce;

■ a prospectus that meets the requirements of the act be provided to prospective buyers; and

■ penalties (civil, criminal, or administrative) be imposed for violations of this act.

1. 2   EXEMPTED SECURITIES UNDER THE SECURITIES ACT OF 1933

The Securities Act of 1933 makes it unlawful to sell or deliver a security through any instrument of interstate commerce unless a registration statement is in effect. However, certain securities are exempted from the registration requirements of the act. The following issues qualify as exempted securities:

■ Any security issued or guaranteed by the United States, any state, or any political subdivision of a state (all federal government issues and municipal securities are exempted securities)

■ Any commercial paper that has a maturity at the time of issuance of no more than nine months (270 days), with the stipulation that the proceeds are to be used by the issuer to increase working capital and not for the purchase of fixed assets; there is no minimum denomination or rating requirement similar to that found in the Uniform Securities Act (exemptions there will be covered in Session 2)

■ Any security issued by a person organized and operated exclusively for religious, educational, benevolent, fraternal, or charitable purposes and not for pecuniary profit

- Any interest in a railroad equipment trust (for purposes of the law, *interest in a railroad equipment trust* means any interest in an equipment trust, lease, or other similar arrangement entered into, guaranteed by, or for the benefit of a regulated common carrier to finance the acquisition of rolling stock, including motive power)
- Any security issued by a federal or state bank, savings and loan association, building and loan association, or similar institution

TAKE NOTE   The exemption described for banks does not apply to bank holding companies. Most of the large U.S. banks today are owned by holding companies.

The following issue qualifies as an exempt security under federal law but is not exempt under the Uniform Securities Act and will probably have to register with the state:

- Rule 147 issue: any security offered and sold only to persons resident within a single state or territory, where the issuer of such security is a person resident and doing business within such state or territory

The Rule 147 exemption is available only if the entire issue is offered and sold exclusively to residents of a single state. If any sales take place to non-residents, the entire issue loses its exemption. The purpose of this exemption is to allow issuers to raise money on a local basis, provided the business was operating primarily within that state. The following conditions must be met in order to have a distribution qualify as an intrastate offering exempt from federal registration.

- The securities must be offered or sold exclusively to persons resident in one state; persons purchasing the securities must have their principal residence within the state.
- For nine months from the date of the last sale by the issuer of any part of the issue, resales of any part of the issue by any person will be made only to persons resident within the same state or territory. This will satisfy requirements that the issue come to rest in the state in order to claim the exemption.
- At least 80% of the issuer's gross revenue must be derived from operations within the state.
- At least 80% of the proceeds of the offering must be used for business purposes within the state.
- At least 80% of the issuer's assets must be located within the state.

TEST TOPIC ALERT   Do you see why this is sometimes referred to as the "80-80-80 Rule"?

TAKE NOTE   No waivers may be granted by the purchaser agreeing to the seller's failure to comply with the Securities Act of 1933. It is important to remember that any such waivers are null and void.

1. 3 EXEMPTED TRANSACTIONS UNDER THE SECURITIES ACT OF 1933

In addition to exempting certain securities, the act also exempts:

■ transactions by any person other than an issuer, underwriter, or dealer; and

■ transactions by an issuer that do not involve a public offering (private placement under Regulation D).

1. 4 REGISTRATION OF SECURITIES

The Securities Act of 1933 protects investors who buy new issues by:

■ requiring registration of new issues that are to be distributed interstate;

■ requiring an issuer to provide full and fair disclosure about itself and the offering;

■ requiring an issuer to make available all material information necessary for an investor to judge the issue's merit;

■ regulating the underwriting and distribution of primary and secondary issues; and

■ providing criminal penalties for fraud in the issuance of new securities.

1. 4. 1 THE REGISTRATION STATEMENT

An issuer must file a *registration statement* with the SEC disclosing material information about the issue. The registration statement must be signed by the principal executive officer (usually designated the CEO), the principal financial officer (usually designated the CFO), and a majority of the board of directors.

All of the signers are subject to criminal and civil penalties for willful omissions and misstatements of material facts. The information required in the registration statement may be summarized as follows:

■ Purpose of issue

■ Public offering price (anticipated range)

■ Underwriter's commissions or discounts

■ Promotion expenses

■ Expected use of the net proceeds of the issue to the company

■ Balance sheet

■ Earnings statements for the last three years

■ Names, addresses, and bios of officers, directors, underwriters, and stockholders owning more than 10% of the outstanding stock (i.e., control persons)

■ Copy of underwriting agreements

■ Copies of articles of incorporation

1. 4. 2   THE COOLING-OFF PERIOD

After the issuer files a registration statement with the SEC, a 20-day **cooling-off period** begins. After the issuer (with the underwriter's assistance) files with the SEC for registration of the securities, the cooling-off period begins before the registration becomes effective. The registration can become effective as early as 20 calendar days after the date the SEC has received it. In practice, however, the cooling-off period is seldom the minimum 20 days; the SEC usually takes longer to clear registration statements.

The Three Phases of an Underwriting

Issuer files registration statement with the SEC

Cooling-off period

Effective date—offering period may begin

Prior to the filing of the registration statement, no sales can be solicited and no prospectus can circulate.

No one can solicit sales during the cooling-off period, but indications of interest can be solicited with a red herring.

Sales can now be solicited, but the firm must use a final prospectus.

The cooling-off period can last several months because of the time it takes to make additions and corrections. If the SEC finds something is not stated properly, is missing, or needs further explanation, a **deficiency letter** will be sent describing what needs to be done in order for the registration to proceed. The SEC sometimes issues a **stop order**, which demands that all underwriting activities cease. This may be done if requirements of the 1933 Act have not been met or if fraud is suspected. The SEC may issue a stop order to suspend the effectiveness of the registration even after the effective registration date. The SEC will take this action if they feel the registration statement includes any untrue statement of a material fact. The SEC may subpoena the issuing corporation's records to determine whether a stop order is necessary.

1. 4. 3   PRELIMINARY (RED HERRING) PROSPECTUS

The preliminary prospectus must be made available to any prospective purchaser who expresses interest in the security from the time the issue is filed with the SEC until it becomes publicly available for sale, the effective date (the previously described cooling-off period).

A red herring is used to acquaint investors with essential facts concerning the new issue. It is also used to solicit indications of buyer interest. However, it cannot be used:

■ as a confirmation of sale;

■ in place of a registration statement; or

■ to declare the final public offering price.

However, along with stating the expected number of shares to be sold, a bona fide estimate of the price range per share is required to be included.

Under no circumstances may a broker-dealer or one of its agents accept money or orders prior to the effective date.

A communication sent or delivered to any potential investor that is accompanied or preceded by a preliminary prospectus, including a price range where required by rule, may solicit from the recipient of the communication a non-binding indication as to whether she might be interested in the security, if the communication contains substantially the following statement:

> No offer to buy the securities can be accepted and no part of the purchase price can be received until the registration statement has become effective, and any such offer may be withdrawn or revoked, without obligation or commitment of any kind, at any time prior to notice of its acceptance given after the effective date.

The term *red herring* was given to the preliminary prospectus because the front page contains the following statement printed in red ink.

> A Registration Statement relating to these securities has been filed with the Securities and Exchange Commission but has not yet become effective. Information contained herein is subject to completion or amendment. These securities may not be sold nor may offers to buy be accepted prior to the time the Registration Statement becomes effective.

No person connected with the offering is allowed to make marks on a preliminary prospectus under any circumstances. They cannot write short summaries or reviews on the preliminary prospectus. The preliminary prospectus must be given to customers without any alterations because, as stated above, information is subject to change.

TAKE NOTE

Two items missing from the preliminary prospectus (red herring) are the public offering price (expected range may be shown) and the effective date.

TEST TOPIC ALERT

During the cooling-off period, underwriters may not:

- take orders; or

- distribute sales literature or advertising material.

However, they may:

- take indications of interest;

- distribute preliminary prospectuses; or

- publish tombstone advertisements to provide information about the potential availability of the securities.

1. 4. 4   THE FINAL (EFFECTIVE) PROSPECTUS

A registration statement is normally a very long and complex document for an investor to read. The act requires the preparation of a shorter document called a **prospectus**. The prospectus summarizes the information contained in the registration statement. It must contain all the material facts in the registration statement, but in shorter form. The prospectus must be given to every person who purchases no later than with confirmation of the sale. The purpose of a prospectus is to provide the investor with adequate information to analyze the investment merits of the security. Even if an investor does not intend to read a prospectus, it still must be given to him. It is unlawful for a company to sell securities before the effective date of the registration statement.

1. 4. 4. 1   Rule 482 (Omitting) Prospectus

There is a specific SEC rule permitting investment companies to use what is known as an **omitting prospectus**. The rule is SEC Rule 482, which describes mutual fund advertisements. To comply with this rule, an omitting prospectus must meet the following conditions.

- Any information in the advertisement must be taken substantially from the regular prospectus.
- The advertisement must state conspicuously from whom a prospectus may be obtained.
- The advertisement must urge investors to read the prospectus carefully before investing.
- Any past performance data, such as yields or return, that are quoted in the advertisement must be accompanied by appropriate disclaimers and disclosures of load, if any.
- The advertisement cannot be used to purchase the shares; purchase may be made only via an application found in the prospectus.

1. 4. 5   EFFECTIVE DATE OF REGISTRATION STATEMENT

On the date a registration statement becomes effective, securities may be sold to the public by the investment bankers.

A copy of the final (effective) prospectus must be delivered to each purchaser. This is normally accomplished by including the prospectus along with a confirmation of the trade, although it would certainly be permitted to deliver it earlier. Additional sales literature may be used by the firm as long as the sales literature is preceded or accompanied by a prospectus. Just as with a preliminary prospectus, no markings of any kind may be placed on the prospectus. No areas of special interest may be highlighted or have attention drawn to them by any other method. Money may be accepted by the broker-dealer from customers at this time.

Every prospectus always has the following statement in bold print on the front page.

THESE SECURITIES HAVE NOT BEEN APPROVED OR DISAPPROVED BY THE SECURITIES AND EXCHANGE COMMISSION NOR HAS THE COMMISSION PASSED UPON THE ACCURACY OR ADEQUACY OF THIS PROSPECTUS. ANY REPRESENTATION TO THE CONTRARY IS A CRIMINAL OFFENSE.

This statement is known as the **SEC disclaimer** and should be self-explanatory.

If an underwriter pays for the publication of any description of a security offered (other than a tombstone), the act requires that the publisher disclose the fact that payment was made and the amount of the payment.

1. 4. 6   LIABILITIES UNDER THE SECURITIES ACT OF 1933

The Securities Act of 1933 provides penalties for false and misleading statements contained in the registration statement or prospectus. If misrepresentations were intentionally made, the individuals responsible are subject to criminal prosecution. The civil liabilities codes allow a purchaser of a security under a registration statement containing a false statement of a material fact or omission of a material fact to sue:

- every person who signed the registration form;
- all directors of the issuer;
- attorneys;
- accountants;
- appraisers or other experts;
- underwriters; and
- parent companies.

A person would be exempt from liability if he could prove he had reasonable grounds to believe, after investigation, that the statements contained in the registration statement are accurate. The statute of limitations for bringing action is the earlier of one year after discovery of the violation or three years after the date of the action. Compare this statute with the statute of limitations in Session 2, which is almost the same, except that the time limit is two years after discovery. This is one of the rare cases where the time period in the Uniform Securities Act is greater than that in federal law.

Other powers of the SEC include the ability to:

- make, amend, and rescind rules;
- administer oaths;
- subpoena witnesses and other records for evidence;
- seek injunctions or restraining orders in the appropriate court; and
- turn over evidence to the attorney general of the United States for possible criminal prosecution.

If a person is found guilty in court, civil penalties can be severe, including a substantial fine as well as being barred from serving as an officer or director of a public corporation for a number of years. If the case involves criminal prosecution, the penalties may include a fine, a prison term, or both.

1. 5   SEC REGULATION D (PRIVATE PLACEMENT EXEMPTION) RULE 506

In a major effort aimed at facilitating the capital formation needs of small businesses, the SEC adopted Regulation D, the private placement exempt transaction. Securities offered and sold in compliance with Regulation D are exempt from registration with the SEC and, as we will learn in the next session, are considered federal covered securities exempt from registration on the state level as well. Our primary concern is with **SEC Rule 506,** a private placement where there is no dollar limit on the amount sold.

The Jumpstart Our Business Startups Act of 2012, or **JOBS Act**, made several important changes to Rule 506 of Regulation D. These changes became effective September 23, 2013. It is unlikely that the new information will be tested for some time, but when it is, we will post that to the Exam-tips & Contents Updates and revise our practice questions.

Rule 506 now consists of two sections, 506(b) and 506(c). A company seeking to raise capital through a private placement under Rule 506(b) can sell the offering to an unlimited number of accredited investors (defined below) and up to 35 non-accredited investors. In addition, no advertising may be done on behalf of the offering.

On the other hand, Section 506(c) permits the offering to be advertised. There are two primary (and interrelated) requirements in order to do this.

■ All purchasers are accredited investors, or the issuer reasonably believes that they are accredited investors.

■ The issuer takes reasonable steps to verify that all purchasers are accredited investors, which could include reviewing documentation, such as W-2s, tax returns, bank and brokerage statements, credit reports and the like.

An issuer can elect to make a typical Rule 506 offering without general solicitation or advertising under Section 506(b) in order to include non-accredited investors in the offering or to avoid the heightened verification procedures.

The JOBS Act also included a provision that an issuer is disqualified from using Rule 506 under their "bad actor," sometimes called "bad boy," provisions. Simply, if the issuer or other relevant persons, (such as underwriters, directors, officers, or significant shareholders of the issuer) have been convicted of securities fraud or certain other securities violations, an offering under Rule 506 may not take place.

1. 5. 1   SEC RULE 501 ACCREDITED INVESTORS

SEC Rule 501 classifies an accredited investor for the purposes of Regulation D into separate categories. Investors are considered to be accredited under the rule only if the issuer or any person acting on the issuer's behalf has reasonable grounds to believe, and does believe after reasonable inquiry, that the investors are included in one of the categories in the definition.

The separate categories of accredited investors under Regulation D include:

■ a bank, insurance company, or registered investment company;

■ an employee benefit plan if a bank, insurance company, or registered investment adviser makes the investment decisions, or if the plan has total assets in excess of $5 million;

■ a charitable organization, corporation, or partnership with assets exceeding $5 million;

■ directors, executive officers, and general partners of the issuer;

■ any natural person whose individual net worth, or joint net worth with that person's spouse, excluding the net equity in his primary residence, exceeds $1 million at the time of his purchase;

■ any natural person who had an individual income in excess of $200,000 in each of the two most recent years or joint income with that person's spouse in excess of $300,000 in each of those years and has a reasonable expectation of reaching the same income level in the current year; and

■ entities made up of accredited investors.

The term *accredited investor* applies only to private placements. The dollar amount of the net worth requirement has not changed since the introduction of this rule in 1982, but particularly due to increased real estate values, the Dodd-Frank Act of 2010 declared that the net worth had to exclude the net equity in the primary residence. A favorite phrase of the regulators is, "eligibility does not equal suitability." Therefore, just because one meets the financial requirements of an accredited investor does not mean that suitability standards are ignored.

TEST TOPIC ALERT

Can assets in an account or property held jointly with another person who is not the purchaser's spouse be included in determining whether the purchaser satisfies the net worth test in Rule 501?

Answer: Yes, assets in an account or property held jointly with a person who is not the purchaser's spouse may be included in the calculation for the net worth test, but only to the extent of his or her percentage ownership of the account or property.

TAKE NOTE

For purposes of Rule 506(b), in counting the number of non-accredited investors, the following rules apply:

■ Any relative, spouse or relative of the spouse of a purchaser who has the same primary residence as the purchaser counts as a single purchaser; and

■ A corporation, partnership, or other entity is counted as one purchaser. If, however, the entity was organized for the purpose of acquiring the securities, each owner will be counted separately.

Q

QUICK QUIZ 1.B

1. Which of the following statements about accredited investors is TRUE?

    A. Taxpayers who report an income in excess of $200,000 on a joint return in each of the last two years and who reasonably expect the same for the current year are included in the definition.

    B. An officer, director, or greater than 10% shareholder of any company listed on the NYSE would be considered an accredited investor for purposes of acquiring a private placement your firm is selling.

    C. The term includes an employee benefit plan with assets in excess of $2 million.

    D. Purchases of securities by accredited investors do not count toward the 35-investor limitation found in Rule 506(b) of Regulation D.

1. 5. 2   FORM D

What is Form D, and when does it have to be filed? Under Rule 503 of Regulation D, an issuer that is issuing securities in reliance on Regulation D must file Form D with the SEC no later than 15 days after the first sale (defined as the time when an investor has delivered an irrevocable commitment to invest) of securities in the offering. Form D requires certain basic information about the issuer and the offering, including total size of the offering, amount sold to date, the use of proceeds, and the names of any persons paid commissions.

TAKE NOTE

One other point worth mentioning is that there is a proposal that the Form D be filed 15 days **prior** to the first sale for those offerings made under 506(c) rather than the 15 days after as is the case with 506(b) offerings.

1. 5. 3   RESTRICTED SECURITIES

Restricted securities are unregistered securities purchased by an investor in a private placement and are generally *restricted* from resale for a stated period of time. They are also called **letter securities** (or **legend securities**), which refers to the fact that purchasers must sign an investment letter attesting to their understanding of the restriction upon resale and to the legend placed on the certificates indicating restriction upon resale.

1. 5. 3. 1   Control Person

A corporate director, officer, greater than 10% voting stockholder, or the spouse of any of the preceding is a **control person**. They are loosely referred to as **insiders** or **affiliates** because of their unique status within the issuer.

1. 5. 3. 2   Control Stock

Control stock is stock held by a control person. What makes it control stock is who owns it, not how it was acquired. In general, purchases and sales of control stock must be reported to the SEC.

1. 5. 3. 3   Nonaffiliate

An investor who is not a control person and has no other affiliation with the issuer other than as an owner of securities is a **nonaffiliate**.

1. 5. 3. 4   SEC Rule 144 (Sale of Restricted and Control Securities)

SEC Rule 144 was created so that certain resales of already existing securities could be made without having to file a complete registration statement with the SEC. The time and money involved in having to file such a registration are usually so prohibitive as to make it uneconomical for the individual seller. In almost all cases, those who wish to sell control stock or restricted stock must do so by filing a Form 144.

QUICK QUIZ 1.C

1. A man owns 15% of the stock of a company. His wife owns 5% of the stock of the same company. If the wife wishes to sell the stock she owns, which of the following statements are TRUE?

   I. Both the husband and the wife are affiliates.
   II. He is an affiliate, but she is not.
   III. She must file under Rule 144.
   IV. She does not have to file under Rule 144.

   A. I and III
   B. I and IV
   C. II and III
   D. II and IV

---

1. 6   THE SECURITIES EXCHANGE ACT OF 1934

The Securities Exchange Act created the **SEC**. The act grants the SEC authority over all aspects of the securities industry, including the power to register, regulate, and oversee brokerage firms, transfer agents, and clearing agencies as well as the nation's securities self-regulatory organizations (SROs).

The various stock exchanges, such as the New York Stock Exchange (NYSE), Chicago Stock Exchange (CHX), and Nasdaq, are SROs. The largest SRO is FINRA, the organization to which virtually all broker-dealers belong.

The act also identifies and prohibits certain types of conduct in the markets and confers to the SEC disciplinary powers over regulated entities and the persons associated with them.

The act also empowers the SEC to require periodic reporting of information by companies with publicly traded securities.

1. 6. 1   THE SECURITIES AND EXCHANGE COMMISSION (SEC)

The SEC consists of five people, with one serving as chair, appointed by the president with the advice and consent of the Senate. The SEC administrates all federal laws regulating the securities industry except those regulating the extension of credit. SEC commissioners are appointed for five-year terms and may have no other business or employment other than this job. The terms are staggered so that a new commissioner is appointed each year. To minimize political shenanigans, no more than three of the five commissioners may belong to the same party. Therefore, if there are three Republicans and two Democrats and a Democrat's term expires, the president must appoint another Democrat. Because of the sensitive nature of the employment, SEC commissioners may not engage in any personal securities transactions other than in U.S. government issues. All securities positions they had when appointed are placed into a blind trust.

1. 6. 2   DEFINITIONS

The act defines many important terms, such as *broker, dealer,* and *exchange.* Many of these terms are also used in the Uniform Securities Act, which is model legislation that the states use to draft their securities laws.

1. 6. 2. 1   Broker

A **broker** is any person engaged in the business of effecting transactions in securities for the account of others. Banks are not included in this definition.

1. 6. 2. 2   Dealer

A **dealer** is any person regularly engaged in the business of buying and selling securities for his own account. Banks, insurance companies, investment companies, and any persons engaged in investing, reinvesting, or trading in securities for their own account, either individually or in some fiduciary capacity, but not as part of a regular business, are not included in this definition.

1. 6. 2. 3   Associated Person

A **person associated with a broker-dealer** is any partner, officer, or director of the broker-dealer (or any person performing similar functions) or any person directly or indirectly controlling or controlled by the broker-dealer, including any employees of the broker-dealer, except that any person associated with a broker or dealer whose functions are solely clerical or ministerial, shall not be included in the meaning of the term.

TEST TOPIC ALERT   Even "outside" directors or partners whose only connection to the firm is the contribution of capital are considered associated persons of the broker-dealer.

1. 6. 2. 4   Market Maker

A **market maker** is a dealer who holds himself out as being willing to buy and sell a particular security for his own account and on a regular or continuous basis. This holding out may be by entering quotations in an interdealer communications system or otherwise.

1. 6. 2. 5   Securities Information Processor

A **securities information processor (SIP)** is any person engaged in the business of:

- collecting, processing, or preparing for distribution or publication information with respect to transactions in, or quotations for, any nonexempt security; or
- distributing or publishing (whether by means of a ticker tape, a communications network, a terminal display device, or otherwise), on a current and continuing basis, information with respect to such transactions or quotations.

Some of the obvious securities information processors are:

- The Consolidated Ticker Tape;
- OPRA (Options Price Reporting Authority);
- SIAC (Securities Industry Automation Corporation); and
- The OTC Markets Group Inc. (owners of OTC Link, formerly known as the *Pink Sheets*).

The term *securities information processor* does not include:

- a bona fide newspaper, news magazine, or business or financial publication of general or regular circulation, such as *The Wall Street Journal*;
- any SRO;
- any bank or broker-dealer supplying quotation and transaction information as part of its customary banking or brokerage business; or
- any common carrier subject to the jurisdiction of the Federal Communications Commission or a state commission (radio and television stations).

1. 6. 2. 6   Transfer Agent

A **transfer agent** is any person who engages on behalf of an issuer of securities in:

- countersigning the certificates;
- registering the transfer of the issuer's securities;
- exchanging or converting the issuer's securities; and
- transferring record ownership of securities by bookkeeping entry without physical issuance of securities certificates.

The term *transfer agent* does not include:

- any insurance company or separate account that performs these functions solely with respect to variable annuity contracts or variable life policies that it issues; or
- any registered clearing agency (e.g., Options Clearing Corporation) that performs these functions solely with respect to options contracts that it issues.

1. 6. 2. 7   Exchange

An **exchange** is an organization, association, or group of persons providing a marketplace or facilities for bringing together purchasers and sellers of securities. The term includes the marketplace and the facilities.

Exchanges must be registered. Registration is accomplished by filing an application with the SEC, which will be accepted or denied within 90 days of application. The exchange must be prepared to demonstrate the following.

- Formation of the exchange is in the public interest.
- The exchange will have compliance enforcement ability—that is, the ability to enforce both the SEC's and its own rules.
- The board of directors will be represented by at least one member representing the investing public and at least one member representing listed companies. The balance of the board is usually made up of directors representing the membership of the exchange.
- Membership in the exchange may only be offered to registered broker-dealers or associated persons.

1. 6. 2. 8   Self-Regulatory Organization

A **self-regulatory organization (SRO)** is a national securities exchange or a registered securities association, such as FINRA.

1. 6. 2. 9   Security

The definition of a security is similar to the definition given in the Securities Act of 1933 and in the Uniform Securities Act, which will be discussed in Session 2.

1. 6. 2. 10   Equity Security

Equity security is defined as a stock or similar security. **Stock** means common or preferred stock. **Similar security** would include:

- a security convertible into stock (e.g., convertible bond);
- any security with a warrant or right attached to subscribe to or buy stock (e.g., a bond with warrants attached); and
- any warrant or right to purchase stock.

1. 6. 2. 11   Municipal Securities

Municipal securities are securities that are direct obligations of, or obligations guaranteed as to principal or interest by, a state or any political subdivision thereof, or any agent or instrumentality of a state or any political subdivision thereof. The most common example of municipal securities are municipal bonds.

1. 6. 2. 12   Government Securities

Government securities are securities that are direct obligations of, or obligations guaranteed as to principal or interest by, the U.S. government. The term also includes government agency securities, such as those issued by the Federal National Mortgage Association (Fannie Mae).

1. 6. 2. 13   Statutory Disqualification

A person is subject to a **statutory disqualification** with respect to membership or participation in, or association with a member of, an SRO if that person:

- has been or is expelled or suspended from membership or being associated with a member of any SRO, commodities market, or futures trading association;
- is subject to an order of the SEC or other appropriate regulatory agency denying, suspending for a period not exceeding 12 months, or revoking his registration as a broker-dealer, or barring or suspending for a period not exceeding 12 months his association with a broker or dealer;
- by his conduct while associated with a broker or dealer, has been found to be a cause of any effective suspension, expulsion, or order of the type described in the two points above;
- has associated with any person who is known, or with the exercise of reasonable care should be known, to him to be a person described by one of the three points above;
- has been convicted within the past 10 years of a securities violation or a misdemeanor involving finance or dishonesty, bribery, embezzlement, forgery, theft, and so forth, or any felony;
- is subject to a temporary or permanent injunction from a competent court of jurisdiction prohibiting him from engaging in any phase of the securities business;
- has willfully violated any federal securities law; or
- has made a false or misleading statement in any filing with information requested by an SRO (omitting important facts is cause as well).

Loss of a civil lawsuit, even involving securities, is not a cause for statutory disqualification.

The effect of statutory disqualification is a prohibition against association of any kind with a member firm or any investment adviser.

1. 6. 2. 14   Appropriate Regulatory Authority

The SEC is the appropriate regulatory agency for the following:

- National securities exchanges
- Registered securities associations
- Members of an exchange or association
- Persons associated with a member
- Applicants to become a member or person associated with a member

The SEC is also the appropriate regulatory agency for the Municipal Securities Rulemaking Board (MSRB). However, the SEC has no jurisdiction over banks and other similar financial institutions that are regulated by their functional regulators, such as the Office of the Controller of the Currency (not tested).

TAKE NOTE

One of the provisions of the Securities Exchange Act was that the board of governors of the Federal Reserve was authorized by the act to establish regulations governing the use of credit for the purchase or carrying of securities. The Federal Reserve has issued Regulation T covering such credit.

1. 6. 2. 15 Investment Discretion

A **discretionary account** is an account set up with preapproved authority for a securities professional to make transactions without having to ask for specific approval.

Discretion is defined as the authority to decide:

- which security;
- the number of shares or units; or
- whether to buy or sell.

TAKE NOTE

Discretion does not apply to decisions regarding the timing of an investment or the price at which it is acquired.

EXAMPLE

An order from a customer worded "Buy 100 shares of ABC for my account whenever you think the price is right" is not a discretionary order because the client has specified the action (buy), the amount (100 shares) and the asset (ABC). Time and/or price are not considered discretion.

TEST TOPIC ALERT

To identify a discretionary order, try this method: an order is discretionary if any one of the **three A's** is missing. The three A's are:

- Activity;
- Amount; and
- Asset.

1. 6. 2. 15. 1 Discretion—Time and/or Price

Both state and federal law prohibit the exercise of any discretionary power in a customer's account unless the customer has given prior written authorization (a power of attorney/trading authorization) to a stated individual or individuals and the account has been accepted by the member firm, as evidenced in writing by the firm.

There is an exception to this requirement that applies to the exercise of time and price discretion—which is discretion orally granted by the customer to purchase or sell a specific amount of a particular security (e.g., "Buy 100 shares of ABCD and get the best price you can").

An oral grant of time and price discretion is limited to the end of the business day on which the customer grants it. An extension of such time and price discretion requires explicit signed and dated customer instructions. Any exercise of time and price discretion must be reflected on the order ticket (as is the case with regular discretion).

Why is it necessary to have written instructions if the discretion is to carry beyond the date of the order? The concept of time and price discretion has been subject to abuse and/or misunderstanding. At one time, there was no time limit placed on a grant of oral time and price discretion by a customer. This became problematic in instances where an agent was granted such discretion but did not exercise it for an extended period of time, sometimes several weeks. This led to claims of unauthorized trading by customers who may have forgotten that they granted the discretion, or who assumed it was not valid for such an extended period of time. The written extension requirement under the rules is intended to prevent such misunderstandings.

1. 6. 2. 16 Discretionary Authority

Customers can give discretionary power over their account(s) only by filing a written trading authorization or a limited power of attorney with the broker-dealer. No discretionary transactions can take place without this document on file. Once authorization is given, the firm is legally empowered to make trading decisions for the account, although the customer may also continue to enter orders.

In addition to requiring the proper documentation, discretionary accounts are subject to the following rules.

- Each discretionary order must be identified as such when it is entered for execution.
- An officer or a partner of the firm must approve each order promptly and in writing, not necessarily before order entry.
- A record must be kept of all transactions.
- No excessive trading may occur in the account when considering the clients financial resources and investment objectives.
- To safeguard against the possibility of churning, a designated supervisor or manager must review all trading activity frequently and systematically.

QUICK QUIZ 1.D   1.   An agent receives instructions from a client to buy 100 shares of KAPCO common stock at what the agent thinks is the best price. Two days later, the agent enters the order. In this case, the agent has

A.   acted appropriately

B.   acted inappropriately

C.   failed to follow the customer's instructions

D.   potentially become subject to statutory disqualification

2. Alice Allison is the president of Podunk University and sits on the board of directors of KAPCO Securities, a broker-dealer registered with the SEC. President Allison

    A. would be considered an associated person of KAPCO
    B. would not be considered an associated person of KAPCO
    C. would be required to register as an agent of KAPCO
    D. must resign her position at Podunk University in order to remain on KAPCO's board

3. A securities order that is initiated by a client is what type of order?

    A. Nondiscretionary
    B. Unsolicited
    C. Discretionary
    D. Solicited

1. 6. 3   REGISTRATION UNDER THE SECURITIES EXCHANGE ACT OF 1934

The Securities Exchange Act of 1934 requires many different groups and organizations to register with the SEC. Among them are:

■ brokers and dealers operating in interstate commerce, including those operating on exchanges and in the over-the-counter markets (broker-dealers file application for membership on **Form BD**, and the SEC has 45 days to accept or deny the registration);

■ securities exchanges (as mentioned earlier, the SEC has 90 days to accept or deny registration of an exchange);

■ national securities associations, such as FINRA and the MSRB (the Maloney Act of 1938 amended the Securities Exchange Act of 1934 and led to the creation of the NASD, which became FINRA, and the MSRB was created out of the Securities Amendments Act of 1975, which means that both associations were created by the Securities Exchange Act of 1934, as amended);

■ corporations with listed securities (a security may be registered on a national securities exchange by the issuer filing an application with the exchange and filing with the SEC as well). The application for registration must include:

— the organization, the financial structure, and nature of the business,

— the terms, position, rights, and privileges of the different classes of outstanding securities,

— the terms on which their securities are to be, and during the preceding three years have been, offered to the public,

— the directors, officers, and underwriters, and each security holder of record holding more than 10% of any class of equity security of the issuer, including their remuneration and their interests in the securities and their material contracts with the issuer and any person directly or indirectly controlling or controlled by the issuer,

— certified balance sheets for the previous three fiscal years prepared by independent public accountants, and

— certified profit and loss statements for the preceding three fiscal years prepared by independent accountants; and

■ securities Information Processors (SIPs); and

■ transfer agents

1. 6. 4 INSIDER TRANSACTIONS UNDER THE SECURITIES EXCHANGE ACT OF 1934

This act regulates securities transactions by insiders who generally own large amounts of their companies' stock. Certain persons must file a statement with the SEC concerning the amount of equity securities owned. These persons are:

■ every person who is directly or indirectly the beneficial owner of more than 10% of any class of equity security (other than exempt securities) registered on a national securities exchange; and

■ officers or directors of the issuers of such securities.

The SEC must be notified of any changes in the ownership of such securities. Such individuals are prohibited from selling short and from engaging in short-term transactions, usually called short-swing profits. These are defined as gains made when both the purchase and sale take place within a 6-month period. Stockholders are permitted to sue to recover any short-term profits improperly realized by such insiders. Exercise of stock options is not prohibited.

1. 6. 4. 1 Schedule 13D Filings

Section 13(d)—5% Beneficial Owners generally requires a beneficial owner of more than 5% of a class of equity securities registered under the Securities Exchange Act of 1934 (equity securities of publicly traded companies) to file a report with the issuer, SEC, and the securities markets where those securities trade within 10 days of any transaction that results in beneficial ownership of more than 5%. The reporting requirement of this section is fulfilled by filing Schedule 13D.

Schedule 13D requires information about the acquiring person, including:

■ the name and background of the person or entity (including partners, executive officers, directors, and controlling persons);

■ the origin of the money for the acquisition of the securities; and

■ the purpose of acquiring the securities, such as to acquire control of the business of the issuer, and plans or proposals that such persons may have to liquidate the issuer, to sell its assets to or merge it with any other persons, or to make any other change to its business or corporate structure.

1. 6. 4. 2 Section 13(f) Filings

Section 13(f) of the Securities Exchange Act of 1934 requires that any institutional investment manager that uses the mail or any means or instrumentality of interstate commerce in the course of its business as a institutional investment manager, and that exercises investment discretion over an equity portfolio with a market value on the last trading day in any of the preceding 12 months of $100 million or more in 13(f) securities, must file a **Form 13F** with the SEC quarterly, within 45 days of the end of each quarter.

The purpose of this rule is to require institutional investment managers who exercise investment discretion over accounts holding certain levels of securities to make periodic public disclosures of significant portfolio holdings.

1. 6. 4. 2. 1 What are 13(f) Securities?

At the end of each calendar quarter, a list of these securities—called the Official List of Section 13(f) Securities—may be found on the SEC's website.

Generally, the list includes exchange-traded (e.g., NYSE, CHX) or Nasdaq-quoted stocks, equity options and warrants, shares of closed-end investment companies, and certain convertible debt securities. Shares of open-end investment companies (i.e., mutual funds) are not included. Shares of exchange-traded funds (ETFs), however, are on the official list and would be reported on Form 13F.

1. 6. 4. 3 Schedule G Filings

Regulation 13G was adopted to ease the beneficial ownership requirements for passive investors. Rather than filing a Schedule 13D, a passive investor whose beneficial ownership exceeds 5% of any registered security may file a Schedule 13G. A **passive investor** is defined as any person who can certify that they did not purchase or do not hold the securities for the purpose of changing or influencing control over the issuer and hold no more than 20% of the issuer's securities. Investment companies and large pension funds are good examples of those that might have to file a Schedule 13G. Passive investors who choose to file a Schedule 13G must do so within 10 calendar days after crossing the 5% threshold just as with a Schedule 13D. Passive investors must amend their Schedule 13G within 45 days after the end of the calendar year to report any changes in the information previously reported.

1. 6. 4. 4 Section 16 Filings

Section 16(a) of the Securities Exchange Act of 1934 requires executive officers, directors and greater than 10% stockholders (i.e., control persons) to file transaction reports before the end of the second business day following the day on which a transaction has been executed in an equity security where they are considered an insider.

1. 6. 5 CREDIT REQUIREMENTS (MARGIN)

As mentioned earlier, Regulation T of the Federal Reserve Board came about as a result of the Act of 1934. It delegates the board of governors of the Federal Reserve System to set margin requirements. These margin requirements determine how much credit may be extended by broker-dealers to their customers to purchase certain securities. During the stock market crash of 1929, the margin requirements were 10%. Today they are 50%. This means that, in 1929, an investor could purchase $20,000 worth of stock with cash equity of only $2,000. Today, that same purchase of $20,000 of stock would require a cash down payment of $10,000. It should be obvious from this example that one of the purposes of Regulation T is to prevent the excessive use of credit.

One specific type of security on which credit may not be extended is a new issue. The underwriting syndicate must receive full payment for any new issue within 35 days of the purchase. Since mutual funds are a continuous new issue, their shares may NOT be purchased on margin. However, as with all new issues, once the shares have been owned in the account for 30 days, they may be used as collateral for a margin loan.

Although there are exceptions (which won't be tested), another case where margin is not permitted is on the purchase of options.

1. 6. 6   REGULATION OF THE USE OF MANIPULATIVE AND DECEPTIVE DEVICES

The act outlaws the use of any manipulative, deceptive, or other fraudulent devices. The intent is to prevent any deception in or manipulation of securities markets. Some of the specific devices prohibited are listed below. The first item below is considered a form of deception and the other two, market manipulation.

- **Churning** can be described as a broker-dealer effecting transactions in a discretionary account that are excessive in size or frequency, in view of the financial resources, objectives, and character of the account.

- **Wash trades** are prohibited under the act. A wash trade is a securities transaction that involves no change in the beneficial ownership of the security. For example, an investor might simultaneously buy and sell shares in one company through two different brokerage firms in order to create the appearance of substantial trading activity, and that is misleading to other investors. A wash sale for tax purposes is not related to this in any way. A wash sale for tax purposes occurs when a person sells a security and repurchases it within 30 days prior to or after the sale and is covered in Unit 4 of this course.

- **Matched orders** are illegal under the act. A matched order is the entering of a sell (or buy) order knowing that a corresponding buy (or sell) order of substantially the same size, at substantially the same time and at substantially the same price, either has been or will be entered. As is the case with wash trades, no real change in ownership takes place as a result of the transaction.

Accurate recording of orders and subsequent trades is one way the regulators monitor for attempts to manipulate the market.

1. 6. 6. 1   Order Tickets

SEC rules require preparation of order tickets before order entry. Required disclosures include:

- the account number;
- whether the order is solicited, unsolicited, or discretionary (including time or price);
- if a sale, whether long or short;
- the terms and conditions of the order (market or limit);
- the number of shares if a stock and if a bond, aggregate par value (but not rating or current yield);
- the time of order entry and execution, and the execution price; and
- the name of the broker-dealer and identity of the registered individual who accepted the order or is responsible for the account.

TEST TOPIC ALERT Two items that would *not* be on an order ticket are the current market price of the security and the client's name or address.

1. 7 INSIDER TRADING AND SECURITIES FRAUD ENFORCEMENT ACT OF 1988 (ITSFEA)

An **insider** or **control person** is defined as an officer, director, or owner of more than 10% of the voting stock of the company, or the immediate family of any of these persons. After the tremendous insider abuses of the mid-1980s, the SEC took steps to beef up its enforcement of insider trading, hence this act. This act incorporated all of the other prohibitions against the activities of insiders and the use of inside information and also increased the penalties that could be levied and made the recipient of inside information as guilty as the insider who passed on that information. In other words, the tippee would be just as guilty as the tipper.

An insider is in violation of SEC rules when he trades securities on the basis of material, nonpublic information (MNPI), or when he passes on this information to another who subsequently acts on this information. It is critical to remember that no chargeable violation has occurred unless a transaction has taken place.

Even persons who do not meet the definition of an insider are subject to the rules governing the use of nonpublic information and could be liable for any actions taken. When it comes to who could potentially be an insider—that is, who could possibly possess material inside information—the list is virtually endless. One could therefore say that a potential insider could be anyone coming across information dealing with a company, other than those individuals who, by virtue of their title or other circumstance, are definitely insiders.

The Insider Trading and Securities Fraud Enforcement Act of 1988 gave the SEC authority to seek *civil* penalties against persons violating the provisions of the act in amounts up to the greater of $1 million or treble damages. **Treble damages** means that the guilty party could be fined up to three times any ill-gotten gains or up to three times any losses avoided by using inside information to get out before a market drop. These civil penalties are in addition to any disgorgement of profits made or losses avoided as a result of the insider trading. From this fine, the SEC is authorized to award bounties to informants. If the SEC should elect to pursue *criminal* action, then penalties would include potential jail time with a maximum sentence of 20 years.

1. 7. 1 PRIVATE RIGHTS OF ACTION FOR CONTEMPORANEOUS TRADING

Any person who violates the rules or regulations by purchasing or selling a security while in possession of material, nonpublic information shall be liable in an action in any court of competent jurisdiction to any person who, contemporaneously with the purchase or sale of securities that is the subject of such violation, has purchased (where such violation is based on a sale of securities) or sold (where such violation is based on a purchase of securities) securities of the same class.

■ **Limitations on liability**

— The total amount of damages imposed will not exceed the profit gained or loss avoided in the transaction or transactions that are the subject of the violation. In other words, the person who lost can recover his money, but there is no claim for treble damages—that is reserved for SEC actions.

■ **Statute of limitations**

— No action may be brought under this section more than five years after the date of the last transaction that is the subject of the violation.

1. 7. 2   CHINESE WALL DOCTRINE

It is plain that the regulators wish to maintain a level playing field for all and if those with material nonpublic information were to let it leak out to favored interests, a prohibited activity would be taking place. This is particularly an issue with those broker-dealers who engage in investment banking, especially mergers and acquisitions. In order to do their job, they must have access to confidential information that is not publically available—at least not yet. Therefore, in order to ensure that this information does not become available, for example, to the research department or the retail sales staff, these firms must erect (figuratively) a wall as impenetrable as the Great Wall of China between these departments. In essence, a Chinese Wall is the term used to describe the procedures followed by these firms to insulate information from reaching the wrong hands.

TAKE NOTE
Although you might see the term *Chinese Wall* on your exam, the preferred term in the industry is *Information Barriers*.

1. 8   POWERS OF THE SEC

The SEC has the authority to investigate possible violations of the federal securities laws. In addition, the SEC may also investigate possible violation of the rules of the SROs, specifically those of:

■ a national securities exchange;

■ the FINRA; and

■ the MSRB.

The fact that these SROs have their own procedures for enforcing the rules in no way limits the SEC's powers to investigate and/or obtain a court injunction.

In the course of these investigations, the SEC has the power to:

■ administer oaths;

■ subpoena witnesses;

■ compel attendance;

■ require books and records to be produced;

- summarily suspend trading in any nonexempt security for up to 10 days without prior notice; and
- suspend trading on an entire exchange for up to 90 days (in order to do this, the SEC must give prior notification to the president of the United States).

1. 8. 1 FINANCIAL RESPONSIBILITY RULES UNDER THE SECURITIES EXCHANGE ACT OF 1934

The SEC adopted SEC Rule 15c3-1 **(Uniform Net Capital Rule)**, which establishes minimum net capital requirements for broker-dealers. The term *net capital* refers to net liquid assets of a firm. In other words, a broker-dealer must at all times maintain a minimum amount of net capital for the protection of its customers. If a firm does not have the required net capital under the rule, the SEC does not allow it to operate. Therefore, the purpose of the net capital rule is to protect the customers of the firm by imposing minimum net capital requirements.

The SEC also requires all broker-dealers to maintain a fidelity bond to protect against misappropriation, forgery, and similar violations of the firm and its associated persons. In the next session, you will learn testable information about surety bonds required under state law.

1. 9 SECURITIES AMENDMENTS ACT OF 1975

The Securities Amendments Act of 1975 was signed into law by President Ford on June 4, 1975. The act amended certain parts of the Securities Exchange Act of 1934 and the Securities Act of 1933. This act represents the most important changes in the regulation of securities markets since the Securities Exchange Act was passed by Congress in 1934.

The main purpose of the act was to remove any barriers to competition in the securities industry. The SEC was given much greater power to regulate the securities industry. The following is a summary of the main provisions of the Securities Amendments Act of 1975.

- Fixed-commission rates were abolished in favor of negotiated commissions on public orders.
- The act required registration of municipal securities dealers with the SEC. Previously, these broker-dealers were exempt from registration with the SEC. This amendment gave rise to the MSRB. It is important to remember that the existence of the MSRB does not in any way limit the power of the SEC to regulate the securities business. However, many MSRB members are banks that are beyond the jurisdiction of the SEC and are regulated by the various banking authorities.
- The SEC was given the power to regulate the activities of transfer agents.

QUICK QUIZ 1.E

1. Under the Securities Exchange Act of 1934, as amended, registration with the SEC would be required of

    I. a broker-dealer whose business is strictly municipal securities
    II. a broker-dealer whose business is strictly in non-Nasdaq over-the-counter securities
    III. a banking institution dealing in municipal bonds

    A. I and II
    B. I and III
    C. II and III
    D. I, II and III

2. Provisions under the Securities Exchange Act of 1934 include all of the following EXCEPT

    A. requiring that all issues listed on a national securities exchange be registered with the SEC
    B. prohibiting manipulative practices such as wash trades and misleading statements
    C. requiring full disclosure regarding an upcoming IPO
    D. requiring registration of transfer agents

1. 10   INVESTMENT COMPANY ACT OF 1940

Under the Investment Company Act of 1940, an **investment company** is defined as any issuer that is or holds itself out as being engaged primarily in the business of investing in securities. It is important for you to know that the definition of investment company does not include:

- broker-dealers and underwriters;
- banks and savings and loans;
- insurance companies;
- holding companies;
- issuers whose securities are beneficially owned by no more than 100 persons; and
- issuers who trade in investments other than securities.

1. 10. 1   TYPES OF INVESTMENT COMPANIES

The Investment Company Act of 1940 defines three types of investment companies.

- **Face-amount certificate company:** a face-amount certificate company is an investment company that issues face-amount certificates on the installment plan. A face-amount certificate is a security that represents an obligation on the part of its issuer to pay a stated sum at a fixed date more than 24 months after the date of issuance, in consideration of the payment of periodic installments of a stated amount. If the investor discontinues the plan and cashes in the certificate before maturity, he will probably lose money.

- **Unit investment trust:** a unit investment trust (UIT) is an investment company that does not have a board of directors and issues only redeemable securities, each of which represents an undivided interest in a unit of specified securities. In other words, without an investment adviser (management), once compiled, the portfolio remains fixed. An example of a UIT is the municipal bond trust.

- **Management company:** a management company is any investment company other than a face-amount certificate company or a UIT. These companies are managed by advisers with a fee generally based on the amount of assets under management.

QUICK QUIZ 1.F

1. Which of the following would be considered investment companies under the Act of 1940?

   I.   Face-amount certificate company
   II. Unit investment trust
   III. Management company
   IV. Holding company
   V.   Insurance company

   A. I, II and III
   B. I, II, III and IV
   C. I, II, III and V
   D. I, II, III, IV and V

1. 10. 2 SUBCLASSIFICATION OF INVESTMENT COMPANIES

For the purpose of the Investment Company Act of 1940, management companies are divided into **open-end** and **closed-end** companies as follows.

- An **open-end** company is a management company that is continuously offering for sale, or has outstanding, any redeemable security of which it is the issuer. The term *open-end company* is synonymous with *mutual fund*. The redemption price is the net asset value, which is calculated every business day as of the close of the market. Purchases of mutual funds are always at net asset value plus a sales charge (if any). Redemptions are made at the next computed NAV, minus a redemption charge, if any, and must be made within seven days of receipt of the redemption request.

- A **closed-end** company is any management company other than an open-end company. Closed-end companies generally have a onetime offering of shares and do not redeem their outstanding shares. Pricing of closed-end companies is not like that of open-end companies. The pricing is not based on net asset value—it is based on supply and demand. Therefore, shares may be purchased or sold in the marketplace at a price above, below, or at the net asset value. When a closed-end company is selling at a price above the net asset value, it is said to be selling at a premium; selling below the net asset value is called selling at a discount.

Management companies are further subclassified into **diversified** and **nondiversified** companies based on meeting certain diversification levels.

1. 10. 2. 1 Management Company Prospectus Delivery Requirements

Because open-end investment companies are continuously offering new shares, a current fund prospectus must be delivered prior to or concurrent with the sale. In the case of a closed-end company, a prospectus is only required on the IPO; all trading subsequent to that is in the secondary market and does not require delivery of a prospectus.

QUICK QUIZ 1.G

1. How do closed-end investment companies differ from open-end investment companies?

   I.   Closed-end companies register their shares with the SEC; open-end companies do not.
   II. The only time a prospectus is used with the sale of a closed-end company is on the IPO; sales of open-end shares must always be preceded or accompanied by a prospectus.
   III. Closed-end companies issue a fixed number of shares; open-end companies continuously issue new shares.
   IV. Closed-end companies may only sell shares to institutional investors; open-end companies can sell to any investor.

   A. I and II
   B. I and IV
   C. II and III
   D. III and IV

2. A financial reporter notices that the quoted price of one investment company's shares is at a 22% discount from the NAV. From this information, it can be deduced that the company must be a(n)

   A. closed-end investment company
   B. contractual plan of a mutual fund
   C. open-end investment company
   D. unit investment trust

1. 10. 3 REGISTRATION OF INVESTMENT COMPANIES

Investment companies must register as such by filing with the SEC as would any other company under the Securities Act of 1933. In addition, they register specifically as investment companies under the Investment Company Act of 1940. In the registration statement, the registrant describes all of the important information, such as objective, sales loads, whether they will be concentrating investments in a particular industry or group of industries, and so on.

1. 10. 4 INELIGIBILITY OF CERTAIN AFFILIATED PERSONS AND UNDERWRITERS

The Investment Act of 1940 prohibits people who have committed certain acts from serving in certain sensitive positions with an investment company, its adviser, or its principal underwriter. Specifically, no one may serve as a director, employee, investment adviser, member of an advisory board, officer, or principal underwriter if that person has been:

- convicted, within the previous 10 years, of any felony or misdemeanor involving the purchase or sale of any security or arising out of that person's conduct as an underwriter, broker-dealer, investment adviser, or affiliated person, salesman, or employee of any investment company; or

- permanently or temporarily enjoined by order, judgment, or decree of any court of competent jurisdiction from acting in any phase of the securities business.

Any person who is ineligible, because of a conviction for felony or misdemeanor, to serve or act as stated above may file with the SEC an application to become eligible again. The SEC may grant the request, either unconditionally or on an appropriate temporary or other conditional basis, if it feels that it is not against the public interest or protection of investors to allow that person back into the business.

In general, investment companies cannot have a board of directors that consists of more than 60% of persons who meet the definition of interested persons of the investment company.

TAKE NOTE

Another way of stating that no more than 60% of the directors may be interested persons is to say that at least 40% must be non-interested, that is, "outside" directors. These are individuals who have no connection to the fund other than a position on the board (and maybe owning some shares of the fund as would any investor).

1. 10. 5 RULE 12b-1

Rule 12b-1 is titled Payment of Asset-Based Sales Loads by Registered Open-End Management Investment Companies. This rule permits a mutual fund to act as a distributor of its own shares without the use of an underwriter and with an asset-based sales load. An **asset-based sales load** is any direct or indirect financing by a mutual fund of sales or promotional services or activities in connection with the distribution of shares. This basically permits no-load funds to pay commissions (sometimes called **trails**) to broker-dealers who sell or otherwise promote the sale of their fund shares. The mutual fund may not use the term *no-load* if its 12b-1 fee exceeds .25% (25 basis points). Under any circumstances, the maximum 12b-1 charge may not exceed .75% (and FINRA allows another .25% to be added on as a servicing fee).

The mutual fund may act as a distributor of the shares of which it is the issuer, provided that any asset-based sales load paid by the company is paid according to a written plan describing all material aspects of the financing of the distribution. This written plan must meet the following requirements.

- The plan has been approved initially by a vote of at least a majority of the outstanding voting securities of the investment company.

- The plan, together with any related agreements, has been approved initially and reapproved at least annually by a vote of the board of directors of the company, and of the directors who are not interested persons of the company and have no direct or indirect financial interest in the operation of the 12b-1 plan or in any related agreements.

The directors who vote in favor of implementation or continuation of the plan must believe that:

■ it is likely that the plan will benefit the company, existing shareholders, and future shareholders;

■ given the circumstances, the amounts payable under the plan and related agreements represent charges within the range of what would have been negotiated at arm's length as payment for the specific sales or promotional services and activities to be financed under the plan; and

■ the plan may be terminated at any time by a vote of the majority of the members of the board of directors of the company who are not interested persons of the company and have no direct or indirect financial interest in the operation of the plan or in any related agreements, or by a vote of the majority of the shareholders of the company.

QUICK QUIZ 1.H

1. All of the following statements regarding a 12b-1 company are true EXCEPT

   A. the plan must be initially approved by at least a majority of the out-standing voting securities of the investment company
   B. the plan must be renewed by a majority of the fund's directors
   C. the plan may be terminated by a vote of the majority of shareholders or a majority of the board of directors
   D. the rule only applies to open-end investment companies

1. 10. 6 PROHIBITED ACTIVITIES OF INVESTMENT COMPANIES

Investment companies are prohibited from engaging in several activities. Investment companies may not:

■ purchase any security on margin;

■ participate on a joint basis in any trading account in securities (i.e., an investment company cannot have a joint account with someone else);

■ sell any security short; or

■ acquire more than 3% of the outstanding voting securities of another investment company.

There are exceptions to the above prohibitions, but, for the purposes of the exam, you may disregard any exceptions.

QUICK QUIZ 1.I

1. The Investment Company Act of 1940 prohibits registered investment companies from engaging in any of the following practices EXCEPT

   A. issuing common stock
   B. selling short or purchasing securities for the company's portfolio on margin
   C. owning more than 3% of the outstanding voting securities of another investment company
   D. opening a joint account with another investment company

1. 10. 7 CHANGES IN INVESTMENT POLICY

In order for an investment company's board to make fundamental investment policy changes, a majority vote of the outstanding voting stock is required. Examples of fundamental changes would include:

■ a change in subclassification, such as from an open-end to a closed-end company or from a diversified to a nondiversified company;

■ deviation from any fundamental policy in its registration statement, including a change in investment objective; and

■ changing the nature of its business so as to cease to be an investment company.

In other words, since the investment company is supposed to function for the benefit of the shareholders, any of these changes would require the vote of a majority of the shareholders.

1. 10. 8 SIZE OF INVESTMENT COMPANIES

No registered investment company is permitted to make a public offering of securities unless it has a net worth of at least $100,000.

1. 10. 9 INVESTMENT ADVISORY AND UNDERWRITER CONTRACTS

No registered investment company shall, unless authorized by a majority of its outstanding voting securities, engage any person to serve or act as investment adviser of a registered investment company, or as principal underwriter, except pursuant to a written contract that:

■ precisely describes all compensation to be paid;

■ will be approved at least annually by the board of directors or by majority vote of the shareholders if it is to be renewed after the first two years;

■ provides that it may be terminated at any time, without penalty, by the board of directors or by majority vote of the shareholders on not more than 60 days' written notice to the investment adviser; and

■ provides for its automatic termination in the event of its assignment.

In addition, it is unlawful for any registered investment company to enter into or renew any contract with an investment adviser or principal underwriter unless the terms have been approved by majority vote of directors who are not parties to such contract as affiliated persons (i.e., directors who are not affiliated with the adviser or the underwriter, who in the aggregate must comprise at least 40% of the directors).

TAKE NOTE   The effect of this final paragraph is that no advisory contract, whether initial or renewal, may take effect without approval of the noninterested members of the board.

1. 10. 9. 1 Transactions of Certain Affiliated Persons and Underwriters

It is unlawful for any affiliated person of, or principal underwriter for, a registered investment company to:

■ knowingly sell any security to that investment company unless it is a sale only of shares issued by that company itself (redemption of the fund's shares) or a sale of securities of which the seller is the issuer and which are part of a general public offering;

■ borrow money or any other property from the fund; or

■ knowingly purchase from that investment company any security other than the fund's shares.

Any person may file with the SEC an application for an order exempting a proposed transaction of the applicant from one or more of the above provisions, which may or may not be granted depending on the circumstances.

TEST TOPIC ALERT

An **affiliated person** is defined as any person directly or indirectly owning, controlling, or holding with power to vote, **5%** or more of the outstanding shares of the investment company. An affiliated person also includes any person directly or indirectly controlling, controlled by, or under common control with the investment company or any officer, director, partner or employee of the investment company. However, while technically considered an affiliated person, no person is deemed to be an "interested person" for purposes of the maximum percentage of interested persons on the board solely by reason of his being a member of the fund's board of directors or an owner of its securities. A person is deemed to be a **control** person when owning or controlling more than **25%** of the outstanding shares.

1. 10. 9. 2 Custodian

In the same section of the Act where the SEC put limitations on the activities of certain affiliates of the fund, it acted to erect a firewall of sorts to make it more difficult for those persons to have access to assets of the fund. As a result, it is required that every registered investment company keeps its assets with a custodian. In the majority of cases, that custodian is a bank, hence the common use of the term *custodian bank*. Although the Act specifies certain financial requirements for that bank, it does not require that the bank have FDIC coverage. Alternatively, the investment company may use a broker-dealer that is a member firm of a national securities exchange.

1. ABC is an FINRA member broker-dealer. Among other functions, it serves as the principal underwriter of the XYZ Mutual Fund. Which of the following transactions of ABC would be prohibited unless exemptive relief was offered by the SEC?

   A. ABC tenders, from its investment account, 500 shares of the XYZ Mutual Fund for redemption.
   B. ABC purchases, for its investment account, 500 shares of XYZ Mutual Fund.
   C. ABC purchases some securities directly from XYZ's portfolio.
   D. All of the above.

2. Which of the following statements correctly expresses requirements under the Investment Company Act of 1940?

   I. A registered open-end investment company using a bank as custodian must choose one that has FDIC coverage.
   II. If an affiliated person of a registered investment company wishes to borrow money from the fund, there must be at least 300% asset coverage.
   III. No investment advisory contract may be entered into that does not provide for termination with no more than 60 days notice in writing.
   IV. No registered investment company may acquire more than 3% of the shares of another investment company.

   A. I and II
   B. I and IV
   C. II and III
   D. III and IV

1. 10. 10 SALE OF REDEEMABLE SECURITIES

This section deals with prices at which mutual fund shares may be sold. The rule basically requires that the public offering price, as stated in the prospectus, be upheld for all buyers. There are, however, several ways in which fund shares may be sold to investors at a reduced sales charge and even at no sales charge.

The most important way in which a reduction of sales charge may be made available is by use of a **breakpoint**. This is the quantity level stated in the prospectus at which investors receive a reduction in load. This breakpoint is available to any person who purchases in the stated quantity. In this case, however, the definition of any person is somewhat limited. Most commonly, it includes:

■ an individual, spouse, and dependent children under age 21 purchasing in one or more accounts;

■ any legitimate entity purchasing for its own account, as long as the entity was not formed for the purposes of making this purchase; and

■ the trustee purchasing on behalf of a qualified employee benefit plan, such as a pension or profit-sharing plan.

It does not include:

■ purchases made for the account of an investment club; and

■ purchases made on behalf of any entity or group that does not have a common purpose, other than making this investment.

Under what circumstances are the shares available at no sales charge?

■ Sales made to related persons of the fund, such as officers and other employees of the fund, the adviser, or the principal underwriter.

■ Shares purchased through automatic reinvestment of dividends and capital gains distributions. Although no tax benefit accrues, the investor is able to enjoy compounding without expense.

TEST TOPIC ALERT   This rule may appear on your exam in a question asking if an investment adviser (IA) is permitted to reduce his fees because of commissions earned on the sale of mutual funds. Commissions earned on any product, such as mutual funds, insurance, and so forth, may be used either in full or in part as a credit against advisory fees. What the IA cannot do is rebate or reduce commissions on products offered with a stated offering price, such as mutual funds or insurance company products. While they appear to result in the same outcome, legally, there is a difference.

TEST TOPIC ALERT   Engaging in sales practices that prevent clients from reaching breakpoints not only is a violation of federal law but also is considered an unethical business practice by NASAA (as you will see in the next session). It is critical that you know that when an agent makes an initial sale of shares of an open-end investment company in a quantity just below a published breakpoint, the agent is in violation for failing to indicate that with a small amount added to the purchase, a substantial savings in sales charge will result.

QUICK QUIZ 1.K   1.   Under which of the following circumstances would a purchase of mutual fund shares at a price below the public offering price be allowable?

I.   The purchase is made by the designated agent of an incorporated investment club that reaches the breakpoint.

II.   A parent buys enough to reach the breakpoint but places half the order in his account and the other half in an account for which his wife is designated as custodian for their son.

III.   The receptionist for the XYZ Growth Fund purchases $100 of that fund.

IV.   A financial planner bunches his clients' orders and turns them in as one in an amount sufficient to reach the breakpoint.

A.   I and II

B.   I and III

C.   II and III

D.   II, III and IV

1. 10. 11 PERIODIC AND OTHER REPORTS

All investment companies must file annual financial reports with the SEC. These reports contain an audited balance sheet and income statement.

1. 10. 11. 1 Shareholder Reports

At least semiannually, shareholders must be mailed reports, including:

- a balance sheet;
- an income statement;
- a listing of the amounts and values of securities owned;
- a statement of purchases and sales; and
- a statement of the remuneration paid by the investment company during the period covered by the report to officers and directors, as well as any person of whom any officer or director of the company is an affiliated person.

1. 10. 12 UNLAWFUL REPRESENTATIONS AND NAMES

It is unlawful for any person, in issuing or selling any security of which a registered investment company is the issuer, to represent or imply in any manner whatsoever that such security or company has been guaranteed, sponsored, recommended, or approved by the U.S. government or any agency thereof. This is a parallel requirement to the SEC disclaimer found on the front of every prospectus.

1. 10. 13 LARCENY AND EMBEZZLEMENT

Whoever steals, unlawfully and willfully converts to his own use or to the use of another, or embezzles any of the monies, funds, securities, or assets of any registered investment company will be deemed guilty of a crime and, upon conviction thereof, will be subject to the penalties of a fine of a maximum of $10,000, imprisonment for up to five years, or both. In addition to these penalties, officers and directors of investment companies may be subject to civil action by the SEC for various violations of the Investment Company Act of 1940. If found guilty, you have the right to appeal within 60 days to the Federal Court of Appeals for the District in which the case was heard.

1. 10. 14 COMPUTING RETURNS ON MUTUAL FUND SHARES

In order to avoid misrepresentation or misunderstanding, the SEC stipulates the methods that are to be used when computing returns on an investment in open-end investment company shares. There are two types of return used: current and total.

1. 10. 14. 1 Current Return on Mutual Fund Shares

To calculate a fund's current yield (return), divide the yearly dividend paid from net investment income by the current offering price. Current yield calculations may only be based on dividend distributions for the preceding 12 months. Capital gains distributions may not be included in yield calculations. Most mutual funds with income objectives distribute dividends quarterly, although they can be with any frequency, even monthly.

EXAMPLE

The KAPCO Income Fund has a current public offering price of $10.50 and a net asset value per share of $10.00. During the past 12 months, the fund has made four quarterly distributions from net investment income of $.15 and one distribution from capital gains in the amount of $.25. The fund's current yield would be?

   A.   1.5%
   B.   5.7%
   C.   6.0%
   D.   1.1%

Answer: B. It is computed by dividing the annual income (4 x $.15 = $.60) by the POP (not the NAV) of $10.50. Only the dividends are used for current yield.

1. 10. 14. 2 Total Return on Mutual Fund Shares

Total return for a mutual fund is computed by adding the capital gains to the dividends distributed. Total return always assumes reinvestment of all distributions (dividends and capital gains). This is the only time that dividends and capital gains are combined.

1. 11   MONEY LAUNDERING

Money laundering involves disguising financial assets so they can be utilized without detecting the illegal activity that produced them. Through money laundering, a criminal transforms the proceeds of illicit activities into funds that appear to have been generated by legal means. Money laundering enables criminals to hide and legitimize the proceeds derived from illegal ventures.

1. 11. 1   CURRENCY TRANSACTION REPORTS (CTRS)

The Bank Secrecy Act requires every financial institution to electronically file through the Department of the U.S. Treasury, a currency transaction report (CTR) on FinCEN Form 112 for each cash transaction that exceeds $10,000. This requirement applies to cash transactions used to pay off loans, the electronic transfer of funds, or the purchase of certificates of deposit, stocks, bonds, mutual funds, or other investments. The act also requires the reporting of wire transfers in excess of $3,000.

1. 12   THE NATIONAL SECURITIES MARKETS IMPROVEMENT ACT OF 1996 (NSMIA)

In October, 1996, Congress passed the National Securities Markets Improvement Act of 1996 (NSMIA). That bill became law and extensively amended various provisions of the Securities Act of 1933, the Securities Exchange Act of 1934, and the Investment Advisers Act of 1940. As we will cover in Session 3, the law effectively bifurcated (split in two) the regulation of investment advisers by creating a new definition: Covered Adviser (sometimes referred to under state securities laws as "Federal Covered Adviser"). Relevant to Session 2, a new definition was created: Covered Security (sometimes referred to under state securities laws as "Federal Covered Security"). State securities registration requirements were preempted with respect to federal covered securities.

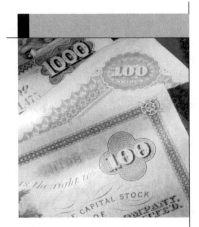

2

State Regulation Under the Uniform Securities Act (USA)

The Uniform Securities Act (USA) is model legislation that arose in an effort to unify numerous state securities laws, known as **blue-sky laws**. Under the USA, the state Administrator has jurisdiction over securities transactions that originate in, are directed into, or are accepted in the Administrator's state. For those persons or transactions that fall within the jurisdiction of the Administrator, the Administrator has power to make rules and orders; conduct investigations and issue subpoenas; issue cease and desist orders; and deny, suspend, cancel, or revoke registrations.

The USA provides both civil liabilities and criminal penalties for violating the act. Civil liabilities enable an investor to recover attorney's fees, court costs, and losses resulting from securities sold in violation of the USA. Criminal penalties may be levied in addition to the civil liabilities against those who engage in fraudulent activities under the act.

The Series 65 exam will include approximately 19 questions on the material presented in this session.

When you have completed this session, you should be able to:

- **recognize** the jurisdiction of the state securities Administrator;

- **list** the powers of the Administrator within its jurisdiction;

- **discuss** the different methods of state securities registration;

- **identify** instruments that are defined under the USA as securities;

- **identify** securities that are defined as exempt under the USA;

- **define** exempt transactions and provide examples;

- **define** and understand the differences between broker-dealer, agent, investment adviser, and investment adviser representative;

- **identify** for each category of professional, the procedures and requirements for registration in a state;

- **understand** the antifraud provisions of the USA;

- **recognize** specific fraudulent activities, unethical practices prohibited practices, and various forms of deceptive market manipulation;

- **identify** what is and what is not considered a person;

- **understand** the differences between exclusions from a definition and exemptions from provisions of the USA;

- **recognize** what is and what is not a security;

- **determine** who is and is not a security issuer;

- **describe** the requirements for exemption from registration for private placements;

- **understand** the relationship between state and national securities laws;

- **describe** the civil rights of recovery for a security's sale or for investment advice purchased in violation of the USA; and

- **contrast** civil and criminal penalties for violation of the act.

2. 1   DEFINITIONS UNDER THE UNIFORM SECURITIES ACT

2. 1. 1   THE UNIFORM SECURITIES ACT OF 1956 (USA)

2. 1. 1. 1   The USA is Model State Securities Legislation

With the enactment of numerous state securities laws, commonly referred to as blue-sky laws, the need for uniformity in securities laws among the states arose. In 1956, the **National Conference of Commissioners on Uniform State Laws (NCCUSL)**, a national organization of lawyers devoted to unifying state laws, drafted the original Uniform Securities Act **(USA)** as model legislation for the separate states to adopt. As model legislation, the USA is not actual legislation; the USA is a template or guide that each state uses in drafting its securities legislation. The securities laws of most states follow the USA very closely, and, in many cases, almost exactly.

TEST TOPIC ALERT   The exam will test your knowledge of the Uniform Securities Act, not the specifics of your state's securities legislation. The USA is periodically updated to adjust to developments in the securities markets through the passage of Model Rules. You will be tested on the 1956 version of the USA used by the **North American Securities Administrators Association (NASAA)**, the advisory body of state securities regulators responsible for the content of the exam. The Series 65 exam requires that you not only know what the USA says, but also are able to apply the law to concrete situations. General knowledge of the law is not enough to pass the exam; you will be asked to apply the law to situations that may arise in the course of business.

2. 1. 2   ADMINISTRATOR

Although some states may use other terms to describe this position, the exam will only use the word **Administrator** to refer to the office or agency that has the complete responsibility for administering the securities laws of the state.

Therefore, the Administrator has jurisdiction over all securities activity that emanates from his state as well as that received in his state. The Administrator has jurisdiction over the registration of securities professionals and securities. He has the power to make rules and issue orders. He can deny, suspend, or revoke registrations. Yes, there are some limitations on the Administrator's powers (and those will be covered in this session and Session 3), but overall, this is one very powerful person.

When it comes to legal issues, terminology is critical. For example, there are three terms that will be used in this section that can become quite confusing. Let's try to explain them here, and they will make more sense as you go through this manual.

2. 1. 2. 1   Cease and Desist Order

This is used by the Administrator whenever it appears to him that any registered person has engaged or is about to engage in any act or practice constituting a violation of any provision of this act or any rule or order hereunder. The Administrator may issue a cease and desist order, with or without a prior hearing against the person or persons engaged in the prohibited activities, directing them to cease and desist from further illegal activity. Note that this only applies to registered persons, not securities.

2. 1. 2. 2   Stop Order

A **stop order** is used to deny effectiveness to, or suspend or revoke the effectiveness of, any registration statement. This applies only to securities, not professionals such as broker-dealers, agents, investment advisers and investment adviser representatives.

2. 1. 2. 3   Summary Order (Acting Summarily)

The dictionary defines "summarily" as acting without prior notice. This is one of the powers of the Administrator with regard to registration of both persons and securities. There are three specific cases where this power applies in the USA:

- Postponing or suspending the registration of any securities professional pending a final determination of a proceeding related to a problem
- Postponing or suspending the registration of a security pending a final determination of a proceeding relating to a problem
- Denying or revoking a specific security or transaction exemption

In each of these cases, upon the entry of the order, the Administrator must promptly notify all interested parties that it has been entered, the reasons for the order, and that within fifteen days after the receipt of a written request a hearing will be granted.

2. 1. 2. 4   Final Orders

A **final order** is one that ends litigation (usually). Under the Uniform Securities Act, it is when the Administrator (or a court) renders a judgment in an action (guilty or innocent). Regardless of whether we're referring to persons, exemptions, or registration, other than in the case of a summary order, no final order may be entered without:

- appropriate prior notice to the interested parties;
- opportunity for hearing; and
- written findings of fact and conclusions of law.

2. 1. 3   BLUE-SKY LAWS

The common term used to refer to state securities laws.

2. 1. 4   PERSON

The term **person** means any individual, (sometimes known as a *natural person*), corporation, partnership, association, joint stock company, or trust where the interests of the beneficiaries are evidenced by a security, an unincorporated organization, a government, or a political subdivision of a government. This is a very broad definition.

TEST TOPIC ALERT

Although there are a wide variety of entities that may be defined as persons, on the exam, there are only three nonpersons. Those are:

- minors (anyone unable to enter into contracts under the laws of the state);

- deceased individuals; and

- individuals legally declared mentally incompetent.

Person includes any entity such as:

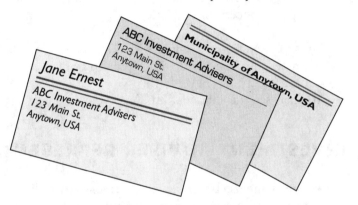

Individual   or   Business   or   Government

2. 1. 5   BROKER-DEALER

The term **broker-dealer** means any person engaged in the business of effecting transactions in securities for the account of others or for his own account. When acting on behalf of others, they are acting as brokers; when acting on behalf of themselves, they are acting as dealers. For exam purposes, it is critical to remember that the primary function of a broker-dealer is making securities transactions. In almost all cases, broker-dealers register with both the SEC and the state(s). This term is sometimes abbreviated to BD on the exam.

2. 1. 6   AGENT

Agent means any **individual**, other than a broker-dealer, who represents a broker-dealer or issuer in effecting or attempting to effect purchases or sales of securities. You must know that these are always individuals (natural persons) and their function is to be involved in securities sales or supervising those who do. On FINRA exams, these individuals are referred to as registered representatives.

Almost always, these individuals work for broker-dealers, but, there can be instances when the individual is selling securities on behalf of the issuer of those securities.

2. 1. 7   INVESTMENT ADVISER

The term **investment adviser** means any person:

- who, for **compensation**, engages in the **business of advising** others, either directly or through publications or writings, as to the value of **securities** or as to the advisability of investing in, purchasing, or selling securities; or
- who, for compensation and as part of a regular business, issues or promulgates analyses or reports concerning securities.

Under the National Securities Markets Improvements Act of 1996 (NSMIA), investment advisers are registered with either the SEC (covered advisers) or the state (state registered adviser), but never both.

You may see the abbreviation IA on your exam.

2. 1. 8   INVESTMENT ADVISER REPRESENTATIVE

An **investment adviser representative** is any individual who represents a state-registered investment adviser or federal covered investment adviser performing duties related to the giving of or soliciting for advisory services. Just as with agents, these can only be individuals (natural persons). You may see the abbreviation IAR on your exam.

2. 1. 9   ISSUER

The term **issuer** means any person who issues or *proposes* to issue any security. Issuers primarily include corporations and governments. However, the exam will want you to know that under the USA, with respect to certificates of interest or participation in oil, gas, or mining titles or leases, or in payments out of production under such titles or leases, there is not considered to be any "issuer."

2. 1. 10   NONISSUER

The term **nonissuer** means not directly or indirectly for the benefit of the issuer.

2. 1. 11 SECURITY

The definition of **security** is quite broad and includes those items one normally thinks of as securities (e.g., stocks, bonds, debentures, mutual funds, variable annuities, etc.), but also includes a number of unusual items, such as an investment contract and a pre-organization certificate. We will cover securities in greater detail later in this session.

2. 1. 12 EXEMPT SECURITY

First, you must understand the meaning of the term **exempt**. When something is exempt, it means that it is excused from certain requirements. When a security is exempt under the USA, it does *not* have to be registered in order to be sold, and there are no requirements to file advertising about the security with the Administrator. You will see more later in this session.

2. 1. 13 EXEMPT TRANSACTION

Under the USA, an **exempt transaction** is one in which the nature of the sale is such that registration with the Administrator and filing of advertising material is *not* required in order for that transaction to take place. More to follow later in this session.

2. 1. 14 GUARANTEED

The term **guaranteed** means guaranteed as to payment of principal, interest, or dividends, but *not* capital gains.

2. 1. 15 OFFER/OFFER TO SELL

The terms **offer** and **offer to sell** include every attempt or offer to dispose of, or solicitation of an offer to buy, a security or interest in a security for value.

2. 1. 16 SALE

The term **sale** or **sell** includes every contract of sale of, contract to sell, or disposition of, a security or interest in a security for value. In other words, the offer is the attempt, the sale is when it is successful.

2. 1. 17 FRAUD

The term **fraud** means an intentional effort to deceive someone for profit; not limited to common-law deceit.

2. 1. 18 SRO

This is the abbreviation for **Self-Regulatory Organization**. The most prominent of these is FINRA, but there are others such as the Municipal Securities Rulemaking Board (MSRB), the Chicago Board Options Exchange (CBOE), and the Investment Industry Regulatory Organization (IIRO) of Canada.

2. 1. 19 SOLICITOR

The term **solicitor** means any individual who, for compensation, acts as an agent of an investment adviser in referring potential clients. The next session will discuss when solicitors must be registered as investment adviser representatives.

2. 1. 20 ACCREDITED INVESTOR

The term **accredited investor** is found in Rule 501 of the federal Securities Act of 1933. It refers to a person who is not counted when computing the number of investors purchasing a private placement under Regulation D of that Act.

Because it is a federal term, not one found in the Uniform Securities Act, on this exam, the term is basically used to confuse you as you will see when you go through our practice questions.

2. 1. 21 REGISTRANT

The term **registrant** is used in legal circles to refer to those securities professionals (BDs, IAs, agents, and IARs), or securities issuers, who are in the process of, or who have registered with the Administrator.

2. 1. 22 INSTITUTION

The term **institution** would include banks, trust companies, savings and loan associations, insurance companies, investment companies, employee benefit plans with assets of not less than one million dollars ($1,000,000), and governmental agencies or instrumentalities. Institutions are included in the term *person*, defined previously. The Act generally affords less protection to these investors owing to their greater investment sophistication.

2. 1. 23 RETAIL CLIENT

As you know, terminology is very important on this exam. A few questions use the term, *retail client* instead of noninstitutional client. Look for it and remember that retail clients need far more protection than institutional ones. Also, individuals who meet the standard of accredited investor are still retail rather than institutional clients.

2. 1. 24 NATIONAL SECURITIES MARKETS IMPROVEMENTS ACT OF 1996 (NSMIA)

Congress enacted the NSMIA in 1996 to promote efficiency in capital formation in the financial markets. In effect, the act generally preempts states' blue-sky laws, eliminating the dual system of state and federal registration of certain securities and investment advisers.

2. 1. 25 STATE

The term **state** means any of the 50 states, any territory or possession of the United States (such as American Samoa , Guam, and the Virgin Islands), the District of Columbia, and Puerto Rico.

2. 2   EXCLUSION FROM DEFINITIONS AND EXEMPTION FROM REGISTRATION

Understanding terms is not a mere semantic exercise. Definitions create jurisdiction. Jurisdiction means that a person or security is covered or subject to the law. Exemptions and exclusions affect persons covered by the act but provide for exemptions and exclusions from provisions of the act. These distinctions must be kept in mind.

2. 2. 1   EXCLUSION FROM A DEFINITION

Exclusion means excluded from, or not included in, a definition. For the purposes of the USA, if a person is excluded from the definition of an agent, that person is not subject to provisions of state law that refer to agents. *Agent,* as defined above, is any individual other than a broker-dealer who represents a broker-dealer or issuer in effecting transactions in securities.

There are, however, situations in which a person who is representing an issuer in securities transactions is not, by definition, an agent for purposes of the USA. How is this accomplished? By excluding that person from the definition. Later in this session, we will discuss the cases where this occurs.

2. 2. 2   EXEMPTION FROM REGISTRATION UNDER THE ACT

Exemption in the USA means not being subject to a registration provision of the act even though that person is otherwise covered by the act. For example, a person defined as an investment adviser can be exempt from state registration requirements as an investment adviser because that person enjoys an exemption from state registration under federal law, such as in the case of a federal covered adviser.

QUICK QUIZ 2.A

True or False?

_____ 1. A final order may be entered only after opportunity for a hearing has been granted.

_____ 2. If an administrator determines that a registration statement for a security is incomplete, he may issue a cease and desist order.

_____ 3. Under the Uniform Securities Act, the city of Atlanta would be included in the definition of the term *person*.

_____ 4. The GEMCO Employees Retirement Plan currently has assets of $750,000. Under the Uniform Securities Act, the plan would be considered an institutional investor.

5. What is the official designation of the person or agency that enforces the USA in each state?

A. Administrator
B. Transfer agent
C. Registrar
D. Issuer

Quick Quiz answers can be found at the end of the unit.

2. 3   PERSONS SUBJECT TO STATE REGISTRATION

Now that the basic terms used in the exam have been addressed, attention must now be directed to those persons who are not excluded or exempted from provisions of the act. The following are the four classes of persons that fall under the jurisdiction of state securities laws:

- Broker-dealers—generally legal persons, such as corporations or partnerships
- Agents—always individuals (natural persons)
- Investment advisers—generally legal persons, such as corporations or partnerships
- Investment adviser representatives—always individuals (natural persons)

In this session, we will focus on broker-dealers and their agents with investment advisers and their representatives receiving the attention in the next session.

TEST TOPIC ALERT

On your exam, always keep in mind which of the four categories of persons is the subject of the question. Rules that apply to agents, for example, are not the same as those that apply to broker-dealers. You will be tested on your understanding of the distinctions between each class of person defined in this session.

2. 3. 1   BROKER-DEALER

A **broker-dealer** is defined in the USA as any person (think back to the broad definition we gave you a few pages ago) engaged in the business of effecting transactions in securities for the accounts of others or for its own account. Any person (e.g., a securities firm, even one organized as a sole proprietorship) with an established place of business (an office) in the state that is in the business of buying and selling securities for the accounts of others (customers) and/or for its own proprietary account is a broker-dealer and must register in the state as such.

In other words, broker-dealers are firms for which agents (registered representatives) work. They are firms that engage in securities transactions, such as sales and trading. When acting on behalf of their customers—that is, buying and selling securities for their clients' accounts—broker-dealers act in an agency capacity. When broker-dealers buy and sell securities for their own accounts, called proprietary accounts, they act in a principal capacity as dealers.

TAKE NOTE   Individuals who buy and sell securities for their own accounts are not broker-dealers because they are engaged in personal investment activity, not the business of buying and selling securities for others. They are individual investors, not securities dealers.

TEST TOPIC ALERT   One of the roles of a broker-dealer is underwriting (distributing) shares of new securities for issuers. When they do that, they generally earn a spread (the difference between the public offering price and what they pay the issuer) or receive a commission on the sales, which they then use to pay their agents who actually made the sales to the clients.

As we covered in the previous session, broker-dealers, unless exempt, must register with the SEC. In addition, registration with the state(s) in which the broker-dealer does business is required unless qualifying for an exemption. The procedure is different for investment advisers, as you will learn in the next session. Investment advisers either register on the state *or* the federal level, never both. If registered with the SEC as a federal covered adviser, the states have no jurisdiction over the activities of the adviser other than in the case of fraudulent activity.

2. 3. 1. 1   Exclusions from the Definition of Broker-Dealer

Broker-dealers are firms that buy and sell securities for others or themselves as a business. There are, however, many persons, legal and natural, that effect securities transactions that are excluded from the definition of broker-dealer for purposes of state regulation. Persons not included in the definition of broker-dealer are:

- agents;
- issuers; and
- banks, savings institutions, and trust companies (not engaged in broker-dealer activities).

Domestic commercial banks and other financial institutions are generally excluded from the definition of a broker-dealer. However, with the adoption of the Gramm-Leach-Bliley Act in 1999, also known as the Financial Modernization Act, federal securities law adopted a functional approach to the regulation of financial institutions. Under the functional approach, those financial institutions that engage in brokerage-related securities activities are subject to SEC registration as broker-dealers as well as to applicable provisions of state securities law—the USA—that relate to broker-dealers.

Today most banks and other financial institutions engage in securities activities through broker-dealer subsidiaries. The broker-dealer subsidiaries of banks are, as a result, not excluded from the definition of a broker-dealer and therefore subject to the same securities regulations as other broker-dealers. Keep in mind that formation of these subsidiaries eliminates the need for the bank holding companies to register as broker-dealers. Their broker-dealer subsidiaries must, of course, register.

TAKE NOTE   Keep in mind the distinction between a bank holding company and a wholly owned commercial bank subsidiary. Commercial banks, the subsidiaries of bank holding companies, do not have to register because they are excluded from the definition of broker-dealer. When engaged in securities transactions with the public, bank subsidiaries are subject to securities legislation as any other broker-dealer.

2. 3. 1. 1. 1 No Place of Business in the State

There is another exclusion from the definition of broker-dealer. This exclusion relates to the location of the broker-dealer's place of business. States exclude from the definition of broker-dealer those broker-dealers that:

- have no place of business in the state and deal exclusively with the issuers of the security involved in the transactions, other broker-dealers, and other financial institutions, such as banks, savings and loan associations, trust companies, insurance companies, investment companies, and pension or profit-sharing trusts; and

- have no place of business in the state, but are licensed in a state where they have a place of business, and offer and sell securities in the state only with persons in the state who are existing customers and who are not residents of the state. This is sometimes referred to as the *snowbird exemption* and applies as well to agents, investment advisers, and investment adviser representatives.

In other words, the USA excludes broker-dealers with no place of business in the state from the definition of a broker-dealer to allow those firms that deal exclusively with other financial institutions to engage in securities transactions in the state without registering. The reason for this exclusion is that the regulators understand that this category of investor has a high level of investment sophistication and expertise and does not need the same degree of protection as the so-called little guy.

The USA also allows broker-dealers to do business with existing customers who are temporarily in a state to avoid unnecessary multiple registrations. In most states, when an existing client legally changes residence to another state in which the broker-dealer (and/or the agent) is not registered, the firm (and/or agent) has 30 days during which it may continue to do business with that client without registration in the new state. Should it wish to continue to maintain that client, the broker-dealer (and/or agent) would have to register in that state.

As long as your client has not changed state of residence, there is no time limit. For example, many "snowbirds" spend the entire winter in Florida, which is no problem for the firms they do business with "up North." Or many people, after a couple of years in the workforce, decide to get an MBA. If they go out of state to a resident program for a year or two, that does not mean they've changed their state of residence, merely that they are not commuter students. Only when official residency is changed (new driver's license or voter registration) does the 30-day rule apply.

Notice how important language is here: If broker-dealers with no place of business in the state were defined as broker-dealers, they would be subject to state registration. But if such broker-dealers with no place of business in the state are not defined as broker-dealers, those broker-dealers are not subject to the registration requirements of that state. Language and definitions determine jurisdiction. If a person or entity is defined as a broker-dealer, that person is covered by (subject to) the provisions of the act. If a person or entity is excluded from a definition, that person is not subject to (covered by) the act.

TAKE NOTE

Under the USA, you are a broker-dealer if:

1. you have a place of business in the state

2. you have even 1 retail client in the state

Under the USA, you are *not* a broker-dealer if:

1. you have no place of business in the state AND

2. your only clients are: other BDs, institutions, and issuers of the security involved in the transaction

2. 3. 1. 1. 2   *Using the Internet*

Another example that has recently been addressed by NASAA is broker-dealers and investment advisers using the internet. A firm's website, considered advertising, can be seen everywhere. Does that mean the firm has a place of business in the state? Without getting too technical, there are several requirements to insure that the person is not deemed to be in the state.

■ The communication clearly states that the person may only do business in this state if properly registered or exempt from registration.

■ Any follow-up individualized responses with prospects in this state that involve either the effecting or attempting to effect transactions in securities, or the rendering of personalized investment advice for compensation, as may be, will not be made without compliance with state broker-dealer, investment adviser, agent or IA representative registration requirements, or an applicable exemption or exclusion.

■ The site may only make available general information, not specific advice or recommendations.

■ In the case of an agent or IAR

— the affiliation with the broker-dealer or investment adviser of the agent or IAR is prominently disclosed within the Communication,

— the broker-dealer or investment adviser with whom the agent or IAR is associated retains responsibility for reviewing and approving the content of any internet communication by an agent or IAR,

— the broker-dealer or investment adviser with whom the agent or IAR is associated first authorizes the distribution of information on the particular products and services through the internet communication, and

— in disseminating information through the internet communication, the agent or IAR acts within the scope of the authority granted by the broker-dealer or investment adviser.

What this basically means is that if you just generally advertise on the internet, you don't have to be registered in the state. BUT, if you follow-up with advice (IAR) or offering securities (agent), you either have to register or find some kind of exemption.

TEST TOPIC ALERT

The exam focuses more on the exclusions from the definition of broker-dealer than on the definition itself. Know these exclusions well.

CASE STUDY

Exclusion from the Definition of Broker-Dealer

Situation: First Securities Corporation is a registered broker-dealer with offices in Illinois. Mr. Thompson, a registered agent in the Illinois office of First Securities, recommends the purchase of ABC Shoes stock to his customer, Mr. Bixby, an Illinois resident, who is temporarily on vacation in Hawaii. Mr. Bixby agrees to the purchase of ABC Shoes, as well as other securities, while in Hawaii.

The Hawaiian state securities Administrator does not issue a cease and desist order against First Securities for unlawfully selling securities as an unregistered broker-dealer in Hawaii.

Analysis: The Hawaiian securities Administrator acted correctly by not issuing a cease and desist order against First Securities. Under the USA, First Securities is not required to register as a broker-dealer in Hawaii because it limits its business to an existing customer, Mr. Bixby, who is temporarily in the state. Because First Securities is properly registered in Illinois, it need not register in Hawaii, provided, of course, Mr. Bixby does not take up permanent residence there. In this case, First Securities does not fall under the definition of broker-dealer in Hawaii because it does not do business in Hawaii other than with one existing customer temporarily in the state. In this situation, First Securities is not defined as a broker-dealer in the state of Hawaii and therefore does not have to register as a broker-dealer in Hawaii. Definitions determine jurisdiction.

2. 3. 1. 2   Broker-Dealer Registration Requirements

Under the USA, if a person is included in the definition of a broker-dealer, that person must register as a broker-dealer in the states where it does business. The USA is clear about broker-dealer registration. It states, "It is unlawful for any person to transact business in this state as a broker-dealer . . . unless he is registered under this Act."

This means every person (legal entity) that falls within the definition of a broker-dealer must register with the Administrator of the state. Again, keep in mind that if a person falls under one of the exclusions from the definition, that person or legal entity does not have to register in the state.

In most jurisdictions, registration is accomplished by filing the SEC's Form BD modified to meet the needs of the state. If any material information on the BD becomes inaccurate, *prompt* notice must be given to the Administrator.

TAKE NOTE

In addition, at the time of registration of a broker-dealer, any partner, officer, or director of the broker-dealer who is active in the broker-dealer's securities business, is automatically registered as an agent of the broker-dealer. This does not mean that the individual doesn't have to take an exam. It just means that when a new broker-dealer is organized or an existing broker-dealer registers in a state for the first time, these individuals submit information on the BD's application that enables the Administrator to determine their eligibility for registration so a separate application does not have to be filed. It is also important to note that, unlike FINRA, there is no separate principal registration category for those in supervisory positions—they are all agents.

CASE STUDY

Who Is a Broker-Dealer?

Situation: First Securities Corporation of Illinois, (FSCI), sells municipal bonds and equity securities to both the general public and other securities firms. FSCI sells many of its municipal bonds to its biggest customer, Indiana Institutional Services, Inc., (IISI), a broker-dealer located in Indiana. IISI has no offices in Illinois and limits its business to banks and insurance companies.

First Securities Corporation discovers that Indiana Institutional Services is not registered in Illinois. The president of First Securities Corporation asks the president of IISI why his firm is not registered in Illinois. The president of IISI answers that it is because they are not broker-dealers in Illinois. The president of FSCI is baffled—it appears to him that IISI is indeed a broker-dealer.

Analysis: First Securities Corporation sells both exempt securities (municipal bonds) and nonexempt securities (equities) to the general public and to other broker-dealers. First Securities is a broker-dealer because it is a legal entity with a place of business in the state that effects securities transactions for itself and for the accounts of others and so must register in Illinois.

Like First Securities, IISI conducts broker-dealer activities. However, in Illinois it confines the business to transactions between itself and institutional clients. The USA specifically excludes from the definition of *broker-dealer* out-of-state broker-dealers who deal exclusively with institutions and have no place of business in the state.

Although IISI is, in fact, conducting operations of a broker-dealer in Illinois, it does not meet the definition as stated in the USA and, therefore, is not subject to registration with the Illinois securities Administrator. If IISI were located or had an office in Illinois, it would be a broker-dealer by definition and have to register as such in Illinois.

What about the Indiana Administrator? Which of the firms must register? Even though IISI only does business with institutions , because it has an office in the state of Indiana, it would meet the definition of broker-dealer and would have to register as such. What about First Securities? Well, it depends on several factors we haven't been told. Does First Securities maintain an office in Indiana? If it does, registration is required. If it doesn't and the only securities business it does is with other broker-dealers and financial institutions, then it does not have to register in Indiana. However, if any of its clients are individuals (sometimes called retail clients on the exam), then registration is required.

2. 3. 1. 3   Financial Requirements

The Administrator may establish **net capital requirements** for broker-dealers. Think of net capital as the broker-dealer's liquid net worth. Net capital requirements of the states may not exceed those required by federal law, in this case, the Securities Exchange Act of 1934. The Administrator of a state may, however, require those broker-dealers that have custody of, or discretionary authority over, clients' funds or securities to post **surety bonds**. Just as with net capital, the amount of surety bonds required by the states is limited to the amount set by the Securities Exchange Act of 1934. No bond may be required of any broker-dealer whose net capital exceeds the amounts required by the Administrator.

The NSMIA amended the Securities Exchange Act of 1934 to add section 15(h)(1) which reads as follows:

"No law, rule, regulation, or order, or other administrative action of any State or political subdivision thereof shall establish capital, custody, financial responsibility, making and keeping records, bonding, or financial or operational reporting require-ments for broker-dealers, that differ from, or are in addition to, the requirements in those areas established under the Exchange Act."

Stated simply, when it comes to broker-dealers, regardless of how many states in which they are registered, other than enforcing anti-fraud statutes, the Administrator has relin-quished most control to the SEC.

TEST TOPIC ALERT

You will have to know that broker-dealers who meet the SEC's net capital or bonding requirements cannot be required to meet higher ones in any state in which they do business.

TEST TOPIC ALERT

In lieu of a surety bond, the Administrator will accept deposits of cash or securities.

QUICK QUIZ 2.B

True or False?

_____ 1. In general, a person who effects transactions in securities for itself or for the account of others in the course of business must register in the state as a broker-dealer.

_____ 2. Under the Uniform Securities Act, an out-of-state firm that transacts business with an established customer who is on vacation is not considered a broker-dealer in the state in which the customer is on vacation.

_____ 3. A person not defined as a broker-dealer in the state under the USA need not register as such.

_____ 4. A broker-dealer registered with the SEC and several states must meet the net capital standard of the state with the most stringent requirements.

5. Under the Uniform Securities Act, a broker-dealer is defined as any person who

A. buys securities
B. sells securities
C. is in the business of effecting securities transactions for its own account or for the accounts of others
D. is registered with the SEC

2. 3. 2   AGENT

The USA defines an **agent** as any individual who represents a broker-dealer (legal entity) or an issuer (legal entity) in effecting (or attempting to effect) transactions in securities.

Agents are individuals in a sales capacity who represent broker-dealers or issuers of securities. As agents, they act, usually on a commission basis, on behalf of others. Other than on this exam, agents are often referred to as **registered representatives**, whether they sell registered securities or securities exempt from registration.

The use of the term _individual_ here is important. Only an individual, or a natural person, can be an agent. A corporation, such as a brokerage firm, is not a natural person—it is a legal entity. The brokerage firm is the legal person (legal entity) that the agent (natural person) represents in securities transactions.

2. 3. 2. 1   Exclusions from Definition of Agent for Administrative Personnel

Clerical and administrative (sometimes referred to as _ministerial_) employees of a broker-dealer are generally not included in the definition of agent and, therefore, are not required to be registered. The logic for this exclusion from the definition should again be obvious. Clerical and administrative employees do not effect securities transactions with the public. They attend to the administration of the broker-dealer as a business organization. Under these circumstances, they are like employees of any other corporation. In fact, if the broker-dealer they work for wishes to pay their employees, including this group, a year-end bonus based on company profits (not related to any individual's sales efforts), it would be allowable.

The situation changes when administrative personnel take on securities-related functions. When they do so, they lose their exemption and must register as an agent.

TAKE NOTE

Secretaries and sales assistants (known as ministerial personnel) are not agents if their activities are confined to administrative activities, including responding to an existing client's request for a quote. However, if secretaries or sales assistants accept customer transactions or take orders over the phone, they are engaging in securities transactions and are subject to registration as agents.

TEST TOPIC ALERT

Cold callers working for a broker-dealer would have to register as an agent if they did any more than ask if clients wanted to receive information. For example, if they prequalified clients or suggested ways to receive more money for their stocks or bonds, they would have to register as agents.

As is customary in other industries, broker-dealers frequently hire summer interns. If these interns received any selling related compensation, such as $10 for each existing client solicited, they would be considered agents and would have to register.

2. 3. 2. 2   Exclusions from the Definition of Agent for Personnel Representing Issuers

In many cases, individuals who represent issuers of securities are agents and therefore must register as such in the states in which they sell the issuers' securities. When does something like this occur? In many cases, a local company is looking to raise some additional capital—something in the range of several million dollars. Instead of going through the normal investment banking procedure (and paying all of those fees and commissions to the investment bankers), the company (known under the USA as the issuer) either uses its own employees or hires an outside sales force to sell the new security. However, individuals are excluded from the definition of agent and, therefore, are exempt from registration in a state when representing issuers in effecting transactions:

■ in certain exempt securities;

■ exempt from registration; or

■ with existing employees, partners, or directors of the issuer if no sales-related commission or other remuneration is paid or given directly or indirectly for soliciting any person in this state.

2. 3. 2. 2. 1   Effecting Transactions in Exempt Securities

Securities exempt from registration are called **exempt securities**. Although there are almost a dozen different securities that qualify for exemption under the Uniform Securities Act (they will be discussed later in this session), an individual is excluded from the term *agent* only when that individual represents an issuer in effecting transactions for the following five exempt securities:

- Any security issued or guaranteed by the United States, any state, any political subdivision of a state, or any agency of one or more of these or any security issued or guaranteed by Canada, any Canadian province, or any political subdivision of any such province
- Securities of governments with which the United States has diplomatic relationships
- Any security issued by, or guaranteed by, any bank organized under the laws of the United States, or any bank, savings institution, or trust company organized and supervised under the laws of any state
- Commercial paper rated in the top three categories by the major rating agencies with denominations of $50,000 or more with maturities of nine months or less
- Investment contracts issued in connection with employee's stock purchase, savings, pensions, or profit-sharing plans

2. 3. 2. 2. 2   Effecting Exempt Transactions

An employee of an issuer is not an agent when representing an issuer in exempt transactions. Transactions exempt from registration are called **exempt transactions**. Some examples are:

- unsolicited brokerage transactions;
- transactions between the issuer and underwriters;
- transactions with financial institutions; or
- private placements.

Exempt securities and exempt transactions will be covered in thorough detail later in this session.

TAKE NOTE

An employee of an issuer is not an agent when representing an issuer if the issue is exempt from registration, as long as it is one of the five listed above. Additionally, the employee is not an agent when representing an issuer in exempt transactions (e.g., transactions between an underwriter and issuer).

TAKE NOTE

Keep in mind that an individual who works for an issuer of securities is excluded from the definition of agent when engaging in transactions with employees involving the issuer's securities, provided that the individual is not compensated for such participation by commissions or other remuneration based either directly or indirectly on the amount of securities sold. In other words, salaried employees engaged in distributing their employers' shares as part of an employee benefit plan would not be required to register as agents because they are, by definition, excluded from the definition. If such employees were compensated on the basis of the number of shares sold, they would be defined as agents and therefore would be subject to registration.

TEST TOPIC ALERT

Individuals representing *broker-dealers* in a sales capacity must register as agents whether they sell registered securities or securities exempt from registration.

2. 3. 2. 3   Agent Registration Requirements

The registration requirements for an agent that is not exempt are similar to those for a broker-dealer. An application, generally the Form U-4, must be completed. One thing, however, that is on the agent's application that does not apply to a broker-dealer is disclosing *citizenship*.

The USA states, "It is unlawful for any person to transact business in this state as an agent unless he is registered under this act." In other words, an individual may not conduct securities transactions in a state unless that person is properly registered in the state where he conducts business. This is true even when receiving unsolicited orders. If an agent does business in a state, she must be registered in that state, even if there is only one client. This is not like investment advisers and their representatives who, as we will learn in the next session, enjoy a de minimis exemption. Furthermore, the act makes it unlawful for any broker-dealer or issuer to employ an agent unless the agent is registered.

So, what can an individual who has been hired to become an agent of a broker-dealer do while registration is pending? After all, one does not fill out the Form U-4 and become an agent immediately. Permitted activities would be those allowed to any other employee of the broker-dealer who is not required to be registered. That would include clerical functions, such as posting trade details to client accounts, or administrative activities, like assisting with research. As long as it does not involve customer contact relating to selling/offering securities or opening accounts, these "newbies" can hang around the office and try to make themselves useful. Of course, most of their time should be spent preparing to pass the exam.

An agent's registration is not effective during any period when the agent is not associated with a broker-dealer registered in the state. Therefore, if the broker-dealer's registration is terminated, the agent is no longer considered licensed. The terminology depends on the specific state. In some cases, the agent's license is placed in *suspense*. In other states, it is put on *hold* or some such similar language. Whatever the phrase, when the broker-dealer closes up shop, either voluntarily or involuntarily (think revocation of registration by the Administrator), the agent cannot function because there is no broker-dealer affiliation. When an agent begins or terminates a connection with a broker-dealer or issuer, or begins or terminates those activities that make him an agent, the agent and the broker-dealer or issuer must promptly notify the Administrator.

When an agent shifts employment from one broker-dealer or issuer to another, all three persons—the agent, the old employer, and the new employer—must promptly notify the Administrator.

2. 3. 2. 4   Financial Requirements

There are no financial requirements, or **net worth requirements**, to register as an agent. The Administrator may, however, require an agent to be bonded, particularly if the agent has discretion over a client's account.

CASE STUDY   **Agent as Defined by the USA**

Situation: The City of Chicago issues bonds for the maintenance of local recreational facilities. Purchasers have two choices: they can purchase the bonds directly from the city through Ms. Stith (an employee of the city responsible for selling the bonds), or they can purchase them from Mr. Thompson (an employee of First Securities Corporation of Chicago). Neither Ms. Stith nor Mr. Thompson charges a commission, although First Securities is remunerated with an underwriting fee.

Analysis: The City of Chicago is an issuer of exempt securities (municipal bonds). Ms. Stith, as an employee of the issuer (City of Chicago), is not an agent as defined in the USA because she is representing the issuer in the sale of an exempt security. Therefore, Stith does not need to register as an agent with the Administrator of Illinois. However, Thompson, as a representative of First Securities, must register with the Administrator because he represents a broker-dealer in effecting securities transactions in the state. Representatives (agents of broker-dealers) must register in the states where they sell securities.

Exemptions from registration as an agent generally apply to representatives of issuers, rather than to representatives of broker-dealers.

2. 3. 2. 5   Multiple Registrations

An individual may not act at any one time as an agent for more than one broker-dealer or for more than one issuer, unless the broker-dealers or issuers for whom the agent acts are affiliated by direct or indirect common control or the Administrator grants an exception. In the event an agent does wish to affiliate with a second broker-dealer, the agent would have to go through the registration process with the second firm in the same manner as the original application (filing another Form U-4).

2. 3. 2. 6   Limited Registration of Canadian Broker-dealers and Agents

Provided the limited registration requirements enumerated below are met, a broker-dealer domiciled in Canada that has no office in this state may effect transactions in securities with or for, or attempt to induce the purchase or sale of any security by:

- a person from Canada who is temporarily a resident in this state who was already a client of the broker-dealer; or
- a person from Canada who is a resident in this state, whose transaction is in a self-directed, tax-advantaged retirement plan in Canada of which the person is the holder or contributor. In Canada, the equivalent of an IRA is called a Registered Retirement Savings Plan (RRSP).

An agent who will be representing a Canadian broker-dealer who registers under these provisions may effect transactions in securities in this state on the same basis as permitted for the broker-dealer.

For the Canadian broker-dealer to register in this fashion, it must:

- file an application in the form required by the jurisdiction where it has its principal office in Canada;
- file a consent to service of process;
- provide evidence that it is registered in good standing in its home jurisdiction; and
- be a member of an SRO or stock exchange in Canada.

Requirements for agents are the same, except that membership in an SRO or stock exchange is not relevant.

However, just as with domestic broker-dealers, if there is no place of business in the state, there are no registration requirements if the only securities transactions are with issuers, other broker-dealers, and institutional clients.

TAKE NOTE   Renewal applications for Canadian broker-dealers and agents who file for limited registration must be filed before December 1 each year.

QUICK QUIZ 2.C   Here are examples of questions you might see on the exam:

1. Under the Uniform Securities Act, the term *agent* would include an individual who represents an issuer in effecting non-exempt transactions in

    A.   a city of Montreal general obligation bond
    B.   common stock offered by a commercial bank
    C.   a New Jersey Turnpike Revenue bond
    D.   non-exempt securities

2.   Under the Uniform Securities Act, the term *agent* would include
   A.   an individual who represents an issuer in an exempt transaction
   B.   an individual who represents a broker-dealer in a transaction in an exempt security
   C.   a receptionist for a broker-dealer who directs calls for trade information to the appropriate individual
   D.   the vice president of personnel for a national brokerage firm

Write A if the person is an agent and B if not.

_____   3.   Person who effects transactions in municipal securities on behalf of a broker-dealer

_____   4.   An agent's salaried secretary who takes orders

_____   5.   An employee of a bank that is issuing shares who receives a commission for selling the bank's securities

_____   6.   An individual who represents her nonexempt employer in the sale of its securities to existing employees for a commission

_____   7.   A person who represents an issuer in effecting transactions with underwriters

8.   Under the Uniform Securities Act, an individual licensed as an agent by the state may NOT
   A.   simultaneously represent two different unrelated broker-dealers in the same transaction
   B.   be licensed by both an independent insurance company and a securities broker-dealer
   C.   be registered with two broker-dealers under common control
   D.   be registered with a licensed real estate broker as well as with a licensed securities broker-dealer

2. 3. 3   INVESTMENT ADVISER

Under the USA, an **investment adviser** is defined as any person who, for compensation and as part of a regular business, engages in the business of advising others as to the value of securities or as to the advisability of investing in or selling them. The advice can be delivered in person, through publications or writings, or through research reports concerning securities.

Advice given on investments not defined as securities, such as rare coins, art, and real estate, is not investment advice covered by the USA or other securities legislation. As a result, persons providing such advice are not investment advisers. Again, definitions are crucial for determining whether an activity is subject to securities law or not.

To be an investment adviser under both state and federal securities law, a pe;rson must:

■   provide advice about securities (not about jewelry, rare coins, or real estate);

■   provide that advice as part of an ongoing business (hang out a shingle and have an office for conducting business); and

■   receive compensation (actually get paid for the advice).

TAKE NOTE

In most cases, investment advisers are legal persons—that is, partnerships or corporations that provide investment advice or portfolio management services on an ongoing basis. Investment adviser representatives work for investment advisers, just as registered agents work for a broker-dealer. An individual can be an investment adviser if he operates as a sole proprietorship and is registered as both an investment adviser and the only investment adviser representative of the business.

2. 3. 3. 1   Investment Adviser Representative

An **investment adviser representative** is any individual who represents a state-registered investment adviser or federal covered investment adviser performing duties related to the giving of or soliciting for advisory services.

TAKE NOTE

The subject of investment advisers and their representatives will be covered in greater detail in the next session.

In our many years of preparing applicants for this exam, one thing we have observed is that many students do not have a clear idea of the difference between a broker-dealer and an investment adviser and, similarly, between an agent and an investment adviser representative. Perhaps the following will help:

Broker-dealer	Investment Adviser
■ Primary business function is executing transactions in securities ■ Compensation is earned in the form of commissions and markups (markdowns)	■ Primary business function is giving advice ■ Compensation is earned in the form of fees or other charges, generally based on the amount of assets managed
Agents	**IARs**
■ Individuals employed by brokers/dealers to handle their customer orders to buy or sell securities ■ Separate function from an IAR (although many in large firms wear both hats)	■ Individuals employed by investment advisers to give advice to their clients ■ After an IAR advises a client about a specific security, the next step is to contact the broker-dealer where that client maintains a brokerage account to give the buy/sell order to an agent

TAKE NOTE
Broker-dealers and investment advisers perform two separate functions (although many large firms do wear both hats): that of giving the advice and then executing the transaction.

2. 4   GENERAL REGISTRATION PROCEDURES

Any person who meets the definition of broker-dealer, agent, investment adviser, or investment adviser representative must register with the state. To register with the state securities Administrator, a person must:

- submit an application;
- provide a consent to service of process;
- pay filing fees;
- post a bond (if required by the Administrator); and
- take and pass an examination if required by the Administrator. The examination may be written, oral, or both.

2. 4. 1   SUBMITTING AN APPLICATION

All persons must complete and submit an **initial application** (as well as renewals) to the state securities Administrator. The application must contain whatever information the Administrator may require by rule, and may include:

- form and place of business (broker-dealers and investment advisers);
- proposed method of doing business;
- a list of all jurisdictions in which the applicant is registering (or already registered);
- qualifications and business history (broker-dealers and investment advisers must include the qualifications and history of partners, officers, directors, and other persons with controlling influence over the organization);
- court-issued injunctions and administrative orders;
- adjudications by the SEC or any securities SRO within the past 10 years;
- convictions of misdemeanors involving a security or any aspect of the securities business;
- felony convictions, whether securities related or not;
- financial condition and history (broker-dealers and investment advisers only, but only of the firm—no credit reports on the officers);
- any information to be furnished or disseminated to any client or prospective client, if the applicant is an investment adviser; and
- in the case of an individual registrant (agent or investment adviser representative), citizenship information.

The Administrator also may require that an applicant publish an announcement of the registration in one or more newspapers in the state.

TEST TOPIC ALERT

Please note that, unlike FINRA (NASD) registration requirements, fingerprints do not have to be submitted.

TAKE NOTE

If an agent terminates employment with a broker-dealer, both parties must notify the Administrator promptly. If an agent terminates employment with one broker-dealer to join another broker-dealer, all three parties must notify the Administrator. One way to remember this is that in the case of an agent, the first letter, **A**, tells us that **A**ll the parties involved must notify the Administrator.

2. 4. 2 PROVIDE A CONSENT TO SERVICE OF PROCESS

New applicants for registration must provide the Administrator of every state in which they intend to register with a **consent to service of process**. The consent to service of process appoints the Administrator as the applicant's attorney to receive and process non-criminal securities-related complaints against the applicant. Under the consent to service of process, all legal documents (e.g., subpoenas or warrants) received by the Administrator have the same legal effect as if they had been served personally on the applicant.

TAKE NOTE

The consent to service of process is submitted with the initial application and remains in force permanently. It does not need to be supplied with each renewal of a registration.

TEST TOPIC ALERT

If a securities professional is registering in six states, the Administrator of each state must receive a consent to service of process.

2. 4. 3 PAYMENT OF INITIAL AND RENEWAL FILING FEES

States require **filing fees** for initial applications as well as for renewal applications. If an application is withdrawn or denied, the Administrator is entitled to retain a portion of the fee. Filing fees for broker-dealers, investment advisers, and their representatives need not be identical. A registered broker-dealer, covered adviser, or state registered investment adviser may file an application for registration of a successor, whether or not the successor is then in existence, for the unexpired portion of the year. There is no filing or registration fee until renewal of the firm's license, but the successor firm would have to file a new consent to service of process.

The renewal date for all registrations is December 31, and there is no proration of fees.

TEST TOPIC ALERT

One of the tricks the exam likes to play is asking about a person who registers in November. When does that registration come up for renewal? Well, even if it is only a month or so later, every registration of a securities professional comes up for renewal on the NEXT December 31, so your first year is always a short one.

2. 4. 4   EFFECTIVENESS OF REGISTRATION

Unless a legal proceeding is instituted or the applicant is notified that the application is incomplete, the license of a broker-dealer, agent, investment adviser, or investment adviser representative becomes effective at noon, 30 days after the later of the date an application for licensing is filed and is complete or the date an amendment to an application is filed and is complete. An application is complete when the applicant has furnished information responsive to each applicable item of the application. The Administrator will notify the employing firm of effectiveness, and they will tell the new registrants when they are "good to go." By rule or by order, the Administrator may authorize an earlier effective date of licensing. In other words, there could be an occasion where, in effect, a person was the subject of a rush order.

In the same manner as a registration becomes effective on the 30th day after application, a request to withdraw registration also becomes effective on the 30th day after submission. However, should there be any legal proceedings in progress, the withdrawal will be held up until resolution of the issue. In any event, once withdrawal has taken place, the Administrator has jurisdiction of the former registrant for a period of one year.

TEST TOPIC ALERT

Although withdrawal of registration normally takes 30 days, the Administrator has the power to shorten that period, in effect permitting a rush order.

TEST TOPIC ALERT

Although successful completion of the Series 65 examination may satisfy a portion of the requirements of a particular state, it does not convey the right to transact business prior to being granted a license or registration by that state.

TEST TOPIC ALERT

While registration as an agent (or IAR) is pending, the individual may not take part in any activity that would require registration. Clerical work (filing customer records) or assisting internally with research would be permitted.

True or False?

_____ 1. A consent to service of process must be submitted with each renewal application.

_____ 2. A Canadian broker-dealer, properly registered with the Administrator of the province in which he is headquartered and with no office in the state, may do business with his customers who are on a skiing vacation in Vail without registering with the Colorado Administrator.

_____ 3. When a securities professional registers in a state, he must provide the state Administrator with a list of all the states where he intends to register.

4. According to the Uniform Securities Act, a consent to service of process must accompany which of the following?

   I. Agent's initial registration application
   II. Civil complaint against a broker-dealer
   III. Broker-dealer's initial registration application
   IV. A cease and desist order
   A. I and III
   B. I and IV
   C. II and III
   D. II and IV

2. 4. 5   POSTREGISTRATION REQUIREMENTS

Once registered, broker-dealers are subject to numerous administrative requirements to keep their registrations current and in good order.

2. 4. 5. 1   Books and Records

Every registered broker-dealer must make and keep such accounts, blotters (records of original entry), correspondence (including emails), memoranda, papers, books, and other records as the state Administrator by rule prescribes. All records so required must be preserved for three years (the first two years easily accessible in the principal office) unless the Administrator specifies otherwise. These records must be current, complete, and accurate. Broker-dealers are obligated to promptly file correcting amendments. State securities Administrators cannot impose recordkeeping requirements that are in excess of those prescribed by the SEC.

The records broker-dealers are required to maintain are subject to periodic, special, or other examinations by representatives of the Administrator of the state where the broker-dealer's principal office is located or of any other state in which the broker-dealer is registered as the Administrator deems necessary or appropriate in the public interest.

If the information contained in any document filed with the Administrator is or becomes inaccurate or incomplete in any material respect, the registrant must file a correcting amendment *promptly*.

TEST TOPIC ALERT   Included in the recordkeeping requirements are electronic communications, particularly emails. However, it is not required to maintain emails of a personal nature sent to non-clients (e.g., "Honey, I'm stuck at the office and will be late for dinner").

2. 4. 5. 1. 1   *Website Storage*

Websites are treated as would be any other advertisement. So, the original site design is kept for three years and, whenever revised, the new copy is maintained and starts a new retention requirement for that copy. Therefore, you will likely have several different versions in your advertising file at the same time.

TEST TOPIC ALERT   Although it is required to keep all records relating to customers, there are no requirements to keep copies of their tax returns.

2. 5   WHAT IS A SECURITY UNDER THE UNIFORM SECURITIES ACT?

Perhaps the most important term in the USA is the term *security*. Why is it so important? The reason is simple: the USA applies only to those financial instruments that are securities. The purchase, sale, or issuance of anything that is not a security is not covered by the act. The definition of a security, however, is complex. Over the years, courts have determined case by case what constitutes a security. The U.S. Supreme Court, in the Howey decision, defined the primary characteristics of what constitutes a security. For an instrument to be a security, the court held, it must constitute (1) an investment of money, (2) in a common enterprise, (3) with the expectation of profits, (4) to be derived primarily from the efforts of a person other than the investor. A **common enterprise** means an enterprise in which the fortunes of the investor are interwoven with those of either the person offering the investment, a third party, or other investors.

TAKE NOTE   If you think about it, the Howey decision sounds very much like it is describing a mutual fund or other pooled investment vehicle.

2. 5. 1   LIST OF SECURITIES UNDER THE UNIFORM SECURITIES ACT

The USA does not define the term but provides a comprehensive list of financial instruments that are securities under the act and therefore covered by its provisions. Under the USA, *securities* include:

- notes;
- stocks;

- treasury stocks;

- bonds;

- debentures;

- evidence of indebtedness;

- certificates of interest or participation in a profit-sharing agreement;

- collateral trust certificates;

- preorganization certificates or subscriptions;

- transferable shares;

- investment contracts;

- voting trust certificates;

- certificates of deposit for a security;

- certificate of interest or participation in an oil, gas, or mining title or lease;

- puts, calls, straddles, options, or privileges on a security;

- any interest or instrument commonly known as a security; or

- certificates of interest or participation in, receipts of, guarantees of, or warrants or rights to subscribe to or purchase, any of the above.

The following six items are not securities under the act:

- An insurance or endowment policy or annuity contract under which an insurance company promises to pay a fixed sum of money either in a lump sum or periodically (this is basically any product from a life insurance company that does not use the word "variable")

- Interest in a retirement plan, such as an IRA or Keogh plan

- Collectibles

- Commodities such as precious metals and grains, including futures contracts

- Condominiums used as a personal residence

- Currency

TEST TOPIC ALERT   The exam will want you to know what is and what is not a security. We suggest that you concentrate on learning the six that are NOT securities because they are much easier to remember, and you will still be able to answer the questions correctly.

2. 5. 1. 1   Nonsecurity Investments

Although collectibles, fixed annuities, precious metals, grains, real estate, and currencies can be attractive investments, they are not securities. Because these items are not securities, their sale is not regulated by state securities law. Furthermore, if a registered agent commits fraud in the sale of any of these items, he has not committed a violation of any state securities law. He has violated the antifraud provisions of another act prohibiting fraudulent commercial transactions.

EXAMPLE

An individual farmer's direct ownership of a cow is not a security—it is just ownership of a cow. However, if the farmer makes an investment of money in a tradable interest in a herd of cattle, on which he expects to earn a profit solely as the result of the breeder's efforts, he has purchased a security. In the same manner, if a condominium is purchased in a resort area with the goal of renting it out most of the year, and it is used only for personal vacation time, the condo is considered a security because there is a profit motive, typically reliant on the efforts of a third party—the rental agent. On the other hand, if you have chosen to live in a condominium as a personal residence, that's a home, not a security.

TAKE NOTE

Annuities with fixed payouts are not securities, but variable annuities are because they are dependent on the investment performance of securities within the annuity.

2. 5. 2   NONEXEMPT SECURITY

A nonexempt security is a security subject to the registration provisions mandated by the USA. *Exempt* means not subject to registration. Therefore, unless the nonexempt security is registered, it may not be sold in a state unless it is sold in an exempt transaction (more about that in the following). As you will see, the sale of an unregistered nonexempt security is a prohibited practice under the USA and may subject an agent to civil and possibly criminal penalties.

TAKE NOTE

The methods of registration discussed in this session refer to nonexempt securities. Think of what the legal terms actually mean in everyday usage. For example, a registered nonexempt security is most likely a common stock properly registered for sale in a state.

2. 5. 3   ISSUER

An **issuer** is any person who issues (distributes) or proposes to issue a security. The most common issuers of securities are companies or governments (federal, state, and municipal governments and their agencies and subdivisions). However, under the USA, with respect to certificates of interest; participation in oil, gas, or mining titles or leases; or in payments out of production under such titles or leases, there is not considered to be any issuer.

If an issuer is nonexempt, it must generally register its securities in the states where they will be sold under one of the registration methods described in the session.

ABC Shoe Co. (a retail chain store) issues shares to the public. Mr. Bixby (an investor) buys the shares through his broker, Mr. Thompson, at First Securities Corporation. ABC Shoe is the issuer; Mr. Bixby is the investor; First Securities is the broker-dealer; and Mr. Thompson is the registered representative, known under the USA as an agent.

2. 5. 3. 1   Issuer Transaction

An **issuer transaction** is one in which the proceeds of the sale go to the issuer. All newly issued securities are issuer transactions. In other words, when a company raises money by selling (issuing) securities to investors, the proceeds from the sale go to the company itself.

2. 5. 3. 2   Nonissuer Transaction

A **nonissuer transaction** is one in which the proceeds of the sales do not go, directly or indirectly, to the entity that originally offered the securities to the public. The most common instance of this is everyday trading on exchanges such as the New York Stock Exchange or Nasdaq. In a nonissuer transaction, the proceeds of the sale go to the investor who sold the shares. Because the shares are not new, we refer to this as *secondary trading*.

T A K E   N O T E   If Mr. Bixby, an investor, sells 100 shares of stock he owns in ABC Shoe Co. (the securities issuer) on the New York Stock Exchange (NYSE), Mr. Bixby receives the proceeds from the sale, not ABC Shoes. This is a nonissuer transaction.

Nonissuer transactions are also referred to as **secondary transactions** or transactions between investors.

2. 5. 4   INITIAL OR PRIMARY OFFERING

An issuer transaction involving new securities is called a **primary offering**. If it is the first time an issuer distributes securities to the public, it is called an **initial public offering (IPO)**. Any subsequent issuance of new shares to the public is called an **SPO (subsequent public offering)** or APO (additional public offering). All primary offerings, IPOs and SPOs, are issuer transactions because the issuer (the company) receives the proceeds from the investor investing in the company.

E X A M P L E   The first time that ABC Shoe Co. issued shares to the public, ABC Shoe engaged in an IPO or a primary offering because it received the proceeds from distributing its shares to the public. After ABC Shoe went public, transactions between investors executed on exchanges through brokerage agents were secondary transactions in nonissuer securities.

TEST TOPIC ALERT   When investors purchase shares of an open-end investment company (mutual fund), that is always an issuer transaction because the fund is continuously offering new shares. However, when the investment company sells shares out of its portfolio, that is a nonissuer transaction in the secondary markets.

QUICK QUIZ 2.E

1. Which list of instruments below is NOT composed of securities?

    A. Stock, treasury stock, rights, warrants, and transferable shares
    B. Voting trust certificates and interests in oil and gas drilling programs
    C. Commodity futures contracts and fixed payment life insurance contracts
    D. Options on securities and interests in multilevel distributorship arrangements

2. The U.S. Supreme Court defined an investment contract as having four components. Which of the following is NOT part of the four-part test for an investment contract?

    A. An investment of money
    B. An expectation of profit
    C. Management activity by owner
    D. Solely from the efforts of others

3. Nonexempt securities

    A. need not be registered in the state in which they are sold
    B. must always be registered in the state in which they are sold
    C. need not be registered if sold in an exempt transaction
    D. need not be registered if sold in a nonexempt transaction

4. A nonissuer transaction is a transaction

    A. between two corporations where one is issuing the stock and the other is purchasing
    B. in which the issuer of the security will not receive the proceeds from the transaction
    C. where a mutual fund purchases a Treasury bond directly from the government
    D. where registration is always required

5. Prompt notification to the Administrator must be made when

    A. a federal covered adviser with a place of business in the state relocates that office to a different city in the state
    B. there is a change to the marital status of an agent
    C. a non-exempt issuer's dividend is reduced
    D. there is a material change to any information contained in a broker-dealer's application for registration that is on file with the state

2. 6 REGISTRATION OF SECURITIES UNDER THE UNIFORM SECURITIES ACT

Under the USA, it is unlawful for any person to offer or sell an unregistered security in a state unless (1) it is registered under the Act, (2) the security or transaction is exempted from registration under the Act, or (3) it is a federal covered security. If the security or transaction is not exempt or is not a federal covered security as defined by the National Securities Markets Improvement Act, it must be registered in the state or it cannot be lawfully sold in the state.

2. 6. 1 NATIONAL SECURITIES MARKETS IMPROVEMENT ACT OF 1996 (NSMIA)

We introduced you to the NSMIA in the previous session. This law effectively divided the responsibility for regulating investment advisers between the states and the SEC by creating the category of registration known as a federal covered adviser. We'll have more to say about that in the next session.

Of importance to this session, the NSMIA also created the term *federal covered security*, a security that was exempt from registration on the state level. State securities registration requirements were preempted with respect to federal covered securities. However, states may require Notice Filings, consisting of filing fees and copies of documents filed with the Securities and Exchange Commission (SEC), primarily in the case of registered investment companies.

2. 6. 2 CATEGORIES OF FEDERAL COVERED SECURITIES

The major categories of covered securities (securities covered by federal securities laws), which therefore cannot be regulated by state securities Administrators, include:

- securities issued by an open-end or closed-end investment company, unit investment trust, or face amount certificate company, that is registered under the Investment Company Act of 1940;

- securities listed on the New York Stock Exchange, the Chicago Stock Exchange, the Nasdaq Stock Market, and (not tested) several other U.S. exchanges [in addition, any security equal in seniority (rights or warrants) or senior to these securities (bonds and preferred stock) is also considered federal covered]; and

- securities offered pursuant to the provisions of **Rule 506(b)** or **506(c) of Regulation D** under the Securities Act of 1933 (qualifying under the private placement transaction exemption).

- most securities exempt from registration under the Securities Act of 1933 (you do not have to know the exceptions other than the one we're going to describe below). If the federal government says the security does not have to register, no state can overstep that. We know from the previous session that securities offered by a U.S. federal government issuer or a municipal issuer are exempt on the federal level (state as well, but that is not relevant to a discussion of a covered security). However, under the NSMIA, if the municipal issuer is located in the state in which the securities are being offered, that security is not considered a *federal covered security*.

Bonds issued by municipalities—for example, the City of New York bonds due 2030—are federal covered securities exempt from registration requirements in the states, but there is an exception to the rule.

Congress felt it unwise to impose upon the states. Even though municipal securities are exempt under the Uniform Securities Act, remember, the USA is only a template and a specific state theoretically could pass legislation removing the exemption from municipal bonds. That could only apply to bonds issued by municipalities of that state. If those securities were federal covered, the state could not do so. However, because municipal securities of other states are federal covered securities, the state cannot overrule federal law and take away their exemption.

EXAMPLE

A bond issued by the city of Columbus, OH, is a federal covered security everywhere but in the state of Ohio. The effect of this is that no state regulator can enforce any of their rules against the bond. But, in the state of Ohio, even though the security is exempt under Ohio's securities laws, the Administrator could request that the issuer (the city) furnish certain details about the issue.

TAKE NOTE

It is important to note that registering a security with the SEC does not automatically make it federal covered. Yes, that is true of investment companies and those securities listed on the exchanges and Nasdaq, but there are thousands of stocks registered with the SEC that trade on the OTC Bulletin Board or the OTC Link, formerly known as the Pink Sheets, and they are *not* federal covered. Furthermore, a security does not have to be registered with the SEC to be included in the definition of federal covered security. For example, U.S. government and municipal securities are federal covered securities and are exempt from registration with the SEC.

TAKE NOTE

Although investment company securities are federal covered securities, the Uniform Securities Act allows states to impose filing fees on them under a process called notice filing, as described below.

2.7 METHODS OF STATE REGISTRATION OF SECURITIES

The USA provides two methods for securities issuers to register their securities in a state, plus a special method for certain federal covered securities. They are:

■ notice filing;
■ coordination; and
■ qualification.

2. 7. 1 NOTICE FILING

As previously mentioned, the National Securities Markets Improvement Act of 1996 (NSMIA) designated certain securities as federal covered and, therefore, removed from the jurisdiction of the state regulatory authorities. Although the states are preempted from requiring registration for federal covered securities, status as a federal covered security is not a preemption of the licensing or anti-fraud laws. Any person that sells a federal covered security must be licensed as a broker-dealer or agent (unless otherwise exempted) and must also comply with the anti-fraud provisions of state laws.

The Uniform Securities Act gives the Administrator the authority to require notice filings with respect to federal covered securities, generally investment companies registered with the SEC under the Investment Company Act of 1940. So, what is this notice filing? Primarily, it is an opportunity for the states to collect revenue in the form of filing fees because, unlike with the two actual methods of registration we are going to discuss, the Administrator has limited powers to review any documentation filed with his department. The fees for notice filing are generally lower than for the two forms of registration.

Under the notice filing procedure, state Administrators may require the issuer of certain federal covered securities to file the following documents as a condition for sale of their securities in the state:

- Documents filed along with their registration statements filed with the SEC
- Documents filed as amendments to the initial federal registration statement
- A report as to the value of such securities offered in the state
- Consent to service of process

TEST TOPIC ALERT

Keep in mind the distinction between federal covered securities and SEC-registered securities. Under the NSMIA, federal covered securities are a narrowly defined group of securities that either trade on certain exchanges or are exempt from SEC registration. There are thousands of SEC-registered securities that do not meet the required standard, including those on the OTC Bulletin Board and the OTC Link of the OTC Markets Group Inc., formerly known as the *Pink Sheets*.

TEST TOPIC ALERT

Before the initial offer of any federal covered security in this state, the Administrator, by rule or order, may require the filing of all documents that are part of a federal registration statement filed with the U.S. Securities and Exchange Commission under the Securities Act of 1933, together with a consent to service of process signed by the issuer. However, unless there is an appearance of fraud, the Administrator does not have the power (because of lack of jurisdiction) to prevent the sale of a federal covered security in his state.

TEST TOPIC ALERT

Even though an issuer of a federal covered security (think about a Fortune 500 company listed on the NYSE) may not have to notice file, that does not mean that the company can make misrepresentations during an offer made in any state. To do so would violate the antifraud provisions of the USA.

2. 7. 2   REGISTRATION BY COORDINATION

The most common form of registration for those securities that are not federal covered (typically securities traded on the OTC Bulletin Board or the OTC Link) is coordination. A security may be **registered by coordination** if a registration statement has been filed under the Securities Act of 1933 in connection with the same offering.

In coordinating a federal registration with state registration, issuers must supply the following records in addition to the consent to service of process:

- Copies of the latest form of prospectus filed under the Securities Act of 1933, if the Administrator requires it

- Copy of articles of incorporation and bylaws, a copy of the underwriting agreement, or a specimen copy of the security

- If the Administrator requests, copies of any other information filed by the issuer under the Securities Act of 1933

- Each amendment to the federal prospectus promptly after it is filed with the SEC

2. 7. 2. 1   Effective Date

Registration by coordination becomes effective at the same time the federal registration becomes effective, provided:

- no stop orders have been issued by the Administrator and no proceedings are pending against the issuer;

- the registration has been on file for at least the minimum number of days specified by the Administrator, a number that currently ranges from 10 to 20 days, depending on the state; and

- a statement of the maximum and minimum offering prices and underwriting discounts have been on file for two business days.

Registration by coordination is by far the most frequently used method and, from a practical standpoint, is the only sensible way to register a multi-state offering.

2. 7. 3   REGISTRATION BY QUALIFICATION

Any security can be **registered by qualification**. Registration by qualification requires a registrant to supply any information required by the state securities Administrator. Securities not eligible for registration by another method must be registered by qualification. In addition, securities that will be sold only in one state (intrastate) will be registered by qualification.

To register by qualification, an issuer must supply a consent to service of process and the following information:

- Name, address, form of organization, description of property, and nature of business

- Information on directors and officers and every owner of 10% or more of the issuers securities, and the remuneration paid to owners in the last 12 months

- Description of issuers' capitalization and long-term debt

- Estimated proceeds and the use to which the proceeds will be put

- Type and amount of securities offered, offering price, and selling and underwriting costs
- Stock options to be created in connection with the offering
- Copy of any prospectus, pamphlet, circular, or sales literature to be used in the offering
- Specimen copy of the security along with opinion of counsel as to the legality of the security being offered
- Audited balance sheet current within four months of the offering with an income statement for three years before the balance sheet date

The Administrator may require additional information by rule or order. The Administrator may require that a prospectus be sent to purchasers before the sale and that newly established companies register their securities for the first time in a state by qualification.

T A K E N O T E

As we've noted previously, in order to register, even by notice filing, there must be a consent to service of process filed with the Administrator. However, a person (remember the broad definition) who has filed such a consent in connection with a previous registration or notice filing need not file another. A practical effect of this is if you leave the firm you are registering with (you've probably already filed the consent to service of process to get this far) and register with another firm, you do not have to file a new consent—the old one remains on file. Or, if a company decides to raise additional capital by issuing more stock, a new consent is not required.

2. 7. 3. 1　Effective Date

Unlike coordination, where the effective date is triggered by SEC acceptance of the registration, a registration by qualification becomes effective whenever the state Administrator so orders.

Regardless of the method used, every registration statement is effective for one year from its effective date. Unlike agent and broker-dealer registrations, the date December 31 is of no consequence. One interesting facet of the law is that the registration may continue in effect past the first anniversary if there are still some unsold shares remaining, as long as they are still being offered at the original public offering price by either the issuer or the underwriter.

Although the above rule applies to all methods of registration, as a practical matter, it would rarely apply other than in a security registered by qualification. Those registered by coordination are also obviously registered with the SEC and therefore are sold by the major investment banking houses. Unless the issue is a real dog, it will sell out rather quickly. Even those that are not popular are usually completely subscribed to in a week or two.

On the other hand, what if the issue, regardless of the method of registration, is in very high demand? Is it possible to increase the number of shares in the offering without having to file a new registration statement? Yes. A registration statement may be amended after its effective date so as to increase the securities specified to be offered and sold if two conditions are met:

■ The public offering price; and
■ The underwriters' discounts and commissions are not changed from the respective amounts stated in the original registration statement.

The amendment becomes effective when the Administrator so orders. Every person filing such an amendment shall pay a late registration fee and a filing fee, calculated in the manner as the original quantity, levied against the additional securities proposed to be offered.

TEST TOPIC ALERT

A registration statement may be amended after its effective date to change the number of shares to be offered and sold if the public offering price and underwriter's discounts and commissions are unchanged.

QUICK QUIZ 2.F

True or False?

_____ 1. ABC Shoe Company, a new retail shoe store chain, has applied for the registration of its securities with the SEC as required by the Securities Act of 1933 and wants to register its securities in the state of Illinois and several neighboring states. ABC would most likely register by coordination.

_____ 2. Any company may register by qualification whether or not it files a statement with the SEC.

3. XYZ Corporation has been in business for over 20 years. They need additional capital for expansion, and determine that a public offering in their home state and neighboring states is appropriate. Which method of securities registration would most likely be used to register this initial public offering?

A. Coordination
B. Notice filing
C. Qualification
D. Registration

4. KAPCO Dividend Yield Fund, a closed-end investment company registered under the Investment Company Act of 1940, wishes to commence offering its shares in States A, B, C, and D. It could be required to

A. coordinate its federal registration with each of the four states
B. notice file
C. register by qualification in each of the states
D. do none of these because investment companies registered under the Investment Company Act of 1940 are federal covered securities and are exempt from registration

2. 8   EXEMPTIONS FROM REGISTRATION

In certain situations, the USA exempts both securities and transactions from registration and filing requirements of sales literature. A security, a transaction, or both, can be exempt.

An **exempt security** retains its exemption when initially issued and in subsequent trading. However, justification as an **exempt transaction** must be established before each transaction.

The USA provides for a number of categories of exempt securities and even more categories of exempt transactions. Those securities that are **nonexempt** must register unless sold in exempt transactions. Federal covered securities do not register with the Administrator but may, especially in the case of investment companies, have to Notice File with the Administrator. As mentioned above, an **exempt security** retains its exemption at its initial issue and in subsequent trading.

An exemption for a transaction, on the other hand, must be established with each transaction. Provided it is in the public interest, the state Administrator can deny, suspend, or revoke any securities transaction exemption other than that of a federal covered security. This action may be taken with or without prior notice (summarily).

TAKE NOTE   A security is exempt because of the nature of the issuer, not the purchaser.

An **exempt transaction** is exempt from the regulatory control of the state Administrator because of the manner in which a sale is made or because of the person to whom the sale is made. A transaction is an action and must be judged by the merits of each instance.

One of the most important statements found in the USA is the following. It is unlawful for any person to offer or sell any security in this state unless:

■ it is registered under the act;

■ the security or transaction is exempted under the act; or

■ it is a federal covered security.

For example, an agent can sell a security that is not exempt from registration in the state if the purchaser of the security is a bank or other institutional buyer. Why is that so? Because the sale of securities to certain financial institutions is an exempt transaction (as will be enumerated shortly), the sale can be made without registration. This means that the securities sold in exempt transactions do not have to be registered in the state. If such securities were not sold in exempt transactions, such as to an individual investor, they would have to be registered in the state.

2. 8. 1   EXEMPT SECURITIES

Securities exempt from state registration are also exempt from state filing of sales literature. Exempt securities include the following.

■ **U.S. and Canadian government and municipal securities**. These include securities issued, insured, or guaranteed by the United States or Canada, by a state or province, or by their political subdivisions.

- **Foreign government securities**. These include securities issued, insured, or guaranteed by a foreign government with which the United States maintains diplomatic relations. However, unlike U.S. or Canadian issues, political subdivisions are not included (unless guaranteed by the sovereign government).

- **Depository institutions**. These include securities that are issued, guaranteed by, or are a direct obligation of a depository institution. The USA divides them into the following categories: (1) any security issued by and representing an interest in or a debt of, or guaranteed by, any bank organized under the laws of the United States, or any bank, savings institution, or trust company organized and supervised under the laws of any state; (2) any security issued by and representing an interest in or a debt of, or guaranteed by, any federal savings and loan association, or any building and loan or similar association organized under the laws of any state and authorized to do business in this state; and (3) any security issued or guaranteed by any federal credit union or any credit union, industrial loan association, or similar association organized and supervised under the laws of this state. Please note that for categories (2) and (3), if the institution is not federally chartered, then it must be authorized to do business in the state (under the supervision of a regulator in that state).

- **Insurance company securities**. These include securities issued, insured, or guaranteed by an insurance company authorized to do business in the state. Insurance company securities refer to the stocks or bonds issued by insurance companies, not the variable life policies and variable annuities sold by the companies. **Public utility securities**. These include any security issued or guaranteed by a public utility or public utility holding company, or an equipment trust certificate issued by a railroad or other common carrier regulated in respect to rates by federal or state authority; or regulated in respect to issuance or guarantee of the security by a governmental authority of the United States, any state, Canada, or any Canadian province.

- **Federal covered securities.** These include any security of that issuer equal to or senior to it. This would include rights, warrants, preferred stock, and any debt security.

- **Securities issued by nonprofit organizations**. These include securities issued by religious, educational, fraternal, charitable, social, athletic, reformatory, or trade associations. Nonprofit is the key word.

- **Securities issued by cooperatives**. These include securities issued by a nonprofit membership cooperative to members of that cooperative.

- **Securities of employee benefit plans**. This includes any investment contract issued by an employee stock purchase, saving, pension, or profit-sharing plan.

- **Certain money market instruments.** Commercial paper and banker's acceptances are the two most common examples.

The distinction between exemptions and exceptions (or exclusions) from definitions is important in view of the fact that an exempt security is not exempt from the anti-fraud provisions of the Uniform Securities Act.

For example, as we covered earlier in this session, the typical life insurance policy or fixed annuity is not a security, and is not covered under the anti-fraud statutes of the Uniform Securities Act. On the other hand, we have just seen that securities issued by insurance companies are exempted from registration under the conditions of the Act. Even though these securities are exempt from registration and the filing of advertising and sales literature with the Administrator, they are still subject to the antifraud provisions. Therefore, one cannot be charged with fraudulent behavior under the USA in the sale of a fixed annuity while one could be with the sale of stock in an insurance company (or any other exempt security).

TAKE NOTE

A promissory note (commercial paper), draft, bill of exchange, or banker's acceptance that matures within nine months, is issued in denominations of at least $50,000, and receives one of the three highest ratings by a nationally recognized rating agency is exempt from registration requirements. Please note that this is the only case where a security's rating is part of the registration or exemption under the Uniform Securities Act.

TAKE NOTE

The following, although considered exempt from registration under the Uniform Securities Act, are not exempt from federal registration under the Securities Act of 1933:

- Foreign government securities

- Insurance company securities

- Federal covered securities (those listed on exchanges or Nasdaq and registered investment companies)

TEST TOPIC ALERT

Securities issued by regulated banks are exempt from registration under both state and federal law. However, as stated in the previous session, securities issued by bank holding companies are not exempt, at least not under the *bank* exemption. Most of the major bank holding companies are listed on the exchanges or Nasdaq and, as federal covered securities, are exempt from registration with the states (but not the SEC). Please try to keep these straight because the exam will attempt to confuse you.

QUICK QUIZ 2.G

1. Which of the following securities is(are) exempt from the registration and advertising filing requirements under the USA?

    I. Shares of investment companies registered under the Investment Company Act of 1940
    II. Shares sold on the Nasdaq Stock Market
    III. AAA rated promissory notes of $100,000 that mature in 30 days
    IV. Shares sold on the New York Stock Exchange

    A. I only
    B. II, III, and IV
    C. II and IV
    D. I, II, III, and IV

2.   Which of the following securities is NOT exempt from the registration and advertising requirements of the USA?

   A.   Shares of Commonwealth Edison, a regulated public utility holding company

   B.   Securities issued by the Carnegie Endowment for Peace

   C.   Securities issued by a bank that is a member of the Federal Reserve System

   D.   Variable annuity contracts issued by Metrodential Insurance Company

3.   Which of the following securities is(are) exempt from the registration provisions of the USA?

   I.   Issue of a savings and loan association authorized to conduct business in the state

   II.   General obligation municipal bond

   III.   Bond issued by a company that has common stock listed on the Chicago Stock Exchange

   A.   I only

   B.   II only

   C.   II and III

   D.   I, II, and III

4.   Securities exempt under the Uniform Securities Act are exempt from

   I.   registration requirements

   II.   antifraud provisions of state securities laws

   III.   filing sales and advertising literature with the Administrator

   A.   I and II

   B.   I and III

   C.   II and III

   D.   I, II, and III

2. 8. 2   EXEMPT TRANSACTIONS

Before a security can be sold in a state, it must be registered unless exempt from registration, or traded in an exempt transaction. This section covers exemptions for transactions that take place in a state.

■ There are many different types of **exempt transactions**. We begin by focusing on those most likely to be on your exam and finish with several others.

■ **Isolated nonissuer transactions**. Isolated nonissuer transactions include secondary (nonissuer) transactions, whether effected through a broker-dealer or not, that occur infrequently (very few transactions per agent per year; the exact number varies by state). However, these usually do not involve securities professionals. In the same manner that individuals placing a "for sale by owner" sign on their front lawns do not need a real estate license, one individual selling stock to another in a one-on-one transaction is engaging in a transaction exempt from the oversight of the Administrator, because the issuer is not receiving any of the proceeds, and the parties involved are not trading as part of a regular practice.

■ **Unsolicited brokerage transactions**. These include transactions initiated by the client, not the agent. This is probably the most common of the exempt transactions.

If a client calls a registered agent and requests that the agent buy or sell a security, the transaction is an unsolicited brokerage transaction exempt from state registration. But, the Administrator may by rule require that the customer acknowledge upon a specified form that the sale was unsolicited, and that a signed copy of the form be kept by the broker-dealer for a specified period.

- **Underwriter transactions.** These include transactions between issuer (or any other person on whose behalf the offering is made), and broker-dealers performing in the capacity of an underwriter (such as a firm commitment underwriting) as well as those between underwriters themselves (as when functioning as members of a selling syndicate).

- **Bankruptcy, guardian, or conservator transactions.** Transactions by an executor, administrator, sheriff, marshal, receiver, guardian, or trustee in bankruptcy are exempt transactions. Please note that a custodian under UGMA or UTMA is not included in this list and that the only trustee is one in bankruptcy.

- **Institutional investor transactions.** These are primarily transactions with financial institutions such as banks, insurance companies, and investment companies, and there is no minimum order size used to define these trades.

- **Limited offering transactions.** These include any offering, called a private placement, directed at not more than 10 persons (called *offerees*) other than institutional investors during the previous 12 consecutive months, provided that

  — the seller reasonably believes that all of the noninstitutional buyers are purchasing for investment purposes only,

  — no commissions or other remuneration is paid for soliciting noninstitutional investors, and

  — no general solicitation or advertising is used.

Unlike federal law, where the private placement rule restricts the number of purchasers, the USA restricts the number of offers that may be made.

There is another way in which the USA differs from the federal law on private placements. The federal law will not be tested, but we are referring to it because we know many of our Series 65 students have just completed studying for a FINRA exam where this topic is covered, and we don't want you to choose the wrong answer on this test. Under federal law, any non-institutional purchaser must sign an *investment* letter indicating that purchase was made for investment purposes only and not for immediate resale. However, the USA does not require a written representation by each buyer that he is purchasing for investment but agrees that it would be prudent on the part of the seller to obtain something in writing. All that is required is that the seller *reasonably* believes that the buyer is purchasing for investment only. Moreover, one who, in good faith, buys for investment can later change his mind and resell, although the shorter the interval, the harder it will be to show that there was a bona fide change of mind.

The number 10 is the figure that will be tested. But, an Administrator may want to reduce it, for example, for uranium stocks or oil royalties, or increase it for a closely held corporation that wants to solicit 20 or 30 friends and relatives of the owners for additional capital. As we continue to learn, the Administrator has a great deal of power.

- **Preorganization certificates.** An offer or sale of a preorganization certificate or subscription is exempt if

  — no commission or other remuneration is paid or given directly or indirectly for soliciting any subscriber,

— the number of subscribers does not exceed 10, and

— no payment is made by any subscriber.

You have probably never heard of a preorganization certificate or subscription, so a little explanation is in order. A new corporation cannot receive a charter unless its documents of incorporation provide evidence that minimum funding is assured. Since the purpose of these preorganization certificates is to enable a new enterprise to obtain the minimum amount of capital required by the corporation law of the state, the USA places a limitation on the number of *subscribers* rather than the number of offerees (as in the private placement exemption above). Hence, there may be a publicly advertised offering of preorganization subscriptions. But there may be *no payment* until effective registration unless another exemption is available. This tool itself simply postpones registration; it does not excuse registration altogether.

■ **Transactions with existing security holders**. A transaction made under an offer to existing security holders of the issuer (including persons who are holders of convertible securities, rights, or warrants) is exempt as long as no commission or other form of remuneration is paid directly or indirectly for soliciting that security holder.

■ **Nonissuer transactions by pledgees.** A nonissuer transaction executed by a bona fide pledgee (i.e., the one who received the security as collateral for a loan), as long as it was not for the purpose of evading the act, is an exempt transaction. For example, you pledged stock as collateral for a loan and defaulted on your obligation. The lender will sell your stock to try to recoup his loss and, under the USA, this is considered an exempt transaction.

■ The following are examples of exempt transactions that are unlikely to be on your exam.

■ **Unit secured transactions**. These include transactions in a bond backed by a real mortgage or deed of trust provided that the entire mortgage or deed of trust is sold as a unit.

■ **Control transactions**. This includes mergers, consolidations, or reorganization transactions to which the issuer and the other person or its parent or subsidiary are parties.

■ **Rescission offers**. These include offers made to rescind an improper transaction.

TAKE NOTE
Some students find it helpful to remember that an exempt security is a noun while an exempt transaction is a verb (hence the word "action").

TEST TOPIC ALERT
Remember the distinction between an accredited investor and institutional investor. An **accredited investor** is an investor who meets the accredited investor standards of Regulation D. Rule 501 of Regulation D considers an individual with net worth greater than $1 million on the date of purchase, singly or with a spouse, excluding the net equity in the primary residence, to meet the definition of accredited investor. Alternatively, one may qualify with earnings greater than $200,000 per year ($300,000 if including spouse) in each of the previous two years and a reasonable expectation of reaching that level in the current year. This

term only applies to federal law, not the USA, and will probably never be the correct answer to a USA question.

An **institutional investor** is an investor that manages large amounts of money for other people, such as a mutual fund, an insurance company, a bank, or a pension fund.

TEST TOPIC ALERT

For purposes of meeting the net worth requirements of Rule 501, assets in an account or property held jointly with a person who is not the purchaser's spouse may be included in the calculation, but only to the extent of his or her percentage ownership of the account or property.

2. 8. 2. 1   Administrator's Powers Over Exemptions

The USA grants the Administrator the authority, by rule or order, to exempt a security, a transaction, or an offer from the USA's registration and filing requirements. In addition, the Administrator may waive a requirement for an exemption of a transaction or security.

Try to follow this next point because it is a bit tricky. The Administrator may, by rule or order, deny or revoke the registration exemption of:

- any security issued by any person organized and operated not for private profit but exclusively for religious, educational, benevolent, charitable, fraternal, social, athletic, or reformatory purposes, or as a chamber of commerce or trade or professional association (your basic nonprofit exemption); and

- any investment contract issued in connection with an employees' stock purchase, savings, pension, profit sharing, or similar benefit plan.

Please note that a few pages ago, we gave you a list of 10 different exempt securities, from U.S. and Canadian government issues through certain money market instruments. However, the Administrator can only deny exemption to the two specified above. On the other hand, with the exception of those involving federal covered securities qualifying for the designation due to being listed on an exchange or Nasdaq, the Administrator may deny any exempt transaction. That means that, for example, just because an agent solicited a transaction with an insurance company of a security that was not federal covered, the Administrator has the power, if he feels it is justified, to consider that transaction nonexempt.

Under the USA, the burden of providing an exemption or an exception from a definition falls upon the person claiming it.

TAKE NOTE

There are only two securities exemptions that the Administrator may revoke, while all exempt transactions, other than in federal covered securities, may be revoked.

2. 8. 3   SUMMARY OF EXEMPTIONS FROM REGISTRATION

Let's start our summary with the key statement from the USA:

> It is unlawful for any person to offer or sell any security in this state unless (1) it is registered under this act or (2) the security or transaction is exempted under this act; or (3) it is a federal covered security.

We must point out that these exemptions apply to the security or transaction only, not to the securities professional. So if a security is exempt, such as a government security, it can be sold in this state without any registration. But, the person who sells it must be properly registered in this state (unless that person qualifies for an exemption). Are you confused? Remember, we learned earlier in this session that broker-dealers with no place of business in the state, dealing exclusively with other broker-dealers or institutional clients, are not considered to be a BD in the state (as long as they are properly registered in at least one state—the location of their principal office). Let's apply that to the following situation.

ABC Securities is a broker-dealer registered in State A. They have no place of business in State B, but they do effect transactions on behalf of a number of banks and insurance companies located in State B. Therefore, they are not considered BDs in State B and are exempt from registering. Should ABC Securities sell some government securities to these clients, neither ABC nor the agents making the sale are required to be registered. This is not because the government securities are exempt (that just means that *they* don't have to register with the Administrator), but because, under the USA, ABC does not meet the definition of a broker-dealer in State B.

However, should ABC decide to have any of their agents sell these government bonds to individual (sometimes referred to as *retail*) clients in State B, then, even though the bonds are exempt securities, both ABC and the selling agents must register in that state.

The same applies to exempt transactions. One of the most common cases is when a client calls an agent to purchase a security that is not exempt and not registered in your state. But, because the transaction has been initiated by the client, as an unsolicited trade, it is an exempt transaction and, therefore, the trade may be made even though the security is not registered.

One way the exam will try to trick you is by asking about an individual calling an agent from a state in which the agent is not registered. The broker-dealer is registered in that state, and the individual is a client of the firm, but not that particular agent. The individual wishes to enter an unsolicited order—can the agent accept it? No! Although the transaction is exempt (which only means that the security does not have to be registered in that state), an agent can only do business with a resident of a state if the agent is properly licensed in that state. In this case, the agent would have to turn the order over to an agent who is licensed in that other state.

QUICK QUIZ 2.H

Indicate an exempt transaction with **Y** and a nonexempt transaction with **N**.

_____   1. Mr. Thompson, an agent with First Securities, Inc. (a broker-dealer), receives an unsolicited request to purchase a security for Mary Gordon, a long-time client

_____   2. The sale of an unregistered security in a private, nonpublicly advertised transaction, offered to 10 or fewer retail investors over the previous 12 months

_____   3. The sale of unclaimed securities by sheriff of Santa Fe, New Mexico

_____   4. Sale of stock of a privately owned company to the public in an initial public offering

5. Which of the following are exempt transactions?

    I.   A nonissuer transaction with a bank in a Nasdaq Capital Market Security

    II. An unsolicited request from an existing client to purchase a nonexempt security

    III. The sale of an unregistered security in a private, nonpublicly advertised transaction to 10 noninstitutional purchasers over a period not exceeding 12 months

    IV. The sale of unlisted securities by a trustee in bankruptcy

    A. I and II

    B. I, II, and III

    C. I, II, and IV

    D. I, II, III, and IV

6. All of the following describe exempt transactions EXCEPT

    A. ABC, a broker-dealer, purchases securities from XYZ Corporation as part of an underwriting commitment

    B. First National Bank sells its entire publicly traded bond portfolio to Amalgamated National Bank

    C. Amalgamated National Bank sells its publicly traded bond portfolio to ABC Insurance Company

    D. Joe Smith, an employee of Amalgamated National Bank, buys securities from ABC Brokerage Corporation

7. Under the USA, all of the following are exempt securities EXCEPT

    I.   U.S. government securities

    II. unsolicited transactions

    III. transactions between issuers and underwriters

    IV. securities of federally chartered credit unions

    A. I, II and IV

    B. I and IV

    C. II and III

    D. IV only

8. Under the rules of the Uniform Securities Act, an agent who sells shares of a Nasdaq Stock Market security to an insurance company has engaged in (a/an)

    A. issuer transaction
    B. unsuitable transaction
    C. unlawful transaction
    D. sale exempt from the registration and advertising provisions of the USA

2. 9   STATE SECURITIES REGISTRATION PROCEDURES

The first step in the registration procedure is for the issuer or its representative to pick up a registration statement or application from the state securities Administrator. The person registering the securities is known as the **registrant**. There are some provisions applicable to all registrations regardless of the method used. The exam will want you to know these well.

2. 9. 1   FILING THE REGISTRATION STATEMENT

State Administrators require every issuer to supply the following information on their applications:

- Amount of securities to be issued in the state
- States in which the security is to be offered, but not the amounts offered in those other states
- Any adverse order or judgment concerning the offering by regulatory authorities, court, or the SEC

When filing the registration statement with the Administrator, an applicant may include documents that have been filed with the Administrator within the last five years, provided the information is current and accurate. The Administrator may, by rule or order, permit the omission of any information it considers unnecessary.

TEST TOPIC ALERT   Although most registration statements are filed by the issuer, the exam may require you to know that they may also be filed by any selling stockholder, such as an insider making a large block sale, or by a broker-dealer.

2. 9. 1. 1   Filing Fee

The issuer (or any other person on whose behalf the offering is to be made) must pay a filing fee, as determined by the Administrator, when filing the registration. The filing fees are often based on a percentage of the total offering price.

If the registration is withdrawn or if the Administrator issues a stop order before the registration is effective, the Administrator may retain a portion of the fee and refund the remainder to the applicant.

2. 9. 1. 2   Ongoing Reports

The Administrator may require the person who filed the registration statement to file reports to keep the information contained in the registration statement current and to inform the Administrator of the progress of the offering.

TEST TOPIC ALERT   These reports cannot be required more often than quarterly.

2. 9. 1. 3   Escrow

As a form of investor protection, the Administrator may require as a condition of registration by qualification or coordination:

- that any security issued within the past three years or to be issued to a promoter for a consideration substantially different from the public offering price, or to any person for a consideration other than cash, be deposited in escrow; and

- that the proceeds from the sale of the registered security in this state be impounded until the issuer receives a specified amount from the sale of the security either in this state or elsewhere.

2. 9. 1. 4   Special Subscription Form

The Administrator may also require, as a condition of registration, that the issue be sold only on a form specified by the Administrator and that a copy of the form or subscription contract be filed with the Administrator or preserved for up to three years.

2. 9. 1. 5   Withdrawal of Registration Statement

A registration statement may not be withdrawn until one year after its effective date, if any securities of the same class are outstanding, and may be withdrawn only with the approval of the Administrator.

QUICK QUIZ 2.1

1. With regard to the registration requirements of the Uniform Securities Act, which of the following is NOT a correct statement?

    A. Only the issuer itself can file a registration statement with the Administrator.
    B. An application for registration must indicate the amount of securities to be issued in the state.
    C. The Administrator may require registrants to file quarterly reports.
    D. The Administrator may require the proceeds of an offering be placed into an escrow account until the issuer receives a specified amount from the sale of the security.

2. 10   ANTIFRAUD PROVISIONS OF THE USA

Fraudulent activity may occur when conducting securities sales or when providing investment advice. Each of these categories is discussed separately. In general, **fraud** means the deliberate or willful attempt to deceive someone for profit or gain. Any security, or transaction involving a security, exempt or nonexempt, is covered under the USA's anti-fraud provisions. However, these provisions only apply to securities. Therefore, if the inappropriate activity occurs during the offer or sale or rendering of advice relating to something that is *not* a security, these anti-fraud provisions do not apply.

2. 10. 1   FRAUDULENT AND PROHIBITED PRACTICES

Although there is a legal difference between a fraudulent practice and one that is unethical or prohibited, it is highly unlikely that you will have to know that for the exam. About the only significant testable concern is that you can go to jail for committing fraud (a criminal offense) while engaging in a practice that is prohibited or unethical is generally limited to a fine, and/or suspension or revocation. Most of the exam will deal with practices that are unethical, but let's point out what the Uniform Securities Act considers fraud.

State securities laws modeled on the USA address fraud by making it unlawful for any person, when engaged in the offer, sale, or purchase of any security, directly or indirectly, to:

- employ any device, scheme, or artifice to defraud;
- make any untrue statement of a material fact or omit to state a material fact necessary to make a statement not misleading; or
- engage in any act, practice, or course of business that operates as a fraud or deceit on a person.

With regard to investment advice, it is unlawful for any person who receives, directly or indirectly, any consideration from another person for advising the other person as to the value of securities or their purchase or sale, whether through the issuance of analyses or reports or otherwise, to:

- employ any device, scheme, or artifice to defraud the other person; or
- engage in any act, practice, or course of business which operates or would operate as a fraud or deceit upon the other person.

There are other more specific examples related to investment advice, but we will cover them as they arise.

TAKE NOTE

As long as it involves a security, there are no exceptions to the antifraud provisions of state securities laws. They pertain to any person or transaction whether the person or transaction is registered, exempt, or federal covered. Prevention of fraud is one of the few areas of securities law over which the states have full authority to act.

The following is a list of the fraudulent acts most likely to be tested on your exam.

2. 10. 1. 1 Misleading or Untrue Statements

Securities laws prohibit any person from making misleading or untrue statements of a material fact in connection with the purchase or sale of a security. Not all facts are material. The law defines **material** as information used by a prospective purchaser to make an informed investment decision. In other words, when selling securities to their clients, agents must not deliberately conceal a material fact to encourage a client to buy or sell a security. Such act would constitute deceit for personal gain.

An agent providing a client with an inaccurate address of a company whose shares the client was interested in purchasing would not be making an untrue statement of a material fact. Investors do not purchase shares on the basis of the company's street address. On the other hand, investors do make investment decisions on the basis of the qualifications of a company's management. Those qualifications would therefore be material fact. To misstate them is fraud. An example would be claiming that the chief operating officer (COO) of a biotech company had a Ph.D. in biochemistry when, in fact, the doctorate was in sociology. It is important to note that it is the responsibility of the agent to determine what is and what is not a material fact.

The following are examples of material facts that constitute fraud if misstated by agents knowingly and willfully.

- **Inaccurate market quotations**—Telling a client a stock is up when the reverse is true is obviously an improper action. However, it would not be considered fraud if the inaccuracy resulted from a malfunction of the quote machine or an unintended clerical error. To be considered fraud, the action must be deliberate.

- **Misstatements of an issuer's earnings or projected earnings or dividends**—Telling a client that earnings are up, or that the dividend will be increased when such is not the case, is a fraudulent practice. However, it would not be fraud if you were quoting a news release that was incorrect.

TEST TOPIC ALERT   You might see a question where you have to know that it could be considered fraudulent activity for an agent or IAR to use social media to make a false announcement about a company in order to affect the stock price.

- **Inaccurate statements regarding the amount of commissions, markup, or markdown**—There are circumstances where the amount of commission or markup may be higher than normal. That is permissible, as long as it is disclosed properly. However, telling a client that it costs him nothing to trade with your firm because you never charge a commission, and not informing him that all trades are done on a principal basis with a markup or markdown, is fraud.

TEST TOPIC ALERT   It is important to understand that, other than in the above circumstance where commissions may be higher than normal, a broker-dealer is not obligated to disclose the amount of commission on any offer to sell before the transaction. However, commissions are always required to be disclosed on the trade confirmation.

- **Stating or implying that the agent has inside information when such is not the case**—As we will see shortly, the use of non-public material *inside* information is a fraudulent practice. But, what about the agent who attempts to boost her credibility to clients by inferring that what she is about to tell them is "inside info" and, once released, will have a major impact on the stock? Since it isn't true, she isn't acting on inside information, but, she is still guilty of making untrue statements.

- **Telling a customer that a security will be listed on an exchange without concrete information concerning its listing status**—Years ago, before the Nasdaq Stock Market became the home for so many leading companies, an announcement that a stock was going to be listed on the NYSE invariably caused its market price to jump. Even though it does not have the same significance today, any statement of this type relating to a change in marketplace for the security is only permitted if, in fact, you have knowledge that such change is imminent.

- **Informing a client that the registration of a security with the SEC or with the state securities Administrator means that the security has been approved by these regulators**—Registration never implies approval.

- **Misrepresenting the status of customer accounts**—This behavior is fraudulent. Many people are not motivated to pay strict attention to their monthly account statements, making it relatively easy for an unscrupulous agent to fraudulently claim increasing values in the account when the opposite is true. Doing so would be a fraudulent action.

- **Promising a customer services without any intent to perform them or without being properly qualified to perform them**—You say, "Yes, I can" to your client, even if you know you cannot deliver. For instance, the client asks you to analyze his bond portfolio to determine the average duration. Even though you do not know how to do that, you agree to do so. Under the USA, you committed fraud.

- **Representing to customers that the Administrator approves of the broker-dealer's or agent's abilities**—This is another case of using the word *approve* improperly. A broker-dealer or agent is registered, not approved.

TEST TOPIC ALERT   Merely learning the terms is not enough to get you through the exam. On the exam, you must be able to identify situations in which the above violations occur. Be able to apply the concepts of fraud and unethical behavior to scenarios that are likely to occur in everyday business.

CASE STUDY   **Making Leading or Untrue Statements**

Situation: Mr. Thompson, a registered securities agent in Illinois, informs a long-standing client, Ms. Gordon, that her largest equity holding, First Tech Internet Services, Inc., will be listed on the NYSE upon completion of its application for listing. In addition, he exaggerates the earnings by $1 per share to make her more comfortable and encourage her to buy more shares. Mr. Thompson is convinced the earnings will rise to that amount and does not want Ms. Gordon to sell because he believes the stock will appreciate in price once listed on the Exchange. He also tells her that his firm will not be charging her any commission on the trade as they already have the stock in inventory, so she will be ahead from the start.

Analysis: Mr. Thompson violated the USA by deliberately misrepresenting the earnings of First Tech Internet Services. Although Mr. Thompson's motives may have been good, he must be truthful in his effort to encourage clients to purchase more stock—his conviction that the stock would rise upon its listing on the NYSE is not sufficient. No violation of the act occurred with respect to First Tech's Exchange listing because Mr. Thompson knew that the stock had a pending application to be listed on the NYSE. To state that she will be ahead from the start because the firm will not charge a commission, but failing to state that a sale from inventory would include a markup, is a fraudulent act.

2. 10. 1. 2 Failure to State Material Facts

The USA does not require an agent to provide all information about an investment, but only information that is material to making an informed investment decision. However, the agent must not fail to mention material information that could affect the price of the security. In addition, the agent may not state facts that in and of themselves are true but, as a result of deliberately omitting other facts, render the recommendation misleading under the circumstances.

TEST TOPIC ALERT

Full disclosure also applies when filling out an order to purchase or sell securities, referred to as an order ticket. Each order ticket must disclose the account ID, a description of the security including the number of shares if a stock and total par value if a bond, the terms and conditions of the order (market or limit), the time of order entry and execution, the execution price, and the identity of the agent who accepted the order or is responsible for the account. We do not need the client's name or address on the order ticket.

CASE STUDY

Failure to State Material Facts

Situation: Upon NYSE acceptance of the listing application, there is an announcement that First Tech Internet Services will publish its financial statements in a newspaper advertisement. Mr. Thompson deliberately failed to mention this advertisement to Ms. Gordon.

After its listing on the NYSE, the research department in Mr. Thompson's firm prepares a negative report on First Tech. The research department discovered a change in accounting practices that will have a detrimental effect on subsequent earnings reported by First Tech. Mr. Thompson continues to recommend the stock to Ms. Gordon because he believes the increased exposure gained by the Exchange listing will outweigh the future decline in earnings. As a result, Mr. Thompson neglects to inform Ms. Gordon of the change before her purchase of additional shares.

Analysis: Mr. Thompson violated the USA even though he made no misleading statements to Ms. Gordon with respect to First Tech. Mr. Thompson did not have to mention the advertisement in the newspaper because it is not material, yet he violated the act when he failed to mention the accounting change that would result in significantly lower earnings. Although an accounting change is not ordinarily a material fact, in this case it was because it would have a detrimental impact on the company's earnings and its market price. An informed investor must have such information.

2. 10. 1. 3   Using Inside Information

Making recommendations on the basis of material inside information about an issuer or its securities is prohibited. Should an agent come into possession of inside information, the agent must report the possession of the information to a supervisor or compliance officer. However, the use of a broker-dealer or investment adviser's internally generated research report prior to public release is not considered use of inside information.

TAKE NOTE

Material inside information under securities law is any information about a company that has not been communicated to the general public and that would likely affect the value of a security. Even if you acquire the information "accidentally," you cannot use it until it becomes public.

TEST TOPIC ALERT

The exam may ask you to identify who is guilty of insider trading violations—a corporate officer of the issuer who divulges material inside information to a friend, but no transaction takes place, or an agent who executes a trade for a client who is acting on inside information? Simply giving someone inside information, although imprudent, is not a violation of the law. Only when the information is used for trading does a violation occur. In our question, the agent is in violation for accepting an order on the basis of material nonpublic information that results in a trade.

CASE STUDY

Using Inside Information

Situation: Mr. Thompson is a friend and neighbor of Mr. Cage, president and owner of more than half of First Tech's securities. Mr. Cage discloses to Mr. Thompson that the company has just discovered a new technology that will double First Tech's earnings within the next year. No one outside of the company, except for Mr. Thompson, knows of this discovery. On this basis, Mr. Thompson buys additional shares of First Tech for Ms. Gordon.

Analysis: The information on First Tech's new technology is material inside information that has not been made public. It is material information that only Mr. Thompson and company officials know. Mr. Thompson violated the USA by acting on this information. Mr. Thompson should have communicated the possession of the information to his compliance officer and refrained from making recommendations on the basis of this information.

2. 11   DISHONEST AND UNETHICAL BUSINESS PRACTICES OF BROKER-DEALERS AND AGENTS

In 1983, NASAA released a Statement of Policy enumerating a large number of business practices that, when engaged in by broker-dealers or agents, they deemed dishonest or unethical. Subsequently, they have issued several Model Rules that have expanded the list. Most students report seeing at least five questions on their Series 65 exam that are drawn from the following material, especially those relating uniquely to agents. In most cases, the listed prohibition is logical common sense, "don't lie, don't cheat, and don't steal". However, due to the nature of this exam and their legal interpretations, particularly for those of you without a securities or law background, further explanations will be supplied.

The premise of the Policy is that each broker-dealer and agent shall observe high standards of commercial honor and just and equitable principles of trade in the conduct of their business. Acts and practices, including but not limited to those enumerated below, are considered contrary to such standards and may constitute grounds for denial, suspension or revocation of registration or such other action authorized by the Uniform Securities Act. You will need to know that it is a dishonest or unethical business practice if a broker-dealer is doing any of the following (those that apply to agents as well are prefaced with an **(A)**).

2. 11. 1   DELIVERY DELAYS

Engaging in a pattern of unreasonable and unjustifiable delays in the delivery of securities purchased by any of its customers and/or in the payment upon request of free credit balances reflecting completed transactions of any of its customers. A free credit balance is just like a credit balance on your charge card—it is your money and must be sent to you upon request. In the event that the client requests a certificate for the security purchased, it would be considered an unethical business practice for the firm to delay delivering it to the client.

2. 11. 2   CHURNING

(A) Inducing trading in a customer's account which is excessive in size or frequency in view of the financial resources, objectives, and character of the account. A key here is the word *excessive*. By definition, anytime something is excessive, it is too much. The regulators understand that different clients have different needs and ability to take risks, so what is excessive for the 80-year-old pensioner is probably not going to be so for the 40-year-old partner in a major law firm.

TEST TOPIC ALERT   *Excessive trading* may be used on the exam instead of the word *churning*.

2. 11. 3   UNSUITABLE RECOMMENDATIONS

(A) Recommending to a customer the purchase, sale, or exchange of any security without reasonable grounds to believe that such transaction or recommendation is suitable for the customer based upon reasonable inquiry concerning the customer's investment objectives, financial situation and needs, and any other relevant information known by the broker-dealer.

Agents must always have reasonable grounds for making recommendations to clients. Before making recommendations, the agent must inquire into the client's financial status, investment objectives, and ability to assume financial risk. What about the client who refuses to give any financial information or discuss objectives? In that case, all the agent can do is accept unsolicited orders because there is no basis for making any recommendation.

The following practices violate the suitability requirements under the USA as well as the rules of fair practice that regulatory agencies have developed. A securities professional may not:

■ recommend securities transactions without regard to the customer's financial situation, needs, or investment objectives;

■ induce transactions solely to generate commissions (**churning**), defined as transactions in customer accounts that are excessive in size or frequency in relation to the client's financial resources, objectives, or the character of the account;

■ recommend a security without reasonable grounds;

■ make blanket recommendations. That is, it will almost always be unsuitable if the same security is recommended to the majority of your clients. How could all of them have the same needs? Some are looking for income, some for growth, and some for safety, and no one security can provide all three; and

■ fail to sufficiently describe the important facts and risks concerning a transaction or security.

CASE STUDY   Making Unsuitable Investment Recommendations

Situation: Mr. Thompson has a wide variety of clients: high-net-worth individuals, trusts, retirees with limited incomes and resources, and college students. Mr. Thompson has strong beliefs about First Tech, a growth stock that pays no dividends. He aggressively recommends the stock to all his clients without informing them of the volatility of First Tech and the firm's research department's pending downgrade in earnings.

Analysis: Mr. Thompson has violated the USA on several counts. First, he made a recommendation without regard to the separate financial conditions, needs, and objectives of his diverse client base. The recommendation is unsuitable for the investment objectives of his retired clients with fixed incomes and limited financial resources. In addition, he made the recommendation in an unsuitable manner by failing to reveal the earnings volatility or risk and the downgrade in earnings.

TAKE NOTE

So, what do you do when you think you've made a totally appropriate recommendation to your client, but your client is not happy with it. Upon reflection, you realize the client's problem is a lack of understanding of both the recommendation and the marketplace. What should you do? Most would agree that the first step would be to attempt to impart some education to the client in an effort to make your recommendation clearer. However, as with all customer issues, the client is the one who has to make the final decision.

2. 11. 3. 1 Free Lunch Seminars

Although not specifically included in the NASAA Statement of Policy, recent rules regarding unfair business practices, especially with regard to seniors, may be included on your exam. The most common instance is the so-called free lunch seminar. These seminars are widely offered by financial services firms seeking to sell financial products and they often include a free meal for attendees. Even though many of these seminars are promoted as being educational or workshops accompanied by the statement, "nothing will be sold at this meeting," the seminars are clearly intended to result in the attendees' opening new accounts with the sponsoring firm and, ultimately, in the sale of investment products, if not at the seminar itself, then in follow-up contacts with the attendees.

If not clearly presented, NASAA will consider that both the sponsoring firm and those agents involved in the delivery of the seminar are committing a prohibited business practice.

2. 11. 4 UNAUTHORIZED TRANSACTIONS

(A) Executing a transaction on behalf of a customer without authorization to do so. Unless discretionary authorization (see following) has been received, broker-dealers and their agents may never enter an order for a client on their own volition, even when it is in the best interest of the client. You may be asked a question where a spouse of a client or other person with a strong personal relationship contacts the agent with transaction instructions, allegedly on behalf of the client. Unless there is a written third-party trading authorization on file, no activity can take place.

Somewhat related to this activity is deliberately failing to follow a customer's instructions. In this case, the client has given the terms of the order and if the agent decides to purchase more or less than ordered, or in any other way change the nature of the order, it is a prohibited practice.

2. 11. 5 EXERCISING DISCRETION

(A) Exercising any discretionary power in effecting a transaction for a customer's account without first obtaining written discretionary authority from the customer, unless the discretionary power relates solely to the time and/or price for the executing of orders.

Agents of broker-dealers may not exercise discretion in an account without prior written authority (power of attorney) from the client. Prior written authority is also known as trading authorization.

Discretion is given to an agent by the client when the client authorizes (in writing) the agent to act on his own and use his discretion in deciding the following for the client:

■ Asset (security)

■ Action (buy or sell)

■ Amount (how many shares)

However, merely authorizing an agent to determine the best price or time to trade a security is not considered to be discretion for purposes of the financial requirements, such as bonding or, in the case of an investment adviser, minimum net worth.

CASE STUDY   **Discretionary Trading Authorization**

Situation: Mr. Thompson's client, Mr. Bixby, has indicated over the phone that he authorizes Mr. Thompson to make trades for him. Mr. Bixby's family lawyer, Mr. Derval, has specific power of attorney over some of Mr. Bixby's businesses. Mr. Bixby promised Mr. Thompson that he would send in the trading authorization within the next day or two to give Mr. Thompson discretion over the account. However, Mr. Thompson immediately executed trades in First Tech for Mr. Bixby to take advantage of its impending NYSE listing.

The following week, Mr. Thompson received Mr. Bixby's written discretionary trading authorization. On the day after the authorization arrived, Mr. Bixby's attorney, Mr. Derval, indicated that Mr. Bixby would like to buy shares in General Electric. Because Mr. Derval has power of attorney for Mr. Bixby, Mr. Thompson bought the shares.

Analysis: Mr. Thompson violated the USA by trading in Mr. Bixby's account before receipt of the written trading authorization. Having authorization in the mail is not sufficient. Mr. Thompson also violated the USA by accepting the order from Mr. Derval because although he is Mr. Bixby's attorney, he was not specifically authorized to trade in Mr. Bixby's securities account. The trading authorization signed by Mr. Bixby only gave authority to Mr. Thompson. Had Mr. Derval provided Mr. Thompson with specific written third-party trading authorization from Mr. Bixby, Mr. Thompson then could have accepted the order for General Electric without a violation of the act.

2. 11. 6 MARGIN DOCUMENTS

(A) Executing any transaction in a margin account without securing from the customer a properly executed written margin agreement promptly *after* the initial transaction in the account.

2. 11. 7   COMMINGLING OF CUSTOMER AND FIRM ASSETS

Failing to segregate customers' free securities or securities held in safekeeping. Customer "free" securities are those which have no lien against them (just like one might have a lien against your car). Securities are pledged as collateral in a margin account.

Securities that are held in a customer's name must not be **commingled** (mixed) with securities of the firm.

If a firm has 100,000 shares of General Electric stock in its own proprietary account and its clients separately own an additional 100,000 shares, the firm may not place customer shares in the firm's proprietary account.

To mix shares together would give undue leverage or borrowing power to a firm and could jeopardize the security of client securities in the event of default.

One area of particular concern is brokerage firms maintaining margin accounts for their clients. In a margin account, the broker-dealer extends credit for the purchase of eligible securities and then uses those securities as collateral for the margin debt (loan). The pledging of these margin securities is known as **hypothecation**. There are strict rules regarding how much of the client's securities may be hypothecated and requiring that the balance be segregated from the firm's own securities.

2. 11. 8   IMPROPER HYPOTHECATION

Hypothecating a customer's securities without having a lien thereon unless the broker-dealer secures from the customer a properly executed written consent promptly after the initial transaction, except as permitted by rules of the Securities and Exchange Commission. As indicated previously, there are strict rules to be followed, the details of which will not be tested.

2. 11. 9   UNREASONABLE COMMISSIONS OR MARK-UPS

(A) Entering into a transaction with or for a customer at a price not reasonably related to the current market price of the security or receiving an unreasonable commission or profit.

There is one way that a broker-dealer might make a very large profit and it would *not* be considered unreasonable. When acting in a dealer (or principal) capacity, broker-dealers sell out of inventory. What would be the situation if a firm bought some securities for their inventory and, several months later, the value of those securities had doubled or tripled? What would be a fair price to charge customers? The rules make it clear that quotes are always based on the current market so, in this case, the broker-dealer would make a substantial profit. By the way, this "sword cuts both ways." If the firm had stock in inventory that decreased greatly in value, the firm would not be able to pass any of the loss to clients—any sales would take place based on the current depressed market prices.

2. 11. 10 TIMELY PROSPECTUS DELIVERY

(**A**) Failing to furnish to a customer purchasing securities in an offering, no later than the due date of confirmation of the transaction, either a final prospectus or a preliminary prospectus.

Here is further detail from the USA that might answer a question on the exam: The Administrator may, by rule or order, require as a condition of registration under Coordination, that a prospectus be sent or given to each person to whom an offer is made no later than with confirmation of the trade. Of course, one must always be sent to a person who actually purchases the security. The Administrator may require that a prospectus for a security registered under Qualification be sent or given to each person to whom an offer is made prior to the sale of the security rather than prior to the offer.

2. 11. 11 UNREASONABLE SERVICING FEES

Charging unreasonable and inequitable fees for services performed, including miscellaneous services such as collection of monies due for principal, dividends or interest, exchange or transfer of securities, appraisals, safekeeping, or custody of securities and other services related to its securities business. However, as long as these charges are not unreasonable, they would be permitted for performing these services.

2. 11. 11. 1 Higher Than Normal Commissions

NASAA recognizes that not all broker-dealers offer the same level of services and that those who offer a large array of services to their clients may charge more without it being considered an unethical business practice. In other cases, a particular transaction may involve more expense to the broker-dealers, particularly in a thinly traded security, and that too would justify a charge that is higher than normal. Of course, all charges must be clearly disclosed to clients. If not, a violation has occurred.

2. 11. 12 DISHONORING QUOTES

Offering to buy from or sell to any person any security at a stated price unless such broker-dealer is prepared to purchase or sell, as the case may be, at such price and under such conditions as are stated at the time of such offer to buy or sell.

In other words, if a broker-dealer quotes a stock at 20.60 to 20.75, he had better be ready to sell at least the minimum trading unit (usually 100 shares) to a client at $20.75 per share (his ask or offering price), or buy from a client at $20.60 (his bid price).

2. 11. 13 MARKET MANIPULATION

(**A**) Effecting any transaction in, or inducing the purchase or sale of, any security by means of any manipulative, deceptive, or fraudulent device, practice, plan, program, design, or contrivance.

Securities legislation is designed to uphold the integrity of markets and transactions in securities. However, market integrity is violated when transactions misrepresent actual securities prices or market activity. The most common forms of market manipulation are matched orders and wash trades.

Matched orders occur when an order to buy or sell securities is entered with knowledge that a matching order on the opposite side of the transaction has been or will be entered for the purpose of (1) creating a false or misleading appearance of active trading in any publicly traded security or (2) creating a false or misleading appearance with respect to the market for any such security.

Increased volume in a security can induce unsuspecting investors to purchase the security, thereby bidding up the price. As the price rises, participants who initiated the matched orders sell their securities at a profit.

A **wash trade** is an order to buy or sell securities resulting in no change of beneficial ownership for the purpose of (1) creating a false or misleading appearance of active trading in any publicly traded security; or (2) creating a false or misleading appearance with respect to the market for any such security. This is typically done by an investor buying in one brokerage account and simultaneously selling through another. No real change in ownership has occurred, but to the marketplace, it appears that volume and/or price is increasing.

TAKE NOTE

So, what is the difference between a matched order and a wash trade? Keeping it simple (because the exam only wants you to know they're both prohibited), *wash trades* are trades in which the (natural or legal) person who is the beneficial owner of the traded securities does not change, even though this is the impression conveyed to the public. In other words, in a wash sale, it is the same investor trading in two or more accounts owned or controlled by that single investor. In the case of *matched orders*, these are pre-arranged entries of equal but opposite buy and sell orders in the same security made between different parties with the intention to distort the public impression of actual liquidity or prices. There is a change in ownership, but the attempt is to deceive.

TAKE NOTE

Arbitrage is the simultaneous buying and selling of the same security in different markets to take advantage of different prices; it is not a form of market manipulation. Simultaneously buying a security in one market and selling it in another forces prices to converge and, therefore, provides uniform prices for the general public.

2. 11. 14 GUARANTEEING AGAINST LOSS

(A) Guaranteeing a customer against loss in any securities account of such customer carried by the broker-dealer or in any securities transaction effected by the broker-dealer or in any securities transaction effected by the broker-dealer with or for such customer.

Securities professionals may not guarantee a certain performance, nor may they guarantee against a loss by providing funds to the account.

The term *guaranteed* under the USA means "guaranteed as to payment of principal, interest, or dividends." It is allowable to refer to a guaranteed security when an entity other than the issuer is making the guarantee. However, the regulatory agencies of the securities industry prohibit securities professionals from guaranteeing the performance returns of an investment or portfolio.

2. 11. 15 DISSEMINATING FALSE TRADING INFORMATION

(A) Publishing or circulating, or causing to be published or circulated, any notice, circular, advertisement, newspaper article, investment service, or communication of any kind which purports to report any transaction as a purchase or sale of any security unless such broker-dealer believes that such transaction was a bona fide purchase or sale or such security; or which purports to quote the bid price or asked price for any security, unless such broker-dealer believes that such quotation represents a bona fide bid for, or offer of, such security.

2. 11. 16 DECEPTIVE ADVERTISING PRACTICES

(A) Using any advertising or sales presentation in such a fashion as to be deceptive or misleading. An example of such practice would be a distribution of any nonfactual data, material or presentation based on conjecture, unfounded or unrealistic claims or assertions in any brochure, flyer, or display by words, pictures, graphs, or otherwise designed to supplement, detract from, supersede, or defeat the purpose or effect of any prospectus or disclosure.

One way in which this violation occurs is when a broker-dealer or agent prepares a sales brochure for a new issue but includes only the positive information from the prospectus. Leaving out risk factors and other potential "deal-killing" information is prohibited. Somewhat related, and also prohibited, is **highlighting** or making any other marks on a prospectus to draw attention to key points.

2. 11. 17 FAILING TO DISCLOSE CONFLICTS OF INTEREST

Failing to disclose that the broker-dealer is controlled by, controlling, affiliated with or under common control with the issuer of any security before entering into any contract with or for a customer for the purchase or sale of such security, the existence of such control to such customer, and if such disclosure is not made in writing, it shall be supplemented by the giving or sending of written disclosure at or before the completion of the transaction. One of the most common examples of a conflict of interest that must be disclosed is when the agent is offering a proprietary product, such as a *house* fund (a mutual fund where the underwriter or adviser is affiliated with the broker-dealer) or a limited partnership offering (DPP) where the sponsor is an affiliate of the broker-dealer.

Suppose you were selling shares of a company where your sister was a control person? Do you think you'd have to disclose that potential conflict to your clients? Yes!

2. 11. 18 WITHHOLDING SHARES OF A PUBLIC OFFERING

Failing to make a bona fide public offering of all of the securities allotted to a broker-dealer for distribution, whether acquired as an underwriter, a selling group member, or from a member participating in the distribution as an underwriter or selling group member. If the firm is fortunate to be part of the underwriting of one of these IPOs that rockets in price because the issue is oversubscribed, they better be sure to allocate the shares to clients in an equitable manner and not keep any for themselves.

2. 11. 19 RESPONDING TO COMPLAINTS

(A) Failure or refusal to furnish a customer, upon reasonable request, information to which he is entitled, or to respond to a formal written request or complaint.

When a written complaint is received by the firm (and only written complaints are recognized), action must be taken. The complainant (customer) would be notified that the complaint had been received and an entry would be made in the firm's complaint file. If an agent were the subject of the complaint, the agent would be notified, but would *not* be given a copy of the complaint (agents do not have recordkeeping requirements). If the complaint is received by the agent rather than the firm, the agent must report the complaint to the appropriate supervisor. In the unusual case (except on the exam) where a customer files a written complaint and then withdraws it, the firm makes a copy of the communication, places it in their complaint file, and then returns the original to the client.

2. 11. 19. 1 Reporting errors

In order to keep from generating complaints, any trade or other operational error, once discovered, must be reported by the agent to the appropriate supervisory person.

TEST TOPIC ALERT   A complaint received by electronic means (email) is considered a written complaint.

2. 11. 20 FRONT RUNNING

(A) Front running is the unethical business practice of a broker-dealer or one of its representatives placing a personal order ahead of a previously received customer order. It occurs most frequently when the firm has received an institutional order of sufficient size to move the market. By running in front of the order, the firm or representative can profit on that movement.

CASE STUDY   Practices—Customer Complaints and Front Running

Situation: Mr. Thompson, an agent with First Securities, a broker-dealer, recommends to his client, Mr. Byers, that he purchase ABC Shoe Co., a thinly traded chain store that First Securities's analysts have highly recommended subsequent to its initial public offering. Mr. Byers agrees. Just before entering Mr. Byers's order, Mr. Thompson purchases several hundred shares for himself. Mr. Byers learned of Mr. Thompson's purchase and wrote him a stinging letter of complaint about it. Because Mr. Thompson considered the transaction a private matter, he did not think it necessary to bring the letter to the attention of First Securities. A few days later, Mr. Thompson personally apologized to Mr. Byers and took him out for a drink.

Analysis: Mr. Thompson has engaged in two practices that violate industry practice. First, although the recommendation of ABC Shoe Co. was perfectly appropriate, it was not appropriate for Mr. Thompson to enter his personal order for the same shares before completing Mr. Byers's purchase. This is known as front running, a prohibited practice. Additionally, Mr. Thompson (as a registered agent) must bring all written complaints to the attention of his employer. Had Mr. Byers simply lodged an oral complaint, Mr. Thompson would not have been under an obligation to bring it to the attention of the manager of his office. Taking Mr. Byers out for a drink did not violate industry standards.

2. 11. 21 SPREADING RUMORS

(A) Any agent hearing a rumor must report it to the appropriate supervisor. Broker-dealers must insure that rumors they become aware of are not spread or used in any way, particularly not as the basis for recommendations.

2. 11. 22 BACKDATING RECORDS

(A) All records and documents must reflect their actual dates. Although there can be tax or other benefits to clients when their trade confirmations are backdated, it is an unethical business practice to do so.

2. 11. 23 WAIVERS

The USA makes it clear that any condition, stipulation, or provision binding any person acquiring any security or receiving any investment advice to waive compliance with any provision of the Act or any rule or order hereunder is void. For exam purposes, if you are given a question where clients agree to waive their rights to sue, the agreement is null and void.

2. 11. 24 INVESTMENT COMPANY SALES

(A) In 1997, NASAA adopted the NASAA Statement of Policy titled Dishonest or Unethical Business Practices by Broker-Dealers and Agents in Connection with Investment Company Shares. Several of those items are currently being tested. Under this Policy, any broker-dealer or agent who engages in one or more of the following practices shall be deemed to have engaged in "dishonest or unethical practices in the securities business" as used in the Uniform Securities Act, and such conduct may constitute grounds for denial, suspension, or revocation of registration or such other action authorized by statute.

2. 11. 24. 1 Sales Load Communications

In connection with the solicitation of investment company shares, stating or implying to a customer that the shares are sold without a commission, are "no load" or have "no sales charge" if there is associated with the purchase of the shares:

- a front-end load;
- a contingent deferred sales load (CDSC); or
- a Rule 12b-1 fee or a service fee if such fees in total exceed .25% of average net fund assets per year.

2. 11. 24. 2 Breakpoints

In connection with the solicitation of investment company shares, failing to disclose to any customer any relevant:

- sales charge discount on the purchase of shares in dollar amounts at or above a breakpoint; or
- letter of intent feature, if available, which will reduce the sales charges.

2. 11. 24. 3 Selling Dividends

In connection with the solicitation of investment company shares, stating or implying to a customer that:

- the purchase of such shares shortly before an ex-dividend date is advantageous to such customer unless there are specific, clearly described tax or other advantages to the customer; or
- a distribution of long-term capital gains by an investment company is part of the income yield from an investment in such shares.

2. 11. 24. 4 Share Classes

In connection with the solicitation of investment company shares, recommending to a customer the purchase of a specific class of investment company shares in connection with a multi-class sales charge or fee arrangement without reasonable grounds to believe that the sales charge or fee arrangement associated with such class of shares is suitable and appropriate based on the customer's investment objectives, financial situation and other securities holdings, and the associated transaction or other fees.

2. 11. 24. 5 Switching Funds

In connection with the solicitation of investment company shares, recommending to a customer the liquidation or redemption of investment company shares for the purpose of purchasing shares in a different investment company portfolio having similar investment objectives and policies without reasonable grounds to believe that such recommendation is suitable and appropriate based on the customer's investment objectives, financial situation and other securities holdings, and any associated transaction charges or other fees.

2. 11. 24. 6 Proper Yield Disclosures

In connection with the solicitation of investment company shares, stating or implying to a customer the fund's current yield or income without disclosing the fund's most recent average annual return, calculated in a manner prescribed in SEC Form N-1A, for 1-, 5- and 10-year periods and fully explaining the difference between current yield and total return; provided, however, that if the fund's registration statement under the Securities Act of 1933 has been in effect for less than 1, 5, or 10 years, the time during which the registration statement was in effect shall be substituted for the periods otherwise prescribed.

2. 11. 25 LENDING OR BORROWING

(A) Engaging in the practice of lending to or borrowing money or securities from a customer.

Securities professionals may not borrow money or securities from a client unless the client is a broker-dealer, an affiliate of the professional, or a financial institution engaged in the business of loaning money.

Securities professionals may not loan money to clients unless the firm is a broker-dealer or financial institution engaged in the business of loaning funds or the client is an affiliate.

CASE STUDY   **Borrowing Money or Securities from Clients**

Situation: On occasion, Mr. Thompson borrows cash from his discretionary client, Mr. Bixby, when Mr. Bixby's account is not fully invested. Mr. Bixby has given Mr. Thompson much latitude because Mr. Thompson has done well in managing the account and Mr. Thompson always repays the money in time to reinvest Mr. Bixby's funds in new securities purchases. Mr. Thompson justifies these borrowings as within the discretionary power Mr. Bixby had granted him. The First National Bank is also a client of Mr. Thompson, but he does not borrow from the bank because it charges unusually high interest rates.

Analysis: Mr. Thompson has engaged in a prohibited practice because securities professionals may not borrow from customers who are not in the business of lending money. Furthermore, Mr. Thompson violated the USA in exceeding the specific discretionary authority that Mr. Bixby had authorized. Mr. Bixby had authorized Mr. Thompson to trade in securities—not to take his money for personal use. Had Mr. Thompson decided to borrow from The First National Bank, it would have been permitted because it is an entity engaged in the business of lending money.

TEST TOPIC ALERT

As a former President of the United States once said, "Let me make one thing perfectly clear." When it comes to borrowing or lending money, you cannot borrow from *any* client (including your mother), unless that client is a lending institution such as a bank or credit union. Likewise, as an agent, you can never lend money to any client unless the client has some kind of affiliation with your firm. If your broker-dealer handles margin accounts, then, of course, money can be loaned to clients. Don't take this personally, just get the questions right on the exam.

2. 11. 26 PRACTICES RELATING SOLELY TO AGENTS

2. 11. 26. 1 Selling Away

Effecting securities transactions not recorded on the regular books or records of the broker-dealer which the agent represents, unless the transactions are authorized in writing by the broker-dealer prior to execution of the transaction.

CASE STUDY   **Practices—Trades Not on the Books**

Situation: Mr. Thompson, a registered agent for First Securities, Inc., of Illinois, is also a part owner of Computer Resources, Inc., a privately held company in the state. Mr. Thompson is also a friend of Mr. Byers, the chairman of Aircraft Parts, Inc., a large manufacturing company traded on the NYSE. Mr. Byers has an account with Mr. Thompson at First Securities.

Mr. Thompson decides to sell his shares in Computer Resources to one of his clients. Because the shares are not publicly traded, Mr. Thompson completes the trades without informing First Securities or recording the transaction on their books. Mr. Thompson believes there is no need to inform his employer because the transaction was private. On the following day, Mr. Byers calls Mr. Thompson and indicates that he would like to sell his shares in Aircraft Parts. Mr. Thompson, who now has plenty of liquid assets from the sale of his shares in Computer Resources, decides to buy the shares directly from Mr. Byers. Mr. Thompson does not record the trade on the records of First Securities because he considers it a private transaction between himself and Mr. Byers.

Analysis: In both cases, Mr. Thompson has engaged in a prohibited practice. A registered agent may not conduct transactions with customers of his employing broker-dealer that are not recorded on the books without prior written consent. It makes no difference whether the shares Mr. Thompson sold were privately held; when an agent effects trades with clients of the firm, the transactions must be recorded on the books of the firm unless prior written authorization is obtained from the firm.

TEST TOPIC ALERT
The exam may refer to this as a trade made off the books of the broker-dealer. Just remember that it is considered to be a prohibited practice anytime an agent effects securities transactions not recorded on the regular books or records of the broker-dealer the agent represents, unless the transactions are authorized in writing by the broker-dealer before execution of the transaction.

2. 11. 26. 2 Fictitious Accounts

Establishing or maintaining an account containing fictitious information in order to execute transactions which would otherwise be prohibited. Examples of this kind of conduct sometimes given on the exam are "beefing up" a client's net worth to enable him to engage in margin or options trading, or making him appear to have more investment experience than is true.

2. 11. 26. 3 Sharing in Accounts

Sharing directly or indirectly in profits or losses in the account of any customer without the written authorization of the customer and the broker-dealer which the agent represents.

Agents cannot share in the profits or losses of client accounts unless the client and the broker-dealer supply prior written approval. In such a situation, it would be permissible to commingle the agent's and the customer's funds because they have a joint account.

TEST TOPIC ALERT
Unlike agents, broker-dealers, investment advisers, and investment adviser representatives are never permitted to share in the profits or losses in their client's accounts.

2. 11. 26. 4 Splitting Commissions

Dividing or otherwise splitting the agent's commissions, profits, or other compensation from the purchase or sale of securities with any person not also registered as an agent for the same broker-dealer, or for a broker-dealer under direct or indirect common control. It is not necessary to disclose to an agent's client that he is splitting commissions with another agent *unless* it increases the transaction cost to the client. This is one of the very rare cases where disclosure is not necessary.

QUICK QUIZ 2.J   Write **U** for unlawful or prohibited activities and **L** for lawful activities.

_____   1. An agent guarantees a client that funds invested in mutual funds made up of government securities cannot lose principal.

_____   2. A nondiscretionary customer calls his agent and places a buy order for 1,000 shares of any hot internet company. Later in the day, the agent enters an order for 1,000 shares of Global Internet Services.

_____   3. An agent receives a call from his client's spouse, advising him to sell her husband's securities. Her husband is out of the country and requested that his wife call the agent. The agent refuses because the wife does not have trading authorization, and she complains vigorously to his manager.

_____   4. A client writes a letter of complaint to his agent regarding securities that the agent had recommended. The agent calls the client to apologize and then disposes of the letter because the client seemed satisfied.

_____   5. A registered agent borrows $10,000 from a credit union that is one of her best customers.

_____   6. An agent is convinced that Internet Resources will rise significantly over the next 3 months. She offers to buy the stock back from her customers at 10% higher than its current price at any time during the next 3 months.

_____   7. An agent receives an order for the purchase of an obscure foreign security. The agent informs the client that the commissions and charges on this purchase will be much higher than those of domestic securities.

_____   8. An agent who works for a small broker-dealer that employs no securities analysts assures her clients that she can analyze any publicly traded security better than any analyst and that she will do it personally for each security purchased by a client, regardless of the industry.

_____   9. An agent recommends that her client buy 1,000 shares of Internet Consultants, Inc., an unregistered nonexempt security with a bright future.

10. Market manipulation is one of the prohibited practices under the Uniform Securities Act. Which of the following is an example of a broker-dealer engaging in market manipulation?
    I.   Churning
    II. Arbitrage
    III. Wash trades
    IV. Matched orders
    A.   I and II
    B.   I, III, and IV
    C.   III and IV
    D.   IV only

11. All of the following are prohibited practices under the USA EXCEPT
    I.   borrowing money or securities from the account of a former banker with express written permission of the bank
    II. failing to identify a customer's financial objectives
    III. selling rights instead of exercising them
    IV. supplying funds to a client's account only when or if it declines below a previously agreed-upon level
    A.   I and II
    B.   I, II, and III
    C.   II and IV
    D.   III only

12. A customer is upset with her agent for not servicing her account properly and sends him a complaint letter about his actions. Under the Uniform Securities Act, the agent should
    A.   call the customer, apologize, and attempt to correct the problem
    B.   tell the customer he is willing to make rescission
    C.   do nothing
    D.   bring the customer complaint to his employer immediately

13. An agent hears a rumor concerning a security and uses the rumor to convince a client to purchase the security. Under the USA, the agent may
    A.   recommend the security if it is an appropriate investment
    B.   recommend the investment if the rumor is based on material inside information
    C.   recommend the security if the source of the rumor came from a reliable source
    D.   not recommend the security

14. It is permitted under the USA for an individual licensed as an agent in the state to tell a client that
    A.   a registered security may lawfully be sold in that state
    B.   an exempt security is not required to be registered because it is generally regarded as being safer than a nonexempt security
    C.   her qualifications have been found satisfactory by the Administrator
    D.   a registered security has been approved for sale in the state by the Administrator

15. Which of the following is(are) prohibited under the USA?
    I.   Recommending tax shelters to low-income retirees
    II. Stating that a state Administrator has approved an offering on the basis of the quality of information found in the prospectus
    III. Soliciting orders for unregistered, nonexempt securities
    IV. Employing any device to defraud
    A. I only
    B. I and II
    C. I, II and III
    D. I, II, III, and IV

2. 12   JURISDICTION AND POWERS OF THE STATE ADMINISTRATOR

The jurisdiction and powers of the Administrator extend to activities related to securities transactions originated in the state, directed to the state, or accepted in the state.

2. 12. 1   SALE OR SELL AND OFFER OR OFFER TO SELL

2. 12. 1. 1   Sale or Sell

The USA defines **sale** or **sell** as every contract of sale, contract to sell, and disposition of a security or interest in a security for value. This means that any transfer of a security in which money or some other valuable consideration is involved is covered by this definition and subject to the act.

2. 12. 1. 2   Offer or Offer to Sell

The USA defines **offer** or **offer to sell** as every attempt or offer to dispose of, or solicitation of an offer to buy, a security or interest in a security for value. For test purposes, you should know that:

- any security given or delivered with, or as a bonus on account of, a purchase of securities or anything else (a car, jewelry, and so forth) is considered to constitute part of the subject of the purchase and to have been offered and sold for value;

- a purported gift of assessable stock is considered to involve an offer and a sale (assessable stock is stock issued below par for which the issuer or creditors have the right to assess shareholders for the balance of unpaid par); or

- a sale or offer of a warrant or right to purchase or subscribe to another security of the same or another issuer, as well as every sale or offer of a security which gives the holder a present or future right or privilege to convert into another security of the same or another issuer, is considered to include an offer of the other security.

If a car dealer, as an essential part of a car sale, offers $1,000 in corporate bonds as an incentive, this would be considered a bonus under the act and, therefore, this now becomes a securities sale and falls under the jurisdiction of the state securities Administrator. As a result, to do this, and I know it is hard to believe, the car dealer would have to register with the state as a broker-dealer.

2. 12. 1. 3 Assessable Stock

When assessable stock is given as a gift, the Administrator has jurisdiction over the transaction because there is a potential future obligation in that either the issuer or, more likely, creditors can demand payment for the balance of the par value.

TAKE NOTE

If an individual owned assessable stock and felt that the issuer was on the verge of bankruptcy, that person could give the stock as a present. If the bankruptcy occurred, the new owner would then be subject to the assessment.

2. 12. 1. 4 Exclusions From the Definition of Sale/Sell and Offer/Offer to Sell

The terms *sale* or *sell* and *offer* or *offer to sell* do not include any:

- bona fide pledge or loan;
- gift of nonassessable stock;
- stock dividend, whether the corporation distributing the dividend is the issuer of the stock or not, if nothing of value is given by stockholders for the dividend (and this would include stock splits);
- class vote by stockholders, pursuant to the certificate of incorporation or the applicable corporation statute, or a merger, consolidation, reclassification of securities, or sale of corporate assets in consideration of the issuance of securities of another corporation; or
- act incident to a judicially approved reorganization with which a security is issued in exchange for one or more outstanding securities, claims, or property interest, or partly in such exchange and partly for cash.

2. 13 LEGAL JURISDICTION OF THE ADMINISTRATOR

Under law, for any agent of a state (e.g., the Administrator) to have authority over an activity such as a sale or offer of securities, it must have **legal jurisdiction** to act. Jurisdiction under the USA specifically means the legal authority to regulate securities activities that take place in the state.

The USA describes those activities considered to have taken place in the state as any offer to buy or sell a security, as well as any acceptance of the offer, if the offer:

- **originated in** the Administrator's state;
- is **directed to** the Administrator's state; or
- is **accepted in** the Administrator's state.

TAKE NOTE

Because securities transactions often involve several states, more than one Administrator may have jurisdiction over a security or a transaction.

CASE STUDY

Offer Originated in Administrator's State

Situation: Mr. Thompson (a registered agent in Illinois and Indiana), on the recommendation of his best client (Mr. Bixby), phones a friend of Mr. Bixby's in Indiana. Mr. Thompson sells a security to Mr. Bixby's friend, Ms. Gordon, who then mails payment to Mr. Thompson's office in Illinois.

Analysis: The Administrators of both Illinois and Indiana have jurisdiction— the Administrator of Illinois has jurisdiction because the call (offer) originated in Illinois, and the Administrator of Indiana has jurisdiction because the offer was accepted by Ms. Gordon in Indiana.

CASE STUDY

Offer Directed to Administrator's State

Situation: The day after he completes his first transaction with Ms. Gordon, Mr. Thompson mails sales offering materials to her home address in Indiana. Ms. Gordon is not in a position to buy any more securities, so she discards the material without reading it.

Analysis: By sending sales materials to Ms. Gordon's home address in Indiana, Mr. Thompson directed the offer to Indiana. Even though Ms. Gordon discarded the information, the Administrator in Indiana has jurisdiction because the sales offer was directed to Indiana. The Administrator of Illinois also has jurisdiction because the offer originated in Illinois.

CASE STUDY

Offer Accepted in an Administrator's State

Situation: Mr. Thompson sends additional offers to Ms. Gordon in Indiana, who is now on a three-month summer vacation in Florida. Ms. Gordon has her mail forwarded to her in Florida. Upon receiving Mr. Thompson's materials in Florida, she decides to purchase the securities. She pays for the securities by mailing a check to Mr. Thompson drawn on her local bank in Indiana.

Analysis: The offer is accepted by Ms. Gordon while she was in Florida; therefore, the Administrator of Florida has jurisdiction. Additionally, the Administrator in Illinois has jurisdiction because the offer originated in Illinois, and the Administrator in Indiana has jurisdiction because the offer was directed to Indiana. This is a situation where the Administrators of three different states have jurisdiction.

TAKE NOTE
The Administrator's authority does not stop at the state line. The Administrator of any state where the registrant is registered may demand an inspection during reasonable business hours with whatever frequency the Administrator deems necessary.

TAKE NOTE
To avoid unnecessary duplication of examinations, the Administrator may cooperate with the securities administrators of other states, the SEC, and any national securities exchange or national securities association registered under the Securities Exchange Act of 1934.

2. 13. 1   PUBLISHING AND BROADCAST EXCEPTIONS TO JURISDICTION

There are special rules regarding the Administrator's jurisdiction over offers made through a TV or radio broadcast or through a bona fide newspaper.

The USA specifies that an offer would not be made in an Administrator's state and, therefore, the Administrator would not have jurisdiction if it were made in:

■ a television or radio broadcast that originated outside of the state;

■ a bona fide newspaper or periodical published outside of the state; or

■ a newspaper or periodical published inside the state but with more than two-thirds (66%) of its circulation outside the state in the last year.

TAKE NOTE
A bona fide newspaper is a newspaper of general interest and circulation, such as *The New York Times*. Private investment advisory newsletters, usually distributed by subscription, are not bona fide newspapers and therefore do not fall under the publishing exception.

TEST TOPIC ALERT
A radio or television program is considered to originate in the state where the microphone or television camera is located.

CASE STUDY   **Publishing and Broadcast Exemptions**

Situation: First Securities & Co., broker-dealers with offices in New York state and Illinois, offers to sell shares in a new retail shoe chain store located in New York. First Securities advertises the offering to residents of New York in the local newspaper, the *New York Gazette*. First Securities also advertises through the *Gazette's* wholly owned radio station. The *Gazette* and its radio station are both located in western New York near the Pennsylvania border. About 55% of the *Gazette's* readers and listeners live in Pennsylvania.

Analysis: Although more than half the readers and listeners of the *Gazette* live in Pennsylvania, under the terms of the publishing and broadcasting exemption of the USA, the offer is not made in Pennsylvania because the paper is not published in Pennsylvania, so the Administrator of New York state has sole jurisdiction over the offering. No dual or multiple jurisdiction applies in this case unless the offer is actually accepted in Pennsylvania. The fact that First Securities is registered in Illinois in addition to New York is not relevant to this offering because no securities were sold there, nor were any offers or advertising directed to the state.

QUICK QUIZ 2.K

1. A state's securities Administrator has jurisdiction over a securities offering if it was
   A. directed to residents of that state
   B. originated in that state
   C. accepted in that state
   D. all of the above

2. An Administrator has jurisdiction over an offer to sell securities if it is made in a newspaper published within the state with no more than
   A. $1/3$ of its circulation outside the state
   B. $1/2$ of its circulation outside the state
   C. $2/3$ of its circulation outside the state
   D. 90% of its circulation outside the state

3. What is the difference between an offer and a sale of a security?
   A. An offer can be made only by a customer and a sale can be made only by a broker-dealer.
   B. An offer is a binding proposal to sell and a sale is a nonbinding proposal to sell.
   C. An offer is the attempt to sell and a sale is a binding contract to transfer a security for value
   D. An offer must be approved by a designated supervisory person and a sale needs no such approval.

2.14 ACTIONS TO BE TAKEN BY THE ADMINISTRATOR

The USA not only establishes the jurisdiction of the Administrator but also outlines the powers that the Administrator has within his jurisdiction.

The four broad powers the Administrator has to enforce and administer the act in its state are to:

- make, amend, or rescind rules and orders;
- conduct investigations and issue subpoenas;
- issue cease and desist orders and seek injunctions; and
- deny, suspend, cancel, or revoke registrations and licenses.

Although the Administrator has powers to enforce the act for the benefit of the public, the Administrator and his employees have the obligation not to misuse the office for personal gain. Administrators are, as a result, prohibited from using for their own benefit any information derived from their official duties that has not been made public.

2. 14. 1   RULES, ORDERS, AND FORMS

To enforce the USA, the Administrator has the authority to make, amend, or rescind rules, forms, and orders necessary to administer the act. The Administrator may also issue interpretive letters. The USA requires that all rules and forms be published. A rule or order of the Administrator has the same authority as a provision of the act itself, but these rules and orders are not part of the USA itself. The difference between a rule and an order is that a rule applies to everyone, whereas an order applies to a specific instance.

EXAMPLE   The Administrator may decide to issue a rule requiring all agents to pay an annual registration fee of $250. This *rule* applies to everyone. Or, the Administrator may find that a specific agent has violated a provision of the law and orders a 30-day suspension. This *order* applies only to that particular agent.

A person may challenge an order of the Administrator in court within 60 days of order issuance.

Although the Administrator has the power to make and amend rules for compliance with his state's blue-sky laws, he does not have the power to alter the law itself.

The composition or content of state securities law is the responsibility of the state legislature and not that of administrative agencies. Rules for administration and compliance with the law are the responsibility of the securities Administrator.

CASE STUDY   **Rules and Orders of the Administrator**

Situation: The Iowa state securities Administrator requires by rule that all companies registering their securities in Iowa must supply financial statements in a specific form and with content prescribed by the Administrator. However, the Administrator does not publish the rule because the rule is too long and complex.

Analysis: The USA allows state Administrators to issue rules and orders in carrying out their regulatory functions, and the Iowa Administrator acted properly in designing the form and content for financial reports. However, it is required by the USA that Administrators publish all rules and orders. The Administrator, despite the latitude given him in administering the USA, cannot suspend any provision of the USA itself. The Iowa Administrator acted within his authority in designing the forms but acted without authority—that is, he violated the USA— by suspending the requirement that all rules and orders be published.

2. 14. 2 CONDUCT INVESTIGATIONS AND ISSUE SUBPOENAS

The Administrator has broad discretionary authority to **conduct investigations** and **issue subpoenas**. These investigations may be made in public or in private and may occur within or outside of the Administrator's state. Normally, these investigations are open to the public, but when, in the opinion of the Administrator and with the consent of all parties, it is felt that a private investigation is more appropriate, that investigation will be conducted without public scrutiny.

In conducting an investigation, the Administrator, or any officer designated by him, has the power to:

■ require statements in writing, under oath, as to all matters relating to the issue under investigation;

■ publish and make public the facts and circumstances concerning the issue to be investigated;

■ subpoena witnesses and compel their attendance and testimony; and

■ take evidence and require the production of books, papers, correspondence, and any other documents deemed relevant.

TEST TOPIC ALERT   If the Administrator of State A wishes to investigate a BD registered in State A, but whose principal office is located in State B, does he need the okay of the State B Administrator? No! When can he go in? The Administrator can go in during normal business hours and doesn't need to make an appointment.

2. 14. 2. 1 Contumacy

So, what happens if a person who is the subject of an investigation refuses to furnish the required evidence or just ignores the subpoena? After all, the Administrator is not a police officer—he doesn't wear a badge and cannot arrest anyone. There is a legal term that describes this type of disobedience. That term is *contumacy* and here is what the USA says about that:

> *In case of contumacy by, or refusal to obey a subpoena issued to, any person, the Administrator may apply to the appropriate court in his state and ask for help. Upon application by the Administrator, the court can issue an order to the person requiring him to appear before the Administrator, or the officer designated by him, to produce documentary evidence if so ordered or to give evidence touching the matter under investigation or in question. Failure to obey the order of the court may be punished by the court as a contempt of court.*

Contempt of court can, of course, lead to jail time.

In addition to having the power to conduct investigations, the Administrator may enforce subpoenas issued by Administrators in other states on the same basis as if the alleged offense took place in the Administrator's state. However, the Administrator may issue and apply to enforce subpoenas in his state at the request of a securities agency or administrator of another state only if the activities constituting an alleged violation for which the information is sought would be a violation of the USA if the activities had occurred in his state.

2. 14. 3 ISSUE CEASE AND DESIST ORDERS

Whenever it appears to the Administrator that any person has engaged or is about to engage in any act or practice constituting a violation of any provision of this act or any rule or order hereunder, she may in her discretion bring either or both of the following remedies:

(a) issue a cease and desist order, with or without a prior hearing, against the person or persons engaged in the prohibited activities, directing them to cease and desist from further illegal activity; or

(b) bring an action in the appropriate court to obtain enforcement of the order through the issuance of a temporary or permanent injunction. If necessary, the court may appoint a receiver or conservator for the defendant or the defendant's assets.

The Administrator is granted this power to prevent potential violations before they occur. It is sometimes said that the Administrator can act when she "smells the smoke, even without seeing the fire." Sometimes a tipster or whistleblower will divulge information to the Administrator that might be relevant to a serious infraction. To prevent any further damage to investors, a cease and desist order can be entered.

Although the Administrator has the power to issue cease and desist orders, she does not have the legal power to compel compliance with the order. To compel compliance in the face of a person's resistance, the Administrator must apply to a court of competent jurisdiction for an injunction. Only the courts can compel compliance by issuing injunctions and imposing penalties for violation of them. You will need to know that **enjoined** is the legal term that is used to refer to a person who is the subject of an injunction. If a temporary or permanent injunction is issued, upon request of the Administrator, a receiver or conservator may be appointed over the defendant's assets.

Cease and desist orders are not the same as stop orders. **Cease and desist orders** are directed to persons, requiring them to cease activities. Stop orders are directed to applications regarding registration of a security.

CASE STUDY   **Cease and Desist Orders**

> **Situation:** Mr. Thompson is registered to conduct business in the state of Illinois and makes plans to sell a security within the next few days. The Administrator considers this security ineligible for sale in the state. The Administrator orders Mr. Thompson to stop his sales procedures immediately.
>
> **Analysis:** The Administrator of Illinois issued a cease and desist order to Mr. Thompson because there was insufficient time to conduct a public hearing before the sale to determine whether the security was eligible for sale in the state.

Frequently, before a final determination of proceedings under the act, the Administrator will act summarily to suspend a registration. However, no formal order may be issued without the Administrator:

- giving appropriate prior notice to the affected persons;
- granting an opportunity for a hearing; and
- providing findings of fact and conclusions of law.

2. 14. 4 DENY, SUSPEND, CANCEL, OR REVOKE REGISTRATIONS

The Administrator has the power to deny, suspend, cancel, or revoke the registration of broker-dealers, investment advisers, and their representatives as well as the registration of securities issues.

2. 14. 4. 1 Broker-dealers, Advisers, and Their Representatives

To justify a denial, revocation, or suspension of the license of a **securities professional**, the Administrator must find that the order is in the public interest and also find that the applicant or registrant, or in the case of a broker-dealer or investment adviser, any partner, officer, or director, or any person occupying a similar status or performing similar functions:

- has filed an incomplete, false, or misleading registration application;
- has willfully violated the USA;
- has been disqualified from membership in any securities or commodities regulatory body due to a conviction of a securities-related misdemeanor as a result of action brought within the last 10 years;
- has been convicted of any felony within the last 10 years;
- has been enjoined by law from engaging in the securities business;
- is subject to another Administrator's denial, revocation, or suspension;
- is engaged in dishonest or unethical securities practices;
- is insolvent;
- is the subject of an adjudication that the broker-dealer has willfully violated the Securities Act of 1933, the Securities Exchange Act of 1934, the Investment Advisers Act of 1940, the Investment Company Act of 1940, or the Commodities Exchange Act;
- has failed to reasonably supervise his agents or employees;

- has failed to pay application filing fees; or
- is not qualified on the basis of training, lack of experience, and knowledge of the securities business.

TEST TOPIC ALERT

Because of a lack of uniformity in state criminal laws, it can happen that a person is convicted of a misdemeanor in one state and then moves to a state where that same crime is a felony. If the person were to then apply for registration, the Administrator must consider the crime under the statutes of the state where it occurred, not his own. In other words, the Administrator may only consider what is on the person's record.

TEST TOPIC ALERT

If a person is subject to a disqualification by any SRO, even the NASD (before it became FINRA), for something that was *not* a violation of the Uniform Securities Act, that would still be a cause for denial.

TAKE NOTE

The public's best interest is not reason enough for the denial, suspension, or revocation of a registration. There must be a further reason, as described above.

Other than when acting summarily, no order to deny, suspend, or revoke may be entered without:

- appropriate prior notice to the applicant or registrant (as well as the employer or prospective employer if the applicant or registrant is an agent or investment adviser representative);
- opportunity for hearing; and
- written findings of fact and conclusions of law.

The Administrator may not suspend or revoke a registration on the basis of facts that were known to the Administrator at the time the registration became effective (unless the proceedings are initiated within 90 days).

2. 14. 4. 1. 1 Lack of Qualification

An Administrator may not base a denial of a person's registration solely on his lack of experience. However, the Administrator may consider that registration as a broker-dealer does not necessarily qualify one for a license as an investment adviser and may restrict that applicant's registration as a broker-dealer conditional upon its not functioning as an investment adviser.

To better understand these two points, let's look at the wording in the Act itself:

1. The Administrator may not enter an order denying registration solely on the basis of lack of experience if the applicant or registrant is qualified by training or knowledge or both.

Obviously, a new applicant for registration as an agent is not going to have any experience selling securities. So, the Act says that this lack of experience by itself is not enough to deny the registration as long as the Administrator feels assured that the individual will receive adequate training and/or has the requisite knowledge. One could suppose that passing this exam demonstrates the necessary knowledge.

> *2. The Administrator may consider that an investment adviser is not necessarily qualified solely on the basis of experience as a broker-dealer or agent. When he finds that an applicant for initial or renewal registration as a broker-dealer is not qualified as an investment adviser, he may, by order, condition the applicant's registration as a broker-dealer upon his not transacting business in this state as an investment adviser.*

In this case, the Act is dealing with a person who has experience, albeit not necessarily in the giving of advice. Just because a person has been a broker-dealer, or an agent for a broker-dealer, does not mean that the person is qualified to be an investment adviser. So, the registration will be limited to acting only in their stated capacity as long as one does not cross over the line and give investment advice.

2. 14. 4. 1. 2 Summary Powers

One of the powers of the Administrator is known as acting **summarily**. This means that he may order, without having to go through the hearing process, a postponement or suspension of a registration pending final determination of any proceeding based upon actions described above. Once the summary order is entered, the Administrator will promptly notify the applicant or registrant, as well as the employer or prospective employer if the applicant or registrant is an agent or investment adviser representative, that it has been entered and of the reasons for it. If the applicant wishes a hearing, written request must be made and, within fifteen days after the receipt of the written request, the matter will be set down for hearing. If no hearing is requested and none is ordered by the Administrator, the order will remain in effect until it is modified or vacated by the Administrator.

As stated previously (and repeated because it is likely to be on the exam), other than when the Administrator has acted summarily as described above, no final order may be issued without the Administrator:

■ giving appropriate prior notice to the affected persons;

■ granting an opportunity for a hearing; and

■ providing findings of fact and conclusions of law.

QUICK QUIZ 2.L

1. With regard to the powers of the Administrator, which of the following statements are NOT true?

   I. The Administrator must seek an injunction to issue a cease and desist order.

   II. The USA requires an Administrator to conduct a full hearing, public or private, before issuing a cease and desist order.

   III. The USA grants the Administrator the power to issue injunctions to force compliance with the provisions of the act.

   A. I and II

   B. I and III

   C. II and III

   D. I, II and III

2. Although the Administrator has great power, the USA does place some limitations on the office. Which of the following statements regarding those powers are TRUE?

    I. In conducting an investigation, an Administrator can compel the testimony of witnesses.

    II. Investigations of serious violations must be open to the public.

    III. An Administrator in Illinois may only enforce subpoenas from South Carolina if the violation originally occurred in Illinois.

    IV. An administrator may deny the registration of a securities professional who has been convicted of any felony within the past 10 years.

    A. I, II and IV

    B. I, III and IV

    C. I and IV

    D. II and III

3. To protect the public, the Administrator may

    I. deny a registration if the registrant does not have sufficient experience to function as an agent

    II. consider that an applicant for registration as an investment adviser is not necessarily qualified solely on the basis of experience as a broker-dealer or agent and, therefore, when he finds that an applicant for initial or renewal registration as a broker-dealer is not qualified as an investment adviser, he may by order condition the applicant's registration as a broker-dealer upon his not transacting business in this state as an investment adviser

    III. take into consideration that the registrant will work under the supervision of a registered investment adviser or broker-dealer in approving a registration

    IV. deny a registration, although denial is not in the public's interest, if it is prudent in view of a change in the state's political composition

    A. I and II

    B. II and III

    C. III and IV

    D. I, II, III, and IV

4. Under powers granted by the Uniform Securities Act, the Administrator may take all of the following actions EXCEPT

    A. issue a cease and desist order against a broker-dealer

    B. issue an arrest warrant for an investment adviser representative

    C. refer evidence concerning violations of this act to the attorney general or the proper district attorney who may then institute the appropriate criminal proceedings

    D. file a civil complaint against an agent

2. 14. 4. 2 Securities Issues

The Administrator has the power under the USA to deny, suspend, or revoke the registration of a security by issuing a stop order; however, the Administrator can invoke these powers only if it is in the public's interest and:

■ the applicant files a false or incomplete statement;

- the applicant is in violation of the USA;
- the applicant is engaged in a method of business that is illegal;
- the applicant has prepared a fraudulent registration;
- the underwriter charges unreasonable fees;
- the issue is subject to a court injunction; or
- the registrant is subject to an administrative stop order of any other state.

In addition, the Administrator may deny a registration if the applicant fails to pay the filing fee. When the fee is paid, the denial order will be removed provided the applicant is in compliance with all registration procedures.

Unless the Administrator is acting summarily, no stop order may be entered to deny, suspend, or revoke the registration of a security without:

- appropriate prior notice to the applicant or registrant, the issuer, and the person on whose behalf the securities are to be or have been offered;
- opportunity for hearing; and
- written findings of fact and conclusions of law.

TEST TOPIC ALERT   When the conditions that led to the issuance of the stop order have changed for the better, the legal term (remember, this is a law exam) used to describe the lifting of the stop order is **vacated** (e.g., "the order has been vacated").

2. 14. 5 NONPUNITIVE TERMINATIONS OF REGISTRATION

A registration can be terminated even if there has not been a violation of the USA. A request for withdrawal and lack of qualification are both reasons for cancellation.

2. 14. 5. 1 Withdrawal

A person may request on his own initiative a withdrawal of a registration. The withdrawal is effective 30 days after the Administrator receives it, provided no revocation or suspension proceedings are in process against the person making the request. In that event, the Administrator may institute a revocation or suspension proceeding within one year after a withdrawal becomes effective.

2. 14. 5. 2 Cancellation

If an Administrator finds that an applicant or a registrant no longer exists or has ceased to transact business, the Administrator may cancel the registration.

TEST TOPIC ALERT   Once your registration has been withdrawn, the Administrator still retains jurisdiction over you for a period of one year.

TEST TOPIC ALERT

You may encounter this type of question regarding cancellation: "What would the Administrator do if mailings to a registrant were returned with no forwarding address?" The answer is, "Cancel the registration."

The Administrator may also cancel a registration if a person is declared mentally incompetent.

TAKE NOTE

Be familiar with the distinctions between cancellation and denial, suspension, or revocation. Cancellation does not result from violations or a failure to follow the provisions of the act. Cancellation occurs as the result of death, dissolution, or mental incompetency.

TEST TOPIC ALERT

Because an agent's (or IAR's) registration is dependent on being associated with a broker-dealer (or IA), when the employer's registration is suspended or revoked, that of the registered individual is placed into suspense or some other term with essentially the same effect. When the period of suspension of the firm is over, registration of the individuals is reactivated. If the firm's registration has been revoked, then the individual will either have to find a new affiliation or the license will be canceled. Individual agents or IARs who withdraw their registration must re-affiliate within two years or will be required to retake the exam to re-qualify.

QUICK QUIZ 2.M

1. Which of the following statements relating to termination of registration is TRUE?

   A. A registration, once in effect, may never be voluntarily withdrawn.
   B. An Administrator may not cancel a registration of a securities professional who is declared mentally incompetent.
   C. An Administrator may revoke the registration of a securities professional who is declared mentally incompetent.
   D. An Administrator may cancel the registration of a registrant no longer in business.

2. 15   PENALTIES FOR VIOLATIONS OF THE UNIFORM SECURITIES ACT

The USA provides both civil liabilities and criminal penalties for persons who violate the USA. In addition, the act provides for recovery by a client of financial loss that results from the fraudulent sale of a security or investment advice. In many cases, when an agent or IAR is found civilly liable for improper behavior, officers or other supervisory personnel of the firm may be liable as well if failure to supervise can be proven.

2. 15. 1 CIVIL LIABILITIES

Persons who sell securities or offer investment advice in violation of the USA are subject to **civil liabilities** (as well as possible criminal penalties).

The purchaser of securities sold in violation of the act may sue the seller to recover financial loss.

The purchaser may sue for recovery if:

- a sale was made of an unregistered nonexempt security in violation of the registration provisions of USA;
- the securities professional omits or makes an untrue statement of material fact during a sales presentation;
- the agent was named along with the broker-dealer for a civil infraction;
- the securities were sold by an agent who should have been but was not registered under the act; or
- the securities were sold in violation of a rule or order of the securities Administrator.

2. 15. 1. 1 Statute of Limitations

The time limit, or statute of limitations, for violations of the civil provisions of the USA is three years from the date of sale (or rendering of the investment advice) or two years after discovering the violation, whichever comes first.

2. 15. 1. 2 Rights of Recovery from Improper Sale of Securities

If the purchaser of securities feels that the sale has been made in violation of the USA, that purchaser may file a complaint with the Administrator. If the Administrator investigates the claim and finds it has merit, then a case will be opened against the offending broker-dealer and/or agent.

If the client's case is proven, at the direction of the Administrator, the client may recover:

- the original purchase price of the securities ("made whole"); plus
- interest at a rate determined by the Administrator (generally referred to as the state's *legal rate*); plus
- all reasonable attorney's fees and court costs; minus
- any income received while the securities were held.

TAKE NOTE

The exam may refer to the interest paid to the client as being at the state's legal rate.

2. 15. 1. 3 Rights of Recovery from Improper Investment Advice

A person who buys a security as the result of investment advice received in violation of the USA also has the right to file a complaint. In the case of securities purchased as a result of improper investment advice, if the client's case is proven, at the direction of the Administrator, the advisory client may recover:

- cost of the advice; plus
- loss as a result of the advice; plus
- interest at a rate determined by the Administrator; plus
- any reasonable attorney's fees minus
- the amount of any income received from the advice.

When securities are sold improperly, the buyer can recover the original purchase price in addition to other losses. When improper investment advice is offered, the purchaser of the advice is entitled to recover the cost of the advice and losses incurred but is not entitled to recover the original purchase price from the adviser.

TEST TOPIC ALERT   The USA provides that every cause of action under this statute survives the death of any person who might have been a plaintiff or defendant. Therefore, any bond required must provide that suit may be brought for the specified statute of limitations even though the person who is bonded dies before the expiration of that period.

2. 15. 1. 4 Right of Rescission

If the seller of securities discovers that a sale has been made in violation of the USA, the seller may offer to repurchase the securities from the buyer. In this case, the seller is offering the buyer the **right of rescission**. To satisfy the buyer's right of rescission, the amount paid back to the buyer must include the original purchase price and interest, as determined by the Administrator.

By offering to buy back the securities that were sold in violation of the act, the seller can avoid a lawsuit (and legal fees and court costs) through a **letter of rescission**. The buyer has 30 days after receiving the letter of rescission to respond. If the buyer does not accept or reject the rescission offer within 30 days, the buyer gives up any right to pursue a lawsuit at a later date.

To further explain the reason for the 30 days to accept or reject, the purpose of that is to take care of the case where the buyer has already disposed of the security before the rescission offer is made to him. In such a case, the buyer is not denied the ability to bring suit if he is not satisfied with the seller's computation of damages, but in order to do so he must reject the rescission offer within 30 days so that the seller may know where he stands.

TEST TOPIC ALERT   Unlike some federal laws, there is no provision for receiving treble damages. That is, in addition to receiving back your investment, you receive payment equal to three times what you lost. That is primarily found in the federal laws regarding insider trading, but that is not relevant to the Uniform Securities Act.

2. 15. 1. 5 Claims Against the Surety Bond

Earlier in this session, we discussed the need for securities professionals to post a surety bond under certain conditions. The USA states:

> *Every bond shall provide for suit thereon by any person who has a cause of action under this Act and, if the Administrator by rule or order requires, by any person who has a cause of action not arising under this act. Every bond shall provide that no suit may be maintained to enforce any liability on the bond unless brought within the time limitations of the Act.*

TEST TOPIC ALERT

In other words, in order for a surety bond to meet the requirements of the USA, it must provide that any customer who can prove a violation (and does so within the statute of limitations) is entitled to collect against the bond.

TAKE NOTE

Because this is an exam based on the law, it is sometimes necessary for us to delve into the legalities more than we would like. The USA states: "Any person who offers or sells a security in violation of the Act is liable to the person buying the security from him." What this does is impose civil liability when the offer violates one of the specified provisions even though the sale does not. The making of a nonexempted offer before the effective date can create no civil rights on behalf of the offeree (the potential buyer) unless the offer results in a sale. When it does, however, this language means that the buyer may recover even though no contract was made until after the effective date.

2. 15. 2 CRIMINAL PENALTIES

Persons found guilty of a fraudulent securities transaction are subject to criminal penalties (as well as possible civil liabilities). Upon conviction, a person may be fined, imprisoned, or both. The maximum penalty is a fine of $5,000, a jail sentence of three years, or both. It is important to note that no person may be imprisoned for the violation of any rule or order if he proves that he had no knowledge of the rule or order. In other words, you have to know that you are willingly in violation in order to get jail time. It is also important to note that while the Administrator does not have the power to arrest anyone, he may apply to the appropriate authorities in his state for the issuance of an arrest warrant. The appropriate state prosecutor, usually the State Attorney General, may decide whether to bring a criminal action under the USA, another statute, or, when applicable, common law. In certain states, the Administrator has full or limited criminal enforcement powers. To be convicted of fraud, the violation must be willful and the registrant must know that the activity is fraudulent.

TAKE NOTE

Fraud is the deliberate or willful concealment, misrepresentation, or omission of material information or the truth to deceive or manipulate another person for unlawful or unfair gain. Under the USA, fraud is not limited to common-law deceit.

2. 15. 2. 1 Statute of Limitations

The statute of limitations for criminal offenses under the USA is five years from the date of the offense.

TAKE NOTE

Remember the sequence 5-5-3 for the application of criminal penalties: 5-year statute of limitations, $5,000 maximum fine, and/or imprisonment of no more than 3 years.

Under the civil provisions, the statute of limitations runs for 2 years from the discovery of the offense or to 3 years after the act occurred, whichever occurs first.

CASE STUDY

Fraudulent Sale of Securities

Situation: Mr. Thompson, the registered sales agent, knowingly omitted the fact that the shares of a company he sold to his client, Mr. Bixby, were downgraded to speculative grade and that their bonds were placed on a credit watch by one of the major credit rating agencies. A month after the sale, the shares became worthless.

Analysis: Mr. Thompson sold these securities to Mr. Bixby in violation of the USA because he deliberately or knowingly failed to mention material information—information that was important for Mr. Bixby to know for him to make an informed investment decision. Mr. Bixby has the right to recover the financial losses that result from the sale.

Under the USA, the actual seller of the securities or the advice is not the only person liable for the violation of the act. Every person who directly or indirectly controls the person who sold the securities or the advice, or is a material aid to the transaction, is also liable to the same extent as the person who conducted the transaction unless that supervisor could not have reasonably known about the improper activity.

2. 15. 3 JUDICIAL REVIEW OF ORDERS (APPEAL)

Any person affected by an order of the Administrator may obtain a review of the order in an appropriate court by filing a written petition within 60 days. In general, filing an appeal does not automatically act as a stay of the penalty. The order will go into effect as issued unless the court rules otherwise.

2. 16 SALES OF SECURITIES AT FINANCIAL INSTITUTIONS

The 1990s saw a proliferation of broker-dealer services being offered on the premises of financial institutions, particularly banks. In response to the potential for confusion as well as conflicts of interest, NASAA prepared Model Rules for sales of securities at financial institutions which were adopted October 6, 1998. Here are the key points for you to know.

No broker-dealer shall conduct broker-dealer services on the premises of a financial institution where retail deposits (that means from ordinary customers like you and me) are taken unless the broker-dealer complies initially and continuously with the following requirements.

2. 16. 1 SETTING

Wherever practical, broker-dealer services shall be conducted in a physical location distinct from the area in which the financial institution's retail deposits are taken. In those situations where there is insufficient space to allow separate areas, the broker-dealer has a heightened responsibility to distinguish its services from those of the financial institution. The broker-dealer's name shall be clearly displayed in the area in which the broker-dealer conducts its services.

2. 16. 2 CUSTOMER DISCLOSURE AND WRITTEN ACKNOWLEDGMENT

At or prior to the time that a customer's securities brokerage account is opened by a broker-dealer on the premises of a financial institution where retail deposits are taken, the broker-dealer must:

■ disclose, orally and in writing, that the securities products purchased or sold in a transaction with the broker-dealer

— are not insured by the Federal Deposit Insurance Corporation (FDIC),

— are not deposits or other obligations of the financial institution and are not guaranteed by the financial institution, and

— are subject to investment risks, including possible loss of the principal invested; and

■ make reasonable efforts to obtain from each customer, during the account opening process, a written acknowledgment of the disclosures.

2. 16. 3 COMMUNICATIONS WITH THE PUBLIC

The following logo format disclosures may be used by a broker-dealer in advertisements and sales literature, including material published, or designed for use, in radio or television broadcasts, Automated Teller Machine (ATM) screens, billboards, signs, posters, and brochures, to comply with the requirements, provided that such disclosures are displayed in a conspicuous manner:

■ Not FDIC Insured

■ No Bank Guarantee

■ May Lose Value

As long as the omission of the disclosures would not cause the advertisement or sales literature to be misleading in light of the context in which the material is presented, such disclosures are not required with respect to messages contained in:

- radio broadcasts of 30 seconds or less;

- electronic signs, including billboard-type signs that are electronic, time, and temperature signs and ticker tape signs, but excluding messages contained in such media as television, online computer services, or ATMs; and

- signs, such as banners and posters, when used only as location indicators.

QUICK QUIZ 2.N

1. Which of the following statements relating to penalties under the USA is TRUE?

   A. Unknowing violation of the USA by an agent is cause for imprisonment under the criminal liability provisions of the act.

   B. A purchaser of a security where an agent committed a violation of the USA may recover the original purchase price plus legal costs plus interest, less any income already received.

   C. A seller who notices that a sale was made in violation of the act may offer a right of rescission to the purchaser; this must be accepted within the sooner of two years after notice of the violation or three years after the sale.

   D. Any person aggrieved by an order of the Administrator may request an appeal of the order within 15 days, which, in effect, functions as a stay of the order during the appeal period.

2. When making an offer of a new issue that is in registration to a prospective client, an agent claims that his registration with the Administrator is proof of his qualifications. Under the USA

   A. claiming his registration is approved by the Administrator while making an offer of a security undergoing registration subjects this agent to a civil liability claim

   B. claiming his registration is approved by the Administrator while making an offer of a security does not subject this agent to a civil liability claim until the registration becomes effective

   C. claiming his registration is approved by the Administrator subjects this agent only to civil liability if a sale results

   D. regardless of whether a sale takes place, an agent making a misleading statement of this type subjects himself to possible civil liability

3. If convicted of a willful violation of the Uniform Securities Act, an agent is subject to

   A. imprisonment for 5 years

   B. a fine of $5,000 and/or imprisonment for 3 years

   C. a fine of $10,000

   D. disbarment

4. The Administrator has authority to
   I. issue a cease and desist order without a hearing
   II. issue a cease and desist order only after a hearing
   III. suspend an effective securities registration upon discovering an officer of the registrant has been convicted of a nonsecurities related crime
   IV. sentence violators of the USA to 3 years in prison
   A. I only
   B. I and IV
   C. II and III
   D. II and IV

5. If a broker-dealer wishes to conduct operations on the premises of a financial institution, it is required to
   I. disclose both in writing and orally to customers that the investments being sold are not FDIC insured, may lose value, and are not obligations of the financial institution
   II. make a reasonable attempt to be in a location physically distinct from that where retail deposits are taken
   III. attempt to obtain written acknowledgement from customers that they have received and read the disclaimers
   IV. be under common control with the institution
   A. I and IV
   B. I, II, and III
   C. II and III
   D. I, II, III, and IV

6. An agent of a broker-dealer who willfully violates the Uniform Securities Act may be subject to which of the following?
   I. Civil liabilities
   II. Criminal penalties
   III. Action taken by the Administrator to deny, suspend, or revoke the agent's registration
   A. I only
   B. I and II
   C. II and III
   D. I, II, and III

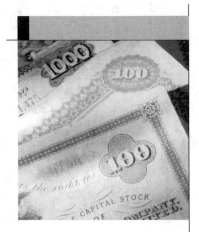

3

Federal and State Regulation of Investment Advisers and Their Representatives

Investment advisers and their representatives are defined by federal and state securities laws. A person that performs the functions of an investment adviser, as the term is defined in the Investment Advisers Act of 1940 and more fully described in SEC Release IA-1092, is by definition an investment adviser. Advisers and their representatives must conduct business within the regulatory framework prescribed in federal and state securities laws.

The Series 65 exam will include approximately 15 questions on the material presented in this session.

When you have completed this session, you should be able to:

■ **define** federal covered investment adviser and list exemptions and exclusions under the Investment Advisers Act of 1940 and the Uniform Securities Act;

■ **describe** the investment adviser registration process, required post registration filings, and business activities;

■ **identify** required elements of the investment advisory contract, client disclosure brochure, wrap-fee programs, and solicitor's brochure;

■ **list** the important ethical considerations and fiduciary responsibilities in providing investment advisory services;

■ **explain** the impact of SEC Release IA-1092 on the definition of investment advisers and their activities; and

■ **understand** the implications of the NASAA Model Rule on Unethical Business Practices of Investment Advisers, Investment Adviser Representatives, and Federal Covered Advisers.

3. 1   INVESTMENT ADVISERS ACT OF 1940

The **Investment Advisers Act of 1940** is the federal legislation that defines the term *investment adviser* and requires persons that fall within the definition to register with the **Securities and Exchange Commission (SEC)** or with the **states** in which they do business. As we have discussed earlier, under the **National Securities Markets Improvement Act of 1996 (NSMIA)**, investment advisers who are registered with the SEC under the Investment Advisers Act of 1940, (federal covered advisers), do not register with state securities Administrators.

The two primary purposes of the Investment Advisers Act of 1940 are:

■ the regulation of persons, both natural and legal, in the business of giving investment advice; and

■ the establishment of standards of ethical business conduct for the industry.

3. 1. 1   DEFINITIONS

To understand the application of this act, it is necessary to understand the definitions that follow. Although these definitions come from the Investment Advisers Act of 1940—federal legislation—the same terms are used in the Uniform Securities Act (USA), model legislation that most states use for drafting state securities laws, known as blue-sky laws, as discussed in Session 2.

3. 1. 1. 1   Broker

A **broker** means any person engaged in the business of effecting transactions in securities for the account of others.

3. 1. 1. 2   Dealer

A **dealer** is any person regularly engaged in the business of buying and selling securities as principal for his own account, but does not include a bank, insurance company, or an investment company.

3. 1. 1. 3   Fiduciary

A **fiduciary** is a person legally appointed and authorized to hold assets in trust for another person. The fiduciary manages the assets for the benefit of the other person rather than for his or her own profits and must exercise a standard of care imposed by law. Examples include an executor of an estate, a trustee, and, in this exam, an investment adviser.

3. 1. 1. 4   Person

Although the definition of person (see Session 2) under the USA is somewhat broader than that found in federal law, for purposes of the exam, the slight differences are not relevant.

3. 1. 1. 5   Person Associated with an Investment Adviser

Person associated with an investment adviser means any partner, officer, or director of the investment adviser (or any person performing similar functions) or any person directly or indirectly controlling or controlled by the investment adviser, including any employees of the investment adviser, except that as far as registration requirements are concerned, persons associated with investment advisers whose functions are clerical or administerial are not included in the meaning of the term. Most students taking this course are included in the definition of an investment adviser representative.

3. 1. 1. 6   Supervised Person

Supervised person means any partner, officer, director (or other person occupying a similar status or performing similar functions), or employee of an investment adviser, or other person who provides investment advice on behalf of the investment adviser and is subject to the supervision and control of the investment adviser.

What is the difference between an associated person and a supervised person? The supervised person includes all employees, even those who perform clerical functions and are not required to become registered.

QUICK QUIZ 3.A

1. Seven Seas Strategic Advisers (SSSA) maintains a place of business in 11 states and is registered with the SEC. As defined in the Investment Advisers Act of 1940, the office from which control of the activities of SSSA takes place is known as the

   A. Office of Supervisory Jurisdiction (OSJ)
   B. Principal office and place of business
   C. Home office
   D. Executive office

Quick Quiz answers can be found at the end of the unit.

3. 1. 1. 7   Principal Office and Place of Business

Both state and federal law define this as "the executive office of the investment adviser from which the officers, partners, or managers of the investment adviser direct, control, and coordinate the activities of the investment adviser."

3. 2 WHO ARE INVESTMENT ADVISERS?

An **investment adviser** is defined under both the Investment Advisers Act of 1940 and the USA as "any person who, for compensation, engages in the business of advising others as to the value of securities or the advisability of investing in securities or, as part of a regular business, issues analyses or reports concerning securities."

3. 2. 1   SEC RELEASE IA-1092

As a result of the proliferation of persons offering investment advice, Congress directed the SEC to define the activities that would subject a person to the 1940 Investment Advisers Act. The SEC did so in SEC Release IA-1092.

SEC Release IA-1092 interprets the definition of investment adviser under the Investment Advisers Act of 1940 to include financial planners, pension consultants, and others who offer investment advice as part of their financial practices.

Release IA-1092, in short, identifies as an investment adviser anyone who:

- provides investment advice, reports, or analyses with respect to securities;
- is in the business of providing advice or analyses; and
- receives compensation, directly or indirectly, for these services.

TAKE NOTE

If a person engages in these three activities, that person is an investment adviser subject to the Investment Advisers Act of 1940. As an investment adviser, this person must register with either the SEC or the states.

3. 2. 1. 1   Provide Investment Advice

In Release IA-1092, the SEC maintains that a person who gives advice, whether in written or oral form, and issues reports, analyses, and recommendations about specific securities is an investment adviser if that person is in the business of doing so and receives compensation for the advice. This definition of an investment adviser includes financial planners, pension consultants, and sports and entertainment representatives.

3. 2. 1. 1. 1   Financial Planners

Financial planners who make recommendations regarding a person's financial resources or perform analyses that concern securities are investment advisers if such services are performed as part of a business and for compensation. Under this interpretation, the SEC holds that there is no such thing as a *comprehensive financial plan* that does not involve securities.

3. 2. 1. 1. 2   Pension Consultants

Consultants who advise employee benefit plans on how to fund their plans with securities are also considered investment advisers by the SEC. In addition, under Release IA-1092, the SEC considers pension consultants who advise employee benefit plans on the selection, performance, and retention of investment managers to be investment advisers. A bit later in this session you will learn the conditions under which pension consultants become eligible to register with the SEC rather than the states.

3. 2. 1. 1. 3   Sports and Entertainment Representatives

Persons who provide financially related services to entertainers and athletes that include advice related to investments, tax planning, budgeting, and money management are also investment advisers. As earnings for these celebrities continue to climb, more and more of them use personal managers to handle all of their finances, and those individuals or firms are generally going to be considered investment advisers.

TAKE NOTE

A sports agent who secures a favorable contract for a football player and receives a commission of 10% of the player's salary is not necessarily an investment adviser. However, if the sports agent advises the football player to invest his money in specific securities, the agent is then in the business of offering investment advice and would then be subject to the Investment Advisers Act of 1940 or the Uniform Securities Act.

3. 2. 1. 2   In the Business of Providing Advice

A person is in the business of providing advice and subject to regulation as an investment adviser if he:

- gives advice on a regular basis such that it constitutes a business activity conducted with some regularity (although the frequency of the activity is a factor, it is not the only determinant in whether one is in the business of giving advice, and providing advice does not have to be the person's principal activity); and
- advertises investment advisory services and presents himself to the public as an investment adviser or as one who provides investment advice.

TAKE NOTE

A person is in the business of giving investment advice if he receives separate compensation that represents a charge for giving the advice.

A person is in the business if he provides investment advice or issues reports on anything other than rare, isolated, and nonperiodic instances. In this context, a person is an investment adviser if he recommends that a client allocate funds to specific assets, such as high-yield bonds, technology stocks, or mutual funds.

A person whose business is to offer only nonspecific investment advice, through publication of a general newsletter, for instance, is not covered by the act. That exclusion will be covered shortly.

3. 2. 1. 3   Compensation

A person who receives any economic benefit as a result of providing investment advice is an investment adviser. Compensation includes advisory fees, commissions, or other types of fees relating to the service rendered. A separate fee for the advice need not be charged; the fee can be paid by a third party on behalf of the beneficiary of the advice. No matter what the source, all compensation must always be disclosed to the client.

EXAMPLE

Fees that an investment adviser receives from a corporation for advice given to the corporation's employees or retirees are considered compensation. A financial planner who designs a comprehensive financial plan for the corporation's employees without charging a fee but receives commissions on insurance policies sold as part of the plan is acting as an investment adviser representative. Even though that compensation is indirect, it meets the release's definition of compensation for investment advice.

3. 2. 2   EXCLUSIONS FROM DEFINITION OF INVESTMENT ADVISER UNDER FEDERAL LAW

Although the definition of an investment adviser is broad, certain exclusions apply. There are six primary exclusions from the definition of an investment adviser.

- Any bank as defined in the Bank Holding Company Act of 1956, is excluded.
- Any **lawyer, accountant, teacher,** or **engineer** whose advice is solely incidental to the practice of his profession is excluded. This exclusion is not available to any of these who have established a separate advisory business. Also, the exclusion would not be available to any of these who holds himself out as offering investment advice.
- Any broker-dealer whose performance of such services is solely incidental to the conduct of his business as a broker or dealer and who receives no special compensation (such as when offering wrap fee programs) is excluded. The exclusion also applies to registered representatives of broker-dealers.

TAKE NOTE

Special compensation for investment advice is compensation to the broker-dealer or salesperson in excess of that which he or she would be paid for providing a brokerage or dealer service alone. Consequently, *special compensation* exists where there is a clearly definable charge for investment advice.

- The definition of investment adviser encompasses publishers as well as authors. However, the act excludes from the definition of investment adviser a "publisher of any bona fide newspaper, news magazine, or business or financial publication of general and regular circulation."

To qualify for this exclusion, the publication must be (1) of a general and impersonal nature, in that the advice provided is not adapted to any specific portfolio or any client's particular needs; (2) bona fide, or genuine, in that it contains disinterested commentary and analysis as opposed to promotional material; and (3) of general and regular circulation, in that it is not timed to specific market activity or events affecting, or having the ability to affect, the securities industry.

For example, newspapers of general circulation would be eligible for the exclusion.

TEST TOPIC ALERT   An investment newsletter is being published for a subscription fee. Rather than being published on a regular basis (weekly, monthly, quarterly, and so forth), issues are released in response to market events. How does federal law view this publisher? In this case, registration would be required as you will see in the following Supreme Court case.

In 1985, a cause célèbre, *Lowe v. SEC*, made it to the U.S. Supreme Court, which ruled that registration of publishers of investment newsletters as financial advisers was not required provided that the activities of a person or company were limited to the issuance of general advice; that is to say, the advice was given without regard to the particular circumstances of the investor, and the publication was published with some sort of regular schedule rather than being timed to specific market events.

■ Any person whose advice, analyses, or reports are related only to securities that are direct obligations of, or obligations guaranteed by, the United States, or by certain U.S. government-sponsored corporations designated by the Secretary of the Treasury (e.g., FNMA, GNMA) is excluded.

■ Any nationally recognized statistical rating organization (e.g., Standard & Poor's or Moody's), unless such organization engages in issuing recommendations as to purchasing, selling, or holding securities or in managing assets, consisting in whole or in part of securities, on behalf of others is excluded.

3.2.3   EXCLUSIONS FROM THE DEFINITION OF INVESTMENT ADVISER UNDER STATE LAW

Below are the exclusions from the definition of investment adviser under state law.

■ Banks, savings institutions, and trust companies are excluded.

■ Any lawyer, accountant, teacher or engineer whose advice is solely incidental to the practice of his profession is excluded. This exclusion is not available to any of these who have established a separate advisory business. Also, the exclusion would not be available to any of these who holds himself out as offering investment advice.

■ Any broker-dealer or its agents whose performance of such services is solely incidental to the conduct of his business as a broker-dealer and who receives no special compensation (wrap fees) is excluded.

■ The definition of investment adviser encompasses publishers as well as authors. However, the act excludes from the definition of investment adviser a publisher of any bona fide newspaper, news column, newsletter, news magazine, or business or financial publication or service, whether communicated in hard copy form, or by electronic means, or otherwise, that does not consist of the rendering of advice on the basis of the specific investment situation of each client.

■ Investment adviser representatives are excluded.

■ Any person who is a federal covered adviser is excluded.

■ Any person excluded by the Investment Advisers Act of 1940 is also excluded.

■ Any other person the Administrator specifies is excluded.

As you can see, the first four exclusions are virtually identical under both federal and state law. The only real difference is that under the USA, publishers will only be considered investment advisers if their advice is specific to each and every subscriber.

Then we have some important differences. There is no stated exclusion under the USA for those giving advice solely on U.S. government securities, but, they are excluded because they are federal covered advisers. The state law specifically excludes investment adviser representatives and, of course, federal covered advisers.

TAKE NOTE

An individual may act as both an investment adviser and an investment adviser representative. This is typically the case when the business is organized as a sole proprietorship. However, an individual who acts solely as an investment adviser representative is excluded from the definition of investment adviser.

TAKE NOTE

For purposes of the exclusion, under both state and federal law, the term "bank" does not include a savings and loan association or a foreign bank.

TAKE NOTE

For purposes of incidental, look at this example. The Maryland Securities Act sets that, "[a] lawyer, certified public accountant, engineer, or teacher whose performance of investment advisory services is solely incidental to the practice of the profession will be excluded from the definition of investment adviser. However, the performance of such services is not solely incidental unless the investment advisory services rendered are connected with and reasonably related to the other professional services rendered; the fee charged for the investment advisory services is based on the same factors as those used to determine the fee for other professional services; and the lawyer, certified public accountant, engineer, or teacher does not hold out as an investment adviser."

QUICK QUIZ 3.B

1. The Investment Advisers Act of 1940 excludes certain persons from the definition of an investment adviser if their performance of advisory services is solely incidental to their professions. This exclusion would apply to all of the following EXCEPT

    A. an accountant
    B. an economist
    C. an electrical engineer
    D. a college professor teaching a course on economics

2. Which of the following would be excluded from the definition of investment adviser under the Investment Advisers Act of 1940?

    I.   A bank offering advice through its trust department

    II. A geologist giving advice on the potential prospects of an oil and gas limited partnership program

    III. A person whose only clients are individuals and whose only advice deals with securities which are direct obligations of the U.S. government

    A. I and II

    B. I and III

    C. II and III

    D. I, II and III

3. Which of the following would meet the definition of investment adviser under the Uniform Securities Act?

    I.   A broker-dealer making a separate charge for investment advice

    II. The publisher of a weekly magazine, sold on newsstands, that contains at least 5 stock recommendations per issue

    III. A civil damages attorney who advertises that she is available to assist clients in suggesting appropriate investments for their successful claims

    IV. A finance teacher at a local community college who offers weekend seminars on comprehensive financial planning at a very reasonable price

    A. I only

    B. I, II, and III

    C. I, III, and IV

    D. I, II, III, and IV

4. Registration as an investment adviser is required for any firm in the business of giving advice on the purchase of

    A. apartments undergoing a conversion to condominiums

    B. convertible bonds

    C. gold coins

    D. rare convertible automobiles

3. 3 REGISTRATION REQUIREMENTS UNDER THE INVESTMENT ADVISERS ACT OF 1940

The Investment Advisers Act of 1940 makes it unlawful for a nonregistered investment adviser to use the mail or any instrumentality of interstate commerce in connection with his business. Unless an exemption is available, registration with the SEC or with a state is required.

TAKE NOTE

In the following section, *exemption from registration* refers to persons who meet the definition of investment advisers but who do not have to register.

3. 3. 1   EXEMPTION FROM THE REGISTRATION REQUIREMENTS UNDER FEDERAL LAW

The Investment Advisers Act of 1940 exempts the following classes of investment advisers from the registration requirements.

3. 3. 1. 1   Intrastate Advisers

Advisers whose clients, other than an investment adviser who acts as an investment adviser to any private fund (defined below), are residents of the state in which the adviser has its principal office and place of business and who do not give advice dealing with securities listed on any national exchange are exempt. For example, an adviser would be exempted under this provision if all of its clients were Georgia residents, its only places of business were in Georgia, and it did not give advice on securities listed on any national exchange.

3. 3. 1. 2   Advisers to Insurance Companies

Advisers whose only clients are insurance companies are exempt.

3. 3. 1. 3   Private Fund Advisers

Title IV of the Dodd-Frank Act, known as the Private Fund Investment Advisers Registration Act of 2010, contains a comprehensive overhaul of the registration process for investment advisers. The bill provided for the following new exemptions from registration under the Advisers Act:

- An exemption for advisers solely to private funds with less than $150 million in assets under management in the United States, without regard to the number or type of private funds (the private fund adviser exemption)
- An exemption for certain non-U.S. advisers with no place of business in the United States and minimal assets under management (less than $25 million) attributable to U.S. clients and investors (the foreign private adviser exemption)
- An exemption for advisers solely to venture capital funds (the venture capital fund exemption)

3. 3. 1. 3. 1   Definition of a Private Fund

Although it is highly unlikely you will be tested on the technical definition, Section 402 of the Dodd-Frank Act defines a private fund as "an issuer that would be an investment company, as defined in section 3 of the Investment Company Act of 1940, but for section 3(c)(1) or 3(c)(7) of that Act."

In more straightforward terms, a 3(c)(1) issuer is one whose outstanding securities are beneficially owned by not more than 100 persons and which is not making and does not presently propose to make a public offering of its securities. With no more than 100 shareholders and no public offering, the term *private fund* seems quite logical.

A 3(c)(7) issuer is one whose outstanding securities are owned exclusively by persons who, at the time of acquisition of such securities, are qualified purchasers (at least $5 million in investments for individuals and generally $25 million in investments for business entities), and which is not making and does not at that time propose to make a public offering of such securities. In this case, the lack of a public offering is logically private, and the fact that the invested wealth requirement limits the potential universe of investors is a factor as well.

The point is, regardless of how it's defined, if one is an adviser solely to private funds, it is possible to qualify for an exemption from registration with the SEC.

Well, what about NASAA? As we will discuss shortly, their model rule closely parallels the federal exemption with two differences.

TEST TOPIC ALERT   Based on 3(c)(1), an investment adviser with discretion over more than 100 accounts using pooled client funds might be considered to be running an investment company and that could require registration under both the Investment Company Act of 1940 and the Advisers Act.

3. 3. 1. 3. 2 Assets Under Management Threshold for Registration of Investment Advisers to Private Funds

Even though those qualifying for the private fund exemption are exempt from the registration requirements under the Advisers Act, the Dodd-Frank Act directs the SEC to require those advisers to maintain records and provide to the SEC any reports that the SEC determines are "necessary or appropriate in the public interest or for the protection of investors". In order to rely upon this exemption, U.S. investment advisers (i.e., investment advisers with their principal office and place of business in the United States) must include the value of assets for each private fund that they manage, regardless of where those private funds are organized.

Under Dodd-Frank, investment advisers must determine the amount of private fund assets on a quarterly basis, based upon the fair value of such assets. Investment advisers will have one calendar quarter after exceeding the $150 million threshold to register with the SEC.

3. 3. 1. 3. 3 Exemption for Foreign Private Advisers

A foreign private adviser is defined in the Dodd-Frank Act as any investment adviser that:

- has no place of business in the United States;
- has, in total, fewer than 15 clients and investors in the United States in private funds advised by the adviser;
- has aggregate assets under management attributable to clients in the United States and investors in the United States in private funds advised by the adviser of less than $25 million; and
- does not hold itself out to the public in the United States as an investment adviser or act as an investment adviser to an investment company registered under the Investment Company Act of 1940.

3. 3. 1. 3. 4   Exemption for Investment Advisers to Venture Capital Funds

The rules define a venture capital fund as a private fund that:

- has limited leverage;
- does not, except in certain limited circumstances, offer its investors redemption rights or other similar liquidity rights;
- represents itself as a venture capital fund to investors; and
- is not registered under the Investment Company Act of 1940.

Please note that these exemptions are granted on the basis of who you advise, not on what types of securities are the subject of your advice. Note also that **exclusion** means exclusion from a definition, whereas **exemption** means not subject to registration. All of the cases mentioned here involve investment advisers; it's just that they qualify for an exemption from registration under federal law.

QUICK QUIZ 3.C

1. Which of the following investment advisers are exempt from registration under the Investment Advisers Act of 1940?

    I. An adviser whose only clients are insurance companies
    II. An adviser who maintains offices in only one state, advises only residents of that state (none of whom is a private fund), and gives advice relating to only tax-exempt municipal bonds
    III. An adviser whose only clients are banks

    A. I and II
    B. I and III
    C. II and III
    D. I, II and III

3. 3. 2   FEDERAL COVERED ADVISERS

The National Securities Markets Improvement Act of 1996 (NSMIA) made major changes in the way investment advisers register. The NSMIA divided registration responsibilities between the SEC and the states' securities departments. Basically, the largest firms are required to register with the SEC, and the smaller ones, unless qualifying for an exception, are required to register with the states.

Who are **federal covered investment advisers**? In most cases, they are investment advisers registered with the SEC. The most tested examples are:

- those required to be registered or registered as an investment adviser with the SEC because they meet the minimum threshold of assets under management (currently $110 million);
- those under contract to manage an investment company registered under the Investment Company Act of 1940, regardless of the amount of assets under management; or
- those not registered with the SEC because they are excluded from the definition of an investment adviser by the Investment Advisers Act of 1940.

✓

TAKE NOTE

Because so much of this exam deals with interpreting the laws, it is sometimes necessary to review some legal concepts with you. For example, if a person is excluded from the definition of investment adviser under the Investment Advisers Act of 1940, the states, under the NSMIA, cannot define such person as an investment adviser because federal law excluded that person from the definition. In other words, if the separate states could define those persons who were excluded from the federal definition as investment advisers, the federal law would have no meaning.

3. 3. 2. 1   Dodd-Frank and Assets Under Management

As stated previously, the NSMIA eliminated state registration requirements for federal covered advisers, largely based upon assets under management. Dodd-Frank has created three thresholds: one for the "large" adviser, one for the "mid-size" adviser, and, logically, one for the "small" adviser. Let's examine each of these; their requirements and their exceptions, if any.

3. 3. 2. 1. 1   Large Investment Advisers

"Large advisers," those advisers with at least $100 million or more in assets under management, are eligible for SEC registration; once AUM reach $110 million, registration with the SEC is mandatory. Unless covered by one of the exemptions mentioned previously, all large IAs must register with the SEC. State registration is not required because the Advisers Act preempts state registration.

3. 3. 2. 1. 2   Small Investment Advisers

This category includes advisers with assets under management of less than $25 million. Unless the investment adviser is an adviser to an investment company registered under the Investment Company Act of 1940, registration with the SEC is prohibited and, unless exempted under state rules, registration with the state is required. In addition, if the adviser would be required to register in 15 or more states, registration with the SEC would be permitted instead. The only other specific exception is that if the IA has its principal office in a state that does not call for registration of IAs (only Wyoming at the date of this printing), then registration with the SEC would be permitted. That is such a rare exception that, unless specifically mentioned in the test question, it is suggested that you don't consider it as a possibility.

3. 3. 2. 1. 3   Mid-size Advisers

This is a new category added by Dodd-Frank. It includes those with AUM of at least $25 million but not $100 million. Generally, these advisers are prohibited from SEC registration and must register with the state. However, there are more extensive exceptions than exist with the small advisers. Just as with any other category, those who are an adviser to an investment company registered under the Investment Company Act of 1940, register with the SEC. That is true regardless of their size.

There are several other ways for a mid-size firm to qualify for SEC registration. A mid-sized adviser is not prohibited from registering with the SEC:

- if the adviser is not required to be registered as an investment adviser with the securities Administrator of the state in which it maintains its principal office and place of business;

- if registered, the adviser would not be subject to examination as an investment adviser by that securities Administrator;

- if the adviser is required to register in 15 or more states; or

- the adviser elects to take advantage of the buffer (described in the following paragraph).

3. 3. 2. 1. 4   Exceptions Under Dodd-Frank

The SEC is permitted to grant exceptions to advisers from the prohibition on Commission registration, including small and mid-sized advisers, if the application of the prohibition from registration would be "unfair, a burden on interstate commerce, or otherwise inconsistent with the purposes" of the Act. Under this authority, they have adopted several exemptions from the prohibition on registration, including:

- pension consultants, but only those with at least $200 million under control—the SEC picked that number to ensure that, in order to register with the SEC, the consultant's activities are "significant enough to have an effect on national markets";

- those mid-size advisers with at least $100 million in AUM, but less than $110 million in AUM who elect to register with the SEC rather than the state(s) (this buffer will be described below);

- investment advisers affiliated with an adviser already registered with the SEC;

- investment advisers expecting to be eligible for SEC registration within 120 days of filing Form ADV;

- multistate investment advisers (required to register in 15 or more states); and

- internet advisers.

TAKE NOTE
Based on prior history, it is unlikely that the test will ask about any of the above except for the pension consultant and the IA expecting to reach $100 million within 120 days.

3. 3. 2. 1. 5   The $20 million Buffer

The SEC recognized that market conditions (or obtaining or losing clients) can cause AUM to fluctuate so they established a buffer to keep advisers from having to switch back and forth. The numbers work like this: A state registered adviser may, once it has assets under management of at least $100 million (subject to certain of the exceptions previously mentioned, everyone needs at least $100 million to initiate registration with the SEC), may choose to remain state registered or may register with the SEC. Once AUM reach $110 million, registration with the SEC is mandatory—they can no longer stay state registered. Then, once registered with the SEC, an investment adviser need not withdraw its SEC registration unless it has less than $90 million of assets under management. This means that an investment adviser can register with the SEC with AUM of as little as $100 million, but must once AUM reach $110 million. Having become SEC registered, the IA can remain so as long as AUM remain at or above the $90 million level. Likewise, those investment advisers registered at the state level can choose to remain there until they reach the $110 million level. This buffer is designed to avoid the expense and hassle involved in potentially annual changes to where the investment adviser is registered.

3. 3. 2. 1. 6   Time for Measuring AUM

These numbers are based on the AUM reported on the IA's annual updating amendment. The effect of this is that a federal covered adviser's AUM could drop below $90 million during the year without triggering the need to change to state registration, just as long as the annual update showed at least the minimum $90 million required. Of course, the same would be true of a state registered adviser whose AUM peaked above $110 million during the year but then fell at the time of the update. If, at the time of filing the annual updating amendment to the Form ADV by an SEC registered IA, the reported AUM is less than $90 million, it is necessary for the investment adviser to withdraw its SEC registration and register with the appropriate state(s) within 180 days. On the other hand, if a state registered adviser's reported AUM exceed $110 million, registration with the SEC must take place within 90 days.

3. 4   EXEMPTION FROM REGISTRATION FOR INVESTMENT ADVISERS UNDER THE UNIFORM SECURITIES ACT

The USA exempts from registration certain persons who, although they fall within the definition of an investment adviser, do not have to register as such in the state.

The advisers exempt from registration with the state Administrator are those who have no place of business in the state but are registered in another state, provided their only clients in the state are:

■ broker-dealers registered under the act;

■ other investment advisers;

■ institutional investors, including employee benefit plans with assets of not less than $1 million;

■ existing clients who are not residents but are temporarily in the state;

■ limited to five or fewer clients, other than those listed above, resident in the state during the preceding 12 months (called the de minimis exemption); or

■ any others the Administrator exempts by rule or order.

TAKE NOTE

Although we try to minimize the legal phraseology in this manual, sometimes seeing the exact wording in the law can actually help clarify things. Here is what the Uniform Securities Act has to say:

It is unlawful for any person to transact business in this state as an investment adviser or as an investment adviser representative unless

(1) he is so registered under this act; or

(2) he has no place of business in this state; and

> (A) his only clients in this state are investment companies as defined in the Investment Company Act of 1940, other investment advisers, federal covered advisers, broker-dealers, banks, trust companies, savings and loan associations, insurance companies, employee benefit plans with assets of not less than one million dollars ($1,000,000), and governmental agencies or instrumentalities, whether acting for themselves or as trustees with investment control, or other institutional investors as are designated by rule or order of the Administrator, or

> (B) during the preceding twelve-month period has had no more than five clients, other than those specified in subparagraph (A), whether or not he or any of the persons to whom the communications are directed is then present in this state.

TAKE NOTE

For purposes of the de minimis rule, how do we count clients? Do Mr. and Mrs. Jones count as one or as two? The best way to tell is to read what the law says:

Rule 203(b)(3)-1 – Definition of "Client" of an Investment Adviser

The following are deemed a single client:

(1) A natural person, and:

(i) Any minor child of the natural person;

(ii) Any relative, spouse, or relative of the spouse of the natural person who has the same principal residence;

(iii) All accounts of which the natural person and/or the persons referred to in this paragraph (a)(1) are the only primary beneficiaries; and

(iv) All trusts of which the natural person and/or the persons referred to in this paragraph (a)(1) are the only primary beneficiaries.

TEST TOPIC ALERT

Because these exemptions all apply when the investment adviser does not have an office in the state, it is relevant to understand that an investment adviser or one of its representatives who advertises to the public, in any way, the availability of meeting with prospective clients in a hotel, country club, seminar, or any other location in the state is considered to have an office in the state. However, an investment adviser representative who contacts existing clients who happen to be in the state and notifies them that he will be passing through the state and will be available to meet with them in his hotel room is not considered to have an office in the state because the announcement is being made only to existing clients and not to the public.

CASE STUDY   **Out-of-State Advice**

Situation: A California-registered investment adviser with no offices located in any other state has directed investment advice on five separate occasions over the past year to individual residents of the state of Nevada. Is the investment adviser required to register in the state of Nevada?

Analysis: The answer is no. Registration is not required because the investment adviser does not have an office in Nevada and directs business to five or fewer individual residents of the state during the year. If the firm had an office in Nevada, registration would be required in that state. Also, even if the firm had no office in Nevada, registration would be required if business had been transacted with six or more individual residents of the state during the previous 12 months.

If the business had been transacted with other investment advisers, broker-dealers, or institutional investors, there is no limit as long as there is no office in the state.

TAKE NOTE

Federal covered investment advisers exempt from state registration are not exempt from paying state filing fees and giving notice to the Administrator. The procedure followed is called **notice filing**. As part of the notice filing, the Administrator can require a federal covered adviser to file a copy of whatever has been filed with the SEC, and, of course, pay a filing fee.

TAKE NOTE

If a federal covered adviser only deals with institutions, other IAs, other BDs, and so forth, notice filing is not required. This is a similar concept to the USA not requiring registration of state registered advisers who have no place of business in the state and deal with this same group of clients. We have not heard of this ever being asked on the exam, but, you never know what NASAA has up their sleeve.

Exclusion from Definition and Exemptions from Registration

Situation: Charles & Goode, a partnership located in Illinois, has been in the business of selling investment advice in the form of research reports and managing securities portfolios for the past 20 years. The partnership has earned a good reputation among investors and has managed less than $25 million until this year. This year they gained several new clients and now have $115 million in assets under management.

Most of Charles & Goode's clients are wealthy individuals and residents of Illinois, but they have three clients who are residents of Wisconsin and 30 clients who live in Indiana. The principals of Charles & Goode have also formed a nonaffiliated partnership called C&G Mutual Fund Advisers, Inc., which manages a small investment company with assets of $15 million. The partners in Charles & Goode are uncertain about what they must do to be in compliance with the Uniform Securities Act.

Analysis: As a partnership in the business of managing money for individual clients, Charles & Goode falls within the definition of an investment adviser and must so register with the Illinois securities Administrator until it manages $100 million or more in assets. However, with the addition of new clients as of the current year, Charles & Goode will be exempt from registration with Illinois, because it is now a federal covered adviser that must register with the SEC because it has crossed the threshold of $110 million of assets under management.

Before becoming a federal covered adviser, Charles & Goode need not register in Wisconsin because they have five or fewer clients in the state; however, they would have to register in Indiana because they have more than five clients there. After becoming a federal covered adviser, Charles & Goode does not have to register in Indiana, Wisconsin, or Illinois—after it manages $110 million or more, it only has to register with the SEC, not the state Administrator.

The separate partnership, C&G Mutual Fund Advisers, Inc., which manages only $15 million, is exempt from registration in Illinois (or any other state) because those persons who operate as investment advisers to investment companies registered under the Investment Company Act of 1940, regardless of the size of the investment company, are included in the definition of federal covered adviser. Both C&G Mutual Fund Advisers Inc. and the fund they manage may have to pay state filing fees under a procedure called *notice filing*.

TAKE NOTE

As a general rule, the SEC or federal rules involve bigger numbers than the state rules—that is, large investment advisers must register with the SEC, whereas small investment advisers must register with the state.

Adviser managing . . .

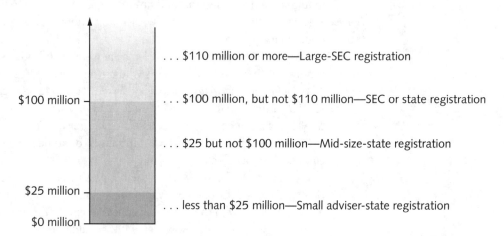

. . . $110 million or more—Large-SEC registration

. . . $100 million, but not $110 million—SEC or state registration

. . . $25 but not $100 million—Mid-size-state registration

. . . less than $25 million—Small adviser-state registration

$100 million

$25 million

$0 million

TEST TOPIC ALERT

An investment adviser registered under state law whose assets reach $110 million under management has 90 days to register with the SEC. A federal covered investment adviser whose assets under management fall below $90 million no longer qualifies for SEC registration and has 180 days to register with the state(s).

3. 4. 1   PRIVATE FUND ADVISER EXEMPTION UNDER STATE LAW

NASAA amended its Model Rule for the Registration Exemption for Investment Advisers to Private Funds, on October 8, 2013, to make it almost identical to the federal exemption described at 3.3.1.3. There are only two differences that might be testable.

■ If qualifying for the exemption as a 3(c)(1) issuer, (no more than 100 investors), NASAA's Model Rule requires that all investors be "qualified." That is, they must have either at least $1 million in assets managed by the investment adviser, or a net worth, excluding the value of the primary residence, of at least $2 million. Remember, "value of primary residence" means the fair market value of a person's primary residence, minus the amount of debt secured by the property up to its fair market value (net equity). Note that "qualified" for NASAA is significantly less than "qualified" under federal law.

■ Neither the private fund adviser nor any of its advisory affiliates are subject to an event that would disqualify an issuer under Rule 506(d)(1) of SEC Regulation D, (the "bad actor" provisions).

3. 4. 2   EXEMPT REPORTING ADVISER

As long as the adviser continues to qualify for the exemption on either the federal or state level, registration will not be required. However, certain reports will have to be filed with either the SEC or the state(s) as appropriate. These firms are known as Exempt Reporting Advisers (ERAs).

QUICK QUIZ 3.D

Write **A** if the phrase describes an investment adviser that must register under the Uniform Securities Act and **B** if it does not.

_____ 1. Publisher of a newspaper that renders general financial advice

_____ 2. Broker-dealer that charges a fee for providing investment advice over and above commissions from securities transactions

_____ 3. Investment adviser that manages $10 million in assets

4. The Uniform Securities Act contains a number of definitions. A person who is in the business of rendering investment advice for compensation is known as

   A. a broker-dealer
   B. a fiduciary
   C. an investment adviser
   D. an issuer

5. Which of the following is required to register as an investment adviser with the state securities Administrator?

   A. The author of a book on money and banking that was sold to residents of the state in which it is published.
   B. An investment advisory firm with $85 million in assets under management that opens an office in the state.
   C. A person with no office in the state whose only advisory clients are investment companies and banks in the state.
   D. A newly formed investment advisory firm with $145 million in assets under management that has two offices in the state and serves exclusively individual clients.

3. 5   REGISTRATION PROCEDURES UNDER FEDERAL LAW FOR AN INVESTMENT ADVISER

With only a few differences, the procedures for registering as an investment adviser are the same, whether registering with the SEC or with the states. Those differences will be pointed out as we go along.

Registration is accomplished using the Form ADV. In 2010, there were significant changes made to the ADV all of which are now in effect. In particular, they are no longer Part I and Part II—it is now Part 1 and Part 2. Of greater importance is the fact that Part 2, which used to be a "check off the blank" form, has now become an open narrative.

Remember how you had tests in school that contained both multiple-choice and essay questions (and how you hated writing those essays)? That is basically what has happened here—the old form was multiple choice and the new one is essay.

Investment advisers use Form ADV to:

■ register with the Securities and Exchange Commission;

■ register with one or more state securities authorities; or

■ amend those registrations.

Filing in almost all cases is done through the IARD.

TAKE NOTE

The Investment Adviser Registration Depository (IARD) is an electronic filing system that facilitates investment adviser registration, regulatory review, and the public disclosure information of investment adviser firms. FINRA is the developer and operator of the IARD system. The system has been developed according to the requirements of its sponsors, the Securities and Exchange Commission (SEC) and the North American Securities Administrators Association (NASAA), along with those of an Industry Advisory Council representing the investment adviser firms. For those of you with a securities license, this is the adviser's version of the CRD (Central Registration Depository).

3. 5. 1   HOW IS FORM ADV ORGANIZED?

Form ADV contains four parts: Part 1A asks a number of questions about the investment adviser, its business practices, the persons who own and control the firm, and the persons who provide investment advice on behalf of the firm. All advisers registering with the SEC or any of the state securities authorities must complete Part 1A.

Part 1A also contains several supplemental schedules. These include:

■ Schedule A, which asks for information about the direct owners and executive officers (control persons);

■ Schedule B, which asks for information about the indirect owners; and

■ Disclosure Reporting Pages (or DRPs), which are schedules that ask for details about disciplinary events involving the adviser or advisory affiliates.

Part 1B asks additional questions required by state securities authorities. Investment advisers applying for registration or who are registered only with the SEC do not have to complete Part 1B.

Part 2A requires advisers to create narrative **brochures** containing information about the advisory firm. The requirements in Part 2A apply to all investment advisers registered with or applying for registration with the SEC and almost all states.

Part 2B requires advisers to create **brochure supplements** containing information about certain supervised persons. The requirements in Part 2B apply to all investment advisers registered with or applying for registration with the SEC and almost all states.

It may help you remember that the **A** in Part 2A tells us that that part is for the **A**dviser and the **B** in Part 2 is about the **B**odies (the people) who work there.

We will cover the brochures and brochure supplements in greater detail later in this session.

TEST TOPIC ALERT

Control means the power, directly or indirectly, to direct the management or policies of an investment adviser, whether through ownership of securities, by contract, or otherwise. Under the Investment Advisers Act of 1940 as well as NASAA's Model Rule, each of the firm's officers, partners, or directors exercising executive responsibility (or persons having similar status or functions) is presumed to control the firm.

A person is presumed to control an IA organized as a corporation if the person directly or indirectly has the right to vote 25% or more of a class of the corporation's voting securities; a person is presumed to control one that is a partnership if the person has the right to receive upon dissolution, or has contributed, 25% or more of the capital of the partnership.

Please note that this is a different percentage from the definition of control person under the Securities Exchange Act of 1934, where having more than 10% of the voting power makes one a control person. Remember that control person is defined three different ways: the Exchange Act requires more than 10%, the Investment Company Act requires *more than* 25%, and the Advisers Act requires 25% *or more*.

3. 5. 1. 1   Form ADV

The application for registration as an investment adviser is on the Form ADV. Part 1 contains information about the IA, including:

- location of principal office;
- location of books and records (if not at the principal office);
- form of business organization (sole proprietorship, partnership, corporation, LLC, and so forth);
- method of business;
- other business activities [broker-dealer, registered representative (agent) of a BD];
- maintaining custody of customer assets or exercising discretion;
- details relating to all control persons (officers, directors, partners, etc.);
- disciplinary history; and
- for state registered IAs, states in which the IA intends to or is already registered.

Part 1B asks additional questions required by state securities authorities. Federal covered advisers do not complete the Part 1B.

Part 2A is known as the investment adviser's brochure and tends to focus on customer related information, such as:

- compensation arrangements (fees, commissions, hourly charge);
- types of clients (individuals, institutions, pension plans);
- type of investments (equities, corporate debt, municipal securities, U.S. treasuries, investment companies);
- types of strategies employed (buy and hold, value, growth);
- methods of analysis used (technical, fundamental);

■ educational and business background of those who render advice; and

■ an audited balance sheet if a federal or state registered adviser requires or solicits *substantial* prepayment of fees (defined shortly) or if a state registered adviser maintains custody (also discussed shortly).

The brochure is arranged in a narrative form using plain English.

Part 2B requires advisers to create brochure supplements containing information about certain supervised persons. Together, Part 2A and Part 2B are delivered to the client as described later in this session.

State registered advisers file *both* Part 1 and Part 2 with the Administrator of each state in which they are registering.

TEST TOPIC ALERT   Under the USA, if a federal covered investment adviser has an office in the state, the Administrator may require, by rule or by order, that the IA submit any documents that have been filed with the SEC. A federal covered IA submits only Part 1A of the Form ADV. Therefore, if the Administrator requests the Form ADV, all that will be sent is the Part 1A. This is known as notice filing. If it is a state registered adviser, then investment adviser must file Parts 1A and 1B with the appropriate state(s).

3. 5. 2   UPDATING THE FORM ADV

The Form ADV must be updated each year by filing an annual updating amendment within 90 days after the end of the adviser's fiscal year. This annual updating amendment is used to update the responses to all items on the ADV. Of critical importance is the verification of assets under management (AUM) ensuring that the adviser is eligible to continue being registered with the SEC. One of the requirements relating to the brochure described in Part 2 is that submission must be made of a summary of material changes either in the brochure (cover page or the page immediately thereafter) or as an exhibit to the brochure.

3. 5. 2. 1   Amendments for Material Changes

In addition to the annual updating amendment, the IA must amend the Form ADV by filing additional amendments promptly if information relating to any of the following changes or becomes inaccurate in any way:

■ Change of the registrant's name

■ Change in the principal business location

■ Change in the location of books and records, if they are kept somewhere other than at the principal location

■ Change to the contact person preparing the form

■ Change in organizational structure, such as from partnership to corporation and so on

■ Information provided in the brochure becomes materially inaccurate

■ Change to any of the questions regarding disciplinary actions

■ Change in policy regarding custody of the customer funds and/or securities

3. 5. 3   FEES

Even though registration under Form ADV remains in effect until it is withdrawn by the registrant or canceled or revoked by the SEC (or the state), there is a requirement for annual renewal. There are fees for the initial filing and renewals. If an investment adviser changes its form of business organization (e.g., from a sole proprietorship to a corporation), a new ADV, but no fees, would be required.

TEST TOPIC ALERT

Successor firm:

Under both federal and state law, a successor firm registers by filing a new application and, in the case of the SEC, paying the appropriate fee and, under the USA, without additional fee. Please note the difference—one case involves a fee, the other does not.

3. 5. 3. 1   Effective Date of Registration

Assuming there are no irregularities in the application, registration with the SEC takes effect on the 45th day after filing of a complete application and, as with all securities professionals, at noon of the 30th day in the case of state registered investment advisers.

3. 5. 4   FORM ADV-W

If an adviser no longer desires to engage in the business, application to withdraw registration is accomplished by filing **Form ADV-W**. Form ADV-W must be filed in order to withdraw the registration voluntarily. The request to withdraw from registration accompanied by properly filed Form ADV-W becomes effective 60 days after filing with the SEC and after 30 days in the case of state registered advisers.

QUICK QUIZ 3.E

1. ABC Advisers is a federal covered IA. John Oldman has been responsible for keeping the firm's Form ADV updated for the last 40 years. John has suddenly announced his immediate retirement. This would require

   A. prompt filing of an amended ADV with the SEC indicating the change in contact person

   B. prompt filing of an ADV-W with the SEC indicating the change of contact person

   C. filing of amended ADV within 90 days of the end of the adviser's fiscal year giving notice of the change of contact person

   D. filing of the ADV-W within 90 days of the end of the adviser's fiscal year giving notice of the change of contact person

2. The Investment Advisers Act of 1940 would permit an ADV to be filed by a(n)

   I. corporation
   II. partnership
   III. sole proprietorship
   IV. unincorporated association
   A. I and II
   B. I, II, and III
   C. II and III
   D. I, II, III, and IV

3. 5. 4. 1   Cancellation of Registration

The SEC has the power to cancel the registration of any adviser upon finding that the adviser is no longer in existence, is not engaged in business as an investment adviser, or does not meet the necessary dollar standards to remain SEC registered. If not withdrawn by the adviser or canceled or revoked by the SEC, registration continues indefinitely as long as the proper renewal procedures are followed. In the case of state registered advisers, the Administrator has similar powers and may also cancel when mental incompetence has been proven.

3. 5. 5   INVESTMENT COUNSEL

One of the terms that may appear on the exam is that of **investment counsel**. Questions dealing with this topic require the student to know that there are two criteria specified in the Investment Advisers Act of 1940 that must be met in order to use the term to describe the nature of the IA's business. They are as follows:

■ *The IA's principal business must be giving investment advice.* This basically excludes financial planners and others for whom investment advice is only a part of what they do.

■ *Provide investment supervisory services.* This one is a bit harder for most to understand so I thought I would give some details as issued by the SEC.

Continuous and Regular Supervisory or Management Services.

General Criteria. *You provide continuous and regular supervisory or management services with respect to an account if:*

(a) you have discretionary authority over and provide ongoing supervisory or management services with respect to the account; or

(b) you do not have discretionary authority over the account, but you have ongoing responsibility to select or make recommendations, based upon the needs of the client, as to specific securities or other investments the account may purchase or sell and, if such recommendations are accepted by the client, you are responsible for arranging or effecting the purchase or sale.

(c) you are compensated based on the average value of the client's assets you manage over a specified period of time, that suggests that you provide continuous and regular supervisory or management services for the account. If you receive compensation in a manner

similar to either of the following, that suggests you do not provide continuous and regular supervisory or management services for the account—

(i) you are compensated based upon the time spent with a client during a client visit; or

(ii) you are paid a retainer based on a percentage of assets covered by a financial plan.

You do not provide continuous and regular supervisory or management services for an account if you:

(a) provide market timing recommendations (i.e., to buy or sell), but have no ongoing management responsibilities;

(b) provide only impersonal investment advice (e.g., market newsletters);

(c) make an initial asset allocation, without continuous and regular monitoring and reallocation; or

(d) provide advice on an intermittent or periodic basis (such as upon client request, in response to a market event), or on a specific date (e.g., the account is reviewed and adjusted quarterly).

QUICK QUIZ 3.F

1. Which of the following investment advisers would be permitted to use the term *investment counsel*?

   A. A financial planner offering a wide range of services to his clients, including tax planning, estate planning, and insurance planning, as well as investment advice

   B. A professional providing a market timing service with an annual subscription fee of $495 (this service attempts to maximize profits by suggesting entry and exit points for over 100 listed stocks)

   C. A firm whose exclusive business is placing their client's assets into model portfolios

   D. All of the above

2. Under which of the following circumstances would the SEC be permitted to cancel or revoke an investment adviser's registration?

   I. A registered investment adviser with no place of business in the state has fewer than 6 clients.

   II. The annual updating amendment has not been filed for the current fiscal year, and mail addressed to the investment adviser is returned with a notation "no forwarding address available."

   III. An investment adviser doing business in 10 states has been enjoined by a competent court of jurisdiction in one of those states from engaging in the securities business.

   IV. A registered investment adviser is insolvent.

   A. I and II

   B. II and III

   C. II, III, and IV

   D. I, II, III, and IV

3. 5. 6   QUALIFICATIONS OF MANAGEMENT PERSONNEL

Although there are no minimum educational or experience requirements, there is a specific area on the Form ADV Part 2 where state registered advisers must identify each of the principal executive officers and management persons, and describe their formal education and business background. If this information has been supplied elsewhere in the Form ADV, it is not necessary to repeat it in response to this question.

3. 6   FINANCIAL REQUIREMENTS FOR REGISTRATION AS AN INVESTMENT ADVISER

Under the Investment Advisers Act of 1940, no specific financial requirements, such as a minimum net worth, are spelled out. However, as we will see, there are financial disclosures that must be made to clients under certain conditions.

Under the Uniform Securities Act, the Administrator may, by rule or order, establish minimum financial requirements for an investment adviser registered in the state. Those will be discussed shortly.

3. 6. 1   SUBSTANTIAL PREPAYMENT OF FEES

Both state and federal law offer extra protection to those clients of investment advisers who have made substantial advance payment of fees for services to be rendered in the future. The term used is *substantial prepayment of fees*. In the case of a federal covered adviser, it is considered substantial if the IA collects prepayments of more than $1,200 per client, six months or more in advance. Under the USA, it is more than $500, and again, six months or more in advance.

TEST TOPIC ALERT

Under the USA, when an investment adviser accepts prepayments of fees of *more* than $500 for a contract period of six months OR more, it is known as a substantial prepayment. However, under the Investment Advisers Act of 1940, it does not become a substantial prepayment until it exceeds $1,200.

3. 6. 2   BALANCE SHEET REQUIREMENT FOR FEDERAL COVERED ADVISERS

Any federal covered investment adviser who requires or solicits clients for *substantial prepayment of fees* (as defined at 3.6.1) must include a balance sheet with the adviser's ADV Part 2A for the adviser's most recent fiscal year. The balance sheet must be prepared in accordance with generally accepted accounting principles (GAAP), audited by an independent public accountant, and accompanied by a note stating the principles used to prepare it, the basis of securities included, and any other explanations required for clarity.

3. 6. 3   BALANCE SHEET REQUIREMENTS FOR STATE REGISTERED ADVISERS

An audited balance sheet must be included in the brochure for any state registered investment adviser who requires or solicits clients for *substantial prepayment of fees* (as defined at 3.6.1). In addition, those who maintain custody of client funds and/or securities must include an audited balance sheet with their ADV Part 2A for their most recent fiscal year with the same requirements. The audited balance sheet is also required when the custodian is a related (affiliated) broker-dealer. Furthermore, state registered advisers who exercise discretionary authority over client accounts but do not maintain custody must file with the Administrator within 90 days of the end of the adviser's fiscal year a balance sheet, but this one does not have to be audited. However, it must follow GAAP and be true and accurate.

3. 6. 4   DISCLOSURE OF FINANCIAL IMPAIRMENT

Any investment adviser that has *discretionary* authority or *custody* of client funds or securities, or requires or solicits *substantial prepayment of fees*, *must* disclose any financial condition that is reasonably likely to impair their ability to meet contractual commitments to their clients. As an example, the SEC has indicated that disclosure may be required of any arbitration award "sufficiently large that payment of it would create such a financial condition."

Here is the way it is stated in the Form ADV Part 2:

"If you have discretionary authority or custody of client funds or securities, or you require or solicit prepayment of more than $1,200 in fees per client, six months or more in advance, disclose any financial condition that is reasonably likely to impair your ability to meet contractual commitments to clients."

3. 6. 5   SPECIFIC FINANCIAL REQUIREMENTS FOR STATE REGISTERED ADVISERS

The Administrator may require an adviser who has *custody* of client funds or securities or has *discretion* over a client's account to post a surety bond or maintain a minimum net worth. Usually, the requirement is higher for custody than for discretion. Typically, the net worth required of investment advisers with discretionary authority is $10,000 and that for those taking custody is $35,000. If the adviser is using a surety bond instead, the requirement in either case is $35,000. An adviser who does not exercise discretion and does not maintain custody, but does accept prepayment of fees of more than $500, six or more months in advance, must maintain a positive net worth at all times.

TAKE NOTE

Because the USA is only a template, some states have higher net worth or bonding requirements. The exam may want you to know that if an IA meets the net worth or surety bonding requirements of the state where its principal office is located, that is sufficient in any other state in which it may be registered.

TEST TOPIC ALERT   One of the effects of the NSMIA is to limit the powers of an Administrator over a federal covered adviser. Section 222 of the Investment Advisers Act of 1940 states that when it comes to federal covered advisers, any financial or bonding requirements, as well as rules relating to recordkeeping, are solely under federal jurisdiction.

TEST TOPIC ALERT   The proper term to use when referring to the financial requirements of an investment adviser is *net worth*, while for broker-dealers it is *net capital*. However, we have heard from a number of students that NASAA is using net capital where they should be using net worth in questions about IAs. So, if you want to get the question right, answer it the way they give it to you. You will see several examples of this in our practice questions.

3. 6. 5. 1   Failure to Maintain Minimum Net Worth

The USA specifies the action to be taken by a registered investment adviser whose net worth falls below the required minimum. By the close of business on the next business day, the adviser must notify the Administrator that the investment adviser's net worth is less than the minimum required. After sending that notice, the adviser must file a financial report with the Administrator by the close of business on the next business day. When the adviser's net worth is below the minimum requirement, the adviser must obtain a bond in an amount of the net worth deficiency rounded up to the nearest $5,000.

EXAMPLE   A state registered investment adviser discovers on *Monday* that its net worth is below the minimum requirement. No later than the close of business on *Tuesday*, notice must be sent to the Administrator of the state in which the investment adviser has its principal office. Then, no later than the close of business on *Wednesday*, the investment adviser must file a detailed report with the Administrator of its financial condition. Included in the report must be a statement as to the number of client accounts.

EXAMPLE   An investment adviser who maintains custody of customer funds and securities discovers that their net worth is only $23,000. Even though the adviser only needs a net worth of $35,000, this would require immediate surety bonding in the amount of $15,000 because it must be rounded up to the nearest $5,000.

3. 6. 5. 2   Computing Net Worth

For NASAA purposes, the term net worth means an excess of assets over liabilities, as determined by generally accepted accounting principles, but shall not include the following as assets:

- Goodwill
- Patents
- Copyrights
- All other assets of an intangible nature, home, home furnishings, automobile(s), and any other personal items not readily marketable in the case of an individual; advances or loans to stockholders and officers in the case of a corporation; and advances or loans to partners in the case of a partnership

However, furniture used in the office, such as a sofa in the reception room, or bookcases in the company research library, are considered assets for the purpose of the computation.

QUICK QUIZ 3.G

1. All of the following statements regarding the USA's minimum financial requirements of an investment adviser are correct EXCEPT

    A. advisers maintaining custody of customer funds and/or securities must have a net worth of $35,000
    B. advisers maintaining discretion over client accounts must have net worth of $35,000
    C. advisers accepting substantial prepayments of fees must have a positive net worth
    D. advisers whose only custody of client funds is the ability to have direct deduction of fees are exempt from the net worth and bonding requirements

2. A registered investment adviser has discretionary authority over client accounts. Its accounting department has just discovered that the firm's net worth is $8,500. Under the Uniform Securities Act, they

    I.   must notify the administrator of the net worth deficiency by the close of that day
    II. must notify the administrator of the net worth deficiency by the close of the next business day
    III. must file a financial report with the Administrator by the first business day following notice
    IV. may no longer exercise discretion until they increase their net worth

    A. I and III
    B. I and IV
    C. II and III
    D. II and IV

3. XYZ Advisers has its principal office in State A. XYZ maintains custody of customer securities and they wish to open an office in State B. They have been informed that the Administrator of State B requires all investment advisers that take custody to maintain a minimum net worth of $65,000. Which of the following statements is CORRECT?

   A. XYZ will have to meet State B's net worth requirements if it wishes to register there.
   B. XYZ can register in State B only if they cease taking custody.
   C. As long as XYZ meets the net worth requirements of State A, it can register in any other state.
   D. In lieu of meeting State B's requirements, a surety bond may be posted.

3. 7 INVESTMENT ADVISER REPRESENTATIVE

Investment adviser representative (IAR) means any partner, officer, director (or an individual occupying a similar status or performing similar functions), or other individual employed by or associated with an investment adviser that is registered or required to be registered under the Uniform Securities Act (state registered IA). If employed by or associated with a federal covered adviser, this individual only comes under the registration requirements by having a place of business in the state. In both cases (state or federal), the individual meets the definition of an IAR by doing any of the following:

- Makes any recommendations or otherwise renders advice regarding securities
- Manages accounts or portfolios of clients
- Determines which recommendation or advice regarding securities should be given
- Solicits, offers or negotiates for the sale of or sells investment advisory services
- Supervises employees who perform any of the foregoing

TAKE NOTE The use of the term *individual* here is important. Only an individual, or a natural person, can be an investment adviser representative. The investment advisory firm is the legal person (entity) that the IAR (natural person) represents in performing the above listed functions.

3. 7. 1 REGISTRATION REQUIREMENTS FOR INVESTMENT ADVISER REPRESENTATIVES

It is unlawful for any state registered investment adviser to employ an investment adviser representative unless the investment adviser representative is registered under this act. However, the registration of an investment adviser representative is not effective during any period when he is not employed by an investment adviser registered under this act. The same holds true for a federal covered adviser to employ, supervise, or associate with an investment adviser representative having a place of business located in this state, unless such investment adviser representative is registered under this act, or is exempt from registration.

The effect of the previous statement (found in Section 203A of the Investment Advisers Act of 1940), is that for those performing as IARs for federal covered advisers, state registration is required only in those states where that individual has a place of business. Place of business of an investment adviser representative means:

(1) an office at which the investment adviser representative regularly provides investment advisory services, solicits, meets with, or otherwise communicates with clients; and

(2) any other location that is held out to the general public as a location at which the investment adviser representative provides investment advisory services, solicits, meets with, or otherwise communicates with clients.

Registration of an investment adviser also leads to automatic registration of partners, officers, or directors functioning as investment adviser representatives. What does that really mean? An investment adviser representative can only be registered as a representative of a registered adviser, so individuals holding the positions mentioned above are in limbo until the adviser's registration becomes effective. At that time, their individual registrations go into effect. Instead of filing a Form U-4 or Form U-10, their personal information is included in the Form ADV Part 1 filed by the investment adviser. And, just like any other IAR, they must take and pass the appropriate qualification exam(s) and wait for notice of effectiveness.

For those of you who have taken a FINRA exam, you know there is a supervisory level of registration—registered principal. No such gradations apply under NASAA rules. So, no matter how high ranking the officer (of either a BD or IA), he just registers as either an agent or an IAR.

Many independent financial planners operate as independent contractors, not employees of investment advisory firms or broker-dealers. Regardless, they are required to be registered as investment adviser representatives of the firm and must be placed under the same level of supervisory scrutiny as employees. Their business cards may contain the name of their separate planning entity, but must also disclose the name of the entity registered as the investment adviser.

Registered investment advisers are responsible for the supervision of individuals registered as investment adviser representatives, but acting in the capacity of independent contractors, to the same extent that they supervise those who are actual employees of the firm.

Investment Adviser: Business or Individual

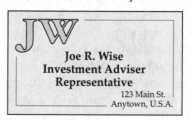

Investment Adviser Representative:
Individual Only

Registration as an IAR is done solely on a state basis. IARs never register with the SEC, even when they are representing a federal covered adviser. That is why it is NASAA who has the responsibility for this exam, rather than FINRA or the SEC.

3. 7. 1. 1   Financial Requirements of IARs

Unlike an investment adviser, there are no financial requirements, or net worth requirements, to register as an investment adviser representative. However, as with the other securities professionals, insolvency (bankruptcy) is a cause for denial or revocation of registration.

3. 7. 2   EXCLUSIONS FROM THE DEFINITION OF INVESTMENT ADVISER REPRESENTATIVE

Certain employees of investment advisory firms are excluded from the term *investment adviser representative*, provided their activities are confined to clerical duties or those activities that are solely incidental to the investment advisory services offered, such as mailing out a research report to an advisory client when directed by an IAR. Should the investment advisory employee "step over the line" as the saying goes, and perform any activity that makes one an IAR, the employee would then have to register as an investment adviser representative. Exclusion criteria for administrative employees of investment advisers are much the same as those for administrative personnel of broker-dealers.

In addition, an individual is not an investment adviser representative if the person does not on a regular basis solicit, meet with, or otherwise communicate with clients of the investment adviser or provides only impersonal investment advice.

Let's define that last term because you're going to see it a number of times in this course. "Impersonal investment advice" means investment advisory services provided by means of written material or oral statements that do not purport to meet the objectives or needs of specific individuals or accounts.

3.7.3   IAR TERMINATION PROCEDURES

If an investment adviser representative terminates employment with an investment adviser, notification requirements depend on how the investment adviser is registered.

If the investment adviser is a state-registered adviser, the firm must notify the Administrator. If the investment adviser is a federal covered adviser, the investment adviser representative must notify the Administrator.

Please note how this is different from an agent's termination where all of the parties involved notify the Administrator. Just as we gave you a clue to use the *a* in agent to represent all, visualize the *I* in IAR as the number 1 to remember that only one person gives notification.

The one area in which termination of agents and IARs is the same is that in both cases, termination is accomplished by filing the Form U-5.

QUICK QUIZ 3.H

True or False?

_____   1.   An investment adviser representative must register with the SEC if she has clients with assets of $110 million or more under management.

_____   2.   A state-registered investment adviser maintaining custody of a customer's securities or funds and exercising discretion in the account is generally required to maintain a minimum net worth of $35,000.

_____   3.   An employee of an investment advisory firm is an investment adviser representative if his duties are confined to clerical activities.

_____   4.   An administrative employee who receives specific compensation for offering investment advisory services is not an investment adviser representative.

_____   5.   An employee of an investment advisory firm is an investment adviser representative if his duties involve making investment recommendations.

6.   Under the Uniform Securities Act, registration with the state could be required of which of the following?

A.   A financial planner or other person who provides investment advisory services to others for compensation

B.   A publisher of a bona fide newspaper, news magazine, or business or financial publication of general and regular circulation

C.   A federal covered investment adviser

D.   Any person who the Administrator excludes by rule or order

7. Under the Uniform Securities Act, which of the following is NOT an investment adviser representative?

A. A director of a state registered investment advisory firm who determines specific recommendations for clients

B. An associate in an SEC-registered investment advisory firm who has a place of business in the state and manages the account of only one individual client

C. A clerk employed by a state registered investment advisory firm

D. A vice president of a state registered investment advisory firm who supervises employees who solicit clients for the firm

3. 8   BOOKS AND RECORDS REQUIRED BY FEDERAL AND STATE LAW

The Uniform Securities Act virtually duplicates the first 12 items of the recordkeeping requirements of the Investment Advisers Act of 1940. The major exception is that on the eleventh bullet (a copy of each notice), NASAA's Model Rule requires a copy when the material is distributed to two or more persons(other than persons connected with the investment adviser), not 10 or more as is the case under federal law.

The Investment Advisers Act requires every adviser (other than one specifically exempted from registration) to make, keep, and preserve such records, and for such periods as the SEC may prescribe as necessary or appropriate in the public interest or for the protection of investors. By rule, the SEC has set forth various recordkeeping requirements for investment advisers. Moreover, the act makes it unlawful for any person to willfully make any untrue statement of a material fact in any report filed with the SEC or to willfully omit to state in a report any material fact required to be stated therein.

The SEC and the states require investment advisers to maintain the following books and records:

■ A journal, including cash receipts and disbursement records

■ General and auxiliary ledgers reflecting asset, liability, reserve, capital, income, and expense accounts

■ A memorandum of each order given by the adviser for the purchase or sale of any security, or any instruction received by the adviser from the client concerning the purchase, sale, receipt, or delivery of a security, and of any modification or cancellation of any such order or instruction

■ All checkbooks, bank statements, canceled checks, and cash reconciliations

■ All bills or statements (or copies thereof) paid or unpaid

■ All trial balances, financial statements, and internal audit working papers

■ Originals of all written communications received and copies of all written communications sent by the adviser related to any recommendation or advice given or proposed to be given; any receipt, disbursement, or delivery of funds or securities; or the placing or execution of any order to purchase or sell any security (provided, however, that if the investment adviser sends any notice, circular, or other advertisement offering any report, analysis, publication, or other investment advisory service to more than 10 persons, the investment adviser shall not be required to keep a record of the names and addresses of the persons to whom it was sent; except that if the notice, circular, or advertisement is distributed to persons named on any list, the investment adviser shall retain with the copy of the notice, circular or advertisement a memorandum describing the list and its source.)

■ A record of all accounts in which the adviser is vested with any discretionary power with respect to the funds, securities, or transactions of any client

■ All powers of attorney and other evidences of the granting of any discretionary authority by any client to the adviser, or copies thereof

■ All written agreements (or copies thereof) entered into by the adviser with a client or otherwise relating to his investment advisory business

■ A file containing a copy of each notice, circular, advertisement, newspaper article, investment letter, bulletin, or other communication, including by electronic media (email), that the investment adviser circulates or distributes, directly or indirectly, to 10 or more persons (other than persons connected with the investment adviser); if the item, including communications by electronic media recommends the purchase or sale of a specific security and does not state the reasons for the recommendation, the adviser must prepare a memorandum indicating the reasons for that recommendation

■ A file containing a copy of all written communications received or sent regarding any litigation involving the investment adviser or any investment adviser representative or employee, and regarding any written customer or client complaint

■ With certain exceptions, a record of all securities transactions in which an investment adviser or any advisory representative has, or by reason of such transaction acquires, any direct or beneficial ownership

In practice, the recordkeeping rule has served as a deterrent to the practice of scalping because it requires all advisory representatives to report all of their security transactions to their affiliated advisory firms on a regular basis; these reports are subject to SEC examination. **Scalping** is the practice whereby an investment adviser, before the dissemination of a securities recommendation, trades on the anticipated short-run market activity that may result from the recommendation.

TEST TOPIC ALERT   Under the NASAA Model Rule on Recordkeeping of Investment Advisers, if a state-registered investment adviser has custody because it advises a pooled investment vehicle, the adviser must also keep true, accurate, and current audited account statements. The records required to be made and kept include:

■ the date(s) of the audit;

■ a copy of the audited financial statements; and

■ evidence of the mailing of the audited financial statements to all limited partners, members or other beneficial owners within 120 days of the end of its fiscal year.

The adviser is not required to keep a copy of the minutes of the board of directors, bank statements, or the trust agreement.

3. 8. 1   TIME PERIOD FOR MAINTENANCE OF RECORDS

The Investment Advisers Act of 1940, as well as the Uniform Securities Act, requires that an investment adviser's books and records be maintained in a readily accessible place for five years. The five-year period will run from the end of the fiscal year during which the last entry was made on the record. During the first two years of the five-year period, the rule requires that the records be maintained in the principal office of the adviser. However, after this initial two-year period, the records may be preserved in electronic or microfilm format or any other form of data storage in compliance with the act. Even though the recordkeeping requirements are almost identical, it is important to remember for the test that federal covered advisers only comply with the SEC's requirements while state registered advisers need only meet the requirements of the state where their principal office is located.

Partnership articles and any amendments thereto, articles of incorporation, charters, minute books, and stock certificate books of the investment adviser and of any predecessor must be maintained in the principal office of the investment adviser and preserved until at least three years after termination of the enterprise.

TEST TOPIC ALERT   A few pages ago, we gave you a Test Topic Alert that emphasized that as long as state registered investment advisers met the net worth or surety bond requirements of their home state, that was sufficient for any state in which they are registered. The same is true regarding recordkeeping requirements and the proof is in the following statement copied from the Form ADV:

2. State-Registered Investment Adviser Affidavit

If you are subject to state regulation, by signing this Form ADV, you represent that, you are in compliance with the registration requirements of the state in which you maintain your principal place of business and are in compliance with the bonding, capital, and recordkeeping requirements of that state.

3. 8. 2   STORAGE REQUIREMENTS

The records required to be maintained and preserved may be maintained and preserved for the required time by an investment adviser on:

- paper or hard copy form, as those records are kept in their original form;
- micrographic media, including microfilm, microfiche, or any similar medium; or
- electronic storage media, including any digital (computer disk) storage medium or system as long as the investment adviser establishes and maintains procedures

    — to maintain and preserve the records, so as to reasonably safeguard them from loss, alteration, or destruction,

    — to limit access to the records to properly authorized personnel and the Administrator, and

    — to reasonably ensure that any reproduction of a non-electronic original record on electronic storage media is complete, true, and legible when retrieved.

In all cases, the investment adviser must arrange and index the records in a way that permits easy location, access, and retrieval of any particular record and provide the Administrator with the means to access, view, and print the records.

QUICK QUIZ 3.1

1. Under the Investment Advisers Act of 1940, all of the following are true regarding adviser recordkeeping EXCEPT

    A. the IA must keep records of transactions made for its own account as well as the account of investment adviser representatives to lessen the likelihood of scalping
    B. computer-generated records may be stored in that format
    C. client account records must be maintained, including a list of recommendations made
    D. records must be maintained for a period of 2 years from the end of the fiscal year in which the last entry was made

2. An investment adviser registered in State G is obligated to maintain certain books and records as specified by the Uniform Securities Act. Which of the following statements regarding adviser recordkeeping is NOT true?

    A. Records originally created on computer may be stored in electronic media.
    B. Records are subject to surprise audits by the State G Administrator.
    C. Written records may be reduced to microfilm.
    D. Records must be kept for six years.

TEST TOPIC ALERT
You will need to remember that the record retention requirement for investment advisers is five years while that for broker-dealers is three years.

3. 9   INVESTMENT ADVISER CODE OF ETHICS

There are some additional recordkeeping requirements under federal law because of the need for federal covered advisers to institute a code of ethics. This text will include the most testable items relating to that code. Rule 204A-1, Investment Adviser Code of Ethics, requires:

■ a copy of the investment adviser's code of ethics adopted and implemented pursuant to the Investment Advisers Act of 1940;

■ a record of any violation of the code of ethics and of any action taken as a result of the violation;

■ a record of all written acknowledgments, as required by the code of ethics rule, for each person who is currently, or within the past five years was, a supervised person of the investment adviser; and

■ each adviser's code of ethics to require an adviser's access persons (defined below) to periodically report their personal securities transactions and holdings to the adviser's chief compliance officer or other designated persons. The code of ethics must also require the adviser to review those reports. Reviewing these reports will allow advisers as well as the SEC's examination staff to identify improper trades or patterns of trading by access persons.

3. 9. 1   PERSONAL TRADING PROCEDURES

Advisory firms should include the following elements, or address the following issues, when crafting their procedures for employees' personal securities trading:

■ Prior written approval before access persons can place a personal securities transaction (i.e., preclearance)

■ Maintenance of lists of issuers of securities that the advisory firm is analyzing or recommending for client transactions, and prohibitions on personal trading in securities of those issuers

■ Maintenance of restricted lists of issuers about which the advisory firm has inside information, and prohibitions on any trading (personal or for clients) in securities of those issuers

■ Reminders that investment opportunities must be offered first to clients before the adviser or its employees may act on them, and procedures to implement this principle

There are several exceptions where access persons may be permitted to trade in securities, such as when the person is participating in a DRIP (and does not alter the program to take advantage of the IA's recommendations or other information), but it is unlikely that these will be tested.

3. 9. 1. 1   Access Person

An **access person** is any of the adviser's supervised persons who (1) has access to nonpublic information regarding any clients' purchase or sale of securities, or nonpublic information regarding the portfolio holdings of any reportable fund, or (2) is involved in making securities recommendations to clients, or who has access to such recommendations that are nonpublic. If providing investment advice is the adviser's primary business, all of the firm's directors, officers and partners are presumed to be access persons.

The following records are required under Rule 204A-1, Investment Adviser Code of Ethics:

■ A record of each report made by an access person

■ A record of the names of persons who are currently, or within the past five years were, access persons of the investment adviser

■ A record of any decision, and the reasons supporting the decision, to approve the acquisition of securities by access persons, for at least five years after the end of the fiscal year in which the approval is granted

---

TAKE NOTE

Long before this Code of Ethics was promulgated, NASAA had its version, now titled the *NASAA Model Rule on Unethical Business Practices of Investment Advisers, Investment Adviser Representatives and Federal Covered Advisers*. Many of those practices will be covered later in this session and the entire model rule is included as Appendix B to this manual. It is critical that you study that appendix—many questions on the exam are pulled directly from it.

3. 10 BROCHURE RULE

As mentioned earlier, the Form ADV Part 2 is a disclosure document that, under state and federal securities laws, is required to be given to clients. On July 28, 2010, the Securities and Exchange Commission adopted amendments to Part 2 of Form ADV and related rules that require investment advisers registered under the Investment Advisers Act of 1940 to provide new and prospective clients with a brochure and brochure supplements written in plain English.

The new Part 2 consists of the following three parts:

■ Part 2A of Form ADV: Firm Brochure

■ Part 2A Appendix 1 of Form ADV: Wrap Fee Program Brochure

■ Part 2B of Form ADV: Brochure Supplement (describes certain supervised persons)

Under SEC and similar state rules, investment advisers are required to deliver to clients and prospective clients a brochure disclosing information about the firm. They also may be required to deliver a brochure supplement disclosing information about one or more of their supervised persons. Part 2 of Form ADV sets out the minimum required disclosure that the brochure (Part 2A for a firm brochure, or Appendix 1 for a wrap fee program brochure) and brochure supplements (Part 2B) must contain. Here are some of the key points of which you should be aware:

■ *Narrative Format.* Part 2 of Form ADV consists of a series of items that contain disclosure requirements for the firm's brochure and any required supplements. The items require narrative responses. The IA must respond to each item in Part 2. They must include the heading for each item provided by Part 2 immediately preceding their response to that item and provide responses in the same order as the items appear in Part 2. If an item does not apply to their business, they must indicate that item is not applicable. There are 18 items on the ADV Part 2 (with a 19th one for state registered advisers only). Remember, this is for clients to use to understand what the IA does so the information disclosed relates to the way the IA operates the business. Some of the items include

— a description of the types of advisory services provided,

— fees and compensation,

— methods of analysis, investment strategies, and risk of loss,

— disciplinary information,

— how you select or recommend broker-dealers for client transactions,

— custody practices; and

— investment discretion.

■ *Plain English.* The items in Part 2 of Form ADV are designed to promote effective communication between the firm and their clients. The brochure and supplements must be written in plain English, taking into consideration the clients' level of financial sophistication. Specifically, the SEC states that the brochure should be concise and direct. In drafting the brochure and brochure supplements, the IA should: (1) use short sentences; (2) use definite, concrete, everyday words; (3) use active voice; (4) use tables or bullet lists for complex material, whenever possible; (5) avoid legal jargon or highly technical business terms unless you explain them or you believe that your clients will understand them; and (6) avoid multiple negatives. The brochure should discuss any conflicts the adviser has or is reasonably likely to have and practices in which it engages or is reasonably likely to engage. If a conflict arises or the adviser decides to engage in a practice that it has not disclosed, supplemental disclosure must be provided to clients to obtain their consent. If the IA has a conflict or engages in a practice with respect to some (but not all) types or classes of clients, advice, or transactions, such should be indicated rather than disclosing that the firm may have the conflict or engage in the practice.

■ *Disclosure Obligations as a Fiduciary.* Under federal and state law, IAs act in a fiduciary capacity and must make full disclosure to their clients of all material facts relating to the advisory relationship. As a fiduciary, they also must seek to avoid conflicts of interest with their clients, and, at a minimum, make full disclosure of all material conflicts of interest between them and their clients that could affect the advisory relationship.

■ *Full and Truthful Disclosure.* Obviously, all information in the brochure and brochure supplements must be true and may not omit any material facts.

■ *Filing.* The investment adviser must file the brochure(s) (and amendments) through the IARD system. If the IA is federal covered or in the process of registering with the SEC, it is not required to file the brochure supplements through the IARD or otherwise. However, a copy of the supplements must be preserved and made available to SEC staff upon request. If the IA is registered with or is in the process of registering with one or more state securities authorities, a copy of the brochure supplement (Part 2B) must be filed for each supervised person doing business in that state.

TAKE NOTE

Only in the case of state registered investment advisers is it required to file the brochure supplements. If you think about it, it makes sense because virtually all of the supervised persons described in the supplements are investment adviser representatives and they are always registered on a state level only, not with the SEC.

The cover page of the brochure must state the name, business address, contact information, website address (if there is one), and the date of the brochure. Furthermore, the cover page of the brochure must state the following (or other clear and concise language conveying the same information) and identify the document as a brochure:

This brochure provides information about the qualifications and business practices of [firm name]. If you have any questions about the contents of this brochure, please contact us at [telephone number and/or email address]. The information in this brochure has not been approved or verified by the United States Securities and Exchange Commission or by any state securities authority.

Additional information about [firm name] also is available on the SEC's website at **www.adviserinfo.sec.gov***.*

3. 10. 1   BROCHURE SUPPLEMENT DISCLOSING INDIVIDUAL ADVISORY PERSONNEL

As has been mentioned earlier, Part 2B is a brochure supplement that must contain certain information about "advisory personnel on whom clients rely for investment advice." The brochure supplement is also a narrative format in plain English and includes six required disclosure categories:

- **Cover page** identifying the supervised person (or persons) covered by the supplement as well as the advisory firm
- **Educational background and business experience**, including disclosing if the supervised person has no high school education, no formal education after high school, or no business background
- **Disciplinary information** about material events within the past 10 years, although the SEC says that even if more than 10 years have passed since the date of the event, you must disclose the event if it is so serious that it remains currently material to a client's or prospective client's evaluation
- **Other business activities**, including disclosing if the supervised person receives commissions, bonuses, or other compensation based on the sale of securities or other investment products, including as a broker-dealer or registered representative (agent), and including distribution or service (trail) fees from the sale of mutual funds
- **Additional compensation** beyond that paid by the client (such as a sales award or other prize)
- **Supervision**, including providing the name, title, and telephone number of the individual responsible for supervising the supervised person's advisory activities on behalf of the firm

3. 10. 1. 1   Supervised Persons Included in the Brochure Supplement

The investment adviser must prepare a brochure supplement for the following supervised persons:

- Any supervised person who formulates investment advice for a client and has direct client contact
- Any supervised person who has discretionary authority over a client's assets, even if the supervised person has no direct client contact

TAKE NOTE

No supplement is required for a supervised person who has no direct client contact and has discretionary authority over a client's assets only as part of a team. In addition, if discretionary advice is provided by a team comprised of more than five supervised persons, brochure supplements need only be provided for the five supervised persons with the most significant responsibility for the day-to-day discretionary advice provided to the client.

3. 10. 2 WRAP FEE PROGRAMS

The rules on disclosure are somewhat different for wrap fee programs. A **wrap fee program** is a program under which a client is charged a specified fee, or fees, not based directly on transactions in a client's account, for investment advisory services (which may include portfolio management or advice concerning the selection of other investment advisers) and for execution of client transactions.

Any registered investment adviser compensated under a wrap fee program for sponsoring, organizing, or administering the program, or for selecting, or providing advice to clients regarding the selection of, other investment advisers in the program, does not use the normal brochure or Part 2A of the ADV. Instead, that adviser furnishes clients and prospective clients Part 2A, Appendix 1.

If the investment adviser sponsors a wrap fee program, it must deliver a wrap fee program brochure to their wrap fee clients. The disclosure requirements for preparing a wrap fee program brochure appear in Part 2A, Appendix 1 of Form ADV. If the entire advisory business is sponsoring wrap fee programs, the firm does not need to prepare a firm brochure separate from the wrap fee program brochure(s). In other words, if all the IA does is sponsor wrap fee programs, it must prepare and deliver a completed Part 2A, Appendix 1, but not a Part 2A.

If the investment adviser sponsors more than one wrap fee program, it may prepare a single wrap fee program brochure describing all the wrap fee programs sponsored, or it may prepare separate wrap fee program brochures that describe one or more of its wrap fee programs. If it prepares separate brochures, each brochure must state that it sponsors other wrap fee programs and must explain how the client can obtain brochures for the other programs.

If the firm provides portfolio management services to clients in wrap fee programs that it does not sponsor, it must deliver the normal brochure prepared in accordance with Part 2A (not Appendix 1) to its wrap fee clients. It also must deliver to these clients any brochure supplements required by Part 2B of Form ADV.

However, if a wrap fee program that you sponsor has multiple sponsors and another sponsor creates and delivers to your wrap fee program clients a wrap fee program brochure that includes all the information required in your wrap brochure, you do not have to create or deliver a separate wrap fee program brochure.

Some of the required disclosures required under Appendix 1 include:

- a statement on the cover page of the wrap fee program brochure must state the following (or other clear and concise language conveying the same information) and identify the document as a wrap fee program brochure:

    This wrap fee program brochure provides information about the qualifications and business practices of [firm name]. If you have any questions about the contents of this brochure, please contact us at [telephone number and/or email address]. The information in this brochure has not been approved or verified by the United States Securities and Exchange Commission or by any state securities authority.

    *Additional information about [firm name] also is available on the SEC's website at **www.adviserinfo.sec.gov**.*

- the amount of the wrap fee charged for the program;
- whether the fees are negotiable;

- the portion of the total fee paid to persons providing advice to clients regarding the purchase or sale of specific securities under the program;

- the services provided under the program, including the types of portfolio management services;

- a statement that the program may cost the client more or less than purchasing these services separately;

- a description of the nature of any fees that the client may pay in addition to the wrap fee;

- if the person recommending the wrap fee program to the client receives compensation as a result of the client's participation in the program, disclose this fact

  — explain, if applicable, that the amount of this compensation may be more than what the person would receive if the client participated in the firm's other programs or paid separately for investment advice, brokerage, and other services, or

  — explain that the person, therefore, may have a financial incentive to recommend the wrap fee program over other programs or services;

- if a wrap fee program imposes any requirements to open or maintain an account, such as a minimum account size, disclose these requirements—if there is a minimum amount for assets placed with each portfolio manager as well as a minimum account size for participation in the wrap fee program, disclose and explain these requirements;

- describe how portfolio managers are selected and reviewed, the basis for recommending or selecting portfolio managers for particular clients, and the criteria for replacing or recommending the replacement of portfolio managers for the program and for particular clients;

- disclose whether any of the firm's related persons act as a portfolio manager for a wrap fee program described in the wrap fee program brochure

  — explain the conflicts of interest faced because of this arrangement and describe how these conflicts of interest are addressed,

  — disclose whether related person portfolio managers are subject to the same selection and review as the other portfolio managers that participate in the wrap fee program, or

  — if they are not, describe how related person portfolio managers are selected and reviewed;

- describe the information about clients that is communicated to the clients' portfolio managers and how often or under what circumstances updated information is provided;

- explain any restrictions placed on clients' ability to contact and consult with their portfolio managers; and

- state registered investment advisers must describe any relationship or arrangement that they or any of their management persons have with any issuer of securities that is not already listed in Part 2A.

TEST TOPIC ALERT   It is generally agreed that "buy and hold" clients are not suitable for a wrap fee account because they don't do enough trading to benefit from the fact that commissions are included in the program fee.

3. 10. 3 BROCHURE DELIVERY REQUIREMENTS

Both federal and state registered advisers must prepare and deliver a brochure to their clients. If the question does not specify federal or state registered (or refer to the Investment Advisers Act of 1940 or the USA), you should assume they are asking about a state registered adviser. It is, after all, NASAA's exam.

3. 10. 3. 1 Delivery Requirements for SEC Registered Advisers

A firm brochure must be delivered to each client. It must be delivered even if the advisory agreement with the client is oral (as we will learn, under federal law, contracts may be oral or in writing; under state law, they must be in writing).

The firm brochure must be given to each client before or at the time an advisory agreement is entered into with that client. Thereafter, each year, within 120 days of the end of the fiscal year, a free, updated brochure must be delivered to each client that either includes a summary of material changes or is accompanied by a summary of material changes, or alternatively, it would be permitted to deliver to each client a summary of material changes that includes an offer to provide a copy of the updated brochure and information on how a client may obtain the brochure.

TAKE NOTE

If there are no material changes, then nothing—not the brochure nor the brochure supplement, nor the summary—is required to be sent.

Although, as we will see below, the brochure must be updated promptly when something becomes materially inaccurate, the only time that an interim amendment must be delivered to clients is when there is a disciplinary action. This interim amendment can be in the form of a document describing the material facts relating to the amended disciplinary event.

3. 10. 3. 2 Delivery Requirements for State Registered Advisers

The brochure delivery requirements for state registered advisers are essentially the same as that for covered advisers with one very important exception. Under the NASAA Model Rule on adviser brochures, advisers are required to deliver the brochure to the client at least 48 hours before entering into an advisory contract or at the time of entering into an advisory contract, if the advisory client has the right to terminate the contract without penalty within five business days after entering into the contract. Some advisers charge a startup or setup fee. Any new client who does not receive a brochure at least 48 hours before entering into an advisory agreement may terminate the agreement and be refunded the setup fee. However, it would not be considered a penalty for the adviser to make a pro rata charge for management services rendered during that five-business-day period.

3. 10. 3. 3 Delivery of the Brochure Supplements

Initially and annually, the investment adviser must deliver to a client the brochure supplements for each supervised person who provides advisory services to that client. However, there are three categories of clients to whom the IA is not required to deliver supplements.

■ Clients to whom the IA is not required to deliver a firm brochure (Part 2A) or a wrap fee program brochure (Appendix 1 to Part 2A). The logic here is that because the supplement is a *supplement* to the brochure, if there is no brochure, why would there be a supplement?

■ Clients who receive only impersonal investment advice, even if they receive a firm brochure. An example of this would include those paying $500 or more per year for a subscription.

■ Individual clients who are any executive officers, directors, trustees, general partners, or people serving in a similar capacity, of that firm; or any employees of that firm (other than employees performing solely clerical, secretarial or administrative functions) who, in connection with their regular functions or duties, participate in the investment activities of that firm and have been performing such functions or duties for at least 12 months.

3. 10. 3. 4 Exemptions from the Brochure Rule

There are two exemptions under both state and federal law from the delivery requirements of the rule.

■ Contracts with a registered investment company are exempted. Section 15 (not testable) of the Investment Company Act of 1940 requires investment advisers to furnish information to the board of directors of a registered investment company to enable the board to evaluate the terms of the proposed contract. As long as the contract meets those requirements, the SEC thought it unnecessary to require the adviser to deliver a brochure to the investment company.

■ Advisers entering into a contract providing solely for impersonal advisory services—that is, publishers of market letters—are exempt from the rule's initial delivery requirements. If the annual charge for this service is $500 or greater, delivery of the brochure must be offered with the same two timing options listed above.

3. 10. 4 UPDATING THE BROCHURE

The brochure must be updated:

■ each year at the time of filing the annual updating amendment; and

■ promptly, whenever any information in the brochure becomes materially inaccurate.

It is not required to update the brochure between annual amendments solely because the amount of client assets under management has changed or because the fee schedule has changed. However, if the brochure is being updated for a separate reason in between annual amendments (a disciplinary action, some other material change, and so forth), and the amount of client assets under management listed in the brochure the fee schedule listed has become materially inaccurate, the IA should update that item(s) as part of the interim amendment.

If, when preparing the annual updating amendment, there are no material changes to the previous brochure, and there have been no interim amendments making material changes to the brochure that was filed with the previous year's annual updating amendment, a summary of material changes does not have to be prepared (because there is nothing to say). Read what the SEC has to say about that: "If you do not have to prepare a summary of material changes, you do not have to deliver a summary of material changes or a brochure to your existing clients that year. If you are a state-registered adviser, you should contact the appropriate state securities authorities to determine whether you must make an annual offer of the brochure." That means that a new brochure doesn't even have to be offered (in the case of federal covered advisers) if there has been no material change.

Try to follow these next two points.

■ Federal covered advisers are required to file amendments to their brochure electronically through IARD. However, they are not required to file amendments to the brochure supplements with the SEC, but must maintain a copy of them in their files.

■ State-registered advisers are required to file amendments to their brochure and amendments to their brochure supplement with the appropriate state securities authorities through IARD.

Why the difference? I think it just makes it easier for NASAA to write a hard test question.

Finally, if the IA has no clients to whom delivery of a brochure is required, they don't have to prepare one.

QUICK QUIZ 3.J

1. With regard to the brochure rule of the Investment Advisers Act of 1940, which of the following are exempt from the delivery requirements of that rule?

   A. An adviser whose only clients are registered investment companies
   B. An adviser whose only clients are insurance companies
   C. An adviser who only provides impersonal advisory services at an annual charge of less than $500
   D. All of the above

2. With regard to a federal covered investment adviser, which of the following statements regarding the Form ADV Part 2A is CORRECT?

   A. It must be delivered no later than 48 hours before entering into an advisory contract.
   B. It must be delivered no later than upon receipt of a client's funds.
   C. It must accompany the ADV Part 1A when being delivered to new clients.
   D. An investment adviser must deliver to each client, a copy of the most recent ADV Part 2A no later than at the time of entering into the advisory agreement.

3. Under the Investment Advisers Act of 1940, an investment adviser is required to

   I. submit justification for continued registration to the SEC if their client base drops below 15 individuals for any consecutive 12-month period

   II. disclose, in their brochure, the number of clients they serve

   III. disclose, in their brochure supplements, the educational background, business experience, and disciplinary history (if any) of the supervised persons who provide advisory services to the clients

   A. I and II

   B. I and III

   C. II and III

   D. III only

4. Smith & Jones is a registered investment adviser under the Investment Advisers Act of 1940. It has 1,000 active clients. The firm maintains custody for 200 of their clients and exercises investment discretion for 400 of them. When preparing its brochure for annual distribution, it would need to include an audited balance sheet prepared by an independent accountant for

   A. the 200 clients for whom it maintains custody

   B. the 200 clients for whom it maintains custody, as well as the 400 for whom it exercises investment discretion

   C. all of its clients because it is an integral part of its brochure once it maintains custody for even 1 client

   D. none of its clients because the balance sheet requirement is only required when the firm collects fees in excess of $1,200, 6 or more months in advance

5. Under the Investment Advisers Act of 1940, a registered investment adviser who provides investment advisory services to individuals must

   A. have a minimum net worth of $100,000

   B. limit the giving of advice to securities listed on major exchanges

   C. avoid maintaining control or custody of client funds and securities

   D. provide each new client with a disclosure statement or brochure no later than when entering into the advisory agreement

3. 11 RULES ON CUSTODY OF FUNDS AND SECURITIES

In April of 2004, compliance with new SEC rules regarding an investment adviser's custody of customer's funds and securities went into effect. NASAA published its rules on custody later that same month. For the most part, the rules are identical. Our text will focus on the rule stated in the Investment Advisers Act of 1940 and, where the NASAA model rule differs, a notation will be made.

Safekeeping required. If you are an investment adviser registered or required to be registered under either federal or state law, it is a fraudulent, deceptive, or manipulative act, practice, or course of business within the meaning of the act for you to have custody of client funds or securities unless the following conditions are met.

◼ You have a qualified custodian. A qualified custodian maintains those funds and securities in a separate account for each client under that client's name, or in accounts that contain only your clients' funds and securities, under your name as agent or trustee for the clients.

■ You give notice to your clients. If you open an account with a qualified custodian on your client's behalf, either under the client's name or under your name as agent, you must notify the client in writing of the qualified custodian's name and address and the manner in which the funds or securities are maintained, promptly when the account is opened and following any changes, such as a change in the location of the assets, to this information.

■ Account statements are delivered to clients, either:

— by qualified custodian: you have a reasonable basis for believing that the qualified custodian sends an account statement, at least quarterly, to each of your clients for which it maintains funds or securities, identifying the amount of funds and of each security in the account at the end of the period and setting forth all transactions in the account during that period; or

— by adviser: you send a quarterly account statement to each of your clients for whom you have custody of funds or securities, identifying the amount of funds and of each security of which you have custody at the end of the period and setting forth all transactions during that period. An independent public accountant must verify all of those funds and securities by actual examination at least once during each calendar year, at a time that is chosen by the accountant without prior notice or announcement to you and that is irregular from year to year, and file a copy of the auditor's report and financial statements with the SEC/Administrator stating that it has examined the funds and securities and describing the nature and extent of the examination: If the independent public accountant finds any material discrepancies during the course of the examination, the accountant must promptly notify the SEC/Administrator.

■ Under the NASAA model rule, in the absence of a rule prohibiting custody, the investment adviser notifies the Administrator promptly in writing on Form ADV that the investment adviser has or may have custody.

Exceptions to this rule. Some exceptions include the following.

■ Shares of mutual funds—with respect to shares of an open-end company (mutual fund), you may use the mutual fund's transfer agent in lieu of a qualified custodian since the mutual fund's transfer agent maintains the securities for the client on the mutual fund's books.

■ Registered investment companies—you need not comply with the rule with respect to clients that are registered investment companies. Registered investment companies and their advisers must comply with the strict requirements of the Investment Company Act of 1940, and the custody rules adopted under that act.

Definitions. For the purposes of this rule **custody** means holding, directly or indirectly, client funds or securities, or having any authority to obtain possession of them. Custody also includes:

■ possession of client funds or securities (but not of checks drawn by clients and made payable to third parties) unless you receive them inadvertently and you return them to the sender promptly but in any case within three business days (might say 72 hours on the exam) of receiving them: therefore, you should remember that the SEC never considers the receipt of a third-party check to constitute custody, while the Administrator will if the check is not sent on within three business days (NASAA—Under state law, the receipt of checks drawn by clients and made payable to unrelated third parties is considered custody unless forwarded to the third party within three business days of receipt and the adviser maintains a record of the event);

■ any arrangement (including a general power of attorney) under which you are authorized or permitted to withdraw client funds or securities maintained with a custodian upon your instruction to the custodian; and

■ any capacity (such as general partner of a limited partnership, managing member of a limited liability company, or a comparable position for another type of pooled investment vehicle, or trustee of a trust) that gives you or your supervised person legal ownership of or access to client funds or securities.

A **qualified custodian** is a bank or savings association that has deposits insured by the Federal Deposit Insurance Corporation under the Federal Deposit Insurance Act, a registered broker-dealer holding the client assets in customer accounts, and a foreign financial institution that customarily holds financial assets for its customers, provided that the foreign financial institution keeps the advisory clients' assets in customer accounts segregated from its proprietary assets.

TEST TOPIC ALERT

Most investment advisers do not take custody and, therefore, are unable to accept direct delivery of customer securities or funds except under the limited conditions described in this section. However, broker-dealers are not constrained by this rule; they are only required to provide receipts anytime they accept customer assets.

TAKE NOTE

There are two major benefits to an investment adviser using a qualified custodian.

■ Since the custodian is sending the quarterly reports to the client, that administrative burden is lifted from the investment adviser.

■ There is no requirement for a surprise annual audit by an independent accountant.

The NASAA model rule also adds language dealing with direct fee deduction. An adviser who has custody because the adviser's fees are directly deducted from client's accounts must also provide the following safeguards.

■ Written authorization—the adviser must have written authorization from each client to deduct advisory fees from the accounts held with the qualified custodian.

■ Notice of fee deduction—each time a fee is directly deducted from a client account, the adviser must concurrently:

— send the qualified custodian notice of the amount of the fee to be deducted from the client's account, and

— send the client an invoice itemizing the fee. Itemization includes the formula used to calculate the fee, the amount of assets under management the fee is based on, and the time period covered by the fee.

■ Notice of safeguards—the investment adviser notifies the Administrator in writing on Form ADV that the adviser intends to use the safeguards provided above.

TAKE NOTE

If the above three requirements are satisfied, then the IA who is only considered to have custody because of direct deduction of fees will receive a waiver from the financial requirements for the net worth and bonding requirements described earlier in this session (usually $35,000). In addition, just as with the IA who uses a qualified custodian, they will be relieved of the obligation to file an audited balance sheet.

EXAMPLE

Let's look at three examples of custody given by the SEC.

■ An adviser that holds clients' stock certificates or cash, even temporarily, puts those assets at risk of misuse or loss. The rule, however, expressly excludes inadvertent receipt by the adviser of client funds or securities, so long as the adviser returns them to the sender within three business days of receiving them. The rule does not permit advisers to forward clients' funds and securities without having custody, although advisers may certainly assist clients in such matters. In addition, the rule makes clear that an adviser's possession of a check drawn by the client and made payable to a third party is not possession of client funds for purposes of the custody definition. (Note, this is only true under NASAA rules if forwarded within three business days).

■ An adviser has custody if it has the authority to withdraw funds or securities from a client's account. An adviser with power of attorney to sign checks on a client's behalf, to withdraw funds or securities from a client's account, or to dispose of client funds or securities for any purpose other than authorized trading has access to the client's assets. An adviser authorized to deduct advisory fees or other expenses directly from a client's account has access to, and therefore has custody of, the client funds and securities in that account. These advisers might not have possession of client assets, but they have the authority to obtain possession.

■ An adviser has custody if it acts in any capacity that gives the adviser legal ownership of, or access to, the client funds or securities. One common instance is a firm that acts as both general partner and investment adviser to a limited partnership. By virtue of its position as general partner, the adviser generally has authority to dispose of funds and securities in the limited partnership's account and thus has custody of client assets.

QUICK QUIZ 3.K

1. Which of the following advisers would be deemed to have custody of customer funds or securities as defined in the Investment Advisers Act of 1940?

    A. The adviser receives the proceeds of sales in the customer's account.
    B. The adviser receives a fee of $1,500 as a prepayment for the next contract year.
    C. The adviser has investment discretion over the account.
    D. All of the above.

2. Which of the following state registered investment advisers would be required to furnish an audited balance sheet as part of its disclosure statement?

    I.   The adviser's fee is automatically debited from the client's account.
    II. The adviser receives its fee each year in advance in the amount of $900.
    III. The client's securities are held by a broker-dealer with whom the adviser has an affiliate relationship.

    A. I and II
    B. I and III
    C. II and III
    D. I, II and III

3. An investment adviser registered with the state wishes to take custody of client's funds or securities. Which of the following statements best describes NASAA rules regarding notification to the Administrator?

    A. The adviser must supply prompt notification to the Administrator by immediately updating its Form ADV.
    B. The adviser must notify the Administrator within 90 days of the end of its fiscal year by updating its Form ADV.
    C. If the adviser will be using a qualified custodian, no notification is necessary.
    D. Prompt notification to the Administrator is made by the independent accounting firm performing the adviser's annual surprise audit.

4. An investment adviser takes custody of client's funds and securities. Client account statements must be sent no less frequently than

    A. monthly
    B. quarterly
    C. semiannually
    D. annually

5. A federal covered investment adviser inadvertently receives securities from a client. The custody rules of the Investment Advisers Act of 1940 would require the adviser to

    A. forward those securities to the qualified custodian within 3 business days after receipt
    B. keep those securities in its vault
    C. notify the SEC promptly
    D. return those securities to the sender within 3 business days after receipt

6. What type of qualified custodians do NASAA rules permit to hold investment advisory clients' funds or securities?

  I.   FDIC insured banks and savings associations
  II. Federal covered investment advisers
  III. Registered broker-dealers
  IV. Transfer agents for NYSE listed corporations

  A. I and III
  B. I and IV
  C. II and III
  D. II and IV

7. Under the NASAA Model Custody Rules, an investment adviser is deemed to have custody of customer funds or securities when

  A. securities inadvertently received are returned to the customer within 3 business days of receipt
  B. checks made payable to the investment adviser are returned to the customer within 3 business days of receipt
  C. checks made payable to an unrelated third party are returned to the customer within 3 business days of receipt
  D. checks made payable to an unrelated third party are forwarded to that third party within 3 business days of receipt

8. If an investment adviser registered under the Investment Advisers Act of 1940 maintains custody of customer funds or securities, which of the following is TRUE?

  A. A surety bond will be required.
  B. The independent public accountant engaged to verify client funds and securities must give appropriate notice to the adviser before doing the verification.
  C. The adviser must, on an annual basis, provide his clients for whom he maintains custody a list of all securities held in custody by the firm.
  D. If the firm changes the location of safekeeping, all affected clients must be notified promptly.

Just because an adviser does not maintain custody or require prepayments and is not required to file the balance sheet with the SEC does not mean it has no obligation to maintain true, accurate, and current books.

TEST TOPIC ALERT   Although the general rule is that state registered investment advisers having custody must maintain a minimum net worth of $35,000 (or an equivalent surety bond), there are two cases where the net worth/bonding requirements are waived:

■ Advisers having custody solely due to direct fee deduction and who keep the required records and make the required notifications to clients

■ Advisers having custody solely due to advising pooled investment vehicles and who keep the required records and make the required notifications to clients

3. 11. 1   FORM ADV-E

In December 2009, the SEC approved amendments to the custody rule under the Investment Advisers Act of 1940. The amendments, among other things, require certain registered investment advisers that have custody of client funds or securities to undergo an annual surprise examination by an independent public accountant to verify client funds and securities. Form ADV-E is used as a cover page for a certificate of accounting of securities and funds of which the investment adviser has custody (surprise exam report). Form ADV-E contains both information about the adviser and the surprise exam conducted.

The Form ADV-E is filled out by the investment adviser and then submitted along with the surprise examination report or statement by the independent public accountant after a surprise inspection of the adviser.

TEST TOPIC ALERT

Filing of the Form ADV-E is required only when the investment adviser, rather than a qualified custodian, maintains custody of customer funds/securities.

3. 12   FIDUCIARY RESPONSIBILITIES OF INVESTMENT ADVISERS

Investment advisers are fiduciaries who owe a duty of undivided loyalty to their clients and must deal fairly and honestly with them. This fiduciary relationship between an adviser and his client imposes on an adviser an affirmative duty of utmost good faith and full and fair disclosure, as well as an affirmative obligation to employ reasonable care to avoid misleading his clients.

Both state and federal law reflect a recognition of the delicate fiduciary nature of an investment advisory relationship, as well as an intent to eliminate or at least expose all conflicts of interest that might incline an adviser to render advice that was not disinterested. A key difference between investment advisers and broker-dealers is that, as fiduciaries, the former have a defined legal obligation to always place the interests of the client first.

Although this relationship requires many things to be disclosed, one exception is that an IAR need not disclose personal transactions that are consistent with those recommended to clients.

3. 12. 1   DISCLOSURE AND CONSENT

To provide some assurance that the disclosure requirements of the acts will not be violated, the regulators have recommended that each of the adviser's advisory clients be given the written statement (brochure previously described) prepared by the adviser that makes all appropriate disclosures.

The securities laws do not prohibit a registered investment adviser representative from being an employee of a registered broker-dealer. However, there would be a duty on the part of both the broker-dealer and the soliciting advisers to inform advisory clients of their ability to seek execution of transactions with broker-dealers other than those who have employed the advisers.

Disclosure must be made to all current clients and to prospective clients regarding material disciplinary action. The broadest definition of *material* would include any actions taken against the firm or management persons by a court or regulatory authority within the past 10 years. Required disclosure would include the following:

■ State or regulatory proceedings in which the adviser or a management person was found to have violated rules or statutes that led to the denial, suspension, or revocation of the firm's or the individual management person's registration

■ Court proceedings, such as a permanent or temporary injunction, against the firm or management person pertaining to an investment-related activity or any felony

■ SRO proceedings in which the adviser or management person caused the business to lose its registration or the firm or individual was barred, suspended, or expelled, or a fine in excess of $2,500 or a limitation was placed on the adviser or management person's activities

During routine inspections, the regulators review an adviser's filings with the SEC or Administrator and other materials provided to clients to ensure that the adviser's disclosures are accurate, timely, and do not omit material information. Examples of failures to disclose material information to clients would include the following.

■ An adviser fails to disclose all fees that a client would pay in connection with the advisory contract, including how fees are charged and whether fees are negotiable.

■ An adviser fails to disclose its affiliation with a broker-dealer or other securities professionals or issuers.

■ If a state registered adviser has discretionary authority or custody over a client's funds or securities, or requires prepayment of advisory fees of more than $500 from a client, six or more months in advance, the adviser fails to disclose a financial condition that is reasonably likely to impair the ability of the adviser to meet contractual commitments to those clients. In the case of a federal covered adviser, the dollar limit is more than $1,200.

■ An adviser may defraud its clients when it fails to use the average price paid when allocating securities to accounts participating in bunched trades and fails to adequately disclose its allocation policy. This practice violates the act if securities that were purchased at the lowest price or sold at the highest price are allocated to favored clients without adequate disclosure.

■ Any material legal action against the adviser must be disclosed to existing clients promptly. If the action occurred within the past 10 years, it must be disclosed by a state registered adviser to prospective clients not less than 48 hours before entering into the contract, or no later than the time of entering into such contract if the client has the right to terminate the contract without penalty within five business days. In the case of a federal covered adviser, the "48 hour rule" does not apply; disclosure is part of the brochure delivered no later than commencing the advisory agreement.

QUICK QUIZ 3.L

1. The BJS Advisory Service maintains no custody of customer funds or securities, requires no substantial prepayments of fees, and does not have investment discretion over clients' accounts. Which of the following would have to be promptly disclosed to clients?

    I.   The SEC has entered an order barring the executive vice president of the firm from association with any firm in the investment business.
    II. BJS has just been fined $3,500 by the NYSE.
    III. A civil suit has just been filed against BJS by one of its clients alleging that BJS made unsuitable recommendations.

    A. I and II
    B. I and III
    C. II and III
    D. None of the above

3. 12. 2 HEDGE CLAUSES

A constant concern of the regulators is any attempt by an investment adviser to waive the implied fiduciary responsibilities inherent in the client/adviser relationship. One of the most common methods of doing so is through the use of the hedge clause. This is not a new issue. In 1951, the SEC addressed it in a release that simply states that "the anti-fraud provisions of the Securities and Exchange Commission statutes are violated by the employment of any legend, hedge clause, or other provision which is likely to lead an investor to believe that he has in any way waived any right of action he may have." This test is consistent with the Investment Advisers Act of 1940 which states that "any condition, stipulation, or provision binding any person to waive compliance with any provision of this Act or with any rule, regulation or order thereunder shall be void."

Several recent investment adviser applications filed with the states have contained advisory contracts with hedge clauses that the Administrator believed would be potentially misleading to clients.

As an example, one state took issue with a contract that stated: "It is understood that we will extend our best efforts in the supervision of the portfolio, but we assume no responsibility for action taken or omitted in good faith if negligence, willful or reckless misconduct, or violation of applicable law is not involved."

So, here's the bottom line for the exam. You will be presented with a question or two containing a statement to the effect of, "the client agrees to waive rule violations by the IA (or other securities professional)." The answer to choose is the one that states that "waivers are never permitted."

This is not to say that the acts prohibit the use of all hedge clauses. For example, the SEC has not objected to clauses that limit the investment adviser's liability for losses caused by conditions and events beyond its control, such as war, strikes, natural disasters, new government restrictions, market fluctuations, communications disruptions, and so forth. Such provisions are acceptable since they do not attempt to limit or misstate the adviser's fiduciary obligations to its clients; but, it is highly unlikely that one of these choices will be on your test.

1. An investment adviser runs an advertisement in the business section of the local newspaper. The ad describes the nature of the firm's model portfolio and indicates that it has outperformed the overall market by 800% over the past 10 years, and, therefore, they guarantee that their clients will more than keep pace with inflation. At the bottom of the ad, in smaller print is the following statement: Results are not guaranteed. Past performance is not indicative of future results. These results are not normal and cannot be expected to be repeated. This is an example of a(n)

   A. properly worded disclaimer
   B. improper hedge clause
   C. violation of an investment adviser's fiduciary responsibility
   D. wrap fee account

2. Which of the following statements regarding the use of a hedge clause by an investment adviser is CORRECT?

   A. The adviser's brochure must always contain at least one hedge clause.
   B. A properly worded hedge clause may be used to minimize the investment adviser's fiduciary responsibility.
   C. A hedge clause that limits the investment adviser's liability for losses caused by conditions and events beyond its control, such as war, strikes, and natural disasters, would generally be acceptable to the Administrator.
   D. A hedge clause that limits liability to acts done in bad faith or pursuant to willful misconduct but also explicitly provides that rights under state or federal law cannot be relinquished would generally be acceptable to the Administrator.

3.12.3 PRINCIPAL OR AGENCY TRANSACTIONS

Under both state and federal law, it is unlawful for any investment adviser, directly or indirectly "acting as principal for his own account, knowingly to sell any security to or purchase any security from a client, or acting as broker for a person other than such client, knowingly to effect any sale or purchase of any security for the account of such client, without disclosing to such client in writing before the completion of such transaction the capacity in which he is acting and obtaining the consent of the client to such transaction." The key point here is that the laws impose a prior consent requirement on any adviser that acts as principal in a transaction with a client, or that acts as broker (that is, an agent) in connection with a transaction for, or on behalf of, an advisory client.

In a principal transaction, an adviser, acting for its own account, buys a security from, or sells a security to, the account of a client. In an agency transaction, an adviser arranges a transaction between different advisory clients or between a brokerage customer and an advisory client. Advisory clients can benefit from both types of transactions, depending on the circumstances, by obtaining a more favorable transaction price for the securities being purchased or sold than otherwise available. Principal and agency transactions, however, also may pose the potential for conflicts between the interests of the adviser and those of the client.

The regulators have recognized that both principal and agency transactions create the potential for advisers to engage in self-dealing. Principal transactions, in particular, may lead to abuses such as price manipulation or the placing of unwanted securities into client accounts. When an adviser engages in an agency transaction on behalf of a client, it is primarily the incentive to earn additional compensation that creates the adviser's conflict of interest. Although recognizing the potential for these abuses, the regulators did not prohibit advisers entirely from engaging in all principal and agency transactions with clients. Rather, they chose to address these particular conflicts of interest by imposing a disclosure and client consent requirement.

It is important to remember that:

■ an adviser may obtain client consent to a principal or agency transaction after execution, but prior to settlement, of the transaction; and

■ an adviser is not "acting as broker" within the meaning of the acts if the adviser receives no compensation (other than its advisory fee) for effecting a particular agency transaction between advisory clients. It is primarily the incentive to earn additional compensation that creates the adviser's conflict of interest when effecting an agency transaction between advisory clients.

TEST TOPIC ALERT   What happens if the investment adviser is also registered as a broker-dealer? The requirements just described do not apply to any transaction with a customer of a broker-dealer if such broker-dealer is not acting as an investment adviser in relation to such transaction. In other words, the transaction is not as a result of a recommendation from the adviser.

3. 12. 3. 1 Time of Consent

As stated, both acts prohibit any adviser from engaging in or effecting a principal or agency transaction with a client without disclosing in writing to the client, "before the completion of such transaction," the capacity in which the adviser is acting and obtaining the client's consent to the transaction. It has been determined that a securities transaction is completed upon settlement, not upon execution. Implicit in the phrase "before the completion of such transaction" is the recognition that a securities transaction involves various stages before it is "complete." The phrase "completion of such transaction" on its face would appear to be the point at which all aspects of a securities transaction have come to an end. That ending point of a transaction is when the actual exchange of securities and payment occurs, which is known as "settlement." The date of execution (i.e., the trade date) marks an earlier point of a securities transaction at which the parties have agreed to its terms and are contractually obligated to settle the transaction. Thus, an adviser may comply with the rules either by obtaining client consent prior to execution of a principal or agency transaction, or after execution but prior to settlement of the transaction.

When soliciting a client's post-execution, pre-settlement consent to a principal or agency transaction, an adviser should be able to provide the client with sufficient information regarding the transaction, including information regarding pricing, best price, and final commission charges, to enable the client to make an informed decision to consent to the transaction. The regulators agree that, if after execution but before settlement of the transaction, an adviser also provides a client with information that is sufficient to inform the client of the conflicts of interest faced by the adviser in engaging in the transaction, then the adviser will have provided the information necessary for the client to make an informed decision for purposes of the rule.

This consent is required for each transaction of this type. In a 1945 decision, federal law determined that "blanket" approval is not permitted.

TAKE NOTE

What is really going on here? As stated previously, the function of an investment adviser is to be compensated for giving investment advice, not trading securities. Buying and selling securities is the job of a broker-dealer. This discussion deals with the odd case where an investment adviser wears "two hats" as it were and, in addition to giving advice, also trades the security.

3. 13   ADVERTISING

Under both laws, it is unlawful for an adviser to engage in any act, practice, or course of business that is fraudulent, deceptive, or manipulative. These prohibitions apply to advertising. The USA's rule on investment adviser advertising merely states that it is unlawful for any investment adviser to publish, circulate or distribute any advertisement that does not comply with the rules under the Investment Advisers Act of 1940.

The SEC has defined the term *advertisement* to include any notice, circular, website, letter, or other written communication addressed to more than *one* person, or any notice or other announcement in any publication or by radio or television, that offers:

■ any analysis, report, or publication concerning securities;

■ any graph, chart, formula, or other device to be used in making any determination concerning securities; or

■ any other investment advisory service with regard to securities.

The term *advertisement* has generally been broadly construed. For example, an investment adviser's proposed publication of lists of past securities recommendations for a specific period constitutes an advertisement. Similarly, investment advisory material that promotes advisory services for the purpose of inducing potential clients to subscribe to those services is advertising material. In keeping with the changing times, an investment adviser's website is considered advertising.

The act provides that it is unlawful for an investment adviser to publish, circulate, or distribute any advertisement that:

■ makes use of testimonials, including any statement of a client's experience with the adviser or a client's endorsement of the adviser (testimonials are prohibited under the Advisers Act);

■ represents or implies that the adviser has been sponsored, recommended, or approved, or that its abilities or qualifications have in any respect been passed upon by the SEC or the Administrator (the SEC has taken the position that the use of the initials *R.I.A.* following a name on printed materials would be misleading because, among other things, it suggests that the person to whom it refers has a level of professional competence, education, or other special training, when in fact there are no specific qualifications for becoming a registered investment adviser; the term *registered investment adviser* may be used, but not the initials);

TEST TOPIC ALERT   In the same manner that the use of the designation, RIA is prohibited, investment adviser representatives may not use the initials IAR on business cards or any other literature. Yes, the exam will frequently use IAR, but you can't. What you can use on your business card are certain recognized professional or academic designations (assuming you've earned them). Examples would include CPA, CLU®, CFA®, CFP®, MBA, JD, or PhD.

- makes reference to past, specific, profitable recommendations made by the adviser, without the advertisement setting out a list of all recommendations made by the adviser, both profitable and unprofitable, within the preceding period of not less than one year, and cautions the reader that it should not be assumed that recommendations made in the future will be profitable or will equal the performance of previous recommendations;

- represents that any graph, chart, formula or other device can, in and of itself, be used to determine which securities to buy or sell, or when to buy or sell such securities, or can assist persons in making those decisions, without the advertisement prominently disclosing the limitations and the difficulties regarding its use;

- represents that a report, analysis, or other service, such as tax preparation, was provided without charge, when the report, analysis, or other service was provided with some obligation; or

- fails to disclose any ownership position in securities being recommended by the investment adviser.

TEST TOPIC ALERT   Although use of the initials *RIA* or *IAR* is unethical, the exam may refer to investment advisers as *IAs* and adviser representatives as *IARs*.

QUICK QUIZ 3.N

1. Which of the following statements is(are) TRUE regarding advertising by an investment adviser?

    I.   Free offers must be free of cost or any other obligation.
    II. All advertisements where the copy will be seen by 10 or more people must be filed with the SEC.
    III. Past specific recommendations may be shown, but only if they include all recommendations for at least the previous 12 months and make very clear that past performance is not any assurance of the future.

    A. I only
    B. I and II
    C. I and III
    D. II and III

2. Ponzi Planning Associates (PPA), is an investment adviser registered in the tri-state area of New York, New Jersey, and Connecticut. PPA's principal office is located in Jersey City, NJ. Which of the following statements is CORRECT?

   A. PPA must meet the bonding requirements of the SEC.
   B. PPA must meet the bonding requirements of whichever of the three states is the most stringent.
   C. The Connecticut Administrator can require PPA to submit advertisements placed in his state.
   D. If the New York Administrator wishes to examine the records of PPA, advance written notice must be given.

3. Which of the following are unlawful or prohibited practices for an investment adviser under the Investment Advisers Act of 1940?

   I. Making an untrue statement of a material fact in a registration application with the SEC
   II. Stating that the firm's ability and qualifications have been approved by the U.S. government
   III. Stating that the firm is registered under the Investment Advisers Act of 1940
   IV. Representing that the firm is an investment counselor when it does not normally render investment advice
   A. I, II, and IV
   B. I and III
   C. II and IV
   D. I, II, III, and IV

4. Under the Investment Advisers Act of 1940, an investment adviser would be prohibited from engaging in which of the following practices, even if disclosed in writing to the customer?

   A. Putting the adviser's own interests before those of the customer
   B. Providing advice to the customer and receiving compensation for the resulting sale of products
   C. Employment with a broker-dealer and also serving as an investment adviser
   D. Using advice she provides to customers regarding securities transactions as a basis for her own investment account trades

5. An investment adviser has engaged a website designer. What may the designer include on the website?

   A. Client testimonials
   B. A general description of the types of investment advisory programs offered by the firm
   C. Recommendations on specific stocks
   D. Recommendations on specific managed investments such as mutual funds

3. 14   INVESTMENT ADVISORY CONTRACTS

The primary relationship between a client and an investment adviser is evidenced by an investment advisory contract. There are three major differences between federal and state law. The USA prohibits entering into, extending, or renewing any advisory services, unless the contract is in writing, while federal law permits the contract to be written or oral. Another difference concerns the amount of the fees. The USA requires that fees be competitive while federal law only requires that they be reasonable in view of the services rendered. Finally, the NASAA Model Rule on performance-based compensation is a bit more stringent than that of the SEC as we will cover in this section.

Under both acts, the contract must disclose:

- the services to be provided, including custody if appropriate;
- the term of the contract (contracts can be of any length, not necessarily annual, but all renewals under **state law**, just as with initial contracts, must be in **writing**);
- the amount of the advisory fee or the formula for computing the fee;
- the amount or manner of calculation of the amount of any prepaid fee to be returned in the event of contract termination;
- whether the contract grants discretionary power to the adviser or its representatives;
- that no assignment of the contract may be made by the adviser without the consent of the other party to the contract (the client); and
- that, if the adviser is organized as a partnership, any change to a minority interest in the firm will be communicated to advisory clients within a reasonable period of time. A change to a majority of the partnership interests would be considered an assignment.

The acts also prohibit certain performance fee arrangements contingent on capital gains or appreciation or waiving fees in the event of losses in the client's account. There is an exception, however, from the performance fee provisions for contracts with a qualified client defined as:

- a natural person or company that immediately after entering into the contract has at least $1 million under the management of the investment adviser;
- a natural person or company that the IA has reason to believe that immediately prior to entering into the contract has a net worth exclusive of the primary residence (in the case of individuals, assets held jointly with a spouse, but no one else, can be used) in excess of $2 million; or
- a natural person who is an officer or director of the investment adviser or one of their IARs who has been employed in the industry at least 12 months. (Did you notice that 12 months is the same as we showed you with the non-delivery requirement for the brochure supplement?)

TAKE NOTE

Please notice the inconsistency in the rule. It is *at least* $1 million in AUM with the adviser or, net worth *in excess* of $2 million. Why couldn't they both be *at least*, or *in excess* of? Makes the test tougher, doesn't it?

A fee based on the average amount of money under management over a particular period is not considered to be a performance fee.

There is one significant difference between the rules for state registered IAs and federal covered IAs. In order for a state registered IA to enter into, extend, or renew an investment advisory contract that provides for compensation to the investment adviser on the basis of a share of capital gains upon or capital appreciation of the funds, or any portion of the funds, of the client, to the extent not otherwise disclosed on Form ADV Part 2, the investment adviser must disclose in writing to the client, all material information concerning the proposed advisory arrangement, including the following:

■ That the fee arrangement may create an incentive for the investment adviser to make investments that are riskier or more speculative than would be the case in the absence of a performance fee

■ Where relevant, that the investment adviser may receive increased compensation with regard to unrealized appreciation as well as realized gains in the client's account

■ The periods that will be used to measure investment performance throughout the contract and their significance in the computation of the fee

■ The nature of any index that will be used as a comparative measure of investment; and performance, the significance of the index, and the reason the investment adviser believes that the index is appropriate

None of these disclosures apply to federal covered advisers; although, from a practical standpoint (not on the exam), most of these are made to clients.

The most common type of performance fee is known as a fulcrum fee. In this case, the fee is averaged over a specified period (at least 12 months) with an increase or decrease in proportion to the investment performance in relation to the performance of a specified securities index (usually the S&P 500). For example, for each 5% that the client's account outperforms the specified index, the adviser would receive an increase to the fee of 10 basis points. Of course, negative performance would have the same results.

TEST TOPIC ALERT   There are two additional points related to performance-based compensation that you must know. Firstly, the adviser must use net performance, that is, consider both gains and losses. Secondly, as with so many other rules, the Administrator has the power to authorize this type of fee even when the stated conditions are not met.

TAKE NOTE   It is necessary for you to understand the technical definition of *assignment* as used in the acts. When an advisory firm is sold, what do you think its major asset is? Furniture? Computers? No. It is the advisory contracts with clients and, legally, that sale means the contracts have been assigned to the new buyer. This does not mean that the clients have to approve of the sale; they only have to approve of letting the new owner(s) manage their money. They can decide to take their money elsewhere. Assignment also includes any direct or indirect transfer or pledge of an investment advisory contract by the adviser or of a controlling block of the adviser's outstanding voting securities by a stockholder of the adviser. If the investment adviser is a partnership, no assignment of an investment advisory contract is considered to result from the death or withdrawal of a minority of the partners or from the admission to the adviser of one or more partners who, after admission, will be only a minority interest in the business while a change to a majority would be considered an assignment. However, a reorganization or similar activity that does not result in a change of actual control or management of an investment adviser is not an assignment.

QUICK QUIZ 3.0

1. The Investment Advisers Act of 1940 would permit investment advisory contracts to provide for

   I. assignment without the client's consent
   II. changes to be made in a partnership with notification to clients within a reasonable period of time
   III. compensation based on average assets of the management over a particular time period

   A. I and II
   B. I and III
   C. II and III
   D. I, II and III

2. Which two of the following statements regarding investment advisory contracts demonstrate compliance with the Uniform Securities Act?

   I. ABC Investment Advisers, organized as a partnership with 5 equal partners, admits 2 additional partners on a proportionate basis, but fails to obtain consent of its clients.
   II. DEF Investment Advisers, organized as a partnership with 7 equal partners, has 4 of those partners simultaneously leave, but the firm continues to operate as before while failing to obtain consent of its clients.
   III. GHI Investment Advisers, organized as a corporation with 5 equal shareholders, has 3 of them pledge their GHI stock as collateral for a bank loan, but the firm fails to obtain consent of its clients.
   IV. JKL Investment Advisers, organized as a corporation with 5 equal shareholders, has 3 of them sell their shares to the remaining 2 owners, but the firm fails to obtain consent of its clients.

   A. I and III
   B. I and IV
   C. II and III
   D. II and IV

3. Which of the following fee arrangements is legal under the Investment Advisers Act of 1940?

   A. Adviser A charges an annual fee of 0.05% of the value of the client's account, due on the first day of the client's fiscal year.
   B. Adviser B charges an annual fee of 0.075%, guaranteed to be waived if the value of the account does not increase during the year.
   C. Adviser C charges an annual fee of 0.05% to be waived if the account does not grow by at least 5% during the year.
   D. Adviser D guarantees the annual fee will be waived if the account decreases in value while under his management.

4. Foster Advisers operates as an investment adviser that is registered in a state where the Administrator, by rule, prohibits investment advisers from holding custody of client funds and securities. This means that Foster Advisers may NOT

A. refer clients to an affiliated broker-dealer
B. manage client accounts on a discretionary basis
C. examine customers' stock certificates
D. have physical custody over its clients' monies and certificates

---

CASE STUDY   **Assignment and Notification of Change in Membership**

Situation: Mr. Bixby withdrew $10 million from his account at the end of the year, leaving less than $250,000 under management with Market Tech Advisers, Inc., an advisory company incorporated in Illinois. During the course of the year, three officers left the firm. As a matter of corporate policy, Market Tech did not advise Mr. Bixby of these changes.

The following year, Market Tech (without notifying Mr. Bixby) assigned his account to Associated Investment Partners, a small partnership located in California, and Mr. Bixby was happy with the new partnership. Shortly after the assignment, Mr. Bixby learned of the death of one of the major partners through an article in the newspaper. He retained his account at Associated even though he had not been informed by them of the partner's death.

Analysis: Market Tech Advisers, Inc., was under no obligation to inform Mr. Bixby of the change in officers because it is a corporation and not a partnership. However, they did violate the USA by assigning Mr. Bixby's account to Associated Partners without his consent. Additionally, the USA requires partnerships to inform clients of any change in partner membership within a reasonable amount of time after the change, which means that Associated Partners violated the USA by not informing Mr. Bixby of the partner's death.

CASE STUDY   **Investment Advisory Fees**

Situation: Using the same client information as above, Market Tech Advisers, a registered investment advisory company, charges clients a fee of 1% of their assets managed by the firm, on the basis of the average amount of funds in the account each quarter. In addition, for some of their high net worth clients, Market Tech charges a fee based on the degree to which their performance exceeds that of the S&P 500. Last quarter, Market Tech's performance was extremely good, and, as a result, the fees of one of its largest clients, Mr. Bixby, more than doubled. Next quarter, the value of the account dropped by 25%, and so did the fee. Mr. Bixby complained that Market Tech was sharing in his capital appreciation in violation of the USA, because he no longer had the required funds on deposit in the account.

Analysis: Market Tech is in compliance with the USA. Market Tech charged Mr. Bixby a 1% fee based on the total assets in the account over a designated period as well as the stated performance fee. Because the assets increased and the performance beat the benchmark, so did the fee. Market Tech based its fees on the average value of funds under management and on a percentage of Mr. Bixby's capital gains—a practice in compliance with the USA for investors with a net worth at his level. Even though he no longer had the required minimum assets managed by the firm, his net worth was still in excess of the statutory minimum. In the subsequent quarter, Market Tech's fee declined by 25% as a result of market deterioration. More than likely, there was no incentive fee earned in this quarter.

3. 15   AGENCY CROSS TRANSACTIONS

In an **agency cross transaction**, the adviser (or IAR acting on behalf of the firm) acts as agent for both its advisory client and the party on the other side of the trade. Both state and federal law will permit an adviser to engage in these transactions provided the advisory client executes a written consent prospectively (in advance) authorizing the investment adviser to effect agency cross transactions for such client and the adviser discloses the following:

- The adviser will be receiving commissions from both sides of the trade.
- There is a potential conflict of interest because of the division of loyalties to both sides.
- On at least an annual basis, the adviser will furnish a statement or summary of the account identifying the total number of such transactions and the total amount of all remuneration from these transactions.
- In a conspicuous manner, indicates that this arrangement may be terminated at any time.
- No transaction is effected in which the same investment adviser or an investment adviser and any person controlling, controlled by, or under common control with that investment adviser recommended the transaction to both any seller and any purchaser.

These requirements do not relieve advisers of their duties to obtain best execution and best price for any transaction.

In addition to the prior written consent, at or before the completion of each agency cross transaction, the client must be sent a written trade confirmation which includes:

- a statement of the nature of the transaction;
- the date, and if requested, the time of the transaction; and
- the source and amount of any remuneration to be received by the IA (or IAR) in connection with the transaction.

EXAMPLE   An adviser has a client who is conservative and another who generally looks for more aggressive positions. The conservative client calls and expresses concerns about the volatility of First Tech Internet Services, Inc., stating that he thinks this may be the best time to exit his position. The adviser agrees and mentions that he has a risk-taking client for whom First Tech is suitable and he'd like to "cross" the security between the two clients, charging a small commission to each of them. He then contacts the other client and recommends the purchase of First Tech. With the prior written consent of both parties, this is not a violation because the recommendation was only made to one side (the buyer).

TEST TOPIC ALERT   In an agency cross transaction, the adviser may not recommend the transaction to both parties of the trade.

TAKE NOTE   In the case of agency cross transactions, permission to engage in them must be obtained in writing prior to the first transaction. In essence, the client is giving blanket authority to engage in this activity. In the case of acting as a principal or agent, as described several pages ago, no blanket authorization is permitted and oral, rather than written consent must be obtained prior to the completion of the transaction.

3. 16   CASH REFERRAL FEES

The SEC has not prohibited payment of cash referral fees by investment advisers to persons who solicit business for them. The Investment Advisers Act of 1940 permits payment of cash referral fees to solicitors providing four conditions are met. The first three conditions apply to all cash referral fee payments.

The first condition requires that the investment adviser be registered under the Advisers Act. Thus, the rule prohibits cash referral fee payments to a solicitor by an investment adviser required to be registered but who is not registered. The second condition prohibits payment of cash referral fees to a solicitor who is subject to a statutory disqualification (e.g., a solicitor who is subject to an SEC order or convicted of certain crimes within a 10-year period). The third condition requires cash referral fees to be paid pursuant to a written agreement to which the investment adviser is a party.

Even if the first three conditions are satisfied, cash referral fee payments are prohibited unless they are made in one of three circumstances. In the first circumstance, payments are for the provision of impersonal advisory services. The second circumstance is where the adviser pays a referral fee to a person affiliated with the adviser (e.g., a partner, officer, director, or employee of the adviser and this is likely the only case where the individual will be registered as an investment adviser representative of the IA). The third circumstance in which cash referral fees may be paid involves third-party solicitors who are not persons affiliated with the adviser.

When the cash referral fees are paid to third-party solicitors who are not affiliated with the adviser, the following disclosures must be made:

■ Unless for impersonal advisory services, the fact that it is a third party must be disclosed (this is usually accomplished by requiring that a separate solicitor brochure be delivered along with the adviser's brochure).

■ Any script or sales approach used by the third party is the responsibility of the adviser.

According to the SEC staff, failure to adequately inform clients of a referral fee arrangement may violate the act. The amount of the remuneration and the basis on which it is paid must be disclosed, together with the fact that the finder is being compensated specifically for referring clients to the adviser.

Finally, the SEC requires investment advisers to keep copies of the following material pertaining to solicitors and referrals:

- The separate written disclosure document required to be furnished by the solicitor to the client (e.g., the Solicitor's Written Disclosure Document).

- Copies of the investment adviser's disclosure documents (e.g., Form ADV Part 2A) delivered to the solicited client by the solicitor.

The rules are much simpler for state registered advisers. Under the Uniform Securities Act, in almost every case, anyone who solicits on behalf of an investment adviser must be registered as an IAR. One point made by most of the states is that the solicitor does not have to be registered as an IAR of the IA for whom the solicitations are being made. It sounds kind of strange that you would solicit business for another investment adviser, but that is the way they rule.

TEST TOPIC ALERT

Many good investment advisers are successful at networking. As a result, they may refer to, and/or receive referrals from, other professionals, such as attorneys, accountants, and insurance agents. Depending on the nature of the relationship, there may even be a fee paid by the investment adviser for the referral. The rules we've previously discussed regarding cash referral fees deal with those who are focused on soliciting clients for an investment adviser. However, when a lawyer, accountant, or insurance agent refers a client to an IA, it would be permitted for the IA to offer a nominal fee (something in the range of several hundred dollars) as a thank you. What would be prohibited would be to have the size of the fee based on the size of the client account or the fees generated by managing that account.

QUICK QUIZ 3.P

1. Which of the following statements regarding cash referral fees to solicitors are CORRECT under the Investment Advisers Act of 1940?

    I. If the solicitation involves anything other than impersonal advisory services, disclosure must be made to the client regarding any affiliation between the adviser and the solicitor.
    II. The agreement must be in writing.
    III. The solicitor must not be subject to a statutory disqualification.
    IV. The adviser's principal business activity must be the rendering of investment advice.

    A. I and II
    B. I, II and III
    C. III and IV
    D. I, II, III and IV

2. Omerta Transparent Advisers, Inc., (OTA), registered with the SEC as an investment adviser, wishes to pay an individual to act as a third party solicitor to solicit or refer new advisory clients. Under the provisions of the Investment Advisers Act of 1940, which of the following statements is TRUE regarding this relationship?

    A. The individual would be required to register as an IAR of OTA, Inc.
    B. The individual would not be required to register as an IAR of OTA, Inc.
    C. The individual would be prohibited from registering as an IAR of OTA, Inc.
    D. The individual would only be required to register as an IAR of OTA, Inc. if compensated for the solicitation activities.

3. 17   FRAUDULENT AND PROHIBITED PRACTICES WHEN PROVIDING INVESTMENT ADVICE

Both acts make it unlawful for any person who receives compensation (directly or indirectly) for advising another person (whether through analyses or reports) as to the value of securities to use any device, scheme, or artifice to defraud the other person. Additionally, they may not engage in any act, practice, or course of business that operates or would operate as a fraud or deceit upon the other person or engage in dishonest or unethical practices.

The following are examples of prohibited practices when providing investment advice:

■   Making a recommendation to an advisory client that is not suitable for that client based on the financial objectives and goals, financial situation, non-financial considerations, and specific needs. Much of the rest of this course will be devoted to ways to determine suitability.

■   Disclosing the identity or investments of a client without consent of the client, unless required by law (an example of forced disclosure would be a subpoena to testify in a divorce case or a demand by the IRS to provide information about a client who is the subject of an audit). Please note that if it is a joint account, permission from one owner, such as a spouse, suffices for both.

■   Using third-party prepared materials without proper attribution. Reports that are purely statistical in nature are excluded from this requirement, but a research report or market letter prepared by another entity could only be used if its authorship were disclosed. However, use of someone else's research report when formulating your own report does not require disclosure of the source. It is sort of like when you wrote a term paper in school. If you "lifted" something directly from someone else, you'd better have disclosed it, because if the teacher found out, you just flunked that paper. But, if you went to the library and did some research on your own, viewed many different sources, and then put together a report using your own words, that was yours and was OK.

■   Use of any advertisement (defined as a communication to more than one person) that uses any testimonial (an advertisement may make reference to specific past performance of the adviser's recommendations as long as all recommendations of the same type of security for at least the past 12 months are included—not only the winners, but the losers as well). One of the more common testable points is that any advertisement that promotes the use of a charting system or formula must disclose the *limitations* and *difficulties* of using the system.

- Calculating advisory fees using a methodology different than that agreed to in the contracts

- Failing to comply with clients' wishes concerning directed brokerage arrangements

- Causing clients to invest in securities that are inconsistent with the level of risk that clients have agreed to assume

- Allocating client brokerage to a broker in exchange for client referrals without full disclosure of either the practice or the fact that clients pay higher brokerage commissions and do not obtain the best price and execution

- Allocating client brokerage to a broker in exchange for research or other products without disclosure

- Trading in securities for personal accounts, or for accounts of family members or affiliates, shortly before trading the same securities for clients (i.e., front-running), and thereby receiving better prices

- Directing clients to trade in securities in which the adviser has an undisclosed interest, causing the value of those securities to increase to the adviser's benefit

- Guaranteeing that a specific recommendation will result in a profit (this would include a promise to reimburse a client for any losses)

- Engaging in the practice of lending to or borrowing money or securities from a customer (Investment advisers [or their IARs] may not borrow money or securities from a client unless the client is a broker-dealer, an affiliate of the adviser, or a financial institution engaged in the business of loaning money. Likewise, they may not loan money to clients unless the firm is a financial institution engaged in the business of loaning funds or the client is an affiliate. [It is the same as covered in the previous session with agents. Remember, you can't even lend money to your mother if she is your client.])

- Indicating in an advisory contract, any condition, stipulation, or provisions binding any person to waive compliance with any provision of the Uniform Securities Act or the Investment Advisers Act of 1940 (e.g., the use of certain hedge clauses or the client and IA agreeing to engage in performance-based compensation even though the client's assets are below the mandated minimum)

- Unfairly criticizing work done by a client's professional advisers, such as accountants and lawyers (e.g., "Your attorney drew up a very poor estate plan", or "Your CPA missed many tax saving opportunities on your income tax return" are statements that may be considered unethical)

- Recommending the same security to clients without regard to individual suitability. This is sometimes referred to as blanket recommendations

- For state registered advisers, relying on oral discretionary authority for transactions in a customer's account beyond the first 10 business days after the date of the initial transaction

If you are an investment adviser registered or required to be registered under the Investment Advisers Act of 1940, it is unlawful for you to provide investment advice to clients unless you:

- adopt and implement written policies and procedures reasonably designed to prevent violation, by you and your supervised persons, of the act and the rules that the SEC has adopted under the act;

- review, no less frequently than annually, the adequacy of the policies and procedures established pursuant to this act and the effectiveness of their implementation; and

- designate an individual (who is a supervised person) responsible for administering the policies and procedures that you adopt, as noted above.

For a complete listing of those practices considered unethical, please review Appendix B, which contains NASAA's Model Rule on Unethical Business Practices of Investment Advisers and Investment Adviser Representatives. Pay particular attention to NASAA's comments since they use those to derive actual test questions.

3. 18   SECTION 28(E) SAFE HARBOR

Research is the foundation of the money management industry. Providing research is one important, long-standing service of the brokerage business. Soft-dollar arrangements have developed as a link between the brokerage industry's supply of research and the money management industry's demand for research. What does that mean and how does it work? To find the answers, we must review the provisions of Section 28(e) of the Securities Exchange Act of 1934.

Broker-dealers typically provide a bundle of services, including research and execution of transactions. The research provided can be either proprietary (created and provided by the broker-dealer, including tangible research products as well as access to analysts and traders) or third party (created by a third party but provided by the broker-dealer). Because commission dollars pay for the entire bundle of services, the practice of allocating certain of these dollars to pay for the research component has come to be called *soft dollars*. The SEC has defined soft-dollar practices as arrangements under which products or services other than execution of securities transactions are obtained by an adviser from or through a broker-dealer in exchange for the direction by the adviser of client brokerage transactions to the broker-dealer, frequently referred to as *directed transactions* on the exam. Under traditional fiduciary principles, a fiduciary cannot use assets entrusted by clients to benefit itself. As the SEC has recognized, when an adviser uses client commissions to buy research from a broker-dealer, it receives a benefit because it is relieved from the need to produce or pay for the research itself.

Because of the conflict of interest that exists when an investment adviser receives research, products, or other services as a result of allocating brokerage on behalf of clients, the SEC requires advisers to disclose soft-dollar arrangements to their clients. Section 28(e) provides that a person who exercises investment discretion with respect to an account will not be deemed to have acted unlawfully or to have breached a fiduciary duty solely by reason of his having caused the account to pay more than the lowest available commission if such person determines in good faith that the amount of the commission is reasonable in relation to the value of the brokerage and research services provided.

In adopting Section 28(e), Congress acknowledged the important service broker-dealers provide by producing and distributing investment research to money managers. Section 28(e) defines when a person is deemed to be providing brokerage and research services, and states that a person provides brokerage and research services insofar as he:

- furnishes advice directly or through publications or writing about the value of securities, the advisability of investing in, purchasing, or selling securities, or the availability of purchasers or sellers of securities;

■ furnishes analyses and reports concerning issuers, industries, securities, economic factors and trends, portfolio strategy, and performance of accounts; or

■ effects securities transactions and performs functions incidental thereto (such as clearance, settlement, and custody).

An adviser is obligated under both the Investment Advisers Act of 1940 and state law to act in the best interests of its client. This duty generally precludes the adviser from using client assets for its own benefit or the benefit of other clients, without obtaining the client's consent based on full and fair disclosure. In such a situation, the antifraud provisions of the federal securities laws also would require full and fair disclosure to the client of all material facts concerning the arrangement. As the SEC has stated, "the adviser may not use its client's assets for its own benefit without prior consent, even if it costs the client nothing extra." Consent may be expressly provided by the client; consent also may be inferred from all of the facts and circumstances, including the adviser's disclosure in its Form ADV.

Section 28(e) does not relieve investment advisers of their disclosure obligations under the federal securities laws. Disclosure is required whether the product or service acquired by the adviser using soft dollars is inside or outside of the safe harbor. Advisers are required to disclose, among other things, the products and services received through soft-dollar arrangements, regardless of whether the safe harbor applies.

Registered investment advisers must disclose certain information about their brokerage allocation policies to clients in Item 12 of Part 2A of Form ADV. Specifically, if the value of products, research, and services provided to an investment adviser is a factor in selecting brokers to execute client trades, the investment adviser must describe in its Form ADV:

■ the products, research, and services;

■ whether clients may pay commissions higher than those obtainable from other brokers in return for the research, products, and services;

■ whether research is used to service all accounts or just those accounts paying for it; and

■ any procedures that the adviser used during the last fiscal year to direct client transactions to a particular broker in return for products, research and services received.

The purpose of this disclosure is to provide clients with material information about the adviser's brokerage selection practices that may be important to clients in deciding to hire or continue a contract with an adviser and that will permit them to evaluate any conflicts of interest inherent in the adviser's policies and practices. In this respect, the SEC and courts have stated that disclosure is required, even when there is only a potential conflict of interest.

Here is an example of a statement found in one adviser's brochure:

> *"We may direct transactions for your account to registered broker-dealers in return for research products and services that assist us in making decisions about investments. The research products will be used to generally service all of our clients, so the brokerage commissions you pay may be used to pay for research that is not used in managing your account."*

Finally, the SEC believes that an adviser accepting soft dollar benefits must explain that:

■ the adviser benefits because it does not have to produce or pay for the research or other products or services acquired with soft dollars; and

■ the adviser therefore has an incentive to select or recommend brokers based on the adviser's interest in receiving these benefits, rather than on the client's interest in getting the most favorable execution.

TEST TOPIC ALERT

What this all comes down to is knowing what is and what is not included in the safe harbor. Here are some of the items that, if received as soft-dollar compensation, would likely fall under 28(e)'s safe harbor:

■ research reports analyzing the performance of a particular company or stock;

■ financial newsletters and trade journals could be eligible research if they relate with appropriate specificity;

■ quantitative analytical software;

■ seminars or conferences with appropriate content; and

■ effecting and clearing securities trades.

Likely to fall out of the safe harbor would be:

■ telephone lines;

■ office furniture, including computer hardware;

■ travel expenses associated with attending seminars;

■ rent;

■ any software that does not relate directly to analysis of securities;

■ payment for training courses for this exam; and

■ internet service.

QUICK QUIZ 3.Q

1. Which of the following would NOT be included in the safe harbor provisions of Section 28(e) of the Securities Exchange Act of 1934?

    A. Proprietary research
    B. Third-party research
    C. Rent
    D. Seminar registration fees

2. When an investment adviser with discretion over a client's account directs trade executions to a specific broker-dealer and uses the commission dollars generated to acquire software that analyzes technical market trends, it is known as

   A. hard-dollar compensation
   B. indirect compensation
   C. investment discretion
   D. soft-dollar compensation

3. One respect in which NASAA treats the handling of discretionary authorization by an investment adviser differently from the SEC is that

   A. NASAA has a requirement that all discretionary orders be approved before entry
   B. NASAA allows use of oral discretion for the first 10 business days after the date of the first transaction
   C. an investment adviser is prohibited from opening discretionary accounts without prior notification to the Administrator
   D. a federal covered adviser may not be cited for churning a discretionary account by an Administrator

4. Which of the following would justify an investment adviser's use of a full-service broker?

   I. Obtaining special reports dealing with economic projections from the broker
   II. Expense-paid business trips paid for by the broker
   III. The use of the research analysis provided by the broker
   A. I and II
   B. I and III
   C. II and III
   D. I, II, and III

QUICK QUIZ 3.R

1. An investment advisory contract need NOT include

   A. the fees and their method of computation
   B. a statement prohibiting assignment of client accounts without client consent
   C. the states in which the adviser is licensed to conduct business
   D. notification requirement upon change in membership if an investment partnership

   True or False?

   _____ 2. An Administrator may not prevent custody of securities or funds if an adviser notifies the Administrator before taking custody.

   _____ 3. An adviser may not sell securities to its customers from its own proprietary account.

   _____ 4. Under USA antifraud provisions, an investment adviser is bound by the restrictions that apply to sales practices when engaged in sales activities.

3. 19   OTHER BROKERAGE PRACTICES

In addition to disclosing how soft dollars are handled, there are several other practices involving broker-dealers and investment advisers where disclosure is required. Investment advisers must describe the factors that they consider in selecting or recommending broker-dealers for client transactions and determining the reasonableness of the broker-dealer's compensation.

3. 19. 1   CLIENT REFERRALS

It is not an uncommon practice for broker-dealers to recommend their clients to investment advisers. Naturally, the investment adviser is happy to receive the referral, and the broker-dealer hopes to continue to execute the client's trades. This is considered as if the IA is compensating the broker-dealer for the referral. It is not illegal, but the IA must disclose the practice and, as a fiduciary, take steps to insure that the charges for the services being rendered by the broker-dealer are reasonable.

3. 19. 2   DIRECTED BROKERAGE

Directed brokerage is the practice of asking or permitting clients to send trades to a specific broker-dealer for execution When the IA suggests the client use a specific broker-dealer(s), disclosure of any possible conflicts of interest must be made. There is nothing wrong with urging clients to use specific firms because of the quality of service received, even if the IA is doing so in response to referrals or soft dollars. As long as it is disclosed and the services rendered bear a reasonable relationship to their cost, directed brokerage should be a good deal for both the client and the IA. On the other hand, if the adviser permits the client to direct the brokerage firm to use, certain other disclosures are required. For example, the IA must explain that it may be unable to achieve most favorable execution of client transactions or that directing brokerage may cost clients more money. For example, in a client-directed brokerage account, the client may pay higher brokerage commissions because the IA may not be able to aggregate orders to reduce transaction costs, or the client may receive less favorable prices because the IA has arranged a preferred commission rate with a preferred broker-dealer. Here is an example of how that might appear in the brochure:

> "It is important to note that if you do not give KAPCO Advisers discretion to direct trades, you may limit our ability to negotiate favorable commissions and seek best execution for trades in your account. You may also be excluded from block trades and average price transactions."

3. 19. 3   TRADE AGGREGATION AND ALLOCATION

This is the practice of bundling (sometimes called *bunching*) trades to obtain volume discounts on execution costs. It occurs most often when an IA with discretion over accounts has several of them for whom the same security is appropriate and, instead of entering separate orders, enters them as one larger order. This invariably saves on execution costs. Sometimes, the order cannot be filled in one transaction or at a single price. In that case, it is generally considered that the fairest method of allocating the security's cost is on an average basis.

3. 20   VOTING CLIENT SECURITIES

In many client accounts with investment advisers, voting proxies come to the investment adviser instead of to the clients themselves. Therefore, there may be questions regarding how those proxies are voted. Included in the adviser's brochure, Part 2A of the Form ADV, must be information about the adviser's policy on voting client securities. If the IA has, or will accept, authority to vote client securities, a brief description must be given to describe those voting policies and procedures. This summary must describe:

- whether (and, if so, how) clients can direct the IA's vote in a particular solicitation;
- how the IA addresses conflicts of interest between himself and his clients with respect to voting their securities;
- how clients may obtain information from the IA about how he voted their securities; and
- how clients may obtain a copy of the firm's proxy voting policies and procedures upon request.

If the adviser does not have authority to vote client securities, this fact must be disclosed. An explanation must be given as to whether clients will receive their proxies or other solicitations directly from their custodian or a transfer agent or from the adviser, and they must be informed whether (and, if so, how) clients can contact the adviser with questions about a particular solicitation.

3. 21   COMPLIANCE PROGRAMS

We have just completed a very comprehensive description of the many rules and regulations imposed upon investment advisers. How do the regulators ensure compliance with these rules? Effective October 2004, the Investment Advisers Act of 1940 was amended to require each investment adviser registered with the SEC to adopt and implement written policies and procedures designed to prevent violation of the federal securities laws, review those policies and procedures **annually** for their adequacy and the effectiveness of their implementation, and designate a **chief compliance officer** (CCO) to be responsible for administering the policies and procedures. An adviser's chief compliance officer should be competent and knowledgeable regarding the Advisers Act and should be empowered with full responsibility and authority to develop and enforce appropriate policies and procedures for the firm. Thus, the compliance officer should have a position of sufficient seniority and authority within the organization to compel others to adhere to the compliance policies and procedures. In fact, the CCO's identity must be disclosed on the Form ADV. However, the SEC does not set a standard of competency such as a specific qualification exam or number of years of experience.

Under rule 206(4)-7, it is unlawful for an investment adviser registered with the Commission to provide investment advice unless the adviser has adopted and implemented written policies and procedures reasonably designed to prevent violation of the Advisers Act by the adviser or any of its supervised persons. The rule requires advisers to consider their fiduciary and regulatory obligations under the Advisers Act and to formalize policies and procedures to address them.

Each adviser, in designing its policies and procedures, should first identify conflicts and other compliance factors creating risk exposure for the firm and its clients in light of the firm's particular operations, and then design policies and procedures that address those risks. The SEC expects that an adviser's policies and procedures, at a minimum, should address the following issues to the extent that they are relevant to that adviser:

■ Portfolio management processes, including allocation of investment opportunities among clients and consistency of portfolios with clients' investment objectives, disclosures by the adviser, and applicable regulatory restrictions

■ Trading practices, including procedures by which the adviser satisfies its best execution obligation, uses client brokerage to obtain research and other services ("soft-dollar arrangements"), and allocates aggregated trades among clients

■ Proprietary trading of the adviser and personal trading activities of supervised persons

■ The accuracy of disclosures made to investors, clients, and regulators, including account statements and advertisements

■ Safeguarding of client assets from conversion or inappropriate use by advisory personnel

■ The accurate creation of required records and their maintenance in a manner that secures them from unauthorized alteration or use and protects them from untimely destruction

■ Marketing advisory services, including the use of solicitors

■ Processes to value client holdings and assess fees based on those valuations

■ Safeguards for the privacy protection of client records and information

■ Business continuity plans

Although the rule requires only annual reviews, advisers should consider the need for interim reviews in response to significant compliance events, changes in business arrangements, and regulatory developments.

3. 22   ENFORCEMENT

Enforcement and administration of the Investment Advisers Act of 1940 is the responsibility of the SEC. As of the date of publication, there is no self-regulatory organization (SRO) for investment advisers. If that situation should change and become testable, it will be posted in both the Exam-tips Blog & Content Updates. In other words, FINRA, the NYSE, and the like have no jurisdiction over federal covered investment advisers; only the SEC does. If the SEC suspects a violation of the law or its rules, it may take the following actions:

■ Subpoena witnesses

■ Acquire evidence

■ Subpoena books and records

■ Administer oaths

■ Go to a competent court of jurisdiction to obtain an injunction enjoining a person from continued activity until the results of a hearing

■ Refer to the appropriate court for criminal prosecution

The SEC has the power to censure, place limitations on the activities, functions, or operations of, suspend for a period not exceeding 12 months, or revoke the registration of any investment adviser if it finds, after a hearing, that the penalty is appropriate. If it is necessary to go to court, all hearings are held in the federal court system. If a defendant is found guilty, he may appeal an SEC order against him by filing that appeal in the U.S. Court of Appeals with jurisdiction where the violation occurred.

If the violation is one in which the SEC seeks criminal penalties, the act provides for a fine of no more than $10,000, imprisonment for no more than five years, or both.

Enforcement and administration of the USA is the responsibility of each individual Administrator. If the Administrator suspects a violation of the law or its rules, he may take all of the actions listed above.

However, there is nothing in the USA that specifies a maximum suspension as there is in the federal law. Another difference is that, in the case of an appeal, it is made through the state court system, not the federal one. In both cases, the appeal must be filed within 60 days of the court's decision.

Another difference is in the level of penalties. Under the USA, the maximum penalties for a criminal infraction are a fine of up to $5,000, or a prison sentence not to exceed three years, or both. However, imprisonment is only an option when the violation is committed knowingly.

TEST TOPIC ALERT

You will be asked about either or both of these penalties on your exam and must be able to keep them straight. Federal law is $10,000 and five years. State law is $5,000 and three years.

UNIT TEST

1. The Securities Act of 1933 covers which of the following?

   I.   The sale of new issues to the public
   II. The use of deficiency letters
   III. Insider trading
   IV. Trading on national securities exchanges

   A. I and II
   B. I, III and IV
   C. III and IV
   D. I, II, III and IV

2. All of the following are exempt from registration under the Securities Act of 1933 EXCEPT

   A. an intrastate offering
   B. a Regulation D offering
   C. a U.S. government security
   D. an interstate offering of preferred stock

3. A broker-dealer effecting transactions in a discretionary account that are excessive in size or frequency in view of the financial resources and character of the account is considered to be

   A. churning
   B. matching orders
   C. pegging, fixing, and stabilizing
   D. successful

4. Under which of the following cases could an agent offer a security for sale?

   I.   A registration statement has been filed with the SEC but has not yet become effective.
   II. A registration statement has been filed with the SEC and has become effective.
   III. The agent is aware of negotiations going on between an issuer and the employing broker-dealer's investment banking department.

   A. I and II
   B. I and III
   C. II only
   D. II and III

5. Under the Securities Act of 1933, the SEC

   A. approves securities registered with it
   B. attempts to make certain that all pertinent information is fully disclosed
   C. passes on the investment merit of the security
   D. guarantees that the statements made in the prospectus and registration statement are accurate

6. An exemption from registration under the Securities Act of 1933 is available to securities that are

   A. offered to the public only when the total amount is more than $4 million
   B. sold in more than one state by persons resident in those states
   C. sold only to persons resident in one state when the issuer is a resident doing business within that state
   D. listed on national exchanges

7. Among the groups and organizations required to register with the SEC by the Securities Exchange Act of 1934 are

   A. corporations with listed securities
   B. securities exchanges and securities traded on exchanges
   C. brokers and dealers operating in interstate commerce and national securities associations
   D. all of the above

8. A principal purpose of the Securities Exchange Act of 1934 is generally considered to be to

   A. establish specific statutory standards for contractual agreements between corporations issuing bonds and the representatives of investors who own the bonds
   B. protect the public against unfair and inequitable practices in the over-the-counter market and on stock exchanges
   C. reimburse customers of failed broker-dealers
   D. establish standards to govern activities of organizations that engage in the business of providing securities investment advice

9. Under federal law, an application for becoming an associated person of a broker-dealer would be denied for an individual

 I. convicted of a felony 122 months ago
 II. pleading no contest to a misdemeanor involving a financial matter 65 months ago
 III. accused of a securities-related felony 110 months ago

 A. I and II
 B. I and III
 C. II only
 D. II and III

10. A manufacturing company whose debt securities are consistently rated AAA wishes to issue $20 million in 6-month commercial paper. The proceeds will be used to acquire the latest in computer-controlled lathes. Under the Securities Act of 1933, this issue

 A. is exempt from registration
 B. is not exempt from registration
 C. would only be exempt from registration if the denominations were a minimum of $50,000
 D. is straddling a commingled arbitrage

11. The Investment Company Act of 1940 permits a reduction in sales charge when reaching a breakpoint for

 A. a designated agent of an investment club
 B. purchasers meeting the definition of *any person*
 C. clients of fee-only investment advisers
 D. a mother and her 35-year-old son purchasing separate accounts

12. Among the provisions of the Investment Company Act of 1940 designed to protect the interests of investors is the provision that

 A. any change in fundamental investment policy must be approved by stockholders
 B. communications with the public must be approved by FINRA before its use
 C. selection of company investments must be approved by SEC
 D. for diversification purposes, an investment company may own up to 10% of the shares of another investment company

13. Which of the following statements under the Investment Company Act of 1940 are TRUE?

 I. Holding companies are not included in the definition of an investment company.
 II. Investment companies are prohibited from owning more than 3% of another investment company's shares.
 III. Mutual funds must file semiannual reports with their shareholders and the SEC.

 A. I and II
 B. I and III
 C. II and III
 D. I, II and III

14. A securities salesperson may indicate to a prospective customer that the SEC has approved a securities issue if

 A. the SEC has not initiated action against either the company or the underwriters of the issue
 B. the SEC has not opened an investigation of the company, the underwriter, or the market makers of the security
 C. a registration statement is in effect with the SEC
 D. none of the above

15. It would be most CORRECT to state that, as defined in the Securities Exchange Act of 1934, a securities information processor

 A. clears trades made on regulated stock exchanges
 B. distributes information on trades or quotations for nonexempt securities
 C. processes information provided by the SEC
 D. secures the information necessary to process a trade

16. Which of the following terms are defined in the Securities Exchange Act of 1934?

 I. Securities information processor
 II. Transfer agent
 III. Market maker
 IV. Prospectus

 A. I and II
 B. I and III
 C. I, II and III
 D. I, II, III and IV

17. Which of the following statements may NOT be made by an agent in regard to a security registered with the SEC under the Act of 1933?

A. "The SEC has approved of this issue and that's why I'm so glad to be able to offer it to you."
B. "This issue is lawful for sale."
C. "This issue is suitable for you on the basis of your objectives and the personal profile you have provided me."
D. None the above.

18. Under the Securities Exchange Act of 1934, the term *municipal security* would include a(n)

I. New Jersey Turnpike revenue bond
II. Illinois Tool Company debt issue backed by their full faith and credit
III. State of Texas general obligation bond

A. I and II
B. I and III
C. II and III
D. I, II and III

19. Under the Securities Exchange Act of 1934, the term *municipal security* would NOT include a(n)

I. City of Chicago school district bond
II. U.S. Treasury Bill
III. Province of Ontario library construction bond

A. I and II
B. I and III
C. II only
D. II and III

20. There are certain circumstances under which clients might wish to give their agents discretionary power over their account. An agent empowered to do which of the following would be considered using discretion?

A. Determining the specific price
B. Determining the specific time
C. Making the decisions in the account while awaiting delivery of the proper paperwork
D. Picking the specific security

21. Which of the following would be an agent as the term is defined in the Uniform Securities Act?

I. A representative of a licensed broker-dealer who sells securities to the general public
II. An assistant to the president of a broker-dealer who accepts orders on behalf of the senior partners
III. A subsidiary of a major commercial bank registered as a broker-dealer that sells securities to the public
IV. An issuer of nonexempt securities registered in the state and sold to the general public

A. I and II
B. I, II and III
C. III and IV
D. I, II, III and IV

22. A publicly traded corporation offers its employees an opportunity to purchase shares of the company's common stock directly from the issuer. A specific employee of the company is designated to process any orders for that stock. Under the USA, the employee

A. must register as an agent of the issuer
B. need not register as an agent of the issuer under any circumstances
C. may receive commissions without registration
D. must register as an agent if commissions or other remuneration will be received by the employee, either directly or indirectly

23. Which of the following persons is defined as an agent by the Uniform Securities Act?

A. Silent partner of a broker-dealer
B. Secretary of a branch office sales manager
C. Clerk at a broker-dealer who is authorized to take orders
D. President of the state university who sits on the broker-dealer's board of directors

24. Under the Uniform Securities Act, an agent is

A. a broker-dealer who sells registered securities to the general public
B. an individual who represents an issuer of a security issued by a Canadian province
C. an individual representing a broker-dealer who sells federal covered securities
D. an individual who represents an issuer in an exempt transaction

25. GEMCO Securities, a registered broker-dealer, has a policy of hiring unpaid interns from top business schools. GEMCO is currently the lead underwriter on a new issue and has assigned three of its interns to specific tasks. One is doing entering the data as indications of interest are received, the second is calling clients to offer to deliver their prospectus via email instead of mail, and the third is calling clients to offer the new issue and accept indications of interest. Which of the interns would need to register as agents?

   A. Because they are not being compensated, none of the interns need to register.
   B. The second and third interns would be required to register.
   C. Only the third intern would have to register.
   D. All of the interns would need to register.

26. Under the USA, which of the following is considered a broker-dealer in a state?

   A. First Federal Trust Company
   B. XYZ broker-dealer with an office in the state whose only clients are insurance companies
   C. An agent effecting transactions for a broker-dealer
   D. A broker-dealer with no place of business in the state who only does business with other broker-dealers in the state

27. Which of the following is defined as a security under the Uniform Securities Act?

   A. A guaranteed, lump-sum payment to a beneficiary under a modified endowment policy
   B. Fixed, guaranteed payments made for life or for a specified period under an annuity contract
   C. Commodity futures contracts
   D. An investment contract

28. Under the Uniform Securities Act, which of the following persons is responsible for proving that a securities issue is exempt from registration?

   A. Underwriter
   B. The person requesting the exemption
   C. State Administrator
   D. There is no need to prove eligibility for an exemption.

29. Registration is effective when ordered by the Administrator in the case of registration by

   A. coordination
   B. integration
   C. notice filing
   D. qualification

30. Under the Uniform Securities Act, which of the following would be considered an exempt transaction?

   I. An existing client calls you to purchase 1,000 shares of a common stock that is not registered in this state
   II. At the suggestion of the agent handling her account, a client purchases some U.S. Treasury bonds for inclusion in her IRA
   III. Shares of a bank's IPO are sold to an institutional client
   IV. Shares of an insurance company's IPO are sold to an individual client

   A. I and III
   B. I, III, and IV
   C. II and IV
   D. I, II, III, and IV

31. A transactional exemption would be available under the USA when an agent for a broker-dealer

   A. sells a large block of an unregistered nonexempt security to an individual who meets the definition of an accredited investor
   B. sells a large block of an unregistered nonexempt security to an insurance company that is not authorized to do business in this state
   C. sells a retail client $10,000 of U.S. Treasury bonds
   D. receives an unsolicited order from a client to purchase heating oil contracts

32. In general, registration statements for securities under the Uniform Securities Act are effective for

   A. a period determined by the Administrator for each issue
   B. 1 year from the effective date
   C. 1 year from the date of issue
   D. 1 year from the previous January 1

33. Under the Uniform Securities Act, an issuer is any person who issues, or proposes to issue, a security for sale to the public. According to the USA, which of the following is NOT an issuer?

    I. The City of Chicago, which is involved in a distribution of tax-exempt highway improvement bonds

    II. A partner in the AAA Oil and Gas Partnership sells his interest in the investment

    III. The AAA Manufacturing Company, which proposes to offer shares to the public but has not completed the offering

    IV. The U.S. government, which proposes to offer Treasury bonds

    A. I only
    B. II only
    C. I, II, and III
    D. I, II, and IV

34. Which of the following transactions are exempt from registration under the USA?

    I. A trustee of a corporation in bankruptcy liquidates securities to satisfy debt holders.

    II. An offer of a securities investment is directed to 10 individuals in the state during a 12-month consecutive period.

    III. A sale of securities by the trustee of the Lorgan Family Children's Trust.

    IV. Agents for an entrepreneur offer pre-organization certificates to fewer than 10 investors in the state for a modest commission.

    A. I and II
    B. I, III, and IV
    C. II and IV
    D. I and IV

35. Which of the following is(are) issuer transactions?

    I. John inherited securities of the XYZ Corporation from his father who, as a founder to the company, received the shares directly from the company as a result of stock options.

    II. John sold the securities he had inherited from his father to his neighbor, Peter, at the market price without charging a commission.

    III. John's father, a founder of XYZ corporation, purchased shares of XYZ directly from the corporation subsequent to its founding without paying a commission.

    IV. John purchased shares in XYZ Corporation in a transaction made in the over-the-counter market.

    A. I only
    B. I and II
    C. III only
    D. I, II, III, and IV

36. Section 402 of the USA contains a listing of those securities that are granted an exemption from the registration and advertising filing requirements of the Act. Included in that listing would be

    I. corporate debentures
    II. bonds issued by a Canadian province
    III. bonds issued by the District of Columbia
    IV. securities issued by a credit union authorized to do business in the state

    A. I, II, III, and IV
    B. I and IV
    C. II, III, and IV
    D. II and IV

37. Under the USA, the Administrator may bring an action against an agent's registration if the agent

    I. borrows money from his wealthy clients' accounts
    II. solicits orders for nonexempt unregistered securities
    III. buys and sells securities in accounts to generate a high level of commissions
    IV. alters market quotations to induce a client to invest in an attractive growth stock

    A. I, II, and III
    B. I and III
    C. I and IV
    D. I, II, III, and IV

38. According to the USA, which of the following is an example of market manipulation?

    A. Creating the illusion of active trading
    B. Omitting material facts in a presentation
    C. Guaranteeing performance of a security
    D. Transactions in excess of a customer's financial capability

39. Which of the following practices is prohibited under the Uniform Securities Act?

    A. Actively trading a security in which an unusually high trading volume has occurred
    B. Offering services that an agent cannot realistically perform because of his broker-dealer's limitations
    C. Altering the customer's order prior to execution at the request of a customer, which subsequently results in a substantial loss
    D. Failing to inform the firm's principal of frequent oral customer complaints

40. If an agent thought that a technology stock was undervalued and actively solicited all customers, the agent

    A. did not violate the USA if all material facts were disclosed
    B. committed an unethical sales practice because the firm has not recommended this technology stock
    C. committed an unethical business practice
    D. did not commit a violation if all clients were accurately informed of the price of the stock

41. Which of the following actions taken by an agent are prohibited?

    I. Borrowing money or securities from a high net-worth customer
    II. Selling speculative issues to a retired couple of modest means on a fixed income
    III. Failing to follow a customer's orders so as to prevent investment in a security not adequately covered by well-known securities analysts
    IV. Backdating confirmations for the benefit of the client's tax reporting

    A. I and II
    B. I, II, and III
    C. II and III
    D. I, II, III, and IV

42. Fearing loss of a potential sale, an agent omits facts that a prudent investor requires to make informed decisions. Under the Uniform Securities Act, this action is

    A. fraudulent for nonexempt securities only
    B. fraudulent for exempt securities only
    C. fraudulent for both exempt and nonexempt securities
    D. not fraudulent if there was willful intent to omit the information

43. According to the USA, which of the following is a prohibited activity?

    A. An agent enters into an agreement to share in the profits/losses of the customer's account without prior written consent of the employing broker-dealer.
    B. An agent and spouse jointly own their own personal trading account at the firm.
    C. An agent, with the written authorization of the customer and the broker-dealer that the agent represents, participates in the profits and losses of the account.
    D. An agent refuses a client's request to share in the performance of the client's account.

44. Under the Uniform Securities Act, broker-dealers are required to prepare and maintain certain records. Which of the following statements reflects the position of the act?

    I. A firm registered in more than one state must meet the recordkeeping requirements of the state where its principal office is located, even if those are less comprehensive than those of some of the other states where it is registered.
    II. A firm must maintain records of every email sent from the office by agents.
    III. A broker-dealer's website is considered advertising.
    IV. Once a broker-dealer's trade blotter has been posted, it may be discarded.

    A. I and II
    B. I and III
    C. II and IV
    D. III and IV

45. Aaron is a client of XYZ Financial Services. Over the past several years, Aaron has been suspicious of possible churning of his account, but has taken no action because account performance has been outstanding. After reviewing his most recent statement, Aaron suspects that excessive transactions have occurred. He consults his attorney, who informs him that under the USA, any lawsuit for recovery of damages under the USA must be started within

    A. 1 year of occurrence
    B. 2 years of occurrence
    C. 3 years of occurrence or 2 years of discovery, whichever occurs first
    D. 2 years of occurrence or 3 years of discovery, whichever occurs last

46. Which of the following accurately describes a cease and desist order as authorized by the USA?

    A. An Administrator's order to an issuer to suspend sale of its security as a result of improper disclosures in the registration statement
    B. An Administrator's order to refrain from a practice of business believed by that Administrator to be unfair
    C. A court-issued order requiring a business to stop an unfair practice
    D. An order from one brokerage firm to another to refrain from unfair business practices

47. A resident of Albany, NY, is visiting relatives in Albany, GA. While there, she receives a phone call from her agent in the Troy, NY, office of Capital City Investments who offers a security that the client immediately agrees to purchase. The next day, she sends her payment from Georgia. The agent sends the trade confirmation to the purchaser's residence address in New York. This agent is registered in 12 states, including New York and Georgia. The security is not exempt and was not registered. Which Administrator has the authority to pursue action against the agent?

    A. Georgia
    B. New York
    C. Both Georgia and New York
    D. The Administrator of any of the 12 states in which the agent is registered

48. If it is in the public interest, the Uniform Securities Act provides that the state Administrator may deny the registration of a person for all of the following reasons EXCEPT

    A. the applicant is not qualified owing to lack of experience
    B. a willful violation of the Uniform Securities Act has taken place
    C. the applicant is financially insolvent
    D. the applicant is enjoined temporarily from engaging in the securities business

49. If an agent chooses to appeal an Administrator's order, when must the agent file for review of the order with the appropriate court?

    A. Immediately
    B. Within 30 days after the entry of the order
    C. Within 60 days after the entry of the order
    D. Within 180 days after the entry of the order

50. An Administrator may summarily suspend a registration of an agent or an IAR pending final determination of proceedings under the USA. However, the Administrator may not enter a final order without

    I. appropriate prior notice to the applicant as well as the employer or prospective employer of the applicant
    II. opportunity for a hearing
    III. findings of fact and conclusions of law
    IV. prior written acknowledgment of the applicant

    A. I only
    B. I and II
    C. I, II, and III
    D. I, II, III, and IV

51. A state-registered investment adviser maintains custody of client funds and securities. On Thursday, the chief financial officer of the firm informs the chief compliance officer that their net worth is $31,578. Under the provisions of the Uniform Securities Act, the firm would

    A. do nothing, as their net worth is far in excess of the minimum requirement of $10,000
    B. send a detailed financial report to the Administrator by the close of business Friday
    C. send a detailed financial report to the Administrator by the close of business Monday
    D. need to increase the amount of their surety bond

52. An investment adviser owes an undivided loyalty to its clients and therefore is considered to be a(n)

    A. agent
    B. fiduciary
    C. principal
    D. custodian

53. Which of the following statements regarding provisions of the Investment Advisers Act of 1940 is TRUE?

    A. Big Gains Registered Investment Advisers must disclose its sources of information for specific recommendations they make to their clients.
    B. An investment adviser must obtain client permission to accept a buyout offer for all of the adviser's stock.
    C. Five Partners Advisers, Ltd., must inform all clients that one of the 5 partners has retired and been replaced by a new partner.
    D. Pledging a client's contract as collateral for a loan to the adviser would not be considered an assignment of the contract.

54. Under the NASAA Model Custody Rule, an investment adviser would be considered to have custody of client assets if that adviser inadvertently receives

    I. a check from a client made out to the IA and does not return the check within 24 hours
    II. a check from a client made out to a third party and does not forward the check within 3 business days
    III. stock certificates from a client and does not forward them within 3 business days
    IV. stock certificates from a client and does not return them within 3 business days

    A. I and IV
    B. I, II and IV
    C. II and IV
    D. II and III

55. Which of the following would be deemed to be an assignment of an investment advisory contract?

    I. All of the stock in NLT Advisers, a corporation, is acquired by MMS Advisers, Inc.
    II. The Lucky Seven Partnership is an investment adviser with 7 partners. Four of the partners make a fortune and decide to retire. They are replaced by new partners.
    III. Albert is an investment adviser. His clients' accounts are automatically debited monthly for his fee. Because of this steady cash flow, his banker readily accepts a pledge of these accounts as collateral for a loan.

    A. I and II
    B. I and III
    C. II and III
    D. I, II and III

56. Who of the following are exempt from registration as an investment adviser under the Investment Advisers Act of 1940?

  I. An adviser whose clients consist solely of insurance companies
  II. An adviser to 7 private funds with total assets under management in the U.S. of $125 million
  III. An adviser whose only office is in Georgia who deals only with Georgia residents, none of whom is a private fund, and does not deal in securities listed on any national securities exchange
  IV. An adviser in Florida with only 10 Florida clients who advertises in telephone and business directories and specializes in dealing in New York Stock Exchange issues

  A. I and II
  B. I, II and III
  C. III and IV
  D. I, II, III and IV

57. Which of the following statements concerning investment advisers are true?

  I. An investment adviser who is exempt from registration is also exempt from the antifraud provisions of the Uniform Securities Act.
  II. The SEC can cancel the registration of a federal covered investment adviser if it finds that the adviser is no longer in business.
  III. An investment adviser who represents that their qualifications and methods of security analysis have been passed on by the SEC has violated the act.

  A. I and II
  B. I and III
  C. II and III
  D. I, II and III

58. All of the following statements regarding investment advisers are NOT true EXCEPT

  A. there are specific educational requirements that all investment advisers must meet
  B. the term scalping is the practice whereby an investment adviser, before the dissemination of a securities recommendation, trades on the anticipated short-run market activity that may result from the recommendations
  C. an investment adviser's books and records must be maintained in an easily accessible place for 3 years under the act
  D. federal covered advisers may not maintain custody of funds and securities of clients residing in a state if custody is prohibited by the Administrator of that state

59. Which of the following people would NOT meet the definition of a person associated with an investment adviser?

  A. An individual who solicits potential clients to open advisory accounts
  B. A vice president of a registered investment adviser
  C. A brokerage firm that is considered to be the parent of a registered investment adviser
  D. The typist responsible for operating the desktop publishing system that prepares the investment adviser's weekly research bulletins

60. A firm is registered as an investment adviser under the Investment Advisers Act of 1940. It has decided to raise its annual management fee from $1,500 to $1,800 and require that it be paid 1 year in advance instead of quarterly. The firm would

  A. need client permission to make this change
  B. need SEC permission to make this change
  C. now come under the balance sheet requirements of the ADV
  D. be in violation of the law that prohibits prepayments more than 6 months in advance

61. Which of the following statements regarding the SEC's power to revoke the registration of an investment adviser is TRUE?

A. If it is determined that an investment adviser is insolvent, the SEC may revoke the registration.

B. Failure to adequately supervise a person associated with the adviser could be cause for the SEC to revoke the firm's registration.

C. Revocation would occur, with appropriate notice, when a firm's annual updating amendment was received by the SEC 120 days after the end of the registrant's fiscal year.

D. An investment adviser receiving substantial prepayment of fees from 50% of its clients that fails to include a copy of its balance sheet in its brochure delivered to all clients would give the SEC cause for beginning revocation proceedings.

62. An investment adviser registered with the SEC could use the term *investment counsel* if

I. their principal business consists of rendering investment advice

II. a substantial portion of their business involves investment supervisory services

III. they maintains full investment discretion

A. I and II
B. I and III
C. II and III
D. I, II and III

63. Which of the following is NOT a prohibited practice under the Investment Advisers Act of 1940?

A. Scalping
B. Failure to maintain a file of all advertisements circulated to 10 or more persons
C. Maintaining required records easily accessible for only 5 years
D. Maintaining required records easily accessible for only 2 years

64. A registered investment adviser runs a promotion offering free information to all who request it. Which of the following statements to people who respond do not comply with the advertising interpretation of the Uniform Securities Act?

I. "The offer is yours, free of charge; all I need are the names of 5 friends who might be able to use our service."

II. "Such a deal; our information about the market is free to anyone who makes only one trade with our broker-dealer affiliate."

III. "Thank you for responding; if we can help you after you read our information, please let us know."

A. I and II
B. I and III
C. II and III
D. I, II and III

65. Which of the following statements made by an investment adviser would be fraudulent?

A. "We believe that fundamental analysis is the best way to select stocks for our clients."

B. "Our fees are nonnegotiable" (when ADV Part 2A clearly indicates otherwise).

C. "We require any associated person determining general investment advice to be a CFA."

D. "We have over $40 billion in assets under management representing both institutional and retail clients."

66. A federal covered investment adviser is one who

I. has $110 million or more in assets under management

II. manages an investment company registered under the Investment Company Act of 1940

III. limits his advice to securities listed on the NYSE

IV. is affiliated with a federally chartered bank

A. I and II
B. I and III
C. II and III
D. I, II, III and IV

67. Under the Uniform Securities Act, which of the following would be included in the definition of an investment adviser representative?

    A. An employee, highly skilled in evaluating securities, who performs administrative or clerical functions for an investment adviser
    B. An individual who renders fee-based advice on precious metals
    C. A solicitor for an investment advisory firm who is compensated for the service rendered
    D. An agent who offers incidental advice on securities whose sole compensation is from commissions on transactions

68. Under the Uniform Securities Act, all of the following may provide investment advice incidental to their normal business without requiring registration as an investment adviser EXCEPT

    A. a teacher
    B. an economist
    C. a lawyer
    D. an engineer

69. Under the Uniform Securities Act, any partner, officer, or director of a registered investment adviser is an investment adviser representative if a function of the position involves

    I. offering advice concerning securities
    II. managing client accounts or portfolios
    III. determining securities recommendations for representatives to disseminate
    IV. supervising personnel engaged in advisory activities but not directly dealing with the public

    A. I only
    B. I and II
    C. I, II and III
    D. I, II, III and IV

70. As defined in the Uniform Securities Act, an investment adviser is all of the following EXCEPT

    I. a broker-dealer who charges for investment advice
    II. a publisher of a financial newspaper
    III. a person who sells security analysis
    IV. a CPA who, as an incidental part of his practice, suggests certain tax-sheltered investments to his affluent clients

    A. I and II
    B. II and III
    C. II and IV
    D. III and IV

71. An Administrator can deny an individual's application for registration as an investment adviser representative for all of the following reasons EXCEPT

    A. lack of experience
    B. conviction for a securities-related misdemeanor within the past 10 years
    C. failure to pass a written exam
    D. submitting an incomplete application

72. Under the Uniform Securities Act, an investment adviser may legally have custody of money or securities belonging to a client if the

    I. investment adviser has insufficient net worth or is not appropriately bonded
    II. Administrator has not issued a rule prohibiting custody
    III. investment adviser does not also have discretionary authority over the account
    IV. investment adviser has notified the Administrator that custody is maintained

    A. I and III
    B. II only
    C. II and IV
    D. IV only

73. According to the Uniform Securities Act, an investment adviser may have custody of a customer's funds and securities if

A. it has received the permission of the Administrator
B. it has received permission from the SEC
C. it does not share in the capital gains of the account
D. the Administrator has been informed of the custody

74. Which of the following are prohibited practices?

I. An investment advisory firm organized as a partnership fails to inform its clients of the departure of a partner with a very small interest in the partnership.
II. An investment advisory firm charges an annual fee equal to 2% of the first $250,000 in assets under management; 1% of the next $500,000; and .5% for everything in excess of $750,000.
III. The majority stockholder of a registered investment adviser pledges his stock as collateral for a loan taken out by the firm to expand its services without obtaining client consent for assignment of their contracts.
IV. An investment advisory firm engages in agency cross transactions.

A. I and III
B. I and IV
C. III and IV
D. I, II, III and IV

75. The head of research for your firm has just prepared a very positive report on DEF Industries, Inc. The report will be placed on the firm's website later today and copies mailed to clients for whom the security is deemed appropriate. Tonight, this analyst will be appearing on CNBC and will be describing why he has issued this "strong buy" recommendation. As an investment adviser representative, you would

A. be permitted to contact your clients with this recommendation right now
B. be permitted to contact your clients with this recommendation tomorrow
C. not be permitted to contact your clients until it was ascertained that the report was general public knowledge
D. be required to send your clients to the firm's website before making any comments regarding this security

ANSWERS AND RATIONALES

1. **A.** Insider trading is covered primarily in the Insider Trading and Securities Fraud Enforcement Act of 1988, as well as the 10(b) sections of the Securities Exchange Act of 1934. Of course, it is the Securities Exchange Act of 1934 that deals with securities exchanges. A deficiency letter is used by the SEC to extend the 20-day cooling-off period when something is missing from the registration statement.

2. **D.** Intrastate issues are exempt from the Securities Act of 1933 under Rule 147. U.S. government securities are always exempt. Regulation D is the private placement exemption.

3. **A.** This is the definition of churning.

4. **C.** An offer can only be made with an effective prospectus. A red herring is neither an offer to sell nor an offer of a solicitation to buy; it may only be used to obtain indications of interest.

5. **B.** Every prospectus carries the SEC disclaimer on the front cover in bold type. All the SEC can hope for is full disclosure of the pertinent information.

6. **C.** These securities are eligible for the intrastate exemption afforded under Rule 147. They might have to register in that particular state, depending on whether they met the exemption requirements in that state for that type of issue. Only under the NSMIA and the Uniform Securities Act do securities listed on a national stock exchange receive a registration exemption, as will be covered in the next session.

7. **D.** The Securities Exchange Act of 1934 requires registration of securities exchanges, as well as the securities listed on those exchanges. It also requires registration of corporations whose securities are listed. All broker-dealers (other than intrastate) must register, as well as SROs, such as FINRA and the MSRB.

8. **B.** Choice A relates to the Trust Indenture Act of 1939 (not tested); Choice C relates to SIPA of 1970, which created SIPC (also not tested); and Choice D relates to the Investment Advisers Act of 1940.

9. **C.** An individual who is convicted of, or has pleaded guilty or no contest to, any felony or certain misdemeanors in the previous 10 years (120 months) is subject to statutory disqualification. A conviction made more than 10 years ago is part of the record but not cause for disqualification. A misdemeanor involving a financial matter within the past 10 years is a cause for disqualification. Accusation is not the same as conviction.

10. **B.** Under the Securities Act of 1933, there are two requirements for commercial paper to be exempt from registration: maturity may not exceed nine months and proceeds must be used for current operational needs.

    Acquiring machinery would not be considered current because the result is new fixed assets. Rating and denominations are only important under the Uniform Securities Act.

11. **B.** The term *any person* does not include the designated agent of an investment club. Groups put together for the purpose of investing together, such as an investment club or clients of an investment adviser, do not qualify. Although there are exceptions, the exam will deal with accounts for minor children only.

12. **A.** An investment company may own up to 3% of another investment company. Even though FINRA rules do require approval of investment company communications with the public, such approval is not part of the Investment Company Act of 1940.

13. **A.** Section 30(d) of the act requires semiannual reports from the fund. Although filing is required with the SEC, the company does not file with its shareholders. In the description of the types of investment companies, holding companies (which invest in other companies for the purpose of management control) are not included.

14. **D.** The SEC does not approve securities.

15. **B.** Securities information processors (SIPs) are regulated under the Securities Exchange Act of 1934. They include any person engaged in the business of collecting, processing, or preparing for distribution or publication information dealing with transactions in, or quotations for, any nonexempt security; or distributing or publishing (whether by means of a ticker tape, a communications network, a terminal display device, or otherwise), on a current and continuing basis, information with respect to such transactions or quotations.

16. **C.** A prospectus deals with new issues, so the term is defined in the Securities Act of 1933.

17. **A.** The SEC never approves of an issue. The other statements are permissible.

18. **B.** The Illinois Tool Company is a corporation, even though it has a state in its name.

19. **D.** Treasury bills are defined as government securities, not municipal securities. Under federal law, Canadian cities (or provinces) are not municipal securities.

20. **D.** An agent exercising discretion is picking the specific security, and/or the specific amount, and/or the specific action (buy or sell). Time and price are excluded from the definition of discretion. An agent cannot make any discretionary decisions in the account until the proper authorizations have been received and approved.

21. **A.** Under the USA, only individuals can be agents. A person who sells securities for a broker-dealer is an agent. An administrative person, such as the assistant to the president of a broker-dealer, is considered an agent if he takes securities orders from the public. Corporate entities are excluded from the definition of an agent. Broker-dealers and issuers are not agents.

22. **D.** Under the USA, an individual is an agent when effecting transactions with an issuer's existing employees if commissions are paid. Therefore, Choice B is not correct because there are cases where the employee would have to register as an agent.

23. **C.** Anyone who solicits or receives an order while representing a broker-dealer is an agent. Silent partners, administrative personnel, and executives of broker-dealers, such as outside directors, who have nothing to do with the sales end of the business are not agents under the terms of the USA because they do not solicit or receive orders or supervise those who do. Remember, broker-dealers are not agents; agents represent broker-dealers. If, however, any of these individuals were authorized to accept orders, or supervise those that do, registration as an agent would be required.

24. **C.** An individual employed by a broker-dealer who sells securities to the public is an agent under the Uniform Securities Act. The USA defines an agent as "any individual other than a broker-dealer who represents a broker-dealer or issuer in effecting or attempting to effect purchases or sales of securities." The law excludes those individuals from the definition of an agent who represent an issuer in exempt transactions, selling certain exempt securities (Canadian provincial securities are on that list), and transactions with issuers' employees when no commission is paid. There is virtually no case in which a salesperson representing a broker-dealer is not an agent.

25. **C.** An employee of a broker-dealer, permanent or temporary, compensated or not, does not have to register if their only function is clerical or administrative. Compiling data is clerical and following up with clients to determine how they wish to receive documents for a purchase they've already made is simply an administrative task. However, making an offer of a security clearly requires registration.

26. **B.** Any broker-dealer with an office in the state, regardless of the nature of its clients, is defined as a broker-dealer under the USA. If the firm did not have an office in the state and its only clients were institutions such as insurance companies, or other broker-dealers as in Choice D, it would be excluded from the definition. Banks or trust companies and agents are never broker-dealers.

27. **D.** Investment contracts are defined as a security under the Uniform Securities Act. In fact, the term is often used as a synonym for a security. A guaranteed, lump-sum payment to a beneficiary is an endowment policy excluded from the definition of a security. Fixed, guaranteed payments made for life or for a specified period are fixed annuity contracts not defined as securities. Commodity futures contracts and the commodities themselves are not securities. It is much easier to remember what is not a security than what is.

28. **B.** The burden of proof for claiming eligibility for an exemption falls to the person claiming the exemption. In the event the registration statement was filed by someone other than the issuer (such as selling stockholders or a broker-dealer), that person must prove the claim.

29. **D.** Registration by qualification is the only registration method where the Administrator sets the effective date. The effective date under registration by coordination is set by the SEC, and notice filing is merely the filing of certain documents by certain federal covered securities.

30. **A.** A client calling to purchase stock is an unsolicited transaction, probably the most common of the exempt transactions. Any sale to an institutional client is an exempt transaction, whereas those to individuals, unless unsolicited, generally are not. Please note, even though the Treasury bonds are an exempt security, because the transaction was solicited by an agent to an individual client, it is not an exempt transaction.

31. **B.** The sale of a security to an institution, such as an insurance company, is considered an exempt transaction. The fact that the company is not authorized to do business in the state only means that its securities would not be exempt, but that does not change the fact that this is a sale to an institution and is, therefore, exempt. The term accredited investor is meaningless here, only institutions qualify for exempt treatment, not rich people. The T-bonds are an exempt security, but the sale to a retail client is not an exempt transaction. Heating oil contracts are a commodity, not a security.

32. **B.** On the state level, securities registration statements are generally effective for 1 year from the effective date. However, the effective date may be extended for a longer period during which the security is being offered or distributed in a nonexempt transaction by the issuer or other person on whose behalf the offering is being made or by any underwriter who is still offering part of an unsold allotment or subscription taken by him as a participant in the distribution.

33. **B.** Under the Uniform Securities Act, an issuer is any person who issues, or proposes to issue, a security. The resale of a partnership interest by an investor is a nonissuer sale because the investor is not the issuer. Examples of issuers are a municipality such as the city of Chicago, which issues tax-exempt highway improvement bonds; the AAA Manufacturing Company, which proposes to offer shares to the public even though it has not completed the offering; and the United States government, when it proposes to offer Treasury bonds.

34. **A.** Transactions by fiduciaries, such as a trustee in a bankruptcy reorganization, are exempt from registration. But only a trustee in bankruptcy is afforded this exemption, not for a family trust. An offer of a securities investment to 10 or fewer individuals (called a private placement) is also exempt from registration. Offers of pre-organization certificates are not exempt when compensation is paid.

35. **C.** An issuer transaction is one where the issuer of the securities receives the proceeds of the sale. John's father, although a founder of the company, purchased shares directly from the company. This transaction is an issuer transaction because the firm received the funds from the sale of the shares. In all the other instances, the firm, the original issuer of the securities, did not receive the proceeds of the transaction. These transactions are called nonissuer transactions.

36. **C.** Bonds issued by states (under the USA, the District of Columbia is considered a state) and Canadian provinces are exempt. Any security issued by a federally chartered credit union or one that is authorized to do business in the state is exempt. However, unless some other condition is given, such as the issuer's common stock is listed on an exchange or Nasdaq (making it federal covered), a corporate debenture is not an exempt security. Don't make any assumptions on the exam.

37. **D.** An Administrator may commence an action against an agent's registration if the agent engages in prohibited practices such as those described in each of the choices in the question.

38. **A.** Creating the illusion of trading activity is market manipulation. Guaranteeing performance of a security and omitting material facts are prohibited practices but do not constitute market manipulation. Trades too large for a customer are also prohibited because they are not suitable.

39. **B.** An agent may not offer services that he cannot perform. An agent may participate actively in trading a security in which an unusually high trading volume has occurred, provided the trading is not designed to create a false appearance of high volume. At the client's request, an agent can alter a client's order, even if the change results in a loss. An agent is only required to report written complaints to his employing principal, although it would be wise to report repeated oral complaints.

40. **C.** Agents must always determine suitability before soliciting purchases or sales. The key here is that the agent recommended this stock to all clients. One investment cannot be suitable for all of your clients.

41. **D.** All of the practices are prohibited. An agent may not borrow money or securities from a customer unless that customer is a bank or broker-dealer in the business of lending money and/or securities. Selling speculative issues to a retired couple of modest means is an unsuitable transaction because it is not consistent with the objectives of the client. An agent must follow legal orders of the customer, even if the agent believes the order is an unwise one. An agent may not backdate confirmations for the benefit of the client.

42. **C.** Material facts are facts that an investor relies on to make investment decisions. The willful omission of a material fact in the sale, purchase, or offer of a security is fraudulent. This applies whether the security offered is exempt or nonexempt.

43. **A.** It is a prohibited practice under the USA for an agent to share in the profits or losses of a customer's account unless the customer and employing broker-dealer have given prior written authorization. An agent is permitted to jointly own, with spouse, a personal account at the firm and can refuse to share in a customer's account.

44. **B.** Regardless of the requirements of other states, the only requirements that must be met are those of the state where the principal office is located. Among the items of advertising requiring maintenance of records is a firm's website. Personal email sent by agents that is not business related does not have to be retained. Trade blotters have a 3-year retention requirement. Please note that in most cases, broker-dealers are registered with the SEC in addition to the states in which they do business. In that case, the recordkeeping requirements of the SEC trump those of any state.

45. **C.** Under the USA, the lawsuit for recovery of damages must commence within the sooner of 3 years of occurrence of the offense or 2 years of its discovery.

46. **B.** A cease and desist order is a directive from an administrative agency to immediately stop a particular action. The order can come from a federal, state, or judicial body; it is not exclusive to anyone. Administrators may issue cease and desist orders with or without a prior hearing. Brokerage houses cannot issue cease and desist orders to each other. An order issued by the Administrator to halt the sale of a security is known as a stop order, not a cease and desist order.

47. **C.** Let's start with the legal stuff first. Under the Uniform Securities Act, an offer to sell or to buy is made in a state when the offer (1) originates from the state or (2) is directed by the offeror (the agent) to the state and received at the place to which it is directed (or at any post office in the state in the case of a mailed offer). Furthermore, an offer to buy or to sell is accepted in a state when acceptance is communicated to the offeror orally or in writing, inside, or outside the state. The offer originated in New York and was directed to Georgia where it was accepted. The mailing of the confirmation is of no consequence. Therefore, the Administrators of both New York and Georgia would have jurisdiction over this activity. If the check had been mailed from another state while the client was on her way home, that would have no impact on this question.

48. **A.** If the person qualifies by virtue of training or knowledge, registration cannot be denied for lack of experience only. Registration may be denied if the applicant willfully violates the Uniform Securities Act, is financially insolvent, or has been enjoined from engaging in the securities business. In certain cases, an applicant for registration as an investment adviser may have his license restricted to only acting as a broker-dealer, but that is not considered a denial.

49. **C.** Under the USA, a registered person has up to 60 days to appeal any disciplinary finding by the state Administrator.

50. **C.** With the exception of those proceedings awaiting final determination, the Administrator must provide an appropriate prior notice to the applicant as well as the employer or prospective employer of the applicant and provide the opportunity for a hearing. In addition, the Administrator may only issue a final order after findings of fact and conclusions of law. An applicant is not required to provide written acknowledgment before an order is issued.

51. **C.** A state-registered investment adviser who maintains custody of client assets must maintain net worth of at least $35,000 or a bond of the same amount (not both). If the net worth should fall below the minimum, by the close of the next business day after discovery (Friday in our example), notice of the deficiency must be sent to the Administrator of the state in which the principal office of the adviser is located. Then, by the close of business the day after that (Monday in our example), a detailed financial report, including the number of clients served by the adviser, must be sent to the Administrator. The firm would need to increase their net worth, not the bond.

52. **B.** Both federal and state law consider the relationship to be a fiduciary one.

53. **C.** Both state and federal law require advisers operating as partnerships to notify their clients of changes in partners where it represents a minority interest in the firm. No adviser is required to disclose the sources for a particular recommendation. An advisory firm can be sold without client permission. However, if the transaction results in a change that would be deemed to be an assignment, the adviser must obtain the consent of the clients to maintain their contracts. The regulatory bodies consider a pledge of clients' contracts to be an assignment.

54. **C.** Checks made out to a third party must be *forwarded* to that party within 3 business days of receipt or the IA will be considered to be maintaining custody. In the case of certificates or checks made out to the IA, *return* must be made within 3 business days of receipt in order to avoid custody issues; they are never forwarded.

55 **D.** It is deemed to be an assignment whenever a majority interest in an adviser changes hands. Pledging a client's contract is considered to be an assignment.

56. B. To qualify for the intrastate exemption, there is no numerical limitation, none of the clients can be private funds, and advertising on an intrastate basis is permitted. However, no advice may be given on securities traded on a national stock exchange. Under the federal law, an exemption from registration applies if the adviser's only clients are insurance companies. And, if an adviser's only clients are private funds (regardless of how many) and AUM in the United States is less than $150 million, that adviser is exempt as well.

57. C. As long as a security is involved, no one is ever exempt from the USA's antifraud provisions on the exam. The SEC may cancel the registration of an adviser for one of several reasons, no longer being in business is one of them. It is always a violation to claim that the SEC (or the Administrator) has approved of your methods of doing business.

58. B. First of all, let's get rid of the negatives. By stating all are not true except, the question is looking for the true statement. The correct choice describes scalping, a prohibited practice. There are no educational requirements for investment advisers and books and records must be kept easily accessible for a period of 5 years, the first 2 years in an appropriate office (generally the principal office of the IA). State Administrators have no jurisdiction over federal covered advisers; if the state prohibits custody, that would only impact state-registered IAs.

59. D. People in strictly clerical or administrative positions are not considered to be associated persons of an investment adviser. Expect to see several variations of this theme on the exam.

60. C. For federal covered investment advisers, a prepayment in excess of $1,200 and for periods of 6 months or more in advance (substantial prepayment) requires the adviser to submit an annual audited balance sheet as part of its ADV Part 2 (and brochure). Previously, even though the firm's fee was in excess of $1,200, because it was collected on a quarterly basis, the firm did not fall under the balance sheet rule. Had this been a state registered IA, the answer would have been the same, even though the dollar limit is $500 rather than $1,200. That is for the reason given above—the former fee was charged quarterly and the substantial prepayment definition requires both exceeding a stated dollar amount ($500 or $1,200) and it being for 6 months or more in advance.

61. B. Failure to supervise, if proven, is one of the most common causes for disciplinary action against a broker-dealer or investment adviser. Insolvency is not a cause for revocation under the Investment Advisers Act of 1940, but it is for a state registered investment adviser (it tough to keep these straight; please see Appendix A). A late ADV annual updating amendment might be cause for some action but almost certainly not a revocation. It is not that serious an offense. The balance sheet would only have to be part of the disclosure statement (brochure) given to those from whom substantial prepayment of fees is received.

62. A. These are the 2 requirements for use of the term *investment counsel*. Although it can be a factor, exercising discretion is not a requirement of the definition.

63. C. Both state and federal law require that records be kept easily accessible for a period of no less than 5 years. What might have tricked you here is that these laws require that the records be kept in the principal office of the IA for the first 2 years.

64. **A.** If an advertisement claims to offer something for free, it must be free of any obligation. Choices I and II have strings attached and are not free.

65. **B.** Stating an untruth would be considered fraud. If the Form ADV Part 2 says that the fees are negotiable, you can't state that they are not. An adviser may certainly state which method of analysis he thinks is best. A firm can also set whatever standards it wishes, even though none are required by the regulatory bodies. As far as bragging about the amount of AUM, if you've got them, it is okay to flaunt them.

66. **A.** Federal registration is generally required of any investment adviser managing at least $110 million in assets. The NSMIA provides that any investment adviser under contract to a registered investment company under the Investment Company Act of 1940 is required to register with the SEC as a federal covered adviser. Providing advice on federal covered securities listed on the NYSE does not make the adviser a federal covered adviser. Determining if one is a federal covered investment adviser is not based on affiliations; it is generally a function of AUM or managing an investment company.

67. **C.** A solicitor is considered an investment adviser representative under the Uniform Securities Act. An employee who performs only clerical or administrative functions is not an investment adviser representative. Precious metals are not securities and, therefore, a person advising on them is not considered an investment adviser representative. An agent is a representative of a broker-dealer, and as long as the only form of compensation is sales commissions based upon transactions, registration as an investment adviser representative is not required.

68. **B.** The Uniform Securities Act does not exclude economists from the definition of investment adviser as it does lawyers, accountants, teachers, and engineers who give advice that is incidental to the practice of their profession. Remember the acronym LATE—lawyers, accountants, teachers, and engineers. Do not be fooled by the E in *economist*.

69. **D.** The Uniform Securities Act defines persons associated with an investment adviser as an investment adviser representative, including any partner, officer, or director who offers advice concerning securities. Persons who manage client accounts or portfolios, determine securities recommendations, or supervise personnel engaged in the above activities are investment adviser representatives.

70. **C.** A publisher of a financial newspaper and a CPA who, as an incidental part of his practice, suggests tax-sheltered investments are not investment advisers. Once a broker-dealer is compensated for investment advice, usually referred to as *special compensation* in the rules, the exclusion from the definition is lost. This answer would be the same under either the USA or federal law.

71. **A.** Lack of experience, by itself, is not cause for registration denial.

72. **C.** The Administrator may, by rule, prohibit advisers from having custody of client funds or securities. If no such prohibition applies, the Administrator must be notified in writing if an adviser has custody. In almost all jurisdictions, a bond or sufficient net worth is required to maintain custody. Discretionary authority does not affect an adviser's ability to have custody.

73. **D.** As long as retaining custody of funds is not prohibited, an investment adviser may have custody of a customer's account after providing notice to the Administrator.

74. **A.** Any change in the ownership of an investment advisory firm organized as a partnership, no matter how small, requires notification to all clients within a reasonable amount of time. If the firm is structured as a corporation, pledging a controlling interest in the company's stock is viewed as an assignment of the contracts. This may not be done without the approval of the clients. Agency cross transactions—that is, where the adviser represents both sides of the trade—are permitted as long as the adviser makes the proper written disclosures and does not make the buy/sell recommendations to both parties.

75. **A.** A firm's internal research is not considered inside information. Clients may be contacted as soon as the IAR has access to the report. What is prohibited would be for the IAR to purchase this stock personally, prior to release of the report, and then contact clients.

QUICK QUIZ ANSWERS

Quick Quiz 1.A

1. **A.** An issuer is a person who issues a security, whether or not the security is exempt. In the question, the antique dealer is issuing collectibles, not securities.

2. **D.** A security is any note, stock, bond, certificate of interest, or participation in any profit sharing arrangement, investment contract, certificate of deposit for a security, interest in oil, gas, or mining rights, or any investment commonly considered a security. (Generally, it is an investment contract wherein the investor is passive and expects a return on the investment through the efforts of others.) The definition of a security does not include direct ownership of real estate, commodities futures contracts (e.g., corn, wheat), collectibles, precious metals, or life insurance or annuity contracts that have fixed payouts.

Quick Quiz 1.B

1. **D.** One of the benefits of this term is that these investors do not count in the numerical limitation placed on private placements made under Rule 506(b). Note that for offerings made under Rule 506(c), *all* investors must be accredited. When filing a joint return, the income requirement is $300,000, and an employee benefit plan must have assets in excess of $5 million. Insiders are only considered accredited investors when it is that issuer's security being offered.

Quick Quiz 1.C

1. **A.** His 15% ownership is control. Her 5% is not, but the fact that she is the spouse of an affiliate makes her one, causing this to be a sale of control stock. All sales of control stock (unless an exemption applies) must be accompanied by a Rule 144 filing.

Quick Quiz 1.D

1. **B.** Whenever the order calls for time/price discretion, it is considered a *day* order and must be executed that day. Waiting two days is inappropriate.

2. **A.** University presidents are a popular choice for serving as outside directors. Under the Securities Exchange Act of 1934, the term *associated person* of a broker-dealer would include an outside director of a broker-dealer and all registered personnel but not employees who are strictly clerical and administrative.

3. **B.** This is the definition of an unsolicited transaction.

Quick Quiz 1.E

1. **A.** The 1975 Amendments required, for the first time, that any firm engaged in the municipal securities business be registered with the SEC. Ever since 1934, broker-dealers engaged in any phase of the securities markets have been required to register with the SEC. Banks (financial institutions) are members of the MSRB but are exempt from SEC registration.

2. **C.** The disclosure requirement for new issues (IPOs) is found in the Securities Act of 1933.

Quick Quiz 1.F

1. **A.** Holding companies and insurance companies are specifically excluded from the definition of an investment company.

Quick Quiz 1.G

1. **C.** Closed-end companies issue a fixed number of shares, whereas open-end companies do not specify the number of shares to be issued. Both types of company register issues with the SEC, and any investor may invest in either type of company. Open-end shares must always be sold with a prospectus because each is a newly issued share.

2. **A.** If the selling price of an investment company is less than the NAV, the fund must be a closed-end investment company.

Quick Quiz 1.H

1. **C.** The plan may be terminated by a majority vote of the shareholders or a majority vote of the board of directors who are noninterested directors of the fund. A 12b-1 plan wouldn't work with anything other than an open-end investment company.

Quick Quiz 1.I

1. **A.** The one thing that all investment companies must do is issue common stock. That is the form of ownership. All of the other activities are prohibited.

Quick Quiz 1.J

1. **C.** Without an exemptive order from the SEC, it would be a violation of the Investment Company Act of 1940 for any affiliated person to purchase any security from an investment company other than shares of the fund itself.

2. **D.** The Investment Company Act of 1940 requires that all advisory contracts contain a provision that the contract may be terminated upon no more than 60 days notice in writing. The Act prohibits any registered investment company from owning more than 3% of the shares of another investment company. There are no circumstances under which an affiliated person can borrow from the fund, and it is not a requirement that the custodian bank have FDIC insurance.

Quick Quiz 1.K

1. **C.** Any family unit may combine purchases in as many accounts as it wishes to reach the breakpoint for reduced sales charges. Most often, this is spouses and custodial accounts for minor children (there are exceptions—not tested). If an employee of the fund (the receptionist) purchases for his own account, the sales charge is usually eliminated altogether. A purchase made for a group, such as an investment club or multiple clients with no common purpose other than investment, is not eligible for a reduction.

Quick Quiz 2.A

1. **T.** A final order, such as a suspension or revocation, may only be entered after the opportunity for a hearing has been granted.

2. **F.** Cease and desist orders are directed at securities professionals. Stop orders are used for securities offerings.

3. **T.** Governments and political subdivisions are considered persons under the act. Remember there are only three choices that are not a person—minors, persons since deceased, and those judged mentally incompetent.

4. **F.** In order for an employee benefit plan to be included in the definition of institution, it must have assets of not less than $1 million.

5. **A.** The USA specifies that a state's securities Administrator has the authority to enforce the act in that state. A transfer agent is the person or corporation responsible for recording the names and holdings of registered security owners.

Quick Quiz 2.B

1. **T.** A person who effects transactions in securities for itself or for the account of others must register in the state as a broker-dealer unless specifically excluded from the definition or exempt from registration.

2. **T.** A firm with an out-of-state registration is not considered a broker-dealer in that state if transacting business with a customer who is passing through the state on vacation.

3. **T.** If a person is excluded from the definition, that person need not register as a broker-dealer; however, if they are not excluded (or exempt), they must register.

4. **F.** When a broker-dealer is registered with both the SEC and several states (the usual case), the financial and operational requirements to be met are those of the SEC.

5. **C.** A broker-dealer is any person, partner, officer, director, or securities firm engaged in the business of effecting securities transactions for the accounts of others (broker) or for its own account (dealer).

Quick Quiz 2.C

1. **D.** There is a special group of five exempt issuers (U.S. and Canadian government and municipal issuers; foreign governments; banks; commercial paper; and investment contracts related to employee benefit plans) where an individual representing that issuer is not an agent. This is true whether the transaction is exempt or non-exempt. In addition, when representing any exempt issuer (not just the five listed), in an exempt transaction, the individual is not an agent. However, when representing a non-exempt issuer, if the transaction is non-exempt, then the individual must register as an agent of that issuer.

2. **B.** All of the exclusions from the term *agent* refer to an individual representing an issuer. As long as the transaction is exempt, the individual is not deemed to be an agent. There is no case on the exam where an individual performing a sales function for a broker-dealer is not an agent. Clerical persons are not agents, nor are officers with no apparent sales function.

3. **A.** Persons must be registered as agents when they effect transactions on behalf of broker-dealers whether or not the securities are exempt.

4. **A.** Any individual taking orders on behalf of a broker-dealer must be registered whether or not they receive a commission.

5. **B.** Employees of a bank engaging in retail sales of securities issued by that bank are not agents regardless of how they are compensated.

6. **A.** A person who represents an employer in selling securities to employees must register as an agent if the person receives a commission. If no commission is paid, registration is not necessary.

7. **B.** Persons who represent issuers in exempt transactions, such as with underwriters, need not register as agents.

8. **A.** A registered agent may not simultaneously represent two different unrelated broker-dealers in the same transaction. Under current regulations, only a few states allow agents to have dual registrations with more than one broker-dealer, unless those broker-dealers are under common management. In those cases, the agent may only represent one of the broker-dealers in any single transaction. Agents of broker-dealers may be simultaneously registered with real estate agencies, insurance companies, and with two broker-dealers, provided the broker-dealers are under common ownership or control or the arrangement has been authorized by the Administrator.

Quick Quiz 2.D

1. **F.**   A consent to service of process is filed with the initial application and permanently remains on file with the Administrator.

2. **F.**   In order to do business with their Canadian customers who are temporarily in any state(s), Canadian broker-dealers (and their agents) must obtain a form of limited registration.

3. **T.**   Whether the Form BD for a broker-dealer or the Form U-4 for an agent, the registrant must check the box(es) listing all jurisdictions in which the applicant is registering (or already registered). This is also required for investment advisers and their representatives.

4. **A.**   A broker-dealer, an agent, an investment adviser representative, or a state registered investment adviser must file a consent to service of process with the Administrator upon filing a registration application. The consent to service of process gives the Administrator the right to process legal complaints against the applicant. In some states, a federal covered adviser may also be required to furnish a consent to service of process.

Quick Quiz 2.E

1. **C.**   Commodity futures contracts and fixed payment life insurance contracts are included in our list of 6 items that are not securities.

2. **C.**   Management activity on the part of the owner is not part of the Howey, or four-part, test for an instrument to be a security. The four parts are: (1) an investment of money in (2) a common enterprise with (3) an expectation of profit (4) solely from the effort of others.

3. **C.**   Nonexempt means the security is not exempt from the state's registration requirements. However, if the nonexempt security is sold in an exempt transaction, registration is not required.

4. **B.**   A nonissuer transaction is one where the company that is the issuer of the security does not receive the proceeds from the transaction. A nonissuer transaction is a transaction between two investors and may or may not require the security to be registered depending on whether the security or the transaction (or both) are exempt. Whenever the proceeds go to the issuer, it is an issuer transaction.

5. **D.**   Whenever there is a material change to the information contained in the registration application of a securities professional, the Administrator must be promptly notified. Marital status is not included on the Form U-4. Federal covered investment advisers are not under the Administrator's jurisdiction.

Quick Quiz 2.F

1. **T.**   Registration by coordination involves coordinating a state registration with that of a federal registration.

2. **T.**   Any company may register by qualification. However, in virtually all cases, qualification is only used when it is the only choice, such as for intrastate offerings.

3. **A.**   Because this offering is being made in more than one state, SEC registration is necessary. The state registration method would be coordination, which is the simultaneous registration of a security with both the SEC and the states.

4. **B.**   Although these are federal covered securities and exempt from traditional registration, it could, at the discretion of the Administrator, be required to engage in a notice filing.

Quick Quiz 2.G

1. **D.** Securities issued by registered investment companies and those sold on the NYSE and Nasdaq Stock Market are federal covered securities and, therefore, do not register with the states. Commercial paper with a maximum maturity of 270 days, in denominations of no less than $50,000 and a top three rating are exempt under the Uniform Securities Act.

2. **D.** Variable annuities (whose performance depends on the securities in a segregated fund) are nonexempt, which means they are covered by the act and have to register. Shares in public utilities, charitable foundations, and banking institutions that are members of the Federal Reserve System are included in our list of exempt securities.

3. **D.** The USA exempts from registration a number of different issues. Included in that group are securities issued by depository institutions including a savings and loan association that is authorized to do business in the state. Securities issued by a governmental unit are always exempt. Any security senior to a common stock that is a federal covered security is itself considered federal covered and, therefore, exempt from state registration.

4. **B.** An exempt security is exempt from the registration requirements and the provisions that require the filing of advertising and sales literature. Exempt securities are never exempt from the antifraud provisions of the act.

Quick Quiz 2.H

1. **Y.** Mr. Thompson's receipt of an unsolicited order from Ms. Gordon is an exempt transaction.

2. **Y.** The sale of an unregistered security in a private, nonpublicly advertised transaction to 10 or fewer offerees over the previous 12 months is an exempt transaction under the *limited offering* exemption (a private placement).

3. **Y.** Any transaction by an executor, administrator, sheriff, marshal, receiver, trustee in bankruptcy, guardian, or conservator (but not a custodian for a minor under UTMA) is considered an exempt transaction under the Uniform Securities Act.

4. **N.** The sale of stock of a previously privately owned company to the public in an initial public offering is not an exempt transaction.

5. **C.** Choice III is not an exempt transaction because the private placement exemption is limited to 10 offerees, not 10 purchasers. The Administrator would be suspicious of anyone with a 100% closing ratio. All of the others are included in our list of exempt transactions.

6. **D.** The purchase of securities from a broker-dealer by an employee of a bank is a nonexempt transaction—it is a sale of a security by a broker-dealer to a member of the public and is therefore not exempt. Transactions between broker-dealers and issuers as part of an underwriting commitment; transactions between banks; and transactions between banks and insurance companies are exempt because they are transactions between financial institutions. Exempt transactions are most often identified by who the transaction is with rather than what type of security is involved.

7. **C.** Both unsolicited transactions and transactions between issuers and underwriters are exempt transactions, not exempt securities. U.S. government securities and securities of credit unions are exempt securities, not exempt transactions.

8. **D.** An agent who sells any security to an insurance company is engaged in an exempt transaction that is not bound by the advertising and registration requirements of the USA. Any sale to certain institutional customers, such as banks, investment companies, and insurance companies, is an exempt transaction. Neither exempt securities nor exempt transactions must adhere to the registration and advertising provisions of the USA. This is an exempt transaction because of the nature of the purchaser, not the type of security being sold.

Quick Quiz 2.I

1. **A.** A registration statement may be filed by the issuer, any other person on whose behalf the offering is to be made, or a registered broker-dealer.

Quick Quiz 2.J

1. **U.** It is unlawful to guarantee the performance of any security. Even though repayment of the principal of the government securities at maturity is assured, the same cannot be said about the mutual fund.

2. **U.** It is unlawful to exercise discretion without prior written authorization. Because the client was a nondiscretionary client, the agent could not, on his own initiative, select which internet company to invest in.

3. **L.** An agent must refuse orders from anyone other than the customer unless that person has prior written trading authority.

4. **U.** All written customer complaints must be forwarded to a designated supervisor of the agent's employing broker-dealer.

5. **L.** Agents may borrow from clients who are banks or financial institutions that are in the business of lending money to public customers. Agents may not borrow money from customers who are not in the business of lending money.

6. **U.** An agent may not guarantee the performance of a security.

7. **L.** It is lawful to charge extra transaction fees when justified as long as the customer is informed before the transaction.

8. **U.** It is unlawful to promise services that an agent cannot reasonably expect to perform or that the agent is not qualified to perform.

9. **U.** It is unlawful to solicit unregistered nonexempt securities.

10. **C.** A wash trade, the practice of attempting to create the appearance of trading activity by entering offsetting buy and sell orders, is a form of market manipulation. Matched orders or matched purchases occur when market participants agree to buy and sell securities among themselves to create the appearance of heightened market activity; this is also a form of market manipulation. Although churning is a prohibited practice, it does not involve manipulating the market, and arbitrage is the perfectly legal practice of buying a security in one marketplace and simultaneously selling it in another to benefit from a price disparity.

11. **D.** It is permissible to sell rights, which are securities. Borrowing money or securities from other than a bank or broker-dealer in the business of lending, failing to identify a customer's financial objectives, and guaranteeing a customer's account against losses are all prohibited practices.

12. **D.** Failure to bring customers' written complaints to the attention of the agent's broker-dealer is prohibited.

13. **D.** The use of information, such as a rumor, that has no basis in fact is prohibited.

14. **A.** An agent may indicate that a security is registered or is exempt from registration. All of the other statements are prohibited.

15. **D.** Recommending tax shelters to low-income retirees is an example of an unsuitable transaction. Stating that an Administrator has approved an offering on the basis of the quality of information in the prospectus, soliciting orders for unregistered nonexempt securities, and employing a device to defraud are all prohibited practices under the USA.

Quick Quiz 2.K

1. **D.** The Administrator has jurisdiction over a security offering if it was directed to, originated in, or was accepted in that state.

2. **C.** A state Administrator has jurisdiction over a securities offering made in a bona fide newspaper published within the state, but only whose circulation is not more than ⅔ outside the state.

3. **C.** An offer is made in an attempt to sell; a sale is the binding contract to sell a security for value. An offer will not require prior approval, but a designated supervisory individual must approve all sales on the date the order is executed.

Quick Quiz 2.L

1. **D.** The Administrator need not seek an injunction to issue a cease and desist order. The USA does not require that an Administrator conduct a public or private hearing before issuing a cease and desist order. When time does not permit, the Administrator may issue a cease and desist before a hearing to prevent a pending violation. The USA does not grant the Administrator the power to issue injunctions to force compliance with the act. The act permits the Administrator to issue cease and desist orders, and, if they do not work, the Administrator may seek an injunction from a court of competent jurisdiction. A cease and desist order is an administrative order, whereas an injunction is a judicial order.

2. **C.** An Administrator may compel the testimony of witnesses when conducting an investigation. Investigation of serious violations need not be held in public. An Administrator in Illinois may enforce subpoenas from South Carolina whether or not the violation occurred in Illinois. Conviction for any felony within the past 10 years is one of a number of reasons that the Administrator has for denying a license.

3. **B.** The Administrator can deny, suspend, or revoke a registration for many reasons, but they must be in the interest of the public. The Administrator may not deny the registration simply because it is prudent. The Administrator may determine that an applicant is not qualified to act as an adviser and thus limit the registration to that of a broker-dealer; the Administrator can also take into consideration whether the registrant will work under the supervision of a registered investment adviser or broker-dealer when approving an application. Lack of experience is insufficient for denial.

4. **B.** An arrest warrant can only be issued by a court of law.

Quick Quiz 2.M

1. **D.** An administrator may cancel the registration of a registrant that is no longer in existence. A person may request a withdrawal of a registration. Withdrawals become effective after 30 days if there are no revocation or denial proceedings in process. An Administrator does not revoke the registration of a person who is declared mentally incompetent but instead cancels his registration; this is a nonpunitive administrative action.

Quick Quiz 2.N

1. **B.** To be subject to time in prison, a sales agent must knowingly have violated the USA. A client who purchased a security in violation of the USA may recover the original purchase price plus costs involved in filing a lawsuit. In addition, the purchaser is entitled to interest at a rate stated by the Administrator, less any earnings already received on the investment. The right of rescission must be accepted within 30 days of receipt of the letter of rescission. Although any person aggrieved by an order of the Administrator may request an appeal of the order within 60 days, such appeal does not function as a stay order during the appeal process. The person who is the subject of the order must comply with the order during the period unless a stay is granted by the court.

2. **C.** For an agent to have civil liability, a sale must take place. If the offer is made using a statement like the one in this question and a sale subsequently occurs, a client suffering a loss would be able to sue. Even though one may never claim approval by the Administrator, there is no civil liability unless the client has some kind of a claim. However, even though the client cannot bring a case, the Administrator could bring a disciplinary action against the agent for making this claim. On a law exam, you must be careful to understand who has a claim and when they do.

3. **B.** Under the USA, the maximum penalty is a fine of $5,000 and/or 3 years in jail.

4. **A.** The Administrator may issue a cease and desist order without a hearing, but does not have the authority to convict violators of the 1933 Securities Act in criminal prosecutions or sentence violators of the USA. The Administrator may suspend a security's effective registration upon subsequently discovering that an officer of the firm has been convicted of a securities-related crime, not a nonsecurities-related one.

5. **B.** It is a NASAA Model Rule that broker-dealers operating on the premises of a financial institution make certain disclosures. Every attempt should be made to locate separately from the banking operation and to obtain something in writing from the clients indicating that they have received the disclosures. It is not necessary that there be any relationship between the BD and the institution other than a business one.

6. **D.** Persons who are convicted of violating securities laws may find themselves subject to criminal penalties, civil liabilities, and suspension, denial, or revocation of registration.

Quick Quiz 3.A

1. **B.** This is the term used in both the federal and state law. OSJ is a FINRA term and has no relevance to investment advisers. In fact, it may be the home office or executive office, but the exam will be looking for their definition.

Quick Quiz 3.B

1. **B.** The act specifically excludes accountants, lawyers, any professional engineer (aeronautical, civil, mechanical, or others), and teachers. Economists are not included in this listing.

2. **B.** There is an exclusion from the definition for all banks, regardless of what they do. Also excluded are persons whose advice relates only to securities that are direct obligations of or guaranteed by the United States—it makes no difference who their clients are. A geologist is not excluded because the law only specifies 4 professional exclusions: accountants, attorneys, engineers, and teachers.

3. **C.** Publishers of general circulation newspapers and magazines are excluded from the definition of investment adviser, even if the entire publication is devoted to investment advice. An important key here is that it is published regularly, not upon market events. A broker-dealer loses its exclusion the moment it offers advice for a separate charge, as does an attorney who holds herself out as offering investment advice. Normally, a teacher is excluded, but not when charging for advice as would appear to be the case here. On this examination, the term *comprehensive financial planning* always includes securities advice.

4. **C** Only those individuals in the business of giving advice on securities are required to register as investment advisers; only the convertible bonds are securities.

Quick Quiz 3.C

1. **A.** Advisers who only service insurance companies are exempt, as are advisers performing intrastate who do not give advice on listed securities (municipal bonds are not listed). Advising banks only does not qualify one for the exemption.

Quick Quiz 3.D

1. **B.** Publishers of newspapers and magazines of general circulation that offer general financial advice need not register.

2. **A.** Broker-dealers must register as investment advisers if they receive special or separate compensation for giving investment advice.

3. **A.** An investment adviser that manages less than $100 million in assets must register as an investment adviser under the USA. If the client is an investment company registered under the Investment Company Act of 1940, registration with the SEC is mandatory regardless of amount under management.

4. **C.** This is the straightforward definition of an IA. Yes, an IA does act in a fiduciary capacity, but are all fiduciaries investment advisers? No.

5. **B.** Unless some kind of exemption applies, an investment adviser must register on the state level if it manages less than $100 million in assets. Publishers of general circulation books are exempt from state registration, as are advisers with no offices in the state whose only customers are institutions, such as banks and investment companies, in the state. Investment advisers with $110 million or more in assets under management must register with the SEC, not the state Administrator regardless of offices in the state and the type of clientele being served.

Quick Quiz 3.E

1. **A.** Because Mr. Oldman has been responsible for updating the ADV, it is logical to assume that he is the contact person for information regarding the form. His sudden retirement means the firm would have to appoint a new contact person. This is a change that the SEC deems necessary to promptly amend of the Form ADV. Amendments to the ADV may not be done using Form ADV-W—that is for withdrawal only.

2. **D.** Any entity meeting the definition of a person would be eligible to file for registration as an investment adviser on Form ADV.

Quick Quiz 3.F

1. **C.** In order to use the term *investment counsel*, 2 criteria must be met— the principal business must be giving investment advice and the adviser must provide investment supervisory services. Running model portfolios for clients would meet both requirements. The financial planner is not principally in the business of offering investment advice because he describes his service as offering a wide range of services, of which advice is only one part. The exam frequently uses that wording to indicate that advice is not the principal activity. While the publisher's principal business activity may be offering advice, nothing about the description indicates that individual client accounts are being monitored.

2. **B.** Reasons for cancellation do not include dropping below a minimum number of clients. Revocation of registration is usually connected with some form of disciplinary action. Insolvency is not cause for revocation or cancellation under the Investment Advisers Act of 1940, although it is cause under the Uniform Securities Act.

Quick Quiz 3.G

1. **B.** Advisers maintaining discretion over client accounts are required to have a minimum net worth of $10,000. No, we haven't covered the information dealing with choice D yet, but this is a good opportunity to learn a test-taking technique. You will sometimes find an answer choice you have never heard of before. It might be correct, especially if it is an "all of these are true except" question. But, don't pick an answer just because you don't know what it means. And, in a question like this, where you should have easily spotted that the correct net worth is $10,000 instead of $35,000, before you go on to the next question, make a mental note (or write down on the pad given to you), the fact you learn from choice D—it might show up on another question.

2. **C.** Under the USA, an investment adviser exercising discretion over client accounts must maintain minimum net worth of $10,000. If the adviser falls below that minimum, it must notify the Administrator by the close of business the following day. Then, a complete financial report must be furnished to the Administrator by the close of business the day following the sending of the notice. Unless otherwise instructed by the Administrator, the firm may continue to exercise discretion.

3. **C.** The USA requires advisers who take custody to maintain a minimum net worth of $35,000. Any Administrator is empowered to change that number, higher or lower. As long as an investment adviser meets the net worth requirements of the state where its principal office is located, there is no need to be concerned about any other state's requirements.

Quick Quiz 3.H

1. **F.** An investment adviser (not the investment adviser representative) must register with the SEC if the firm manages assets of $110 million or more. As a representative of a federal covered investment adviser, the individual would have to be registered as an investment adviser representative in each state where she maintains a place of business.

2. **T.** An adviser maintaining custody, whether or not discretion is involved, is generally required to maintain a net worth of $35,000.

3. **F.** An employee of an investment advisory firm is not an investment adviser representative if his duties are confined to clerical activities.

4. **F.** Any administrative employee who receives specific compensation for offering investment advisory services is considered an investment adviser representative.

5. **T.** Any employee of an investment advisory firm is an investment adviser representative if his duties involve making investment recommendations.

6. **A.** A financial planning firm or other person that, as an integral component of other financially related services, provides investment advisory services for compensation is an investment adviser. A publisher of a bona fide newspaper, news magazine, or business or financial publication of general and regular circulation and a federal covered investment adviser are excluded from the definition of an investment adviser. Obviously, if the Administrator excludes a person from the definition, they're not going to have to register. Likewise, if the Administrator were to include that person, registration would be required.

7. **C.** Clerical and ministerial personnel are specifically excluded from the definition of investment adviser representative. Specifically included in the definition are directors, officers, partners, associates, and employees of state registered advisers who carry out investment advisory or solicitation functions or who supervise those functions. Also included in the definition are persons who perform similar functions for SEC-registered advisers and who have a place of business in the state. Once there is a place of business in the state, the de minimis rule no longer applies.

Quick Quiz 3.I

1. **D.** This is the exception, since the records must be kept for 5 years. Nothing in the question asked about the 2-year requirement in the office. The 5-year requirement is that records be easily accessible whether in the office or not.

2. **D.** Records of an investment adviser must be maintained for five years. Records are subject to surprise audits by the state Administrator, written records may be reduced to microfilm, and records originally created on a company's computer may be stored in electronic media.

Quick Quiz 3.J

1. **D.** An adviser to investment companies and an adviser who provides only impersonal advisory services are specifically listed as being exempt from the delivery requirements of the brochure rule (impersonal advice with a charge of $500 or more would require an offer to deliver). An adviser who provides advice only to insurance companies is exempt from registration as an investment adviser and therefore would also be exempt from the requirements of the brochure.

2. **D.** Delivery of the ADV Part 2A, or brochure, must be made to each client no later than the commencement of the advisory agreement. If the adviser wishes to deliver prior to that, there is no problem, but it is not required. For a state registered adviser, there is a requirement to deliver the brochure at least 48 hours in advance, unless the contract calls for a penalty-free termination. The ADV Part 1 is used when registering and is not furnished to clients.

3. **D.** This is one of the purposes of ADV Part 2B, the brochure supplement. Justification for SEC registration is based on assets under management, not the number of clients, and the brochure is not required to disclose the number of clients served by the investment adviser.

4. **D.** The balance sheet is required only when the adviser receives prepayments in excess of $1,200 for periods of 6 months or longer—not for those maintaining custody. If this had been a state registered adviser, the conditions are different in that the substantial prepayment amount requiring a balance sheet is $500 instead of $1,200 and NASAA Model Rules also require a balance sheet to all clients for whom the IA maintains custody.

5. **D.** The brochure rule requires that each client be given a written disclosure statement by the adviser no later than the time of entering into the advisory agreement. It may consist of a copy of Part 2A and 2B of Form ADV or another document providing similar information. There are no minimum net worth requirements for SEC registered investment advisers.

Quick Quiz 3.K

1. **A.** Under the Investment Advisers Act of 1940, discretion and substantial prepayments are not considered custody. Access to funds in the client's account is one of the standard tenets of custody.

2. **C.** If an IA is registered or is registering with one or more of the state securities authorities, the dollar amount reporting threshold for including the required balance sheet is more than $500 in fees per client, six months or more in advance. Unlike the federal law, under state law, a balance sheet is also required whenever the IA maintains custody of client assets. When the custodian is an affiliated broker-dealer (as in this case), the balance sheet requirement is triggered. When the only reason one is considered to have custody is automatic debiting of fees, the balance sheet is not normally required. Yes, there are certain conditions to be met to qualify for this exception, but on the exam, in a question like this, you may assume they're met.

3. **A.** Taking custody is considered to be of such significance that it requires prompt notification to the Administrator by the investment adviser by updating the Form ADV. Using a qualified custodian still constitutes a form of custody and requires notification to the Administrator.

4. **B.** Whether custody is maintained by the investment adviser itself or by a qualified custodian, statements must be sent at least quarterly.

5. **D.** If the adviser does not return the securities to the sender within 3 business days, the adviser not only has actual custody, but has also violated the rule's requirement that client securities be maintained in an account with a qualified custodian.

6. **A.** NASAA lists 3 acceptable qualified custodians. They are (1) a bank or savings association that has deposits insured by the Federal Deposit Insurance Corporation under the Federal Deposit Insurance Act; (2) a registered broker-dealer holding the client assets in customer accounts; and (3) a foreign financial institution that customarily holds financial assets for its customers, provided that the foreign financial institution keeps the advisory clients' assets in customer accounts segregated from its proprietary assets.

7. **C.** Under the NASAA Model Custody Rule, whenever an investment adviser receives customer checks made payable to an unrelated third party, failure to forward the check to that third party within 3 business days of receipt is considered to be maintaining custody. Unlike the other cases where the money or securities are returned to the client, third party checks must be forwarded.

8. **D.** Surety bonds are never required under the Investment Advisers Act of 1940, although they may be required under the Uniform Securities Act. The audit must be a surprise. The adviser only informs the client about the client's securities, not everybody else's securities held by the adviser.

Quick Quiz 3.L

1. **A.** Material disciplinary violations must be reported by all investment advisers, regardless of whether they keep custody. The first 2 answers fit the definition of material actions, but not the third. If the suit goes in favor of the client and the adviser is found guilty, disclosure would need to be made. However, there is something that investment advisers who do not maintain custody or receive substantial prepayments avoid having to do. What is that? They do not have to notify their clients about any financial situation that might impair their ability to meet contractual commitments to clients.

Quick Quiz 3.M

1. **B.** Hedge clauses may not be used to disclaim statements that are inherently misleading.

2. **C.** The regulators have not objected to clauses that limit the investment adviser's liability for losses caused by conditions and events beyond its control, such as war, strikes, natural disasters, new government restrictions, market fluctuations, communications disruptions, and so forth. Such provisions are acceptable since they do not attempt to limit or misstate the adviser's fiduciary obligations to its clients. Limiting liability to acts done in bad faith might cause the unsophisticated client to fail to understand that he still has a right to take action, even when the acts are committed in good faith. Fiduciary responsibility cannot be limited by hedge clauses.

Quick Quiz 3.N

1. **C.** Investment advisers never file anything with the SEC unless it relates to Form ADV. Past specific recommendations may be shown as long as they include all recommendations covering at least the prior 12-month period and contain a disclaimer regarding any assurance of future results.

2. **C.** With its principal office in New Jersey, PPA only has to meet the financial and recordkeeping requirements of that state. However, any business done in Connecticut, including advertising, comes under that state's jurisdiction. SEC requirements are bogus because this is not a federal covered adviser and the Administrator of any state in which the IA is registered can pull a surprise visit during business hours.

3. **A.** One of the criteria for using the term *investment counsel* is that the adviser's primary business is providing investment advice. It is always prohibited to make an untrue statement, whether or not the fact is material, and one can never imply government approval of one's abilities.

4. **A.** An investment adviser may never put his own interests before those of customers. The Investment Advisers Act of 1940 does not prohibit employment with a broker-dealer and serving as an investment adviser. Any conflict of interests must be disclosed to the client. An adviser is not prohibited from investing in the same securities transactions as recommended to clients.

5. **B.** It is permissible to post general information about an investment adviser on a public website, which comes under the definition of advertising. Advertising implies that the publisher of the material has no control over who may view it. Thus, recommendations of specific securities, including managed products, are prohibited because it is not possible to determine the suitability of specific investments for unknown viewers. The SEC and NASAA prohibit client testimonials in investment adviser advertising.

Quick Quiz 3.O

1. **C.** A client's contracts, whether written or oral (technically, the Investment Advisers Act of 1940 does not require written contracts), may not be assigned without the client's consent under any circumstances. If the adviser is a partnership, notice must be made to clients of any changes in the membership of the partnership within a reasonable period. It is always permitted to charge a fee based on the average value of assets under management.

2. **B.** The addition of 2 equal partners to a 5-person firm does not constitute a majority change so all that is necessary is notice within a reasonable period of time, not consent. In the case of a corporation, a change in stock ownership is never required to be disclosed unless there is an actual change to the control or management of the adviser and such is not indicated here. Pledging a majority stock interest in an adviser structured as a corporation is considered an assignment and, therefore, requires client consent.

3. **A.** An adviser's fee may not be based on portfolio appreciation or capital gains, except under certain circumstances that are not detailed in the question. Advisory fees may be based on a percentage of assets under management. There should be no question on the exam where "waiving" something will be permitted.

4. **D.** Under the Uniform Securities Act, custody indicates that the adviser has physical possession over its clients' certificates and monies. If there is a rule prohibiting it, no investment adviser registered in that state can act in contravention of that rule. A prohibition against custody in a given state does not prohibit the adviser from holding investment discretion over clients' accounts, provided such discretion is granted under a suitable authorization or power of attorney. Merely examining customers' stock certificates is certainly not the same as holding custody or possession of such certificates. As long as the affiliation is disclosed, there is nothing improper about an IA referring advisory clients to that affiliated BD.

Quick Quiz 3.P

1. **B.** To make cash payments to solicitors, the agreement must:

   - be in writing;
   - provide for disclosure of any affiliations between the adviser and the solicitor (unless the solicitation is being made for impersonal advisory service);
   - provide that no one subject to statutory disqualification be compensated;
   - follow a script approved by the adviser; and
   - provide that, in addition to the adviser's brochure, a solicitor brochure be delivered as well (3rd party).

   Nothing in the rules refers at all to how much of the adviser's time must be spent giving advice. The only time there is a requirement that a substantial portion of the adviser's business be giving investment advice is when using the term *investment counsel*.

2. **B.** The Investment Advisers Act of 1940 and the associated SEC rules do not require the solicitor to register as an investment adviser representative as long as the solicitor's activities are strictly limited to merely referring clients to a registered investment adviser in compliance with SEC rules. However, the majority of state securities regulators define the solicitation or referral of investment advisory clients as an investment advisory activity requiring the registration of the solicitor as an investment adviser or investment adviser representative. But remember to read the question—it only asks about the federal law.

Quick Quiz 3.Q

1. **C.** Section 28(e) provides a safe harbor for those expenses paid with soft dollars that offer a direct research benefit. Rent is not included in the list of acceptable items coming under that safe harbor.

2. **D.** Soft-dollar compensation is when an investment adviser derives an economic benefit from the use of a client's commission dollars. Software of the type mentioned here is allowable under the safe harbor provisions of Section 28(e) of the Securities Exchange Act of 1934. It is true that this is indirect compensation and that this is a discretionary account, but the answer that best matches the question is soft dollar. Many times on the exam, you have to select best of the choices given.

3. **B.** The SEC requires prior written discretionary authorization, whereas The NASAA Model Rule on Unethical Business Practices Of Investment Advisers, Investment Adviser Representatives, and Federal Covered Advisers only requires that the written document be received no later than 10 business days after the first transaction in the account. Discretionary orders must be promptly reviewed, but not before placing the order. Even with the NSMIA, the Administrator has the power to take action against any federal covered adviser operating in the state where there is a belief that fraudulent action has taken place.

4. **B.** Full-service brokerage firms often provide research reports, securities and portfolio analysis, and special reports without specific charges, but are usually compensated by their higher commissions. Nothing in industry rules prevents an adviser from using a full-service broker to effect customer transactions. However, it would be unethical if the adviser were to benefit personally from the direction of the client business.

Quick Quiz 3.R

1. **C.** The USA does not require investment advisers to include in their contracts a list of those states in which they are licensed to do business. The USA does require advisers to include their method of computing fees, a statement prohibiting assignment without client consent, and notification of change in membership of the investment partnership.

2. **F.** An Administrator may, by rule or order, prevent an adviser from taking custody. If an Administrator prevents custody, an adviser cannot overrule the Administrator by notifying the Administrator first.

3. **F.** An adviser may sell securities to clients from its own account provided disclosure is made upon receipt of consent from the client before completion of the trade.

4. **T.** Investment advisers are bound by the regulations that apply to sales activities as well as those that apply to advisory activities.

Unit 2

Investment Vehicle Characteristics

This unit consists of six sessions:

In total there will be 31 questions on this material, representing 24% of the Series 65 exam.

4

Types and Characteristics of Equity Securities Including Methods Used to Determine Their Value

The investment world is divided between owners (represented by stock or equity securities) and lenders (represented by bonds or debt securities).

Investors who buy stock in a company are its owners. Owners receive dividends. Investors who buy bonds in a government or corporation are lenders. Lenders receive interest payments.

The Series 65 exam will include approximately 7 questions on the material presented in this session. ■

When you have completed this session, you should be able to:

■ **compare** and contrast the basic features of common and preferred stock;

■ **evaluate** the methods used to determine the value of equity securities;

■ **explain** how incentive stock options differ from non-qualified ones;

■ **describe** and evaluate the basic features of rights and warrants; and

■ **identify** the unique features of American depositary receipts (ADRs) and the risks of investing in foreign securities.

4. 1   EQUITY SECURITIES

When individual investors become owners of a corporation by purchasing stock in that company, they can participate in the company's prosperity by sharing in earnings through the receipt of dividends and, particularly in the case of common stock, benefit from an increase in the price of the shares.

4. 1. 1   COMMON STOCK

Common stock is equity ownership in a corporation. A company issues stock to raise business capital, and investors who buy the stock are buying a share of ownership in the company. Whatever a business owns (its assets) less its creditors' claims (its liabilities) belongs to the businessowners (its stockholders).

Each share of stock entitles its owner to a portion of the company's earnings and dividends and a proportionate vote in major management decisions. Most corporations are organized in such a way that their stockholders regularly vote for and elect a few individuals to a **board of directors** to oversee company business. By electing a board of directors, stockholders have a say in the company's management but are not involved in the day-to-day details of its operations.

EXAMPLE   If a corporation issues 100 shares of stock, each share represents an identical 1/100—or 1%—ownership position in the company. An investor who owns 10 shares of stock would own 10% of the company; an investor who owns 50 shares of stock would own 50% of the company.

Corporations may issue two types of stock: **common** and **preferred**. When speaking of stocks, people generally mean common stock. **Preferred stock** also represents equity ownership in a corporation but usually does not have the same voting rights or appreciation potential as common stock. Preferred stock normally pays a fixed quarterly dividend and has **priority claims** over common stock; that is, the preferred is paid first if a company goes bankrupt, and common stockholders will never receive a dividend until the preferred shareholders have been paid theirs.

4. 1. 2   BENEFITS OF OWNING COMMON STOCK

4. 1. 2. 1   Growth (Capital Gains)

An increase in the market price of securities is **capital appreciation**. Historically, owning common stock has provided investors with returns in excess of the inflation rate. For this reason, most investors with a long-term investment horizon have included common stock in their portfolios as a hedge against inflation. Of course, it must be mentioned that stock prices can decline, particularly over the short run.

EXAMPLE   An investor buys shares of RST for $60 per share on January 1, 2015. On December 31, 2015, the shares are worth $90, an increase of 50% in the market price.

4. 1. 2. 2   Income

Many corporations pay regular quarterly cash dividends to stockholders. A company's dividends may increase over time as profitability increases. Dividends, which can be a significant source of income for investors, are a major reason many people invest in stocks. Issuers may also pay **stock dividends** in additional shares in the issuing company, or **property dividends**, shares in a subsidiary company, or in product.

EXAMPLE   RST paid a dividend of $2 per share during 2015, which provided the investor with a dividend yield of 3.3% ($2 ÷ $60 = 3.33%) in addition to the price appreciation.

TAKE NOTE   The increase in the price of RST stock in the example above is an **unrealized gain** until the stock is sold; when it is sold, it becomes a **realized gain**. Capital gains are not taxed until they are realized. Under current tax law, most dividends and long-term capital gains are taxed at a rate not in excess of 15%. Taxation will be covered in more detail in Unit 4.

4. 1. 2. 3   Rights of Stockholders

As mentioned earlier, common stockholders have the right to vote for the corporation's board of directors at the corporation's annual meeting. They have the right to sell or give away their shares without permission of the corporation. Common stock is freely transferable to anyone who wants to buy it or receive it as a gift. Without this feature, there would be no stock markets. Common stockholders have a right to limited access to the corporation's books. For the most part, common stockholders have the right to examine the minutes of meetings of the board of directors and the right to examine the list of the stockholders. Usually, this right is not exercised unless the performance of the corporation's management declines seriously. They also have the right to receive an audited set of financial statements of the company's performance each year (annual reports). Common stockholders usually have the preemptive right to maintain their proportionate share of ownership in the corporation. The word *preempt* means to put oneself in front of another.

4. 1. 2. 4   Limited Liability

One of the most important features of equity ownership (common stock or preferred stock) is limited liability. In the event of the bankruptcy of a corporation, when corporate assets are not adequate to meet corporate obligations, the stockholder's personal assets are not at risk. One cannot be forced to sell any personal assets to help pay the debts of the business.

An individual investing $5,000 in the stock (common or preferred) of a corporation that goes bankrupt may lose the entire $5,000 if the company is not salvaged, but will not be forced to pay out any more money to take care of the corporation's debts. That investor is personally at risk only for the amount that was invested. This is different from a business organized as a sole proprietorship or partnership where the owner's personal assets are placed at risk should the business not be able to pay off its obligations. This concept will be discussed later in Unit 4.

4. 1. 2. 5   Liquidity

In almost all cases, shares of common stock are freely transferrable. That means that shareholders do not need the permission of the issuer, or anyone else, in order to sell their stock in the open market. This is especially true in the case of shares traded on the major stock exchanges. One exception is restricted stock (covered in Unit 1, Session 1), where sales are contingent upon meeting the requirements of SEC Rule 144.

4. 1. 3   RISKS OF OWNING COMMON STOCK

Regardless of their expectations, investors have no assurances that they will receive the returns they expect from their investments.

4. 1. 3. 1   Market Risk

The chance that a stock will decline in price is one risk of owning common stock (known as **market risk**). A stock's price fluctuates daily as perceptions of the company's business prospects change and influence the actions of buyers and sellers. Investors have no assurance whatsoever that they will be able to recoup the investment in a stock at any time. The concept of market risk will be dealt with in more detail in Unit 3.

4. 1. 3. 2   Decreased or No Income

A risk of stock ownership is the possibility of dividend income decreasing or ceasing entirely if the company loses money.

4. 1. 3. 3   Low Priority at Dissolution

If a company enters bankruptcy, the holders of its bonds and preferred stock have priority over common stockholders. A company's debt and preferred shares are considered **senior securities**. Common stockholders have **residual rights** to corporate assets upon dissolution.

TAKE NOTE

In owning common equity, the investor stands to lose current income through dividend reduction or suspension, as well as capital loss, should the market price decline. In return, however, the shareholder has limited liability; that is, the liability is limited to the amount invested.

In summation, why would you include common stock in a client's portfolio?

- Potential capital appreciation
- Income from dividends
- Hedge against inflation

In doing so, the client would be incurring the following risks:

- Market
- Business difficulties leading to possible reduction or elimination of the dividend and even bankruptcy leading to loss of principal

QUICK QUIZ 4.A

1. Which of the following represent(s) ownership in a company?

    I.   Corporate bonds
    II. Common stock
    III. Preferred stock
    IV. Mortgage bonds

    A. I and IV
    B. II only
    C. II and III
    D. I, II, III and IV

2. Among the benefits of owning common stock are

    I.   it has historically been a hedge against inflation
    II. voting rights
    III. access, as owners, to information about corporate earnings before the general public
    IV. dividends

    A. I and II
    B. I, II and IV
    C. II and IV
    D. I, II, III and IV

3. A corporation may distribute which of the following as a dividend?

    I.   Cash
    II. Stock
    III. Stock of a subsidiary

    A. I only
    B. I and II
    C. II and III
    D. I, II and III

4. Limited liability regarding ownership in a U.S. corporation means all of the following EXCEPT

   A. investors might lose more than the amount of their investment
   B. investors might lose their investment
   C. creditors of the corporation cannot seek relief from the shareholders
   D. investors are not liable to the full extent of their personal property

5. Common stockholder rights include a

   I. residual claim to assets at dissolution
   II. vote for the amount of stock dividend to be paid
   III. vote in person at the annual meeting of shareholders
   IV. claim against dividends that are in default

   A. I only
   B. I and III
   C. II and III
   D. III and IV

6. All of the following are considered to be risks of owning common stock EXCEPT

   A. market risk
   B. possible decrease in dividend payments
   C. removal of voting rights
   D. low priority of claim at dissolution

Quick Quiz answers can be found at the end of the unit.

4. 1. 4   PREFERRED STOCK

Preferred stock is an equity security because it represents a class of ownership in the issuing corporation. However, it does share some characteristics with a debt security. Just as with debt securities, the rate of return on a preferred stock is fixed rather than subject to variation as with common stock. As a result, its price tends to fluctuate with changes in interest rates rather than with the issuing company's business prospects unless, of course, dramatic changes occur in the company's ability to pay dividends. This concept, known as interest rate or money rate risk, will be covered in greater detail later in the next session covering fixed-income securities.

TAKE NOTE

Unlike common stock, most preferred stock is nonvoting.

TEST TOPIC ALERT

Like common stock, preferred stock represents ownership in a company, but its price reacts to the market more like a bond because with its fixed dividend payment, its price is sensitive to interest rate changes.

4. 1. 4. 1   Benefits of Preferred Stock

Although preferred stock does not typically have the same growth potential as common stock, preferred stockholders have four advantages over common stockholders.

- When the board of directors declares dividends, owners of preferred stock must be paid prior to any payment to common stockholders.

- A preferred stock's fixed dividend is a key feature for income-oriented investors. Normally, a preferred stock is identified by its annual dividend payment stated as a percentage of its **par value**. A preferred stock with a par value of $100 that pays $6 in annual dividends would be known as a **6% preferred**. The dividend of preferred stock with no par value is stated in a dollar amount (e.g., a **$6 no-par preferred).**

- If a corporation goes bankrupt, preferred stockholders have a priority claim over common stockholders on the assets remaining after creditors have been paid.

- Although it is generally regarded as a fixed-income investment, preferred stock, unlike debt securities, usually has no preset date at which it matures and no scheduled redemption date. Preferred stock is thus a perpetual security.

TEST TOPIC ALERT

Because the primary objective met by investing in preferred stock is *income*, when analyzing a specific preferred stock, the most important determination should be the ability of the company to meet its dividend payments.

4. 1. 4. 2   Types of Preferred Stock

There are several different types of preferred stock starting with straight preferred (think of "plain vanilla") and expanding depending on which and how many adjectives we use to describe the security. However, all maintain preference over common stock. Remember, preferred stock is an equity security and, just as with common stock, dividends are paid at the discretion of the Board of Directors. What is special about preferred stock is that no dividend can ever be paid to the common stockholders unless the preferred is satisfied first. Preferred stock may have one or more of the following characteristics.

4. 1. 4. 2. 1   Straight (Noncumulative)

Straight preferred has no special features beyond the stated dividend payment. Missed dividends are not paid to the holder.

4. 1. 4. 2. 2   Cumulative Preferred

Cumulative preferred stock accrues payments due its shareholders in the event dividends are reduced or suspended.

Dividends due cumulative preferred stock accumulate on the company's books until the corporation's board of directors decides to pay them. When the company resumes dividend payments, cumulative preferred stockholders receive current dividends plus the total accumulated dividends—dividends **in arrears**—before any dividends may be distributed to common stockholders.

EXAMPLE   In 2010, RST Corp. had both common stock and cumulative preferred stock outstanding. The common paid a dividend of $1, and the preferred paid a $2 dividend. Because of financial difficulties, the company stopped paying dividends after 2010. Having resolved its problems in 2015, the company resumed dividend payments and paid the cumulative preferred holders an $8 dividend for the arrears in years 2011, 2012, 2013, and 2014 plus the current year's (2015) $2 dividend before paying any dividends to the common stockholders.

TEST TOPIC ALERT   Because of this unique feature, found only with cumulative preferred stock, an investor seeking steady income would find this to be the most suitable of the different types of preferred stock.

4. 1. 4. 2. 3   Callable Preferred

Corporations often issue **callable** (or **redeemable**) **preferred**, which a company can buy back from investors at a stated price after a specified date. The right to call the stock allows the company to replace a relatively high fixed dividend obligation with a lower one when the cost of money has gone down. This is similar to refinancing a mortgage.

When a corporation calls a preferred stock, dividend payments cease on the call date. In return for the call privilege, the corporation may pay a premium exceeding the stock's par value at the call, such as $103 for a $100 par value stock. This can create a problem for your client who purchased callable preferred shares issued at a time when market conditions dictated relatively high dividend rates. If the cost of new money comes down, the company will call in the preferred and the investor will now have to reinvest the proceeds at a lower rate.

Having the call price at a premium over par is one way to compensate for this additional risk (and inconvenience). Another is that the dividend rate on callable preferred stock is generally a bit higher than other preferred stock issued by the corporation.

4. 1. 4. 2. 4   Convertible Preferred

A preferred stock is **convertible** if the owner can exchange the shares for a fixed number of shares of common stock of the issuing corporation.

TAKE NOTE   Because the value of a convertible preferred stock is linked to the value of a common stock, the convertible's preferred price tends to fluctuate in line with the common.

Convertible preferred is generally issued with a lower stated dividend rate than nonconvertible preferred of the same quality because the investor may have the opportunity to convert to common shares and enjoy greater capital gain potential. The concept of a convertible security will be discussed in greater detail later in the next session when we cover convertible bonds.

4. 1. 4. 2. 5   Adjustable-Rate Preferred

Some preferred stocks are issued with adjustable (or variable) dividend rates. Such dividends are usually tied to the rates of other interest rate benchmarks, such as Treasury bills and money market rates, and can be adjusted as often as quarterly. Because the payment adjusts to current interest rates, the price of the stock remains relatively stable.

TEST TOPIC ALERT

For investors looking for income through preferred stocks, this would be their least appropriate choice.

TAKE NOTE

A preferred stock could be cumulative and callable, callable and convertible, or any combination of these adjectives. If none are listed, it is just a straight preferred.

QUICK QUIZ 4.B

1. Which of the following types of preferred stock typically has the highest stated rate of dividend (all other factors being equal)?
   A. Convertible
   B. Straight
   C. Cumulative
   D. Callable

2. An investor who has purchased preferred stock with the goal of receiving steady quarterly income would be most interested in the
   A. seniority of the stock compared to other securities
   B. ability of the company to continue paying the stated dividend
   C. voting power of the shares
   D. parity price of the shares

3. Which of the following types of preferred stock is most influenced by the price of an issuer's common stock?
   A. Cumulative
   B. Straight
   C. Convertible
   D. Callable

4. A company that has issued cumulative preferred stock
   A. pays past and current preferred dividends before paying dividends on common stock
   B. pays the preferred dividend before paying the coupons due on its outstanding bonds
   C. pays the current dividends on the preferred, but not the past dividends on the preferred, before paying a dividend on the common
   D. forces conversion of the preferred that is trading at a discount to par, thereby eliminating the need to pay past-due dividends

4. 1. 4. 3   Risks of Owning Preferred Stock

In summation, why would you include preferred stock in a client's portfolio?

- Fixed income from dividends
- Prior claim ahead of common stock
- Convertible preferred sacrifices income in exchange for potential appreciation

In doing so, the client would be incurring the following risks:

- Market risk—in an economic downturn, fear of an inability to maintain the dividend will cause the price to drop
- Possible loss of purchasing power
- Interest rate (money rate) risk
- Business difficulties leading to possible reduction or elimination of the dividend and even bankruptcy leading to loss of principal

4. 1. 5   FOREIGN INVESTMENTS: AMERICAN DEPOSITARY RECEIPTS (ADRs)

American Depositary Receipts (ADRs), also known as **American Depositary Shares (ADSs)**, facilitate the trading of foreign stocks in U.S. markets because everything is done in English and in U.S. dollars. ADRs are bought and sold (traded) in U.S. dollars, and dividends are paid out in U.S. dollars.

An **ADR** is a negotiable security that represents a receipt for shares of stock in a non-U.S. corporation, usually from to shares. ADRs are bought and sold in the U.S. securities markets like any stock.

4. 1. 5. 1   Rights of ADR Owners

Most of the rights that common stockholders normally hold, such as the right to receive dividends, also apply to ADR owners.

4. 1. 5. 2   Currency Risk

In addition to the normal risks associated with stock ownership, ADR investors are also subject to currency risk. **Currency risk** is the possibility that an investment denominated in one currency (such as the Mexican peso) could decline if the value of that currency declines in its exchange rate with the U.S. dollar. Because ADRs represent shares of stock in companies located in foreign countries, currency exchange rates are an important consideration. There will be more on currency risk in Unit 3.

4. 1. 5. 3   Custodian Bank

Domestic branches of large commercial U.S. banks issue ADRs. A custodian, typically a bank in the issuer's country, holds the shares of foreign stock that the ADRs represent.

The stock must remain on deposit as long as the ADRs are outstanding because the ADRs are the depositary bank's guarantee that it holds the stock.

4. 1. 5. 4   Registered Owner

ADRs are registered on the books of the U.S. banks responsible for them. The individual investors in the ADRs are not considered the stock's registered owners. Because ADRs are registered on the books of U.S. banks, dividends are sent to the custodian banks as registered owners. The banks collect the payments, convert them into U.S. funds for U.S. owners, and withhold any required foreign tax payments.

TAKE NOTE
Although portions of dividends may be withheld to pay local taxes, owners of ADRs can claim a U.S. tax credit for these withholdings.

TEST TOPIC ALERT
The exam will want you to know that ADRs are issued by domestic branches of American banks and that, even though they are traded in U.S. dollars, they still bear currency risk.

4. 1. 6   RISKS OF INVESTING IN FOREIGN MARKETS

Although foreign securities offer investors the potential for substantial gains, they bear a variety of risks that are not present with domestic investments. There are two broad market classifications of foreign markets: emerging and developed.

4. 1. 6. 1   Emerging Markets

Emerging markets are markets in lesser developed countries. They are generally associated with:

- low levels of income, as measured by the **country's gross domestic product (GDP);**
- low levels of equity capitalization;
- questionable market liquidity;
- potential restrictions on currency conversion;
- high volatility;
- prospects for economic growth and development;
- stabilizing political and social institutions;
- high taxes and commission costs for foreign investor;
- restrictions on foreign ownership and on foreign currency conversion; and
- lower regulatory standards resulting in a lack of transparency.

Despite primitive market infrastructures, many emerging markets have rapid growth rates that make their securities attractive to foreign investors whose local markets experience more modest growth.

4. 1. 6. 2   Developed Markets

Developed markets are those associated with countries that have highly developed economies with stable political and social institutions. These are characterized by:

- large levels of equity capitalization;
- low commission rates;
- few, if any, currency conversion restrictions;
- highly liquid markets with many brokerage institutions and market makers;
- many large capitalization securities; and
- well-defined regulatory schemes leading to transparency similar to that enjoyed by those investing in U.S. securities.

In summation, why would you include foreign securities in a client's portfolio?

- You have expanded the potential investment universe leading to greater diversification.
- Foreign securities sometimes outperform domestic ones.
- Foreign securities are usually not highly correlated with domestic ones (correlation is covered in Unit 3) and, as a result, the overall risk of the portfolio is reduced.

In doing so, whether investing in the securities of emerging or developed foreign markets, the investor faces, in addition to the normal risks involved in investing, the following risks not present in domestic investing:

- Country risk
- Exchange controls
- Currency risk
- Withholding taxes and fees

4. 1. 6. 3   Country Risk

Country risk is a composite of all the risks of investing in a particular country. These may include political risks, such as revolutions or military coups, and structural risks, such as confiscatory policies toward profits, capital gains, and dividends. Economic policies, interest rates, and inflation are also elements of risk of investing in emerging countries.

4. 1. 6. 4   Exchange Controls

Foreign investors can also be subject to restrictions on currency conversion or movement.

4. 1. 6. 5   Withholding, Fees, and Taxes

Some foreign countries may withhold a portion of dividends and capital gains for taxes. Some also impose heavy fees and taxes on securities that the investor must bear in addition to generally higher brokerage commissions.

QUICK QUIZ 4.C

1. ADRs are used to facilitate

    A. foreign trading of domestic securities
    B. foreign trading of U.S. government securities
    C. domestic trading of U.S. government securities
    D. domestic trading of foreign securities

2. Which 2 of the following risks would be of greatest concern to the holder of an ADR?

    I.   Currency
    II. Liquidity
    III. Market
    IV. Purchasing power

    A. I and II
    B. I and III
    C. II and IV
    D. III and IV

4. 1. 7   RIGHTS AND WARRANTS

Rights and warrants allow investors to buy additional shares of stock under defined circumstances.

4. 1. 7. 1   Rights

Preemptive rights entitle existing common stockholders to maintain their proportionate ownership shares in a company by buying newly issued shares before the company offers them to the general public.

A **rights offering** allows these stockholders to purchase common stock below the current market price. The rights are valued separately from the stock and trade in the secondary market during the **subscription period**.

A stockholder who receives rights may:

■ **exercise the rights** to buy stock by sending the rights certificates and payment for the required amount to the rights agent;

■ **sell the rights** and profit from their market value (rights certificates are negotiable securities); or

■ **let the rights expire** and lose their value.

4. 1. 7. 2   Warrants

A **warrant** is a certificate granting its owner the right to purchase securities from the issuer at a specified price, normally higher than the current market price. Unlike a right, a warrant is usually a long-term instrument that gives the investor the option of buying shares at a later date at the exercise price.

4. 1. 7. 2. 1   Origination of Warrants

Warrants are usually offered to the public as sweeteners in connection with other securities, such as debentures or preferred stock, to make those securities more attractive. Such offerings are often bundled as **units**.

TEST TOPIC ALERT

Because the value of rights and warrants is dependent upon the value of the underlying stock into which the right or warrant may be exchanged, these are considered derivatives (more about them coming up later).

4. 1. 8   EMPLOYEE STOCK OPTIONS

Employee stock options give an employee the right to purchase a specified number of shares of the common stock of his employer at a stated price over a stated time period. Unlike qualified retirement plans (discussed in Unit 4, there are no non-discrimination requirements for these plans. For publicly traded stock, the "strike" price (also called the grant or exercise price) is usually the market price of the stock at the time the option is granted. In most cases, there is a minimum time the employee must remain with the company in order to be able to use the option (the vesting period). The hope of the employee is that the market price of the employer's stock will increase in value. Then, the employee will be able to purchase the stock by exercising the option (purchasing the stock) at the lower strike price and then sell the stock at the current market price. There are two principal kinds of stock option programs, each with their own rules and tax consequences: nonqualified stock options (NSOs) and incentive stock options (ISOs). Don't confuse these with publicly traded puts and calls described later in another session of this unit—these are available only to employees of the issuing company.

4. 1. 8. 1   Nonqualified Stock Options

These are the most common of the two varieties of employee stock options. NSOs are basically treated as a form of compensation. When NSOs are exercised, the difference between the current market price at the time of exercise and the strike price is reported as wages on the tax returns of the employer and the employee. Therefore, instead of capital gains treatment, the employee is taxed as ordinary income while the company receives a tax deduction as salary expense for the difference between the current market price and the strike price.

T A K E   N O T E

Because the spread between the market price and the strike price is considered salary, it is subject to payroll taxes as well as income tax.

4. 1. 8. 2   Incentive Stock Options

An ISO is granted as part of a formal plan adopted by the company's board of directors and approved by the shareholders. There are generally no tax consequences to the employer, but, if done properly, they can be more advantageous than NSOs to the employee. As mentioned above, the employee's profits from NSOs are taxed as ordinary income. However, as long as stock purchased through exercise of an ISO is held at least two years after the date of grant and one year after the date of exercise, any profits are reported as long-term capital gains. If these time limits are broached, the ISO is taxed like an NSO. There is one other time stipulation—there is a maximum 10-year limit for exercise.

But, there is a catch. When an ISO is exercised, the difference between the market value at time of purchase and the strike price is a preference item used in calculating the Alternative Minimum Tax (AMT) (covered in Unit 4).

Incentive Stock Options (ISOs)
No income recognized when option is granted
No tax due when option is exercised
Tax is due when stock is sold ■ Gain is capital if held at least one year and sold at least two years after grant ■ Otherwise—ordinary income
Difference between option price and the FMV on date of exercise is an add back for AMT purposes

E X A M P L E

Jeff's employer grants him an incentive stock option (ISO) on January 1, 2012, with an exercise (strike) price of $25 per share. Jeff exercises the option on January 1, 2013, when the market price of the stock is $40 per share. Because this is an ISO and the stock has not yet been sold, there is no "salary" income or capital gains taxation. But, there is a $15 per share adjustment for purposes of computing the AMT.

Jeff sells the stock two years later for $60 per share. Now that the sale has been recognized and Jeff has followed the required holding periods, the $35 per share profit is taxed as long-term capital gain.

1. Which of the following statements regarding warrants is TRUE?

   A. Warrants are only offered to current shareholders.
   B. Warrants have longer terms than rights.
   C. Warrants do not trade in the secondary market.
   D. At the time of issuance, the exercise price of a warrant is typically below the market value of the underlying stock.

2. Which of the following statements regarding rights is TRUE?

   A. Common stockholders would not generally receive preemptive rights
   B. Preferred stockholders would not generally receive preemptive rights
   C. Both common and preferred stockholders would generally receive preemptive rights
   D. Neither common nor preferred stockholders would generally receive preemptive rights

3. On July 15, 2013, an employee of KAPCO Manufacturing Company receives an incentive stock option to purchase 100 shares of KAPCO common stock at $21 per share when the current market price is $19. She exercises the option on June 30, 2014 and sells her shares on August 4, 2015 at $30 per share. For tax purposes, she has a

   A. $900 short-term capital gain
   B. $1,100 short-term capital gain
   C. $900 long-term capital gain
   D. $1,100 long-term capital gain

4.1.9   METHODS USED TO DETERMINE THE VALUE OF EQUITY SECURITIES—FUNDAMENTAL ANALYSIS

The two approaches most commonly used to select investments are fundamental and technical analysis. Both fundamental and technical analysts attempt to forecast prices or values of securities and markets.

Fundamental analysts evaluate broad-based economic trends, current business conditions within an industry, and the quality of a particular corporation's business, finances, and management. **Technical analysts** attempt to predict the direction of prices on the basis of charts reflecting price and trading volume patterns of specific securities without regard to the issuer's profitability. We will limit our discussion to fundamental analysis because that is the focus of the exam.

Fundamental analysis is the study of the business prospects of an individual company within the context of its industry and the overall economy. They do this by examining the company in detail, including the financial statements and company management. We could compare this to an individual receiving a full physical examination which, in addition to all kinds of tests, would include a detailed family medical history. With a company, the financial statement analysis is like the blood tests, x-rays, stress test, and so forth, and the evaluation of the company's management is like the medical history. One of the ways these analysts attempt to determine the value of common stock is through the use of dividend models.

4. 1. 9. 1   Dividend Models

Some analysts believe that the value of a stock can be determined based upon current or anticipated dividends. The models work best with a company with dividends that are paid with regularity, so it is more popular with larger, well-established organizations than smaller companies with irregular dividend distributions. Two models used are the dividend discount model and the dividend growth model.

4. 1. 9. 1. 1   Dividend Discount Model

This model states that the value of a stock should be equal to the present value of all future dividends. There are several methods to use, such as assuming constant or variable dividends, but the concept is still the same. We take the investor's expected future returns (the dividends), and then discount that amount to compute the present value. It is not necessary to know the formula for the exam; however, it can be calculated by dividing the annual dividend by the expected return, sometimes referred to as the required rate of return. For example, if a stock pays a $1.20 dividend and the required rate of return in the marketplace is 6%, the stock should be worth $20 (1.20/.06).

This tool may also be used to value preferred stock. Let's take a look at the following example:

EXAMPLE   If you have a $100 par, 6% preferred stock and the required rate of return is 8%, what should the current market price of the stock be? You might encounter a question similar to this on the exam and you solve it by dividing the $6 dividend (6% of the $100 par) by the 8% required rate of return: $6.00/.08 = $75. In other words, if this preferred stock is selling for $75 per share, the $6 annual dividend will produce an 8% return on your investment.

4. 1. 9. 1. 2   Dividend Growth Model

This model assumes that the amount of the annual dividend will grow at a constant rate. Since projections of future growth can be hazy, this model is best used in conjunction with other forecasting tools. It is not necessary to know the formula for the exam; however, it can be calculated by taking the current dividend, multiplying it by 1+ the dividend growth, and then dividing it by the remainder of the required rate of return less the expected growth rate. For example, if a stock pays a $1.20 dividend that is expected to grow at a 3% rate each year with a required rate of return of 6%, the stock should be worth $41.20 (1.236/.03). This is significantly higher than a stock with dividends that are expected to remain constant.

TEST TOPIC ALERT   If you are asked on the exam, "Which model forecasts a higher stock price?" it should be common sense the answer that factors in "growth" is the correct answer. Remember, you will never have to do this computation on the test.

TAKE NOTE

There are other fundamental tools used to value equity securities and we will cover them in Unit 3 when we discuss financial statement analysis and the business cycle.

QUICK QUIZ 4.E

1. Among the popular methods of valuing equity securities is the dividend growth model. One could expect to see an analyst using this to value any of these EXCEPT

   A. common stock
   B. ADRs represent common stock in a foreign company
   C. preferred stock
   D. none of these are exceptions

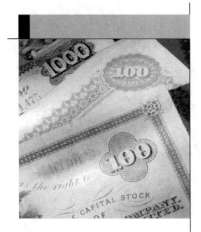

5

Types and Characteristics of Fixed Income (Debt) Securities and Methods Used to Determine Their Value

I n addition to raising capital through the issuance of equity securities (stock), many corporations fund their business efforts through borrowing by issuing debt securities. Long-term borrowing is usually in the form of bonds and debentures, while the money market is used for short-term needs. Governmental bodies can only issue debt securities (you cannot buy stock in the U.S. Treasury or your state).

The Series 65 exam will include eight questions on the material presented in this session.

When you have completed this session, you should be able to:

- **recognize** the unique features of U.S. Government and Agency issues;

- **differentiate** between secured and unsecured corporate debt;

- **compute** the tax-equivalent yield of a municipal bond;

- **describe** the advantages and disadvantages of investing in foreign bonds;

- **compute** the parity price of a convertible bond;

- **compare** current yield, yield to maturity and yield to call;

- **explain** how TIPS bonds work;

- **evaluate** the effect of a bond's duration on its market price; and

- **list** the components of a discounted cash flow computation.

5. 1   FIXED INCOME (DEBT SECURITIES)

Debt capital represents money loaned to an issuer by investors purchasing that issuer's bonds. A **bond** represents the issuer's indebtedness. There is, in essence, a contract between the borrower (the issuer) and the lender (the investor). The terms of the loan are expressed in a document known as the bond's **indenture**. The indenture, sometimes also referred to as the deed of trust, states the issuer's obligation to pay back a specific amount of money on a specific date. The indenture also states the issuer's obligation to pay the investor a specific rate of interest for the use of the funds as well as any collateral pledged as security for the loan and all other pertinent details. An investor purchasing a bond is lending the issuer money for a set period of time at a fixed annual interest rate.

It is important to understand that debt capital refers to **long-term debt** financing. Long-term debt is money borrowed for a minimum of five years, although more frequently the length of time is 20–30 years.

There are three major issuers of debt securities. The largest issuer of debt securities is the U.S. government. Corporations issue bonds to finance their operations and substantial sums are also borrowed by state governments and those political entities that are subdivisions of a state, such as cities, counties, towns, and so forth. These issues from state and local political entities are called **municipal bonds**. Whenever the word "government" is used in conjunction with a security on the exam, it means the federal government. Whenever the phrase "municipal security" is used on the exam, it is referring to a security issued by a state or other municipality.

Let us begin this adventure by explaining the different types of bonds and their issuers.

5. 1. 1   U.S. GOVERNMENT SECURITIES

U.S. Government bonds are the safest of all. There are two primary types of backing; direct government backing or guarantee, as in the case of Treasury issues, and the moral guarantee as in the case of federal agencies.

Although most government issues trade in what is known as the capital market—that is, the market for long-term securities, stocks, and bonds—there are several issues that trade in the money market. The money market is where short-term instruments, those that mature in one year or less, are traded. The money market will be discussed in the next session. No discussion of Treasury issues would be possible, however, without describing the widely held bellwether of the money market known as U.S. Treasury bills.

5. 1. 1. 1   U.S. Treasury Bills

Treasury bills are direct short-term debt obligations of the U.S. government. They are issued every week by using a competitive bidding process. Each week, T-bills, as they are known, with maturities of 4 weeks, 13 weeks, 26 weeks, are issued and once per month, 52 week bills are issued.

Treasury bills pay no interest; they are issued at a discount from their par value. An investor might purchase a $10,000, 26-week T-bill at a price of $9,800. No interest would be received, but, at maturity, the Treasury would send the investor a check for $10,000. The difference between the $9,800 paid and the $10,000 received would be considered interest income even though a separate interest check was never received.

Key points to remember regarding T-bills include: (1) Treasury bills are the only Treasury security issued at a discount; (2) Treasury bills are the only Treasury security issued without a stated interest rate; (3) Treasury bills are highly liquid; and (4) 13-week (also referred to as 90-day) Treasury bills are used in market analysis as the stereotypical "risk-free" investment.

5. 1. 1. 2   U.S. Treasury Notes

U.S. Treasury notes are direct debt obligations of the U.S. Treasury with the following characteristics.

- They pay semiannual interest as a percentage of the stated par value.
- They have intermediate maturities (2, 3, 5, 7, and 10 years).
- They mature at par value.

5. 1. 1. 3   U.S. Treasury Bonds

U.S. Treasury bonds are direct debt obligations of the U.S. Treasury with the following characteristics.

- They pay semiannual interest as a percentage of the stated par value.
- They have long-term maturities, generally 10–30 years.
- Older 30-year bonds are usually callable at par beginning 25 years after issue. However, the last callable 30-year bond was issued in November 1984.
- They mature at par value.

When doing any calculations relating to bonds on the exam, the par or face value will always be $1,000. This is true even though the above three Treasury issues are available in denominations as low as $100.

5. 1. 1. 4   Treasury Inflation Protection Securities (TIPS)

A special type of Treasury issue, **Treasury Inflation Protection Securities (TIPS)**, helps protect investors against purchasing power risk. These notes are issued with a fixed interest rate, but the principal amount is adjusted semiannually by an amount equal to the change in the Consumer Price Index (CPI), the standard measurement of inflation. They are issued with maturities of 5, 10, and 30 years.

The interest payment the investor receives every six months is equal to the fixed interest rate times the newly adjusted principal. During times of inflation, the interest payments increase, while during times of deflation, the interest payments fall. These notes are sold at lower interest rates than conventional fixed-rate Treasury notes because of their adjustable nature.

Like other Treasury notes, TIPS are exempt from state and local income taxes on the interest income generated, but are subject to federal taxation. However, in any year when the principal is adjusted for inflation, that increase is considered reportable income for that year even though the increase will not be received until the note matures.

EXAMPLE

If you have a TIPS bond with a 3% coupon and the annual inflation rate is 4% for the next two years, here is what happens:

Each six months, you will receive 1.5% (half of the annual 3% coupon) of the principal value as adjusted for the inflation rate. If the inflation rate is 4% per year, that is 2% each six months. So, after the first semiannual period, the principal value of the bond is now $1,020 ($1,000 + 2% of $1,000, or 102% × $1,000). Therefore, the first interest check will be 1.5% × $1,020, or $15.30. Six months later, the adjusted principal value is $1,040.40 (102% × $1,020), so that interest check will be for $15.61 ($1,040.40 × 1.5%). As we continue into the next year, the principal will increase to $1,061.21 ($1,040.40 × 102%) and the interest check will be for $15.92. Since we're only looking at two years, the ending principal value will be $1,082.43 with the final interest check of $16.24. As you can see, both the income from the TIPS and its principal value are increasing at a compounded rate based upon inflation.

We know that some of you may be mathematically challenged so here is a shortcut that will always work. The key to the increased principal value of the TIPS is that the interest is compounding. But, you don't have to do that. In this example, the inflation rate is 4%. Using just simple interest would mean that the principal would increase by $40 (4% of $1,000) per year. After two years, that would be $80 or a new principal amount of $1,080. However, we know that compounding will give us more so we choose the first number given in the answers that is above $1,080. The same "trick" can be used to determine the final interest payment. We take 1.5% of $1,080 ($16.20) and look for an answer choice that is slightly higher.

TEST TOPIC ALERT

The Series 65 exam may ask questions similar to the following.

1. A customer wishes to buy a security providing periodic interest payments, safety of principal, and protection from purchasing power risk. The customer should purchase

    A. TIPS
    B. TIGRS
    C. CMOs
    D. STRIPS

    Answer: A. TIPS offer inflation protection and safety of principal because they are backed by the U.S. government.

2. A client has a TIPS with a coupon rate of 4.5%. The inflation rate has been 7% for the last year. What is the inflation-adjusted return?

    A. –2.5%
    B. 4.5%
    C. 7.0%
    D. 11.5%

Answer: B. Treasury Inflation Protection Securities (TIPS) adjust the principal value every 6 months to account for the inflation rate. Therefore, the real rate of return will always be the coupon.

5. 1. 1. 5   U.S. Federal Agency Securities

U.S. federal agency securities are issued by U.S. government agencies that have been authorized by Congress to issue debt securities to help meet their financial needs. Although the securities do not have direct Treasury backing, they are considered moral obligations of the U.S. government. Most of the agency bonds are described by their titles.

5. 1. 1. 5. 1   Federal National Mortgage Association

The Federal National Mortgage Association (Fannie Mae) was a government-owned corporation that was converted into a privately owned corporation in 1968. The common stock of the private corporation was traded on the New York Stock Exchange but, after the economic crisis of 2008, the stock now trades on the OTCBB (Over-The-Counter Bulletin Board). Fannie Mae purchases and sells real estate mortgages—primarily those insured by the Federal Housing Administration (FHA) or guaranteed by the Veterans Administration (VA). Fannie Mae issues mortgage-backed bonds that can be purchased by individual investors. All Fannie Mae securities are considered to be quite safe. They are issued at par and pay semiannual interest. Like the other federal issues, they come out in book entry form.

5. 1. 1. 5. 2   Government National Mortgage Association

In the late 1960s, when the Federal National Mortgage Association was split into two corporations, one privately owned, the other wholly owned by the federal government, the privately owned corporation retained the original name. The new federally owned corporation became known as the Government National Mortgage Association (Ginnie Mae). Ginnie Maes are known as modified pass-through certificates. They represent an interest in pools of FHA-insured mortgages or VA or Farmers Home Administration-guaranteed mortgages. The term *pass-through* is used because, as the homeowners make their monthly mortgage payments, those payments are collected in the pool and the shares passes through to the investor. This payment received by the investor differs from most other securities in two respects.

First, payments are received monthly, because underlying the security is a pool of home mortgages, which are paid for monthly. Second, each monthly payment the investor receives consists partly of interest and partly of principal. Because payments on home mortgages consist of principal and some interest and, because that money goes into the pool for all the investors, as it is paid out monthly, some of each monthly payment to the investor represents principal, and the balance of each payment represents interest. Ginnie Maes carry a minimum denomination of $25,000 and, unlike the other agencies are backed by the full faith and credit of the federal government. The interest on both the Fannie Maes and Ginnie Maes is subject to state and local taxation and, of course, federal income tax as well. Ginnie Mae investors receive monthly, not semiannual, payments.

5. 1. 1. 5. 3 Tennessee Valley Authority (TVA)

On May 18, 1933, Congress passed the TVA Act. The Tennessee Valley Authority is the nation's largest public power provider and a corporation of the U.S. government. TVA bonds are not backed by the U.S. government. Instead, they're backed by the revenues generated by the agencies' projects. Even though the U.S. Treasury does not officially guarantee the debt of TVA, as the Government Accountability Office puts it, credit-rating agencies perceive that there is an "implicit government guarantee of TVA bonds." If push came to shove, it's a good bet that Uncle Sam would make that guarantee explicit.

TVA issues a variety of debt securities. TVA Discount Notes have maturities of less than one year. TVA may issue long-term bonds with final maturities of up to 50 years. Just as most other agency issues that are not backed by mortgages, interest on TVA securities is exempt from state and local income tax and subject to federal income tax.

QUICK QUIZ 5.A

1. All of the following debt instruments pay interest semiannually EXCEPT

   A. Ginnie Mae pass-through certificates
   B. U.S. Treasury notes
   C. U.S. Treasury bonds
   D. TIPS

Quick Quiz answers can be found at the end of the unit.

5. 1. 2 CORPORATE BONDS

Corporate debt securities, like any other loan, may be either secured or unsecured. **Secured debt securities** are backed by various kinds of assets of the issuing corporation, whereas **unsecured debt securities** are backed only by the reputation, credit record, and financial stability of the corporation.

5. 1. 2. 1 Mortgage Bonds

Just as the owner of a home pledges a real asset (the home and land) as collateral for the mortgage, a corporation will borrow money backed by real estate and physical assets of the corporation. Just as a home ordinarily would have a market value greater than the principal amount of its mortgage, the value of the real assets pledged by the corporation will be in excess of the amount borrowed under that bond issue. If the corporation develops financial problems and is unable to pay the interest on the bonds, those real assets pledged as collateral are generally sold to pay off the mortgage bondholders.

The principle is no different from having a mortgage on a home. Does the lender of a home mortgage feel his loan to a buyer is secure? If the buyer couldn't pay, could he sell the home for more than the mortgage? Probably so. A purchaser of a mortgage bond is in the same position of safety. However, as we have seen recently, there may be a situation where foreclosing on the property results in a sale below the outstanding mortgage balance. In that case, the mortgage holder becomes a general creditor for the unsatisfied balance.

5. 1. 2. 2   Equipment Trust Certificate

Corporations, particularly railroads and airline companies, finance the acquisition of their rolling stock, locomotives, or airplanes by issuing an equipment trust certificate. The company makes a down payment, usually 20% of the cost of the rolling stock, and finances the balance over the course of time, for example, 15 years. Because the equipment does wear out, the railroad will pay off a portion of the loan on an annual basis. At no time, theoretically, is the value of the assets (the rolling stock, locomotives, or planes) worth less than the amount of the principal remaining on the loan. When the company has finished paying off the loan, it receives clear title to its equipment from the trustee. If the company does not make the payments, the lender repossesses the collateral and sells it for his benefit.

5. 1. 2. 3   Collateral Trust Bonds

Sometimes a corporation wants to borrow money and has neither real estate (for a mortgage) nor equipment (for an equipment trust) to use as collateral. Instead, it deposits securities it owns into a trust to serve as collateral for the lenders. The securities it deposits can be securities in that corporation or any other securities as long as the securities are marketable, that is, readily liquidated. Obviously, the better the quality of the securities deposited as collateral, the better the quality and rating of the bond.

5. 1. 2. 4   Debenture

A **debenture** is a debt obligation of the corporation backed only by its word and general creditworthiness. Debentures are written promises of the corporation to pay the principal at its due date and interest on a regular basis. Although this promise is as binding as a promise for a mortgage bond, debentures are not secured by any pledge of property. They are sold on the general credit of the company; their security depends on the assets and earnings of the corporation. Although debentures are unsecured, there are issuers whose credit standing is so good that their debentures are safer than mortgage bonds of less creditworthy companies.

5. 1. 2. 5   Guaranteed Bonds

A **guaranteed bond** is a bond that is guaranteed as to payment of interest, or both principal and interest, by a corporate entity other than the issuer. The value of the guarantee is only as good as the strength of the company making that guarantee. Guaranteed bonds were particularly popular in the railroad industry in which a major railroad seeking to lease trackage rights from a short line would guarantee that smaller company's debt. A more recent example is the ExxonMobil Corporation guaranteeing the debt issues of the Exxon Pipeline Company.

5. 1. 2. 6   Senior

The word *senior* is used to describe the relative priority of claim of a security. Every preferred stock has a senior claim to common stock. Every debt security has senior claim to preferred stock. Secured bonds have a senior claim to unsecured debt, such as debentures. The term *senior securities* means bonds and preferred stock, because they have a claim senior to common stock. If an exam question described a corporation as having issued senior bonds, the answer would have to state that there were mortgage bonds and/or collateral trust bonds and/or equipment trust certificates issued by that corporation with prior claim ahead of unsecured creditors.

5. 1. 2. 7   Subordinated

The term *subordinated* means "belonging to a lower or inferior class or rank; secondary." It is usually describing a debenture. A subordinated debenture has a claim that is behind (junior to) that of any other creditor. However, no matter how subordinated the debenture, it is still senior to any stockholder.

TEST TOPIC ALERT

When examining the capital structure of a corporation, it is important to know the liquidation priority:

■ Secured creditors, (e.g., mortgage bonds, equipment trust certificates, collateral trust bonds)

■ Unsecured creditors, (e.g., general creditors including debenture holders)

■ Subordinated debt holders

■ Preferred stockholders

■ Common stockholders

However, the exam may want you to know about the priority of items that are not securities. Even though they are not legally considered secured assets, highest priority is given to wages (up to about $12,000 earned in the 180 days prior to the employer's declaration of bankruptcy) followed by taxes.

Features of Various Securities Issues

	Common Stock	Preferred Stock	Bonds
Ownership and control of the firm	Belongs to common stockholders through voting rights and residual claim to income	Limited rights, may include a participation feature	Limited rights under default in interest payments
Obligation to provide return	None	Must receive before common stockholder	Contractual obligation
Claim to assets in bankruptcy	Lowest claim of any security holder	Bondholders and creditors must be satisfied first	Highest claim
Risk-return trade-off	Higher risk, higher return	Moderate risk, moderate return (dollar amount of dividend is known before stock purchase)	Low risk, moderate return
Tax status of payment to recipient	Taxable as dividend in most cases	Taxable as dividend in most cases	Taxable as ordinary income in most cases

5. 1. 3 MUNICIPAL BONDS

The record of safety of principal of municipal bonds is second only to that of government issues. There are two basic types of municipal bonds.

5. 1. 3. 1 General Obligation Bonds (GOs)

General obligation bonds are backed by a pledge of the issuer's full faith and credit for prompt payment of principal and interest. Most city, county, and school district bonds have the further distinction of being secured by a pledge of unlimited ad valorem (property) taxes to be levied against all taxable property. Because GOs are geared to tax resources, they are normally analyzed in terms of the size of the resources being taxed. They are generally very safe.

5. 1. 3. 2 Revenue Bond

Revenue bonds are payable from the earnings of a revenue-producing enterprise, such as a water, sewer, electric or gas system, toll bridge, airport, college dormitory, or other income-producing facility.

Authorities and agencies are created by states or their subdivisions to perform specific functions, such as the operation of water, sewer, or electric systems, bridges, tunnels, or highways and in some states, to construct schools or public facilities. In some cases, the authority has the right to levy fees and charges for its services. In other cases, it receives lease rentals, which may be payable from specific revenues or may be general obligations of the lessee. They are usually analyzed in terms of their earnings, historical or potential, compared with bond requirements. The yield, generally, is higher for this type of bond than for a GO (taxes are more secure than revenues), although many have built up a good record over a long period of time and are sometimes rated higher than GOs.

QUICK QUIZ 5.B

1. In the event of a company's insolvency, which of the following has first claim on assets?

    A. Bondholders.
    B. Preferred stockholders.
    C. Common stockholders.
    D. Members of the board of directors.

2. Corporate bonds are considered safer than common stock issued by the same company because

    A. the par value of bonds is generally higher than that of stock
    B. bonds and similar fixed-rate securities are guaranteed by SIPC
    C. bonds place the issuer under an obligation but stock does not
    D. if there is a shortage of cash, dividends are paid before interest

5. 1. 4   RATINGS

The purchase of a debt security is only as safe as who the borrower is and what is received for collateral. Because safety of the bond will frequently be a very important consideration for clients, consult the rating services. The two primary rating organizations for debt securities are Standard & Poor's and Moody's. Both organizations have highly qualified personnel who analyze all the details of the debt issue and arrive at a letter rating indicating their opinion of the debt's quality (safety). The following chart should give you all the information you need for the exam.

Standard & Poor's Bond Ratings		Moody's Ratings	
AAA	Bonds of highest quality	Aaa	Bonds of highest quality
AA	High-quality debt obligations	Aa	Bonds of high quality
A	Bonds that have a strong capacity to pay interest and principal but may be susceptible to adverse effects	A	Bonds whose security of principal and interest is considered adequate but may be impaired in the future
BBB	Bonds that have an adequate capacity to pay interest and principal but are more vulnerable to adverse economic conditions or changing circumstances	Baa	Bonds of medium grade that are neither highly protected nor poorly secured
BB	Bonds of lower medium grade with few desirable investment characteristics	Ba	Bonds of speculative quality whose future cannot be considered well assured
B	Primarily speculative bonds with great uncertainties and major risk if exposed to adverse conditions	B	Bonds that lack characteristics of a desirable investment
CCC	Bonds in poor standing that may be defaulted	Caa	Bonds in poor standing that may be defaulted
C	Income bonds on which no interest is being paid	Ca	Speculative bonds that are often in default
D	Bonds in default	C	Bonds with little probability of any investment value (lowest rating)

Note:
Plus (+) and minus (−) are used to show relative strength within a rating category.

Note:
For ratings Aa through B, 1 indicates the high, 2 indicates the middle, and 3 indicates the low end of the rating class.

5. 1. 4. 1   Investment-Grade Debt

In the industry, bonds rated in the top four categories (BBB or Baa and higher) are referred to as investment grade. Investment-grade bonds are generally the only quality eligible for purchase by the institutions (e.g., banks or insurance companies) and by fiduciaries and therefore have greater liquidity than lower grade instruments.

Some bonds are not rated. There are two major reasons a debt security is not rated.

■ The issuer does not want to pay the cost of receiving the rating.

■ The issuer does not have a sufficient credit history to enable the rater to make a fair judgment.

5. 1. 4. 2   High-Yield Bonds

Lower-grade bonds, known in the industry as junk bonds, are now more commonly called high-yield bonds. Because of their lower ratings (BB or Ba or lower) and additional risk of default, high-yield bonds may be subject to substantial price erosion during slow economic times or when a bond issuer's creditworthiness is questioned. Their volatility is usually substantially higher than investment-grade bonds, but they may be suitable for sophisticated investors seeking higher returns and possible capital appreciation from speculative fixed-income investments.

The cost of money is determined by supply and demand and inflation expectations. The most popular measurement of this supply and demand is the prime rate. This is the rate charged by major banks to their most creditworthy customers and is a leading indicator of money rates. In order for the lender to enjoy a real rate of return, nominal interest rates must be above the inflation rate.

There is a critical relationship in all investments known as the risk-reward relationship. The more risk an investor takes, the greater must be his reward. When a bank is loaning money to a major corporation, such as AT&T or IBM, it takes little risk, and therefore it is willing to rent out the money at the lowest possible rates given the supply and demand situation at that time. The less creditworthy the borrower, the more risk to the lender, so the greater reward the lender must receive to compensate for that risk. That is why lower-rated bonds carry higher rates of return.

To make its creditworthiness a little more attractive, an issuer can pledge collateral. It is important to understand that when the raters evaluate a bond they look at all the factors, including collateral. A mortgage bond is not necessarily safer than any debenture.

5. 1. 4. 3   Yield Spread

It should be obvious that the greater the risk, the higher the yield on the bond. Many analysts compare the difference between yields on bonds with the same maturity, but different quality (rating) to get a sense of the market sentiment. One common measurement is the difference in yields between Treasuries and corporate bonds. This difference is called the yield spread and tends to widen when economic conditions sour and narrow when they get better.

Yield spread can also be used between issues of the same issuer. For example, one of the most popular measurements of attitudes regarding future economic conditions is the yield spread between the 2-year Treasury note and the 10-year Treasury bond. When investors are feeling optimistic about the economy, the yield spread narrows; when pessimistic, the yield spread widens.

5. 1. 5   FOREIGN BONDS

Many investors choose to diversify their portfolios by investing in bonds issued by sovereign foreign governments. Some, such as the gilts (a gilt is a UK liability issued by the British Treasury and listed on the London Stock Exchange), are extremely safe. Others, especially those issued by countries with a less established financial structure, can be very risky and may even carry a rating equivalent to a junk bond. In addition, it is also possible to invest in corporate debt securities issued by foreign business entities. Once again, there is a great variation in risk. The advantages of investing in foreign bonds include:

- Potentially higher returns

- Diversification
- Hedging against a drop in value of the U.S. dollar

Risks would include those found with all debt securities plus:
- Currency risk (if the foreign currency falls in value against the dollar)
- Potentially higher risk of default
- Generally less liquidity
- Generally higher trading costs

In a later session, we will discuss how most investors use pooled investment vehicles, such as mutual funds, to invest in foreign debt securities.

5. 1. 5. 1   Eurobonds and Eurodollar Bonds

A **eurobond** is any long-term debt instrument issued and sold outside the country of the currency in which it is denominated. A U.S. dollar-denominated eurobond, or Eurodollar bond, is a bond issued and sold outside the United States, but for which the principal and interest are stated and paid in U.S. dollars. Foreign corporations, foreign governments, domestic corporations, and domestic governments (including municipalities) can issue Eurodollar bonds. The U.S. government does not issue Eurodollar bonds. These bonds are not limited to European issuers; that's just where they originated. For example, if an Indian bank held dollar-denominated bonds issued by a Korean company, the term *Eurodollar bond* would still apply.

TEST TOPIC ALERT

Test questions sometimes ask you to contrast eurobonds and Eurodollar bonds. The name of the instrument tells you how principal and interest is paid. Eurodollar bonds pay in U.S. dollars; eurobonds pay in foreign currency. Note that these instruments must be issued outside of the United States.

TEST TOPIC ALERT

What is a Yankee bond? There are a number of cute names given to bonds in an attempt to signify where they are issued, in what currency they are denominated, and by whom they are issued. The Yankee bond is a first cousin to the Eurodollar bond discussed above.

Just as a Eurodollar bond is a U.S. dollar-denominated bond issued by a non-U.S. entity outside the United States, a Yankee bond is a U.S. dollar-denominated bond issued by a non-U.S. entity in the U.S. market. Another example of this is the Maple bond, a Canadian dollar-denominated bond issued by a non-Canadian entity in the Canadian market. Can you guess what a Matilda bond is? (Clue—it takes its name from a song that had "waltzing" in the title.) The answer will be found later in this course.

✓

TAKE NOTE

If you purchase a bond issued in a foreign currency, you will receive your fixed rate of interest in that currency. However, when converting to U.S. dollars, you will be subject to currency risk. The same is true at maturity. For example, if you purchase £100,000 of UK gilts (the term given to their government bonds) with a 4% coupon, you would always receive £4,000 per year in interest. At the exchange rate in effect when this is being written (£1 = $1.59), the bonds would cost you $159,000 and you would be receiving the equivalent of $6,360 in interest. At maturity you would receive £100,000, but if the value of the pound had fallen, say to $1.49, then the value of the matured bonds would only be $149,000. The same would be true about your interest payments if, during the holding period, the pound changed in value. Remember, currency values can fluctuate up or down; that is the nature of currency risk.

The primary reason for issuing these bonds is that they are free from the requirement to register with the SEC resulting in lower issuance costs. However, because the liquidity is not as great as with domestic issues and because the political and country risks tend to be higher, yields are generally higher.

TEST TOPIC ALERT

Three advantages of Eurodollar bonds to investors are:

■ because they are U.S.-dollar denominated, they bear no currency risk to U.S. investors;

■ they are rated by U.S. rating agencies so the risk is clear; and

■ they may offer higher yields than domestic bonds from the same issuer.

Disadvantages of Eurodollar bonds (as with foreign bonds in general) are:

■ since they are not registered with the SEC, there may be a lack of transparency;

■ they have political and country risk (taken into consideration by the rating agencies);

■ they have less liquidity than domestic issues; and

■ currency risk (if denominated in a currency other than one's home country).

5. 1. 6   BRADY BONDS

Brady bonds, named after former U.S. Treasury Secretary Nicholas Brady initiated a plan in 1989 to exchange defaulted commercial bank loans issued in less-developed countries, particularly in Latin America, with a security that could be carried on the bank's books as a performing asset. The first Brady agreement was reached with Mexico and the bonds were first issued in March, 1990. Partners in the program were the International

Monetary Fund (IMF) and the World Bank. Most are denominated in U.S. dollars. Maturities range from 10 to 30 years and may be interest bearing or discounted or even zero coupon. The safety of a Brady bond largely depends on the pledged collateral, frequently a U.S. Treasury zero-coupon bond. The Brady bond market was the largest and most actively traded emerging market asset class, but, as most of the countries involved have matured, they are only a small fraction today. Because of their relatively high safety, Brady bonds are generally more liquid than other debt issues from emerging markets.

The Brady Plan offered several important benefits:

- Those countries who participated were able to reduce both their overall debt level as well as the debt servicing cost
- For the bank's portfolio, their sovereign risk was diversified
- The Plan encouraged emerging markets countries to undertake economic reforms
- With the added safety and promise of economic reforms, emerging markets countries would now have a broader access to the financial markets.

TEST TOPIC ALERT   No Brady bond carries a U.S. government guarantee.

5. 2   REPAYMENT OF PRINCIPAL

As stated in the beginning of this session, in addition to receiving regular income from the investment, the investor does want to receive a return of the loan principal. Normally, one expects to be paid off when the debt matures. However, there are cases when the issuer pays off the debt prior to maturity.

5. 2. 1   CALLABLE BONDS

Most of the questions on the exam dealing with early payback of principal are about callable bonds. Bonds can be either callable or noncallable. Callability is a feature that permits the issuer to redeem its bonds (pay off the principal) before maturity if it so desires. The call feature is most often exercised when interest rates (borrowing costs) have declined. In this case, the issuer could take advantage of the lower cost of borrowing by issuing new bonds at the lower rate prevailing in the market and using those proceeds to call in the old bonds with their higher coupons. This is similar to refinancing a home mortgage, but in this business we use the term refunding. An issuer would not be interested in redeeming its bonds when interest rates have gone up and the bond prices have gone down; the cheapest way for the issuer to retire its debt is to buy it in the open market.

5. 2. 1. 1   Call Protection

Before purchasing a bond, determine the extent of its call protection. **Call protection** is the number of years into the issue before the issuer may exercise the call provision. The best call protection a bond may have is if a bond is noncallable; in other words, the issuer cannot call it early, and the investor has the best protection against a call.

5. 2. 2   CONVERTIBLE BONDS

The exam also deals with bonds paid off before maturity that have a convertible feature. These convertible bonds are issued by corporations only. Since they may be converted or exchanged for the company's common stock, there are no convertible municipal or government bonds. The conversion privilege is exercised at the discretion of the investor. The ratio of conversion varies from one company's bond to another according to the terms set forth in the indenture at the time the bonds are issued. The exact number of shares (or method of computing the number) that a particular bond will be convertible into at any point is printed in the bond indenture at the time of issue. Most convertibles are debentures.

In many cases, the indenture merely tells you the number of shares into which the bond is convertible. For example, the bond may be convertible into 50 shares; thus, it would have a conversion ratio of 50:1, 50 shares for 1 bond. If a bond is convertible into 25 shares, it would have a conversion ratio of 25:1.

Frequently, instead of telling the number of shares into which the bond is convertible, the indenture will give the conversion price. That conversion price is the price per share that the corporation will sell their stock in exchange for the bond one is holding. Regardless of the current market price of the bond, the bond always represents a debt of the corporation of $1,000. Therefore, if the conversion price is given, to compute the number of shares into which the bond is convertible, always divide the par value ($1,000) by the conversion price. For example, a bond convertible at $20 per share is convertible into 50 shares ($1,000 ÷ $20 = 50 shares).

If the bond has a conversion price of $50, the conversion ratio is 20 shares ($1,000 ÷ $50 = 20 shares). If the JRP 6s of '31, currently selling at 120, were convertible at $40, how many shares would one get when one converted the bond? The answer is not 30. The current market has nothing to do with the computation. The bond conversion is fixed at issuance, and the market fluctuates all the time. The correct answer is 25 shares ($1,000 ÷ $40 = 25 shares).

The bond's price will rise along with the stock. Most convertible bonds contain a call provision. If the market price of the bonds becomes sufficiently high, the company can force the investors to convert by exercising the call provision. This is known as forced conversion. The reason the bond price went up was because the underlying stock went up. If a bond is called at a price significantly lower than its current market, it will be to the bondholder's advantage to convert the bond into the stock. Once that occurs, the issuer owes nothing, since there is stock now where there once were bonds.

5. 2. 2. 1   Parity

All of the comments we've made about convertible bonds (or convertible preferred) moving in relation to the underlying common stock is due to the concept of parity. According to the dictionary, when two things are at parity, they are equal. How does that work here? If you think about it, when holding a convertible security, we have a choice of two actions: we can either continue to hold the bond (or preferred), or, we can decide to convert it into the common. If the convertible security and the common stock we would get upon conversion are worth the same, we say they are at parity.

EXAMPLE

A bond is convertible into 50 shares of common stock. If the current market price of the bond is $1,200, what does the market price of each share of common have to be so that upon conversion we'd wind up with the same $1,200? Divide $1,200 by 50 shares and the result is $24. That means if the stock is selling for $24 per share when the bond is selling for $1,200, they are at parity: equal. Usually the convertible security sells for a bit over parity, so in this example we'd expect the stock's actual market price to be something under $24. Or, if the question stated that the market price of the stock was $24, we would expect the bond to be selling for slightly higher than $1,200.

5. 2. 2. 2   Advantages to Investors

Downside Protection. The investor is a creditor. If the company's business does not prosper and the stock does not go up, or declines in value, the investor becomes, as a bondholder, a creditor. Interest must be paid currently, and the principal must be repaid at maturity. The investor has assured income, as long as the company is solvent, and has a bondholder's claim, in the event of financial difficulty. There is a market level to which the bond will drop and then drop no further, because it will sell on the basis of its coupon rate competitively with other bonds. Convertibles carry a lower interest rate than non-convertibles because of the added bonus of the convertibility factor. If the underlying common stock declines to a point where the convertibility factor is worth nothing, then the bond will sell on the basis of its yield alone like any other debt security.

Upside Potential. If the company's business prospers, the underlying stock will increase in market value. Since the bondholder can convert to stock, the bond will go up parallel to the increase in the common stock price.

A convertible bondholder, therefore, has all the upside potential of the common stockholder without all the downside risk.

5. 2. 2. 3   Disadvantages to Investors

The only disadvantages to investors in convertible bonds are that they receive a lower interest rate than a nonconvertible debt and, of course, the possibility that the convertible bond may be called away before one is ready to convert.

5. 2. 2. 4   Anti-Dilutive Protection

One of the concerns of any holder of a convertible security (bond or preferred stock) is protection against the potential dilution resulting from a stock split or a stock dividend. For example, if you owned a bond convertible into 20 shares and the issuer declared a 2-for-1 stock split, in order for you to have the same conversion powers, you would need to be able to convert into 40 shares. If the conversion privilege were expressed as a conversion price, the new price would now be half the former one allowing you to convert into twice as many "new" shares.

TEST TOPIC ALERT

The following are key points to remember about convertible securities:

■ They give the owner the opportunity to participate in the company's growth through the ability to acquire common stock

■ The coupon (interest) rate will invariably be lower than for non-convertibles of the same quality. In other words, investors sacrifice income for the growth opportunity

■ They offer the potential stability of a debt security with the upside potential of an equity security

■ Convertible securities generally sell at price somewhat above the parity price

QUICK QUIZ 5.C

True or False?

___ 1. A resident of France purchasing Eurodollar bonds does not incur currency risk.

___ 2. A country wishing to restructure its debt using Brady bonds would do so to save on debt servicing costs.

___ 3. Call protection is of greatest benefit when interest rates are falling.

___ 4. In most cases, convertible securities sell right at their parity price.

___ 5. One of the benefits of holding convertible debentures is the option to convert into the corporation's common or preferred stock.

6. Which of the following statements is TRUE of a corporate bond with a call feature?

A. The owner of the bond may demand that the issuing corporation redeem the bond before it matures.
B. The issuing corporation may change the coupon rate at any time by giving the owner of the bond written notice.
C. The owner of the bond may exchange it for shares of stock.
D. The issuing corporation has the option to redeem the bond before it matures.

7. When a corporate bond has a convertible feature, it means

A. the owner of the bond may exchange it for a pre-determined number of shares of the issuer's common stock
B. the corporation may redeem the bond before its maturity date
C. the owner of the bond may exchange it for a common stock of the issuer at a discount from the current market value
D. the owner of the bond may exchange it for a bond paying a higher coupon rate

5. 3 METHODS OF VALUING FIXED INCOME SECURITIES

The nature of fixed income, being debt rather than equity, involves somewhat different methodology in determining proper valuation. After all, in most cases, these securities are purchased for their income rather than future capital appreciation. The first thing we will look at is the various yield computations that are applicable to debt securities.

5. 3. 1 YIELD COMPUTATIONS

The interest rate will always be stated as a percentage of the par value. The interest stated on the face of the bond is called the **nominal yield**. Sometimes it is referred to as the coupon rate. To compute the annual interest payments in dollars, multiply this nominal yield by the face amount of the bond ($1,000 unless stated otherwise). A bond with a 5% coupon rate pays $50 per year. One with an 8% nominal yield pays $80 per year. One with a coupon of 13.5% pays $135 per year. Because, on any particular bond, this interest payment is the same every year, it is referred to as a fixed charge.

TEST TOPIC ALERT

When a question states that a bond pays interest at a rate of 6% semiannually, that does not mean two payments of $60 per year. The interest rate is always stated on an annual basis ($60 per year), and it is paid twice per year, $30 every 6 months.

5. 3. 1. 1 Current Yield

Investors always want to know the return on their investment. The most straightforward way to do that is to actually place the return on the investment as follows.

$$\frac{\text{Return}}{\text{Investment}}$$

The return will always be the annual interest in dollars (if referring to a stock, the dividend in dollars) divided by the current market price (the amount of investment required to own the security). This calculation is called current yield or current return.

Although most bonds are issued with a face, or par, value of $1,000, bond prices do fluctuate in the market. As stated earlier, the interest a bond pays is called its coupon rate or nominal yield. Look at this example: The DBL 10s of '29. DBL is the name of the issuer, 10s means the nominal yield is 10%, and '29 means that the bonds mature in 2029. The letter s is added because it is easier to say "the 10s" than to say "the 10." These bonds pay $100 a year ($50 semiannually) for each $1,000 of face value. Regardless of what the market price of the bonds may be, DBL has an obligation to pay annual interest of 10% of the $1,000 face they borrowed.

If an investor were to buy these bonds for more than $1,000 or less than $1,000, the return on the investment would not be 10%. For example, if these bonds had a current market value of $800, their current yield would be 12.5% ($100 ÷ $800). Similarly, someone paying $1,200 for the bonds will receive a current yield of 8.33% ($100 ÷ $1,200).

Please notice, the $100 interest received is the same in all cases regardless of the current market price.

Bond prices and yields move in opposite directions: as interest rates rise, bond prices fall and vice versa. When a bond trades at a discount, its current yield increases; when it trades at a premium, its current yield decreases.

5. 3. 1. 2   Discount and Premium

When a bond is selling at a price above par (or face), it is selling at a premium; when it is selling below par, it is selling at a discount. Two critical statements to remember follow.

If you pay more, you get less.

If you pay less, you get more.

An investor buying a bond at a premium will always receive a rate of return less than the coupon (or nominal) yield stated on the face of the bond (8.33% is less than 10%). Conversely, any time an investor purchases a bond at a discount, the return will be more than the rate stated on the face of the bond (12.5% is greater than 10%).

In addition to being the dollar amount on which the annual interest was based, par value was also the dollar amount that would be returned to the investor at maturity. Therefore, an investor purchasing a bond at a discount knows that holding the bond until maturity date will result in a return of the par value, an amount which will be more than what was paid for the bond. An investor purchasing a bond at a premium and holding it until the maturity date, knows that the par value received will be less than what was paid for the bond. To accurately reflect this gain or loss that an investor will have upon maturity, there is another yield to consider—the yield to maturity, or true yield.

TEST TOPIC ALERT

Another way you may be tested is by giving you a quoted yield and asking you for the price relative to par. For example, if a bond with a 5% coupon is currently yielding 6%, is it selling at a discount, a premium, or par? Well, anytime you are getting a yield higher than the coupon rate, the bond has to be selling at a discount from par. Conversely, if the bond had a 5% coupon, but the current return was 4%, the bond must be selling at a premium to par.

You may also be asked to determine which is higher (or lower), the current yield or the yield to maturity. Since YTM accentuates the return by adding a profit to a bond bought at a discount or subtracting the loss on a bond bought at a premium, the YTM on a discount bond will always be higher than that bond's current yield and the reverse is true regarding a bond bought at a premium.

5. 3. 1. 3   Yield to Maturity or Basis

This measurement takes into account the gain or loss the investor will have when the bonds are redeemed at maturity. The person who buys the bonds mentioned above at $800 will get back $1,000 if he holds the bonds to maturity, in addition to receiving $100 per year interest (a current yield of 12.5% on his money). Consequently, this investor will have a gain of $200 on top of his annual interest. The individual paying $1,200 for the bonds will have a $200 loss at maturity when he gets back face value for them.

Whenever an investor pays less (buys at a discount), there will be a profit in addition to the annual interest, and whenever the investor pays more (buys at a premium), there will be a loss if held to maturity. Try to understand these key facts:

- A bond is issued at par ($1,000) because that is how much the issuer is borrowing.
- The interest paid on the bond is always fixed as a percentage of the par (face) value.
- Regardless of changes in the market value of the bond, the interest checks remain the same.
- The current market price of a bond is determined by supply and demand.
- The current market price will fluctuate.
- The current market price may be at par, above par, or below par.
- A bond always matures at par.
- Purchasing a bond at par will always result in getting back the same as the original investment at maturity.
- Purchasing a bond at a discount (below par) will always result in getting back par, which means more (a profit) than the original investment.
- Purchasing a bond at a premium (above par) will always result in getting back par, which means less (a loss) than the original investment.

Although you will not have to do a yield to maturity computation on the exam, some students find that seeing the numbers played out gives them a better understanding of the concept. Try to follow this example:

EXAMPLE

An investor who buys a 10% coupon bond at 105 ($1,050 per bond) with 10 years remaining to maturity can expect $100 in interest per year. If he holds the bond to maturity, the bondholder loses $50, the amount of the premium. This loss is included in the YTM approximation.

The actual YTM calculation for this premium bond is shown below:

$$\frac{\text{Annual interest} - (\text{premium} \div \text{years to maturity})}{\text{Average price of the bond}}$$

A bond's average price is the price paid plus the amount received at maturity (par) divided by two. Alternatively, the average price is that price midway between the purchase price and par.

$$\frac{100 - (50 \div 10)}{1025} = \frac{95}{1025} = .093, \text{ or } 9.3\%$$

The YTM of a bond bought at a premium is always lower than both the coupon rate (nominal yield) and the current yield. In this example, the nominal yield is 10%, and the current yield is 9.52% (100 ÷ 1,050).

If an investor buys a 10-year bond with a 10% coupon for 95 ($950 per bond), he receives $100 per year in coupon interest payments and a gain of $50 (the amount of the discount) at maturity. This gain is included in the YTM approximation.

The actual YTM calculation for this discount bond is shown below:

$$\frac{\text{Annual interest} + (\text{discount} \div \text{years to maturity})}{\text{Average price of the bond}}$$

$$\frac{100 + (50 \div 10)}{975} = \frac{105}{975} = .1077, \text{ or } 10.77\%$$

The YTM of a bond bought at a discount is always higher than both the coupon rate (nominal yield) and the current yield. In this example, the nominal yield is 10%, and the current yield is 10.53% (100 ÷ 950).

If these calculations seem complicated, do not worry. You will have at most one question requiring a YTM calculation. Focus on the relationship between YTM and CY based on the price of the bond.

TAKE NOTE

YTM is also called the **market-driven yield** because it reflects the internal rate of return (IRR) from the bond investment.

5. 3. 1. 4   Yield to Call (YTC)

A bond with a call feature may be redeemed before maturity at the issuer's option. Unless the bond was bought at par, and is callable at par, yield to call (YTC) calculations reflect the early redemption date and consequent acceleration of the premium loss from the purchase price.

A bond's **yield to call**, similar to YTM, is the rate of return the bond provides from the purchase date to the call date and price. This calculation generates a lower return than does the YTM and should be considered by investors when evaluating a callable bond trading at a premium.

TEST TOPIC ALERT

The reason why we've only referred to a bond selling at a premium being called for redemption is because it is highly unlikely that an issuer would call in a bond that was available in the marketplace at a discount. If that were to happen, the yield to call would be higher than the yield to maturity because the profit resulting from the discount would be accelerated.

The following example and chart will help you follow the discussion of the various bond yields.

Current Yield, Yield to Maturity, and Yield to Call

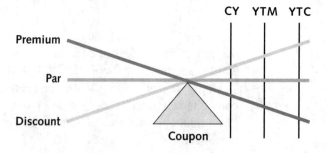

CY = Current Yield   YTM = Yield to Maturity   YTC = Yield to Call

1.   What is the current yield of a 6% bond trading for 80 ($800)?

Current yield = annual income ÷ current market price

Find the solution as follows: $60 ÷ $800 = 7.5%. This bond is trading at a discount. When prices fall, yields rise. The current yield is greater than the nominal yield when bonds are trading at a discount.

2.   What is the current yield of a 6% bond trading for 120 ($1,200)?

Find the solution as follows: $60 ÷ $1,200 = 5%. This bond is trading at a premium. The price is up so the yield is down. The current yield is less than the nominal yield when bonds are trading at a premium.

It is critical to understand the inverse relationship between price and yield. An effective way to visualize it is through the chart. When bonds are at par, coupon and current yield are equal. When bonds are at a premium, the CY is less than the coupon. When bonds are at a discount, the CY is greater than the coupon.

Current market value (CMV) of bond with 10 years to maturity

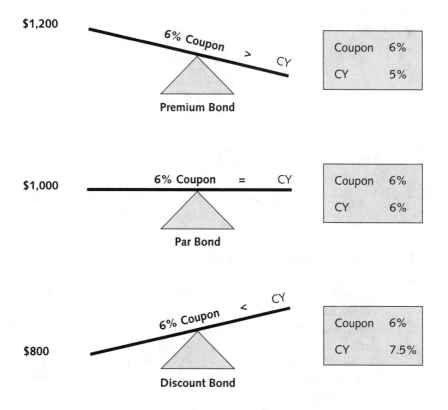

Know how to calculate the CY of a bond or a stock. Expect to see one question on the calculation of CY.

The CY of common stock is calculated by dividing the current dividend by the current price of the stock. For instance, a stock with a $2 dividend trading on the market for $40 has a 5% CY ($2 ÷ $40 = 5%).

EXAMPLE

Answer the following questions with **premium**, **par**, or **discount**.

1. If the bond has a YTC lower than its CY, it is trading at

2. If the bond has a YTM and CY that are equal, the bond is trading at

3. If the bond has a YTM less than its YTC, the bond is trading at

4. If a bond has a YTM greater than its coupon, the bond is trading at

The answers are: 1. premium; 2. par; 3. discount; 4. discount.

TEST TOPIC ALERT

Memorize the following chart for the exam:

Ranking Yields from Lowest to Highest

Discounts	Premiums
Nominal	YTC
CY	YTM
YTM	CY
YTC	Nominal

Once you understand the yield ranking for discounts, the ranking for premium is easy—it is the exact opposite.

5. 3. 1. 5   Tax Equivalent Yield

One final factor to be considered in the analysis of debt securities is taxability. When it comes to taxation, the interest on corporate bonds is taxed as ordinary income on both state and federal tax returns, while the interest on Treasury debt is only taxable on the federal level. Municipal bonds have one important characteristic that sets them apart from all other securities. In most cases, interest received from municipal bonds is free of federal income tax, and if the investor resides in the issuer's state, it is generally free of state income tax as well.

Assume an investor has $2,000 to invest. If he purchases, at par, one corporate or government bond of standard size ($1,000) with a 10% nominal (coupon) yield, he would receive $100 per year paid by two semiannual interest checks of $50. For purposes of this example, assume that he is in the 28% federal income tax bracket. An individual in the

28% tax bracket pays tax on any additional income earned at a rate of 28%. Therefore, on the $100 in interest he received above, he would pay the IRS $28 (28%) and keep the other $72.

The other $1,000 he had available to invest was used to purchase a $1,000-par-value municipal bond with a 7.5% nominal yield. He would receive $75 annually on that bond paid by two semiannual interest checks of $37.50. The 10% bonds, on which the interest is taxable, would net $72 per year after taxes. Of the $75 interest received for the 7.5% municipal, none of it is taxed; the whole amount is kept. Therefore, a client in the 28% bracket should purchase 7.5% municipals before 10% corporates. The taxable equivalent yield of a 7.5% tax-free bond for this investor in the 28% tax bracket would be the tax-free yield divided by (100% minus the tax bracket). In this case, 7.5 ÷ (100 − 28), or .72. That equals 10.42%, so it is obvious that the 7.5% municipal bond will provide a higher after tax return.

There are two ways to work with TEY. The first we've just done. That is, given the coupon on a municipal bond and the investor's tax bracket, divide that coupon by (100 − tax bracket) to determine what a taxable security would have to pay to give the same after-tax return.

Alternatively, we might know the taxable security's coupon and the investor's tax bracket and we want to know what the tax-free bond must yield to give us an equivalent yield. For example, a taxable bond is paying 8% interest and the investor is in the 30% tax bracket. Therefore, the investor will pay taxes equal to 2.4% (30% of the 8%). After paying taxes, the investor will keep the other 5.6% (8% − 2.4%). So, a tax-free bond paying 5.6% will offer a tax-equivalent yield equal to the 8% one.

TEST TOPIC ALERT

The tax equivalent yield for a municipal bond issued by an entity within a state with a state income tax will have a higher tax equivalent yield to a resident of that state due to the "double" tax exemption.

TAKE NOTE

The formula for computing tax equivalent yield (TEY) is

Municipal bond coupon divided by (100% - investor's tax bracket).

Therefore, if the coupon rate (nominal yield) of the municipal bond is 4.2% and the investor is in the 40% tax bracket, you would divide 4.2% by (100%-40%) or 4.2% by 60% and arrive at a TEY of 7%. That is, in order to receive the same after-tax benefit, this investor would have to purchase a taxable bond (corporate or government) with a coupon of 7%. This can be easily proven by taking the 7% yield and reducing it by the 40% tax which results in 7% minus 2.8% tax or 4.2%.

5. 3. 2   BOND PRICING

It is important to understand how the market prices of bonds are quoted. Look at the following examples to see how corporates, municipals, and governments are quoted.

5. 3. 2. 1   Corporates and Municipal

- Corporate and municipal bonds are quoted as a percentage of par.
- Each bond point represents $10, and the fractions are in eighths: each $1/8$ = $1.25.
    - A bond quoted at 90¼ = $902.50.
    - A bond quoted at 101¾ = $1,017.50.

5. 3. 2. 2   Governments

- Government bonds are quoted as a percentage of par.
- Each point is $10, and each 0.1 represents $1/32$ ($.3125).
    - A government bond quoted at 90.8 = $902.50.
    - A government bond quoted at 101.24 = $1,017.50.

5. 3. 2. 3   Price/Yield Relationship

There are many reasons interest rates rise and fall. The main concern for the exam, at this point, is the effect that interest rates have on the price fluctuations of bonds. As a general rule, keep in mind that interest rates and bond prices move counter to each other. That is, when interest rates are going up, the price of older bonds will be going down. When interest rates are going down, the price of older bonds will be going up.

When most people hear this for the first time, they have difficulty understanding it. Simply stated, when newly issued bonds are paying a higher rate of interest than ones currently in the market place, those older bonds are not as attractive. After all, if a new bond came out with a 6% coupon, your 4% or 5% bond would not be as valuable (this always assumes equal quality or rating). Conversely, if you were holding a bond with an 8% coupon, and newly issued bonds were only offering 6%, your bond is more valuable.

5. 3. 2. 4   Zero-Coupon Bonds

The nominal (coupon) rate on a zero-coupon bond is zero. Zero-coupon bonds are issued at a substantial discount from par. They pay no interest, but the difference between the discounted price paid and the par value received at maturity makes up for the lack of a current interest coupon. For example, if an investor were to purchase a new zero-coupon bond for $500 that matured at par in 10 years, he would receive a profit of $500 in 10 years or an average of $50 per year on an out-of-pocket expenditure of $500. Here are the key things to remember about zero-coupon bonds.

- They are always issued at a discount.
- There is no reinvestment risk because there are no interest payments to worry about reinvesting.
- They are more volatile than other bonds of similar quality.

■ Even though no periodic interest payments are received, the IRS requires the issuer to send a Form 1099-OID indicating the taxable interest to be reported each year.

■ This investment is particularly useful when there is a target goal, such as a college education or a qualified retirement plan. This is particularly true because of the tax treatment mentioned above. The child generally incurs little, if any, tax liability, and the earnings in the retirement plan are tax-deferred.

In the case of zero-coupon corporate or municipal securities, there is a somewhat higher level of credit risk. (On a 20-year bond, the investor receives nothing until the maturity date, and if the issuer is insolvent at that time, the investor has received nothing during the entire 20 years.) However, no credit risk exists in the case of zero-coupon treasuries (known as STRIPS for Separate Trading of Registered Interest and Principal of Securities) since the risk of default on a U.S. government security, (at least for purposes of this exam), is nonexistent.

The major attraction of this type of investment is that it allows an investor to lock in a yield (or rate of return) for a predetermined, investor-selected time with no reinvestment risk. Because all zeroes are sold at discounts and have no current return, there is a great deal of price volatility. This point will be reviewed again later in this session at the discussion on duration.

5. 3. 2. 5   Bond Listings

If you were to look up a bond in the newspaper or other source for a quote, you might see something like this:

DEF 5s35 @106. What does that mean? The DEF is the issuer, the 5 is the nominal or coupon rate, the 35 is the maturity date of 2035 and the 106 is the price ($1,060). So, what is the "s"? It is nothing but a separation between the coupon and the maturity date.

QUICK QUIZ 5.D

1. A corporate bond is currently selling in the market at a price of 120. The bond is convertible at $25. The parity price is

    A. $25 per share
    B. $30 per share
    C. $40 per share
    D. $48 per share

2. When a bond with a 6% coupon is selling for 90

    I.   the current yield is approximately 6.67%
    II. the bond is selling at a discount
    III. the bondholder will receive two semi-annual interest payments of $27 each
    IV. the yield to maturity is slightly less than the current yield

    A. I and II
    B. I, II and IV
    C. II and III
    D. III and IV

3. What would likely happen to the market value of existing bonds during an inflationary period coupled with rising interest rates?

    A. The nominal yield of the bonds would decrease.
    B. The price of the bonds would increase.
    C. The price of the bonds would decrease.
    D. The price of the bonds would stay the same.

4. Which of the following statements about zero-coupon bonds are TRUE?

    I.   Zero-coupon bonds are sold at a deep discount from face value.
    II. Zero-coupon bonds pay periodic interest payments.
    III. The owner of a zero-coupon bond receives the face value only at maturity.

    A. I and II
    B. I and III
    C. II and III
    D. I, II, and III

5. A $1,000 bond with a nominal yield of 8% will pay how much interest each year?

    A. $40.00
    B. $80.00
    C. $160.00
    D. There is no way to compute without knowing the current market price of the bond

6. If your clients want to set aside $40,000 for when their child starts college, but do not want to endanger the principal, you should recommend

    A. corporate bonds with high rates of interest
    B. zero-coupon bonds backed by the U.S. Treasury
    C. general obligation municipal bonds for their tax benefits
    D. common stock

7. A bond offered at par has a coupon rate

    A. less than its yield to maturity
    B. less than its current yield
    C. equal to its current yield
    D. greater than its yield to maturity

8. An investor purchasing 5 bonds priced at 102 each would expect to pay a total of (disregard commissions)

    A. $102
    B. $510
    C. $1,020
    D. $5,100

9. Each of the following debt securities would be considered investment grade EXCEPT

    A. corporate subordinated junior unsecured debentures with an A rating
    B. municipal water authority revenue bonds with a Baa rating
    C. corporate first lien mortgage bonds with a BB rating
    D. U.S. Treasury bills

10. An investor in the 25% federal income tax bracket purchasing an unrated public works revenue bond issued by State A that carries a 3% coupon would have a tax equivalent yield of

    A. 2.25%
    B. 3.00%
    C. 4.00%
    D. None of these because it is unlikely that an unrated bond will be able to make timely interest payments

11. Which of the following statements about municipal bonds is NOT true?

    A. The interest on municipal bonds is usually not subject to federal income tax.
    B. Municipal bonds are bonds issued by governmental units at levels other than the federal.
    C. Municipal bonds are generally considered riskier than corporate bonds.
    D. Municipal bonds generally carry lower coupon rates than corporate bonds of the same quality.

5. 3. 3   DURATION

In the financial industry, the term *duration* is used to measure the sensitivity of a debt security when faced with changes in interest rates. The longer the duration, the greater the market price movement, and vice versa.

It is a complicated computation, but, to try to simplify things, it is basically a measurement of the time it takes for the cash flow (interest payments) to repay the invested principal. That being the case, in general the higher the coupon rate, the shorter the duration, or the lower the coupon, the longer the duration.

Just remember that there are two components to the computation: the interest rate and the maturity date. If the maturity dates are about the same (the difference between a 20-year maturity and a 22-year one is almost insignificant), then the bond paying the highest coupon rate will always have the shortest duration and that with the lowest coupon, the longest. However, if the coupon rates are approximately the same, then the bond that will mature first will have the shortest duration, and the one that will mature last will have the longest duration.

TAKE NOTE

One way to keep things straight is to think about the zero-coupon bond. With no periodic interest payments (that's why it's called zero-coupon), the duration of a zero-coupon bond will always equal its length to maturity. In other words, if we're trying to compute how long it will take for the income payments to return your principal, without any interest payments, you can't expect to get your money back until maturity date. If that is the case with a zero-coupon bond, then as we find bonds paying interest, the more they're paying every six months, the quicker the payback.

The general characteristics of duration follow.

- The lower the coupon rate, the longer a bond's duration; the higher the coupon rate, the shorter the duration.

- The longer a bond's maturity, the longer the bond's duration.

- For coupon bonds, duration is always less than the bond's maturity.

- Duration for a zero-coupon bond is always equal to its maturity.

- The longer a bond's duration, the more its value will change for a 1% change in interest rates; the shorter the duration, the less it will change.

The duration of a bond with coupon payments is always shorter than the maturity of the bond. By the same token, the duration of a zero-coupon bond is equal to its maturity.

A five-year zero-coupon bond has a duration of five because it takes five years to make the money back; the buyer gets a single payment (par) at maturity five years after purchase.

5. 3. 3. 1 Convexity

If you took geometry in school, you learned that curves could be convex (bulging to the outside) or concave (curving to the inside). It's been almost 60 years, but I still remember the key to the difference by the statement, "you can hide in a cave." Now, what does that have to do with our discussion?

Convexity is the measurement of the curve that results when plotting a bond's price movements in response to changes in interest rates. It is a more accurate representation than duration of what will happen to a bond's price as interest rates change, especially when the changes are great. Should you have a question about convexity on your exam, here's what you have to know:

- Duration is a linear (straight-line) measurement, while convexity follows a curve.
- Comparing two bonds, the one with the higher convexity will show a greater price increase when yields fall and a smaller decrease when yields rise (that is a good thing).
- If we find two bonds with the same duration, the one with the higher convexity offers greater interest rate risk protection.

If you should be asked, "Which of the following is the most useful in determining the price volatility of a bond to a significant change in interest rates?", the correct choice is *convexity*.

5. 3. 3. 2   Discounted Cash Flow (DCF)

One way of assessing the value of a fixed income security is by looking at the future expected free cash flow (the interest payments plus the eventual return of the principal) and discounting it to arrive at a present value. In its simplest iteration, this is nothing more than taking the all the money you are scheduled to receive over a given future period and adjusting that for the time value of money. The concept is used as well in some equity projections, such as the dividend discount and dividend growth models described previously. Therefore, in order to compute the future value of the cash flow from a bond, you would have to know the:

■ principal amount;

■ coupon rate; and

■ number of interest payments.

TAKE NOTE

The higher the discounted cash flow (DCF), the more valuable the investment.

EXAMPLE

There will be no computations regarding discounted cash flow, but there is a common example that may help you understand the concept better. We all wish we could be a winner of those huge Powerball or Mega Millions jackpots. Winners have the choice of receiving a series of payments over a number of years (about 29 currently), or taking the money in cash. If they take the cash, they'll receive around 70% of the announced total prize. Why is there a difference? The cash represents the *present value* of those future payments and that is why you get less by taking it now instead of over time. In fact, years ago, when interest rates were higher than they are at the time of this printing, the lump sum payment was only about 60% of the "prize." That is because the higher the market interest rates, the higher the *discount rate*. This is the same concept used in valuing a bond using DCF. When you buy a bond, you are expecting semi-annual interest payments (cash flow) until the maturity date. When you compare those interest rates to the current market rates (the *discount rate* in the equation), you get an idea of a fair value of the bond. To better help you understand, take a look at this question.

A client interested in fixed income is viewing different bonds with the same rating and a coupon of 6%. Using the discounted cash flow method, which bond should have the highest market value?

A.   5 year maturity when the discount rate is 4%

B.   5 year maturity when the discount rate is 8%

C.   10 year maturity when the discount rate is 4%

D.   10 year maturity when the discount rate is 8%

The correct answer is: **C**

Remember, the discount rate is just another way of stating the current interest rate in the marketplace. If the discount rate is *higher* than the coupon rate, the present value, the expected market price will be *below* par. Conversely, if the discount rate is *lower* than the coupon rate, the present value will be *above* the par value. Now, there is nothing new for you here – When the current interest rate in the market place (that is what the discount rate represents) is less than the coupon, the bond price is higher (as interest rates go down, bond prices go up). And, if the current market interest rate is higher than the coupon rate, the bond's price will be lower (when interest rates increase, bond prices fall). That would narrow the choices to the two 4% bonds. That is, a bond with a 6% coupon should sell at premium when current interest rates are at 4% and when interest rates are at 8%, the 6% bond should be selling at a discount. Then, as we've just learned with duration, when interest rates change, the longer the time to maturity, the greater the effect on the market price of a bond.

TAKE NOTE

There will be a further discussion of present value in Unit 4 and, after that, you might want to revisit this topic because it should make more sense to you at that time.

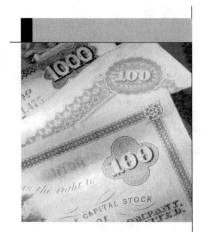

6

Types and Characteristics of Cash and Cash Equivalents

Asset allocation programs (covered later in the course) contain three primary asset classes, equity securities (stock) covered in Session 4, fixed income securities (bonds) covered in Session 5, and cash ("money in the bank" as well as investments that have cash-like liquidity). Cash equivalents, such as commercial paper and Treasury bills, are the primary source of short-term financing for corporations and governments.

The Series 65 exam will include approximately three questions on the material presented in this session.

When you have completed this session, you should be able to:

- **identify** the special characteristics of money market instruments;

- **explain** the risks and benefits of adding cash equivalents to a client's portfolio;

- **summarize** how mortgage-backed securities work; and

- **contrast** DDAs and CDs.

6. 1   CASH AND CASH EQUIVALENTS

As we will learn when discussing asset allocation programs later in this course, one important asset is "cash." Now, we don't mean greenbacks buried in the mattress or the backyard; we're referring to places to keep funds that are in the bank or in securities that are considered to be the same as cash. Although the Financial Accounting Standards Board (FASB) defines cash equivalents as highly liquid securities with maturities of less than three months, when it comes to cash equivalents, the exam will include money market instruments with a maturity of up to one year.

6. 1. 1   MONEY MARKET

The **money market** may be defined as the market for buying and selling short-term loanable funds in the form of securities and loans. It is called the money market because that is what is traded there, money not cash. The buyer of a money market instrument is the lender of the money; the seller of a money market instrument is the entity borrowing the money.

Although there are many different kinds of money market instruments, there are several common factors. For example, they all have a maturity date of one year or less. In fact, the majority of money market instruments mature in less than six months. Another factor that many (but not all) money market instruments share is that they are issued at a discount; they do not pay interest because debt securities generally pay interest semi-annually and since most money market instruments have a maturity of six months or less, the administrative costs of paying out interest would be very high. Therefore, the solution is to issue the security at a discount with the investor being paid back par at maturity, that difference being what he is paid for the use of his money. Money market instruments are safe. Although some are not quite as safe as others (e.g., commercial paper is not as safe as a Treasury bill), they are all considered to be low-risk securities.

6. 1. 1. 1   Treasury Securities

Treasury bills are the bellwether of the money market. Because there is so much Treasury debt outstanding, the level of activity in Treasury bills and other short-term government issues is by far the highest and most carefully watched. Governments with short terms also refer to U.S. Treasury notes or U.S. Treasury bonds that are in their last year before maturity since, at that time, they would trade like any other security with one year or less to maturity. There are a number of advantages to Treasuries. First and foremost, at least for exam purposes, is the absence of credit risk. A second advantage is the extremely high liquidity in the secondary markets: the more active a security, the narrower the spread. The huge market activity in Treasuries keeps the spreads very low, making it easy for the investor to get in and out at a reasonable cost. A third benefit of investing in Treasuries is that the interest is exempt from state income tax. Because of these factors, the yields on these Treasuries are normally the lowest in the money market.

6. 1. 1. 2   Negotiable Certificates of Deposit

Negotiable certificates of deposit (CDs) were created in the mid-1960s because the Federal Reserve Board had restrictions on the amount of money a bank could pay on savings and other time deposits (a time deposit has a fixed maturity) until 1986. Because the Fed's rules were somewhat restrictive, it was impossible for the banks to compete for money. If a corporation had $1 million that they would not need for several weeks, there was no way that a bank could pay them a rate competitive with other money market instruments until the introduction of negotiable CDs. These CDs are unsecured time deposits (no asset of the bank is pledged as collateral), and the money is being loaned to the bank for a specified period of time. A negotiable CD allows the initial investor, or any subsequent owner of the CD, to sell the CD in the open market prior to maturity date. The bank that issues the CD redeems the CD at face value plus interest on maturity date. CDs are the only money market instrument that pays periodic interest, usually semi-annually. To be considered a negotiable CD, such CDs must have a face value of $100,000 or more, with $1 million and more being most common.

TAKE NOTE

In the industry (and sometimes on the exam), these are referred to as Jumbo CDs.

TEST TOPIC ALERT

- Negotiable CDs do not have a prepayment penalty

- FDIC insurance applies up to $250,000

- day jumbo CDs pay interest semi-annually

6. 1. 1. 3   Commercial Paper

Another money market instrument is commercial paper. This is short-term unsecured paper issued by corporations (especially finance companies), primarily to raise working capital. In other words, for current rather than long-term needs. As you saw when we covered securities exemptions in sessions 1 and 2, commercial paper is exempt from registration on both the federal and state level as long as the maximum maturity is nine months.

TEST TOPIC ALERT

Negotiable CDs are interest bearing and issued at face. Commercial paper is generally issued at a discount—instead of receiving interest, the investor receives the face amount at maturity. Finally, yields on commercial paper are usually negotiated between the buyer and issuer.

6. 1. 1. 4   Eurodollars and the Foreign Currency Markets

The cost of raising money and doing business is not restricted by national boundaries. International monetary factors, such as changes in foreign currency exchange rates, Eurodollars, eurosecurities, and the interbank market, can also affect U.S. money markets and businesses.

6. 1. 1. 4. 1 Eurodollars

Eurodollars are U.S. dollars deposited in banks outside the United States; that is, the deposits remain denominated in U.S. dollars rather than the local currency.

EXAMPLE Euroyen are Japanese yen deposited in banks outside Japan. In other words, when a currency is preceded by the prefix *euro*, it refers to a bank deposit outside of the currency's home country.

Eurodollar time deposits tend to be short term, ranging from overnight to 180 days. European banks lend Eurodollars to other banks in much the same way that U.S. banks lend federal funds. The interest rate is usually based on the **London Interbank Offered Rate (LIBOR)**.

6. 1. 1. 4. 2 London Interbank Offered Rate (LIBOR)

LIBOR, sometimes referred to as the ICE LIBOR, is derived from a survey of banks conducted each day in London, UK, on behalf of the Intercontinental Exchange—ICE. Lenders are asked how much it would cost them to borrow from each other for 15 different periods, from overnight to one year, in currencies including dollars, euros, yen, and Swiss francs. Rates are based on actual transactions for which records are kept. After a set number of quotes are excluded, those remaining are averaged and published for each currency by the ICE before noon.

TAKE NOTE The exam may expect you to know that the LIBOR is the world's most widely used benchmark for short-term interest rates.

In summation, why would you place money market securities in a client's portfolio?
- Highly liquid
- Very safe
- The best place to store money that will be needed soon

In doing so, the client would be incurring the following risks:
- Because of their many advantages, the rate of return is quite low so these are not suitable for long-term investors
- Fluctuating income—due to short-term maturities, principal is potentially being reinvested at a different rate each time the instrument matures

1. A company realizes money from the sale of surplus equipment. It would like to invest this money but will need it in 4–6 months and must take that into consideration when selecting an investment. You would recommend

   A. preferred stock
   B. Treasury bills
   C. AAA rated bonds with long-term maturities
   D. common stock

2. Money market instruments are

   A. short-term equity
   B. intermediate debt
   C. short-term debt
   D. long-term debt

Quick Quiz answers can be found at the end of the unit.

6. 1. 2   MORTGAGE-BACKED SECURITIES

These are basically debt obligations backed by a pool of mortgages and usually have a pass-through feature. One of the most popular of all mortgage pass-through securities is the Ginnie Mac. An investor is said to have an undivided interest in the pool. That is, he does not own a specific mortgage, but has a proportionate share in the cash flow generated by the entire pool. That cash flow is passed through to the holder of the security in the form of multiple payments of interest, principal, and frequently prepayments of mortgages. Very few mortgages last the full scheduled term.

Securities guaranteed by the Government National Mortgage Association (GNMA), sometimes referred to as Ginnie Mae, comprise VA-guaranteed or FHA-insured mortgages and are backed by the full faith and credit of the U.S. government. GNMA investors receive monthly payments. GNMA securities are available in minimum denominations of $25,000. Thereafter, the securities are available in increments of $1.

6. 1. 2. 1   Freddie Mac Participation Certificate (PC)

Another type of pass-through is issued by the Federal Home Loan Mortgage Corporation (FHLMC or Freddie Mac). This issue is sometimes called a participation certificate (PC). Freddie Mac PCs comprise qualifying FHLMC, conventional, residential mortgages on single-family homes. These PCs are not backed by the full faith and credit of the U.S. government, but their yield is slightly higher than those of GNMAs.

Fannie Mae also issues mortgage-backed securities. These securities are similar to the Freddie Mac PCs and consist of some conventional mortgages and FHA-insured mortgages. FNMAs are not backed by the full faith and credit of the U.S. government, but it is unlikely that the U.S. government would permit them to default. Their yields are comparable to the PCs and slightly higher than those of GNMAs.

6. 1. 2. 2   Collateralized Mortgage Obligations (CMOs)

Collateralized mortgage obligations (CMOs) were first introduced in June 1983. These are bonds that are collateralized by mortgages or by mortgage-backed securities. A key difference between traditional passthroughs and CMOs is the mechanics of the principal payment process. In a pass-through, each investor receives his proportionate distribution of the monthly principal and interest payments made by the homeowner. This means that the pass-through holder receives some return of his principal each month. He does not get all his principal back, and the pass-through does not mature, however, until the last mortgage in the pool has been paid off. The CMO is issued with a stated maturity: some have short terms, some intermediate, and some long terms. As the principal on the mortgages is being paid, it is used exclusively for the newest maturity in sequence until each maturity has been paid off. Most of the mortgages are private mortgages, not qualified under VA or FHA.

TAKE NOTE

Historically, CMOs were AAA-rated securities with a very low default risk. That changed during the sub-prime mortgage crisis of 2007–2008, but it is possible that the exam will still look at these as relatively free of credit (default) risk. Remember, we're dealing with the test world, which is not always the same as the real world.

6. 1. 2. 3   Benefits to Investors

The primary advantage of investing in mortgage-backed securities is that, compared with other debt securities with similar ratings, they pay a higher rate of return.

6. 1. 2. 4   Risks to Investors

There are a number of risks faced by investors in these securities:

- they are among the most complicated instruments and are, therefore, difficult to understand;
- prepayment risk due to mortgages being refinanced when rates drop;
- default risk, particularly if the mortgages are subprime;
- reinvestment risk; and
- liquidity risk.

6. 1. 2. 5   Cash Flow Analysis

Unlike the other debt securities we've discussed, trying to project your client's cash flow on a portfolio of mortgage-backed securities has its challenges. Although they do have default risk (other than GNMAs), as do other debt securities, the specific risk due to the possible (some would say, likely) prepayments, complicates the computation.

When doing cash flow analysis on a mortgage-backed pass-through security, you would want to know the average maturities.

6. 1. 3   INSURED DEPOSITS

As mentioned, when referring to cash as part of one's asset allocation, in addition to cash equivalents in the form of money market instruments, one might keep the proverbial "cash in the bank." The term *insured* will frequently be used on the exam because, at least up to the legal limits, the funds involved are insured by the FDIC. There are several ways this may be done.

6. 1. 3. 1   Demand Deposits

This is legal term for a checking account. This is the favorite repository for funds that will be needed in the very near term,

What we normally refer to as "cash in the bank" is, in banking terms, known as a **demand deposit**. To bankers, the term *demand deposit* refers to a type of account (usually just shown by the initials DDA) held at banks and financial institutions that may be withdrawn at any time by the customer. Historically, the term referred only to checking accounts, but it now commonly includes savings accounts and money market accounts (not money market mutual funds—those are not banking products).

When analyzing a client's financial profile, it should be understood that these are considered *short-term* funds (readily available) and provide safe, but *low* returns.

6. 1. 3. 2   Certificates of Deposits (CDs)

In the money market segment, we introduced you to the Jumbo (negotiable) CD. Here, we're referring to the non-negotiable (you can't sell it to anyone, you can only redeem it at the bank) certificate of deposit available at your local branch (or online). These are typically available with a minimum deposit of as little as $500 and maturities of anywhere from 3 months to 5 years. In most cases, withdrawal prior to the maturity date will result in a penalty. Here are some key facts to remember for the exam:

■ If capital preservation is the goal with no risk, the answer is an insured bank CD.

■ Insured bank CDs have no interest rate risk (they don't fluctuate in value as interest rates change).

■ Even with the potential early withdrawal penalty, these are considered liquid assets, but certainly not as liquid as a DDA.

QUICK QUIZ 6.B

1. Which of the following are true of GNMA securities but NOT of CMOs?

    A. Backed by the full faith and credit of the U.S. government
    B. Collateralized by mortgages
    C. Yield more than T-bonds
    D. Are pass-through securities

2. One would expect to have checkbook access to a

    A. CMO
    B. DDA
    C. GNMA
    D. LIBOR

7

Pooled Investments

I n addition to equity and debt, other investments related to stocks and
bonds are available to investors. Such investment products include
packaged products such as mutual funds, exchange traded funds (ETFs),
variable contracts of insurance companies (variable annuities and variable
life insurance), and real estate investment trusts (REITs). These packaged
products are generally referred to as pooled investments because they represent a pool of funds contributed by a number of investors.

The Series 65 exam will include approximately 6 questions on the
material presented in this session. ■

When you have completed this session, you should be able to:

- **compare** and contrast the difference between the method of capitalization of open-end investment companies and closed-end investment companies;

- **explain** the difference in pricing between open-end and closed end investment companies;

- **contrast** the different mutual fund share classes;

- **list** the different types of loads charged to fund investors;

- **illustrate** how a letter of intent can be used to reach a breakpoint;

- **name** the distinguishing characteristics of exchange-traded funds (ETFs);

- **identify** the unique features of investment company securities and REITs ; and

- **explain** the use and suitability of these securities in client portfolios.

7. 1   INVESTMENT COMPANY SECURITIES

An **investment company** is a corporation or a trust through which investors may acquire an interest in large, diversified portfolios of securities by pooling their funds with other investors' funds. People often invest in investment companies because they believe a professional money manager should be able to outperform the average investor in the market.

By investing through an investment company, individuals gain some of the advantages large investors enjoy, such as diversification of investments, lower transaction costs, professional management, and more.

Investment companies raise capital by selling shares to the public. Investment companies must abide by similar registration and prospectus requirements imposed by the Securities Act of 1933 on every other issuer.

Investment companies are also subject to regulations regarding how their shares are sold to the public. The **Investment Company Act of 1940** provides for Securities and Exchange Commission (SEC) regulation of investment companies and their activities.

TAKE NOTE

Because of the way many investors combine their investment capital, investment companies are frequently referred to as "pooled investment vehicles."

7. 1. 1   TYPES OF INVESTMENT COMPANIES

The Investment Company Act of 1940 classifies investment companies into three broad types: face-amount certificate (FAC) companies, unit investment trusts (UITs), and management investment companies.

7. 1. 1. 1   Face-Amount Certificate (FAC) Companies

A **face-amount certificate (FAC)** is a contract between an investor and an issuer in which the issuer guarantees payment of a stated (or fixed) sum to the investor at some set date in the future. In return for this future payment, the investor agrees to pay the issuer a set amount of money either as a lump sum or in periodic installments.

■ The only fact you need to know about this security is that it is 1 of the 3 types of investment companies listed in the Investment Company Act of 1940.

7. 1. 1. 2   Unit Investment Trusts (UITs)

A **unit investment trust (UIT)** is an **unmanaged** investment company organized under a trust indenture. UITs:

■ do not have boards of directors;

■ do not employ an investment adviser; and

■ do not actively manage their own portfolios (trade securities).

In its function as a trust for its investors, UIT trustees typically buy other investment company shares (nonfixed UIT) or individual stocks or bonds (fixed UIT) to create the desired portfolio. They then sell redeemable shares, known as **units** or **shares of beneficial interest**, in this portfolio of securities. Each share is an undivided interest in the underlying portfolio. Because UITs are not managed, when securities in the portfolio are liquidated or called, the proceeds must be distributed.

A UIT may be fixed or nonfixed. A **fixed UIT** typically purchases a portfolio of bonds and terminates when the bonds in the portfolio mature. In the past, fixed UITs were almost exclusively a portfolio of bonds. Now, a significant percentage of fixed UITs consist of a portfolio of equities. Since the equities do not have a maturity date, a liquidation date is set in the offering documents. A **nonfixed UIT** purchases shares of an underlying mutual fund. Under the Investment Company Act of 1940, the trustees of both fixed and nonfixed UITs must maintain secondary markets in the units, thus allowing unit holders the ability to redeem their units.

Many exchange-traded funds (ETFs—covered later in this session) are organized as UITs and trade, as the name implies, on exchanges or Nasdaq.

TAKE NOTE

Know the following features of UITs.

- UITs are not actively managed; there is no board of directors (BOD) or investment adviser.

- UIT shares (units) must be redeemed by the trust.

- UITs are investment companies as defined under the Investment Company Act of 1940.

7. 1. 1. 3   Management Investment Companies

The most familiar type of investment company is the **management investment company**, which actively manages a securities portfolio to achieve a stated investment objective. A management investment company is either closed-end or open-end. Initially, both closed- and open-end companies sell shares to the public; the difference between them lies in the type of securities they sell and how investors buy and sell their shares—in the primary or secondary market.

TAKE NOTE

Open-end and closed-end investment companies have far more similarities than differences. One of these is the term, net asset value per share, generally shown as NAV. This value is the result of the fund valuing all of its assets (the largest of which is the portfolio), subtracting its liabilities, and then dividing that by the number of shares outstanding. This NAV per share computation is critical to the purchase and sale of open-end companies, and, as we'll see, has little relationship to the buying and selling price of closed-end funds.

7. 1. 1. 3. 1 Closed-End Investment Companies

To raise capital, a closed-end investment company conducts a common stock offering. For the initial offering, the company registers a fixed number of shares with the SEC and offers them to the public for a limited time through an underwriting group. The fund's capitalization is fixed unless an additional public offering is made. Closed-end investment companies can also issue bonds and preferred stock.

Closed-end investment companies are commonly known as **publicly traded funds**. After the stock is distributed, anyone can buy or sell shares in the secondary market, either on an exchange or over the counter (OTC). Supply and demand determine the **bid price** (price at which an investor can sell) and the **ask price** (price at which an investor can buy). Closed-end fund shares usually trade at a premium or discount to the shares' net asset value (NAV).

TEST TOPIC ALERT

Please remember the following points:

1. Closed-end investment companies trade based upon supply and demand for their shares. As a result, their buying and selling price does *not* have a direct relationship to the NAV of the shares.

2. Country funds are funds that concentrate their investments in the securities of companies domiciled in foreign countries. Well-known examples are the Korea Fund, the New Germany Fund, and the Mexico Fund. These country funds are generally organized as closed-end (rather than open-end) companies because it is often difficult to liquidate the foreign securities to get their value into the United States.

7. 1. 1. 3. 2 Open-End Investment Companies

An open-end investment company, or **mutual fund**, does not specify the exact number of shares it intends to issue. It registers an open offering with the SEC. The open-end investment company can raise an unlimited amount of investment capital by continuously issuing new shares. Any person who wants to invest in the company buys shares directly from the company or its underwriters (or a broker-dealer with a selling agreement) at the public offering price (POP).Unlike closed-end companies, open-end companies only issue common stock.

A mutual fund's **POP** is the NAV per share plus any applicable sales charges. A mutual fund's **NAV** is calculated daily by deducting the fund's liabilities from its total assets. NAV per share is calculated by dividing the fund's NAV by the number of shares outstanding.

An open-end investment company sells **redeemable securities**. When an investor sells shares, the company redeems them at their NAV. For each share an investor redeems, the company sends the investor money for the investor's proportionate share of the company's net assets. Therefore, a mutual fund's capital shrinks when investors redeem shares.

	Open-End	Closed-End
Capitalization	Unlimited; continuous offering of shares	Fixed; single offering of shares
Issues	Common stock only; no debt securities; permitted to borrow	May issue: common stock, preferred stock, debt securities
Shares	Full or fractional	Full only
Offering and trading	Sold and redeemed by fund only Continuous primary offering Must redeem shares	Initial primary offering Secondary trading OTC or on an exchange Does not redeem shares
Pricing	NAV + sales charge Selling price determined by formula in the prospectus; the price can never be below the NAV	Current market value + commission Price determined by supply and demand so it can be above, below, or the same as the NAV
Shareholder rights	Dividends (when declared), voting	Dividends (when declared), voting, preemptive

TEST TOPIC ALERT

We said earlier that closed-end funds also compute NAV; however, because their price is determined by supply and demand and, as a consequence, may be more than, the same as, or less than the NAV, it does not have the relevance that it does with open-end funds. Therefore, instead of daily computation, it is generally only done once per week.

7. 1. 1. 3. 3   Characteristics of Mutual Funds

A **mutual fund** is a pool of investors' money invested in various securities determined by the fund's objective. Open-end investment management companies (mutual funds) have several unique characteristics.

A mutual fund must redeem shares at the NAV. Unlike other securities, mutual funds offer guaranteed marketability because there is always a willing buyer for the shares.

Each investor in the mutual fund's portfolio owns an undivided interest in the entire underlying portfolio. No one investor has a preferred status over any other investor because mutual funds issue only one class of common stock. Each investor shares mutually with other investors in gains and distributions derived from the investment company portfolio.

Each investor's share in the fund's performance is based on the number of shares owned. Mutual fund shares may be purchased in either full or fractional units, unlike stock, which may be purchased in full units only. Because mutual fund shares can be fractional, the investor can think in terms of dollars rather than number of shares owned.

7. 1. 1. 3. 4   Forward Pricing

As mentioned previously, open-end investment companies (mutual funds) must compute their net asset value per share (NAV) at least once per day (very few compute more than that) as of the close of the markets (generally 4:00 pm ET). Price determination for purchases and sales is based upon the forward pricing principle. That is, whenever an order, whether to purchase or redeem shares, is received, the price is based upon the next computed NAV per share. For example, any order received (and time stamped) prior to 4:00 pm ET will be effected at the price computed as of that day's market close. If the order is received at 4:00 pm (or later), it will be executed based upon the NAV computed as of 4:00 pm the next business day.

7. 1. 1. 3. 5   Net Redemptions

It can sometimes happen, particularly during declining markets, that there is an excess of shareholder redemptions over new share purchases. This is known as "net redemptions." When that occurs, the portfolio manager is put in the difficult position of having to decide which assets to liquidate when prices are falling. A fund suffering with net redemptions is probably not going to deliver your clients the performance they are seeking.

EXAMPLE   If NavCo Mutual Fund shares are $15 per share, a $100 investment buys 6.667 shares ($100 ÷ $15 = 6.667).

An investment company's portfolio is elastic. Money is simultaneously invested into the fund and paid out when shares are redeemed. The mutual fund portfolio's value and holdings fluctuate as money is invested or shares redeemed and as the value of the securities held by the portfolio rises and falls. The investor's account value fluctuates proportionately with the mutual fund portfolio's value.

QUICK QUIZ 7.A   Choose **A** for an open-end company or **B** for a closed-end company.

_____ 1. Trades in the secondary market

_____ 2. Investors may purchase fractional shares

_____ 3. Can issue common, preferred, and bonds

_____ 4. Issues a fixed number of shares

_____ 5. Does not trade in the secondary market; shares must be redeemed

_____ 6. Price is set by supply and demand

_____ 7. Usually called mutual funds

Quick Quiz answers can be found at the end of the unit.

7. 1. 2   SALES CHARGES

FINRA prohibits its members who underwrite fund shares from assessing sales charges *in excess of 8.5%* of the POP on the purchase of open-end investment company shares. The actual schedule of sales charges is specified *in the prospectus*.

7. 1. 2. 1   Closed-End Funds

Closed-end funds do not carry sales charges. An investor pays a brokerage commission in an agency transaction or pays a markup or markdown in a principal transaction.

7. 1. 2. 2   Open-End Funds

All sales commissions are paid from the sales charges collected. Sales charges include commissions for the managing underwriter, dealers, brokers, and registered representatives, as well as all expenses incurred in communications with the public.

Mutual fund distributors use three different methods to collect the fees for the sale of shares:

- **Front-end loads** (difference between POP and net NAV)
- **Back-end loads** (contingent deferred sales loads)
- **12b-1 fees** (asset-based fees, technically not a sales charge)

Front-End Loads. Front-end sales loads are reflected in a fund's public offering price. The charges are added to the NAV at the time an investor buys shares. They are frequently referred to as Class A shares and have lower operating expense ratios than other classes.

Back-End Loads. A back-end sales load, also called a *contingent deferred sales charge or load (CDSC)*, is charged at the time an investor redeems mutual fund shares. The sales load, a declining percentage charge that is reduced annually (for instance, 8% the first year, 7% the second, 6% the third, and so forth), is applied to the proceeds of any shares sold in that year. The back-end load is usually structured so that it drops to zero after six to eight years at which time they are converted to Class A shares with their lower operating expense ratios. They are frequently referred to as Class B shares.

12b-1 Asset-Based Fees. Mutual funds cannot act as distributors for their own fund shares except under Section 12b-1 of the Investment Company Act of 1940. This provision permits a mutual fund to collect a fee for promotion or sales-related activities in connection with the distribution of its shares. The fee is determined as a flat dollar amount or as a percentage of the fund's average total NAV during the year. The fee is disclosed in the fund's prospectus.

The percentage of net assets charged must be reasonable (typically .5% of net assets—this annual fee cannot exceed .75% of net assets), and the fee must reflect the anticipated level of distribution services. If the fee exceeds .25%, the fund cannot use the term *no-load*.

The payments represent fees that would have been paid to an underwriter had sales charges been negotiated for sales, promotion, and related activities.

7. 1. 2. 3   Classes of Fund Shares

Mutual funds may offer several classes of shares to allow investors to select how they pay the sales charges. The following is a typical method by which firms may classify fund shares by fee type: Class A, B, and C shares.

- **Class A** shares (*front-end load*): investors pay the charge at the time of purchase.

■ **Class B** shares (*back-end load*): declines over time so investors pay the charge at redemption.

■ **Class C** shares (*level load*): no sales charge to purchase, generally a 1% CDSC for one year, with a continuous 12b-1 charge.

The class of shares determines the type of sales charge as well as operating expenses with Class A having lower costs (usually a low or no 12b-1 fee) than Class B and Class C shares. All other rights associated with mutual fund ownership remain the same across each class.

7. 1. 2. 4 Reductions in Sales Charges

The maximum permitted sales charge is reduced if an investment company does not offer certain features. To qualify for the maximum 8.5% sales charge, the investment company must offer both of the following:

■ Breakpoints—a scale of declining sales charges based on the amount invested

■ Rights of accumulation—permits an investor to aggregate shares owned in related accounts in some or all funds in the fund family to reach a breakpoint discount

7. 1. 2. 5 Breakpoints

The schedule of discounts a mutual fund offers is called the fund's **breakpoints**. Breakpoints are available to any person. For a breakpoint qualification, the term *person* includes married couples, parents and their *minor* children, and corporations. Investment clubs or associations formed for the purpose of investing do *not* qualify for breakpoints.

Sample Breakpoint Schedule

Purchase Amount	Sales Charge
$0–$24,999	6.5%
$25,000–$49,999	5.5%
$50,000–$99,999	5%
$100,000–$249,999	3%
$250,000–$499,999	2%
$500,000–$999,999	1%
$1,000,000 +	0%

An investor can qualify for breakpoints in several ways. A large, lump-sum investment is one method. Mutual funds offer additional incentives for an investor to continue to invest and qualify for breakpoints through a **letter of intent** .

7. 1. 2. 5. 1 Breakpoint Sales

Both state and federal regulators prohibit registered personnel from making higher commissions by selling investment company shares in a dollar amount just below the point at which the sales charge is reduced. This is known as a **breakpoint sale** and this practice is considered contrary to just and equitable principles of trade.

Although not specifically listed as a violation, regulators scrutinize large purchases of Class B shares. A purchase large enough to reach a significant Class A share breakpoint results in a low enough sales charge that, in just a few years, the lower operating expenses of the Class A shares will more than make up the difference in front-end cost. In practice, very few firms will accept an order for Class B shares in excess of $100,000, particularly if the investor intends to maintain the position for a number of years.

7. 1. 2. 6   Letter of Intent (LOI)

A person who plans to invest more money with the same mutual fund company may decrease overall sales charges by signing a **letter of intent (LOI)**. In the LOI, the investor informs the investment company that he intends to invest the additional funds necessary to reach the breakpoint within 13 months.

The LOI is a one-sided contract binding on the fund only. The customer must complete the intended investment to qualify for the reduced sales charge. The fund holds the extra shares purchased as a result of the reduced sales charge in escrow. If the customer deposits sufficient money to complete the LOI, he receives the escrowed shares. Appreciation and reinvested dividends do not count toward the LOI.

EXAMPLE   Using the sample breakpoint schedule displayed above, a customer investing $20,000 is under the $25,000 breakpoint. The customer might sign a letter of intent promising an amount that will qualify for the breakpoint within 13 months from the date of the letter. An additional $5,000 invested in the fund within 13 months qualifies the customer for the reduced sales charge. Each deposit is charged the reduced sales charge at the time of purchase.

If the customer has not completed the investment within 13 months, he will be given the choice of sending a check for the difference in sales charges or cashing in escrowed shares to pay the difference.

7. 1. 2. 6. 1   Backdating the Letter

A fund often permits a customer to sign an LOI as late as 90 days after an initial purchase. The LOI may be backdated by up to 90 days to include prior purchases but may not cover more than 13 months in total. This means that if the customer signs the LOI after 60 days, he has 11 months to complete the letter.

7. 1. 2. 7   Combination Privilege

A mutual fund company frequently offers more than one fund and refers to these multiple offerings as its **family of funds**. An investor seeking a reduced sales charge may be allowed to combine separate investments in two or more funds within the same family to reach a breakpoint.

EXAMPLE

Joe Smith has invested $15,000 in the ACE Growth Fund for retirement and $10,000 in the ACE Income Fund for his children's education. The sponsor may view the two separate expenditures as one investment totaling $25,000 when calculating the sales charge.

7. 1. 2. 7. 1   Exchanges Within a Family of Funds

Many investment companies offer the **exchange** or **conversion privilege** within their families of funds. **Exchange privileges** allow an investor to convert an investment in one fund for an equal investment in another fund in the same family at net asset value without incurring an additional sales charge. For example, someone who started investing when in their 30s or 40s by placing their money into an aggressive growth fund, might consider moving into something more conservative when they reached their 50s. Once they hit their 60s and 70s, they would want to have a greater percentage of their money in income funds. By staying in the same family of funds and using the exchange or conversion privilege, all of these changes could be made free of sales loads.

TEST TOPIC ALERT

Suppose a client had purchased $50,000 of Class B shares of an aggressive growth fund. About a year later, there is a life cycle change requiring that the objective be changed to income. If the growth fund shares are liquidated, there would be a high CDSC. But, what would be the case if you advised the client to use the exchange privilege in that same family? There is no contingent deferred sales charge when shares of one fund in the "family" are exchanged for others. However, if the shares are exchanged within the CDSC period, the original holding period carries over to the newly acquired shares.

TAKE NOTE

Any exchange of funds is considered a sale for tax purposes. Any gains or losses are fully reportable at the time of the exchange.

7. 1. 2. 8   Summary of Key Mutual Fund Characteristics

To assist you in remembering many of the details, here is a list of characteristics that might be tested on the exam:

- A **professional investment adviser** manages the portfolio for investors.
- Mutual funds provide **diversification** by investing in many different companies.
- A **custodian (usually a bank)** holds a mutual fund's assets to ensure safekeeping.
- Most funds allow a low minimum investment, often $500 or less, to open an account and allow additional investment for as little as $25.
- An investment company may allow investments at reduced sales charges by offering **breakpoints,** for instance, through a **letter of intent** .

■ An investor retains voting rights, such as the right to vote for changes in the board of directors of the investment company, approval of the investment adviser, changes in the fund's investment objective, changes in sales charges, and liquidation of the fund.

■ By FINRA rules, all funds created after April 1, 2000 offer automatic reinvestment of capital gains and dividend distributions without a sales charge. To remain competitive, almost all of the old funds do so as well. This has the effect of compounding the investment.

■ An investor can liquidate a portion of his holdings without having to select a specific security—the fund generally has enough cash on hand to process redemption requests.

■ Tax liabilities for an investor are simplified because each year the fund distributes a 1099 form explaining taxability of distributions.

■ A mutual fund may offer various withdrawal plans that allow different payment methods at redemption.

7. 1. 3   INVESTMENT OBJECTIVES

Once a mutual fund defines its objective, its portfolio is invested to match it. The objective must be clearly stated in the mutual fund's prospectus and can be changed only by a majority vote of the fund's outstanding shares.

7. 1. 3. 1   Stock Funds

Common stocks normally provide the growth component of any mutual fund that has growth as a primary objective. Preferred, utility, and large-cap stocks are typically used to provide the income component of any stock mutual fund that has income as a primary objective.

Although there are other categories (to be covered in Unit 4), at this point you need to know the difference between large-cap and small-cap stocks. The term, "cap" refers to the company's market capitalization (the number of outstanding common shares multiplied by the current market price per share). For example, a company with 30 million shares outstanding where the price per share is $30 has a market cap of $900 million. As you will see again in Unit 4, a market cap of $300 million to $2 billion is considered small-cap, while that of more than $10 billion is considered large-cap. It is generally felt that the larger the market cap, the more conservative the investment.

Growth Funds. Growth funds invest in stocks of rapidly growing corporations. Growth companies tend to reinvest all or most of their profits for research and development rather than pay dividends. Growth funds are focused on generating capital gains rather than income. Aggressive growth funds tend to concentrate more in small-cap stocks, while conservative growth funds have a preponderance of large-cap issues.

Income Funds. An income fund stresses current income over growth. The fund's objective may be accomplished by investing in the stocks of companies with long histories of dividend payments, such as utility company stocks, large-cap stocks, and preferred stocks.

Combination Funds. A combination fund (also called a *growth and income fund*) may attempt to combine the objectives of growth and current income by diversifying its portfolio among companies showing long-term growth potential and companies paying high dividends.

Specialized (Sector) Funds. Many funds specialize in particular economic sectors or industries. Others specialize in geographic areas such as the BRIC countries or the Pacific Rim. The funds have 25–100% of their assets invested in their specialties and are more likely than other funds to stick to a relatively fixed allocation.

EXAMPLE

Gold funds (gold mining stocks), insurance funds (insurance company stocks), technology funds, and utility funds are examples of sector funds. Sector funds offer high appreciation potential but may also pose higher risks to the investor because of their lack of diversification among industries or geographic areas.

Special Situation Funds. Special situation funds buy securities of companies that may benefit from a change within the corporations or in the economy. Takeover candidates and turnaround situations are common investments.

Index Funds. Index funds invest in securities to mirror a market index, such as the S&P 500. An index fund buys and sells securities in a manner that mirrors the composition of the selected index. The fund's performance tracks the underlying index's performance. This approach reflects the **passive** style of portfolio management, as opposed to **active** portfolio management.

Turnover of securities in an index fund's portfolio is minimal. As a result, an index fund generally has lower management costs than other types of funds. Furthermore, because index funds have little turnover, they frequently appeal to investors seeking minimal taxable capital gains.

Foreign Stock Funds. Foreign stock funds invest mostly in the securities of companies that have their principal business activities outside the United States. Long-term capital appreciation is their primary objective, although some funds also seek current income. Foreign investments involve foreign currency risks, as well as the usual risks associated with stock investments.

TAKE NOTE

There are two terms generally used to describe funds that invest in foreign securities.

- *International* funds have their entire portfolio invested in securities issued outside of the United States. The way to remember that is if you will be traveling internationally, you'll be outside the United States.

- *Global* funds have the portfolio invested "around the globe," and that includes U.S. securities. Once again, using the travel example, if you were to travel around the globe, a portion of your trip would be in the United States.

7. 1. 3. 2   Bond Funds

Bond funds have income as their primary investment objective. Some funds invest solely in investment-grade corporate bonds. Others, for enhanced safety, invest only in government issues. Others seek capital appreciation by investing in lower-rated issues that may be upgraded in the future.

Tax-Free (Tax-Exempt) Bond Funds. Tax-exempt funds invest in municipal bonds or notes that produce income exempt from federal income tax. Tax-free funds can invest in municipal bonds and tax-exempt money market instruments. Please note that any capital gains distributions from the fund are taxable just as with any other fund.

U.S. Government and Agency Securities Funds. U.S. government funds purchase securities issued by the U.S. Treasury or an agency of the U.S. government, such as Ginnie Mae. Investors in these funds seek current income and maximum safety.

Foreign Bond Funds. These funds invest in foreign sovereign and/or corporate debt issues. Although they carry the same general risks as investing directly into foreign debt, these tend to be reduced because of the professional management and diversification offered by fund investing.

7. 1. 3. 3   Balanced Funds

Balanced funds invest in stocks for appreciation and bonds for income, and different types of securities are purchased according to a formula.

EXAMPLE   A balanced fund's portfolio might contain 60% stocks and 40% bonds.

7. 1. 3. 4   Asset Allocation Funds

Asset allocation funds split investments between stocks for growth, bonds for income, and money market instruments (or cash) for stability. The fund adviser switches the percentage of holdings in each asset category according to the performance, or expected performance, of that group. We will have more to say about asset allocation in Unit 4.

EXAMPLE   A fund may have 60% of its investments in stock, 20% in bonds, and the remaining 20% in cash. If the stock market is expected to do well, the adviser may switch from cash and bonds into stock. The result may be a portfolio of 80% in stock, 10% in bonds, and 10% in cash. Conversely, if the stock market is expected to decline, the fund may invest heavily in cash and sell stocks.

TAKE NOTE

Remember our statement from a few pages ago: *Unlike closed-end companies, open-end companies only issue common stock?* How does that fit into our discussion of these funds that invest solely in bonds, or allocate their assets to various types of securities? Remember, open-end investment companies (mutual funds) raise capital to invest by selling shares of their stock – investors purchase shares of common stock in the fund; the fund is the issuer of that stock. Then, the investment company uses the capital raised from the sale of those shares to invest in whatever the portfolio managers believe will help them meet the fund's objectives. Obviously, in a bond fund, those investments will be in bonds, but the investors are not buying the bonds; the investment company is with the money raised from the sale of its shares.

7. 1. 3. 5 Money Market Funds

Money market funds are no-load, open-end investment companies (mutual funds) that serve as temporary holding accounts for investors' money. The term *no-load* means that investors pay no sales or liquidation fees. Money market mutual funds are most suitable for investors whose financial goals require liquidity above all.

Dividend rates on money market funds are neither fixed nor guaranteed and change often. The interest these funds earn and distribute as dividends is computed daily and credited to customer accounts monthly. In general, money market mutual funds offer check-writing privileges making for extraordinary liquidity.

Investors have a choice of taxable money market funds where the income is treated as a non-qualifying dividend (ordinary income rates) or tax-exempt money market funds where, because the portfolio consists of tax-exempt (municipal) securities, the income is not taxed on a federal basis.

The NAV of money market funds is generally fixed at $1 per share. Although this price is not guaranteed, a fund is managed in order not to "break the buck" regardless of market changes. Thus, the price of money market shares does not fluctuate in response to changing interest rates.

TAKE NOTE

On July 23, 2014, the Securities and Exchange Commission adopted amendments to the rules that govern money market mutual funds. Because there is a two-year transition period before the rules finally take effect, it is unlikely that any of the changes will appear on your exam. Furthermore, the nature of the changes is such that it is possible that questions about them will not ever appear on this test. However, to be safe, here are the most important facts:

■ The new rules require a floating net asset value (NAV) for *Institutional prime money market funds*, which allows the daily share prices of these funds to fluctuate along with changes in the market-based value of fund assets

■ With a floating NAV, Institutional prime money market funds (including institutional municipal money market funds) are required to value their portfolio securities using market-based factors and sell and redeem shares based on a floating NAV. These funds no longer will be allowed to use the special pricing and valuation conventions that currently permit them to maintain a constant share price of $1.00. With liquidity fees and redemption gates, money market fund boards have the ability to impose fees and gates during periods of stress.

■ Two new categories of funds were designated. A *Government money market fund* means a money market fund that invests 99.5% or more of its total assets in cash, U.S. government securities, and/or repurchase agreements that are collateralized fully and a *Retail money market fund* means a money market fund that has policies and procedures reasonably designed to limit all beneficial owners of the fund to natural persons.

■ Government and Retail money market funds may continue to use the previous methods of computing NAV and sell and redeem their shares at a stable price of $1.00.

For funds with a floating NAV, Rule 482 (the tombstone ad rule) requires the following statement:

You could lose money by investing in the fund. Because the share price of the fund will fluctuate, when you sell your shares they may be worth more or less than what you originally paid for them. The fund may impose a fee upon sale of your shares or may temporarily suspend your ability to sell shares if the fund's liquidity falls below required minimums because of market conditions or other factors. An investment in the fund is not insured or guaranteed by the Federal Deposit Insurance Corporation or any other government agency. The fund's sponsor has no legal obligation to provide financial support to the fund, and you should not expect that the sponsor will provide financial support to the fund at any time.

7. 1. 3. 5. 1   *Restrictions on Money Market Funds*

SEC rules limit the investments available to money market funds and require certain disclosures to investors.

Restrictions include the following.

■ Investments are limited to securities with remaining maturities of 397 days or less, with average portfolio maturity not exceeding 60 days.

■ Investments are limited to securities that have received a rating from a recognized rating agency in one of the two highest short-term rating categories.

TEST TOPIC ALERT

Be aware that an investment in a money market fund is not insured or guaranteed by the FDIC or any other government agency. Although a money market fund seeks to preserve the value of the investment at $1.00 per share, it is possible to lose money by investing in a money market fund.

7. 1. 3. 6   Target Date Funds

Although we have yet to hear from students that these funds have been mentioned on the exam, due to their growing popularity, it is only a matter of time before they appear.

What is a target date fund? The Investment Company Institute, the trade organization for investment companies, describes them this way: "Target date funds, which are also called lifecycle funds, are designed to offer a convenient way to invest for a person expecting to retire around a particular date. A target date fund pursues a long-term investment strategy, using a mix of asset classes (or asset allocation) that the fund provider adjusts to become more conservative over time. Fund providers typically offer target date funds with target dates spaced at 5- or 10-year intervals to meet the needs of retirement investors across a wide range of ages. For example, an individual anticipating retirement in 2039 could invest in a 2040 fund, while one expecting to retire in 2017 might choose between a 2015 fund, a 2020 fund, or a combination of the two."

For those familiar with target date funds, although primarily used by investors for retirement purposes, the fund doesn't state its objectives that way. Here is an example of how one target date fund states its objective in its prospectus: "Depending on the proximity to its target date, the fund will seek to achieve the following objectives to varying degrees: growth, income and conservation of capital. The fund will increasingly emphasize income and conservation of capital by investing a greater portion of its assets in bond, equity income and balanced funds as it approaches and passes its target date. In this way, the fund seeks to balance total return and stability over time."

7. 1. 4   COMPARING MUTUAL FUNDS

Investors should select funds that match their personal and financial objectives. When comparing funds with similar objectives, the investor should review information regarding funds':

- costs;
- taxation; and
- services offered.

The suitability of a mutual fund must also be considered once the above information has been determined.

7. 1. 4. 1   Costs

Sales loads, management fees, and operating expenses reduce an investor's returns because they diminish the amount of money invested in a fund. Historically, mutual funds have charged **front-end loads** of up to 8.5% of the money invested (public offering price). This percentage serves as a sales commission to a sales force and other expenses associated with selling the shares.

Many **low-load** funds charge between 2% and 5%. Additionally, funds may charge a **back-end** load when funds are withdrawn. Some funds charge ongoing fees under section 12b-1 of the Investment Company Act of 1940. These funds deduct annual fees to pay for marketing and distribution costs.

A fund's expense ratio expresses the management fees and operating expenses as a percentage of the fund's net assets. All mutual funds, load and no-load, have expense ratios.

The expense ratio is calculated by dividing annual operating expenses by the average dollar value of the fund's assets under management.

The sales charge is not considered an expense when calculating a fund's expense ratio.

EXAMPLE   An expense ratio of 1.72% means that the fund spends $1.72 per year for every $100 of invested assets.

Typically, more aggressive funds have higher expense ratios.

EXAMPLE   An aggressive growth fund's expense ratio is usually higher than that of a AAA bond fund because more trading occurs in the growth fund's portfolio.

7. 1. 4. 2   Taxation

Mutual fund investors pay taxes on income and capital gains distributed by the fund. Dividends that qualify are taxed at 15%; for test purposes, all capital gains distributions are from the fund's long term gains, so they are taxed at 15% to the investor. For investors in higher tax brackets, suggesting municipal bonds funds could be appropriate because their dividends (but not capital gains) are generally free from federal income tax. There are also funds that advertise themselves as *tax efficient funds*, but we don't expect you'll see that term on the exam.

TAKE NOTE   Dividends and capital gains distributions are currently taxable to the shareholder, whether they are taken in cash or reinvested to purchase additional shares. Dividends must be reported as dividend income and will be taxed either as ordinary income or as a qualifying dividend with a maximum rate of 15%; capital gains distributions must be reported as a long-term capital gain.

TAKE NOTE   The American Taxpayer Relief Act of 2012 contained provisions for higher tax rates for very high-income taxpayers. Those are taxpayers with taxable income for 2015 that exceeds $413,200 ($464,850 for married taxpayers filing a joint return). For these taxpayers, instead of a maximum rate of 15%, the capital gains and dividend tax rate is 20% (not including the 3.8% tax on investment income imposed by the Affordable Care Act). Therefore, these folks could be paying a rate as high as 23.8% on qualifying dividends and long-term capital gains. We doubt that this information will be part of the exam, but, if we learn that it is, we will post that information on the Exam Tips and Content Updates.

7. 1. 4. 3   Services Offered

The services mutual funds offer include retirement accounts, investment plans, check-writing privileges, phone transfers, conversion privileges, combination investment plans, withdrawal plans, and others.

7. 1. 5   SUITABILITY

In determining suitability of mutual funds, the first step is to determine the customer's primary objective. In general, the following basic rules apply.

- Investors seeking growth should invest in stock funds.
- Investors seeking income should invest in bond funds.
- Investors who are concerned about safety of principal should invest in government bond funds.

Investors who are concerned with immediate liquidity should invest in money market funds.

- Additional objectives of the investor must also be taken into consideration. Some possibilities are listed below.
- Investors seeking aggressive growth should invest in technology stock funds or stock funds invested in new companies. Aggressive funds or small-cap funds are usually most suitable for investors who have high risk tolerance and/or a long time horizon.
- Investors who are seeking growth but are more conservative should consider balanced funds, which are likely to be large-cap funds. These funds are not as speculative as smaller-cap and aggressive funds.
- Investors seeking both income and safety of principal should invest in a government bond fund.
- Investors seeking higher income who can assume moderate risk should invest in a corporate bond fund.
- Investors with a very high risk tolerance can maximize current income through investing in a high-yield (junk) bond fund.
- High tax bracket investors seeking income should invest in a municipal bond fund.
- Investors seeking income-producing stock should select a large-cap stock fund (a large-cap stock is a large company stock that has a consistently strong performance history and regularly pays dividends), a preferred stock fund, or a utility stock fund (utility stocks historically pay high, consistent dividends).
- Investors seeking safety of principal with high liquidity should consider a money market fund.
- Investors who wish to invest in a portfolio that mirrors the performance of the stock market should consider an index fund.
- Asset allocation funds provide a combination of stocks and cash bonds (as well as other asset classes) and allow the portfolio manager the flexibility to change the portfolio mix to react to market conditions.

Hedge funds (covered later in this Unit) are for the speculative investor. They are not true mutual funds but do provide investors with an undivided interest in a portfolio. They are considered suitable for investors with high risk tolerance.

QUICK QUIZ 7.B

Match the objective with the type of fund.

   A. Balanced fund
   B. Aggressive growth fund
   C. Specialized fund
   D. Large cap stock fund

____   1. Pursues capital growth with less than average risk

____   2. Invests to maximize capital gains quickly with high risk tolerance

____   3. Invests to diversify securities and is conservative

____   4. Invests in medical technology and is not risk averse

---

QUICK QUIZ 7.C

Match the objective with the type of fund.

   A. Conservative growth fund
   B. Money market fund
   C. Small-cap fund
   D. Balanced fund

____   1. Capital gains/income/lower risk

____   2. Capital gains/moderate risk

____   3. Liquidity/low risk

____   4. Capital gains/higher risk

QUICK QUIZ 7.D

Match the objective with the type of fund.

   A. Government bond fund
   B. Large-cap fund
   C. Asset allocation fund

____   1. Capital gains/income/lower risk

____   2. Growth/low risk

____   3. Income/low risk

Match the objective with the type of fund.

  A. Ginnie Mae fund
  B. Special situation fund
  C. Asset allocation fund
  D. Index fund

  ____ 1. Purchase different classes of investments to achieve capital gains, income, and diversification

  ____ 2. Mimic stock market indexes to achieve performance comparable to the market overall

  ____ 3. Achieve safety of principal with yields slightly higher than government bond fund

  ____ 4. Seek investments in companies with unusual opportunities

7. 1. 5. 1 Advantages to Investing in Mutual Funds

■ Diversification: The old saying "don't put all of your eggs in one basket" certainly applies to the benefits of diversifying one's portfolio assets. Mutual funds are probably the easiest way to accomplish this. Although diversification may help to reduce risk, it will never completely eliminate it. It is possible to lose all or part of your investment.

■ Professional management: Those individuals in charge of managing a mutual fund's portfolio must be registered as investment advisers with the SEC. The Investment Company Act of 1940 requires that they follow the stated objectives set forth in the prospectus. Taking into consideration prevailing market conditions and other factors, the mutual fund manager will decide when to buy or sell securities. Rare is the individual who has the time, knowledge, or resources to compete with these professionals.

■ Convenience: With most mutual funds, buying and liquidating shares, changing reinvestment options, and getting information can be accomplished conveniently by going online at the fund's website, by calling a toll-free phone number, or by mail.

 — Although a fund's shareholder is relieved of the day-to-day tasks involved in researching, buying, and selling securities, an investor will still need to evaluate a mutual fund on the basis of investment goals and risk tolerance before making a purchase decision. Investors should always read the prospectus carefully before investing in any mutual fund.

■ Liquidity: The Investment Company Act of 1940 requires that an open-end investment company stand ready to redeem shares at the next computed NAV per share. Payment must be made within 7 days of the redemption request. Although there may be a redemption charge, and, of course, the value of the shares may be less than their cost, liquidity is assured.

■ Minimum initial investment: As mentioned previously, it doesn't take a great deal of wealth to get started investing in funds and, generally, once you are a shareholder, most funds permit additional investments of $100 or even less.

It is generally agreed that the #1 advantage to investing in mutual funds is the *diversification* offered.

7. 1. 5. 2   Disadvantages to Investing in Mutual Funds

- Risks: Even with the benefits offered by diversification and professional management, market prices do fluctuate. Equity funds have market risk, whereas bond funds may be subject to interest rate risk. Unlike an individual bond that ultimately repays principal at maturity, a bond fund doesn't have a maturity date. The only mutual fund that generally does not fluctuate in price is the money market fund, but there is a trade-off in lack of growth and low income. Not only that, but the income of a money market fund will vary, unlike that of a bank CD, which is fixed and insured by the FDIC.

- Fees and expenses: One must carefully analyze all of the costs involved. These include sales charges, -fees, and possible redemption fees. Management fees are probably the largest expense on an ongoing basis. The investor has no control over the manager's timing of purchases and sales, so tax efficiency could become an issue. Prospectuses will not contain all the costs that affect the net return on the fund. This is why it is important to compare net returns after all expenses, including taxes to the investor.

7. 1. 6   EXCHANGE-TRADED FUNDS (ETFs)

An ETF registers with the SEC under the Investment Company Act of 1940 either as a unit investment trust (a "UIT ETF") or as an open-end management company (an "open-end ETF").

This type of fund generally invests in a specific index, such as the S&P 500. Any class of asset that has a published index around it and is liquid can be made into an ETF so that there are ETFs for real estate and commodities as well as stocks and bonds. In this way, an ETF is similar to an index mutual fund. In fact, in recent years, there has been a growth in actively traded ETFs where, instead of attempting to mirror an index, the managers select individual assets based upon expected performance. The difference is that the exchange-traded fund trades like a stock on an exchange or Nasdaq and, in this way, is similar to a closed-end investment company. The investor can take advantage of price changes that are due to the market, rather than just the underlying value of the stocks in the portfolio.

TAKE NOTE

Although, as stated, most ETFs are passive in that they are based on some index, in recent years, there has been a growth in actively traded ETFs where, instead of attempting to mirror an index, the managers select individual assets based upon expected performance. This concept will make more sense after you read Session 16 explaining passive and active portfolio management styles.

ETFs can be purchased on margin and sold short, just like any other listed stock. Expenses tend to be lower than those of mutual funds as well because all the adviser has to do is match up to the specified index, so the fees are minimal. In addition, there can be tax advantages to owning ETFs.

However, because there are brokerage commissions on each trade (in and out), ETFs are generally not competitive with a no-load index fund for the small investor making regular periodic investments such as in a dollar cost averaging plan (described in Unit 4).

TAKE NOTE

There are now some U.S.-listed ETFs that are available for commission-free trading on certain select platforms (these are typically proprietary funds). These products can be bought and sold without traditional brokerage commissions for investors with certain accounts and subject to certain restrictions. For exam purposes, these are the exceptions rather than the rule.

ETFs, along with other investment companies and REITs, are included in the term "pooled investment vehicles." Many exchange-traded funds are legally classified as unit investment trusts (UITs) with the rest as open-end companies (although those cannot be referred to as mutual funds because shares are not redeemable).

Unlike the CEF (close-end fund) where the market price will generally vary quite a bit from the NAV because those prices are determined by supply and demand, there are occasions where persistent small premiums and discounts arise in ETFs, but that is due to a structural inconsistency. Under normal circumstances, the premium and discount that arises between an ETF NAV and its trading price at the end of the day is the result of late in the day market activity and will narrow at the opening on the following trading day.

7. 1. 7   REAL ESTATE INVESTMENT TRUSTS (REITs)

A **real estate investment trust** (**REIT,** pronounced *reet*) is a company that manages a portfolio of real estate investments to earn profits for shareholders. REITs are normally publicly traded and serve as a source of long-term financing for real estate projects. A REIT pools capital in a manner similar to an investment company. Shareholders receive dividends from investment income or capital gains distributions. REITs normally:

■ own commercial property (**equity REITs**);

■ own mortgages on commercial property (**mortgage REITs**); or

■ do both (**hybrid REITs**).

REITs are organized as trusts in which investors buy shares or certificates of beneficial interest either on stock exchanges or in the over-the-counter market.

REITs enjoy a unique hybrid status for federal income tax purposes. A REIT shareholder generally is taxed only on dividends paid by the REIT and on gains upon the disposition of REIT shares. A REIT is a corporation for U.S. tax purposes, but because it receives a dividends paid deduction, the REIT generally is not subject to corporate tax if it distributes to its shareholders substantially all of its taxable income for each year

How much is "substantially" all? Under the guidelines of Subchapter M of the Internal Revenue Code, a REIT can avoid being taxed as a corporation by receiving 75% or more of its income from real estate and distributing 90% or more of its taxable income to its shareholders.

TEST TOPIC ALERT

Four important points to remember about REITs follow.

■ An owner of REITs holds an undivided interest in a pool of real estate investments.

■ REITs are liquid because they trade on exchanges and over the counter.

■ REITs are not investment companies (mutual funds).

■ REITs offer dividends and gains to investors but do not pass through losses like limited partnerships, and therefore are not considered to be direct participation programs (DPPs).

TAKE NOTE

In recent years, there has been substantial growth in the number of "non-traded" REITs (limited liquidity). However, for exam purposes, assume the REIT is publicly traded unless the question states otherwise.

In summation, why would you include REITs in a client's portfolio?

■ The opportunity to invest in real estate without the degree of liquidity risk found in direct ownership

■ A negative correlation to the general stock market (we'll talk more about correlation in Unit 3, but, for now, it means that real estate prices and the stock market frequently move in opposite directions)

■ Reasonable income and/or potential capital appreciation

In doing so, the client would be incurring the following risks:

■ Because the investor has no control, much of the risk in investing in REITs lies with the quality of the management.

■ Problem loans in the portfolio could cause income and/or capital to decrease.

■ Dividends are not considered qualified for purposes of the 15% maximum tax rate and are taxed at full ordinary income rates.

■ If the REIT is not publicly traded, liquidity is very limited. While a portion of total shares outstanding may be redeemable each year, subject to limitations, redemption offers may be priced below the purchase price or current price.

QUICK QUIZ 7.F

1. An open-end investment management company is also referred to as a(n)

A. exchange traded fund

B. face amount certificate company

C. mutual fund.

D. unit investment trust

2. According to the Investment Company Act of 1940, an open-end investment company must compute its NAV

   A. no less frequently than once per day
   B. weekly
   C. monthly
   D. annually

3. A sector fund is one where the assets are

   A. concentrated in a particular industry or geographical area
   B. invested in emerging growth companies
   C. invested in special situations
   D. invested in other mutual funds

4. An investor looking for an open-end investment company with an objective of providing current income to its shareholders, would most likely choose a(n)

   A. common stock fund
   B. growth fund
   C. income fund
   D. venture capital fund

5. If ABC Fund pays regular dividends, offers a high degree of safety of principal, and appeals especially to investors in the higher tax brackets, ABC is a(n)

   A. aggressive growth fund
   B. corporate bond fund
   C. money market fund
   D. municipal bond fund

6. An investor has a portfolio diversified among many different asset classes. If there was an immediate need for cash, which of the following would probably be the most liquid?

   A. Cash value from a universal life insurance policy
   B. CDL Common Stock Mutual Fund
   C. QRS Money Market Mutual Fund
   D. XYZ International Stock Mutual Fund

7. A review of the prospectus of an open-end investment company reveals that its portfolio consists entirely of CDs, Treasury bills, and repurchase agreements. This is probably a(n)

   A. balanced fund
   B. exchange-traded fund (ETF)
   C. index fund
   D. money market fund

8. In the context of purchasing shares in a mutual fund, the term "breakpoint" refers to the point at which the

   A. dollar amount of shares being purchased qualifies the investor for a lower sales charge
   B. mutual fund company stops offering new shares to the public
   C. investor is assured of making a profit on the shares
   D. shares are selling for less than net asset value (NAV)

9. An investor who initially makes a small investment in a mutual fund may have the advantage of a lower sales charge on investments made over a 13-month period through a(n)

   A. breakpoint letter
   B. Class A letter
   C. letter of intent
   D. sponsor's letter

10. A couple in their early 30s has been married for 4 years, their disposable income is relatively high, and they are planning to buy a condominium. If they need a safe place to invest their down payment for about 6 months, which of the following mutual funds is the most suitable for these customers?

   A. LMN Cash Reserves Money Market Fund
   B. ATF Capital Appreciation Fund
   C. ABC Growth & Income Fund
   D. XYZ Investment-Grade Bond Fund

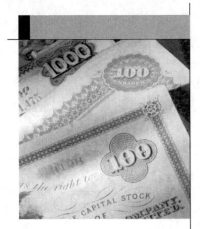

8

Insurance-Based Products

In the previous session, we discussed a number of different pooled investment vehicles. In this session, we're going to cover two more, variable annuities and variable life insurance. But those are not the only insurance-based products that are relevant to this exam. Even though the others we'll discuss are not securities, understanding what they are and their basic features are testable items.

The Series 65 exam will include approximately four questions on the material presented in this session.

When you have completed this session, you should be able to:

- **contrast** the difference between fixed and variable annuities;

- **list** the differences between variable annuities and mutual funds;

- **compute** the account return for an index annuity;

- **compare** the different purchase and settlement options for annuities;

- **calculate** the tax on an early withdrawal from an annuity;

- **give** an example of the major types of life insurance;

- **state** the loan provisions applicable to a variable life policy; and

- **explain** the exchange privilege applicable to a variable life policy.

Although many products offered by insurance companies are not securities, the securities professional should be aware of the features of both securities and non-securities offerings.

8. 1   ANNUITIES

An **annuity** is generally a contract between an individual and a life insurance company, usually purchased for retirement income. An investor, the **annuitant**, pays the premium in one lump sum or in periodic payments. At a future date, the annuitant can either elect to surrender the policy and receive a lump sum payout or begin receiving regular income distributions that will continue for life.

Because all earnings are tax-deferred, many individuals looking to accumulate additional funds for retirement find annuities to be a valuable tool.

Annuity contracts are classified into three types (depending on the payout the annuity makes):

■ fixed annuities;

■ variable annuities; and

■ combination annuities.

8. 1. 1   FIXED ANNUITIES

A **fixed annuity** guarantees a fixed rate of return. When the individual elects to begin receiving income, the payout is determined by the account's value and the annuitant's life expectancy based on mortality tables. A fixed annuity payout remains constant throughout the annuitant's life.

TAKE NOTE

Because the insurance company guarantees the return and the annuitant bears no risk, a fixed annuity is an insurance product and not a security. A salesperson must have a life insurance license to sell fixed annuities but does not need to be securities licensed.

Although principal and interest are not at risk, a fixed annuity risks loss of purchasing power because of inflation.

EXAMPLE

An individual who annuitized a contract in 1990 may have been guaranteed a monthly payout of $800. Decades later, this amount may prove insufficient to live on.

8. 1. 2   VARIABLE ANNUITIES

Instead of purchase payments being directed to the insurance company's general account, money deposited in a variable annuity is directed into one or more subaccounts of the company's separate account. Although the options include money market securities and bonds, purchase payments are frequently invested in a stock portfolio, which has a better chance of keeping pace with inflation than fixed-income investments.

The greater potential gain of a variable annuity involves more potential risk than a fixed annuity because it invests in securities rather than accepting the insurance company's guarantees. Payouts may vary considerably because an annuity unit's worth fluctuates with the securities' value.

Fixed Annuities	Variable Annuities
Monthly payout is fixed	Monthly payout varies
Guaranteed interest rate	Variable rate of return
Investment risk assumed by insurance company	Investment risk assumed by annuitant
Portfolio of fixed-income securities	Portfolio of equities, debt, money market instruments
General account	Separate account
Vulnerable to inflation	Resistant to inflation
Insurance regulation	Insurance and securities regulation

8. 1. 2. 1   Separate Account

The contributions that investors make to a variable annuity are kept in a **separate account** from the insurance company's general funds.

Because the investor rather than the insurance company bears the risk, a variable annuity is considered to be a security. As a consequence, variable annuity salespersons must have both a securities license (registered with FINRA and the applicable state or states) and an insurance license issued by the appropriate state(s).

TEST TOPIC ALERT

It is the performance of the specific subaccount(s) selected by the investor that determines the investment return.

Principal Features of Mutual Funds vs. Variable Annuities

Mutual Funds	Variable Annuities
Investment company	Insurance company
Shares	Units
Investment objectives: varied	Investment objectives: primarily growth and income
No guarantees	Few guarantees
Redeemed by issuer	Redeemed by issuer
Price based on formula	Price based on formula

8. 1. 2. 2   Combination Annuities

A **combination annuity** attempts to provide a monthly payout that consists of guaranteed fixed amounts as well as a payout that might keep pace with inflation.

An investor contributes to both a fixed account and a variable account for a combination annuity. The result is a guaranteed return on the fixed annuity portion and a potentially higher return on the variable annuity portion.

8. 1. 2. 3   Index Annuity

In an effort to overcome the purchasing power risk of fixed annuities, but without the market risk of the variable annuity, the industry developed the index annuity (IA). This product is sometimes called an equity index annuity or a fixed index annuity.

Indexed annuities (IAs) are currently popular among investors seeking market participation but with a guarantee against loss. Unlike a traditional fixed annuity, an index annuity credits interest to the owner's account using a formula based on the performance of a particular stock index such as the S&P 500. If the index does well, the annuitant is credited with a specified percentage of the growth of the index—typically 80% or 90% of the growth. This is known as the participation rate. If, over the life of the annuity, the index does poorly, the annuitant may receive the IA's minimum guaranteed return—typically 3 or 4%.

In addition to the participation rate, there is usually a cap rate. A typical cap might be 12%. This means that if your annuity was pegged to the S&P 500 and that index increased 30% during the year, your gain would be capped at 12%. One other negative characteristic of these products is that they tend to have longer surrender charge periods (as long as 15 years) than other annuities, especially if there is a front-end bonus.

EXAMPLE   To give you an idea of how an index annuity might work, consider one with a participation rate of 80%, a cap rate of 10%, and a minimum guarantee of 3%. If the index shows growth of 9% during the index annuity's measurement period, the annuitant would be credited with 7.2% growth (80% of 9%, which is less than the cap of 10%). In any year where the index declines, the annuitant's account is not credited with any earnings, but, and this is the real benefit, the account does not lose any value either. The 3% guaranteed rate would apply if, over the term of the annuity, performance was less than 3%.

TAKE NOTE   Although *index annuity* is the preferred term in the industry, your exam may refer to this product as an *equity index annuity*.

TEST TOPIC ALERT

In NASAA's never-ending battle to try to baffle potential investment adviser representatives with questions about products they will most likely never handle, we are hearing from students that you should know the different crediting methods used for index annuities.

Without going into the technicalities (it seems all you have to know is the different types, not a lot about how they work), the purchaser can be offered the following choices as to how growth in the underlying index will be credited in the form of interest to the account:

1. Annual reset. In this method, the interest to be credited to the account is computed by comparing the index value at the end of the year to the value at the beginning of the year (hence the term annual).

2. High-water mark. In this method, the highest value reached by the index between anniversary dates of the annuity is compared to the value at the beginning of the year.

3. Point-to-point. In this method, the interest is computed based on the value of the index at the end of the contract compared to the beginning. A variation is annual point-to-point.

8. 1. 3 PURCHASING ANNUITIES

Insurance companies offer a number of purchase options to make it easy for annuity owners to accumulate money.

8. 1. 3. 1 Deferred Annuity

An annuity may be purchased with a single lump-sum investment (with payout of benefits deferred until the annuitant elects to receive them). This type of investment is referred to as a **single-premium deferred annuity**.

8. 1. 3. 2 Periodic Payment Deferred Annuity

A **periodic payment deferred annuity** allows a person to make periodic payments. The contract holder can invest money on a monthly, quarterly, or annual basis (with payout of benefits deferred until the annuitant elects to receive them).

8. 1. 3. 3 Immediate Annuity

An investor may purchase an **immediate annuity** contract by depositing a single lump sum. The insurance company begins to pay out the annuity's benefits immediately—usually within 60 days.

8. 1. 3. 4   Accumulation Stage

The pay-in period for an annuity is known as the **accumulation stage**. During the accumulation stage of an annuity contract, the contract terms are flexible. An investor who misses a periodic payment is in no danger of forfeiting the preceding contributions.

The contract holder can terminate the contract at any time during the accumulation stage, although the contract holder is likely to incur surrender charges on amounts withdrawn in the first five to 10 years after issuance of the contract. To discourage termination of contracts, insurance companies often allow contract holders to borrow from their accounts without having to cancel the contracts.

8. 1. 3. 5   Accumulation Units

An **accumulation unit** is an accounting measure that represents an investor's share of ownership in the separate account. An accumulation unit's value is determined in the same way as the value of mutual fund shares. The unit value changes with the value of the securities held in the separate account and the total number of accumulation units outstanding.

8. 1. 3. 6   Sales Charges on Variable Annuities

Unlike mutual funds, FINRA has not set a maximum sales charge for the sale of variable annuities. However, the SEC has ruled that charges must be reasonable and not excessive.

8. 1. 3. 6. 1   *Variable Annuity Sales and Redemption Practices*

Applications and purchase payments must be promptly transmitted to the issuer of the contract. The insurance company must make prompt payments on any redemption requested by contract holders in accordance with the contract terms.

8. 1. 4   RECEIVING DISTRIBUTIONS FROM ANNUITIES

The payout period for an annuity is known as the **annuity stage**.

8. 1. 4. 1   Annuity Payout Options

It is now time for the contract holder to decide on the **settlement option**. An annuity offers several payout options for amounts accumulated in the annuity contract. The investor can let the money accumulate in the annuity, withdraw the accumulated funds in a lump sum, or withdraw the accumulated funds periodically by **annuitizing** the contract. Annuitizing occurs when the investor converts from the accumulation (pay-in) stage to the distribution (payout) stage.

The decision to annuitize the contract locks in the specified payout option. The contract holder may not change it. Annuity payout options, in order from largest monthly payout to smallest monthly payout, follow.

8. 1. 4. 1. 1 Life Annuity/Straight Life/Pure Life

Under this option, the payout is structured so that the annuitant receives periodic payments (usually monthly) over his lifetime. No added options or benefits exist; therefore, for a given amount of funds, this option provides the largest periodic payment.

8. 1. 4. 1. 2 Life Annuity with Period Certain

Under the life annuity with period certain payout option, an annuitant receives payments for life, with a certain minimum period guaranteed. If the annuitant dies before the period certain expires, payments continue to the annuitant's named beneficiaries for the period certain. If the annuitant lives beyond the period certain, payments continue until the annuitant's death.

EXAMPLE   A client purchases a life annuity with a 10-year period certain payout. The insurance company guarantees payments for the life of the annuitant or 10 years, whichever is longer. If the annuitant lives for only one year after payments begin, the company continues to make payments to the annuitant's beneficiaries for nine more years. If the annuitant dies after receiving payments for 13 years, payments cease at death.

8. 1. 4. 1. 3 Joint Life with Last Survivor Annuity

With this option, the annuity covers two or more people, and payout is conditioned on both (all) lives.

EXAMPLE   A married couple owns an annuity jointly with a last survivor clause. The contract pays benefits as long as one of the annuitants remains alive. The payment may be the same as when both were alive, or it may be reduced for the surviving annuitant, depending on the contract. If this option includes more than two annuitants, payments cease at the last survivor's death.

8. 1. 4. 1. 4 Refund Annuity

Sometimes referred to as a unit refund annuity, under this settlement option, payments will continue after death of the insured until the full value of the initial premium (principal) has been returned. In some cases, the payment to the beneficiary will be a lump sum of cash, in others, a series of monthly payments.

8. 1. 4. 1. 5 Mortality Guarantee

Annuity companies guarantee payments for as long as annuitants live. If a change occurs in life expectancy and annuitants live longer than originally anticipated, the insurance companies assume the increased mortality cost—the **mortality guarantee**.

8. 1. 4. 1. 6   Operating Expense Guarantee

When calculating the amount an annuity company can pay out to a customer, the insurance company must project its own expenses for administering the plan. If for any reason the costs of operation increase, the company sets a ceiling for expenses charged to the separate account. If the actual costs are greater, the company pays the difference. This is known as the **operating expense guarantee**.

8. 1. 4. 2   Annuity Units

When a contract is annuitized, accumulation units become annuity units. An **annuity unit** is a measure of value used only during an annuitized contract's payout period. It is an accounting measure that determines the amount of each payment to the annuitant during the payout period.

The number of annuity units is calculated when an owner annuitizes the contract. The number of annuity units does not change—it is fixed at the time of annuitizing—but each unit's value fluctuates with the separate account portfolio's value. This is, after all, a variable annuity. The number of units credited to the annuitant's account is based on the value of the contract when the payout period begins and on other variables (such as the payout option selected, accumulated value of the annuitant's account, individual's age and sex, and assumed interest rate).

8. 1. 4. 3   Assumed Interest Rate (AIR)

The **assumed interest rate (AIR)** is a basis for determining distributions from a variable annuity. The rate, usually estimated conservatively, provides an earnings target for the separate account. An AIR is used to estimate the value of an account through the annuitant's age at death as forecasted by mortality tables.

The higher the AIR, the higher the projected value of units and the greater the initial payment. The reverse also is true.

8. 1. 4. 3. 1   Effects of Investment Performance on Annuity Payouts

The AIR does not guarantee a rate of return. It is a tool for adjusting an annuity unit's value to reflect changes in the investment performance of the separate account portfolio. As the annuity units change in value, so does the amount of the annuitant's monthly payment. The annuitant always receives a payment equal to the value of one or a specified number of annuity units times the unit value.

8. 1. 4. 4   Variable Annuity Payouts

Variable annuity payments are determined initially by mortality tables and the value of an annuitant's account. Variable annuity plans do not guarantee a payment amount because the insurance company cannot guarantee the separate account's performance. The value of the separate account upon annuitization is used to determine the number of annuity units in the account; future payouts are determined by the annuity units' fluctuating value.

EXAMPLE

An investor who annuitized a variable annuity in 1990 and began with a monthly payout of $375 may now be receiving $1,275 per month.

8. 1. 4. 4. 1   Fluctuating Payouts

After the insurance company determines the number of annuity units used in calculating each payment, the amount of each payment equals the number of units multiplied by the annuity units' current value. The number of annuity units used to calculate future payment remains the same; however, because the units' value depends on the separate account performance, the annuitant's payments may fluctuate if the units' value fluctuates.

QUICK QUIZ 8.A

Matching

A. Accumulation unit
B. Joint and last survivor annuity
C. Deferred annuity
D. Variable annuity

____   1. Delays distributions until the owner elects to receive them

____   2. Determines an annuitant's interest in the insurer's separate account before distribution from the annuity begins

____   3. Performance of a separate account determines value

____   4. Annuity payouts continue as long as one of the annuitants is alive

Quick Quiz answers can be found at the end of the unit.

QUICK QUIZ 8.B

Matching

A. Assumed interest rate
B. Immediate annuity
C. Life income with period certain
D. Separate account

____   1. Contract starts to pay the annuitant approximately one month after its issuance

____   2. The basis for projected annuity payouts, but not guaranteed

____   3. Holds funds paid by variable annuity contract holders

____   4. If the annuitant dies before a specified time expires, payouts go to the annuitant's named beneficiary

8. 1. 5   TAXATION OF ANNUITIES

Contributions to an annuity that is not part of an employer-sponsored retirement plan are made with after-tax dollars. Because contributions have been taxed already, the total amount contributed is not taxable when the account is annuitized. As with other investments, the money invested in an annuity represents the investor's cost basis.

The primary advantage of an annuity as an investment is that the tax on interest, dividends, and capital gains is deferred until the owner withdraws money from the contract. On withdrawal, the amount exceeding the investor's cost basis is taxed as ordinary income.

8. 1. 5. 1   Random Withdrawals

Since 1982, random withdrawals from annuity contracts have been taxed under the **last in, first out (LIFO)** method. Earnings are presumed by the IRS to be the last monies to hit the account. The earnings are considered to be withdrawn first from the annuity and are taxable as ordinary income. After the withdrawal of all earnings, contributions representing cost basis may be withdrawn without tax.

8. 1. 5. 2   Lump-Sum Withdrawals

Lump-sum withdrawals are taken by using the **LIFO** accounting method. This means that earnings are removed before contributions. If an investor receives a lump-sum withdrawal before age 59½, the earnings portion withdrawn is taxed as ordinary income and is subject to an additional 10% tax penalty under most circumstances.

The penalty does not apply if the funds are withdrawn after age 59½, are withdrawn because of death or disability, or are part of a life-income option plan with fixed payouts.

EXAMPLE   A contract with a $100,000 value consists of $40,000 in contributions and $60,000 in earnings. If the investor withdraws all $100,000 at once, the $60,000 in earnings is taxed as ordinary income and the $40,000 cost basis is returned tax free. If the investor is at least 59½, there is no 10% tax penalty; if younger, the 10% tax penalty applies. However, the penalty only applies to the taxable portion ($60,000)—there is never a penalty tax on money that is not taxable.

TEST TOPIC ALERT   Yes, it is true. Even when the distribution is from a non-qualified annuity, if it is made before the age of 59 ½, it is subject to the 10% additional tax (unless it meets one of the exceptions similar to those for an IRA).

8. 1. 5. 3   Annuitized Payouts

Annuitized payouts are typically made monthly and are taxed according to an exclusion ratio. The **exclusion ratio** expresses the percentages of the annuity's value upon annuitization of contribution basis to the total.

EXAMPLE

If $50,000 in after-tax dollars was contributed to an annuity contract worth $100,000 at annuitization, 50% of each payment will be treated as ordinary income, whereas the other 50% of each payment will be treated (for tax purposes) as nontaxable return of basis.

Under certain circumstances, the annuitant's life expectancy may also factor in the exclusion ratio.

TEST TOPIC ALERT

Upon annuitization, there is never a 10% tax penalty, even if annuitization commences prior to age 59½.

TEST TOPIC ALERT

Some additional tax concepts related to annuities are demonstrated below.

1. An annuity contract owner, age 45, surrenders his annuity to buy a home. Which of the following best describes the tax consequences of this action?

    A. Ordinary income taxes and a 10% early withdrawal penalty will apply to all money withdrawn.

    B. Capital gains tax will apply to the amount of the withdrawal that represents earnings; there will be no tax on the cost basis.

    C. Ordinary income taxes and a 10% early withdrawal penalty will apply to the amount of the withdrawal that represents earnings; there will be no tax on the cost basis.

    D. Ordinary income taxes apply to the amount of the withdrawal that represents earnings; the 10% early withdrawal penalty does not apply to surrenders.

    Answer: C. Interest earnings are taxable as ordinary income. They are also subject to the 10% early withdrawal penalty when withdrawn before age 59½. The contract holder recovers his cost basis without tax.

2. After the death of the annuitant, beneficiaries under a life and 15-year period certain option are subject to

    A. capital gains taxation on the total amount of payments received

    B. ordinary income taxation on the total amount of payments received, plus a 10% withdrawal penalty if the annuitant was under age 59½

    C. ordinary income taxation on the amount of the payout that exceeds the cost basis

    D. tax-free payout of all remaining annuity benefits

Answer: C. Payments from the annuity to the beneficiary through a period certain option are taxed in the same way as other periodic annuity payments; benefits over the amount of the cost basis are taxable as ordinary income. However, no 10% penalty applies in this situation.

8. 1. 5. 4   Advantages to Investing in Variable Annuities

The following are advantages to investing in variable annuities.

■ Tax-deferred growth: All income and capital gains generated in the portfolio of the separate account are free from income tax until the money is withdrawn. Over time, this tax-deferred compounding can make a significant difference in the value of the account.

■ Guaranteed death benefit: Most variable annuities contain a provision stating that if the investor dies during the accumulation period, the beneficiary will receive the greater of the current value of the account or the amount invested. Therefore, the estate is assured of getting back at least the original investment.

■ Lifetime income: Although a variable annuity cannot guarantee how much will be paid, choosing a payout option with lifetime benefits gives assurance that there will be a check every month as long as the annuitant is alive. This benefit protects against *longevity risk*, the uncertainty that one will outlive one's money. Be sure that you don't refer to this as guaranteed income—that would be an incorrect statement on the exam, because the income is variable.

■ IRS Section 1035 transfers: If you don't like the annuity you're in, you can transfer to another one without any tax consequences. However, it is possible there will be a surrender charge. This is unlike mutual funds, for which use of the exchange privilege is a taxable event.

■ No age 70½ restrictions or requirements: Unlike traditional retirement plans that have required minimum distributions after the age of 70½, an investor can delay withdrawals as desired and, in fact, can continue to contribute.

■ No contribution limits: Unlike retirement plans, where the annual contribution is limited, no IRS ceiling is placed on the amount that may be invested into a fixed or variable annuity.

■ A choice of separate account objectives with professional management: Some variable annuity companies offer 25–30 different subaccounts, each with a slightly different objective and all managed by professionals.

■ Tax-free transfer between subaccounts: Unlike mutual funds where the exchange between funds is a taxable event, the investor can transfer from one subaccount to another without any current tax liability.

■ No probate: Since the annuity calls for direct designation of a beneficiary, upon death, the asset passes directly without the time and expense of probate.

8. 1. 5. 5   Disadvantages to Investing in Variable Annuities

■ Earnings are taxed as ordinary income: Even though it is possible that the majority of the increase in value is generated through long-term capital gains, all earnings will be taxed at the higher ordinary income rate.

■ The administrative and insurance-related expense fees are typically much higher than the fees incurred by owning a mutual fund.

■ Withdrawals made before age 59½ will generally incur a 10% penalty, in addition to the ordinary income tax.

■ Most variable annuities carry a conditional deferred sales charge. Therefore, surrender in the early years will usually involve additional costs.

■ These are variable investments and carry the same investment risks as mutual funds.

TEST TOPIC ALERT
A variable annuity offers an investor the opportunity to have tax-deferred participation in the equity markets, albeit with expenses that are generally higher than for a mutual fund with a similar objective.

8. 2   LIFE INSURANCE

A life insurance policy is a contract between an insurance company and an individual that is designed to provide financial compensation to the named beneficiaries in the event of the insured's death.

Many types of life insurance contracts are available; each type serves a different need. We will focus more attention on those contracts that use separate accounts to fund the death benefits and those that are considered securities, as defined by the Securities Act of 1933.

8. 2. 1   TERM INSURANCE

Term insurance is protection for a specified period, hence the description, "term." Term insurance provides pure protection and is the least expensive form of life insurance. The important facts about term life insurance policies include the following.

■ They provide temporary insurance protection for a specified period of time (the policy term). For example, the term may be 1 year, 5 years, 10 years, 30 years, or to a specified age (such as age 65).

■ They pay the death benefit only if the insured dies during the term of coverage. For example, a person buying a 20 year term policy at age 35 who dies at 56 will receive nothing.

■ They do not accumulate cash value.

8. 2. 1. 1   Uses of Term Insurance

Term insurance has a variety of useful applications. One of the most common uses for term is to provide a substantial amount of coverage at a minimum cost. Since term insurance provides pure protection, it allows a person with a limited income to purchase more coverage than might otherwise be affordable. This is particularly important when there is a clear need for additional protection, particularly in the case of younger people, married with children.

TEST TOPIC ALERT   For test purposes, younger people with children are better off purchasing term insurance because the lower premiums allow significantly more protection. For those age 60 and older, the rates are generally prohibitive.

8. 2. 2   WHOLE LIFE INSURANCE (WLI)

A type of permanent or cash value insurance, **whole life insurance (WLI)** provides protection for the whole of life. Coverage begins on the date of issue and continues to the date of the insured's death, provided the premiums are paid. The benefit payable is the face amount of the policy, which remains constant throughout the policy's life. The premium is set at the time of the policy's issue and it, too, remains level for the policy's life.

8. 2. 2. 1   Cash Values

Unlike term insurance, which provides only a death benefit, whole life insurance combines a death benefit with an accumulation, or a savings element. This accumulation, commonly referred to as the policy's **cash surrender value**, increases each year the policy is kept in force. In traditional whole life insurance, the insurer invests reserves in conservative investments (e.g., bonds, real estate, mortgage loans).

Because of the low risk of such investments, the insurer can guarantee the policy's cash value and the nonforfeiture options that are based on that cash value. Traditional life insurance reserves are held in the insurer's **general accounts**.

8. 2. 2. 2   Policy Loans

Once an insured has accumulated cash value, it cannot be forfeited. An insured may cash in a policy at any time, by surrendering it in exchange for its cash value. An insured may also borrow a portion of the cash value in the form of a **policy loan**, but this must be paid back (with interest) in order to restore policy values. When a policyowner takes a cash value loan, the amount borrowed and any accumulated interest due on the loan become an indebtedness against the policy. If the insured dies before the loan has been repaid, any indebtedness will reduce the face amount of the policy accordingly—it will be subtracted from any death benefit.

8. 2. 2. 3   Uses of Whole Life

The principal advantage of whole life is that it is permanent insurance and accordingly can be used to satisfy permanent needs such as the cost of death, dying, and final burial expenses. The level premium allows the policyowner to always know exactly what the cost of insurance will be, and basically offers a form of forced savings. Whole life builds a living benefit through its guaranteed cash value that enables the policyowner to use some of this cash (through policy loans) for emergencies, as a supplemental source of retirement income, and for other living needs. The principal disadvantages of whole life insurance are that the premium paying period may last longer than the insured's income-producing years, and it does not provide as much protection per dollar of premium as term insurance.

Whole Life vs. Term	
Guaranteed interest rate on cash value buildup	Term insurance will provide the highest face amount for the lowest premium
Builds cash value with ability to borrow	Term insurance does not build cash value
Remains in effect until age 100 as long as premiums are paid	Term insurance provides coverage for a specific period of time; it is pure protection

8. 2. 2. 4   Surrendering the Policy

If the policyowner decides to stop paying the premiums, the policyowner may:

- surrender the policy for its cash value;
- take a reduced paid-up policy where the death benefit is decreased and future premiums are no longer required; or
- take extended term insurance which pays the beneficiaries the full face amount if death occurs within a specified time period.

8. 2. 3   UNIVERSAL LIFE

Universal life insurance was developed in the late 1970s in response to the relatively low interest rates (generally 3.5–5%) earned by traditional whole life insurance cash values, which made the whole life product less attractive during periods of high inflation. In order to be more competitive, insurers introduced universal life policies that might pay higher interest rates (such as 8%, 10%, or even 12%) during inflationary times. These policies also provide greater flexibility, because they allow policyowners to adjust the death benefits and/or premium payments based on current needs assessment.

A universal life policy is similar to a whole life policy in the sense that it has the same two components—death protection and cash value. However, instead of being fixed and guaranteed amounts, the death protection resembles one-year renewable term insurance and the cash value grows according to current interest rates.

8. 2. 3. 1   Characteristics of Universal Life

■ Premium payments are separated first being paid toward the insurance protection, with the remaining balance being used to build the cash value (with interest).

■ The policyowner may increase or decrease the death benefit during the policy term, subject to any insurability requirements.

■ Premium amounts may be changed as long as enough premium is paid to maintain the policy. This is why universal life is known as flexible premium life. In fact, it is even possible to skip premium payments as long as there is sufficient cash value in the policy to keep it in force.

■ The interest earned by the cash account will vary, subject to a guaranteed minimum.

8. 2. 3. 2   Universal Life Interest Rates

Universal life contracts are actually subject to two different interest rates: the current annual rate and the contract rate.

■ The **current annual rate** varies with current market conditions, and may change every year.

■ The **contract rate** is the minimum guaranteed interest rate, and the policy will never pay less than that amount.

For example, if the guaranteed contract rate is 5% and the current rate is 8%, the cash account would grow by the higher 8% during that year. But if the current rate falls below 5%, the cash account would still grow by the minimum rate of 5% during that year.

8. 2. 3. 3   Universal Life Death Benefits

Generally, there are two options available regarding the death benefit payable under a universal life policy.

■ Option 1 (also known as option A) provides a level death benefit equal to the policy's face amount. As the policy's cash value increases, net death protection actually decreases over the life of the policy, which makes the policy structure similar to a whole life contract.

■ Option 2 (also known as option B) provides for an increasing death benefit equal to the policy's face amount plus the cash account. In terms of policy structure, this contract is more like a combination of level term insurance and increasing cash value than whole life insurance.

TAKE NOTE

With the original universal life policies, it was common that the flexibility of premium payments caused policies to lapse with the result that one could not truly say there was a guaranteed death benefit. Because of this, most insurers today offer a guaranteed death benefit universal life where the policy is guaranteed not to lapse if the sum of the premiums paid (less any loans or partial withdrawals and partial withdrawal fees) is greater than or equal to the sum of the minimum monthly premiums required. As a result, one can say that a universal life insurance policy has at least some guaranteed death benefit.

8. 2. 3. 4   Universal Life Policy Loans

Universal life provides for cash value loans in the same manner that whole life or any permanent plan of insurance does. If a loan is taken, it is subject to interest and, if unpaid, both the interest and the loan amount will reduce the face amount of the policy. Many universal life policies will also permit a **cash withdrawal**, also called a partial surrender, from the cash account. This is not treated as a loan. A partial surrender is not subject to any interest and will reduce the total cash value in the account (rather than the face amount). If this withdrawal is later repaid, it will be treated as a premium payment.

8. 2. 3. 5   Uses of Universal Life

This is a form of permanent insurance that can build cash values, hopefully at a rate greater than with traditional whole life. There is typically a guaranteed minimum interest rate stated in the policy (usually around 4%) which means that, no matter how the investments perform, there will be a known minimum return on the investment. The unique feature is the flexibility to adjust the death benefit as needs change, as well as the flexibility to pay smaller or larger premiums as financial conditions dictate.

However, if the premium payments are reduced to the point where they can no longer support the policy, lapse could occur. Additionally, since this is a form of permanent insurance, poor investment results could cause premiums to increase (if the same face amount of coverage was desired).

Another use of the flexibility of the premium payments is to "overfund" the policy. That is, pay premiums in excess of those required with that excess going into the savings portion of the policy. This can have the effect of greatly increasing the cash value—money that may be borrowed out of the policy without tax consequences if done properly. (This is beyond the coverage of this course.)

8. 2. 4   VARIABLE LIFE INSURANCE

Variable life insurance differs from whole life insurance in that the premiums are invested not in the insurance company's general account, whose investments are determined by the insurance company, but in a separate account, in whose investments the insured has some choice—common stock, bonds, money market instruments, and so on. The purpose is to let the customer assume some investment risk in an attempt to get inflation protection for his death benefit.

Cash value in the policy fluctuates with the performance of the separate account and is not guaranteed. Variable life policies provide policy owners with a **minimum guaranteed death benefit**. The benefit may increase above this minimum amount depending on investment results but may never fall below.

Also, remember what was said earlier about variable annuities being securities requiring those who sell them to be dually licensed (insurance and securities); the same is true for those who wish to sell variable life insurance.

8. 2. 4. 1   Scheduled (Fixed) Premium Variable Life

A **scheduled-premium** (or **fixed-premium**) **VLI contract** is issued with a minimum guaranteed death benefit. (The premiums for some variable life contracts are flexible; this is discussed next under Variable Universal Life.) A scheduled-premium VLI contract's death benefit is determined at issue, and evidence of insurability is required.

The premium is calculated according to the insured's age and sex and the policy's face amount (guaranteed amount) at issue. Once the premium has been determined and the expenses have been deducted, the net premium is invested in a separate account the policyowner selects.

8. 2. 4. 2   Flexible Premium Variable Life (Universal)

Universal variable life insurance (UVL or VUL) is a type of variable life insurance with flexible premiums (and thus flexible death benefit). If variable life insurance is analogous to a combination annuity (the death benefit represents the fixed part, the cash value the variable), then UVL is analogous to a variable annuity (nothing is guaranteed). Premiums are invested only in a separate account, and there is only a variable death benefit. The insured has the option to increase, skip, or reduce premium payments, though he must maintain a minimum cash value, and the death benefit is adjusted appropriately.

8. 2. 4. 3   Deductions from the Premium

Deductions from the gross premium normally reduce the amount of money invested in the separate account. The greater the deductions, the less money available for the investment base in the separate account. Charges deducted from the gross premium include:

■ the administrative fee;

■ the sales load; and

■ state premium taxes (if any).

The administrative fee is normally a one-time charge to cover the cost of processing the application.

The maximum allowable sales load on variable life insurance is the equivalent of an average of 9% of premium per year, computed over a 20-year period. The sales charge may be front-end loaded to 50% of the first year's premium, but must average out to 9% over a 20-year period. Because of the front-end loading, there are special sales charge refund rights for the first two years spelled out in the Investment Company Act of 1940.

8. 2. 4. 4   Deductions from the Separate Account

Deductions from the separate account normally reduce the investment return payable to the policy owner. Charges deducted from the separate account include:

■ mortality risk fee (cost of insurance);

■ expense risk fee; and

■ investment management fee.

The **mortality risk fee** covers the risk that the insured may live for a period shorter than assumed. The **expense risk fee** covers the risk that the costs of administering and issuing the policy may be greater than assumed. And, of course, the investment management fee is the cost of the management of the chosen separate account subaccounts.

TAKE NOTE

The exam may ask you which charges are deducted from the gross premium and which are deducted from the separate account (the net premium). Remember the acronym **SAS** to make it simple. The charges deducted from the gross premium are:

- **s**ales load;

- **a**dministrative fee; and

- **s**tate premium taxes.

Any other charges; such as cost of insurance, expense risk fees, and investment management fees, are deducted from the net premium, which is invested in the separate account.

8. 2. 4. 5   Variable Life Insurance Death Benefit

The death benefit payable under a variable life insurance policy consists of two parts: a guaranteed minimum provided by the portion of funds invested in the general account and a variable death benefit provided by those invested in the separate account. The guaranteed minimum does not change, but total benefit, including the variable portion of the death benefit, must be recalculated at least annually.

The effect that a change in earnings has on the contract's variable death benefit depends on a comparison of actual account performance and the performance assumed by the insurance company. If the separate account returns are greater than the assumed interest rate (AIR), additional funds are available to the insured. These extra earnings are reflected in an increase in the death benefit. If the separate account returns equal the AIR, actual earnings meet estimated expenses, resulting in no change in benefit levels. Should the separate account returns be less than the AIR, the contract's death benefit may decrease; however, it may never fall below the amount guaranteed at issue.

TAKE NOTE

If a variable life insurance policy has a minimum death benefit, the premiums necessary to fund this part of the death benefit are held in the insurer's general account. Any policy benefit that is guaranteed is invested in the insurer's general account.

Any premium above what is necessary to pay for the minimum death benefit is invested in the separate account. This portion of the premium is subject to investment risk. The death benefit will grow above the minimum guaranteed amount if the separate account performs positively. The death benefit will never be less than the minimum guarantee, even if the separate account performs poorly.

TAKE NOTE

With positive performance in the separate account, the death benefit will increase. If this is followed by several periods of performance that fails to equal the AIR, the death benefit will decline (but never below the minimum guarantee). If the decline has been steep enough, it may take several periods of positive results before the death benefit increases again.

8. 2. 4. 6 Variable Life Insurance Cash Value

The policy's cash values reflect the investments held in the separate account. Unlike the death benefit, the individual policy's cash value must be calculated at least monthly.

The cash value, like the death benefit, may increase or decrease depending on the separate account's performance. However, because the cash value is not based on any assumed interest rate, AIR, any positive performance will result in cash value growth. If performance has been negative, the cash value may decrease to zero, even if the contract has been in force for several years. The cash value cannot be negative, but the insurance company keeps track of negative performance. Therefore, like the death benefit, the cash value may not increase until prior negative performance has been offset.

TEST TOPIC ALERT

The AIR has no effect on cash value accumulation in a variable life policy. The cash value will grow whenever the separate account has positive performance. The AIR, however, does affect the death benefit. Just remember the rules for variable annuities. The rules for the death benefits are analogous.

- If the separate account performance for the year is greater than the AIR, the death benefit will increase.

- If the separate account performance for the year is equal to the AIR, the death benefit will stay the same.

- If the separate account performance for the year is less than the AIR, the death benefit will decrease (but never below the guaranteed minimum).

TEST TOPIC ALERT

You may see a question that asks about the frequency of certain calculations associated with variable life insurance policies. Know that:

- death benefits are calculated annually;

- cash value is calculated monthly; and

- separate account unit values are calculated daily (in the event there is a withdrawal of cash value).

Comparison of Whole Life and Variable Life Policies

Whole Life	Variable Life (VLI)	Universal Variable Life (UVL or VUL)
Scheduled premium	Scheduled premium	Flexible premium
Fixed death benefit	Minimum guaranteed plus variable death benefit	Variable death benefit
Premiums to general account	Premiums to general and separate account	Premiums to separate account
Guaranteed cash value	No guaranteed cash value	No guaranteed cash value

8. 2. 4. 7   Variable Life Policy Loans

Like traditional WLI, a VLI contract allows the insured to borrow against the cash value that has accumulated in the contract. However, certain restrictions exist. Usually, the insured may only borrow a percentage of the cash value. The minimum percentage that must be made available is 75% after the policy has been in force for three years. If the death benefit becomes payable during any period that a loan is outstanding, the loan amount is deducted from the death benefit before payment. The interest rate charged is stated in the policy.

TEST TOPIC ALERT

Several testable facts about policy loans are as follows.

- A minimum of 75% of the cash value must be available for policy loan after the policy has been in force three years.

- The insurer is never required to loan 100% of the cash value. Full cash value is obtained by surrendering the policy to the insurer.

- If the insured dies with a loan outstanding, the death benefit is reduced by the amount of the loan.

- If the insured surrenders his contract with a loan outstanding, cash value is reduced by the amount of the loan.

8. 2. 4. 7. 1   Variable Life Insurance Contract Exchange

A unique feature of variable life insurance is the ability for the insured to change his mind. During the early stage of ownership, you have the right to exchange a VLI contract for a form of permanent insurance issued by the company with comparable benefits (usually whole life). The length of time this exchange privilege is in effect varies from company to company, but under no circumstances may the period be less than 24 months (federal law).

The exchange is allowed without evidence of insurability. If a contract is exchanged, the new permanent policy has the same contract date and death benefit as the minimum guaranteed in the VLI contract. The premiums equal the amounts guaranteed in the new permanent contract (as if it were the original contract).

TEST TOPIC ALERT

Three testable facts about the contract exchange provision are listed here.

■ The contract exchange provision must be available for a minimum of two years.

■ No medical underwriting (evidence of insurability) is required for the exchange.

■ The new policy is issued as if everything were retroactive. That is, the age of the insured as of the original date is the age used for premium calculations for the new policy.

8. 2. 4. 7. 2   Variable Life Insurance Voting Rights

Contract holders receive one vote per $100 of cash value funded by the separate account. As with other investment company securities, changes in investment objectives and other important matters may be accomplished only by a majority vote of the separate account's outstanding shares or by order of the state insurance commissioner.

TEST TOPIC ALERT

Do not confuse the voting rights of variable annuities and variable life. Variable annuities and mutual funds are the same: one vote per unit (share). Variable life is one vote per $100 of cash value.

8. 2. 4. 7. 3   Uses of Variable Life Insurance

It must be emphasized that variable life insurance must be sold as life insurance, not as an investment. However, the ability to commit a portion of the premium to investor selected separate account subaccounts, makes this form of insurance unique. There is a guaranteed minimum death benefit, but if separate account performance merits such, the death benefit can increase to keep pace with inflation. Cash values, although not guaranteed, can also increase based upon that performance. As with any variable product, the investor bears the investment risk rather than the insurance company.

QUICK QUIZ 8.C

Match each of the following numbers with the best description below.

A. 9
B. 24
C. 75

_____ 1. Minimum percent of cash value that must be available for a policy loan after 3 years

_____ 2. Number of months contract exchange provision must be in place

_____ 3. Maximum sales charge allowed over life of a variable life policy

8. 2. 5   LIFE SETTLEMENTS

Selling a life insurance policy (or the right to receive the death benefit) to any person other than the insurance company that issued the policy, is a transaction known as a viatical or life settlement. NASAA concludes that viatical investments, regardless of the health status or age of the insured, are securities. All persons involved in the offer and/or sale of viatical investments should be aware of the nature and extent of the registration and antifraud provisions of state securities laws, as well as the applicability of these provisions to every offer and/or sale of a security. Because licensing is done on a state by state basis, there is little uniformity. Some states require just a life insurance license, some require both a life insurance and a life settlement license, and some require either or both of these and being licensed as a securities agent.

8. 2. 6   TAX IMPLICATIONS OF LIFE INSURANCE

There are a number of tax implications involved with life insurance policies including both income and estate taxation. These will be covered in Unit 4, Session 7, where we discuss the topic of taxation.

QUICK QUIZ 8.D

Choose **W** for whole life, **V** for variable life, and **U** for universal variable life. More than one may apply to each choice.

_____ 1. Features a stated premium

_____ 2. Always has some guaranteed death benefit

_____ 3. Features a guaranteed cash value

_____ 4. Cash value not guaranteed

_____ 5. Policy loans available

QUICK QUIZ 8.E

1. Which of the following is considered to be an advantage of annuitization?
    A. It guarantees income that will last for the client's lifetime.
    B. Once annuitized, the client's draw from the annuity is limited to the annuity payment.
    C. A fixed, level periodic payment tends to lose buying power over time due to inflation.
    D. Payments under a variable annuity could be reduced if there is a declining market.

2. A 49-year-old customer purchases a single premium deferred variable annuity. She selects a sub-account of the separate account that is composed largely of equity securities. She is assuming all of the following risks EXCEPT

   A. she is not assured of the return of her invested principal
   B. the underlying portfolio is primarily common stocks, which have no guaranteed return
   C. as an investor, she can be held liable for the debts incurred by the insurance company
   D. if she needs to withdraw a portion of her investment prior to reaching age 59½, she may incur a 10% tax penalty

3. The difference between a fixed annuity and a variable annuity is that the variable annuity

   I. offers a guaranteed return.
   II. offers a payment that may vary in amount.
   III. will always pay out more money than the fixed annuity.
   IV. attempts to offer protection to the annuitant from inflation.
   A. I and III
   B. I and IV
   C. II and III
   D. II and IV

4. A 30-year-old client indicates that he needs $500,000 of life insurance coverage for the next 20 years. The lowest out-of-pocket cost would be if he purchased a

   A. 20-pay life policy
   B. 20-year level term policy
   C. whole life policy
   D. variable annuity with an extended death benefit

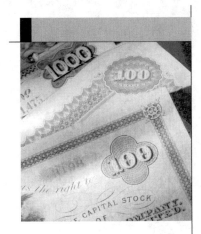

9

Types and Characteristics of Derivative Securities

This session discusses both securities and non-securities derivatives. You can expect to see two questions about derivatives on the Series 65 exam. The term derivative is used to describe investment vehicles that derive their value from an underlying asset, whether that asset be a security, such as a stock, or a physical commodity, such as wheat.

When you have completed this session you should be able to:

■ **explain** the difference between a put option and a call option;

■ **identify** the proper hedging strategies for long stock and short stock positions; and

■ **describe** the difference between futures and forwards contracts.

9. 1   DERIVATIVE SECURITIES—OPTIONS

Options are **derivative securities**, which means that they derive their value from that of an underlying instrument, such as a stock, stock index, interest rate, or foreign currency. Option contracts offer investors a means to **hedge**, or protect, an investment's value or speculate on the price movement of individual securities, markets, foreign currencies, and other instruments.

An **option** is a contract that establishes a price and time frame for the purchase or sale of a particular security. Two parties are involved in the contract: one party receives the right to exercise the contract to buy or sell the underlying security; the other is obligated to fulfill the terms of the contract.

In theory, options can be created on any item with a fluctuating market value. The most familiar options are those issued on common stocks; they are called **equity options**.

The exam is going to deal solely with standardized options traded on an exchange. They are called standardized options because each options contract has three standardized terms:

- The underlying asset. That is, all options on XYZ stock are for 100 shares of the XYZ common stock

- The expiration date. All options that expire in June (or July or whatever month) have the same date and time of expiry

- The exercise or strike price. Strike prices are set at standardized intervals.

It is this standardization that makes secondary trading in options possible.

9. 1. 1   CALLS AND PUTS

There are two types of option contracts: **calls** and **puts**.

- A **call** option gives its holder the right to buy a stock for a specific price within a specified time frame. A call buyer buys the *right to buy* a specific stock, and a call seller takes on the *obligation to sell* the stock.

- A **put** option gives its holder the right to sell a stock for a specific price within a specified time frame. A put buyer buys the *right to sell* a specific stock, and a put seller takes on the *obligation to buy* the stock.

Each stock option contract covers 100 shares (a round lot) of stock. An option's cost is its **premium**. Premiums are quoted in dollars per share.

EXAMPLE

Because a contract covers 100 shares, a premium of $3 means $3 for each share times 100 shares, which equals $300.

9. 1. 1. 1   Leverage

Because an option's cost is normally much less than the underlying stock's cost, option contracts provide investors with leverage: relatively little money allows an investor to control an investment that would otherwise require a much larger capital outlay.

EXAMPLE

An investor can buy the common stock of RST Corporation for $58 per share, investing $5,800, or buy an RST 55 call for $6, an investment of $600. If RST's price increases to $70, the stock investor will see a 20.7% profit, ($12 profit ÷ $58 investment), whereas the option investor, with the call worth a minimum of $15 ($70 – $55), will have more than doubled his money ($9 profit ÷ $6 investment = 150%). The opposite is also true; if RST trades below $55, say at $48, when the option expires, the stock investor has a modest loss, but the option investor loses his whole investment. (What is the value of an option to buy stock at $55 per share when it is currently available to anyone at $48? Nothing.)

9. 1. 2   OPTION TRANSACTIONS

Because two types of options (calls and puts) and two types of transactions (buying and selling) exist, four basic transactions are available to an option investor:

- Buy calls
- Sell calls
- Buy puts
- Sell puts

Option buyers are *long* the positions; option sellers are *short* the positions.

9. 1. 2. 1   Opening and Closing Transactions

An option conveys rights and obligations for a limited time. Therefore, each transaction has a beginning and an end—an open and a close. For instance, an option position opened by an investor buying a call is closed when the call is exercised, is sold, or expires. An option position opened by an investor selling a call is closed when the call is exercised, is bought, or expires.

The owner (long position) of a put or call option contract has three ways to close a position:

- **sell** the option contract before the expiration date.;
- **exercise** the option to buy or sell the security specified in the contract; or
- let the option **expire**.

The simplest and most common way to close an option position is entering the transaction opposite of the opening transaction. The following table summarizes potential opening and closing positions.

Open	To Close
Buy call	Sell call
Sell call	Buy call
Buy put	Sell put
Sell put	Buy put

9. 1. 2. 2   Exercising an Option

In some cases, the holder of the option (only owners can exercise – it is one of their "rights") will decide to exercise the option. Exercising a call means purchasing the underlying stock at the strike price; exercising a put means selling the underlying stock at the strike price. For example, if you were long an ABC 50 Call and the current market price of ABC is 60, you would be able to exercise and purchase stock worth $60 per share at the exercise price of $50. Or, if you were long an XYZ $45 put and the current market price of XYZ is $35, you might wish to purchase 100 shares of XYZ at $35 per share and then exercise your option to "put" the stock at $45. The test may ask you the difference between American- and European-style exercises. American style means the option can be exercised at any time the holder wishes, up to the expiration date. European-style options may only be exercised on the last trading day before the **expiration** date.

TAKE NOTE

A tool for remembering the difference between American and European exercise is to look at the first letter.

A for American means **A**nytime

E for European means **E**xpiration date

TEST TOPIC ALERT

Now that you have become so focused on the exercise date differences between American and European styles, be prepared for a question stem like "A European option is a derivative because," and the first answer choice will probably be "it can only be exercised on the expiration date." Although that is true about exercise, it has nothing to do with why options are derivatives. Please select an answer choice similar to "its value is based on some underlying asset."

TAKE NOTE

Perhaps you noticed an inconsistency. First, we told you that European style means the option can only be exercised on the day prior to its expiration date. Then, we told you it is only exercised on its expiration date. In the industry, there seems to be much confusion about this, and for exam purposes, either statement is correct (and you won't have to choose between them).

9. 1. 2. 3   Options Greeks

Many of our students tell us that when it comes to understanding options, "it is all Greek to me". Maybe that is why options strategists use a number of Greek letters to describe various properties of an option. There are four commonly used *Greeks*, Delta, Gamma, Theta, and Vega. It is highly unlikely that you will have to know anything about them, but we've given a short definition of each in the glossary.

9. 1. 3   OPTIONS STRATEGIES

Options strategies are either **bullish** or **bearish positions** on the underlying stock. Bulls believe the price of a security will go up and bears believe the price of a security will go down. The primary reasons for buying or selling options are to profit from or hedge (protect) against price movement in the underlying security.

A bullish investor may buy calls seeking profit if the price of the underlying stock rises. A bearish investor buy puts seeking profit if the price of the underlying stock declines. Likewise a bullish investor may write (sell) puts which will make money if the stock price is stable or rises and a bearish investor may write (sell) calls which will make money if the stock price is stable or declines.

Bullish and Bearish Options Positions

	Long	Short
Calls	Right to buy Bullish	Obligation to sell Bearish
Puts	Right to sell Bearish	Obligation to buy Bullish
	(Buyer, Holder, Owner)	(Seller, Writer, Grantor)

TAKE NOTE

A phrase that is invaluable for figuring out options questions is "Call Up and Put Down." That is, you would buy a call because you are hoping (or are afraid) the price of the stock will go *up*, and buy a put because you are hoping (or are afraid) the price of the stock will go *down*.

9. 1. 3. 1   Buying Calls

Investors expecting a stock to increase in value speculate on that price increase by buying calls on the stock.

By buying a call, an investor can profit from the increase in the stock's price while investing a relatively small amount of money. The most a call buyer can lose is the money paid for the option. The most a call buyer can gain is unlimited because there is no limit to how high the stock price can go. Owners of options (puts or calls) do not receive dividends on the underlying stock.

As we will show you shortly, buying calls is also a hedging (protection) strategy when the investor is afraid the stock price will rise.

Remember those employee stock options we discussed in Session 4? No, they are not at all like these puts and calls, but the employer (the company issuing the stock) might want to use call options to protect against market risk. You see, when granting employees the option (the right) to buy shares at a set price, the company is obligated to deliver the shares at that agreed upon price. What happens if the company's stock price soars, the employees exercise their options, and the company has to go out into the stock markets and buy stock at a price far in excess of what they're going to be selling it for? That hurts. One way to protect themselves is to buy call options on the stock so that if this were to happen, they could use their options to buy the stock at whatever exercise price was part of the contract.

9. 1. 3. 2   Writing Calls

A neutral or bearish investor can write (sell) a call and collect the premium. An investor who believes a stock's price will stay the same or decline can write a call to:

- generate income from the option premium;
- *partially* protect (hedge) a long stock position by offsetting any loss on the sale of the stock by the premium amount; or
- If the stock price increases, the call may be exercised. In addition to the premium received when the option was sold, the writer will be paid the strike price for the stock, If the option writer owns the stock on which the call is being written, it is known as a covered call and the risk is limited because no matter how high the stock price rises (meaning the call will certainly be exercised), the writer merely uses the stock already owned (which has been deposited with the broker-dealer) to make delivery. However, if the writer does not own the stock, the option is uncovered (usually referred to as "naked" in the industry). That's when the risk is unlimited, because the writer must pay the going market price (and there is theoretically no limit as to how high a stock's price can go) to acquire the stock needed to fulfill the obligation to deliver. That is why naked call writing is the most risky option strategy.

9. 1. 3. 3   Buying Puts

A **bearish investor**—one who believes a stock will decline in price—can speculate on the price decline by buying puts. A put buyer acquires the right to sell 100 shares of the underlying stock at the strike price before the expiration date.

EXAMPLE
Here is how that might work. An investor following ABCD common stock believes that it is grossly overpriced at $75 per share and when the next earnings report is released, the stock will drop at least 10 points. If the investor were to purchase an ABCD 75 put for a premium of $3 and was correct, once the stock was at $65 (the 10 point drop), a purchase could be made at that price for $65 per share and then the put could be exercised at the $75 per share strike price.

This would give the investor a profit of $7 per share (the $10 difference between the cost of $65 and the sale at $75, minus the $3 premium paid). A $700 profit on a $300 investment is a very handsome percentage return on investment.

As we will show you shortly, buying puts is also a hedging (protection) strategy when the investor is afraid the stock price will fall.

9. 1. 3. 4   Writing Puts

Generally, investors who write puts believe that the stock's price will rise or remain stable. A put writer (seller) is obligated to buy stock at the exercise price if the put buyer puts it to the put writer. If a stock's price is above the put strike price at expiration, the put expires unexercised, allowing the put writer to keep the premium. Just as with writing calls, receiving that premium is a source of income. Put writers will lose if the stock price falls (the buyer "wins"), but the loss is limited because the stock price can never fall below zero.

9. 1. 3. 5   Straddles

When an investor is not sure which direction the market will move but has a strong opinion that there will be dynamic movement, a strategy that might be employed is the purchase of a straddle. This is the combining of a put and a call on the same stock with the same exercise price and expiration date. If the stock moves up, a profit is made on the call; if down, a profit is made on the put.

TEST TOPIC ALERT

Those who buy a straddle will profit from volatility while those who sell a straddle will profit if the market is stable because the options will expire unexercised.

QUICK QUIZ 9.A

Matching (each has two answers)

A.   Long call
B.   Short call
C.   Long put
D.   Short put

_____   1.   Which options positions are bearish?

_____   2.   Which options positions are bullish?

_____   3.   Which positions buy stock at exercise?

_____   4.   Which positions sell stock at exercise?

_____   5.   Which positions have rights?

_____   6.   Which positions have obligations?

Quick Quiz answers can be found at the end of the unit.

QUICK QUIZ 9.B

1. Options are best described as

   A. derivatives
   B. substitutes
   C. swaps
   D. futures

2. Your customer is long 10 ABC Jul 50 calls at 4.50. He owns how many options?

   A. 1
   B. 4.50
   C. 10
   D. 100

3. Your customer is long 10 ABC Jul 50 calls at 4.50. What is the name of the underlying instrument?

   A. Call options
   B. Common stock
   C. ABC calls
   D. ABC common stock

4. Your customer is long 10 ABC Jul 50 calls at 4.50. The contract gives him the

   A. right to buy stock
   B. right to sell stock
   C. obligation to buy stock
   D. obligation to sell stock

5. Your customer is long 10 ABC Jul 50 calls at 4.50. How many shares of stock will change hands if he exercises his option?

   A. 10
   B. 100
   C. 1,000
   D. 10,000

6. Which term best describes the following situation: A customer has the right to sell 100 shares of MNO at 60 any time between July and October.

   A. Long call
   B. Long put
   C. Short call
   D. Short put

9.1.4   HEDGING WITH OPTIONS

An investor with an established position in a stock can use options to hedge the position's risks. Remember the term *hedge*, used in this context, means to protect. Normally, investors seek either to increase potential reward or to reduce potential loss.

9. 1. 4. 1   Long Stock and Long Puts

What if the investor is concerned about a potential drop in the price of a stock? An investor who owns a stock can protect against a decline in market value by buying a put. Doing so allows the investor to sell the stock by exercising the put if the stock price declines before expiration, or selling the put at a profit, which will offset the decline in the stock price. This strategy is called **portfolio insurance**. Any profits in the stock are offset by the cost of the put premiums.

EXAMPLE

A concerned (*afraid*) investor who owns 100 shares of stock with a current market value of $50 purchases a 50 put at $2.50 for protection. If the stock goes down to $40 per share, the investor has the ability to exercise the put, deliver the stock, and receive $50 per share. The only cost for this protection is the **premium** of $2.50 paid for the put. So, instead of losing $1,000 the loss was held to only $250.

TEST TOPIC ALERT

This strategy is also useful for managers of large portfolios, such as pension funds. If the portfolio consisted of large-cap stocks, a way to hedge against a down market would be to purchase put options on an index that mirrors the portfolio. In the case of large-cap stocks, that would generally be the S&P 500 index (more about that in Unit 4).

9. 1. 4. 2   Long Stock and Short Calls (Covered Call Writing)

A **covered call** is a call written (sold) on a stock an investor owns. The covered call writer reduces the risk of his long stock position *and generates income* with the dollars received in premiums from selling the call. If the call is not exercised, the call writer keeps the premium. If the call is exercised, the covered call writer can deliver the stock owned. The covered call writer limits potential gain in exchange for the partial protection against a loss.

Partial Protection. By writing a covered call and receiving the premium, an investor, in effect, reduces the stock cost by the premium amount. If the stock price falls below the purchase price minus the premium received, the investor incurs a loss. Should the stock price rise dramatically, the stock will likely be called.

EXAMPLE

An investor buys 100 shares of RST at 53 and writes 1 RST 55 call for 2. The premium offsets the stock price by the $2 per share premium received. The maximum gain equals $400: if the stock price rises above 55, the call will be exercised; thus, the investor will sell the stock for a gain of $200, in addition to the $200 premium received. The maximum loss is $5,100 should the stock become worthless.

TAKE NOTE   A covered call provides partial protection that generates income but reduces the stock's potential gain. Buying puts provides nearly total loss protection that costs money yet does not reduce the stock position's potential gain. The benefit of the covered call is that it does offer some hedging with no cost. In fact, the investor actually receives income in the form of the premium.

9. 1. 4. 3   Short Stock and Long Calls

An investor who sells a stock short sells borrowed stock, expecting the price to decline. The short seller must buy stock to repay the stock loan and hopes to do so at a lower price. A short seller can buy calls to protect against a price rise. If you are not familiar with the concept of short selling, it will be covered in Unit 4, Session 18.

EXAMPLE   An investor sells short 100 shares of RST at 58 and buys an RST 60 call for 3. The maximum loss is no longer unlimited as it would normally be for a short sale. Instead, it is $500: no matter how high the stock price rises above $60, the investor will exercise the call to buy the stock for 60, incurring a $200 loss on the short sale, in addition to the $300 paid for the call.

TEST TOPIC ALERT   The majority of our students report a question on protecting against loss on a short sale. As shown above, the best way to hedge is to buy a call option on the stock underlying the short sale.

9. 1. 5   NON-SECURITIES DERIVATIVES: FORWARD CONTRACTS AND FUTURES

9. 1. 5. 1   Forward Contracts

Forward contracts were developed as a means for commodity users and producers to arrange for the exchange of the commodity at a time agreeable to both. Used in Europe as early as the Middle Ages, typically for agricultural items (grains and so forth), forward contracts evolved to eliminate the problem of finding a buyer or seller for an upcoming cash market transaction. They also reduce the price risk inherent in changing supply and demand relationships. How so? Because the seller knows exactly how much he will receive for his product. Of course, he may wind up contracting to sell too cheaply if market prices at delivery are much higher, but he is protected against receiving too little if the "harvest" is plentiful and prices plunge.

A forward contract is a direct commitment between one buyer and one seller. If the position is held until the closing date, the forward seller is obligated to make delivery; the forward buyer is obligated to take delivery. A forward contract is nonstandardized. Its unique terms are defined solely by the contract parties, without third-party intervention. This arrangement ensures a ready market or supply source because it presumes delivery.

Because forward contracts are direct obligations between a specific buyer and seller (the user and producer), they are not easily transferred and are considered illiquid (there is no secondary market for forward contracts). Further, each party risks the credit and trustworthiness of the other.

The five components of a typical forward contract are:

- quantity of the commodity;
- quality of the commodity;
- time of delivery;
- place for delivery; and
- price to be paid at delivery.

9. 1. 5. 2   Futures

In contrast to forward contracts, futures contracts are exchange-traded obligations. The buyer or seller is contingently responsible for the full value of the contract. A buyer goes long, or establishes a long position, and is obligated to take delivery of the commodity on the future date specified. A seller goes short, or establishes a short position, and is obligated to deliver the commodity on the specified future date. If the seller does not own the commodity, his potential loss is unlimited because he has promised delivery and must pay any price to acquire the commodity to deliver.

As prices change, gains or losses are computed daily for all open futures positions on the basis of each day's settlement price. Gains are credited and losses are debited for each open position, long or short. All accounts for firms and traders must be settled before the opening of trading on the next trading day.

Buyers and sellers benefit from organizations that act as clearinghouses for the contracts. Clearinghouses enable futures positions to be offset easily prior to delivery. To offset, close, or liquidate a futures position before delivery, an investor must complete a transaction opposite to the trade that initiated (opened) the futures position. The offsetting transaction must occur in the same commodity, for the same delivery month, and on the same exchange. About 98% of futures contracts are offset before delivery. Futures may be highly leveraged.

If, at expiration, the settlement price is higher than the delivery price, a long position results in a profit while a short position loses. Conversely, if the settlement price is lower than the delivery price, shorts profit and longs lose.

Typically, there are five standardized parts to an exchange-traded futures contract:

- Quantity of the commodity (e.g., 5,000 bushels of corn or 100 oz of gold)
- Quality of the commodity (specific grade or range of grades may be acceptable for delivery, including price adjustments for different deliverable grades)
- Delivery price (similar to exercise or strike price with options)
- Time for delivery (e.g., December wheat to be delivered)
- Location (approved for delivery)

EXAMPLE

Forwards/futures are commonly used by producers (farmers) to hedge the risk of the price of the commodity falling before it is able to be harvested and sold. For example, if a farmer has planted soybeans and wishes to hedge against a possible decline in the spot or cash price at delivery, the farmer could

    A. buy forward contracts in a size equal to the amount of soybeans expected to be harvested

    B. buy futures contracts in a size equal to the amount of soybeans expected to be harvested

    C. sell futures or forward contracts in a size equal to the amount of the soybeans expected to be harvested

    D. sell the soybeans for cash today

Answer: C. Hedging a commodity yet to be harvested is done by selling a forward or a futures contract on that commodity. In that way, the price is guaranteed in the event of a market decline. However, the producer is giving up any potential gain in the event the prices rise above the futures/forward agreed upon one.

QUICK QUIZ 9.C

Matching (may have more than one answer)

    A. Long call
    B. Short call
    C. Long put
    D. Short put

_____   1. Used to fully protect a long stock position

_____   2. Used to fully protect a short stock position

_____   3. Obligation to buy stock at the strike price if exercised

_____   4. Right to sell stock at the strike price if exercised

_____   5. Used to speculate on the upward movement of a stock's price

_____   6. Used to speculate on the downward movement of a stock's price

_____   7. If uncovered, subjects an investor to unlimited risk

_____   8. The maximum loss is the premium

_____   9. Used to generate income when an investor owns the underlying stock

_____   10. Requires investor to buy stock at a net cost reduced by the amount of premium received, if exercised

1. The term *derivative* could be used to apply to any of the following EXCEPT

   A. forward contracts
   B. futures
   C. options
   D. REITs

2. Commonly traded on a regulated exchange would be any of the following EXCEPT

   A. ETFs
   B. forward contracts
   C. futures
   D. warrants

3. It would be improper to use the term *derivative* to describe

   A. a call option
   B. a closed-end investment company
   C. a futures contract
   D. a warrant

4. One of your clients sells 100 shares of XYZ stock short at $50 per share. Although the client is quite bearish on the stock, she realizes that it is possible that good news in the overall economy could cause a surge in XYZ's price. Which of the following would you recommend to best protect her position?

   A. Buy an XYZ 50 put
   B. Buy an XYZ 50 call
   C. Sell an XYZ 50 put
   D. Sell an XYZ 50 call

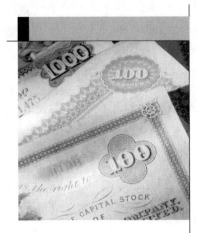

10

Alternative Investments

In the 1990s financial advisers began introducing their wealthy clients to *alternative investments,* now generally referred to as Alts. These included, among other products, hedge funds, private equity, and new, highly sophisticated financial derivatives. One thing that all of these had in common was that they were complex and not easy to understand, for both the investor and the person recommending the investment.

Although investing can be complex, standard investments are fairly easy to comprehend. Even new investors understand that stocks have more risk but hold out the chance of superior returns, while bonds generally have less risk with correspondingly lower returns. All investors dream of scoring a touchdown and not getting tackled for a loss. Alternative investments try to do just that. Some are successful, but many are not. Suitability determinations need to be made on a case-by-case basis considering each customer's objectives, circumstances, and sophistication. Securities professionals must take special care in recommending these complex products to the sophisticated customer and even more so to one with less financial acumen. The Series 65 will have two questions from this session, one on hedge funds and one on direct participation programs (DPPs).

When you have completed this session, you should be able to:

■ **identify** the structure of a hedge fund;

■ **recognize** the unique compensation system of hedge funds;

■ **assess** the special suitability requirements for hedge fund investing;

■ **explain** the concept of "flow-through" as it applies to DPPs;

■ **differentiate** between the roles of the general partners and the limited partners in a DPP;

■ **compute** the taxable effects of passive income and passive loss; and

■ **enumerate** the advantages and disadvantages of DPPs.

10. 1 HEDGE FUNDS

These are a form of fund generally organized as a limited partnership with fewer than 100 investors that does not currently have to register with the SEC, although the portfolio managers generally are required to register as investment advisers. There is pending legislation that would require all hedge funds to register—check the Exam-tips & Contents Updates and we'll post an entry when and if such legislation passes. Such funds are free to adopt far riskier investment policies than those permitted to open and closed-end funds, such as arbitrage strategies and massive short positions during bearish markets. In addition, they may use leverage (borrowed money) and derivatives such as options and futures. Hedge funds are considered to be in the asset class of "alternative" investments. Even though these risky techniques are employed, the primary aim of most hedge funds is to reduce volatility and risk while attempting to preserve capital and deliver positive returns under all market conditions.

Another important factor is that management fees tend to be much, much higher than with other investments. Almost all hedge funds charge performance-based fees. The typical fee structure is known by the vernacular "2 & 20"—most funds take a 2% management fee and 20% of any profits.

Many hedge funds also require that investors maintain the investment for a minimum length of time (e.g., one year) and, to that extent, they can be considered illiquid. These requirements are known as *lock-up* provisions. This provision provides that, during a certain initial period, an investor may not make a withdrawal from the fund—the investor's capital is *locked up*. Generally recognized as one way the manager of the hedge fund portfolio can have capital retained in the fund, it is also seen to be another factor adding to the unique risk of hedge funds—in this case, shares being illiquid for that specified length of time.

Therefore, because of the higher risk, investment in these vehicles is limited to institutional clients and wealthy individuals, known as accredited investors (defined in Unit 1).

TEST TOPIC ALERT   Most hedge funds are organized as limited partnerships with the portfolio managers investing along with the investors. As they say in the industry, they have "skin in the game" so they have a greater motivation to succeed. The partnership is the issuer of the ownership units.

Hedge funds are indirectly available to ordinary investors through mutual funds called funds of hedge funds. Because hedge funds themselves have limited liquidity, purchasing a mutual fund of hedge funds offers not only diversification but also, in many, but not all cases, the liquidity of the mutual fund.

■ In summation, why would you include hedge funds in your client's portfolio?

■ The designed strategy of many hedge funds is to generate positive returns in both rising and falling markets.

■ With a large variety of available investment styles, investors have a plethora of choices to assist them in meeting their objectives.

■ As part of an asset allocation class, hedge funds may reduce overall portfolio risk and volatility and increase returns.

■ A proper selection of hedge funds can create uncorrelated returns, adding a level of diversification. In doing so, the client would be incurring the following risks:

— Expenses can be quite high.

— The risky strategies could backfire leading to significant loss of capital.

— Liquidity risk: during the lock-up period, the investor is locked-in to the investment. Furthermore, even after that period, there is no active secondary market for these unregistered securities. Finally, as is generally the case with limited partnership investments, the sale of partnership interests may require approval of the general partner.

10. 2 DIRECT PARTICIPATION PROGRAMS (DPPs)

This is another class of "alternative" investment. Direct participation programs (DPPs), many of which are limited partnerships, allow the economic consequences of a business to flow through to investors. Unlike corporations, limited partnerships pay no dividends. Rather, they pass income, gains, losses, deductions, and credits directly to investors. Limited partnerships offer investors limited liability. Similar to a stockholder in a corporation, creditors cannot generally come directly to limited partners to collect on defaulted debt. In generally, the maximum potential loss to a limited partner is the amount already invested plus any funds committed for which have not yet been submitted.

Units of ownership in a partnership are called interests, rather than shares.

10. 2. 1 INVESTORS IN A LIMITED PARTNERSHIP

A limited partnership must have at least one general partner and one limited partner. A certificate of limited partnership filed with the Secretary of State lists the status of each investor as a limited or general partner.

10. 2. 1. 1 General Partner (GP)

The GPs are the active investors in a limited partnership and assume responsibility for all aspects of the partnership's operations. A general partner:

■ makes decisions that bind the partnership;

■ buys and sells property for the partnership;

■ manages the partnership property and money;

■ supervises all aspects of the partnership's business; and

■ maintains a minimum 1% financial interest in the partnership.

Unlike LPs, who have limited liability, GPs assume unlimited liability and are therefore personally liable for all partnership business losses and debts. A partnership's creditors may seek repayment from the GPs and may go after their personal assets.

A general partner has a fiduciary relationship to the LPs in that the GP has been entrusted with the LPs' capital and is legally bound to use that capital in the investors' best interests. The GP must manage the business in the partnership's best interest and avoid the appearance of improper use of assets and conflicts of interest. The GP cannot borrow from the partnership, compete with the partnership, or commingle personal funds with partnership funds. Finally, GPs do not generally receive any distributions from profits until after a payment has been made to the LPs.

10. 2. 1. 2 Limited Partner (LP)

LPs are passive investors with no management or day-to-day decision-making responsibilities; therefore, they usually are not held personally responsible for the partnership's indebtedness. LPs may receive cash distributions and capital gains from partnerships. The total yield of a partnership investment takes into account all potential rewards: tax deductions, cash distributions, and capital gains.

Finally, GPs do not generally receive any distributions from profits until after a payment has been made to the LPs.

10. 2. 2 ISSUING PARTNERSHIP INVESTMENTS

DPPs are either public offerings or private placements. In either case, specific documentation is required to form and invest in the partnership.

10. 2. 2. 1 Private Placements

In a private **placement limited partnership**, each of a small number of LPs contributes a large amount of money, such as $100,000 or more. Private placements are usually offered to **accredited investors** or a limited number of other investors and, as were covered in Unit 1 are exempt from registration with the SEC or the states.

10. 2. 2. 2 Public Offerings

In a **publicly offered limited partnership**, a larger number of investors makes relatively small contributions of capital to the partnership, such as $1,000 to $5,000. These partnerships can be publicly advertised, raise relatively large amounts of capital, and may attract investors with smaller budgets and less investment sophistication. Typically, they are more tightly regulated and subject to stringent federal registration and prospectus requirements than private placements. Because private placements are unregistered, they are able to avoid these regulations and registration requirements.

10. 2. 2. 3 Documentation

Subscription Agreement. An investor who buys a limited partnership unit must complete and sign a subscription agreement, which includes a statement of the investor's net worth and annual income and a power of attorney form appointing the GP as the agent of the partnership. The registered representative (agent) is responsible to make certain that the information the potential investor provides in the subscription agreement is complete and accurate.

10. 2. 3 TAX REPORTING FOR PARTNERSHIPS

The partnership files a Form 1065, Statement of Partnership Income. This is really an information return because the partnership does not pay taxes. As we'll learn, the tax consequences fall upon the investors. This information return records the income and then the expenses with the bottom line showing the ordinary business income or, if expenses exceeded revenues, a loss. Each limited partner receives a Schedule K-1 indicating that partner's share of income or loss.

Under current tax law, LPs are classified as **passive investors**. Any income they receive from a partnership is **passive income**, and any loss passed through to them is a **passive loss**. Investors can deduct passive losses against passive income only. Unused passive losses can be carried forward to the next year and used to offset future passive income. Dividend and interest income and wages are not passive income.

TAKE NOTE
An investor may only use a tax loss from a partnership to offset income from another passive investment.

10. 2. 3. 1 Sources of tax benefits

10. 2. 3. 1. 1 Operating Loss

Operating loss passed through to the investors. Partnership losses are apportioned among investors, enabling them to claim those losses as deductions against passive income on their personal tax returns.

10. 2. 3. 1. 2 Operating Income

Operating income passed through to the investors. Unlike the typical corporate form of business, if there is operating income, it passes directly through to the investors and thus avoids double taxation. This is considered passive income and may be offset by any passive losses.

10. 2. 3. 1. 3 Depreciation Expense

Depreciation expense which, in the case of many assets, may be accelerated. This has the effect of creating larger losses in the early years.

10. 2. 3. 1. 4 Tax Credits

Tax credits which permit a dollar for dollar write-off against tax liability. A tax credit is much more valuable than a tax deduction.

In Unit 4, Session 17, we will revisit partnership taxation with a few additional facts relative to all partnerships, not just DPPs.

10. 2. 4   ANALYSIS AND EVALUATION OF DIRECT PARTICIPATION PROGRAMS

The total return of a partnership investment takes into account tax deductions, cash distributions, and capital gains. An investor should choose a limited partnership because:

- it is economically viable;
- the investor can make use of the potential tax benefits;
- the GP(s) has(have) demonstrated management ability and expertise in running similar programs;
- the program's objectives match the investor's objectives and does so within a time frame that meets the investor's needs; and
- the start-up costs and projected revenues are in line with the start-up costs and revenues of similar ventures.

Promoters structure DPPs to meet various objectives. When a promoter's tax stance is too aggressive or is without economic purpose in the view of the IRS, the program is considered an abusive tax shelter. If the IRS judges the program to be abusive, it disallows deductions; assesses back taxes, interest, and penalties; and, in some cases, charges the promoter with criminal intent to defraud.

Investors should try to match their current and future objectives with a program's stated objectives.

EXAMPLE   A person seeking current taxable passive income should not invest in an oil and gas exploratory drilling program. Why not? Because these programs drill where oil (or gas) has never been found before (*exploratory*) and have a low success rate. Even when the do "hit," it may take years before any income is generated.

TAKE NOTE   Because the vast majority of these are privately placed, DPPs are considered illiquid, and investors must commit money for a long period of time.

10. 2. 5   ADVANTAGES AND DISADVANTAGES OF LIMITED PARTNERSHIPS

The DPP investor enjoys several advantages, including:

- an investment managed by others;
- flow-through of income and certain expenses; and
- limited liability—the most the investors can lose is the amount of their investment plus any funds committed for, but not yet remitted.

The exam will probably give more attention to the following disadvantages.

- **Liquidity Risk.** The greatest disadvantage is lack of liquidity. Because the secondary market for DPPs is limited, investors who want to sell their interests frequently cannot locate buyers.

- **Legislative Risk.** When Congress changes tax laws, new rules can cause substantial damage to LPs, who may be locked into illiquid investments that lose previously assumed tax advantages.

- **Risk of Audit.** Statistics from the IRS indicate that reporting ownership of a DPP results in a significantly higher percentage of returns selected for audit.

- **Depreciation Recapture.** One of the tax benefits is the ability to depreciate most fixed assets, especially when that depreciation can be accelerated. The effect of the depreciation deduction is to lower the tax basis of the asset. If that asset is then sold for more than that basis, the excess is "recaptured" and subject to tax, possibly at ordinary income tax rates. You won't need to know anything more than the concept.

QUICK QUIZ 10.A

True or False?

_____ 1. An investor who purchases a limited partnership is generally required to provide a statement of net worth.

_____ 2. One of the greatest advantages of limited partnership investments is that they are readily traded in the secondary market.

_____ 3. DPP investors may deduct passive losses from ordinary income.

_____ 4. The general partner is fully liable for all partnership losses and debts.

_____ 5. Limited partners have limited liability and take an active role in the management of partnerships.

_____ 6. Tax deductions, capital gains, and cash distributions are potential rewards for limited partnership investors.

7. One of your clients wishes to invest in a hedge fund. You should explain which of the following?

   A. Shares of these funds are easy to redeem.
   B. The fund can be expected to generate a profit whether the markets trend up or trend down.
   C. These funds purchase a large amount of preferred stock.
   D. Expenses for these funds tend to be higher than those for traditional mutual funds.

8. The prospectus for a fund states that the minimum initial investment is $500,000. This is most likely what type of fund?

   A. Balanced
   B. Hedge
   C. Small-cap growth
   D. Specialized

Quick Quiz answers can be found at the end of the unit.

UNIT TEST

1. Holders of each of the following are creditors EX-CEPT investors owning
   A. preferred stock
   B. corporate bonds
   C. municipal bonds
   D. government bonds

2. Among the advantages of including preferred stock in an investor's portfolio are
   I. dividends must be paid before any distribution to common stockholders
   II. a rate of return that is likely to keep pace with inflation
   III. the opportunity for increased income if the issuer's profits increase
   IV. a fixed rate of return that is likely higher than that for a debt security offered by the same issuer

   A. I and II
   B. I and IV
   C. II and III
   D. III and IV

3. In general, the type of security offering the greatest degree of safety to an investor is
   A. common stock
   B. debentures
   C. mortgage bonds
   D. preferred stock

4. A debenture is issued based on
   A. the general credit of the corporation
   B. a pledge of real estate
   C. a pledge of equipment
   D. the ability to levy taxes

5. When Treasury bills are issued, they are quoted at
   A. a premium over par
   B. 100% of the par value
   C. par value with interest coupons attached
   D. a discount from principal with no coupons attached

6. According to Standard and Poor's rating system, the 4 highest grades of bonds (from best to lowest grade) are
   A. Aaa; Aa; A; Baa
   B. A; Aa; Aaa; B
   C. B; A; AA; AAA
   D. AAA; AA; A; BBB

7. Municipal bonds are often called tax-exempts. This refers to the exemption of their income from
   A. state, federal, and inheritance taxes
   B. state income taxes
   C. federal income taxes
   D. inheritance taxes

8. The current yield on a bond with a coupon rate of 5.5% selling at 110 is
   A. 2%
   B. 5%
   C. 5.5%
   D. 6%

9. A bond is selling at a premium over par value. Therefore, its
   A. current yield is less than its nominal yield
   B. nominal yield is less than its current yield
   C. yield to maturity is greater than its current yield
   D. none of the above

10. A bond issue that may be retired in advance of maturity at the option of the issuer is said to have
    A. a callable feature
    B. an optional reserve
    C. a conversion feature
    D. a put option feature

11. BFJ Corp's 5% convertible bond is trading at 120. The bond is convertible at $50. An investor buying the bond now and immediately converting into common stock, would receive
    A. 24 shares
    B. 20 shares
    C. 2.4 shares
    D. 20 shares plus cash for fractional shares

12. All of the following are true of government agency bonds EXCEPT

    A. they are considered relatively safe investments
    B. they are direct obligations of the U.S. government
    C. they trade openly
    D. older ones have coupons attached, new ones are book entry

13. All of the following are true about GNMAs EXCEPT

    A. they are backed by the U.S. government
    B. they provide funds for residential mortgages
    C. interest on GNMAs is not exempt from state and local taxes
    D. interest is paid semiannually

14. One of the more popular money market instruments is the negotiable CD. These normally are found in minimum denominations of

    A. $25,000
    B. $100,000
    C. $500,000
    D. $1,000,000

15. Historically, all of the following are risks generally associated with CMOs EXCEPT

    A. credit
    B. liquidity
    C. prepayment
    D. reinvestment

16. Which of the following is NOT a characteristic of owning a limited partnership?

    A. An investment managed by others
    B. Flow-through of income and expenses of a business to the individual limited partner
    C. Legislative risk
    D. Tax-free income

17. Which of the following is NOT an investment objective that must be stated in an investment company's prospectus?

    A. Growth
    B. Income
    C. Tax-advantaged income
    D. Retirement

18. Which of the following statements regarding derivative securities is NOT true?

    A. Derivative securities can be sold on listed exchanges or in the over-the-counter market.
    B. An option contract is a derivative security because it has no value independent of the value of an underlying security.
    C. An option contract's price fluctuates in relationship to the time remaining to expiration as well as with the price movement of the underlying security.
    D. An owner of a put has the obligation to purchase securities at a designated price (the strike price) before a specified date (the expiration date).

19. A client has invested $25,000 into a variable annuity which has grown to $150,000 over the accumulation period. At age 60, the account is liquidated. The tax treatment of the withdrawal would be

    A. capital gains tax on $125,000.
    B. ordinary income tax on $125,000.
    C. ordinary income tax on $125,000 with a 10% tax penalty.
    D. partly ordinary income and partly capital gains depending on the length of time the variable annuity was in force.

20. When advising an investor on the purchase of mutual funds, the registered representative should instruct the client to compare open-end mutual funds with the same objective for all of the following EXCEPT

    A. costs
    B. portfolio turnover
    C. liquidity
    D. services offered

21. Which of the following statements regarding investment companies is NOT true?

    A. The Investment Company Act of 1940 classifies investment companies into three types: face-amount certificate companies, unit investment trusts, and management investment companies.

    B. An investment company can offer investors two ways of participating in the fund under management: through the purchase of closed-end shares, or, if the investor prefers, open-end redeemable shares.

    C. When investors sell or redeem their open-end fund shares, they receive the net asset value (NAV) based on the forward pricing rule.

    D. When investors sell their closed-end fund shares, they may receive an amount below the current net asset value.

22. An owner of an annuitized annuity can do all of the following EXCEPT

    A. receive the benefits on a monthly basis until the time of death

    B. receive the benefits for life with a certain minimum period of time guaranteed

    C. have a joint life with last survivor clause with payments paid until the death of the last survivor

    D. receive monthly payment for a defined period and then 2 years later change the contract to payment for life

23. In a direct participation program, liability for the debts of the business falls upon the

    A. general partner(s)
    B. limited partner(s)
    C. shareholder(s)
    D. sole proprietor

24. Which of the following is NOT a restriction that the SEC has placed on money market mutual funds?

    A. Investments are limited to securities with remaining maturities of 397 days or less, with the average portfolio maturity not to exceed 60 days.

    B. Investments are limited to eligible securities determined to have minimal risk.

    C. No more than 5% of the fund's assets may be invested in below-investment-grade securities.

    D. The prospectus must prominently indicate that the U.S. government does not guarantee the fund and that there is no guarantee that the NAV will be maintained.

25. One way in which closed-end management investment companies differ from open-end investment management companies is that

    A. they trade at a price independent of their net asset value

    B. their portfolio may contain common stock, preferred stock and debt securities

    C. they are federal covered securities

    D. they were in existence prior to 1940

26. Insurance companies selling annuities offer a variety of purchase options to owners. Which of the following definitions regarding these annuity options is NOT true?

    A. Accumulation annuity—an annuity that allows the investor to accumulate funds in a separate account before investment in an annuity

    B. Single premium deferred annuity—an annuity with a lump-sum investment, with payment of benefits deferred until the annuitant elects to receive them

    C. Periodic payment deferred annuity—allows a person to make periodic payments over time. The contract holder can invest money on a monthly, quarterly, or annual basis

    D. Immediate annuity—allows an investor to deposit a lump sum with the insurance company. Payout of the annuitant's benefits starts immediately, usually within 60 days

27. Benefits of investing in a DPP would include
    I. liquidity
    II. flow-through of operating losses
    III. limited liability
    IV. immunization against tax audit
    A. I and II
    B. I and IV
    C. II and III
    D. III and IV

28. Which of the following statements regarding the general partner in a direct participation program (DPP) is NOT true?
    A. The general partner (GP) is the active investor in a limited partnership and assumes responsibility for all aspects of the partnership's operations.
    B. A GP has a fiduciary relationship to the limited partners (LPs).
    C. The GP cannot borrow from the partnership, compete with the partnership, or commingle personal funds with partnership funds.
    D. The GP, as the active manager of the partnership, does not maintain a financial interest in the partnership and only receives income distributions from profits on the business prior to the limited partners.

29. With an annuity
    I. taxes on earned dividends, interest, and capital gains are paid annually, until the owner withdraws money from the contract
    II. random withdrawals are handled under LIFO tax rules
    III. money invested in a nonqualified annuity represents the investor's cost basis
    IV. upon withdrawal, the amount exceeding the investor's cost basis is taxed as ordinary income
    A. I only
    B. I, II and IV
    C. II, III and IV
    D. IV only

30. Covered call writing is a strategy where an investor
    A. sells a call on a security he owns to reduce the volatility of the stock's returns and to generate income with the premium
    B. buys two calls on the same security he owns to leverage the position
    C. buys a call on a security he has sold short
    D. sells a call on an index that contains some of the securities that he has in his portfolio

31. All of the following are advantages of universal life insurance EXCEPT
    A. ability to adjust the amount of premium payments
    B. the policy is guaranteed never to lapse
    C. ability to change death benefit amount
    D. when the cash value is sufficient, no premium payment is required

32. Advantages of Brady bonds to an American investor include all of the following EXCEPT
    A. tax-free interest
    B. greater liquidity than found in most emerging market securities
    C. greater safety than most emerging market debt because of the collateral
    D. higher yields than on U.S. Treasury securities

33. Which of the following is indicative of the primary difference between variable life insurance and straight whole life insurance?
    A. Amount of insurance that can be issued
    B. Cost of the insurance
    C. Tax treatment of the death proceeds
    D. Way in which the cash values are invested

34. Which of the following securities trade on regulated stock exchanges with their prices being determined by supply and demand?
    I. Closed-end investment companies
    II. Exchange-traded funds
    III. Face amount certificate companies
    IV. Mutual funds
    A. I and II
    B. I and III
    C. II and III
    D. III and IV

35. Among the purposes of purchasing derivatives would be all of the following EXCEPT
    A. hedging
    B. income
    C. profits
    D. speculation

36. The term derivative would apply to which of the following?
    A. DPPs
    B. REITs
    C. Warrants
    D. UITs

37. Which of the following indicates a bond selling at a discount?
    A. 7% coupon yielding 6.5%
    B. 7% coupon yielding 7.5%
    C. 10% coupon yielding 9%
    D. 5% coupon yielding 5%

38. When comparing mutual funds and variable annuities, it would be correct to state that
    A. both offer tax-deferred growth of earnings
    B. both require the salesperson possess a securities and an insurance license
    C. the surrender charges on a mutual fund are usually higher than on a variable annuity
    D. the expense ratio of the variable annuity is usually higher than that of a comparable mutual fund

39. A European style option differs from an American style option primarily in that it
    A. derives its value from some underlying asset
    B. can only be exercised on its expiration date
    C. is primarily used for options on foreign securities
    D. is generally offered with a limited number of expiration dates.

40. The term derivative would not include
    A. futures on commodities
    B. interest rate swaps
    C. REITs
    D. LEAPS

41. The LIBOR rate is established on a daily basis in
    A. Liberia
    B. Libya
    C. London
    D. New York

42. On July 15, 2013, your client purchased a variable life insurance policy with a death benefit of $500,000. The November 2015 statement showed a cash value of $30,000. If the client wanted to borrow as much as possible, the insurance company would have to allow a loan of at least
    A. $0
    B. $15,000
    C. $22,500
    D. $27,000

43. Your client who owns a DPP that generated a $10,000 passive loss for the year could
    A. deduct $10,000 against ordinary income
    B. deduct $10,000 against capital gains
    C. deduct $3,000 against ordinary income and carry over the rest
    D. only deduct the passive loss against passive income

44. Which type of investment company is most often organized as a limited partnership?
    A. Face-amount certificate company
    B. Exchange traded fund
    C. Hedge fund
    D. Unit investment trust

45. The Alpha-Gamma Mutual Fund reports a large number of their investors liquidating shares of the fund, so much so that the dollar amount of liquidations exceeds the incoming cash for new purchases. This would lead to a condition known as
    A. cash outflow
    B. net redemptions
    C. improved performance
    D. reduced leverage

46. An employee wishing to obtain long-term capital gain treatment would prefer the employer to offer
    A. incentive stock options
    B. non-qualified stock options
    C. listed stock options
    D. portable stock options

47. GEMCO Manufacturing company, traded on the NYSE, has announced that it will be issuing 10 million new shares of common stock to raise new capital for the purchase of new equipment. Your client owning 1,000 shares of GEMCO common stock would probably receive

    A. an advance invitation to purchase some of the new shares
    B. options to purchase some of the new shares
    C. preemptive rights to purchase some of the new shares
    D. warrants to purchase some of the new shares

48. Which of the following investments would provide the highest after-tax income to your client in the 35% federal income tax bracket?

    A. 6% U.S. Treasury bond
    B. 5% general obligation municipal bond issued by State H
    C. 7% bond issued by Canadian Province M
    D. 8% debenture issued by the LMN Corporation

49. The Wall Street pundits are predicting a substantial increase in interest rates. If they are correct, which of the following bonds would be most sensitive to that increase?

    A. 5s of 2035
    B. 5s of 2040
    C. 5s of 2045
    D. 4s of 2020

50. An important characteristic of mortgage-backed securities not generally found in other debt issues is

    A. a portion of each payment consists of a return of principal in addition to interest
    B. there is collateral pledged for the loan
    C. they are generally convertible
    D. they are rarely paid off prior to their maturity date

ANSWERS AND RATIONALES

1. **A.** Remember all stockholders (even preferred stockholders) are owners of a corporation, not creditors.

2. **B.** Preferred stock carries a fixed dividend that must be paid before any distribution to common stockholders—hence the name preferred. However, unlike the interest on a debt security, there is no obligation to pay the dividend. Therefore, the yield on a company's preferred stock is invariably higher than that on its debt issues. Disadvantages of owning preferred stock are that the fixed return may not keep up with inflation and, regardless of corporate earnings, the dividend will not change, so there is no hope for increased income.

3. **C.** Debt securities, because they are an obligation of the issuer, are generally considered safer than equity securities. The only one of these debt obligations with pledged assets as security for the loan is the mortgage bond.

4. **A.** There are no pledged assets behind a debenture, merely the credit standing of the corporation. It is a corporate IOU.

5. **D.** Treasury bills are always issued at a discount, they pay no interest. The investor profits by receiving back par value and makes the difference between the discounted purchase price and the par received at maturity. All government bonds are now book entry; there has not been a Treasury note or bond issued since July 1986 with interest coupons attached.

6. **D.** Choice A would be correct if the question referred to Moody's.

7. **C.** Although municipal bonds are sometimes exempt from state income tax (if issued in the state of residence of the taxpayer), all references to tax exemption refer to their exemption from federal income taxes.

8. **B.** The current yield of any security, equity, or debt is always the income return (dividend or interest) divided by the current market price. In this case, it is

$$\frac{5.5}{110} = 5\%$$

9. **A.** Any bond selling at a premium will yield less than the coupon rate (nominal yield). Conversely, of course, a bond trading at a discount will certainly yield more. Remember, there is an inverse relationship between bond prices and bond yields. See the previous question for an example of a bond selling at a premium.

10. **A.** A bond that is callable has a provision that the issuer, at its option, may redeem that bond at a specified price known as the call or redemption price.

11. **B.**

$$\frac{par}{conversion\ price} = number\ of\ shares$$

$$\frac{\$1{,}000}{50} = 20\ shares$$

12. **B.** The only government agency that is a direct obligation of the U.S. government is the Ginnie Mae security. All of the others are moral obligations.

13. **D.** GMNAs make payment monthly, unlike virtually all other debt securities, which make payments semiannually.

14. **B.** Negotiable CDs, sometimes referred to as jumbo CDs, have a minimum denomination of $100,000. They are unsecured, interest-bearing obligations of banks.

15. **A.** In the past, CMOs generally carried AAA or AA ratings and, thus, had little credit risk. After the sub-prime meltdown of 2007–2008, we're not sure how NASAA is treating these now. Until we post something different on the Exam-Tips & Contents Updates, stick with the historically correct choice.

16. **D.** The income from limited partnerships is not tax exempt. An investor, however, may use a tax loss from a partnership to offset the income from another passive investment. In limited partnerships, the investor enjoys the advantages and disadvantages of owning a business without having to actually manage one. Limited partnerships are vulnerable to legislative changes that adversely affect ownership of such investments.

17. **D.** Retirement savings and income are objectives of an investor, not of an investment company fund (the fund is not looking to retire when it is 65 years old). Growth, income, and tax-advantaged income are examples of investment company objectives.

18. **D.** An owner of a put has the right, not the obligation, to sell, not purchase, a security at a designated price (the strike price) before a specified date (the expiration date).

19. **B.** Any increase in the value of a variable annuity is taxed as ordinary income, never capital gain. In this case, there is no 10% penalty tax because the client is over 59½ years old.

20. **C.** Shares in an open-end investment company (mutual fund) are liquid. The issuer of the shares is required to redeem them at their net asset value and, therefore, should not be a consideration in comparing mutual funds with the same objective. Sales loads, management fees, and operating expenses reduce an investor's return. Most of these fees continue throughout the holding period and have a significant impact on performance. Portfolio turnover is significant as gains in the portfolio will likely all be short-term gains, which are usually taxable to the investor at a higher rate than long-term capital gains. Services that mutual funds offer include retirement accounts, investment plans, check-writing privileges, telephone transfers, conversion privileges, withdrawal plans, and others.

21. **B.** An investment company cannot offer investors two ways of participating in the fund under management. The fund must either be a closed-end fund with shares traded in the marketplace or an open-end fund with redeemable shares. The Investment Company Act of 1940 classifies investment companies into three types: FACs, UITs, and management investment companies. When investors sell or redeem their open-end fund shares, they receive the NAV as of the close of the day the order was received (i.e., based on the next computed NAV after the order arrives). Because closed-end fund shares are priced based on supply and demand, the price a holder receives when selling might be more, less or the same as the NAV.

22. **D.** The contract is annuitized when the investor converts from the accumulation (pay-in) stage to the distribution (payout) stage. Once a payout option is selected, it cannot be changed. An annuity owner can elect to receive the benefits on a monthly basis until the time of death. An annuity owner can elect to receive the benefits for life with a certain minimum period of time guaranteed. In addition, an annuity owner can have a joint life with last survivor clause with payouts made until the death of the last survivor.

23. **A.** DPPs consist of at least one GP and one LP. The liability of the limited partners is limited to their investment, including commitments made but not yet fulfilled. On the other hand, the general partners bear the liability for the debts of the entity.

24. **C.** The SEC requires that money market mutual funds' investments be limited to securities that are rated in the top two ratings categories by the nationally recognized rating services (e.g., Moody's, Standard & Poor's). Investment in below-investment-grade securities is not allowed.

25 **A.** Unlike open-end companies (mutual funds) where the price is based on the net asset value (NAV), closed-end companies trade at a market price based on supply and demand which could be above, below or the same as the NAV. Both are federal covered, both can have equity and debt in their portfolios (although only closed-end companies can issue senior securities) and both were in existence prior to passage of the Investment Company Act of 1940.

26. **A.** Accumulation does not refer to a purchase option. The pay-in period for an annuity is known as the accumulation stage. A single premium deferred annuity is an annuity with a lump-sum investment, with payment of benefits deferred until the annuitant elects to receive them. Periodic payment deferred annuities allow a person to make periodic payments over time. Immediate annuities allow an investor to deposit a lump sum with the insurance company payout of the annuitant's benefits starting immediately, usually within 60 days.

27. **C.** DPPs are structured as flow-through entities giving their investors to opportunity to receive income without the partnership being taxed first. In addition, if there are losses, they get the opportunity to write-off those losses against income from other DPPs. As limited partnership vehicles, they offer their investors liability limited to their investment. They generally have very low liquidity and, instead of reducing the tax audit risk, they actually increase it.

28. **D.** General partners (GPs) must maintain a financial interest in the partnership and generally do not receive distributions from profits before those paid to the limited partners. The GP is the active investor in a limited partnership and assumes responsibility for all aspects of the partnership's operations and has a fiduciary relationship to the LPs. The GP, as a fiduciary, cannot borrow from the partnership, compete with the partnership, or commingle personal funds with partnership funds.

29. **C.** Money randomly withdrawn (not annuitized) is handled under LIFO tax rules; money invested in an annuity represents the investor's cost basis; and on withdrawal, the amount exceeding the investor's cost basis is taxed as ordinary income. Taxes on earned dividends, interest, and capital gains are not paid annually. They are deferred and paid later, when the owner withdraws money from the contract.

30. **A.** A covered call is simply defined as an investor owning 100 shares of the underlying stock for each option written (sold). The premium received is not only a source of income, but also serves to provide downside protection to the extent of the amount received.

31. **B.** A universal life policy may lapse if the accumulation fund drops below a specified level and an additional premium is not paid.

32. **A.** The interest on Brady bonds is fully taxable to a U.S. investor. All of the other statements are true.

33. **D.** Variable life insurance allows the policyowner to decide how the cash value is invested through a number of subaccounts.

34. **A.** Both closed-end funds and exchange-traded funds (ETFs) trade on stock exchanges with their prices being determined by supply and demand just like any other stock.

35. **B.** Purchase of a derivative, whether an option, a forward, or futures contract, never generates income. Selling one does, but the question refers to a purchaser.

36. **C** A derivative has its value based upon some underlying asset. The value of a warrant is based on the value of the security into which it is exchangeable.

37. **B.** Whenever the yield is higher than the coupon, the bond is selling at a discount from the par value.

38. **D.** It is generally correct to state that variable annuities offer a way to accumulate funds on a tax-deferred basis, although generally with operating expenses somewhat higher than mutual funds with the same investment objective. There is no tax-deferral with mutual funds and no insurance license is required to sell them. Only Class B and C shares have redemption fees, a form of surrender charge, and they are invariable lower than annuity surrender charges.

39. **B.** The single most significant (and tested) difference between these two styles is that an American style option can be exercised anytime while a European style option can only be exercised at expiration. They both derive their value from some underlying asset which is why they are derivative securities. European style has nothing to do with the domicile of the underlying asset behind the option and these are offered with a similar range of expiration dates as are American style options.

40. **C.** A derivative is something which derives its value from something else. REITs represent direct investment into real estate; the asset purchase is the actual asset. Never heard of interest rate swaps? Well, on the real exam, there will occasionally be an answer choice that you've never heard of, but it should not affect your ability to choose the correct one.

41. **C.** LIBOR is the London Interbank Offered Rate (technically the ICE-LIBOR now) and, as shown, the L stands for London, U.K.

42. **A.** Until a variable life policy is in force for a minimum of three years (this one is a bit less than 2½ years), there is no requirement to make the loan provision available. Once the three-year mark is reached, that minimum becomes 75% of the computed cash value.

43. **D.** Passive losses, such as those generated by limited partnership investments (DPPs), are only deductible against passive income.

44. **C.** For various legal reasons, mostly related to the need to avoid registration with the SEC, hedge funds are generally structured as limited partnership entities with the organizers invariably sinking their own funds into a few units.

45. **B.** One of the main features of open-end investment management companies (mutual funds) is that there is a continuous offer of new shares and ready redemption of old ones. When redemptions exceed new purchases, the fund suffers from net redemptions.

46. **A.** Assuming the time limit conditions are met, exercise of an ISO can result in long-term capital gains while non-qualified options are always treated as ordinary income.

47. **C.** Commonly, when a publicly traded company issues new shares of common stock, existing shareholders receive preemptive rights, sometimes called stock rights, enabling them to purchase shares in proportion to their current ownership, usually at a reduced price. These rights rarely last longer than 45 days and must be exercised or sold within that time or they'll just expire worthless. Warrants are not sent to shareholders; they are either purchased in the open market or come attached to a new issue of securities as a "sweetener".

48. **D.** Only the State H bond is exempt from federal income tax. Using the tax equivalent yield formula of the muni coupon divided by (100% minus the investor's tax bracket %) we get 5% divided by 65% or 7.7%. That's a better deal than receiving 6% on the Treasury and paying taxes as well as 7% on the Canadian bond (although you learned that securities issued by Canadian provinces were exempt from registration under the Uniform Securities Act, that has nothing to do with U.S. income taxes). However, with a TEY of 7.7%, your client would take home more with the 8% taxable corporate security. You can also work backward to get the correct answer. Simply subtract 35% tax from each of the choices (other than the muni) and see which is the highest. In this case, 8% minus a 35% tax equals 5.2%—just a bit higher than the 5% coupon on the municipal bond.

49. **C.** The bond with the longest duration will have the greatest sensitivity to change in interest rates. We examine two factors: the coupon rate and the length to maturity. When the coupon rates are the same, as they are for three of these bonds, the one with the maturity date farthest into the future will have the longest duration. Even though the 4% coupon is lower than the others, the maturity date is so much closer that it actually has the shortest duration (least sensitivity to change) of this group.

50. **A.** Because the cash flow is from homeowners paying their mortgages, a portion of each payment is principal with the rest being interest (just like when you pay your home mortgage payment). Yes, there is collateral, but that is also the case with mortgage bonds, collateral trust bonds, and equipment trust certificates. There is nothing for them to be converted into (on this exam, convertible always means into common stock) and, because so few mortgages go full term, these are invariably paid off ahead of the maturity date.

QUICK QUIZ ANSWERS

Quick Quiz 4.A

1. **C.** Owning either common or preferred stocks represents ownership (or equity) in a corporation.

2. **B.** One does not have access to insider information solely by becoming a shareholder. Even if one did receive material nonpublic information, such as prior access to earnings, no benefit may be received from that information. All of the other choices are among the reasons to purchase common stock.

3. **D.** Corporations normally declare cash dividends, but corporations can also declare stock dividends in additional shares of the issuing corporation, shares of a subsidiary, or property dividends (usually products of the company).

4. **A.** An advantage of owning stock is that an investor's liability is limited to the amount of money invested when the stock was purchased.

5. **B.** A residual claim to assets at dissolution and a vote at the annual shareholder's meeting are common stockholder rights.

6. **C.** Owning common stock subjects one to market risk, the possibility that dividends may be reduced, and the fact that they have the last priority in claims against the assets of the corporation. The right to vote cannot be taken away.

Quick Quiz 4.B

1. **D.** Callable preferred. When the stock is called, dividend payments are no longer made. To compensate for that possibility, the issuer must pay a higher dividend.

2. **B.** Investors in preferred stock with the goal of income are most concerned that the company will be able to sustain the dividend.

3. **C.** Because convertible can be exchanged for common shares, its price is closely linked to the price of the issuer's common.

4. **A.** Current and unpaid past dividends on cumulative preferred stock must be paid before common stockholders can receive a dividend. Bond interest is always paid before dividends.

Quick Quiz 4.C

1. **D.** Because everything is in U.S. dollars and in English, ADRs make trading in foreign securities much easier for those who live here.

2. **B.** ADRs represent ownership in a foreign security so there is always going to be currency risk. These ADRs trade in the market and have market risk. Since most ADRs are traded on the exchanges, there is little liquidity risk and, because they represent equity, they are usually a good hedge against inflation.

Quick Quiz 4.D

1. **B.** Warrants are issued with long-term maturities and may be used as sweeteners in an offering of the issuer's preferred stock or bonds. Unlike rights, warrants are not offered to current shareholders; they are attached to a new offering or purchased in the open market. The exercise price of a warrant is typically above the market value of the stock at the time of issue.

2. **B.** Preferred stockholders have no right to maintain a percentage of ownership when new shares are issued (no preemptive rights). However, they do receive preference in dividend payment and company liquidation.

3. **C.** As long as certain time restrictions are met, any difference between the exercise (strike) price and the sale price is considered long-term capital gain. The question is this: did she sell the stock more than two years after granting of the option? Yes, because from July 15, 2008 until August 4, 2010 is more than two years. The second question is this: did she sell the stock more than one year after exercise? Yes, because August 4, 2010 is more than one year after June 30, 2009.

Quick Quiz 4.E

1. **C.** In order to use the dividend growth model, there must be a possibility of dividend growth. Because preferred stock dividends are fixed, this tool would not make any sense.

Quick Quiz 5.A

1. **A.** Ginnie Maes pay interest on a monthly basis, not semiannually.

Quick Quiz 5.B

1. **A.** Bondholders have contractual rights to the assets of a business that must be honored on insolvency before claims of stockholders or directors.

2. **C.** A bond represents a legal obligation to repay principal and interest by the company. Common stock carries no such obligation. SIPC insures broker-dealer client accounts, not bonds.

Quick Quiz 5.C

1. **F.** As the name implies, Eurodollar bonds are denominated in U.S. dollars. That means that someone in France will have the risk that the Euro, the home currency in France, will rise against the dollar and, as a result, interest payments will be worth less as will the ultimate payback at maturity. Only U.S. residents have no currency risk with Eurodollar bonds.

2. **T.** One of the benefits of Brady bonds is the ability of the sovereign government to borrow at a lower cost because of the collateral behind the bond.

3. **T.** When interest rates fall, issuers can borrow at a lower rate so they will be highly motivated to call in the old debt and replace it with debt at a lower interest rate.

4. **F.** Because of the perceived extra safety of the convertible security (either a preferred stock or debenture, both having senior claim over the common), the general case is that convertible securities sell at somewhat of a premium over their parity price.

5. **F.** Convertible debentures are convertible into the issuer's common, not preferred stock.

6. **D.** A callable bond is one that may be redeemed by the issuing corporation before it matures. One reason a corporation might call a bond is because it can now borrow at a lower interest rate.

7. **A.** A convertible bond is usually a debenture that allows the owner to exchange it for a set number of shares of stock as stated in the bond indenture (or contract). This number will change only in response to the anti-dilutive provisions that go into effect in the case of a stock split or stock dividend and has nothing to do with the market price of the stock.

Quick Quiz 5.D

1. **B.** The first step is determining the number of shares upon conversion. That would be found by dividing the $1,000 par value of the bond by the $25 conversion price. This tells us that the bond is convertible into 40 shares. Then, we divide the current market price of $1,200 by the 40 shares to arrive at the parity price (the price as which 40 shares is equal to $1,200).

2. **A.** The current yield on a bond is the coupon divided by the current market price. In this example, 6 divided by 90. The price of 90 represents 90% of par, a discount of $100. Interest payments are based on the $1,000 face amount, so this investor would receive two semiannual payments of $30 each. On a discounted bond, the yield to maturity will always be higher than the current yield.

3. **C.** The market price of outstanding bonds falls when interest rates rise because bond prices have an inverse relationship with interest rates. That is, when an investor can get a higher nominal (coupon) yield on a new bond, the old one paying a lower rate of interest just isn't worth as much so the price goes down. Remember, the nominal yield is the coupon rate stated on the face of the bond and that never changes.

4. **B.** A zero-coupon bond is a type of debt security that pays no periodic interest payments. Instead, they are sold at a deep discount from the maturity value and the investor receives return of that value only when the bonds mature.

5. **B.** The nominal yield (or coupon rate) is the interest rate stated on the bond and is the annual rate the issuer promises to pay on the bond until the bond matures. A $1,000 bond with an 8% nominal yield will pay $80 per year in interest. In all cases on the exam, the interest will be paid in two equal semi-annual installments, in this case, $40 each.

6. **B.** Treasury STRIPS are guaranteed by the U.S. government so there is no chance of default. They are zero-coupon bonds and offer no current income, which is appropriate for a client who wants 100% return paid at a future date for college expenses.

7. **C.** When a bond is selling at par, its coupon or nominal rate, current yield, and yield to maturity are all the same.

8. **D.** A bond price of 102 represents 102% of the $1,000 par value or $1,020. With 5 bonds, the investor would pay a total of 5 × $1,020 or $5,100.

9. **C.** Investment grade is defined as BBB (S&P) or Baa (Moody's) and higher. When giving the rating collateral, or lack of same, it taken into consideration. All you do is look at the letters.

10. **C.** Tax equivalent yield is computed by dividing the coupon rate of the municipal bond by (100% tax bracket). In this case, the calculation is 3% divided by 75% (or 0.75) and results in a TEY of 4%. You can always work backward to check by deducting the 25% tax from each answer to see which one results in the 3% coupon. The fact that the bond is unrated has little or nothing to do with the ability of the issuer to pay the interest.

11. **C.** Municipal bonds are generally considered second only to U.S. Treasury instruments in relative safety. Because of their tax-free yield, their coupon rates are lower than corporate bonds of the same quality.

Quick Quiz 6.A

1. **B.** The appropriate investment for the client is a money market instrument and nothing is safer than a T-bill.

2. **A.** Money market instruments are high-quality debt securities with maturities that do not exceed 1 year.

Quick Quiz 6.B

1. **A.** CMOs are not backed by the full faith and credit of the U.S. government. However, both Ginnie Maes and CMOs are collateralized by mortgages, yield more than T-bonds, and are pass-through securities.

2. **B.** DDA stands for demand deposit account, most often a checking account at a bank.

Quick Quiz 7.A

1. **B.**

2. **A.**

3. **B.**

4. **B.**

5. **A.**

6. **B.**

7. **A.**

Quick Quiz 7.B

1. **D.**

2. **B.**

3. **A.**

4. **C.**

Quick Quiz 7.C

1. **D.**

2. **A.**

3. **B.**

4. **C.**

Quick Quiz 7.D

1. **C.**

2. **B.**

3. **A.**

Quick Quiz 7.E

1. **C.**

2. **D.**

3. **A.**

4. **B.**

Quick Quiz 7.F

1. **C.** Investment companies may be one of three types: unit investment trusts, face amount certificates, or management companies. Within the category of management companies, you will find open- and closed-end companies. Open-end investment management companies are also referred to as mutual funds.

2. **A.** Mutual funds must calculate the value of fund shares at least once per business day; funds may calculate the value more often and will disclose this fact in the prospectus.

3. **A.** Sector funds (specialized funds) target at least 25% of their investments toward a specific industry or geographical location.

4. **C.** Income funds have the goal of producing income; that is why they are named as such. This is a case where you "don't look a gift horse in the mouth".

5. **D.** Municipal bonds are considered second only to U.S. government securities in terms of safety. Furthermore, whenever you see a question about an investor in a high tax bracket, always look for the answer choice with municipal bonds; the tax-free income is the key.

6. **C.** Money market funds generally come with a check-writing privilege offering investors the opportunity to convert the asset to cash at once. Although all mutual funds are readily redeemable, under the Investment Company Act of 1940, the fund has 7 days to redeem. One must request the cash value from the insurance company.

7. **D.** Money market funds hold money market instruments like negotiable CDs, Treasury bills, banker's acceptances, commercial paper, and repurchase agreements.

8. **A.** The term "breakpoint" refers to the point at which the number of shares being purchased is large enough to qualify the investor for a reduced sales load. FINRA and NASAA prohibit broker-dealers and their agents from making a mutual fund sale at just below the breakpoint merely to obtain a larger commission.

9. **C.** Investors who sign a letter of intent stating they will invest a specified amount over a 13-month period may be eligible for breakpoints. Breakpoints entitle investors to reduced sales charges.

10. **A.** These customers are preparing to make a major purchase within the next few months, so they require a highly liquid investment to keep their money safe for a short amount of time. The money market fund best matches this objective.

Quick Quiz 8.A

1. **C.**
2. **A.**
3. **D.**
4. **B.**

Quick Quiz 8.B

1. **B.**
2. **A.**
3. **D.**
4. **C.**

Quick Quiz 8.C

1. **C.**
2. **B.**
3. **A.**

Quick Quiz 8.D

1. **W, V**
2. **W, U, V**

3. **W**
4. **V, U**
5. **W, U, V**

Quick Quiz 8.E

1. **A.** Annuities offer a guarantee of income that will last for a client's lifetime. The other statements, while true, represent disadvantages of annuitization. Annuitization does limit liquidity and flexibility.

2. **C.** Purchasers of variable (or fixed) annuities have no responsibility for obligations of the insurance company. The contract holder bears the investment risk in a variable annuity. This means that the portfolio is not guaranteed to return a specified rate, and the principal invested will also fluctuate in value according to the securities held in the separate account portfolio. Withdrawals of earnings prior to age 59½, (with limited exceptions), are subject to a 10% tax penalty.

3. **D.** Variable annuities differ from fixed annuities because the payments vary and are designed to offer the annuitant protection against inflation.

4. **B.** In almost all circumstances, certainly for short-to-immediate time periods, term life will be the least expensive form of insurance. A 20-pay life is a permanent policy where the premiums are paid in a 20-year period rather than until death. Variable annuities are not life insurance policies even though they are issued by life insurance companies.

Quick Quiz 9.A

1. **B and C.**

2. **A and D.**

3. **A and D.**

4. **B and C.**

5. **A and C.**

6. **B and D.**

Quick Quiz 9.B

1. **A.** Options are a type of derivative because they derive their values from the values of other investment instruments.

2. **C.** 10 options

3. **D.** ABC common stock

4. **A.** Buy; a call is the right to buy stock

5. **C.** 1,000; 100 shares per contract at 10 contracts

6. **B.** The put buyer (long position) has the right to sell stock to a put writer who is obligated to buy that stock.

Quick Quiz 9.C

1. **C.**

2. **A.**

3. **D.**

4. **C.**

5. **A and D.**

6. **B and C.**

7. **B.**

8. **A and C.**

9. **B.**

10. **D.**

Quick Quiz 9.D

1. **D.** REITs are valued based upon their own assets rather than being derived from the value of something else as the other choices are.

2. **B.** A forward contract is a direct commitment between one buyer and one seller. This makes each contract different, and lack of standardization makes exchange trading a virtual impossibility.

3. **B.** The term *derivative* describes an asset whose value is based on something other than itself. Investment companies have their own portfolios—they don't derive their value from some other asset. Options, futures and warrants all base their value on some underlying asset.

4. **B.** A short-seller of stock will lose when the price of the stock rises, and there is no limit to how high that can be. The best protection is to purchase the 50 call because that gives her the ability to buy the stock at the same price she sold it for, thereby limiting the amount she can lose.

Quick Quiz 10.A.

1. **T.** Because of the more stringent suitability requirements for these products, an investor who purchases a limited partnership is generally required to provide a statement of net worth.

2. **F.** Limited partnerships typically have a very limited secondary market. They are generally not liquid.

3. **F.** Passive losses can only offset passive income.

4. **T.** The general partner is fully liable for all partnership losses and debts.

5. **F.** To maintain limited liability, limited partners must not be involved in the day-to-day management of the partnershp.

6. **T.** Tax deductions, capital gains, and cash distributions are potential rewards for limited partnership investors.

7. **D.**   Hedge funds typically use risky strategies to generate profit regardless of market direction, but there is no guarantee that the objective will be realized. Redemption may be difficult with these funds, and the steps management must take to try to generate profits incur higher expenses than traditional mutual funds.

8. **B.**   One of the characteristics of hedge funds is a high minimum investment requirement.

Unit 3

Economic Factors and Business Information

This unit consists of four sessions:

Session 11 Basic Economics and Financial Reporting

Session 12 Methods of Quantitative Analysis

Session 13 Types of Risk

In total there will be 19 questions on this material, representing 14% of the Series 65 Exam.

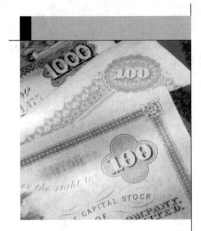

11

Basic Economics and Financial Reporting

Investment decisions are made within the context of the general economic climate and are based on the specific merits of the selected investments. This session will deal with basic economic concepts, such as the business cycle, yield curves, economic indicators and measuring inflation.

The session will then continue with a look at the numbers. There is an old saying popular with sports fans, "You can't tell the players without a scorecard." In that same vein, you can't tell very much about a corporation without examining its financial statements. The conclusion of the session deals with the basics of financial statement analysis including reports required to be filed with the SEC by publicly traded corporations.

The Series 65 exam will include approximately 11 questions on the material presented in this session.

When you have completed this session, you should be able to:

■ **identify** fundamental economic principles and the four stages of the business cycle;

■ **compare** the difference between monetary and fiscal policy;

■ **differentiate** between inflation and deflation;

■ **list** the three types of yield curves;

■ **describe** the major economic indicators;

■ **compare** and contrast balance sheet and income statement items;

■ **compute** various ratios that are used to measure corporate performance; and

■ **distinguish** between the different forms used in SEC reporting.

11. 1   BASIC ECONOMICS

Economics is the social science concerned chiefly with the description and analysis of production, distribution, and consumption of goods and services.

TAKE NOTE

> Economics is about how people choose. From the most important to the most mundane, any decision is economic in nature. Every choice made in terms of the decision maker's utility can be thought of as satisfaction. In every choice we make, we try to find the combination of cost and benefit that maximizes our utility (satisfaction).

There are two major branches of economics: **microeconomics** and **macro-economics**. **Microeconomics** focuses on the economic behavior of narrowly defined units, such as households or business firms.

Macroeconomics is the branch of economics that analyzes aggregates, such as the rate of growth in national economic output as measured by the gross domestic product (GDP), the rate of inflation, and unemployment. Though the two areas overlap in many ways, the Series 65 exam focuses primarily on macroeconomic concepts.

Fiscal policy refers to a government's use of spending and taxation to influence economic activity. The budget is said to be *balanced* when tax revenues equal government expenditures. A **budget surplus** occurs when government tax revenues exceed expenditures, and a **budget deficit** occurs when government expenditures exceed tax revenues.

Monetary policy refers to the central bank's actions that affect the quantity of money and credit in an economy in order to influence economic activity. Monetary policy is said to be **expansionary** (or *accommodative* or *easy*) when the central bank increases the quantity of money and credit in an economy. Conversely, when the central bank is reducing the quantity of money and credit in an economy, the monetary policy is said to be **contractionary** (or *restrictive* or *tight*).Monetary policy is under the control of the Federal Reserve Board (the FED).

TAKE NOTE

> It is important for you to know that the fiscal policy of the United States is determined by the President and Congress through the process of budgeting and taxation. Monetary policy is determined by the Board of Governors of the Federal Reserve System. Unlike monetary policy, the Federal Reserve has nothing to do with fiscal policy.

11. 1. 1   MAJOR SCHOOLS OF ECONOMICS

11. 1. 1. 1   Keynesian Economics

Named after the economist John Maynard Keynes (pronounced, "Canes"), Keynesian economists recognize the importance of government intervention. In 1936, Keynes published *The General Theory of Employment, Interest, and Money* in which he revolutionized the way economists think about macroeconomics. He laid out how and why recessions happen and what must be done to recover from them. His strategy for recovery from a recession was for government to run deficits to stimulate demand and employment. In other words, he suggested lower levels of taxation and more government spending. In this approach, Keynes varied widely from classical economists, such as Adam Smith, who advocated a strict hands-off approach to government. Classical economists argue that market wages and prices will decline quickly enough during a recession to bring about an economic recovery.

11. 1. 1. 2 Classical and Supply-Side Economics

Classical economists favor a school of thought referred to as supply-side economics. The most notable feature of this idea is the belief that lower taxes and less government regulation benefits consumers through a greater supply of goods and services at lower costs. **Supply-side economics** holds that supply creates demand by providing jobs and wages. The prices of goods of which there is excess supply will fall, and the prices of goods in demand will rise. Deficient demand can never be a problem because the production of goods will always generate (through employment) sufficient demand to purchase the goods produced.

Markets will always adjust quickly to direct the economy to full employment. It is argued that if unemployment is temporarily high, wages will fall, which will reduce costs and prices. Reduced prices will increase product demand, which will increase the demand for labor until the excess supply of labor is eliminated.

11. 1. 1. 3 Monetarist Theory

Monetarists, such as the late Milton Friedman, believe that the quantity of money, or **money supply**, determines overall price levels and economic activity. Too many dollars chasing too few goods leads to inflation, and too few dollars chasing too many goods leads to deflation. One of the principal roles of the Federal Reserve Board is monitoring the money supply and making adjustments when necessary.

Monetarists believe a well-controlled, moderately increasing money supply leads to price stability. Price stability allows business managers, who are more efficient allocators of resources than the government, to plan and invest, which in turn keeps the economy from experiencing extremes in the business cycle.

11. 1. 1. 3. 1 Tools of the Federal Reserve Board

Because the Federal Reserve Board (the FED) determines how much money is available for businesses and consumers to spend, its decisions are critical to the U.S. economy. There are three primary tools employed to affect the money supply.

■ **Changes in reserve requirements.** By raising the amount of funds commercial banks must leave on deposit with the FED, the amount of money available for these banks to lend out is decreased. This shrinkage of the money supply generally translates into higher interest rates. The reverse is true when reserve requirements are eased.

■ **Changes in the discount rate.** This is the rate the FED charges member banks when lending them money. Higher rates discourage borrowing, reducing the money supply with lower rates having an opposite effect.

■ **Open market operations.** The FED buys and sells U.S. Treasury securities in the open market under the direction of the Federal Open Market Committee (FOMC). When

Treasuries are purchased, it adds to the money supply. This is because the FOMC is purchasing these securities from commercial banks causing the banks to have greater reserves. When the FOMC sells Treasuries, the money supply is reduced because funds are pulled out of the bank's reserves to pay for those securities.

TEST TOPIC ALERT   Although the FED's actions certainly impact all interests rates, you'll need to know that the FED does not set the prime rate—that is done by the major commercial banks.

11. 1. 2 IMPORTANT TERMS AND CONCEPTS IN ECONOMICS

11. 1. 2. 1 Business Cycles

Business cycles reflect fluctuations in economic activity as measured by the level of activity in such macroeconomic variables as the rate of unemployment and the GDP. Periods of economic expansion have been followed by periods of contraction in a pattern called the **business cycle**. Business cycles go through four stages:

- Expansion
- Peak
- Contraction
- Trough

Expansion. Expansion is characterized by increasing business activity—in sales, manufacturing, and wages—throughout the economy. When GDP increases rapidly and businesses reach their productive capacity, the nation's economy cannot expand further. At this point, the economy is said to have reached its **peak**. When business activity declines from its peak, the economy is **contracting**.

Economists call mild short-term contractions **recessions**. Longer, more severe contractions are **depressions**. When business activity stops declining and levels off, the cycle makes a **trough**.

According to the U.S. Department of Commerce, the economy is in a recession when a decline in real output of goods and services—the **GDP**—continues for two or more consecutive quarters. It defines a depression as a decrease in GDP for six consecutive quarters.

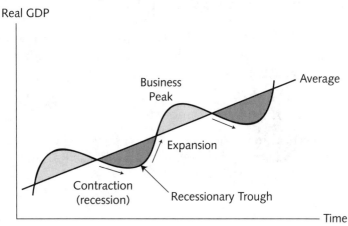

11. 1. 2. 1. 1   The Four Stages of the Business Cycle

To determine the economy's overall direction, economists consider many trends in business activity. Expansions are characterized by increasing consumer demand for goods and services, possibly leading to an:

■ increasing rate of inflation; and

■ increasing industrial production, generally leading to

— a decreasing unemployment rate as hiring accelerates,

— falling inventories,

— rising stock markets,

— rising property values, and

— increasing GDP.

Peaks are characterized by:

■ a decrease to the GDP growth rate;

■ a decrease to the unemployment rate, but a slowdown in hiring;

■ a slower rate of growth in consumer spending and business investment; and

■ an increase to the inflation rate.

Contractions/recessions in the business cycle tend to be characterized by:

■ rising numbers of bankruptcies and bond defaults;

■ decreasing hours worked, increasing unemployment rate;

■ decreasing consumer spending, home construction, and business investment;

■ falling stock markets;

■ a decrease to the inflation rate;

■ rising inventories (a sign of slackening consumer demand); and

■ a negative growth rate for the GDP.

Troughs tend to be characterized by:

■ a change from negative to positive GDP growth rate;

■ a high unemployment rate, increasing use of overtime and temporary workers;

■ spending on consumer durable goods and housing may increase; and

■ a moderate or decreasing inflation rate.

Analysts will frequently make investment decisions based upon where we are in the business cycle. Certain industries outperform while others underperform at different points in the cycle. Following are several examples.

11. 1. 2. 1. 2   Cyclical Industries

Cyclical industries are highly sensitive to business cycles and inflation trends. Most cyclical industries produce durable goods, such as heavy machinery and automobiles, as well as raw materials, such as steel.

During recessions, the demand for durable goods declines as manufacturers postpone investments in new capital goods and consumers postpone purchases of automobiles. On the other hand, **countercyclical industries** tend to turn down as the economy heats up and to rise when the economy turns down. Gold mining has historically been a counter-cyclical industry.

11. 1. 2. 1. 3 Growth Industries

Most industries pass through four phases during their existence: introduction, growth, maturity, and decline. An industry is considered in its growth phase if the industry is growing faster than the economy as a whole because of technological changes, new products, or changing consumer tastes. Social media and bioengineering are examples of current growth industries. Because many growth companies retain nearly all of their earnings to finance their business expansion, growth stocks usually pay little or no dividends.

11. 1. 2. 1. 4 Defensive Industries

Defensive industries are least affected by normal business cycles. Companies in defensive industries generally produce nondurable consumer goods, such as food, pharmaceuticals, tobacco, and energy. Public consumption of such goods remains fairly steady throughout the business cycle.

During recessions and bear markets, stocks in defensive industries generally decline less than stocks in other industries. During expansions and bull markets, defensive stocks may advance less. Investments in defensive industries tend to involve less risk and, consequently, lower investment returns. Those using sector rotation will "rotate" into defensive issues when it appears the business cycle is headed into the contraction phase.

11. 1. 2. 1. 5 Special Situation Stocks

Special situation stocks are stocks of a company with unusual profit potential resulting from nonrecurring circumstances, such as new management, the discovery of a valuable natural resource on corporate property, or the introduction of a new product. In most cases, the phase of the business cycle is irrelevant to this company's near-term prospects.

11. 1. 2. 2 Inflation

Inflation is a general increase in prices as measured by an index such as the **consumer price index (CPI).** The **CPI** reflects the average cost of goods and services (a **market basket**) purchased by consumers, compared with those same goods and services purchased during a base period, currently 1982-84. CPI statistics are published monthly by the Bureau of Labor Statistics (BLS). Mild inflation can encourage economic growth because gradually increasing prices tend to stimulate business investments. High inflation reduces a dollar's buying power, which can reduce demand for goods and services. A term that may appear on your exam is "inflation inertia." This is the concept that the rate of inflation does not immediately react to unexpected changes in economic conditions. Rather, it lags behind, sometimes for several quarters, before there is an effect.

Sometimes the term used is the inertial rate of inflation or *inertial inflation*. This is the persistent rate of inflation that continues at the same rate until an economic shock leads to a change. One of the results of this is that prices rarely go down. After all, what company wants to lower the prices of its goods or services and how many workers are willing to accept wage cuts? So, prices general continue to advance, hopefully at a slow rate.

TEST TOPIC ALERT

Because inflation is a global issue, not just confined to the United States and our dollar, a universal definition would be "a decrease in the value of the monetary unit."

11. 1. 2. 2. 1 Causes of Inflation

Excessive demand occurs when aggregate demand exceeds the aggregate supply and prices rise.

Monetary expansion is a rapid increase in a nation's money stock in excess of the nation's growth rate.

Increased inflation drives interest rates higher and drives bond prices lower. Decreases in the inflation rate have the opposite effect: bond yields decline and bond prices rise.

TAKE NOTE

An increase in real income means the percentage increase in income is greater than the rate of inflation. Buying power has increased.

11. 1. 2. 3 Deflation

Though rare, **deflation** is a general decline in prices. Deflation usually occurs during severe recessions when unemployment is on the rise.

11. 1. 2. 3. 1 Causes of Deflation

Deflation is caused by conditions opposite those that cause inflation. Basically, when the demand for goods and services is substantially below the supply of those goods or services, prices tend to drift downward (certainly not increase) to encourage an increased demand. One other possible cause of deflation is a severe shrinkage in the money supply.

If . . .	And . . .	Then . . .	Thus . . .
inflation increases	interest rates go up	bond prices go down	bond yields go up
inflation decreases	interest rates go down	bond prices go up	bond yields go down

---

TEST TOPIC ALERT

It is not unusual to experience deflation during recessionary periods. At those times, investors tend to flee to safe havens such as U.S. government securities because unlike stocks, real estate, and commodities, Treasuries will likely not only hold their value but may even show some capital appreciation.

QUICK QUIZ 11.A   True or False?

_____ 1. Monetarists believe that the government should take an active role in managing the economy through fiscal policy.

_____ 2. A depression is defined as a decrease in the GDP for 6 or more consecutive months.

_____ 3. Rising inventories are characteristic of an economic expansion.

_____ 4. The CPI is a measurement of inflation.

_____ 5. High consumer debt is characteristic of a downturn in the business cycle.

6. The contraction phase of the business cycle is least likely accompanied by decreasing

A. consumer spending
B. economic output
C. inflation pressure
D. unemployment

Quick Quiz answers can be found at the end of the unit.

11. 1. 2. 4 Top Down Analysis

If we were to draw a picture of top down analysis, it would look like an inverted isosceles triangle: broad on top and narrow on the bottom. The analyst starts with the broadest measure of the overall economy and then successively narrows it down to finally select the company or companies that best fit the objectives.

11. 1. 2. 5 Bottom Up Analysis

This is the direct opposite of top down. In this case, we merely start at the bottom (the point) of the triangle with the specific company and work our way up through the industry and then the economy. This analyst starts with the narrowest indicator and then steadily broadens the search.

11. 2   INTEREST RATES AND YIELD CURVES

Although interest rates in general reflect investor expectations about inflation, short-term rates reflect the policy decisions of the Federal Reserve Board (FRB) as it implements the nation's monetary policy.

11. 2. 1 INTEREST RATES

An **interest rate** is the cost of borrowing money. The rate a borrower pays for funds is determined by the supply and demand for loanable funds, the credit quality of the borrower, and the length of time for which money is borrowed. In addition, the cost of funds is influenced by factors not related to the borrower, such as current and expected inflation and the overall supply and demand for funds in the economy.

When a company borrows money by issuing bonds, the bonds have a fixed interest rate, or coupon payment. As interest rates fluctuate, the price of the bonds in the secondary market also fluctuates. When interest rates increase, the bond prices decrease; when interest rates decrease, bond prices increase. Thus, there is an inverse relationship between interest rates and bond prices.

11. 2. 1. 1 Nominal and Real Interest Rates

The **nominal rate of interest** is the money rate of interest or the actual amount a borrower pays for loanable funds. If inflation is expected, the nominal rate of interest will exceed the real rate of interest on a loan to compensate the lender for the decline in purchasing power. The **real rate of interest** is the nominal rate of interest minus the expected rate of inflation.

TAKE NOTE

If a corporation pays 8% for a 1-year loan and the rate of inflation for the year is 2%, the real rate of interest is 8% − 2% = 6%.

11. 2. 1. 2 Federal Funds Rate

The **federal funds rate** is the rate banks that are members of the Federal Reserve System charge each other for overnight loans of $1 million or more. The rate is considered a barometer of the direction of short-term interest rates. The federal funds rate is listed in daily newspapers and is the most volatile rate; it can fluctuate drastically under certain market conditions.

11. 2. 1. 3 Prime Rate

The **prime rate** is the most preferential interest rate on corporate loans at large U.S. money center commercial banks. Each bank sets its own prime rate, with larger banks generally setting the rate that other banks follow. Banks lower their prime rates when the Fed eases the money supply and raise rates when the Fed contracts the money supply.

11. 2. 1. 4 Discount Rate

The **discount rate** is the rate the New York Federal Reserve Bank charges for short-term loans to member banks.

TAKE NOTE

The Federal Reserve Board establishes the discount rate. The discount rate, unlike the federal funds rate, is a managed rate. It is one of the tools of monetary policy. In contrast, the **federal funds rate** is a market rate determined by the demand for bank reserves on the part of deposit-based financial institutions.

11. 2. 1. 5 Broker Call Loan Rate

The **broker call loan rate** is the interest rate banks charge broker-dealers on money they borrow to lend to margin account customers. The broker call loan rate is also known as the *call loan rate* or *call money rate*. The broker call loan rate usually is slightly higher than other short-term rates. Broker call loans are callable on 24-hour notice.

11. 2. 1. 6 Yield Curve Analysis

Plotted on a graph, the difference between short- and long-term interest rates normally reflects an upward sloping line known as the **yield curve**. When it is an upward sloping curve it is a positive, or normal, yield curve. Long-term interest rates are normally higher than short-term rates for a number of reasons. Lenders must be compensated for the:

- time value of money;
- reduced buying power of money resulting from inflation;
- increased risk of default over long periods; and
- loss of liquidity associated with long-term investments.

The yield curve is also a reflection of investor **expectations** about inflation. If investors expect high inflation rates, they will require higher rates of interest to compensate for the reduction in purchasing power over time.

TAKE NOTE

When the yield curve is normal, long-term interest rates are higher than short-term interest rates. On a graph, the normal yield curve is upward sloping.

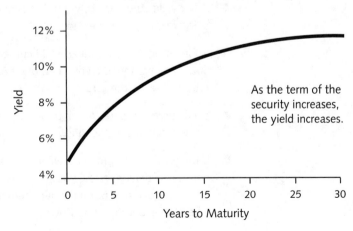

Normal (Positive) Yield Curve

As the term of the security increases, the yield increases.

In unusual circumstances, the yield curve can be inverted, or downward sloping. An inverted or negative yield curve can be the result of high current demand for money relative to the available supply. Short-term interest rates tend to be more sensitive to Fed policy than long-term rates. An inverted yield curve may occur because of a sharp increase in short-term rates. Therefore, when you notice a negative yield curve, you can expect that interest rates have rapidly risen and, according to most analysts, they will soon retreat.

Inverted (Negative) Yield Curve

As the term of the security increases, the yield decreases.

When short-term and long-term rates are the same, it is called a **flat** yield curve.

TEST TOPIC ALERT

You will need to be able to recognize the different yield curves from their "shape." A normal (positive) curve slopes upward. An inverted (negative) curve slopes downward. And, there is such a thing as a flat yield curve which, as the name implies, is level throughout all of the maturities.

TAKE NOTE

The shape of the yield curve varies with changes in the economic cycle.

■ A normal, or ascending, yield curve occurs during periods of economic expansion—it generally predicts that interest rates will rise in the future.

■ A flat yield curve occurs when the economy is peaking, and no change in interest rates is expected.

■ An inverted, or descending, yield curve occurs when the Federal Reserve Board has tightened credit in an overheating economy; it predicts that rates will fall in the future.

■ Yield curves for issuers with different risk levels can be compared to make economic predictions.

■ If the yield curve spread between corporate bonds and government bonds is widening, a **recession** is expected. Investors have chosen the safety of government bonds over higher corporate yields, which occurs when the economy slows down.

■ If the yield curve between corporate bonds and government bonds is narrowing, an economic **expansion** is expected and investors are willing to take risks. They will sell government bonds to buy higher-yielding corporates.

Corporate and Government Bonds

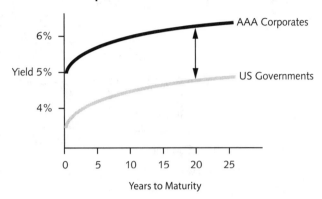

TEST TOPIC ALERT

When constructing a yield curve, the most common method is to use bonds of a single issuer over varying maturities. Specifically, most rely on the curve drawn when plotting yields on U.S. Treasury securities, starting with the 90-day T-bill and ending with anything from the 10-year note to the 30-year bond.

11. 3   ECONOMIC INDICATORS

Certain statistical indicators are used to measure the economic health of a country at a given time. Some of the primary indicators used are discussed below.

11. 3. 1   GROSS DOMESTIC PRODUCT (GDP)

Gross domestic product (GDP) expresses the total value of all final goods and services produced within the United States during the year. GDP includes personal consumption (by far the largest component), government spending, gross private investment, foreign investment, and the total value of net exports. If imports exceed exports, that negatively affects GDP and that net amount is subtracted in our computation. The GDP measures a country's output produced within its borders regardless of who generated it. To account for inflation, GDP is based on a constant dollar, currently the value in 2005.

The **gross national product (GNP)** is another measure of economic activity. In addition to GDP, GNP includes the income a country's citizens earned abroad and excludes the income foreigners earned domestically. GNP measures the output generated by the country's citizens regardless of where they did so. Today, virtually all measurements are in GDP rather than GNP.

EXAMPLE

A U.S.-based firm assembles electronic equipment using parts imported from Singapore. Its income statement looks like this:

Sales:	$60 million
Wages:	30 million
Parts:	16 million
Expenses:	46 million
Net Income:	14 million

What is this firm's contribution to the U.S. GDP?
A. $14 million
B. $30 million
C. $44 million
D. $60 million

Answer: C. The question is how we measure this firm's contribution to U.S. output. At first glance, the answer would seem to be $60 million, the total value of its sales. However, $16 million of this was produced somewhere else, so it shouldn't be counted as part of the firm's—or the United States'—output. Thus, the correct answer is $44 million, the amount of value the firm has added to the imported parts.

TEST TOPIC ALERT

The exam may want you to know that net exports will lead to an **increase** in GDP.

11. 3. 2 EMPLOYMENT INDICATORS

The unemployment level is a key indicator of a country's economic health and bears a relationship to inflation. The two most common employment indicators are the average weekly initial claims for unemployment compensation and the average workweek in manufacturing. Both measures serve to predict the direction of economic activity. Many economists believe an unemployment level of about 4% reflects full employment, the point at which wage pressures do not create undue inflation.

11. 3. 3 CONSUMER PRICE INDEX (CPI)

The **consumer price index (CPI)** is a measure of the general retail price level. By comparing the current cost of buying a basket of goods with the cost of buying the same basket a year ago, we can get an indication of changes in the cost of living. In doing so, the CPI figure attempts to measure the rate of increase or decrease in a broad range of prices, such as food, housing, transportation, medical care, clothing, electricity, entertainment, and services. The CPI is published on a monthly basis by the Bureau of Labor Statistics (BLS) and is the most commonly used measurement of the rate of inflation.

The index for all items, less food and energy, is often unofficially referred to as the *core* CPI, a term created by the media and not the Bureau of Labor Statistics. The reasoning behind excluding food and energy prices when computing *core* inflation is because of their high short-term volatility.

11. 3. 4 BALANCE OF PAYMENTS

The **balance of payments** measures all the nation's import and export transactions with those of other countries for the year. The balance of payments account contains all payments and liabilities to foreigners (debits) and all payments and obligations (credits) received from foreigners.

When you receive interest on your bank account, what happens to that account? It's simple: your balance is credited; it goes up. When foreign money is received here, such as interest received on money loaned to foreign business enterprises, there is a credit to the foreign account balance of the United States. Conversely, a debit to the foreign account balance of the United States occurs when money leaves our shores, such as loans made to foreign governments or dividends paid on foreign investment in the United States.

If the U.S. dollar weakens, meaning it buys less of a foreign currency such as Japanese yen, it makes U.S. exports more competitive in foreign markets. Conversely, if the U.S. dollar strengthens and buys more yen per dollar, it makes U.S. exports less competitive in foreign markets.

One way an investor can protect against a weakening U.S. dollar is to invest in foreign securities. The simplest way to do that is through ADRs. Of course, if the dollar strengthens, the value of the ADR will probably decline.

11. 3. 5 TRADE DEFICIT

A **trade deficit** is an excess of one country's imports over its exports and is reported as part of the balance of payments figures. Over time, an excessive trade deficit can lead to the devaluation of a country's currency because the country will be converting, or selling, its currency to obtain foreign currency to pay for its increasing imports.

11. 3. 6 BAROMETERS OF ECONOMIC ACTIVITY

Certain aspects of economic activity serve as barometers, or **indicators,** of business cycle phases. There are three broad categories of economic indicators: **leading, coincident, and lagging.** These indicators are published on a monthly basis by The Conference Board, a non-governmental, not-for-profit research organization.

11. 3. 6. 1 Leading Indicators

Leading indicators are economic activities that tend to turn down before the beginning of a recession or turn up before the beginning of a business expansion. These indicators are used by economists to predict the future direction of economic activity four to six months hence. The leading economic indicators include the following:

■ Money supply

■ Building permits (housing starts)

■ Average weekly initial claims for unemployment insurance

■ Average weekly hours, manufacturing

■ Manufacturers' new orders for consumer goods

■ Manufacturers' new orders for nondefense capital goods

■ Index of supplier deliveries—vendor performance

■ Interest rate spread between 10-year Treasury bond and the federal funds rate

■ Stock prices (e.g., S&P 500)

■ Index of consumer expectations

Not all leading indicators move in tandem. Positive changes in a majority of leading indicators point to increased spending, production, and employment. This will generally result in an increase to the rate of inflation. Negative changes in a majority of indicators can forecast a recession.

11. 3. 6. 2 Coincident (or Current) Indicators

Coincident, or **current, indicators** are economic measurements that change directly and simultaneously with the business cycle. Widely used coincident indicators include the following:

■ Nonagricultural employment

■ Personal income, minus Social Security, veteran benefits, and welfare payments

■ Industrial production

■ Manufacturing and trade sales in constant dollars

11. 3. 6. 3 Lagging Indicators

Lagging indicators are measurements that change four to six months **after** the economy has begun a new trend and serve to confirm the new trend. Lagging indicators help analysts differentiate long-term trends from short-term reversals that occur in any trend. Lagging indicators include the following:

■ Average duration of unemployment
■ Ratio of consumer installment credit to personal income
■ Ratio of manufacturing and trade inventories to sales
■ Average prime rate
■ Change in the CPI for services
■ Total amount of commercial and industrial loans outstanding
■ Change in the index of labor cost per unit of output (manufacturing)

TAKE NOTE

Simply stated, these indicators attempt to tell us where we're going (Leading), where we are (Coincident), and where we've been (Lagging). As an IAR, we suspect you'd be most interested in knowing where we're going so you'd pay most attention (as everyone else does) to the Leading indicators.

QUICK QUIZ 11.B

Matching

A. Prime rate
B. Lagging indicator
C. Leading indicator
D. Coincident indicator
E. Trade deficit
F. Call money rate

____   1. New orders for consumer goods

____   2. An excess of a country's imports over exports

____   3. Manufacturing inventories

____   4. Rate charged by banks to corporate customers

____   5. GDP

____   6. Rate charged by banks on loans to broker-dealers with securities as collateral

7. Core inflation is best described as an inflation rate
   A. for producers' raw materials
   B. the central bank views as acceptable
   C. that excludes certain volatile goods prices
   D. that represents a market basket of consumer items

8. A bond analyst is plotting a yield curve and notices that short-term maturities have higher yields than intermediate and long-term maturities. This is an example of a(n)

   A. inverted yield curve
   B. positive yield curve
   C. normal yield curve
   D. algorithmic yield curve

9. As current interest rates go up, the market price of existing corporate bonds bearing lower interest rates will

   A. increase
   B. stay the same
   C. decrease
   D. change in unpredictable ways

10. Which of the following statements best describes what will happen when the value of the American dollar rises in relationship to foreign currencies?

    A. Foreign goods and services will become more expensive for Americans.
    B. The risk of stagflation will increase.
    C. Shares of foreign stock will be worth more in terms of American dollars.
    D. Foreign goods and services will become less expensive for Americans.

11. The Conference Board has released information indicating an increase in the Help Wanted Index. Most analysts would take this as a sign of

    A. an impending recession
    B. likely wage inflation in the future
    C. an increase in manufacturing inventories
    D. a rising trade deficit

11. 4   THE TOOLS OF FUNDAMENTAL ANALYSIS: FINANCIAL STATEMENTS

A corporation's **financial statements** provide a fundamental analyst with the information needed to assess that corporation's profitability, financial strength, and operating efficiency. By examining how certain numbers from one statement relate to prior statements and how the resulting ratios relate to the company's competitors, the analyst can determine how financially viable the company is.

Companies issue quarterly and annual financial reports to the SEC. A company's balance sheet and income statement are included in these reports.

11. 4. 1   BALANCE SHEET

The **balance sheet** provides a snapshot of a company's financial position at a specific point in time. It identifies the value of the company's **assets** (what it owns) and its **liabilities** (what it owes). The difference between these two figures is the corporation's **owners' equity**, or **net worth**.

The **balance sheet equation** is:

$$\text{Assets} = \text{liabilities} + \text{owners' equity; or}$$

$$\text{Assets} - \text{liabilities} = \text{owners' equity.}$$

Although it is useful in determining a company's current value, the balance sheet does not indicate whether the company's business is improving or deteriorating. The balance sheet gets its name from the fact that its two sides must balance. The balance sheet equation mathematically expresses the relationship between the two sides of the balance sheet. Simply stated, everything that is owned (assets) minus everything that is owed (liabilities) is equal to the net worth (owners' or shareholders' equity) of the entity.

11. 4. 1. 1   Assets

Assets appear on the balance sheet in order of liquidity, which is the ease with which they can be turned into cash. Assets that are most readily convertible into cash are listed first, followed by less liquid assets. Balance sheets commonly identify three types of assets: **current assets** (cash and assets easily convertible into cash), **fixed assets** (physical assets that could eventually be sold), and **other assets** (usually intangible and only of value to the corporation that owns them).

11. 4. 1. 1. 1 Current Assets

Current assets include all cash and other items expected to be converted into cash within the next 12 months, including the following.

- **Cash and equivalents** include cash and short-term safe investments, such as money market instruments that can be readily sold, as well as other marketable securities.
- **Accounts receivable** include amounts due from customers for goods delivered or services rendered, reduced by the allowance for bad debts.
- **Inventory** is the cost of raw materials, work in process, and finished goods ready for sale.
- **Prepaid expenses** are items a company has already paid for but has not yet benefited from, such as prepaid advertising, rents, insurance, and operating supplies.

11. 4. 1. 1. 2 Fixed Assets

Fixed assets are property, plant, and equipment. Unlike current assets, they are not easily converted into cash. Fixed assets, such as factories, have limited useful lives because wear and tear eventually reduce their value. For this reason, their cost can be depreciated over time or deducted from taxable income in annual installments to compensate for loss in value.

11. 4. 1. 1. 3 Other Assets

Intangible assets are nonphysical properties, such as formulas, brand names, contract rights, and trademarks. Goodwill, also an intangible asset, reflects the corporation's reputation and relationship with its clients.

TAKE NOTE

Although intangible assets may have great value to the corporation owning them, they generally carry little value to other entities.

---

11. 4. 1. 2 Liabilities

Total liabilities on a balance sheet represent all financial claims by creditors against the corporation's assets. Balance sheets usually include two main types of liabilities: **current liabilities** and **long-term liabilities**.

11. 4. 1. 2. 1 Current Liabilities

Current liabilities are corporate debt obligations due for payment within the next 12 months. These include the following:

- **Accounts payable**—amounts owed to suppliers of materials and other business costs
- **Accrued wages payable**—unpaid wages, salaries, commissions, and interest
- **Current long-term debt**—any portion of long-term debt due within 12 months
- **Notes payable**—the balance due on equipment purchased on credit or cash borrowed
- **Accrued taxes**—unpaid federal, state, and local taxes

11. 4. 1. 2. 2 Long-Term Liabilities

Long-term debts are financial obligations due for payment after 12 months. Examples would include bonds and mortgages.

TAKE NOTE

Long-term debts include mortgages on real property, long-term promissory notes, and outstanding corporate bonds.

TEST TOPIC ALERT

Under current accounting practice, deferred tax credits are treated as a liability.

Sample Balance Sheet

Balance Sheet
Amalgamated Widget
as of Dec. 31, 2007

ASSETS			
Current assets	Cash and equivalents	$ 5,000,000	$ 40,000,000
	Accounts receivable	15,000,000	
	Inventory	19,000,000	
	Prepaid expenses	1,000,000	
	Total current assets		
Fixed assets	Buildings, furniture, and fixtures	$40,000,000	
	(at cost less $10 million accumu-	15,000,000	$ 55,000,000
	lated depreciation)		
	Land		
	Total fixed assets		
Other (intangibles, goodwill)		$5,000,000	
Total assets			$100,000,000
LIABILITIES AND NET WORTH			
Current liabilities	Accounts payable	$5,000,000	$ 10,000,000
	Accrued wages payable	4,000,000	
	Accrued taxes payable	1,000,000	
	Total current liabilities		
Long-term liabilities	8% 20-year convertible		$ 50,000,000
Total liabilities	debentures		$ 60,000,000
Net worth	Preferred stock $100 par ($5	$20,000,000	
	noncumulative convertible	1,000,000	
	200,000 shares issued)	4,000,000	
	Common stock $1 par	15,000,000	
	(1 million shares)		
	Capital in excess of par		
	Retained earnings		
Total net worth			$ 40,000,000
Total liabilities and net worth			$100,000,000

11. 4. 1. 3 Shareholder Equity

Shareholder equity, also called **net worth** or **owners' equity**, is the stockholder claims on a company's assets after all of its creditors have been paid. Shareholder equity equals total assets less total liabilities. On a balance sheet, three types of shareholder equity are identified: capital stock at par, capital in excess of par, and retained earnings.

TAKE NOTE

Net worth = assets − liabilities.

11. 4. 1. 3. 1 Capital Stock at Par

Capital stock includes preferred and common stock, listed at par value. **Par value** is the total dollar value assigned to stock certificates when a corporation's owners (the stock-holders) first contributed capital. Par value of common stock is an arbitrary value with no relationship to market price.

11. 4. 1. 3. 2 Capital in Excess of Par

Capital in excess of par, often called **additional paid-in capital** or **paid-in surplus**, is the amount of money over par value that a company received for selling stock.

11. 4. 1. 3. 3 Retained Earnings

Retained earnings, sometimes called **earned surplus** or **accumulated earnings**, are profits that have not been paid out in dividends. Retained earnings represent the total of all earnings held since the corporation was formed less dividends paid to stockholders. Operating losses in any year reduce the retained earnings from prior years.

11. 4. 1. 4 Capital Structure

A company's **capitalization** is the combined sum of its long-term debt and equity securities. The **capital structure** is the relative amounts of debt and equity that compose a company's capitalization. Some companies finance their business with a large proportion of borrowed funds; others finance growth with retained earnings from normal operations and little or no debt.

Looking at the balance sheet, a corporation builds its capital structure with equity and debt including the following four elements:

- Long-term debt
- Capital stock (common and preferred)
- Capital in excess of par
- Retained earnings (earned surplus)

EXAMPLE

(See the table below for reference and explanation of the following terms.) The total capitalization on the sample balance is $90 million ($50 million in long-term debt, $20 million in preferred stock, and $20 million in common shareholders' equity). Remember, capital stock + capital in excess of par + retained earnings = shareholders' equity (net worth).

Total capitalization	$90 million
LT debt	$50 million
+ Pfd.	$20 million
+ Common	$ 1 million
+ Cap. surplus	$ 4 million
+ Ret. earnings	$15 million

If a company changes its capitalization by issuing stock or bonds, the effects will show up on the balance sheet.

11. 4. 1. 4. 1 Issuing Securities

The example balance sheet indicates the company issued 1 million shares of $1 par common stock. If it issues another 1 million shares, the net worth (shareholders' equity) will increase by the additional capital raised, and the amount of cash on the asset side of the balance sheet will increase.

11. 4. 1. 4. 2 Convertible Securities

When an investor converts a convertible bond into shares of common stock, the amount of liabilities decreases, and the owners' equity increases. The changes are on the same side of the balance sheet, so there is no change to the assets.

11. 4. 1. 4. 3 Bond Redemption

When bonds are redeemed, liabilities on the balance sheet are reduced. The offsetting change would be a decrease in cash on the asset side of the balance sheet. The company would have less debt outstanding, but it would also have less cash. The balance sheet balances. Therefore, because the current asset (cash) was used to redeem the long-term liability (bond), working capital is reduced. However, because there would no longer be semiannual interest payments due on the debt, the future effect of the retirement of the bonds would be to increase the company's cash flow.

11. 4. 1. 4. 4 Dividends

When a cash dividend is declared, retained earnings are lowered and current liabilities are increased. The declaration of a cash dividend establishes a current liability until it is paid. Once paid, it reduces cash in current assets and also reduces current liabilities.

Distribution of stock dividends has no effect on corporate assets or liabilities, nor does it change the stockholders' proportionate equity in the corporation. The number of shares each stockholder owns increases, but each single share represents a smaller slice of ownership in the corporation.

11. 4. 1. 4. 5   Stock Splits

Like a stock dividend, a stock split does not affect shareholders' equity. On the balance sheet, only the par value per share and number of shares outstanding change.

11. 4. 1. 4. 6   Financial Leverage

Financial leverage is a company's ability to use long-term debt to increase its return on equity. A company with a high ratio of long-term debt to equity is said to be **highly leveraged**.

Stockholders benefit from leverage if the return on borrowed money exceeds the debt service costs. But leverage is risky because excessive increases in debt raise the possibility of default in a business downturn.

In general, industrial companies with debt-to-equity ratios of 50% or higher are considered highly leveraged. However, utilities, with their relatively stable earnings and cash flows, can be more highly leveraged without subjecting stockholders to undue risk. If a company is highly leveraged, it is also affected more by changes in interest rates.

11. 4. 1. 5   Balance Sheet Computations

11. 4. 1. 5. 1   Working Capital

Working capital is the amount of capital or cash a company has available. Working capital is a measure of a firm's liquidity, which is its ability to quickly turn assets into cash to meet its short-term obligations.

The formula for working capital is:

$$\text{current assets} - \text{current liabilities} = \text{working capital}.$$

Factors that affect working capital include:

- increases in working capital, such as profits, sale of securities (long-term debt or equity), and sale of noncurrent assets; and
- decreases in working capital, such as dividends declared, paying off long-term debt, and net loss.

11. 4. 1. 5. 2   Current Ratio

Knowing the amount of working capital is useful, but it becomes an even better indicator when paired together with the current ratio. This computation uses the same two items, current assets and current liabilities, but expresses them as a ratio of one to the other. Simply divide the current assets by the current liabilities and the higher the ratio, the more liquid the company is.

11. 4. 1. 5. 3 Quick Asset Ratio (Acid Test Ratio)

Sometimes it is important for the analyst to use an even stricter test of a company's ability to meet its short-term obligations (as such, "pass the acid test"). The quick asset ratio uses the company's quick assets instead of all of the current assets. Quick assets are current assets minus the inventory. Then divide these quick assets by the current liabilities to arrive at the quick ratio.

TAKE NOTE

Liquidity measures a company's ability to pay the expenses associated with running the business.

11. 4. 1. 5. 4 Debt-to-Equity Ratio

The best way to measure the amount of financial leverage being employed by the company is by calculating the debt-to-equity ratio. It is really a misnomer—it should be called the debt-to-total capitalization ratio because that is what it is. For example, using the numbers in our capitalization chart above, we see that the total capital employed in the business is $90 million. Of that, $50 million is long-term debt. So, we want to know how much of the $90 million total is represented by debt capital. The answer is simple: $50 million of the $90 million, or 55.55%. That is the debt-to-equity ratio.

11. 4. 1. 5. 5 Book Value Per Share

A fundamental analyst is described as one who focuses on the company's books. Therefore, one of the key numbers computed is the book value per share. The calculation is almost identical to one we have already studied—NAV per share of an investment company.

In the case of a corporation, it is basically the liquidation value of the enterprise. That is, let's assume we sold all of our assets, paid back everyone we owe, and then split what is left among the stockholders. But, remember, before we can hand over anything to the common shareholders, we must take care of any outstanding preferred stock. So, from the funds that are left after we pay off all of the liabilities, we give the preferred shareholders back their par (or stated) value and the rest belongs to the common stockholders.

But, there is one more thing. In the case of liquidation, some of the assets on our books might not really be worth what we're carrying them at. In particular, those that are known as intangible assets (goodwill, patents, trademarks, copyrights, etc.). That is why the analyst uses only the tangible assets, computed by subtracting those intangibles from the total assets.

Expressed as a formula, book value per share is:

$$\frac{\text{tangible assets} - \text{liabilities} - \text{par value of preferred}}{\text{shares of common stock outstanding}} = \text{book value per share.}$$

11. 4. 1. 6 Changes That Affect the Balance Sheet

11. 4. 1. 6. 1 Balancing the Balance Sheet

Balance sheets, by definition, must balance. Every financial change in a business requires two offsetting changes on the company books, known as **double-entry book-keeping**. For example, when a company pays a previously declared cash dividend, cash (a current asset) is reduced while dividends payable (a current liability of the same amount) is eradicated. This results in no change to working capital or net worth because each side of the balance sheet has been lowered by the same amount.

11. 4. 1. 6. 2 Depreciating Assets

Because fixed assets (e.g., buildings, equipment, and machinery) wear out as they are used, they decline in value over time. This decline in value is called **depreciation**. A company's tax bills are reduced each year the company depreciates fixed assets used in the businesses.

Depreciation affects the company in two ways: accumulated depreciation reduces the value of fixed assets on the balance sheet, and the annual depreciation deduction reduces taxable income on the income statement.

Companies may elect either straight line or accelerated depreciation. By use of the straight-line method, a company depreciates fixed assets by an equal amount each year over the asset's useful life. A piece of equipment costing $1 million with a 10-year useful life will generate a depreciation deduction of $100,000 per year.

Accelerated depreciation is a method that depreciates fixed assets more during the earlier years of their useful life and less during the later years.

TAKE NOTE

Compared with straight line, accelerated depreciation generates larger deductions (lower taxable income) during the early years and smaller deductions (higher taxable income) during the later years.

TEST TOPIC ALERT

The Series 65 exam does not generally ask for calculations with balance sheet or income statement items. Make sure to recognize the main components of each of these financial statements. You may be asked about the impact of a certain transaction on the balance sheet.

1. Which of the following choices are affected when a corporation purchases a printing press for cash?

    A. Current assets
    B. Current liabilities
    C. Working capital
    D. Total assets
    E. Total liabilities
    F. Net worth

Answer: A and C. A payment of cash reduces current assets. Whenever either current assets or current liabilities change, working capital is also affected. The new printing press increases the value of the fixed assets. Total assets, however, are unchanged because the decrease in current assets is offset by the increase in fixed assets.

2. Which are affected when a corporation declares a cash dividend?

Answer: B, C, E, and F. The declaration (not payment) of a dividend creates a current liability on the books of the corporation. Because current liabilities are affected, working capital and total liabilities also change. The declaration of a dividend reduces the net worth because the dividend will be paid from retained earnings. When the dividend is paid, current assets will decrease and current liabilities will decrease (this also decreases both total assets and total liabilities). Working capital does not change because both current assets and current liabilities decrease by the same amount.

If a corporation has a stock split, the balance sheet categories above are not affected. A stock split will increase the number of shares and reduce the value of each share, but the total par value as shown in the equity section of the balance sheet is not affected.

QUICK QUIZ 11.C

1. The difference between current assets and current liabilities is called
    A. net worth
    B. working capital
    C. cash flow
    D. quick assets

2. As a result of corporate transactions, a company's assets remain the same and its equity decreases. Which of the following statements is TRUE?
    A. Prepaid expenses decrease.
    B. Total liabilities increase.
    C. Accrued expenses decrease.
    D. Net worth increases.

3. Which of the following is NOT affected by the issuance of a bond?
    A. Assets
    B. Total liabilities
    C. Working capital
    D. Shareholders' equity

4. A company has been experiencing increased earnings but has kept its dividend payments constant. As a result solely of this, the company's balance sheet would reflect
    A. decreased net working capital
    B. decreased net worth
    C. decreased retained earnings
    D. increased shareholders' equity

11. 4. 1. 7 Footnotes

Footnotes to the financial statements identify significant financial and management issues that may affect the company's overall performance, such as accounting methods used, extraordinary items, pending litigation, and management philosophy.

Typically, a company separately discloses details about its long-term debt in the footnotes. These disclosures are useful for determining the timing and amount of future cash outflows. The disclosures usually include a discussion of the nature of the liabilities, maturity dates, stated and effective interest rates, call provisions and conversion privileges, restrictions imposed by creditors, assets pledged as security, and the amount of debt maturing in each of the next five years.

Also disclosed in the footnotes would be *off the books* financing arrangements such as debt guarantees.

TEST TOPIC ALERT
Footnotes are generally found on the bottom of the financial statements and can be several pages long.

TAKE NOTE
The balance sheet reports what resources (assets) a company owns and how it has funded them. How the firm has financed the assets is revealed by the capital structure—for example, long-term debt and owners' equity (preferred stock, common stock, and retained earnings).

11. 4. 2 INCOME STATEMENT

The **income statement,** sometimes referred to as the profit and loss or P&L statement, summarizes a company's revenues (sales) and expenses for a fiscal period, usually quarterly, year to date, or the full year. It compares revenue against costs and expenses during the period. Fundamental analysts use the income statement to judge the efficiency and profitability of a company's operation. Just as with the balance sheet, technical analysts generally ignore this information—it is not relevant to their charting schemes.

11. 4. 2. 1 Components of the Income Statement

The various operating and nonoperating expenses on the income statement are discussed below.

Revenues indicate the firm's total sales during the period (the money that came in).

The **cost of goods sold (COGS)** is the costs of labor, material, and production (including depreciation on assets employed in production) used to create finished goods. Subtracting COGS from revenues shows the gross operating profit. The two major methods of accounting for material costs are the first in, first out method (FIFO) and last in, first out method (LIFO). Under LIFO accounting, COGS normally will reflect higher costs of more recently purchased inventory (last items in). As a result of higher reported production costs under LIFO, reported income is reduced. The opposite is true if the FIFO method is used.

Pretax margin is determined by subtracting COGS and other operating costs (rent and utilities) from sales to arrive at net operating profit. The resulting figure is earnings before interest and taxes (EBIT).

Interest payments on a corporation's debt is not considered an operating expense. However, interest payments reduce the corporation's taxable income. **Pretax income**, the amount of taxable income, is operating income less interest payment expenses.

If dividends are paid to stockholders, they are paid out of net income after taxes have been paid. After dividends have been paid, the remaining income is added to retained earnings and is available to invest in the business.

TEST TOPIC ALERT

Please note the three terms above that we have put in boldface for you. **Revenue** (or sales), **cost of goods sold**, and **pretax income** are the three primary components of an income statement.

Think of simply like this: the income statement shows (1) what came in, (2) what went out, and (3) how much is left (before taxes).

TAKE NOTE

Interest payments reduce a corporation's taxable income, whereas dividend payments to stockholders are paid from after-tax dollars. Because they are taxable as income to stockholders, dividends are taxed twice, whereas interest payments are taxed once as income to the recipient.

11. 4. 2. 2 Accounting for Depreciation

As mentioned earlier when reviewing the balance sheet, fixed assets are shown at their cost minus accumulated depreciation. For these assets, which wear out over a period of time, tax law requires that the loss of value be deducted over the asset's useful life, longer for some assets, shorter for others (you won't have to know depreciation schedules). On the income statement, the allowable portion for the year is shown as an expense and, for our purposes, will generally be part of COGS. Remember, if the company uses accelerated depreciation, the expenses will be higher in the early years resulting in lower pretax income (and lower income taxes) but higher income later on.

11. 4. 2. 3 Fiscal Year Accounting

Many business entities prefer to end their accounting year on a date other than December 31 (calendar year accounting). Any 12-month period used by a business that ends other than on December 31 is known as a fiscal year (the term fiscal is generally defined as something that pertains to financial matters). This term will be used many times when referring to required filings by investment advisers.

QUICK QUIZ 11.D   Matching

Are the following items found on the balance sheet or the income statement?

   A.   Balance sheet
   B.   Income statement

____   1.   Current liabilities

____   2.   Revenues

____   3.   Net worth

____   4.   Retained earnings

____   5.   Cost of goods sold

____   6.   Net income

7.   Potential litigation for patent infringement would appear on a corporation's

   A.   balance sheet as a deferred asset
   B.   footnotes
   C.   income statement as an expense
   D.   statement of potential litigation

8.   The sum of a company's profits, after dividend payments, since the company's inception is called

   I.   accumulated earnings
   II.   cash flow
   III.   earned surplus
   IV.   retained earnings
   A.   III and IV
   B.   II, III, and IV
   C.   I, III, and IV
   D.   I and II

11. 4. 2. 4 Income Statement Computations

There are a number of important ratios that can be computed using information from the income statement. We'll take a look at several of them.

11. 4. 2. 4. 1 Earnings Per Share (EPS)

Among the most widely used statistics, EPS measures the value of a company's earnings for each common share:

$$\text{EPS} = \frac{\text{earnings available to common}}{\text{number of shares outstanding}}$$

Earnings available to common are the remaining earnings after the preferred dividend has been paid. Earnings per share relates to common stock only. Preferred stockholders have no claims to earnings beyond the stipulated preferred stock dividends.

Simplified Income Statement

Net Revenues (Sales)	$10,000,000
− Cost of Goods Sold (including $500,000 of depreciation)	5,500,000
= Gross Profit	4,500,000
− Other Operating Expenses (rent, utilities)	500,000
= Operating Profit (EBIT)	4,000,000
− Interest Expense	750,000
= Income after Interest Expense (Pre-tax Income)	3,250,000
− Income Tax	1,000,000
= Net Income	2,250,000
Earnings per Share (1,000,000 common shares outstanding)	2.25
Dividends per Share ($1.50)	1,500,000
Credited to Retained Earnings	750,000

11. 4. 2. 4. 2 Earnings Per Share After Dilution

EPS after dilution assumes that all convertible securities, such as warrants and convertible bonds and preferred stock, have been converted into the common. Because of tax adjustments, the calculations for figuring EPS after dilution can be complicated and will not be tested.

11. 4. 2. 4. 3 Current Yield (Dividend Yield)

A common stock's **current yield**, like the current yield on bonds, expresses the annual dividend payout as a percentage of the current stock price:

$$\text{current yield} = \frac{\text{annual dividends per common share}}{\text{market value per common share}}$$

11. 4. 2. 4. 4 Dividend Payout Ratio

The **dividend payout ratio** measures the proportion of earnings paid to stockholders as dividends:

$$\text{dividend payout ratio} = \frac{\text{annual dividends per common share}}{\text{earnings per share (EPS)}}$$

In general, older companies pay out larger percentages of earnings as dividends. Utilities as a group have an especially high payout ratio. Growth companies normally have the lowest ratios because they reinvest their earnings in the businesses. Companies on the way up hope to reward stockholders with gains in the stock value rather than with high dividend income.

11. 4. 3   STATEMENT OF CASH FLOW

The cash flow statement reports a business' sources and uses of cash and the beginning and ending values for cash and cash equivalents each year. There are three components generating cash flow:

- operating activities;
- investing activities; and
- financing activities.

TEST TOPIC ALERT

Most financial professionals add revenues and expenses that do not involve cash inflows or outflows (e.g., cost allocations such as depreciation and amortization) back to the company's net income to determine the cash flow. As described previously, the cash flow statement will also reflect money from operations, financing, investing, but not accounting changes.

11. 4. 3. 1   Cash Flow From Operating Activities

Operating activities (all transactions and events that normally enter into the determination of operating income) include cash receipts, (money coming in), from selling goods or providing services, as well as income from items such as interest and dividends. Operating activities also include cash payments, (money going out), such as cost of inventory, payroll, taxes, interest, utilities, and rent. The net amount of cash provided (or used) by operating activities is the key figure on a statement of cash flows. Even though it would seem that interest and dividends would belong in investing activities, the accounting gurus put them here.

EXAMPLE

Sometimes using some numbers makes this concept much easier. If you take a look at the income statement we reviewed a few pages ago, you will see that this company's net income (bottom line, to use the vernacular) was $2,250,000. Among the $6 million in expenses deducted from the total revenues was $500,000 of depreciation. However, the company never "wrote a check" for that money; it is the amount of the original cost that it is allowed to write off as an expense each year as the fixed assets wear out. So, not only does the company have the net income remaining after all expenses and taxes, but also it actually had another $500,000 in funds it could use, giving the company a total cash flow of $2,750,000.

11. 4. 3. 2 Cash Flow From Investing Activities

Investing activities include transactions and events involving the purchase and sale of securities, land, buildings, equipment, and other assets not generally held for resale as a product of the business. It also covers the making and collecting of loans. Investing activities are not classified as operating activities because they have an indirect relationship to the central, ongoing operation of the business (usually the sale of goods or services).

11. 4. 3. 3 Cash Flow From Financing Activities

All financing activities deal with the flow of cash to or from the business owners (equity financing) and creditors (debt financing). For example, cash proceeds from issuing stock or bonds would be classified under financing activities. Likewise, payments to repurchase stock (treasury stock) or to retire bonds and the payment of dividends are financing activities as well.

TEST TOPIC ALERT

Cash flow from operations will only use items from the income statement, while cash flow from financing activities will use balance sheet items. Make sure you know which one the question is asking about.

11. 5   CORPORATE SEC FILINGS

One of the best sources of financial information is found in the reports required to be filed with the SEC by publicly traded companies. This information is available online at the SEC's website. The location is at EDGAR, which stands for Electronic Data Gathering, Analysis, and Retrieval of SEC filings. Among those filings, there are generally three that are used by fundamental analysts.

11. 5. 1   FORM 8-K

This form is used to report newsworthy events to the SEC, thereby making them available to the public. Included are items such as change in management, change in the company's name, mergers or acquisitions, bankruptcy filings, and major new product introductions or sale of a product line. A Form 8-K even has to be filed when a member of the board of directors resigns over a disagreement. The 8-K is filed within four business days of the occurrence. This form is used only by domestic issuers, foreign issuers are exempt. Although ADRs are registered with the SEC, they too are exempt because the underlying security is a foreign issue.

One thing that would not trigger a Form 8-K is the relocation of a wholly owned subsidiary. However, sale of that subsidiary would require a filing and that, like any other Form 8-K filing, must be done within four business days of the event.

11. 5. 2   FORM 10-K

Most domestic public issuers must file an annual report to the SEC on Form 10-K. This report is a comprehensive overview of the company's business and financial condition and includes financial statements that have been audited by an independent accountant. Do not confuse this with the annual report to shareholders, which also contains an audited statement and is sent to shareholders. The Form 10-K will generally contain more detailed financial information than the annual report, while the annual report will have much more detail about the company itself and its future plans.

The filing deadlines depend upon the company's public float. You don't have to know this information for the exam, but, for those companies with a float of $700 million or more, the Form 10-K deadline is 60 days after the close of the fiscal year; $75 million, but not $700 million, it is 75 days; and less than $75 million is due at 90 days.

11. 5. 3   FORM 10-Q

Because one year between filings is a long time and a lot can happen quickly, we also have this form, and it is filed quarterly (Q for quarterly). It contains unaudited financial statements and for all but the companies with a public float of less than $75 million, it must be filed within 40 days of each of the first three fiscal quarters of the year (no 10-Q is filed at the end of the fourth quarter—that information is taken care of by the filing of the 10-K). Those smaller firms file theirs within 45 days of the end of the quarter.

11. 5. 4   ANNUAL REPORTS

When it comes to publicly trade companies, in general, all shareholders must receive a copy of the issuer's annual report. For those too lazy to access EDGAR, this is the most detailed information they can get on the company's financial position. Unlike the Form 10-K, this is usually a professionally prepared piece which is just as much used for marketing purposes as it is for providing information. There is usually a welcoming letter from the CEO and/or Chairman of the Board, and it is generally loaded with beautiful pictures of smiling people (employees and customers) and the company's facilities. New plans for products and programs are discussed and voting proxies are included.

SEC rules provide that a company may provide shareholders with a copy of the Form 10-K instead of sending an annual report.

1. One of the valuation ratios used by fundamental analysts is the price/earnings ratio. The P/E ratio is the current market price of the stock divided by the

    A. book value per share
    B. dividends per share
    C. earnings per share
    D. investor's cost basis per share

2. A corporation's cash flow will increase as a result of

    A. paying dividends to preferred stockholders
    B. collecting on past due receivables
    C. paying overdue bills
    D. increasing inventory on hand

3. XYZ Corporation issues 1 million shares of common stock at a price of $6 per share. As a result of this, all of the following will be true EXCEPT

    A. net worth will increase by $6 million
    B. working capital will increase by $6 million
    C. net income will increase by $6 million
    D. current assets will increase by $6 million

4. A publicly traded corporation keeps its books on a calendar year basis. An investor wanting the most up-to-date financial information in late August would view the company's

    A. June 30 Form 10-Q
    B. June 30 Form 8-K
    C. December 31 Form 10-K
    D. July 31 Form 10-Q

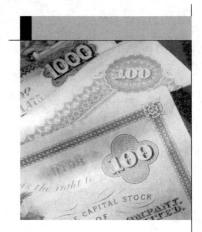

12

Methods of Quantitative Analysis

Quantitative means using numbers and quantitative analysis is the use of various mathematical computations in an attempt to make better investment decisions. Because the testing center only permits the use of a simple four-function calculator, any computations you will be asked to perform will be relatively straightforward. In general, it will be more important to understand the concept than do the computation.

The Series 65 exam will have approximately three questions on the material covered in this session.

When you have completed this session, you should be able to:

- **describe** the difference between present and future value;

- **employ** the Rule of 72 to determine the return on an investment;

- **select** the proper measure of central tendency when presented with a group of numbers;

- **recognize** how standard deviation relates to volatility;

- **explain** the relationship between correlation and diversification;

- **contrast** alpha and beta;

- **calculate** the alpha of a portfolio; and

- **compute** the price to earnings ratio of a common stock.

12. 1   QUANTITATIVE ANALYSIS

There is no question that investing is a "numbers" business. In the previous session, we discussed financial statements as a tool for evaluating a company and those are almost entirely number oriented. In this session, we'll go further by looking at both the overall market and examine some of the tools that quantitative analysts (known as *quants* in the industry) use to assist them in making investment decisions.

12. 1. 1   TIME VALUE OF MONEY

The **time value of money** is the difference between the value of money today (its **present value**) and its value sometime in the future (its future value).

We've all heard the famous saying "time is money." The concept applies to investments. For example, if a person promises to pay a certain sum 10 years from now, what is it worth to have the money today so that the investor will have use of it over the next 10 years instead of having to wait? If the investor could earn 10% on the money, compounded annually, having about $38.55 today would be equivalent in value to receiving $100 in 10 years. The second view of time value relates to computing the amount necessary to be invested today, using an assumed rate of return, so that it will have a defined amount in the future. Using the above case, if the investor were to invest $38.55 today and earn 10% compounded annually, he would have $100 in 10 years.

TAKE NOTE

Although this can be proven in less than 10 seconds using a financial calculator, you may have to do a compound return computation on the exam but won't have the benefit of such a fancy tool. Using the basic four-function calculator issued at the testing center, you would take the initial $38.55 and multiply that by 110% and continue to do that for a total of 10 times. I'll just get you started to show you what it looks like:

38.55 x 110% = 42.405 x 110% = 46.6455 x 110% = 51.31 and so forth seven more times will get to you approximately 100.00. This is the same concept we showed you with the TIPS bond.

12. 1. 1. 1   Future Value

Future value is the formal term that indicates what an amount invested today at a given rate will be worth at some period in the future. The future value of a dollar invested today depends on the:

■ rate of return it earns (r); and

■ number of years over which it is invested (n).

The equation to calculate the FV of an investment is expressed as:

$$FV = PV \times (1 + r)^n.$$

EXAMPLE

In these two examples, we will demonstrate how these values are calculated. However, you will NOT be required to know the formula or how to do these computations. The value of $11,348.54 five years from today, its future value, is calculated using the above formula as follows:

$$FV = \$11{,}348.54 \text{ (the PV)} \times 1.12^5 = \$20{,}000.$$

The future value expressed here reflects a **compound rate of return** on the original $11,348.54 invested. The compound return assumes that the interest earned (12% in this case) in a given period (five years) is reinvested at the identical rate for the number of years in which it is invested.

TAKE NOTE

To find PV, you must already know the FV.

To find FV, you must already know the PV.

12. 1. 1. 2 Present Value

Present value is the formal term for value today of the future cash flows of an investment discounted at a specified interest rate to determine the present worth of those future cash flows.

Intuitively, investors recognize that a dollar in hand is worth more than a dollar in the future. The difference between the value today and sometime in the future is a function of the time elapsed and the rate of interest earned.

The formula used to calculate present value is as follows:

$$PV = FV \div (1 + r)^n.$$

In the formula above, **PV** stands for the present value, **FV** stands for the future value, r is the interest rate, and n is the number of time periods the money is compounded.

This formula says that the present value (PV) of an investment equals the investment's future value (FV) discounted at (divided by) an interest rate over a time period specified by n. The factor $(1 + r)^n$ is known as the **discount factor**.

EXAMPLE

What is the present value of $20,000 that will be received 5 years (n) from today? If the investor requires a 12% return (r) for the $20,000, the value of that $20,000 today (PV) to be received in 5 years is calculated as follows:

$$PV = \frac{FV}{(1 + .12)^5} = \frac{\$20{,}000}{1.7623416} = (\$11{,}348.54).$$

The $20,000 to be received in 5 years discounted by the required 12% interest rate is worth $11,348.54 today.

When computing present value (or future value), we are using an estimated rate of return. What happens if the actual return is different from the estimated? If our actual return is less, we don't make out as well. That means that the present value (the required initial deposit) is going to be higher than we computed. On the other hand, if the actual return was higher than the present value (we did better than we thought), the present value (the amount we would have had to deposit), is less.

The same logic holds true for future value. If the actual return is higher than projected, the future value will be higher (we made more on our money than we thought we would). Logically, if the actual return is lower, our future value winds up lower.

12. 1. 1. 3 Rule of 72

The rule of 72 is a shortcut method for determining the number of years it takes for an investment to double in value assuming compounded earnings. To find the number of years for an investment to double, simply divide the number 72 by the interest rate the investment pays. For example, an investment of $2,000 earning 6% will double in 12 years (72 ÷ 6 = 12).

Here is another example of the rule of 72. A savings account with $1,000 in it bearing 4% compounded per year in interest would double (i.e., the account would be worth $2,000) in 18 years; 72 ÷ 4 = 18.

Suppose an investment of $1,000 was worth $4,000 in 16 years. Under the rule of 72, what is the compounded earnings rate?

You figure this by realizing that the account has quadrupled. That means it has doubled twice. So, if it took 16 years to double twice, it takes 8 years to double one time. Dividing 72 by 8 tells us that our account must be earning 9%.

The Rule of 72 also works in reverse. That is, if you know the number of years you have, you can compute the required earnings rate to double by, once again, using 72 as the numerator and this time the number of years as the denominator. For example, if you have nine years before your child is going to enter college, what will you have to earn in order for a deposit made today to double? Simply divide 72 by 9 and the result is that a 8% earnings rate will have your money double.

12. 1. 1. 4 Net Present Value (NPV)

Net present value (NPV) is the difference between an investment's present value and its cost. An NPV of $10 means that an investment that cost $100 must have a discounted present value of $110, for an NPV of $10. Note that the difference between the cost ($100) and the discounted present value of the investment's future returns ($110) equals the NPV ($10).

NPV is expressed in dollar amounts and not as a rate of return.

NPV is an analytical concept used by corporations to determine whether to invest in a capital project (e.g., a new factory). The anticipated income from the factory is discounted to its present value by using the company's required rate of return as the discount rate.

If the discounted PV of the projected income is greater than the cost of the factory, the project has a positive NPV. If this is the case, the project will add value to the company because its return is more than the company's cost of capital. If the NPV is negative, the project will drain value from the firm.

An investment adviser could use the NPV concept to evaluate a client's investment in any investment vehicle with a projected income stream. The adviser would project the cash flows from the investment and then discount them to their present value at the investor's required rate of return. If the NPV is positive, the investment adds value to the investor's portfolio.

12. 1. 1. 5 Internal Rate of Return (IRR)

The **internal rate of return (IRR)** is the discount rate (r) that makes the future value of an investment equal to its present value. The IRR can be thought of as the r in the present and future value calculations. The IRR is difficult to calculate directly; it must be determined by a trial-and-error process called **iteration**. IRR takes into consideration the time value of money. IRR is not practical for common stock due to uneven cash flow and no maturity date and price.

The IRR calculation can be used to determine whether an investment meets the investor's required rate of return. If an investor requires an investment return of 10% and the IRR for a proposed investment is 12%, the investor will view that investment as attractive because it returns a higher rate than the investor's required rate.

NPV and IRR are far and away the most difficult mathematical concepts you'll encounter on this exam. These are most important points to remember.

- Internal rate of return is the method of computing long-term returns that takes into consideration *time value* of money.

- The yield to maturity of a bond reflects its IRR.

- The investment is a good one if it has a positive NPV; stay away if the NPV is negative.

- NPV is generally considered more important than IRR.

12. 2   DESCRIPTIVE STATISTICS

There are a number of other numerical tools used that do not involve time value. Following are those most likely to appear on your exam.

12. 2. 1   MEASURES OF CENTRAL TENDENCY

We are going to continue this section on quantitative measurements with a discussion dealing with the method of determining how one might approach figuring the logical outcome of a securities investment. Central tendency is usually defined as the center or middle of a distribution. There are many measures of central tendency. Let's take a look at some of them.

12. 2. 1. 1   Mean or Arithmetic Mean

When we use the word average, this is what we are really speaking about. Of all the different measures, this is the one most commonly used to measure central tendency. You've been computing this for years—all you do is take the sum of the variables and divide by the number of occurrences. For example, if a stock returned 5%, then 8%, then 9%, and then 2%, the mean would be 6% (5 + 8 + 9 + 2 = 24 ÷ 4 = 6). Even though is the most used (probably because it is so simple to do), the mean may not be an appropriate measure of central tendency for skewed distributions. As you will soon see, there is also the geometric mean, but the term *mean* by itself will always refer to the arithmetic mean, sometimes referred to as *outliers*.

12. 2. 1. 2   Median

The median is a midpoint of a distribution. That is, there are as many variables below as there are above. To find the median of a number of returns, list them in order and then find the number in the middle. For example, the median of 11, 7, 4, 13 and 8 is 8 (4, 7, 8, 11, 13). If the number of variables is even, then take the average of the middle two. If we use the numbers given above for mean (2, 5, 8, and 9), the average of the middle two is 6.5 (5 + 8 = 13 divided by 2 = 6.5). Note that the median is not the same number as the mean. The median is often more appropriate than the mean in skewed distributions or in situations with variables that fall far outside the normal range.

12. 2. 1. 3   Mode

The mode is determined much differently than the prior two. Mode measures the most common value in a distribution of numbers. For example, the mode of 2, 2, 2, 6, 7, 7, 9 is 2. The mode is likely to be quite unlike the mean or median. For example, using the numbers just shown, the mean is 5 (35 ÷ 7) and the median is 6.

12. 2. 1. 4 Geometric Mean

This one takes some math skills and is, therefore rarely used (and probably won't be a correct choice on the exam and certainly not something you'll have to compute). The geometric mean of any given set of numbers (n) is obtained by multiplying all of them together, and then taking the nth root of them. For example, over the past five years, a stock has annual returns of 10%, 5%, 15%, 8%, and 12%. Its geometric mean is 9.36%. This is computed by multiplying $10 \times 5 \times 15 \times 8 \times 12$ which equals 72,000 and finding the 5th root.

This is not to be confused with the more commonly used arithmetic mean, which, in this case, is $10 + 5 + 15 + 8 + 12 = 50 \div 5 = 10\%$.

TEST TOPIC ALERT   When comparing the arithmetic mean to the geometric mean, the arithmetic mean will always be higher, unless all of the numbers being used are the same (e.g., figuring the mean of 6, 6, and 6), in which case they will be equal. The reason is because the geometric mean uses imputed **compounding**.

12. 2. 1. 5 Range

Range is the difference between the highest and lowest returns in the sample being viewed. When there are many values at either extreme of the range, the results tend to be skewed in that direction. Some look at the mid-range value which, as the name implies, is the number that is exactly in the middle of the range. The simplest way to do this is to reorder the data set from smallest to largest and then subtract the first element from the last element.

For example, if we look at the numbers we used to determine median, we reorder the numbers: 4, 7, 8, 11, and 13. This makes the range 9 (13-4) and the mid-range is 8.5, close to, but not the same as the median. Using our mode example, the range is 7 (9-2) and the mid-range is 5.5.

EXAMPLE   Over the past seven years, a security has produced annual returns of 10%, 4%, –5%, 10%, 12%, –2%, and 6%.

In this example, the mean return (the average) is 5% (adding these seven returns totals +35% and dividing by seven results in an average of 5%). The median return, the one with as many returns above as below, is 6%. The mode, the return with the most occurrences, is 10% and the range, the difference between the lowest and highest returns, is 17% (–5% to +12%).

TEST TOPIC ALERT   You may have a question that shows four portfolios listing the mean, the median and the mode for each one. The question will ask: Which one had some investments that significantly outperformed the average of the other investments? The answer will be the one with the highest mean. (See 7.5.2.11) To show how that works, let's say that you have seven securities in the portfolio with the following returns: A: 5%; B: 5%; C: 8%; D: 10%; E: 12%; F: 40%; and G: 60%. The mode (the number that appears the most frequently) is 5%. The median (the number with the same number of returns above and below it) is 10% and the mean (the average of the seven returns) is 20% (140 divided by 7). The two outliers (F at 40% and G at 60%) caused the mean (average) to be significantly higher than the mode or the median because those two performed significantly better than the other five holdings.

TAKE NOTE

As you review these quantitative evaluation measurements, know that the exam is more concerned with the ability to identify what they measure than how to perform the calculation. One or two questions might require a relatively simple calculation on current yield, after-tax return/yield, inflation-adjusted return, or total return.

12. 2. 2   INCOME IN PERPETUITY

As an investment adviser representative, a client may approach you about a method for providing an annual income "forever" for a relative or perhaps a charity. This is known as income in perpetuity. If you know the average expected rate of return and the desired annual income, divide that income by the rate of return and you will arrive at the lump sum required to throw off that income perpetually.

EXAMPLE

A rich uncle wishes to provide $1,000 per month in perpetuity to his favorite niece. If the account can be invested to earn 5% per annum, what is the required deposit?

    A. $20,000
    B. $24,000
    C. $200,000
    D. $240,000

Answer: D. The first step is to take the monthly income and convert it to a yearly number: $1,000 per month is $12,000 per year. Then, divide that $12,000 by the 5% rate of return, and you arrive at a lump-sum deposit of $240,000.

12. 2. 3   EXHAUSTING THE PRINCIPAL

Unlike the previous example where the income was to last forever, what happens when the client has a fixed sum and wants to know how long money can be withdrawn before it is exhausted?

This is a simple computation when one has a financial calculator available, but all they give you at the test center is a simple four-function one, and that makes the task highly laborious.

Let's take a look at an example of the kind that may be presented on the Series 65 exam.

EXAMPLE

An investor has $100,000 to invest. If the account is estimated to earn at a rate of 5% per year and the investor wishes to withdraw $12,000 per year, approximately how long will the money last?

A. 5 years
B. 8 years
C. 11 years
D. 16 years

Answer: C. Here is the correct math, where BOY means Beginning of the Year and EOY is End of the Year:

Year	BOY Value	EOY Value
1	100,000	105,000
2	93,000	97,650
3	85,650	89,933
4	77,933	81,829
5	69,829	73,321
6	61,321	64,387
7	52,387	55,006
8	43,006	45,156
9	33,156	34,814
10	22,814	23,955
11	11,955	12,552
12	552	580

This shows that one taking the money out at the end of the year, will have exhausted all but a bit over $550 by the end of the 11th year.

You can do this with the calculator furnished at the test center as follows:

■ 100,000 × 105% = 105,000 − 12,000 = 93,000

■ 93,000 × 105% = 97,650 − 12,000 = 85,650

■ 85,650 × 105% = 89,933 − 12,000 = 77,933 and continue

Obviously, this takes a lot of time. Since the answer choices are so far apart, I would suggest taking a shortcut. Take the initial principal, $100,000; divide by the annual withdrawal rate, $12,000 (100 ÷ 12 = 8.33); and choose the next highest number (because you have to realize that the account is earning 5% on whatever assets remain).

1. Present value is a computation that is frequently used to determine the amount of a deposit needed now to meet a future need, such as a college education. If an investor uses an expected return of 8% but the actual return over the period is 10%, the future value will be

   A. lower than anticipated
   B. higher than anticipated
   C. the same as anticipated
   D. too varying to tell

2. Your 50-year-old client has just inherited $50,000 from a relative and wishes to invest it into a single payment deferred variable annuity. What computation would be use to approximate the value of the account when the client reaches 70?

   A. future value
   B. present value
   C. net present value
   D. internal rate of return

3. An investor is looking at the past performance of a security over the past three years. In year one, it returned 10%; year two it returned 15%; and year three it returned –4%. This computes to an average rate of return of 7%. This would be properly referred to as the

   A. arithmetic mean
   B. internal rate of return
   C. median return
   D. range

Quick Quiz answers can be found at the end of the unit.

12. 2. 4 BETA/BETA COEFFICIENT

Beta and *beta coefficient* mean the same thing. In the securities industry, *coefficient* is ordinarily dropped for purposes of convenience. Beta is used to measure the variability between a particular stock's (or portfolio's) movement and that of the market in general. A stock with a beta of 1.00 will tend to have a market risk similar to that of the market as a whole. Most frequently, beta is measured against the Standard & Poor's 500 composite index. A stock with a beta of 1.50 will be considerably more volatile than the market; a stock with a beta of 0.70 will be much less volatile than the market. Although most assets have a positive beta, it is possible to find some with a negative beta. Assets with a negative beta can be an important component when diversifying a portfolio. For example, if beta is –1.2, a 10% up move in the market's return will cause the stock return to decline by 12%. On the other hand, if the general market were to suffer a decline, a stock with a negative beta would generally show positive returns. Know that conservative clients need securities with low positive betas, whereas aggressive clients will find betas in excess of 1.00 to be quite suitable. In the next session, we'll have more to say about beta and **systematic** risk.

TAKE NOTE

If the S&P 500 rises or falls by 10%, a stock with a beta of 1 rises or falls by about 10%, a stock with a beta of 1.5 rises or falls by about 15%, and a stock with a beta of .75 rises or falls by about 7.5%.

12. 2. 5 ALPHA

For portfolio managers, good news is when they can say that they have generated *positive alpha*. Basically, that means that their investment performance is better than what would have been anticipated, given the risk in terms of volatility that was taken. You may be asked to compute how much alpha was generated for a particular stock or portfolio. Alpha can be positive, negative, or zero. If the alpha is negative, then the portfolio is underperforming the market; if higher, the portfolio is outperforming the market (and the manager is doing a good job).

The most common formula for computing alpha goes like this:

(total portfolio return – risk-free rate) – (portfolio beta × [market return – risk-free rate])

In essence, what is being done is comparing performance after eliminating the risk-free rate.

This is one item where it's easier to understand if we show you the numbers.

EXAMPLE

Example #1

Portfolio return 10%
Risk-free rate 2%
Market return rate 8%
Beta 1.2

The computation of alpha would be:

(10% – 2%) = 8%. Then (1.2 times [8 – 2]) which is 1.2 × 6 = 7.2. Plug that into the formula, giving us 8 – 7.2 or an alpha of .8 (positive alpha)

Example #2

Same numbers except the beta is .8

(10% – 2%) – (.8 × 6) = 8 – 4.8 = positive alpha of +3.2

Let's review for a moment. Both portfolios earned the same 12%, but the second one did it with a much lower beta—we would not have expected that portfolio to do as well as the one with the higher beta (remember, more risk, more reward). The fact that it did means the portfolio manager(s) did a great job.

Example #3

Same numbers as example #1 except the portfolio returned 9%

(9% – 2%) – (1.2 × 6) = 7 – 7.2 = alpha of –.2 (negative)

This portfolio underperformed; for the additional risk taken, it should have returned at least 9.2%.

Take a look in the Glossary to see one additional alpha example.

TEST TOPIC ALERT

It is possible on the exam that you will have an alpha computation where the RF (risk-free return) is not given. In that case, the computation is the same, but without the RF being subtracted from both the actual return and the market return. For example, in our first case, the computation would be 10% – (1.2 × 8%) or 10% – 9.6% for an alpha of +.4.

12. 2. 6 STANDARD DEVIATION

Standard deviation is a measure of the volatility of an investment's projected returns, computed by using historical performance data. Standard deviation is a statistical term that measures the amount of variability or dispersion around an average. The larger this dispersion or variability is, the higher the standard deviation. The higher the standard deviation, the larger the security's returns are expected to deviate from its average return, and, hence, the greater the risk.

EXAMPLE

This simple example should give you a basic understanding of the concept behind using standard deviation as a tool to predict price volatility. Let's compare the returns generated by the common stock of two unrelated companies over the past three years.

	2012	2013	2014
Company A	8%	12%	10%
Company B	–4%	25%	9%

For an investor who held shares in Company A for those three years, the mean return on investment was 10%. This is calculated, just like any other average, by adding together the three annual returns (8 + 12 +10 = 30) and dividing that by 3.

For an investor who held shares in Company B for those three years, the mean return on investment was exactly the same 10% (25 + 9 – 4 = 30 ÷ 3). However, which one of the shares had a greater dispersion (or variance) from the mean? Clearly, Company B's. You will not have to compute it, but you should be able to see from this that Company B would have a much higher standard deviation (its returns have deviated far greater from the average) than Company A. If you were asked on your exam to choose which of these two would be more suitable for the conservative investor (the one who likes to sleep well at night), you'd better pick Company A, the one with the lower standard deviation.

Standard deviation is expressed in terms of percentage. It is generally accepted that a security will vary within one standard deviation about two-thirds of the time and within two standard deviations about 95% of the time. A standard deviation of 7.5 means that the return of a stock for a given period may vary by 7.5% above or below its predicted return about two-thirds of the time and within 15% about 95% of the time.

EXAMPLE

A security has an expected return of 12% and a standard deviation of 5%. Investing in a security with an expected 12% return, an investor can expect returns to range within 7% to 17% about 67% of the time and within 2% to 22% about 95% of the time.

TAKE NOTE

An investor can use standard deviation to compare the risk/reward between investments.

EXAMPLE

If an investor had a choice between an investment that historically returned 12% with a standard deviation of 6% and another investment that also returned 12% but had a standard deviation of 10%, the investor would probably choose the first one. In effect, he would expect to receive an equal return in the future return with less risk.

12. 2. 6. 5. 1 Beta vs. Standard Deviation

Beta is a volatility measure of a security compared with the overall market, measuring only systematic (market) risk. Standard deviation is a volatility measure of a security compared with its expected performance and includes both systematic and unsystematic risk. Another way to put that is that standard deviation measures the total risk of a security or portfolio.

12. 2. 7 CORRELATION AND CORRELATION COEFFICIENT

Correlation means that securities move in the same direction. A **strong** or **perfect correlation** means two securities prices move in a perfect positive linear relationship with each other.

EXAMPLE

Two securities are correlated if one security's price rises by 5% and the other security's price then rises by 5%, or if one declines by 4% and the other also declines by 4%.

The correlation coefficient is a number that ranges from –1 to +1. Securities that are perfectly correlated have a correlation coefficient of +1. Securities whose price movements are unrelated to each other have a correlation coefficient of 0. If prices move in perfectly opposite directions, they are negatively correlated or have a correlation coefficient of –1. Generally speaking, correlation coefficients of .80 and up are considered to be a very high correlation.

TAKE NOTE

Index funds attempt to achieve perfect correlation (+1) with the index they are mirroring (e.g., the Standard & Poor's 500). The goal of an index fund manager is to come as close as possible to matching the performance of the underlying index. It is not a goal to exceed the performance, only to match it.

TEST TOPIC ALERT

One of the best ways to increase the diversification of a portfolio is to include investments with a negative correlation. The logic is that those negatively correlated assets will go up when the rest of the portfolio is going down. One of the best examples of a negatively correlated asset is an investment in gold stocks. Bonds frequently have a negative correlation as well which is one of the reasons for creating a balanced allocation.

12. 3 MARKET PRICE RELATED RATIOS

12. 3. 1 PRICE TO EARNINGS RATIO (P/E)

The widely used **price-to-earnings (PE) ratio** provides investors with a rough idea of the relationship between the prices of different common stocks compared with the earnings that accrue to one share of stock:

$$\text{PE ratio} = \frac{\text{current market price of common share}}{\text{earnings per share (EPS)}}$$

Growth companies usually have higher PE ratios than do cyclical companies. Investors are willing to pay more per dollar of current earnings if a company's future earnings are expected to be dramatically higher than earnings for stocks that rise and fall with business cycles. Companies subject to cyclical fluctuations generally sell at lower PEs; declining industries sell at still lower PEs. Investors should beware of extremely high or extremely low PEs. Speculative stocks often sell at one extreme or the other.

If a stock's market price and PE ratio are known, the earnings per share can be calculated as follows:

$$\text{EPS} = \frac{\text{current market price of common stock}}{\text{PE ratio}}$$

TAKE NOTE

A company's stock trades for $30 per share and has earnings of $1.50 per share. It has a PE (multiple) of 20 ($30 ÷ 1.5 = 20). If the average PE of the company's industry is 11, this stock is high priced. If the average PE is 35, this company is low priced.

Some fundamental analysts feel that the company's sales to earnings ratio is more valuable than the PE ratio because different accounting methods can impact earnings much more than sales.

12. 3. 2 PRICE-TO-BOOK RATIO

The **price-to-book ratio** reflects the market price of the stock relative to its **book value** per share. **Book value** is the theoretical value of a company (stated in dollars per share) in the event of liquidation.

TAKE NOTE

A company whose stock sells for $50 per share has a book value of $5 per share. Its price-to-book ratio is 10 ($50 ÷ 5 = 10).

A quick rundown of the most testable points about ratios follows.

- Book value is the company's theoretical liquidation value expressed on a per share basis.

- Speculative companies typically have very high or very low PE ratios.

- Growth companies have higher PE ratios than do cyclical or defensive companies.

- Earnings per share relates only to common stock; it assumes preferred dividends were paid.

QUICK QUIZ 12.B

1. Over a specified time period, the S&P 500 has returned 18%. The manager of a conservative growth portfolio with a beta of .8 reports a return of 16% for that same time period. Assuming a risk-free rate of 4%, the managed portfolio's alpha was
   A. −2.0
   B. −1.6
   C. +0.8
   D. +2.0

2. One of your clients has a portfolio that has a correlation of .91 with the overall market. A stock with which correlation coefficient would most likely offer the greatest diversification to this client?
   A. .91
   B. .51
   C. .01
   D. −.51

3. RMBN common stock is currently selling for $60, which gives the stock a P/E ratio of 20:1. Based on that information, the earnings per share are

   A. $2.00
   B. $3.00
   C. $5.00
   D. $20.00

13

Types of Investment Risks

The quantitative concepts discussed thus far are measures of risk of a security or portfolio. The concepts discussed in this session are types of risk that both businesses and investors bear. Though not a comprehensive list, they are among the most common.

Although we routinely use the term risk, we often have difficulty defining it precisely. In finance, **risk** is defined as the uncertainty that an investment will earn its expected rate of return. There are two basic categories of risk, systematic and unsystematic. We will address both of them and their subcategories one at a time.

The Series 65 exam will include approximately five questions on the material presented in this session.

When you have completed this session, you should be able to:

■ **explain** the difference between systematic and unsystematic risk;

■ **identify** the types of risks faced by investors; and

■ **list** the sequence of priority of claims in the event of a corporate liquidation.

13. 1   SYSTEMATIC RISK

Systematic risk is the risk in the return of an investment that is associated with the macroeconomic factors that affect all risky assets. Stated another way, systematic risk is the risk that changes in the overall economy will have an adverse effect on individual securities regardless of the company's circumstances. It is generally caused by factors that affect all businesses, such as war, global security threats, or inflation. Primary examples would include market risk, interest rate risk, and purchasing power risk, each of which will be dealt with separately. You might also see this referred to as non-diversifiable risk because, as we'll learn, systematic risk cannot be avoided through diversification.

13. 1. 1   MARKET RISK

The first example of systematic risk that generally comes to mind is market risk. When the market tanks, virtually all securities lose value. This is a classic example of a non-diversifiable risk because, regardless of the number of different stocks in your portfolio, when you encounter a stock market such as we had from late 2007 until early 2009, chances are most of those assets will have declined in price. In the previous session, we discussed *correlation*. One way to protect against market risk is to have some negatively correlated securities in your portfolio. Remember, they go up when the others go down.

TAKE NOTE

Market risk is measured by a security's beta.

EXAMPLE

Should a war break out between two major oil-producing countries, the stock market could decline dramatically. The stocks of individual companies would likely decline as well, regardless of whether the war directly affected their businesses.

TAKE NOTE

Market risk cannot be diversified away. However, two strategies that might be used are (1) buy put options on a broad index, such as the S&P 500 (remember, put options become profitable when the underlying asset falls in price), or (2) sell short an ETF based on a broad index (remember, selling short generates a profit when the security falls in price). Furthermore, the longer the investor's time horizon, the better one is able to absorb market risk.

13. 1. 2   INTEREST RATE RISK

Interest rates fluctuate in the market all the time. If market conditions or the Federal Reserve push interest rates higher, the market price of all bonds will be affected. When interest rates rise, the market price of bonds falls and that is why this is a systematic risk.

This risk is sometimes referred to as the market risk for bonds. Rising interest rates can be bearish for some common stock prices as well, particularly those of highly leveraged companies such as public utilities. Having a diversified portfolio of bonds won't help because an increase in interest rates will cause all bonds to decline in price. In the next unit, we'll discuss three strategies that may be used to reduce interest rate risk.

TAKE NOTE

Interest rate risk is intrinsic to all types of fixed-income investments, whether from an emerging market issuer or a triple-A issuer. It is the risk that a debt security's value will decline as a result of an increase in market interest rates.

TEST TOPIC ALERT

The longer the duration, the greater the interest rate risk.

EXAMPLE

If the Federal Reserve increases interest rates dramatically, the market price of all bonds, regardless of credit quality, will decline. Likewise, the stock market could decline as a result of portfolio managers adjusting their valuation models to reflect the revised interest rate environment.

13. 1. 2. 1 Reinvestment Risk

A variation of interest rate risk is reinvestment risk. There is reinvestment risk as to interest and reinvestment risk as to principal.

An investor receiving a periodic cash flow from an investment, such as interest on a debt security, may be unable to reinvest the income at the same rate as the security itself is paying. For example, if an investor purchased a bond with a 10% coupon and several years later comparable securities were only paying 7%, the investor would not be able to compound the investment at the original rate. Zero-coupon bonds avoid this risk because there is nothing to reinvest.

This risk also occurs at maturity. If the fixed income investor was enjoying a 10% return on the above bond, when it matured, the investor was only able to reinvest the principal in a 7% security.

13. 1. 3 INFLATION RISK (PURCHASING POWER RISK)

This is another systematic risk. Inflation reduces the buying power of a dollar (or whatever currency is used where you live). A modest amount of inflation is inherent in a healthy, growing economy, but uncontrolled inflation causes uncertainty among individual investors as well as corporate managers attempting to evaluate potential returns from projects. Treasury Inflation Protection Securities are one investment vehicle designed to protect against inflation risk.

Fixed income securities are the most vulnerable to this risk; equity securities are historically the least susceptible.

EXAMPLE   As we stated, purchasing power risk is a systematic risk, meaning that diversifying your portfolio is of little or no help. Let's assume that an individual nearing retirement took $1 million and, seeking income with safety, invested $100,000 into each of 10 different corporate bonds, all maturing in 20 years. For sure, this diversification does give protection against financial risk (if one of the bonds defaults due to bankruptcy of the issuer, the other nine should still pay off). However, if the cost of living rises, 20 years from now, when each of those bonds pays back the $100,000 principal, the investor will have $1 million, but how much will that $1 million purchase compared to what it would have 20 years earlier?

TEST TOPIC ALERT   Because inflation is a global issue, not just confined to the United States and our dollar, a universal definition would be "a decrease in the value of the monetary unit."

13. 2   UNSYSTEMATIC RISK

Unlike systematic risk which is nondiversifiable, these risks can be reduced through diversification. They are risks that are unique to the specific industry or business enterprise and would include things such as labor union strikes, lawsuits, and product failure. We will cover the most testable examples below.

13. 2. 1   BUSINESS RISK

This is an operating risk, generally caused by poor management decisions (e.g., Edsel, New Coke, or more recently, RIMM failing to pay attention to the success of the iPhone—remember when everybody had to have a Blackberry?). At best, earnings are lowered; at worst, the company goes out of business and common stockholders probably lose their entire investment.

13. 2. 2   FINANCIAL RISK

Often confused with business risk (it is similar), financial risk relates primarily to those companies that use debt financing (leverage). An inability to meet those debt obligations could lead to bankruptcy and, once again, total loss for the stockholders. For that reason, this is sometimes called **credit risk** or **default risk**.

TEST TOPIC ALERT   Unsystematic risk can be minimized through portfolio diversification. For example, a client long 1,000 shares of XYZ selling those shares and investing the proceeds into an S&P Index fund eliminates (or greatly reduces) business risk (but not market risk). In similar fashion, owning a diversified portfolio of bonds, such as is offered in a bond fund, offers protection against financial risk.

TEST TOPIC ALERT   Business risk is highest for investors whose portfolios contain stock in only one issuer or in lower rated bonds.

13. 2. 3 REGULATORY RISK

A sudden change in the regulatory climate can have a dramatic effect on the performance or risk of a business and entire business sectors. Overreaching bureaucrats and court judgments that change the rules a business must comply with can devastate individual companies and industries almost overnight. A very common example of this is rulings by the EPA (Environmental Protection Agency), which can sometime play havoc with the oil and gas industry.

13. 2. 4 LEGISLATIVE RISK

It is common to lump together regulatory and legislative risk, but there is a difference. Whereas regulatory risk comes from a change to regulations, legislative risk results from a change in the law. And, because there is frequently a political agenda behind legislation, this risk is sometimes referred to as political risk, although most consider political risk to be of its own making. A governmental agency, state or federal, may pass certain regulations, but only a legislature can pass a law. Changes to the tax code are the most obvious legislative risks.

13. 2. 5 POLITICAL RISK

It might seem like we are splitting hairs here, but each of these, although potentially interrelated, does have a different basis in the source of the risk. In the case of political risk, most attribute this to potential instability in the political underpinnings of the country (think of a coup). This is particularly true in emerging economies, but, as history has shown, political insurrections can occur even in highly developed societies.

13. 2. 5. 1 Sovereign Risk

Sovereign risk ratings capture the risk of a country defaulting on its commercial debt obligations. Headlines were made several years ago when the credit rating of the United States was reduced from AAA (at the time of this printing, the United States was back up to AAA). That is an example of the perceived increased sovereign risk that existed at the time. More recent examples with Greece point out that even countries can have difficulty paying their obligations.

13. 2. 5. 2 Country Risk

Country risk monitors the political and economic stability of countries. Country risk evaluates the total investment risk of a country, such as risk of default on a bond, risk of losing direct investment, risk to global business dealings, and so forth, by both qualitative and quantitative values. As an example, one would give the qualitative factors a 70% weighting and combine it with three basic quantitative values (30% weighting). Typical factors included in the ranking of countries by risk:

■ Qualitative

— Political risk—30%

— Economic performance/projections—30%

— Structural assessment—10%

■ Quantitative

— Debt indicators—10%

— Credit ratings—10%

— Access to bank finance/capital markets—10%

EXAMPLE   Investments that could be affected by regulatory changes include so-called "green" industries (and those that tend to pollute), oil and gas exploration, airlines, and pharmaceutical manufacturers. The most common regulatory risk comes from governmental agency attempts to control or influence product prices or the competitive structure of a particular industry through the passage and enforcement of regulations.

EXAMPLE   An example of legislative risk is how the domestic boat-building business in the United States was nearly wiped out in the early 1990s after the government instituted a luxury tax for yacht purchases.

EXAMPLE   A recent example of political risk was the actions of the Chavez government in Venezuela several years ago, where nationalization took place in many industries from cement to supermarkets. Those investors in what where previously privately owned (not government) businesses saw much, if not all, of their investment lost.

13. 2. 6 LIQUIDITY RISK

Liquidity measures the speed or ease of converting an investment into cash without causing a price disruption. **Liquidity risk** is the risk that when an investor wishes to dispose of an investment, no one will be willing to buy it, or that a very large purchase or sale would not be possible at the current price. Although there is technically a difference, for exam purposes, you may also refer to this as **marketability risk**.

EXAMPLE

The Treasury bill market is a highly liquid market because investors can sell a Treasury bill within seconds at the quoted prices. Real estate investments, however, can take months or years to sell if you want to get close to your asking price. The longer it takes to convert an investment into cash without having a fire sale, the greater the liquidity risk.

TAKE NOTE

Listed stocks and mutual funds have virtually no liquidity risk. Thinly traded stocks, many municipal bonds, and most tangible assets have a greater degree of inability to liquidate rapidly at your price.

13. 2. 7 OPPORTUNITY COST

Opportunity cost is the foregone return, or the return given up, on an alternative investment. In economic terms, opportunity cost is defined as the highest valued alternative that must be sacrificed as a result of choosing among alternatives. More simply, one can invest in short-term Treasury bills incurring virtually no risk. That is the risk-free alternative that can be earned by basically doing nothing. Any return that deviates from the risk-free return represents your opportunity gained or lost.

EXAMPLE

The 90-day Treasury bill is currently yielding 6%. An investor decides to purchase a stock with an expected return of 11%. If that stock actually returns 2%, the opportunity cost is 4% (6% − 2%) because that is the rate that the investor gave up, risk free, to assume the risk of investing in the alternative choice.

TEST TOPIC ALERT

You may need to know that the three primary systematic risks are:

■ market;

■ interest rate; and

■ inflation or purchasing power.

And, there are five primary unsystematic risks:

■ Business

■ Financial

■ Liquidity

■ Political

■ Regulatory

13. 3   CURRENCY OR EXCHANGE RATE RISK

Purchasers of foreign securities, whether through direct ownership or ADRs, face the uncertainty that the value of either the foreign currency or the domestic currency will fluctuate. For example, as of the date of publication, the euro is down almost 35% against the U.S. dollar in the past 12 months. As a result, someone who invested one year ago in the stock of a company domiciled in the eurozone will find that, even if the stock has remained level or slightly higher on its local market, in terms of dollars, the value has fallen.

TEST TOPIC ALERT   On an individual level, the exam may even ask you about exchange rates and vacationers. For example, you take a trip to Country A and purchase a dinner on your credit card for 200 units of the local currency. Then, on the final night of your stay, you go to the same restaurant, order the same meal and, once again, the bill is for 200 units. When you get home, you check your credit card statement and see that you were billed $100 for the first meal and $110 for the second. What happened? The value of the foreign currency rose against the U.S. dollar from $.50 ($100/200) to $.55 ($110/200). Even though no prices changed in the foreign country, you encountered currency risk.

QUICK QUIZ 13.A   True or False?

_____   1.   Market risk (systematic risk) is the risk associated with the specific business decisions of a company's manager.

_____   2.   The term *risk* refers to the uncertainty that an investment will earn less than its historical return.

_____   3.   Regulatory risk is the risk that the regulatory environment in which a company operates will change as a result of legislation.

_____   4.   Standard deviation is a measure of inflationary pressures on the performance of a company.

5.   All of the following risks are considered diversifiable EXCEPT

   A.   currency risk
   B.   liquidity risk
   C.   purchasing power risk
   D.   sovereign risk

Quick Quiz answers can be found at the end of the unit.

13. 4 CAPITAL STRUCTURE/LIQUIDATION PRIORITY

As discussed in a previous session of this unit, a corporation's capital structure is the way it raises its capital. Think of it like the building blocks of the company. All corporations build the base, as it were, with common stock. They may, or may not issue preferred stock. If they wish to employ leverage, they will borrow money by issuing debt securities. Those securities may be issued with collateral, such as a mortgage bond, or merely on the general credit of the issuer (a debenture). In terms of looking at risks, it is critical to understand where the investor's position is in the event of a bankruptcy.

When examining the capital structure of a corporation, it is important to know the liquidation priority:

- Secured creditors (e.g., mortgage bonds, equipment trust certificates, collateral trust bonds)
- Unsecured creditors (e.g., general creditors including debenture holders)
- Subordinated debt holders
- Preferred stockholders
- Common stockholders

In addition, the exam may want you to know about the priority of items that are not securities. Even though they are not legally considered secured assets, highest priority is given to wages (up to an indexed amount earned in the 180 days prior to the employer's declaration of bankruptcy) followed by taxes.

Regardless of how low on the totem pole a debt security is, such as a subordinated debenture, it still has priority in terms of payment of interest and principal ahead of any equity security. Look for a question asking, in essence, "In the event of a corporate liquidation, who comes first: A senior, prior lien preferred stock or a junior, unsecured subordinated debenture?" Now, you may not see all of those adjectives, but no matter what, a debt security always has priority over an equity security.

UNIT TEST

1. Which of the following is a coincident economic indicator?
   A. Stock market prices as measured by the S&P 500
   B. Machine tool orders
   C. Industrial production
   D. Agricultural employment

2. Which of the following statements about the consumer price index (CPI) is NOT true?
   A. The CPI measures the increase in the general price level of a basket of consumer goods.
   B. The CPI measures the increase or decrease in the level of consumer prices with respect to the level of wholesale prices upon which consumer prices depend.
   C. The CPI is computed monthly.
   D. The CPI measures the rate of increase or decrease in a broad range of prices, such as food, housing, medical care, and clothing.

3. Which of the following statements reflects the monetarist economic position?
   A. The amount of money in the economy is not significant because economic activity reflects the value of real goods and services and, therefore, the Federal Reserve should not attempt to manage the money supply.
   B. The total amount of money in the economy is the result of the level of interest rates.
   C. The amount of money in the economy determines the overall price level over time and, therefore, the Federal Reserve should control the growth in the amount of money in the economy in a gradual and predictable way.
   D. The best way to control the money supply is to raise taxes, which, in turn, will reduce the amount of money in the economy and lower prices.

4. If the U.S. dollar has fallen relative to foreign currencies, which of the following statements are TRUE?
   I. U.S. exports are likely to rise.
   II. exports are likely to fall.
   III. Foreign currencies buy fewer U.S. dollars.
   IV. Foreign currencies buy more U.S. dollars.
   A. I and III
   B. I and IV
   C. II and III
   D. II and IV

5. An upward sloping yield curve represents all of the following EXCEPT
   A. time value of money
   B. increased risk of default over time
   C. inflation expectations
   D. foreign interest rate differentials

6. When discussing employment and production, which of the following industries are typically more affected by a recession?
   I. Capital goods
   II. Consumer durable goods
   III. Consumer nondurable goods
   IV. Services
   A. I and II
   B. I and III
   C. II and IV
   D. III and IV

7. Which of the following statements regarding significant interest rates in the U.S. economy is NOT true?
   A. Federal funds rate is the rate the Federal Reserve charges for overnight loans to member commercial banks.
   B. The prime rate is the interest rate that large U.S. money center commercial banks charge their most creditworthy corporate borrowers.
   C. The discount rate is the rate the New York Federal Reserve Bank charges for short-term loans to member banks.
   D. Broker loan rate is the interest rate banks charge broker-dealers on money they borrow to lend to margin account customers.

8. If the dollar weakens, which of the following statements is TRUE?

    A. The dollar buys more foreign currency.
    B. U.S. exports become less competitive.
    C. Foreign securities denominated in their domestic currency decrease in value to the U.S. investor.
    D. An increase in U.S. interest rates might strengthen the dollar.

9. Your client calls you after reading a story in the business section of his local newspaper. It seems that the article focused on changes to the core CPI and the client wants to know how that is different from the normal CPI. You should explain that it is

    A. the Consumer Price Index excluding energy and food prices
    B. the Consumer Price Index excluding housing and automobiles
    C. the total of the leading indicators, excluding stock prices
    D. the figure used to determine annual increases, if any, to Social Security benefits

10. Which of these is a definition of inflation?

    A. A decrease in consumer demand
    B. An increase in the value of the dollar
    C. An increase in purchasing power
    D. A decrease in the value of the monetary unit

11. Balance sheets contain

    A. gross revenues for the year
    B. the amount of cash and cash equivalents expended during the first half of the fiscal year as opposed to the second half
    C. the net worth of the firm at the end of the reporting period
    D. no reference to the accounting methods used to construct the balance sheet

12. All of the following are considered to be components of cash flow EXCEPT

    A. current asset activities
    B. financing activities
    C. investing activities
    D. operating activities

13. If a publicly traded corporation was going to sell a wholly-owned subsidiary, the information would be made available through the filing of a Form

    A. 8-K
    B. 10-K
    C. 10-Q
    D. 13-F

14. The future value of an invested dollar is dependent on

    I.   the exchange rate of the dollar at the beginning and end of the period
    II.   the interest rate at maturity
    III. the rate of return it earns
    IV.   the time period over which it is invested

    A. I only
    B. II only
    C. II and III
    D. III and IV

15. The present value of a dollar

    A. is the amount of goods and services the dollar will buy in the future at today's rate price level
    B. indicates how much needs to be invested today at a given interest rate to equal a specific cash value in the future
    C. is equal to its future value if the level of interest rates stays the same
    D. cannot be calculated without knowing the level of inflation

16. The terms *mean*, *median*, and *mode* are all measures of

    A. beta coefficient
    B. central tendency
    C. correlation coefficient
    D. standard deviation

17. One of the most common uses of the net present value calculation is for

    A. a parent to compute the amount needed for education funding
    B. a corporation to determine the feasibility of investing in new capital equipment
    C. an investment adviser to compute the expected returns from a portfolio
    D. determining how close a stock's return is to the efficient frontier

18. All of the following statements regarding an investment's internal rate of return (IRR) are true EXCEPT

A. IRR expresses the rate of interest that matches the initial investment with the present value of future cash flows
B. investments are acceptable when their internal rates of return exceed the investor's required rate of return
C. IRR cannot be calculated for investments with uneven cash flows
D. IRR is the one rate of return that results in an investment having a net present value (NPV) of 0

19. The risk to bondholders that bonds may lose value during periods of increasing inflation is known as

A. credit risk
B. reinvestment risk
C. marketability risk
D. interest rate risk

20. Your client has $10,000 to invest today and expects to earn an after-tax return of 8% to send his daughter to college in 12 years. Which of the following is needed to determine whether the investment is likely to satisfy the client's goal?

A. Present value
B. Expected cost of college
C. Consumer Price Index
D. Client's marginal federal income tax bracket

21. What happens to outstanding fixed-income securities when interest rates decline?

A. Yields go up
B. Coupon rates go up
C. Prices go up
D. No change

22. Which of the following describe nonsystematic risk?

I. The risk that an individual stock will not perform well
II. The same as market risk
III. Can be diversified to lower risk
IV. Cannot be diversified to lower risk

A. I and III
B. I and IV
C. II and III
D. II and IV

23. In October 1987, ABC Manufacturing Company showed a strong balance sheet. Nevertheless, its stock lost 15 points in the "crash of 1987." This is an example of

A. business risk
B. beta
C. opportunity risk
D. market risk

24. The risk of not being able to convert an investment into cash at a time when cash is needed is what type of risk?

A. Legislative
B. Liquidity
C. Market
D. Reinvestment

25. Which of the following are considered unsystematic risks?

I. Business
II. Liquidity
III. Market
IV. Purchasing power

A. I and II
B. I and III
C. II and IV
D. III and IV

ANSWERS AND RATIONALES

1. **C.** Industrial production is a coincident indicator. The stock indexes and manufacturing orders are leading indicators. Economists do not use agricultural employment as an indicator.

2. **B.** The CPI does not measure the increase or decrease in the level of consumer prices with respect to the level of wholesale prices. The CPI only measures retail prices whether or not wholesale prices are passed through to the consumer.

3. **C.** Monetarists believe that the economy and inflation are best controlled through the management of the money supply rather than through fiscal policy stimulation.

4. **B.** When the U.S. dollar loses value, compared with a foreign currency, the same amount of the foreign currency now buys more dollars. As a result, U.S. goods are cheaper in terms of that foreign currency, which means that the foreign country tends to buy more U.S. products and U.S. exports rise.

5. **D.** Foreign interest rate differentials are not reflected in an upward sloping yield curve. Interest rate differentials between countries reflect differences in domestic monetary and fiscal conditions. The time value of money is reflected in the upward sloping yield curve. Longer-term rates require higher rates to compensate for loss of current buying power and liquidity. Longer-term funds bear a higher risk of default than do shorter-term funds and, as a result, command higher rates. Increasing inflation expectations cause the yield curve to slope upward to compensate lenders for the loss of future buying power.

6. **A.** Durable goods and capital goods are more affected by a recession than are nondurable goods and services. This is primarily because they are larger items, last for a longer period, and are somewhat discretionary.

7. **A.** The federal funds rate is the rate that member banks charge each other for overnight loans of $1 million or more; it is not the rate that the Federal Reserve charges member banks for overnight loans.

8. **D.** When U.S. interest rates rise, foreign investors invest in U.S. dollar-denominated securities, thereby increasing the demand for dollars and causing the dollar to strengthen.

9. **A.** Because of their high volatility, economists exclude energy and food prices from core inflation figures. Social Security adjustments (and many others as well) are based upon the CPI itself, not the core.

10. **D.** We tend to think solely in terms of our dollar, but inflation can occur worldwide and leads to a decrease in the purchasing power (or value) of the monetary unit in use in any particular jurisdiction. Inflation is commonly caused by increased consumer demand, not a decrease.

11. **C.** The balance sheet provides a snapshot view of the financial condition of the firm at the end of the reporting period. It does not provide information on the flow of expenses, revenues, and cash during the reporting period. Gross revenues are reflected on the income statement, not on the balance sheet. The balance sheet provides a description of the assets, liabilities, and owner's equity at the end of the reporting period. References to accounting methods used are contained in the footnotes of the balance sheet.

12. **A.** There is no such thing as current asset activities. Cash flow is generated through financing (issuing stock or bonds), investing (profits from investments), and, the most significant of all, operations of the entity.

13. **A.** The Form 8-K is filed with the SEC within 4 business days of any one of a number of significant actions, including the sale of a significant asset such as a wholly-owned subsidiary.

14. **D.** The future value of a dollar reflects the interest rate it earns over time. The rate of foreign exchange is not related to or used in the calculation of the future value of a dollar. The foreign exchange rate is not relevant.

15. **B.** The present value of a dollar will indicate how much needs to be invested today at a given interest rate to equal a cash amount required in the future.

16. **B.** Central tendency is usually defined as the center or middle of a distribution. The three most common tools used are mean, median, and mode.

17. **B.** Net present value is frequently used in capital budgeting to determine which of several projects makes the most economic sense. By evaluating future cash flows against initial outlay, the projects with a positive NPV are those that are most likely to offer financial reward.

18. **C.** IRR is the rate of interest that equates the initial investment with the present value of future cash flows; it is the rate of return that results in an investment having a net present value of 0. It is possible, although very difficult, to calculate IRR for investments with uneven cash flows such as common stocks.

19. **D.** Interest rate risk is the risk that as interest rates rise, bond prices fall. Periods of inflation are accompanied by rising interest rates. Another risk in this scenario is purchasing power risk; each semiannual interest payment has less purchasing power due to inflation, and, of course, the purchasing power of the principal at maturity will be far less as well.

20. **B.** To determine whether the investment will satisfy the goal, the investment adviser representative needs to know the amount needed to pay for college. The information we have here will allow us to compute the future value: $25,181.70. This may not be enough to pay for even 1 year of college 12 years from now.

21. **C.** When interest rates drop, prices will rise, decreasing effective yield. Thus, there is an inverse relationship between interest rates and bond prices.

22. **A.** Nonsystematic risk is company risk, the risk that an individual investment will perform poorly. Systematic risk is market risk, the risk that the market will perform poorly, dragging one's portfolio along with it. Diversification will remove most nonsystematic risk. The more stocks owned, the lower the risk that a poor performer will jeopardize the overall value of the portfolio.

23. **D.** Market risk is the risk that a specific stock's price will be driven by factors largely independent of its issuer. Business risk is unique to each business entity. Beta is a measure of a stock's volatility relative to the overall market. The question does not refer to the volatility or sensitivity of the stock to the overall market. Opportunity risk is not among the recognized sources of risk. *Opportunity cost* is a term in economics that refers to the return given up in order to invest in another instrument or project.

24. **B.** Liquidity risk is the measure of how quickly and easily a security can be converted to cash. Legislative risk is a measure of how legal changes (e.g., taxes) affect an investment. Market risk is a measure of the volatility of a stock or the risk of loss as a result of market changes. Reinvestment risk is the risk that an investor will not be able to reinvest interest payments on a bond at the original rate during the life of the bond.

25. **A.** There are 4 general unsystematic risks: business, liquidity, political, and regulatory. Market and purchasing power risk are systematic.

QUICK QUIZ ANSWERS

Quick Quiz 11.A.

1. **F.** Monetarists prefer less government intervention. Keynesian economists believe that the federal government should manage inflation through taxation and spending.

2. **F.** A depression is a decrease in the GDP for at least six consecutive quarters.

3. **F.** Rising inventories are characteristic of a downturn in the business cycle. Inventories accumulate when consumers buy less.

4. **T.** The CPI is a measurement of inflation.

5. **T.** High consumer debt is characteristic of a downturn in the business cycle.

6. **D.** An economic contraction is likely to feature increasing unemployment (i.e., decreasing employment), along with decreasing consumer spending, declining economic output, and decreasing inflation pressure.

Quick Quiz 11.B.

1. **C.**

2. **E.**

3. **B.**

4. **A.**

5. **D.**

6. **F.**

7. **C.** Core inflation is measured using a price index that excludes food and energy prices.

8. **A.** An inverted, or negative, yield curve is one that results when debt with short-term maturities has higher yields than those with maturities that are longer. A positive, or normal, yield curve results when the yields increase as maturities do.

9. **C.** There is an inverse relationship between interest rates and bond prices. This means that as current interest rates go up, the market price of existing bonds will go down.

10. **D.** When the value of the dollar rises, it will buy more foreign money, making foreign goods and services less expensive for Americans. Because foreign securities are valued in foreign currencies, shares of foreign stock will be worth fewer American dollars when the value of the dollar increases.

11. **B.** An increase in the Help Wanted Index signifies that employers are hiring—business is good. Competition for qualified workers will usually result in paying higher wages and that will translate to higher prices for goods and services (inflation).

Quick Quiz 11.C

1. **B.** Working capital (or net working capital) is, by definition, the difference between current assets and current liabilities.

2. **B.** The formula for the balance sheet is as follows: assets = liabilities + shareholders' equity. If assets stay the same and equity (net worth) decreases, liabilities must increase. Prepaid expenses are assets; accrued expenses are liabilities.

3. **D.** On the issuance of a bond, cash is received (thus increasing current assets) and long-term debt increases (increasing total liabilities). Because there is no corresponding increase in current liabilities, working capital will increase; it would have no effect on shareholders' equity.

4. **D.** If earnings increase, retained earnings also increase. If the increased retained earnings are not paid out as dividends, shareholders' equity increases.

Quick Quiz 11.D

1. **A.**

2. **B.**

3. **A.**

4. **A. and B.** Tricky, and this would also be the answer if we had used depreciation.

5. **B.**

6. **B.**

7. **A.** The footnotes to the financial statements carry information such as potential legal actions, accounting methods used (e.g., FIFO or LIFO), and off-book debt.

8. **C.** Although the most common term to describe this important part of a company's net worth is retained earnings, any of them may be used on the exam with the same meaning.

Quick Quiz 11.E

1. **C.** An analyst will compute the P/E ratio by taking the current market price per share and dividing it by the earnings per share.

2. **B.** Cash flow increases when more money comes in than goes out. When receivables are collected, the company receives money. When dividends or bills are paid, someone else receives money. When we buy more inventory, we use cash to do so.

3. **C.** The issuance of common stock brings cash into the company without any offsetting liability. Therefore, current assets, working capital and net worth all increase by the amount of the securities sold. Income is not generated by issuing stock; the company needs sales or revenues for that.

4. **A.** Form 10-Q is the quarterly financial information document filed with the SEC. Because this is a calendar year company, 10-Qs are prepared as of March 31, June 30, and September 30. The Form 10-K is prepared as of December 31 in lieu of another Form 10-Q. Form 8-K is event driven, not a routine financial report.

Quick Quiz 12.A.

1. **B.** Present value is the amount deposited to meet a future goal based on an expected rate of return. If the return is higher than expected, the ending result will be greater (a good thing).

2. **A.** This is what the future value computation is used for. We take a sum of money available now, consider the time the money will be invested, estimate a rate of return, and arrive at the expected value (assuming the earnings are equal to the estimated rate).

3. **A.** When a true average return is shown, that is the arithmetic mean. The median return (the number in the middle of the group of three) is 10%, and the range is 19% (–4 to +15).

Quick Quiz 12.B.

1. **C.** The formula is (portfolio return – RF rate) – (beta × [market return – RF rate). Plugging in the numbers, we have 16% – 4% = 12. Then .8 × [18% – 4%] or .8 × 14%, which equals 11.2%. The final step is 12 – 11.2, giving us a positive alpha of .8. Using these numbers, some find it easier to compare 80% of the market return (after removing the risk-free rate) to the actual return, once again, after the RF rate. In this case, it would be 80% of 14 (that is 11.2) compared to 12 (16% – 4%). We get the same alpha of .8 this way as well.

2. **D.** Adding securities with a negative correlation tends to increase the diversification of a portfolio.

3. **B.** The price-to-earnings ratio compares the market price to the earnings per share of common. What this question is telling us is that the $60 price is 20 times the EPS. Divide $60 by 20 and we arrive at $3.00 per share.

Quick Quiz 13.A.

1. **F.** Market risk is systematic risk, or the risk that the overall market will have an adverse effect on a security independent of the company's circumstances.

2. **F.** In finance, the term *risk* is defined as the uncertainty that an investment will earn its expected rate of return.

3. **F.** Regulatory risk is the risk a company faces that the rules of the game will change as a result of new regulations, not legislation. Remember, regulations are written by government or other agencies while legislation is done by a political body, usually one that has been elected rather than appointed.

4. **F.** Standard deviation is a measure of an investment's volatility. It measures the amount of variance in price or returns from the investment's mean return during an expected period.

5. **C.** Purchasing power risk, also known as inflation risk, is a systematic risk and, as such, is one that cannot generally be lessened through diversification.

Unit 4

Client Investment Recommendations and Strategies

This unit consists of eight sessions

In total there will be 40 questions on this material, representing 31% of the Series 65 Exam.

14

Type of Client

When an individual account is opened, it is registered in the name(s) of one or more individuals; they are the account owners and the only individuals allowed access to and control of the investments in the account. Generally, any competent person of majority age can open an account, and anyone declared legally incompetent cannot. Fiduciary or custodial accounts may be opened for minors or legally incompetent individuals.

In addition to individuals, accounts may be opened for anyone else meeting the definition of a person. That would include business and government entities. Some of these would be considered institutional accounts as defined in Unit 1.

The Series 65 Exam will include four questions on the material covered in this session.

When you have completed this session, you should be able to:

■ **recognize** the different types of clients securities professionals service

■ **distinguish** between the different kinds of business entities capable of opening accounts

■ **explain** the special requirements for trust and estate accounts

14. 1 INDIVIDUAL ACCOUNT

An **individual account** may be for a person, a trust, or a deceased person through an estate account. There is one beneficial owner. When referring to investment advisers, normally an individual client is a natural person whose investments are managed by an adviser for a fee. When a business is organized as a sole proprietorship, that business account is also considered an individual account. The adviser should establish, in consultation with the client, a written statement of objectives and investment strategy before making recommendations to the client. This document is frequently referred to as an Investment Policy Statement (IPS). In the next Session, we will examine the client profile and see the information necessary to prepare the IPS. In Session 20, we will discuss the use of the IPS by those with fiduciary responsibility over qualified retirement plans.

The adviser must periodically review the client's investment profile to determine whether any changes in circumstances could alter the client's objectives.

Unless certain legal documents are procured, the account holder is the only person who can:

- control the investments within the account; or
- request distributions of cash or securities from the account.

14. 1. 1 SUITABILITY FOR INDIVIDUAL ACCOUNTS

Both federal and state regulations require that any investment recommendation be suitable based upon the client's needs, objectives, and financial considerations. In the next session, we will look at a number of those issues.

14. 2 JOINT ACCOUNTS

A **joint account** is owned by two or more persons, and each is allowed control over the account. Generally, suitability information is required on all of the tenants in the account.

On the new account form, the account must be designated as either **tenants in common (TIC)** or **joint tenants with right of survivorship (JTWROS)**. Account forms for joint accounts require the signatures of all owners. Joint account agreements provide that it only takes one of the tenants to transact business in the account. However, checks must be made payable to all of the names in which the account is registered and must be endorsed for deposit by all tenants, although mail need only be sent to a single address. In order for the sale to be effective, all securities sold from a joint account must be signed by all tenants.

14. 2. 1 TENANTS IN COMMON (TIC)

TIC ownership (or JTIC), provides that a deceased tenant's fractional interest in the account is retained by that tenant's estate and is not passed to the surviving tenant(s). Ownership of a TIC account may be divided unequally. At the death of an account owner, that person's proportionate share of the cash and securities in the account is distributed according to the instructions in the decedent's will. If one account owner dies or is declared incompetent, all pending transactions and outstanding orders must be canceled immediately.

EXAMPLE   If a TIC agreement provides for 60% ownership interest by one owner and 40% ownership interest by the other, that fraction of the account would pass into the deceased owner's estate upon death. The TIC agreement may be used by more than two individuals.

14. 2. 2 JOINT TENANTS WITH RIGHT OF SURVIVORSHIP (JTWROS)

JTWROS ownership stipulates that a deceased tenant's interest in the account passes to the surviving tenant(s). Regardless of contributions, each JTWROS account owner has an equal and undivided interest in the cash and securities in the account. Upon the death or declaration of incompetency of any of the account owners, account ownership passes to the survivor(s); a right of succession occurs and the other party or parties becomes sole owner(s) of the account.

TEST TOPIC ALERT   Whenever the test uses the term *joint tenants*, it means JTWROS (not tenants in common).

14. 2. 3 TRANSFER-ON-DEATH ACCOUNTS (TOD)

Using a transfer-on-death (TOD) account is the simplest way to keep assets held in brokerage accounts from becoming subject to probate upon a client's death. However, the TOD account does not avoid estate taxes if applicable. TOD accounts are available for most types of paper assets, such as savings and checking accounts in banks and credit unions, certificates of deposit, stocks, bonds, and other securities.

The owner, while alive, is the only person with any rights to the property. Upon the owner's death, the property is immediately transferred to the named beneficiaries, usually without any added cost. The owner has the right to change beneficiaries at any time and provide for unequal distribution of the assets if desired.

The only types of accounts that may be opened with a TOD designation are individual accounts and JTWROS accounts.

TAKE NOTE   You might also see this as payable-on-death (POD), although the term is used far more frequently for bank accounts.

14. 2. 3. 1 Totten Trust

If you have a really old bank account you might have a Totten trust designation using language similar to "John Doe, in trust for Jane Doe" or perhaps "John Doe as trustee for Jane Doe." Totten trusts, sometimes referred to as a poor man's will, allowed for the transfer of ownership of a bank account to a beneficiary after the owner's death. Totten trusts were the predecessor to POD or TOD designations, but a few states still recognize them.

TEST TOPIC ALERT

Tenants in common can own unequal interests in the account, unlike joint tenants with right of survivorship, who always share equally.

■ TIC: interest can be unequal.

■ JTWROS: all parties must have equal interests.

Checks or distributions must be made payable in the account name and endorsed by all parties.

14. 2. 4 SUITABILITY FOR JOINT ACCOUNTS

The suitability requirements for a joint account follow the same basic rules as all accounts—put the interest of the client first. Because a joint account is really nothing other than a collection of individuals, suitability information must be obtained on all of the account owners and any recommendations must be appropriate based upon that information. An example you might see on the exam has two brothers with a TIC account. One brother is an accredited investor under Rule 501 of the Securities Act, while the other is far from it. Can the account purchase a private placement that is limited to accredited investors with the ownership being allocated 100% to the accredited brother? The answer is no, that wouldn't work.

14. 3 ACCOUNTS FOR BUSINESS ENTITIES

14. 3. 1 SOLE PROPRIETORSHIP

This is the simplest form of business organization and, as mentioned previously, is treated like an individual account. Therefore, the same issues of suitability that apply to individual accounts apply to the management of sole proprietorship accounts. In a sole proprietorship, all income (or loss) is that of the individual. In fact, one of the risks of operating in this fashion is that all of the owner's assets are liable for the debts of the business— you can lose everything. Obviously, this is one of the major considerations when opening an account for this form of business.

14. 3. 2 GENERAL PARTNERSHIP

A general partnership is an unincorporated association consisting of two or more individuals. In a general partnership, the partners manage and are responsible for the operation and debts of the business. Partnerships are easy to form and easy to dissolve, but are generally not suited for raising large sums of capital. Partnerships allow the business' profits and losses to flow directly through to the investors for tax purposes, thus avoiding double taxation of profits at the business and individual levels.

Because the income and losses flow through to the individual partners, an investment policy for a general partnership would have to consider the combined/collective objectives of all of the partners.

14. 3. 3 LIMITED PARTNERSHIP

In the case of an enterprise organized as a limited partnership, the management (and liability) is assigned to the general partner(s) while the limited partner(s) are passive and have liability limited to their investment. This is the typical case with the Direct Participation Programs (DPPs) discussed in Unit 2. Suitability decisions are similar to a general partnership except that the limited partners do not have the full liability of the general partner(s).

14. 3. 4 LIMITED LIABILITY COMPANY (LLC)

A **limited liability company (LLC)** is a business structure that combines benefits of incorporation (limited liability) with the tax advantages of a partnership (flow-through of taxable earnings). The LLC owners are **members** (not shareholders) and are not personally liable for the debts of the LLC.

Just as with the partnership clients described above, the objectives and financial constraints of the individual members must be considered from a suitability standpoint.

14. 3. 5 S-CORPORATION

An **S corporation**, although taxed like a partnership, offers investors the limited liability associated with corporations in general. The profits and losses are passed through directly to the shareholders in proportion to their ownership in the S corporation. Unlike an LLC, which can have an unlimited number of members, an S corporation may not have more than 100 shareholders, none of whom may be a nonresident alien, or more than one class of stock (presumably common).

Losses on S corporation stock may be claimed only to the extent of an investor's basis in the shares. The basis includes money contributed or lent to the corporation.

Any business organization client where the entity itself has no liability and is not subject to tax, such as the partnerships, LLC, and S corporation, requires the adviser to look through the entity to the owners in order to properly meet the suitability standards.

TAKE NOTE

> Geraldine invested $25,000 in an S corporation, along with nine other investors who invested the same amount. Within a year, the corporation needed additional equipment, so Geraldine lent $10,000 to the business from her own funds. Her basis is now $35,000. If the corporation experiences a $400,000 loss, Geraldine's portion is $40,000. However, she may deduct only $35,000 of the loss because that is the amount of her basis.

14. 3. 6   C-CORPORATION

A **C corporation** is a business structure that distinguishes the company as a separate entity from its owners. If a business expects to need significant capital, this form is almost always the preferred choice. Unlike the management of a partnership [the general partner(s)], in most cases, the corporation's officers and directors are shielded from personal liability for the corporation's debts and losses. Shareholders are also shielded from corporate creditors. That is the limited liability benefit of owning stock. Corporate income tax applies to the corporation as an entity rather than being passed through to the shareholder. If your client is a C corporation, you will only look at the corporation's financial needs and objectives when determining suitability.

TAKE NOTE

> C corporation earnings are subject to double taxation. Before distribution, the earnings are taxable to the corporation and then are taxed again to the shareholder when paid out as a dividend. Distributions from LLCs and S corporations are taxed only once because there is no taxation at the business entity level.

14. 3. 7   CHOOSING THE RIGHT BUSINESS STRUCTURE

- Here are some testable points to consider when a person is considering which is the most appropriate business form to use:
- The easiest business to set up, especially if you don't expect much liability, is the sole proprietorship. However, because the business and the owner are inseparable, there is unlimited liability and no limits to the amount of the loss (if any) that may be claimed on the proprietor's tax return.
- Partnerships and LLCs are generally easier to form and dissolve than a C corporation.
- Benefits of structuring a business as a general partnership, an LLC, or an S corporation would include no double taxation as is the case with a C corporation.
- However, a company that expects to be very profitable should be a C corporation instead of a partnership, an LLC, or an S corporation because in those three, all earnings pass to owners—nothing can be retained.
- Only the sole proprietorship and the C corporation are taxed on their income. The sole proprietorship on the owner's personal tax return and the corporation on a Form 1120.
- The only logical choice where a large amount of capital is to be raised is the C corporation.

■ The business entities that have limited liability for owners as well as flow-through of income or loss are the limited partnership, LLC, and S corporation. The C corporation has limited liability but no flow-through; the sole proprietorship and general partnership have flow-through but unlimited liability.

■ Corporations (including LLCs) survive the death of their owners (even if there is only one shareholder in an S corporation or C corporation, or one member of the LLC).

■ When it comes to transferability of ownership, the corporate form, especially the C corporation, is the preferred choice (selling shares is usually pretty straightforward).

QUICK QUIZ 14.A

Match each of the following terms with the appropriate description below.

A. Tenants in common
B. Full power of attorney
C. Discretionary authorization

____ 1. Enables the investment adviser representative to make investment decisions in a client's account

____ 2. A deceased's fractional interest in an account is retained by his estate

____ 3. Legal document that authorizes someone other than the customer to have all privileges in an account

4. A client has an account where, upon her death, she desires that her only son will receive 50% of account value and her 4 daughters will receive 12.5% each. The easiest way to accomplish this would be to title the account

A. TOD
B. JTROS
C. Tenants in common
D. In trust for the children

5. Three friends plan to start a new business. It is anticipated it will be several years before the business turns a profit. Which of the following types of business organization would be best if they wish to limit their liability while, at the same time, being able to receive favorable tax treatment for the expected losses?

A. C corporation
B. S corporation
C. General partnership
D. Sole proprietorship

6. Several investors open an account in joint tenancy. Financial information is required on which of the following investors?

A. The majority of the investors
B. The largest investor only
C. Only the one authorized to trade the account
D. All of the investors

7. A business organized as a sole proprietorship wishes to open an advisory account. When preparing an investment policy statement, the IA would have to consider the objectives of

A. the sole proprietor
B. the partners
C. the stockholders
D. the members

Quick Quiz answers can be found at the end of the unit.

14. 4   TRUST AND ESTATE ACCOUNTS

Two special kinds of accounts that may appear on the exam are those dealing with trusts and estates. What both of these have in common is that the person entering orders on behalf of the account is acting in a fiduciary capacity, whether it be the trustee of the trust or the executor (or administrator) of the estate. These fiduciaries are acting for the benefit of the beneficiary or beneficiaries of the trust or estate so it is necessary to look at the objectives of the trust and the needs of the heirs.

14. 4. 1   TRUST ACCOUNTS

A **trust** is a legal entity that offers flexibility to an individual who wishes to transfer property. Trusts may be established for a variety of personal and charitable property transfers. Trusts are also established as the legal entity for a corporate retirement plan, but that will be covered in a later session.

The subject of trust law is very complicated and should only be addressed by one who is competent in the subject, usually an attorney.

This exam will require you to know the basics of trusts, how trusts are taxed, trustee responsibility, and your obligations when acting as an adviser to the account.

14. 4. 1. 1   Trust Parties

For a trust to be valid, three parties must be specified in the trust document (trust agreement). These parties are a settlor, a trustee, and a beneficiary. Under certain circumstances, the settlor, trustee, and beneficiary may be the same individual. For a trust to be valid, both the settlor and the trustee must be competent parties. However, the beneficiary may be a minor or a legally incompetent adult.

14. 4. 1. 1. 1 The Settlor

The **settlor** is the person who supplies the property for the trust. Trust property is also referred to as its principal or corpus. This party is also known as the maker, grantor, trustor, or donor.

14. 4. 1. 1. 2 Trustee

A **trustee** is an individual or other party holding legal title to property held for the benefit of another person (or persons). The trustee must administer the trust by following directions in a trust agreement or in a will. A trustee must perform certain duties relative to the trust property.

A trustee is a fiduciary and is obliged to perform in the interest of the beneficiaries. The trustee may be one or more adult individuals or an entity in the business of trusteeship that is responsible for investing, administering, and distributing trust assets for benefit of the beneficiary (or beneficiaries).

In many ways, a trustee's duties are like those of an **executor** (for an estate). However, a trustee's duties generally continue for more time than a typical estate settlement, and the trustee is charged with the greater duty of investing trust assets.

14. 4. 1. 1. 3 Beneficiary

A **beneficiary** is a person for whose benefit property is held in trust. A beneficiary is one who receives or who is designated to receive benefits from property transferred by a trustor. Beneficiaries to a trust include only those persons upon whom the settlor intended to benefit from the trust property or those who would succeed their interests.

EXAMPLE   Jill establishes a trust under which her husband, Julian, is to receive all income produced by the trust property for as long as he lives. Upon Julian's death, their daughter, Janet, will receive the trust principal. Julian is a primary beneficiary. However, until Julian's death, Janet is a contingent beneficiary because her benefit depends on the occurrence of an event, in this case, Julian's death.

TEST TOPIC ALERT   Although it doesn't happen often, the grantor of the trust can also be the trustee and/or the beneficiary.

14. 4. 1. 1. 4 Remainderman

When a trust has run its course and all expenses and distributions have been made, the person who receives the remaining balance is called the remainderman (no gender preference here, there's no such term as remainderwoman). The most common case involves real estate. For example, the husband dies and arranges for his wife to have full use of their home until she passes away. At that time, any surviving children inherit the home. They are the remaindermen.

14. 4. 1. 2 Simple Trusts vs. Complex

14. 4. 1. 2. 1 Simple Trusts

All income earned on assets placed into a **simple trust** must be distributed during the year it is received. If the trust does not distribute all of its net income at least annually, the trust is declared a complex trust. The trustee is not empowered to distribute the trust principal from a simple trust.

14. 4. 1. 2. 2 Complex Trust

On the other hand, a **complex trust** may accumulate income. A complex trust is permitted deductions for distributions of net income or principal. Capital gains are deemed part of the distributable net income of a complex trust unless reinvested. Furthermore, the trustee may distribute trust principal according to trust terms.

TEST TOPIC ALERT   The key difference between a simple and a complex trust is that the simple trust must distribute all of its annual income, whereas a complex trust is not obligated to do so.

14. 4. 1. 3 Living vs. Testamentary Trusts

14. 4. 1. 3. 1 Living Trust

A **living trust**, also known as an **inter vivos trust**, is established during the maker's lifetime. A testamentary trust is established according to the instructions of a will—that is, not with the death of the maker.

14. 4. 1. 3. 2 Testamentary Trust

With a **testamentary trust**, the settlor retains control over assets until death (think "last will and testament"). The individual's will stipulates that, at death, the testator's property is to be placed in trust for the benefit of one or more beneficiaries.

The testamentary trust does not reduce the grantor's income or estate tax exposure. Furthermore, assets that pass to a testamentary trust do not avoid probate, because the validity of the will's instructions to pass property to the trust must be substantiated in probate court.

14. 4. 1. 4 Revocable vs. Irrevocable Trusts

Both living and testamentary trusts can be revocable or irrevocable. Terms of a **revocable trust** may be changed during the maker's lifetime. Terms of an irrevocable trust generally cannot be changed.

14. 4. 1. 4. 1 Revocable Trust

A **revocable trust** must be a living trust because only the living grantor has the power to change or revoke (undo) the trust. At the grantor's death, the trust becomes irrevocable because the individual with the power to change or revoke the trust no longer lives.

No estate tax benefit is available for a revocable living trust. The value of any trust assets in which the grantor retains power to revoke the trust and again own the trust property outright is includable in the grantor's gross estate.

14. 4. 1. 4. 2 Irrevocable Trust

For a trust to be considered irrevocable, the settlor must give up all ownership in property transferred into the trust. Property placed in an irrevocable trust is usually not includable in the trustor's estate for federal estate tax purposes. Certain exceptions to the general rule can jeopardize the effectiveness of an irrevocable trust to reduce estate taxes. The exceptions follow.

- The grantor retains a life interest, or life income.
- The grantor retains a reversionary interest in the trust that is considered more than incidental. Reversionary interest means that the grantor may receive property back from the trust. Under tax law, the grantor is treated as the owner of any portion of a trust in which he has a reversionary interest in either the corpus or the income if the value of the interest exceeds 5% of the value of that portion.
- The grantor retains general power to direct to whom trust property will pass.
- The grantor transfers one or more life insurance policies into an irrevocable trust while retaining certain incidents of ownership, including the ability to make loans from policy cash values and/or change beneficiaries.

14. 4. 1. 4. 3 Grantor Retained Annuity Trusts (GRATs)

This is an estate planning tool designed to pass assets to beneficiaries (usually children) in a way to minimize gift and/or estate taxes. The topic is very complicated, but here are the basics you might need to know.

- The grantor transfers property into a trust (a GRAT) that provides that the grantor will receive a fixed annuity each year, usually for a term of years. At the end of the term, the remainder beneficiaries get whatever is left. The gift involved equals the theoretical value of the remainder, determined by using the discount rate (or rate of return) specified in IRS tables.
- If the assets in the trust earn more than the IRS rate (the Section 7520 rate is 1.8% at the time of this printing), any earnings in excess of that rate goes to the beneficiary(s) free of estate and gift taxes. So, if the grantor thinks the transferred property will earn more than 1.8% (the current number is published each month) over the term of the trust, there are major tax benefits.
- However, if the grantor dies during the term of the trust, the remaining assets are considered part of the deceased's estate.
- Even though this is technically an irrevocable trust, because the grantor has a *retained* interest, the tax liability on the trust's income falls upon the grantor.

14. 4. 2 ESTATE ACCOUNTS

An **estate account** is an account that, like a trust account, is directed by fiduciary on behalf of the beneficiary or beneficiaries of an estate. In the case of one who prepares a will, there is a specified executor. In the case of one who dies without a will (intestate), these functions are performed by a court-appointed administrator. The executor or administrator makes the investment, management, and distribution decisions for the account.

14. 4. 2. 1 Per Stirpes

One common way for people to provide for their descendants is to incorporate the phrase, "to my living issue, per stirpes" in their will. In fact, some states automatically distribute in that fashion when one dies intestate. Per stirpes (not a typo—it is not stripes) is from the Latin word meaning branch. When used, per stirpes means that the deceased intended that a beneficiary's share of the inheritance is to go to an heir. For example, a widow (or widower) had three children and wished the estate to be distributed equally. If one of those children died prior to the estate settlement, that child's children (the grand-children of the widow or widower), would receive a one-third share each, while the two living children would each receive a one-third share.

14. 4. 3 SUITABILITY ISSUES

Just as with any other account, recommendations must be suitable when considering all of the relevant information. However, in the case of a trust or estate, there are several considerations that do not arise in other individual accounts. Some of these are as follows.

■ In virtually all cases, the trust document declares the objectives of the trust. Generally, these can only be changed by the grantor or, once in receipt of the assets, the beneficiary. The trustee is obligated to invest the funds in accordance with those objectives. For example, if the objective is income until the death of the grantor, then that is the primary consideration in any recommended transaction. Always follow the terms of the trust.

■ Unless specifically stated in the trust document, margin trading is not permitted.

■ In the case of an estate, the terms of the will must be followed.

■ If the investment adviser managing the account is also the trustee or executor, in addi-tion to the normal fiduciary responsibility assumed by all investment advisers, there are the formal requirements of the Uniform Prudent Investors Act (UPIA). That Act is described in detail in Session 20 dealing with retirement plans. "Wearing two hats" is an allowable practice, but not done very often because of the inherent conflict of interest. This, as with all potential conflicts of interest, must be disclosed to the client.

■ There are unique tax considerations, which will be covered in Session 17.

■ In the case of trusts, conflicts between the grantor and the beneficiary may exist; in the case of estates, conflicts among the beneficiaries may arise.

EXAMPLE   A widow was left a trust with her children as contingent beneficiaries. She is to receive income from the trust, and her two children will receive the principal upon her death. To maximize their value, the children ask you to allocate half of the corpus to growth stocks while leaving the balance in bonds for their mother. Because the trust document calls for the widow to receive income, the adviser must pursue that objective and cannot follow the wishes of the children until the trust's assets become theirs.

14. 5   FIDUCIARY ACCOUNTS

In a fiduciary account, the individual granted fiduciary responsibility enters trades for the account, makes all of the investment, management, and distribution decisions, and must manage the account in the owner's best interests.

Examples of fiduciaries include the following:

- **Trustee** designated to administer a trust
- **Executor** designated in a decedent's will to manage the estate's affairs
- **Administrator** appointed by the courts to liquidate the estate of a person who died intestate (without a will), known as an administrator in intestacy
- **Guardian (conservator)** designated by the courts to handle a minor's affairs
- **Custodian** of an UGMA account
- **Receiver** in a bankruptcy
- **Conservator** for an incompetent person

EXAMPLE   The most familiar fiduciary account is a **trust account**, in which money or securities are placed in trust, and someone else manages the account. The manager, or **trustee**, is a fiduciary.

A **fiduciary** is anyone legally appointed and authorized to represent another person, act on that person's behalf, and make decisions necessary to the prudent management of that person's account. A fiduciary cannot use account contents for personal benefit but may be reimbursed for reasonable expenses incurred in managing the account.

TAKE NOTE   Any trades the fiduciary enters must be consistent with the trust's investment objectives.

14. 5. 1   OPENING A FIDUCIARY ACCOUNT

Opening a fiduciary account may require a court certification of the individual's appointment and authority. An account for a trustee must include a trust agreement detailing the limitations placed on the fiduciary. No documentation of custodial rights or court certification is required for an individual to open an UGMA or UTMA account.

14. 5. 2   POWER OF ATTORNEY

If a person who is not named on an account is to have trading authority, the customer must file written authorization with the broker-dealer giving that person access to the account. Without this power in writing, no matter how tempting the answer on the exam, activity in the account cannot be created by anyone other than the account owner(s). Trading authorization usually takes the form of a power of attorney. Two basic types of trading authorizations are **full** and **limited powers of attorney**.

14. 5. 2. 1 Full Power of Attorney

A full power of attorney allows an individual who is not the owner of an account to:

■ deposit or withdraw cash or securities; and/or

■ make investment decisions for the account owner.

14. 5. 2. 2 Limited Power of Attorney

A limited power of attorney allows an individual to have some, but not total, control over an account. The document specifies the level of access the person may exercise.

TEST TOPIC ALERT

Limited power of attorney, also called limited trading authorization, allows entering of buy and sell orders but not the withdrawal of funds. Entry of orders and withdrawal of funds is allowed if full power of attorney is granted.

14. 5. 2. 3 Durable Power of Attorney

A full or limited power may be made "durable" by the grantor of the power. It is designed to provide that a specifically designated person maintains power over the account even upon the grantor's incapacitation, whether due to physical or mental causes. Its most common use is when providing for aging parents. However, upon the death of either principal to the durable power of attorney, the power is terminated.

TEST TOPIC ALERT

A durable power of attorney survives the physical or mental incompetence of the grantor but not the death of either party.

This means that orders received after the time of death of the grantor, even if the purchase or sale was decided upon prior to death, are not accepted.

QUICK QUIZ 14.B

Match each of the following items with the appropriate description below.

A. Executor
B. Irrevocable trust
C. Fiduciary

_____ 1. Person legally appointed to manage and/or hold assets for the benefit of another person

_____ 2. Once established, changes may not be made

_____ 3. Person authorized by law to manage the estate of a decedent

4. Sam Jones has been a successful businessman and is concerned that his youngest daughter will not be able to live within her means. To protect this

from happening, Mr. Jones places a certain sum of money into a trust for the benefit of the daughter. Because Mr. Jones knows he won't live forever, he arranges for the Fidelity Bank and Trust Company to have control over the assets. In this case:

    I.   Sam Jones is the grantor.

    II.   Sam Jones is the trustee.

    III.   Fidelity Bank and Trust Company is the trustee.

    IV.   Sam Jones's daughter is the beneficiary.

    A.   I, III, and IV

    B.   I and III

    C.   II and III

    D.   II, III, and IV

QUICK QUIZ 14.C

Match each type of account with the appropriate description below.

    A.   Partnership account

    B.   TOD

    C.   TIC

    D.   JTWROS

____ 1.   Each party specifies a percentage interest in the account. If one party dies, her interest in the account passes to her estate.

____ 2.   Parties share an undivided interest in the account. If one party dies, his interest passes to the other owner(s) of the account.

____ 3.   The assets in the account become the property of the beneficiary on the death of the account owner without passing through probate.

____ 4.   An unincorporated interest of two or more individuals. A written agreement specifies which individuals can trade the account.

    5.   The most appropriate term to use when referring to a trust that is established upon the death of the grantor is

    A.   revocable trust

    B.   irrevocable trust

    C.   living trust

    D.   testamentary trust

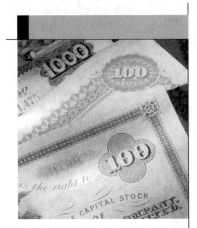

15

Client Profile

An adviser must be familiar with each client's circumstances, financial goals, and needs to formulate suitable investment recommendations. Without suitability information, the account cannot be opened. This is unlike broker-dealers that are permitted to open client accounts without suitability information.

The Series 65 exam will include 4 questions on the material covered in this session.

When you have completed this session, you should be able to:

- **identify** the components of a family balance sheet;

- **contrast** financial and non-financial investment considerations;

- **list** the different goals applicable to investors; and

- **distinguish** between investment objectives and investment constraints.

15. 1   FINANCIAL STATUS

A **financial profile** should include an assessment of the client's:

- current expenditures;
- debt obligations;
- tax status;
- income sources; and
- a balance sheet containing the client's assets, including
  - cash, CDs, and savings accounts (usually looked at as an "emergency fund," generally considered to be a primary requirement for investing in securities),
  - real estate holdings,
  - value and composition of securities holdings,
  - pension and retirement accounts,
  - cash value in life insurance policies, and
  - personal items such as jewelry and automobiles; and
- liabilities, including
  - current debt obligations (credit cards, estimated tax payments, etc.),
  - long-term debt obligations (auto loan, mortgage, etc.),
  - loans against insurance cash value, and
  - loans against 401(k) plan.

Using this information, the adviser will prepare a family balance sheet. This balance sheet reflects all of the client's assets and liabilities in order to determine the overall net worth and liquidity of that client, while a family income statement includes income and expenses and is used to determine the client's cash flow.

Taking into consideration all of this information indicates to the securities professional the extent to which the client is able to make a lump sum investment (the balance sheet shows a large amount of net assets available), and/or periodic investments (the income statement reveals a positive cash flow – there is "money left at the end of the month").

TEST TOPIC ALERT   A family balance sheet only includes assets and liabilities, not income like salary, dividends or interest, or amounts paid for expenses.

15. 2   NONFINANCIAL CONSIDERATIONS

A client's nonfinancial considerations can be more important than the financial information. Relevant nonfinancial information includes the following:

- Age
- Marital status

- Investment experience
- Attitudes and values
- Number and age of dependents
- Employment stability
- Employment of family members
- Demographics (where clients live can affect their investment attitudes)
- Current and future family educational needs
- Current and future family health care needs

15. 2. 1 RISK TOLERANCE

Investor **risk tolerance**—the attitude toward risk and safety—is an important part of a client's profile. Regardless of a person's financial status, the customer's motivation to invest and risk tolerance should shape the portfolio.

Selection of specific types of investments (e.g., stocks, bonds, annuities) depends on three factors:

- Client's objectives
- Amount available for investing (client must use discretionary cash for investing, not the rent money)
- Client's aversion to risk (every investment involves some degree of risk because every investment requires transferring purchasing power from the present to the future and no one knows what the future holds)

To understand a customer's risk tolerance, an adviser should know information such as the following:

- How much of a loss the investor can tolerate (e.g., 5%, 50%, or 100%)
- The liquidity requirements for investments
- The importance of tax considerations
- Investment time horizon, either long-term or short-term
- Investment experience
- Current investment holdings
- Expectations regarding investment returns
- Investment temperament (i.e., is the client bored with stable investments or anxious with volatile ones?)
- Level of tolerance for market fluctuations

A person's risk tolerance is often characterized as either aggressive or conservative.

Aggressive investors are willing to risk greater amounts and withstand market volatility in exchange for the chance to realize substantial returns. An aggressive investor may be willing to sustain losses of 10%, 25%, or even 50% on an investment. **Conservative investors** normally want the relative safety of guaranteed income with low risk to loss of principal. Very conservative investors are unwilling to sustain even modest losses on their investments. There is a full spectrum of risk profiles between these two extremes.

TAKE NOTE
An investor who claims to be aggressive but is unwilling to sustain losses is actually conservative.

A client's tolerance for volatility and risk will often narrow the field of potential investments.

15. 3   FINANCIAL GOALS/OBJECTIVES

Within the parameters determined by a client's circumstances and financial resources, the adviser and client should establish financial goals. The most commonly specified goals include capital preservation, current income, capital growth, and speculation. The objectives behind these goals may be planning for college education, retirement, death, or disability.

However, in attempting to meet these objectives, there may be some obstacles, properly referred to as *investment constraints*, that must be considered. When an investment adviser or IAR prepares a plan for a client, all of these factors are used to prepare an investment policy statement (IPS) we described in the previous session. The following chart may be helpful in your review of objectives and constraints

Investment Policy Statements: Objectives and Constraints

Objectives	Description
Return requirements	Minimum annual income requirements; accumulation amount needed to meet financial goals, and so forth
Risk tolerance	Investor's risk tolerance based on self-evaluation, objective questionnaire, and past experience
Constraints	Description
Time horizon	Time frame in which goals must be attained
Liquidity	What is cash need? For defined-benefit plans, this may be high; for individual retirement plans, this may be low
Taxes	Tax characteristics of investor and desired level of tax management
Laws and regulations	Any legal prohibitions on types of investments or transactions
Unique circumstances and/or preferences	Investor preferences or desires to avoid particular types of assets

15. 3. 1   PRESERVATION OF CAPITAL

Many people are averse to any decline in value of their investments. For such investors, bank insured bonds, CDs, savings accounts, and money market funds offer the safety they seek. However, by reducing market risk (there is little or no market price fluctuation in these instruments), the investor is sacrificing the opportunity for higher income. In addition, as fixed income investments, they are exposed to inflation (purchasing power) risk.

15. 3. 1. 1 Bank Insured Certificates of Deposit (CDs)

In addition to the questions about the jumbo, negotiable CDs that trade in the money market, there are questions on the exam about the certificates of deposit that you can get at your local bank. Here are some points that will help you get the right answer.

- Bank CDs eliminate interest rate risk (their value remains constant, even when interest rates change).

- They are *not* savings accounts with a maturity date.

- They would be included as an asset on a family balance sheet.

- They are the preferred answer when the question asks about a client who wants capital preservation with no risk of loss.

- They are insured by the FDIC up to the current limit (limits are not tested).

- Each bank sets the interest rate it will pay on those CDs with smaller banks typically offering more competitive rates.

TEST TOPIC ALERT   On the exam, the first choice for preservation of capital should always be bank insured CDs. In addition, because they are not marketable (traded in any marketplace), bank CDs (we're referring to the ones retail investors purchase at their local branches—not the jumbo CDs traded in the money market), have no interest rate risk. That is, because their value is fixed, you can always redeem them at face value, regardless of the direction of interest rates. The exam will ignore the fact that there may be a penalty for cashing in before maturity.

15. 3. 2 CURRENT INCOME

Investors seeking current income will normally focus on individual securities or mutual funds that invest in fixed-income investments such as:

- government bonds and notes and agency bonds;

- corporate bonds and notes;

- preferred stock; and

- utility company stock.

Not all income-producing investments are the same. U.S Treasury issues carry the guarantee of the United States and, at least as far as we (and the exam) are concerned, have no default risk. Government agency bonds are only slightly less safe, and few would lose sleep worrying about AAA corporate bonds failing to meet their obligations. All this safety comes at a cost. Based on the risk/reward principle, assuming low risk rewards one with a low return. On the other end of the spectrum are bonds of corporations with very low credit ratings (the high-yield, or junk, bonds). These bonds tend to yield high, if somewhat uneven, income with principal subject to credit (default) risk. The principle here is the same risk/reward; higher risk, greater potential rewards.

In choosing between income-producing investments, the time the investor expects to remain in the holding is a primary consideration. If the client will likely need to use the money invested in less than two years, a money market mutual fund would likely offer a positive return on investment with no fluctuation of principal and ready access to the money through check-writing privileges. Alternatively, the investor might wish to allocate a portion of the funds to T-bills and T-notes. If the client can afford to remain in the investment for 5–10 years, a corporate bond would produce much greater returns. In the three- to five-year range, an intermediate-term government bond can provide relative safety of principal and a competitive interest rate.

15. 3. 3   CAPITAL GROWTH

Stock investments generally provide a means to preserve and increase the buying power of an investor's money over and above the inflation rate. Although subject to short-term volatility, the equity market tends to provide higher investment returns over time.

As with income, the term *growth* refers to a broad spectrum of investments. Aggressive growth stocks may be very appropriate for a person with a very high tolerance for risk and the ability to remain invested for many years. At the other end of the spectrum are large capitalization stock funds that invest in some of the largest and most respected companies. These funds may be a better choice for older investors, who may need to liquidate the investment in three to five years, or investors who are more comfortable knowing they have invested in a fund that is less risky.

15. 3. 4   SPECULATION

A customer may want to speculate with a portion of their investments. Speculative investments offer the opportunity to earn substantial returns but carry a commensurate amount of risk. Speculative investments may include:

- highly volatile stocks;
- high-yield (junk) bonds;
- options on stocks or stock indexes; and
- commodity futures.

15. 3. 5   COLLEGE TUITION

In addition to other types of investments, investors planning for college tuition often invest in zero-coupon bonds that mature when the tuition expenses are due. It may be advisable to establish college tuition investment programs such as Coverdell ESAs (formerly known as Education IRAs) and Section 529 plans because of their tax advantages.

15. 3. 6 RETIREMENT

In determining a client's retirement needs, Social Security, company pensions, retirement savings accounts, and insurance (as well as investments outside of a retirement planning framework) should all be considered.

The earlier an individual begins to save for retirement, the more time the investment assets are able to grow. A long-term retirement planning time horizon may enable an investor to assume additional risk in the portfolio, generally through equities. This helps a client accumulate significant funds to support a long retirement period. As life expectancy has risen, the topic of decumulation has come into focus. How do we make sure that the money accumulated lasts long enough? One way to minimize longevity risk is through the purchase of annuities (fixed, index, and variable) because payout is guaranteed for life. In fact, there is a specialized annuity product known as the longevity annuity, or deferred income annuity, designed specifically to cover that risk.

15. 3. 7 DEATH BENEFITS

Because death can eliminate a family's primary income earner and cause a possible substantial estate tax liability, life insurance is an important component of customer portfolios. Family businesses are often lost as a result of estate taxes insufficiently covered by insurance.

TEST TOPIC ALERT

For test purposes, younger people with children are better off purchasing term insurance because the lower premiums allow significantly more protection. For those age 60 and older, the rates are generally prohibitive.

TEST TOPIC ALERT

In those cases where the estate does have liquid assets such as stocks and bonds, life insurance still may serve a valuable need in that these income producing assets will not have to be sold to cover the estate tax liability or other final expenses.

15. 3. 7. 1 Capital Needs Analysis

A capital needs analysis is used to determine how much life insurance is necessary to meet future needs. At minimum, life insurance coverage should provide for:

- payoff of the client's mortgage and other debts;
- income for the survivor(s) for a reasonable time;
- college tuition; and
- estate taxes if the taxable estate will exceed $5.43 million in 2015.

There are several factors that are used in the computation to evaluate how much is necessary to meet these needs. First, we try to project the client's future earnings. Then, we estimate life expectancy and, of course, we must account for inflation. Because the death benefit in a life insurance policy is generally a fixed amount, we are not concerned about market volatility. Finally, we look at existing assets, such as savings and investments, including those which offer tax deferrals such as IRAs and employer-sponsored plans.

15. 3. 8   DISABILITY

Should a client become disabled, there are three possible sources of replacement income: workers' compensation, Social Security, and disability insurance.

Workers' Compensation. If an employee is injured on the job, workers' compensation can provide protection to cover medical expenses, replace lost income, and provide death benefits to the family. Although the worker's compensation benefits in some states (benefits vary from state to state) are quite generous, payments are made only when the disability results from a work related injury.

Social Security. Like other Social Security benefits, a worker's disability benefit will depend on a number of factors, such as age and income. However, in order to receive payments, you must meet their strict definition of disabled which is:

You must not be able to engage in any substantial gainful activity (SGA) because of a medically-determinable physical or mental impairment(s):

- That is expected to result in death, or
- That has lasted or is expected to last for a continuous period of at least 12 months.

Disability Insurance. Because workers' compensation only covers in limited cases and because Social Security's definition of disabled is relatively strict, most agree that it is wise to purchase a private disability insurance policy. Waiting and benefit periods can be adjusted based on the client's needs and finances.. The amount of insurance can be determined by the information derived from the client's income, assets, and occupation. Many clients are covered under group medical, disability, and life insurance programs supported fully or in part by employers.

15. 3. 9   TAX PLANNING

A client's tax situation is often an important factor in determining suitable investments. Taxes may be reduced by using the following three strategies: asset and income shifting, tax deferral, or tax-free income.

Asset and Income Shifting. A client can shift investment assets and income to a person in a lower tax bracket. Until early 2006, it was common to place income-producing assets in the name of a child aged 14 or older to avoid the "kiddie" tax, but since it now includes all children under age 19 and full-time students under age 24, the practice has lost much of its luster. However, with many of today's baby boomers supporting elderly parents, placing those assets in the parent's name will remove the income from your client and let the parent receive the income directly with little or no tax liability. As mentioned previously, trusts may also be used to shift assets and income.

Tax Deferral. Contributions to a qualified retirement plan or tax-sheltered annuity are not taxed until withdrawn. Investing funds that have not been taxed allows a substantially larger portion of the investor's money to earn income or capital gains, also not taxed until withdrawn.

Tax-Free Income. Most municipal bonds pay interest that is free from federal taxation, although they are generally subject to state income tax unless issued in the taxpayer's state of residence. Municipal bonds generally pay a lower interest rate than taxable bonds but, depending on the investor's tax bracket, may result in higher returns on an after-tax basis.

TAKE NOTE

Although interest income from municipal bonds is tax free, capital gains are fully taxable. Capital gains occur when the bond is sold for a price that is greater than the investor's cost basis (investment) in the bond. This is also true of capital gains distributions from municipal bond mutual funds. While the income distributions may be tax-free, capital gains from any source are always taxable. Other potential sources of tax-free earnings are Section 529 plans, Roth IRAs, and Coverdell ESAs.

15. 3. 10 TIME HORIZON

An investor's time horizon and liquidity needs will determine the level of volatility the client should assume. Over a 20- or 30-year time frame, dramatic short-term volatility is acceptable, even to those who are risk averse. Money that will be needed within three to five years should be invested for safety and liquidity. Time horizon is a particularly important investment constraint when planning for college education and for retirement.

TEST TOPIC ALERT

The longer the time horizon, the more market risk the account can accept and vice versa.

QUICK QUIZ 15.A

1. A married couple is 55 and 57 years old. The older of the two plans to retire at 62 and the younger at 65, and both are healthy. What is the most appropriate estimate of the time horizon for their retirement portfolio?

   A. 5 years
   B. 7 years
   C. 8 years
   D. More than 20 years

2. An individual's net worth is

    A. the difference between the individual's assets and the individual's liabilities

    B. best determined by examining the individual's personal income statement

    C. largely irrelevant in identifying the individual's investment objectives

    D. another term for discretionary income

3. In designing an investment portfolio for a new client, one of the first things to do is determine the client's

    A. home address

    B. Social Security or tax ID number

    C. risk tolerance

    D. beneficiary

4. An 83-year-old widower explains to you that he is risk averse and wishes to find an investment that will provide him with preservation of capital. Which of the following might you recommend?

    A. an index fund

    B. bank-insured CDs

    C. long-term U.S. government bonds

    D. preferred stock

Quick Quiz answers can be found at the end of the unit.

15. 3. 11 LIFE CYCLE CONSIDERATIONS

An investor's goals may change over time. This is especially true as investors move from one phase of life to another. For example, a young couple may have a primary goal of funding a child's education. Later, the same family, having provided for their children's education, may turn their attention to the aggressive accumulation of wealth, perhaps to provide for an early retirement or a dream home. Upon retirement, this couple may need to move toward income-producing investments. Income and net worth change over time, as do investment goals and life cycle considerations. Because the adviser's responsibility to know his client is ongoing, the account form should be updated regularly to reflect the client's new goals and financial considerations.

As the baby boomer generation reaches retirement age, the regulators have increased their focus on protecting senior investors. Among the suggested practices is to take detailed notes of conversations and, when it becomes apparent that the client is not grasping as well as before, recommend that a family member or other competent person participate in all discussions.

TEST TOPIC ALERT

The following chart summarizes common investor objectives and appropriate recommendations. Be ready for a significant number of situational questions that require determining the best solution for the investor.

Investor Objective	Suitable Recommendation
Preservation of capital; safety	Insured bank CDs, money market instruments or funds, T-bills
Growth ■ Balanced/moderate growth ■ Aggressive growth	Common stock or common stock mutual funds ■ Large-cap stocks, defensive stocks ■ Technology stocks, sector funds, or cyclical stocks
Income ■ Greatest safety ■ Tax-free income ■ High-yield income ■ From a stock portfolio	Bonds (but not zero-coupons) ■ U.S. Government bonds ■ Municipal bonds or municipal bond funds ■ Corporate bonds or corporate bond funds ■ Preferred stock and utility stocks
Liquidity	Money market funds ■ (DPPs, real estate, and annuities are not considered liquid)
Speculation	Volatile stocks, high-yield bonds, stock/index options

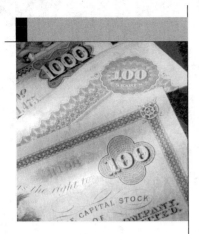

16

Portfolio Management Styles, Strategies, and Techniques

Portfolio managers use a range of investment styles and strategies. Although each style attempts to generate superior investment returns and reduce investment risks, no single style is suited to every investor. Often, an investment adviser's role is to guide clients toward a mutual fund or private money manager that is consistent with the client's objectives and temperament.

The session will conclude with a look at some of the techniques used by the various styles and strategies discussed.

The Series 65 exam will include 11 questions from this session.

When you have completed this session, you should be able to:

■ **list** the major asset classes used in an asset allocation program;

■ **explain** the difference between active and passive management styles;

■ **compute** a rebalancing problem;

■ **name** the three major levels of market capitalization;

■ **compare** the three techniques for minimizing interest rate risk;

■ **compute** the expected return using the security market line;

■ **identify** the three components of the Efficient Market Hypothesis;

■ **illustrate** how dollar cost averaging results in lowering an investor's average cost per share;

■ **explain** the logic behind sector rotating; and

■ **summarize** the risk reduction benefits of diversification.

16. 1 ASSET ALLOCATION

Asset allocation (more accurately, but rarely stated, asset class allocation) refers to the spreading of portfolio funds among different asset classes. Proponents of asset allocation feel that the mix of assets within a portfolio, rather than individual stock selection or marketing timing, is the primary factor underlying the variability of returns in portfolio performance. There are three major types (each with subclasses) of asset classes:

- Stock, with subclasses based on market capitalization, value versus growth, and foreign equity
- Bonds, with subclasses based on maturity (intermediate versus long-term), and issuer (Treasury versus corporate versus non-U.S. issuers)
- Cash, focusing mainly on the standard risk-free investment, the 90-day Treasury bill, but also including other short-term money market instruments

In some instances, tangible assets, such as real estate (usually in the form of REITs), precious metals and other commodities, and certain collectibles (think fine art), are part of the asset allocation because these types of assets tend to reduce inflation risk. Increasingly, institutional investors (and some very high net worth individuals due to the high cost of entry) are using such alternative investment asset classes as hedge funds, private equity, and venture capital.

16. 1. 1 STRATEGIC ASSET ALLOCATION

Strategic asset allocation refers to the proportion of various types of investments composing a long-term investment portfolio.

EXAMPLE

A standard asset allocation model suggests subtracting a person's age from 100 to determine the percentage of the portfolio to be invested in stocks. According to this method, a 30-year-old would be 70% invested in stocks and 30% in bonds and cash; a 70-year-old would be invested 30% in stocks with the remainder in bonds and cash.

16. 1. 1. 1 Rebalancing

A portfolio is **rebalanced** to bring the asset mix back to the target allocations. If the stock market should perform better than expected, the client's proportion of stocks to bonds would be out of balance. So, on some timely basis (perhaps quarterly), stocks would be sold and bonds would be purchased (or funds would be placed in cash) to bring the proportions back to the desired levels.

EXAMPLE

Using the 70% equity/30% debt model described above, the investor's initial investment of $100,000 is split $70,000 into equity securities and $30,000 into debt securities. Let's say the account is to be rebalanced semiannually. Because of a bull market in stocks, six months later, the account value is $120,000. Analysis of the account indicates that the value of the equities is now $90,000, whereas the bonds have remained stable at $30,000. To rebalance—that is, to bring the account back to the 70/30 ratio—it will be necessary to sell $6,000 of the equity and invest those funds into debt. That will make the account $84,000 equity and $36,000 debt, our desired 70/30 ratio. The effect of this is that stocks are sold in a rising market and purchased in a falling market, following the old adage of "buy low and sell high."

16. 1. 1. 1. 1 Constant Ratio Plan

An investment plan that attempts to maintain the type of relationship shown in our example between debt and equity securities (or other asset classes) is sometimes called a constant ratio plan. Periodically, the account is rebalanced to bring it back to the desired ratio.

16. 1. 1. 1. 2 Constant Dollar Plan

Under this investment plan, the goal is to maintain a constant dollar amount in stocks, moving money in and out of a money market fund when necessary. Using the last example, if the investor had a goal of a constant dollar of $70,000 in stock, the other $30,000 would be placed into a money market fund. When the stock value rose to $90,000, $20,000 would be liquidated and placed into the money market account. At this point, the account would have the desired $70,000 in stock and now have $50,000 in money markets. If the stock value should drop to $55,000, the money market fund would be tapped for $15,000 to get back to the $70,000 constant dollar.

16. 1. 2 TACTICAL ASSET ALLOCATION

Tactical asset allocation refers to short-term portfolio adjustments that adjust the portfolio mix between asset classes in consideration of current market conditions.

EXAMPLE

If the stock market is expected to do well over the near term, a portfolio manager may allocate greater portions of a portfolio to stocks. If the market is expected to decline, the portfolio manager may allocate greater portions of the portfolio entirely to bonds and cash.

16. 2   ACTIVE AND PASSIVE MANAGEMENT STYLES

16. 2. 1   ACTIVE MANAGEMENT

An active portfolio manager, using a particular stock selection approach, buys and sells individual stocks. **Active management** relies on the manager's stock picking and *market timing* ability to outperform market indexes. Market timing is the strategy of making buy or sell decisions, generally regarding stocks, by attempting to predict future price movements. Usually, the focus is on timing the overall market rather than a specific security.

EXAMPLE   An active portfolio manager may position the portfolio in stocks within a few market sectors (such as pharmaceuticals and technology) frequently trading in and out of the stocks. An active manager may change the sector focus to capitalize on relative performance of different sectors during different stages of the business cycle.

16. 2. 2   PASSIVE MANAGEMENT

A **passive portfolio manager** believes that no particular management style will consistently outperform market averages and therefore constructs a portfolio that mirrors a market index, such as the S&P 500. Passive portfolio management seeks low-cost means of generating consistent, long-term returns with minimal turnover.

TEST TOPIC ALERT   For purposes of the examination, passive portfolio management is very similar to strategic asset allocation. The same could be said about the relationship between active management and tactical asset allocation. Furthermore, you may be asked about the relative commission expense when comparing active and passive management. It should be obvious that the more active the portfolio, the greater role commissions will play in determining overall portfolio performance.

16. 2. 2. 1   Buy and Hold

The **buy and hold technique** can be used with any investment style. A buy and hold manager rarely trades in the portfolio, which results in lower transaction costs and long-term capital gains taxes. A low expense ratio in a mutual fund often may reflect a buy and hold approach. This is the classic passive strategy used by investors for many years and is probably the easiest of all to implement and follow.

With this strategy, there is always the question, "when do I sell?" As with most investment strategies, there are varying opinions. On an individual investor level, one of the most common reasons for unloading a position is a change in objectives. This is certainly true as one ages, or if one has a windfall, such as an inheritance. Of course, if there is a personal financial need, the asset will be sold to provide the necessary funds. Portfolio managers using this style may sell when the stock's fundamentals have weakened, such as a sharp decrease in earnings, or a change in the competitive arena (think of what digital cameras did to Kodak). Another case would be when the company's price to earnings ratio (P/E) has reached levels well above those for its competitors.

TEST TOPIC ALERT

Maybe you've owned a car that was, so to speak, a lemon. That generally means that you had high maintenance costs. Well, one point to know about the buy and hold style is that it is just the opposite—it is low maintenance.

16. 2. 2. 2 Indexing

Investment portfolios constructed to mirror the components of a particular stock index, such as the S&P 500, will normally perform in line with the index. Because such portfolios are not actively managed, the costs of managing the portfolio are relatively low. With less frequent portfolio turnover, these funds have lower transaction costs and tend to be more tax efficient. Because most professional money managers are unable to consistently outperform market indexes, indexed mutual fund portfolios are a popular investment vehicle for investors. With the advent of index funds and ETFs, this has become a very popular passive strategy.

16. 3 GROWTH VS. VALUE

One of the longest running arguments in investment analysis is, "which is more successful, the growth style or the value style?" The father of value investing was Benjamin Graham and his text Security Analysis (co-authored with David Dodd) is still widely read today. The exam won't ask you about Graham and Dodd, but will want you to know the essential features of both styles.

16. 3. 1 GROWTH STYLE

Portfolio managers using the **growth** style of portfolio management focus on stocks of companies whose earnings are growing faster than most other stocks and are expected to continue to do so. Because rapid growth in earnings is often priced into the stocks, growth investment managers are likely to buy stocks that are at the high end of their 52-week price range. Therefore, in the eyes of some, they might be buying stocks that are overvalued.

TEST TOPIC ALERT

Growth managers are looking for **earnings momentum**.

16. 3. 2 VALUE

Portfolio managers using the **value** style of management concentrate on undervalued or out-of-favor securities whose price is low relative to the company's earnings or book value and whose earnings prospects are believed to be unattractive by investors and securities analysts. In fact, sometimes value managers think they can find a bargain with companies that are currently operating at a loss (no earnings, hence no P/E ratio). Value investment managers seek to buy undervalued securities before the company reports positive earnings surprises. Their primary source of information is the company's financial statements. Value investment managers are more likely to buy stocks that are at the bottom of their 52-week price range.

TEST TOPIC ALERT

In addition to the pricing models expressed above, growth managers expect to see high P/E ratios (price to earnings ratios) with little or no dividends. On the other hand, value managers expect to see a low P/E ratio and dividends offering a reasonable yield. Another sign of a value stock is a large cash surplus, sometimes referred to as a rainy day fund.

EXAMPLE

ABC Co. is a metal processor for parts used in the automotive industry. Earnings per share have grown by a compounded rate of 8% per year for the past 15 years but are somewhat susceptible to downturns in the economy. The stock has paid a quarterly dividend that has increased five times in the past 10 years and the current market price of the stock is 6 times earnings. Conservatively managed, the company owns assets and cash that exceed the market value of its common stock. ABC would be attractive to *value* investors because its intrinsic value is higher than its market value, it appears to pay liberal dividends, and it is selling for a low earnings multiple.

16. 4 OTHER PORTFOLIO MANAGEMENT STYLES

In addition to those already described, there are several other styles you should be familiar with.

16. 4. 1 MARKET CAPITALIZATION

Another portfolio management style is using market capitalization to influence security selection. Although the boundaries are imprecise, micro-cap companies are generally those with a market capitalization of less than $300 million; small-cap companies are generally those with a market capitalization of between $300 and $2 billion; mid-cap companies are those with $2 billion to $10 billion; and large-cap companies are those with more than $10 billion.

It is generally assumed that small companies with a short history, small product line, and limited financial resources represent a larger degree of risk in an economic downturn. As revenues, product diversification, and financial worth increase, the relative risk the company carries in a weak economy diminishes.

TEST TOPIC ALERT

Look out for numbers written in long form. For example, where would you categorize a stock with a market capitalization of $5,000,000,000? Were you able to fight through all of those zeroes to see that this is $5 billion and is a mid-cap security?

TAKE NOTE

In a strong economy, small, fast-moving companies with a concentrated product line in a fast-growing sector can dramatically outperform larger, more bureaucratic companies.

16. 4. 2 CONTRARIAN

A contrarian is an investment manager who takes positions opposite of that of other managers or in opposition to general market beliefs. In essence these managers buy when everyone else is selling and sell when everyone else is buying.

16. 4. 3 INCOME VS. CAPITAL APPRECIATION

At first glance, this might appear to be a rehashing of growth versus value and, although there are some similarities, you should be aware of what each of these styles represents

16. 4. 3. 1 Income

As the term implies, the income style focuses on generating portfolio income. When dividends on common stock offer better income opportunities than interest on debt securities, the portfolio will be overweight in that direction. Frequently, the search for income will lead the portfolio manager to foreign securities and/or high yield bonds. When recommending a manager using this style, it is important to evaluate the risks being taken to provide income. For the most part, an income style relies heavily on debt securities.

Most of the substance of the exam will deal with strategies employed in equity investing, but you may be asked about several popular strategies used by bond buyers. Primarily, the goal in all of these strategies is to mitigate the effects of interest rate fluctuations on the value of the principal, the income received, or both. Three in particular are

■ the barbell strategy;
■ the bullet strategy; and
■ the laddering strategy.

All three of these are considered active rather than passive, and we will look at them individually.

16. 4. 3. 1. 1 Barbells

Envision a barbell—what do you see? A thin bar with heavy weights of equal size on each end. That's what a bond portfolio using the barbell strategy looks like. The investor purchases bonds maturing in one or two years and an equal amount maturing in 10 (or more) years with no bonds in between.

Assuming a normal yield curve, the long-term end of the barbell contains bonds offering the higher long-term interest rates, while the short-term end provides you with soon to be realized cash (as they mature) that may be reinvested at higher rates if that is the direction the market takes. This is not a passive strategy like buy and hold—you will be actively buying new bonds as the old ones get closer to maturity.

16. 4. 3. 1. 2 Bullets

For what do you use a bullet? You use it to hit a target, and that is the concept behind the bullet strategy. Let's say the target is funds for a child's college education, and the child is currently six years old. This strategy would have the investor purchase bonds today that mature in 12 years (assuming college starting when the child is 18). Two years from now, the investor should purchase some more bonds, but those should have a 10-year maturity. In another two years, another purchase is made, this time of bonds that have eight years to go, and so forth. A picture of this strategy would reveal bonds purchased at different times but all maturing at the same time. This tends to allow the investor to capture current interest rates as they change rather than having the entire portfolio locked into one rate.

16. 4. 3. 1. 3 Ladders

Picture a ladder. You see rungs at set intervals going from bottom to top. That is the concept behind a laddered portfolio. Unlike the bullet strategy described previously where the bonds are bought at different times but all mature together, in a laddered strategy, the bonds are all purchased at the same time but mature at different times (like the steps on the ladder). As the shorter maturities come due, they are reinvested and now become the long-term ones. This has also been a very common strategy with those purchasing CDs at their local bank.

16. 4. 3. 2 Capital Appreciation

Capital appreciation can take several forms, from moderate to aggressive. Although growth stocks will frequently be found in these portfolios, the hunt for appreciation will also involve options and/or futures, special situation stocks (potential takeover or merger candidates), futures, IPOs, and day trading. When recommending a manager using this style, it is critical to determine where on the risk scale, from lower to moderate to speculative, this manager's philosophy is. Then, and only then, can you attempt to match it with your clients.

QUICK QUIZ 16.A   Matching

    A. Indexing
    B. Growth investing
    C. Value investing
    D. Tactical asset allocation
    E. Strategic asset allocation

____   1. Balancing portfolio assets for the long term

____   2. Selecting companies currently out of favor on the basis of earnings prospects

____   3. Constructing a portfolio to mirror the performance of the S&P 500

____   4. Constructing a portfolio of companies that are outperforming most other stocks in that industry

____   5. Involves short-term adjustments to portfolio asset class mix

Quick Quiz answers can be found at the end of the unit.

16. 5 CAPITAL MARKET THEORY

There are several capital market theories, all with the goal of maximizing returns while minimizing risks.

16. 5. 1 CAPITAL ASSET PRICING MODEL (CAPM)

CAPM is a securities market investment theory that attempts to derive the expected return on an asset on the basis of the asset's systematic risk. It was William Sharpe who first formulated the CAPM in the 1960s. The basic premise is that every investment carries two distinct risks; systematic, which cannot be diversified away, and unsystematic risk, which can be mitigated through appropriate diversification. As a result of this work, and its further refinements, Professor Sharpe was awarded the Nobel Prize in Economics in 1990 (that isn't tested). You will see several applications of the CAPM in upcoming paragraphs.

16. 5. 2 MODERN PORTFOLIO THEORY

Modern portfolio theory is an approach that attempts to quantify and control portfolio risk. It differs from a traditional securities analysis in that it emphasizes determining the relationship between risk and reward in the total portfolio rather than analyzing specific securities. This is derived from the **capital asset pricing model (CAPM)**, which states that the pricing of a stock must take into account two types of risks: systematic and unsystematic. Under the CAPM, the investor should be rewarded for the risks taken so it is proper to assume that the higher the risk, the higher the return.

Instead of emphasizing particular stocks, **modern portfolio theory (MPT)** focuses on the relationships among all the investments in a portfolio. This theory holds that specific risk can be diversified away by building portfolios of assets whose returns are not correlated.

MPT diversification allows investors to reduce the risk in a portfolio while simultaneously increasing expected returns.

Holding securities that tend to move in the same direction as one another does not lower an investor's risk. Diversification reduces risk only when assets whose prices move inversely, or at different times, in relation to each other are combined.

Harry Markowitz, founder of MPT, explained how to best assemble a diversified portfolio and proved that such a portfolio would likely do well. He proved that, all factors being equal, the portfolio with the least amount of volatility would do better than one with a greater amount of volatility.

TEST TOPIC ALERT

The CAPM is used to provide an expected return on a security or portfolio based on the level of risk.

This is sometimes referred to as designing the optimal portfolio. An **optimal portfolio** is one that returns the highest rate of return consistent with the amount of risk an investor is willing to take. In other words, an optimal portfolio is the portfolio that makes the best trade-off between risk and reward for a given investor's investment profile.

16. 5. 2. 1   Efficient Portfolios/Efficient Frontier

The goal of modern portfolio theory is to construct the most efficient portfolio. One selects the efficient set from the feasible set. The feasible set of portfolios represents all portfolios that can be constructed from a given set of equities. An efficient portfolio is one that offers:

- the most return for a given amount of risk; or
- the least risk for a given amount of return.

The collection of efficient portfolios is called the efficient set or efficient frontier. This efficient frontier is plotted as a curve. The objective is for the portfolio to lie on the curve. Then, by being on the efficient frontier, the optimal portfolio has been created. Any portfolio that is below the curve (not an efficient one) is said to be taking too much risk for too little return.

16. 5. 3   CAPITAL MARKET LINE

One of the offshoots of the CAPM is the capital market line (CML). The CML provides an expected return based on the level of risk. The equation for the CML uses the:

- expected return of the portfolio;
- risk-free rate;

■ return on the market;

■ standard deviation of the market; and

■ standard deviation of the portfolio.

TEST TOPIC ALERT   Please note that alpha and beta are not used in the CML equation while standard deviation is.

The CML provides an expected return for a portfolio based on the expected return of the market, the risk-free rate of return, and the standard deviation of the portfolio in relation to the standard deviation of the market. The CML is generally used to evaluate diversified portfolios. The security market line (SML), which is derived from the CML, allows us to evaluate individual securities for use in a diversified portfolio.

In focusing on a specific asset, the SML uses the following:

■ The expected return for the asset

■ The risk-free rate

■ The return on the market

■ The beta of the asset

The security market line determines the expected return for a security on the basis of its beta and the expectations about the market and the risk-free rate. Basically, we want to determine how much over the risk-free rate we should earn for taking the investment risk.

EXAMPLE   If the beta of ABC Company is 1.2 and the market return is expected to be 13% with a risk-free return of 3%, then the expected return of ABC is 15%, as follows:

We begin with the risk-free rate and then multiply the expected return in excess of that rate by the stock's beta.

3% + 1.2(13% − 3%) = 3% + 1.2(10%) = 3% + 12% = 15%

Therefore, on the basis of the level of systematic risk of ABC Company, it should earn a return of 15%. The SML helps identify how the characteristics of a portfolio will be impacted when a security is added to the portfolio.

16. 5. 4 MONTE CARLO SIMULATIONS

Monte Carlo simulation (MCS) is a risk analysis technique in which probable future events are simulated on a computer, generating estimated rates of return.

MCSs, for example, can be used to randomly generate the behaviors of various asset classes to obtain the range of possible outcomes for a portfolio.

MCSs are well suited to addressing:

- situations where no real-world data exist;
- problems with unknown variables; and
- problems for which no analytical solution exists.

MCSs are commonly used in personal financial planning for wealth forecasting with estimated cash flows.

EXAMPLE   A client might want to know how long a portfolio will last in retirement, or what the odds are that a portfolio will be depleted before he dies.

If there were no cash flows into or out of the portfolio, the time frame was long enough, and we could be assured of receiving the historical average returns for each asset class, it would be fairly easy to forecast the future value of a portfolio without resorting to MCSs. In such an example, we are only solving for the terminal value of the portfolio, so the sequence of returns does not matter.

For an individual entering retirement, the timing of the cash flows out of the portfolio and the sequence of returns are critical.

EXAMPLE   Consider two clients, Mr. Jones and Ms. Smith. Both enter retirement with $1 million, both withdraw $50,000 per year from their portfolios, and both portfolios generate an average return of 10% over the life of the portfolios. Their yearly results are the same, but they come in different sequences. Mr. Jones experiences 15 up years followed by 5 down years. Ms. Smith experiences 5 down years followed by 15 up years. Mr. Jones will be better off than Ms. Smith, because Ms. Smith will deplete her portfolio in the early years, and hence her portfolio will not benefit fully from the positive return years down the line.

The concept of ill-timed cash flows may be easy for experienced advisers to grasp, but it is not one that clients readily understand. Through the use of MCSs, advisers can easily generate charts and graphs to educate clients about sequential return issues.

16. 5. 5 EFFICIENT MARKET HYPOTHESIS

The **efficient market hypothesis** maintains that security prices adjust rapidly to new information with security prices fully reflecting all available information. In other words, markets are efficiently priced as a result. This is sometimes referred to as the **random walk theory**. The random walk theory would suggest that throwing darts at the stock listings is as good a method as any for selecting stocks for investment.

Eugene F. Fama, (announced as a co-winner of the Nobel Prize for economics shortly before publication of this edition), coined the term in a 1965 *Financial Analysts Journal* article entitled "Random Walks in Stock Market Prices":

> In an efficient market, competition among the many intelligent participants leads to a situation where, at any point in time, actual prices of individual securities already reflect the effects of information based both on events that have already occurred and on events which, as of now, the market expects to take place in the future. In other words, in an efficient market at any point in time, the actual price of a security will be a good estimate of its intrinsic value.

There are three versions of the EMH based upon the level of available information. The more information available, the more likely it is that you should be able to beat the market. But, as we will see, under this theory the conclusion is, that under all circumstances, there is no way to accurately predict stock prices, and a passive strategy is probably the most suitable for investment success.

16. 5. 5. 1   Weak-Form Market Efficiency

The weak form of the efficient markets hypothesis (EMH) states that current security prices *fully reflect all currently available security market data*. Thus, past price and volume (market) information will have no predictive power about the future direction of security prices because price changes will be independent from one period to the next. In a weak-form efficient market, an investor cannot achieve positive risk-adjusted returns on average by using technical analysis.

16. 5. 5. 2   Semi-Strong Form Market Efficiency

The semi-strong form of the EMH holds that security prices rapidly adjust without bias to the arrival of all new public information. As such, current security prices *fully reflect all publicly available information*. The semi-strong form says security prices include all past security market information and nonmarket information available to the public. The implication is that an investor cannot achieve positive risk-adjusted returns on average by using fundamental analysis. Therefore, it could be said that fundamental analysts are relying on beating weak-form EMH.

16. 5. 5. 3   Strong-Form Market Efficiency

The strong form of the EMH states that security prices *fully reflect all information from both public and private sources*. The strong form includes all types of information: past security market, public, and private (inside) information. This means that no group of investors has monopolistic access to information relevant to the formation of prices, and none should be able to consistently achieve positive abnormal returns.

Although some would disagree, the prevailing opinion is that the only thing that will work in this case is random walk— just throwing darts because the market is totally efficient with market prices quickly adjusting to reflect new information.

TAKE NOTE

According to the EMH, if a financial market is weakly efficient, technical analysis will be useless, but it is still possible to use fundamental analysis to seek out mispriced investments. On the other hand, if a financial market is semi-strongly efficient, there is no point in using any fundamental analysis tools—all of that information is already in the hands of all investors. If a financial market is strongly efficient, then everything, including information generally only available to insiders is known and, without an edge, there is no benefit to be gained by using any analytical tools.

TAKE NOTE

As a base level knowledge of the EMH, you should know that the weak form is based on past security market information; the semi-strong form is based on all public information (including market information); and the strong form is based on both public information and inside or private information.

The following chart may help you with EMH.

The Three Forms of EHM

Form	Won't Work	Will Work
Weak	Technical Analysis	Fundamental analysis and Insider information
Semi-strong	Technical and Fundamental analysis	Insider information
Strong	Technical and Fundamental analysis and Insider information	Random Walk

TEST TOPIC ALERT

You may have to know that there is no such term as **semi-weak** EMH. Can't imagine what would be weaker than **weak** anyway.

QUICK QUIZ 16.B

1. Followers of the efficient market hypothesis believe that
   A. following the business cycle is the best way to maximize returns
   B. concentration rather than diversification will produce superior returns
   C. by following the pundits on TV, you'll wind up rich
   D. an efficient market is one that produces random results

2. You have a client who has recently retired. A pressing question is, "How much can be withdrawn without running out of money?" One of the popular techniques for approximating an answer is by using
   A. dollar cost averaging
   B. Monte Carlo simulations
   C. LIBOR approximations
   D. portfolio rebalancing

3. The expected return on the market is 15%, the risk-free rate is 8%, and the beta for Stock A is 1.2. Compute the rate of return that would be expected (required) on this stock.

    A. 7%
    B. 8.4%
    C. 16.4%
    D. 18%

16. 6 PORTFOLIO MANAGEMENT TECHNIQUES

The term diversification has been used many times already in this manual. The term is a common one in our everyday life, not restricted to investing. As a technique in portfolio management, **portfolio diversification** (i.e., committing to an array of separate investments) reduces unsystematic risk, such as business risk, and enhances returns. The securities in a diversified portfolio are selected, in part, because they do not tend to move up or down in relation to each other; when some go down, the loss is offset by those that rise. That the concept we covered with correlation coefficient. This kind of diversification is enhanced by the addition of foreign securities to a portfolio because they are usually not highly correlated with domestic equity.

There are many ways to classify investment and financial products. The investment pyramid, for example, categorizes products according to their risk and return potential. Another way is to group similar products into specific classes. These classes are generally defined as the following:

■ **Cash and cash equivalents**—passbook savings and checking accounts; money-market accounts; money-market funds; certificates of deposit; T-bills

■ **Fixed-income investments**—corporate bonds; municipal bonds; Treasury bonds; bond funds; mortgage-backed securities

■ **Equities**—preferred and common stocks of all kinds: growth, income appreciation; stock mutual funds

■ **Hard assets**—real estate, collectibles, precious metals, and stones

Each of these asset classes, as a whole, responds differently to different types of risk; therefore, diversifying or allocating investment resources among these classes is a proven way to reduce risk overall, dampen volatility, and improve the performance of one's portfolio. Fixed-income products, for example, are a hedge against deflation; equities are a hedge against inflation. To minimize market risk, one could diversify among all four asset categories (with additional diversification within the equities category). To minimize interest rate risk, one could diversify within the fixed-income category by staggering bond maturity dates. To minimize business risk, one could allocate among the four categories and purchase mutual funds. To reduce liquidity risk, one would keep a sufficient portion of assets in cash or cash equivalent assets.

16. 6. 1 DIVERSIFYING WITHIN ASSET CATEGORIES

Diversification is not a synonym for asset allocation. For example, an aggressive young professional may invest almost exclusively in common stock. That would be a single asset class. But, within that asset class of common stock, the portfolio might consist the shares of a dozen or more different companies in varied industries.

16. 6. 2 DIVERSIFYING WITHIN ASSET CLASSES

Although asset allocation does not guarantee diversification (it is possible to be concentrated in one or two investments in each class), a proper asset allocation program will generally consist of enough securities in each class to offer broad diversification.

16. 6. 3 SECTOR ROTATING

Sector rotating is sometimes called sector rotation. Different sectors of the economy are stronger at different points in the economic cycle. Each industry sector follows its cycle as dictated by the stage of the economy. Portfolio managers attempt to buy into the next sector that is about to experience a move up. When an industry sector reaches the peak of its move as defined by the business cycle, it is time to start to sell the sector.

Of course, how do you know when to make the switch to a sector that has greater potential? If you jump the gun, your performance will suffer, and you're more likely to have losses. Conversely, waiting too long to make the move will cause you to miss much of the uptrend and most of the profit opportunity.

That is why most advisers recommend being in more than one sector at the same time. The idea is to buy into the sector that is rising toward the top and then hold it until it turns down. As a sector turns down, the advisers rotate their clients to the next sector that is rising toward the top and is expected to outperform. This strategy often means your client will be holding a minimum of three sectors in their portfolio: one sector on the rise, one at the top, and one that is starting to decline.

TAKE NOTE

One way to phrase sector rotation is "overweighting or underweighting industries based on the current phase of the business cycle."

16. 7 AVERAGING TECHNIQUES

One common fear of investors is buying at the top of the market. One can never know when a bull market will reverse its course. Conversely, we all want to get in at the bottom, but how do you know when the bear market is over? Because no one knows all of the answers, one popular technique is time-based investing to average your cost. Popular time-based investment programs used by investors include dollar cost averaging and income reinvestment.

16. 7. 1 DOLLAR COST AVERAGING

Investors use **dollar cost averaging** as a means to invest consistent amounts of money in a mutual fund or stock at regular periodic intervals, such as monthly or quarterly. This form of investing allows the individual to purchase more shares when prices are low and fewer shares when prices are high. This has the effect of reducing timing risk, the risk that all of your money will be invested at a market top. In a fluctuating market, the average cost per share is lower than the average price per share.

EXAMPLE

The following table illustrates how average price and average cost may vary with dollar cost averaging.

Month	Amount Invested	Price per Share	No. of Shares
January	$600	$20	30
February	$600	$24	25
March	$600	$30	20
April	$600	$40	15
Total	$2,400	$114	90

The average cost per share equals $2,400 (the total investment) divided by 90 (the total number of shares purchased), or $26.67 per share, whereas the average price per share is $28.50 ($114 ÷ 4). With any market fluctuations, this strategy will produce a lower cost ($26.67) than average price ($28.50). This average cost of $26.67, not the average price paid of $28.50, is the investor's cost basis when the shares are subsequently sold.

TEST TOPIC ALERT

Although it is unlikely that you will have to compute the average price or average cost per share, a question may ask the purpose of dollar cost averaging. The purpose of dollar cost averaging is to reduce the investor's average cost to acquire a security over the buying period relative to its average price.

16. 7. 2 INCOME REINVESTMENT

Stocks and bonds normally pay dividends and interest in cash, and the investor only realizes a capital gain or loss when the investment is sold. Mutual funds normally allow dividends, interest, and capital gains to be automatically reinvested in the fund shares at the net asset value (NAV) per share.

16. 7. 2. 1 Dividend Reinvestment Plans

Some corporations offer their shareholders the opportunity to purchase additional stock using their cash dividend. Under most **dividend reinvestment plans (DRIPs)**, the shareholder is entitled to purchase the additional shares directly from the issuer paying little or no commission and often at a discount to market price. In fact, most companies permit investors in these plans to add money along with the reinvested dividend.

16. 7. 3 CAPITAL GOAL WITHIN A SPECIFIED TIME PERIOD

When saving for higher education, or retirement, there is a stated goal and a specified time period. In the case of college saving, for example, the investor knows how many years until the child will enter and there are plenty of sources indicating what the costs might be at that time. There may be a lump sum (say from an inheritance), a periodic payment out of cash flow, or both, that is available to save towards the goal. Saving for retirement is a bit trickier because we don't know exactly when the client will retire. Fortunately, there are tax-advantaged plans for both goals and these are covered in Session 20.

17

Tax Considerations

Taxes on income and capital gains diminish the amount of money available to the person who earns it. As a result, personal and business investment decisions are often influenced by the tax implications.

The Series 65 exam will include four questions on the material covered in this session.

When you have completed this session, you should be able to:

- **explain** such terms as marginal tax bracket and effective tax rate;

- **identify** the different types of business taxation;

- **distinguish** between income and capital gain;

- **describe** the fundamentals of estate and gift taxation; and

- **list** the preference items included in the AMT computation.

17. 1   INDIVIDUAL INCOME TAXES

Taxes function as either **regressive** or **progressive** costs. **Regressive taxes** (e.g., sales, excise, payroll, property, and gasoline taxes) are levied at the same rate regardless of income and thus represent a smaller percentage of income for wealthy taxpayers than for taxpayers with lower incomes. Because low-income families spend a larger percentage of their incomes than they save or invest, regressive taxes consume a larger fraction of the income of the poor than of the wealthy. **Progressive taxes** (e.g., estate and income taxes) increase the tax rate as income increases. Progressive taxes are costlier to people with high incomes than to people with low incomes. This session will deal with taxation on the federal level with specific reference to state taxes when necessary.

TEST TOPIC ALERT

In a progressive tax system, the term used to describe the highest rate paid on income (sometimes referred to as the next dollar received, or the last dollar received), is the individual's *marginal tax rate*. For example, in 2011, a single individual with taxable income in excess of $174,400 was taxed on each dollar earned above that amount at a rate of 33% until reaching $379,150, at which time the excess was taxed at 35%. Therefore, if this individual reported earnings of $200,000, it is proper to say that the marginal tax rate is 33%. If the individual earned $400,000, then it would be 35%. Because of changes due to the Affordable Care Act (Obamacare), for 2015, any individual reporting more than $413,200 in taxable income moves into the 39.6% tax bracket (more than $464,850 for those filing jointly).

17. 1. 1   EARNED INCOME

Earned income includes salary, bonuses, and income derived from active participation in a trade or business.

17. 1. 2   ALIMONY

Alimony is payment made under a (divorce) court order (or under a legal separation agreement) to an ex-spouse. Alimony may be paid directly to the ex-spouse or to a third party on the ex-spouse's behalf (e.g., to pay premiums on the ex-spouse's life insurance or contribute to the ex-spouse's IRA). Alimony payments, within limits, are generally deductible to the spouse making the payments and includable in income for tax purposes by the spouse receiving them.

17. 1. 3   CHILD SUPPORT

Alimony should not be confused with child support. **Child support** is a legal obligation of a parent to provide financial support for a child (typically occurring when the parent providing the support is not the parent with whom the child or children lives). Child support is not deductible by the parent who pays it, nor is it includable in income by the recipient, who is often the other parent receiving the support on behalf of the child of the dissolved marriage.

EXAMPLE

Chuck and Alice divorced after a 10-year marriage that produced two children, Tim, age 6, and Kim, age 8. Under a court order, it is decided that Chuck will pay Alice $1,000 per month in alimony and $600 per child per month ($1,200 in total child support). Chuck may deduct $12,000 for the tax year ($1,000 × 12 months) on his federal income tax return. Alice must report $12,000 for the tax year on her federal income tax return. Chuck cannot deduct any of the child support, nor is any of it reportable for income tax by Alice or their children.

TEST TOPIC ALERT

For purposes of an IRA contribution, alimony is considered eligible income while child support is not.

17. 1. 4   PASSIVE INCOME

Passive income and losses come from rental property, limited partnerships, and enterprises (regardless of business structure) in which an individual does not actively participate. For the general partner, income from a limited partnership is earned income; for the limited partner, the income is passive. Passive income is netted against passive losses to determine net taxable income. Passive losses may be used to offset only passive income.

17. 1. 4. 1   Personal Use of Vacation Property

One form of passive income is rental income, particularly rental of real estate. One of the issues that is of concern to those who own rental property, particularly in a resort area, is the number of days the owner may use that property before the IRS will no longer treat it as a business. That means that the deductions that could normally be taken for operating a rental property business (utilities, maintenance, depreciation, and so forth) will be disallowed.

You are considered to use a dwelling unit as a home (and not as a business) if you use it for personal purposes during the tax year for more than the greater of 14 days or 10% of the total days it is rented to others at a fair rental price. It is possible that you will use more than one dwelling unit as a home during the year. For example, if you live in your main home for 11 months, your home is a dwelling unit used as a home. If you live in your vacation home for the other one month of the year, your vacation home is also a dwelling unit used as a home unless you rent your vacation home to others at a fair rental value for 300 or more days during the year.

17. 1. 5   PORTFOLIO INCOME

Portfolio income includes dividends, interest, and net capital gains derived from the sale of securities. No matter what the source of the income, it is taxed in the year in which it is earned.

17. 1. 5. 1 Dividend Income

If the dividend qualifies (you don't need to know the technical points that make a dividend qualify), the tax rate is generally a maximum of 15%. (It can be as high as 20% or more for very high income taxpayers, but that is unlikely to be tested.) Otherwise, the dividend is taxed at ordinary income rates. For test purposes, assume that any dividend from a U.S. corporation is qualified, unless the question states otherwise.

17. 1. 5. 2 Interest Income

Interest on any debt security (other than tax-free municipal issues) is always taxed at ordinary income rates. Please note that interest on U.S. Treasury securities (but not GMNA and FNMA debt) is exempt from state taxation, but not federal. Furthermore, income distributions from bond funds are not qualified dividends and are taxed fully as ordinary income.

TEST TOPIC ALERT

In the case of TIPS, the taxation is a bit different. Being Treasury securities, they are exempt from state and local income tax. However, the annual interest payment received is taxable on a federal basis as ordinary income and, what is reminiscent of the tax treatment of a zero-coupon bond discussed in Session 5, the annual increase to the principal is taxed as well.

17. 1. 5. 3 Taxation of Reinvested Distributions

Distributions are taxable to shareholders whether the distributions are taken in cash or reinvested. The issuer must disclose whether each distribution comes from income or realized capital gains. **Form 1099**, which is sent to shareholders after the close of the year, details tax information related to distributions for the year. Dividends must be reported as dividend income and will be taxed either as ordinary income or as a qualifying dividend, generally with a maximum rate of 15%; capital gains distributions from mutual funds are generally reported as a long-term capital gain.

TEST TOPIC ALERT

One term you might see on the exam refers to an interest-on-interest plan and it will be compared to a dividend reinvestment plan. What is the exam referring to? This is nothing other than a typical bank savings account where your interest compounds, usually quarterly. Therefore, you are earning interest on the interest. From a tax standpoint this interest, just like reinvested dividends, is taxable in the year received.

17. 1. 5. 4 The Effect of Reinvestments on Cost Basis

Because the taxes have already been paid on any income reinvested, when the investor sells the asset, the cost basis is increased so that the income is not taxed again.

An investor purchases 100 shares of KAPCO common stock for $100 per share and elects to participate in KAPCO's Dividend Reinvestment Plan (DRIP). During the next five years, the investor receives dividends totaling $2,200, which has allowed the purchase of 20 additional shares through the DRIP. With KAPCO selling at $110 per share, the investor liquidates the entire position. For tax purposes, the investor has a capital gain of $1,000, even though the proceeds are $3,200 more than the original investment. Here's the math:

Purchase – 100 shares @ $100 = $10,000. Add the reinvested dividends of $2,200 to increase the cost basis to $12,200. Sell all the shares (100 + the 20 acquired through the DRIP) = 120 × $110 = $13,200. The proceeds exceed the adjusted cost basis by $1,000 and that is the amount of capital gain.

Regardless of fluctuations in the market price, as long as a dividend is paid, an investor participating in a DRIP will *always* have more shares in his account at the end of the year than at the beginning.

17. 1. 6   RETIREMENT PLAN DISTRIBUTIONS

Qualified retirement plan distributions are, with few exceptions, taxed at the investor's ordinary income tax rate when funds are withdrawn from the plan. Distributions from a qualified plan before the investor reaches age 59½ are also subject to a 10% early withdrawal penalty). Distributions from a qualified plan must begin by April 1 following the year the participant reaches 70½. More on this in Session 20.

17. 1. 7   ALTERNATIVE MINIMUM TAX

Congress enacted the **alternative minimum tax (AMT)** to ensure that high-income taxpayers do not escape federal income taxes. Certain items that receive favorable tax treatment must be added back into taxable income for the AMT and include the following:

■ Accelerated depreciation on property placed in service after 1986

■ Certain costs associated with limited partnership programs, such as research and development costs and excess intangible drilling costs

■ Local tax and interest on investments that do not generate income

■ Tax-exempt interest on private purpose municipal bonds issued after August 7, 1986. Examples of these private purpose or private activity bonds that makes them subject to the AMT would be those issued to finance sports stadiums, hospitals, housing projects, and so forth.

■ Incentive stock options (ISO) to the extent that the fair market value of the employer's stock is in excess of the strike price of the option, even when the stock is not sold in that year

In addition, the AMT can lead to a loss of:

- personal exemptions;
- deductions for state income tax and property tax; and
- deductions for home equity line interest in some cases.

To determine if you owe AMT, you compute your regular tax and then you compute the AMT and pay whichever is the higher amount. The IRS has an unusual way of stating this. They say that the AMT is the regular tax plus the amount by which the AMT exceeds the regular tax. So, if the AMT computation shows $12,000 due and the regular shows $10,000 due, you take that $10,000 and add the amount by which $12,000 exceeds $10,000 ($2,000) to arrive at $12,000. Wouldn't saying, "Pay the higher of the two," be easier? It sure would, but then that might put some accountants out of business, just like simplifying the tax code would do.

TAKE NOTE

Items that must be added back in for the purpose of the AMT computation are sometimes called **tax preference items**. If the tax liability computed under the AMT computation is greater than the taxpayer's regular tax computation, the taxpayer must pay the AMT amount.

TAKE NOTE

The IRS provides for an exemption amount with AMT being potentially levied only if taxable income exceeds that amount. Like almost every number mentioned, it changes annually and is never tested. But, for your information, the 2015 AMT exemption amouts are:

- $53,600 if filing single or head of household

- $83,400 if married filing jointly

- $41,700 if married filing separately

17. 1. 8 MARGIN EXPENSES

Margin interest is a tax-deductible expense. The one exception is interest expenses incurred in the purchase of municipal securities. Because municipal interest income is federally tax exempt, the IRS does not allow taxpayers to deduct the margin interest expenses for municipal securities. Investors can deduct interest expenses incurred when borrowing money to purchase other securities to the extent those interest expenses do not exceed their net investment income, which includes interest income, dividends, and all capital gains.

17. 1. 9 EFFECTIVE TAX RATE

In an earlier Test Topic Alert, we introduced you to the term *marginal* tax rate. That should not be confused with the individual's effective tax rate. What is the difference? As stated earlier, the marginal tax rate is the rate you pay on each additional dollar you receive as income. The effective tax rate, however, is the overall rate of tax you pay on your total taxable income. The following example should help you visualize the difference.

EXAMPLE

In the Test Topic Alert, we showed you how a single person with $200,000 in taxable income was paying taxes at a marginal rate of 33%. That is, a bonus of $3,000 would result in an additional tax liability of $990, ($3,000 x 33%). That 33% rate was in effect for all income in excess of $174,400. According to the tax tables (and absolutely not tested), the tax on that first $174,400 is $42,449 and then everything above that (until $379,150) is taxed at 33%.

So, for the single individual with $200,000 of taxable income, the total tax bill would be $42,449 + (33% x $25,600) or $42,449 + $8,448, which is a total tax of $50,897. That means that out of $200,000 in income, slightly more than 25% of it ($50,897 divided by $200,000) went to pay tax. This works out to be an *effective* tax rate of 25.45%.

17. 1. 10 TAX FILING STATUS

The choice of filing status one makes has a major impact on the amount of taxes levied. There are five different filing statuses:

- Single
- Married filing jointly
- Married filing separately
- Head of household
- Qualifying widow(er) with dependent child

Filing status is determined by your marital status as of the last day of the year. If more than one filing status applies to the taxpayer, the IRS suggests using the one resulting in the lowest tax obligation. Generally, that will be married filing jointly. For those who are not married, if qualifying, the lowest rate is usually obtained by filing as head of household.

TEST TOPIC ALERT

How you file a return can impact your taxes. Your tax filing status is based on your marital status as of the end of the year (December 31). In the case of a "single" parent with dependent children, it will generally be most advantageous to use the filing status, "head of household."

As you can see, there are a number of ways of generating taxable income—from operating a business, such as a sole proprietorship, being an employee and receiving a salary, being an owner of a business organized as an S corporation or LLC, and receiving dividends and interest from stocks and bonds or other investments. However, when you are the beneficiary of a life insurance policy, death benefit proceeds are *not* taxable as income. As we will see in a few pages, the death benefit might be subject to estate tax, but it is not considered taxable income for purposes of paying income tax.

17. 1. 11 TAXATION AND LIFE INSURANCE

17. 1. 11. 1 Income Tax Implications of Life Insurance

Premiums for individually purchased life insurance are generally nondeductible for income tax purposes. Generally, proceeds from life insurance policies made to a beneficiary are exempt from federal income tax.

17. 1. 11. 2 Estate Tax Implications to Owning Life Insurance

If someone named as the insured individual on a life insurance policy holds incidents of ownership in that policy, the entire death benefit payable under that policy is included for federal estate tax purposes in the insured individual's estate.

If a person retains the right to designate a beneficiary, transfer ownership of an insurance policy (assign), choose how dividends or policy proceeds will be paid out, borrow money from the accumulated cash value of the policy, or perform any other functions that are rights of ownership, then that person has incidents of ownership in the policy.

17. 1. 11. 3 Irrevocable Life Insurance Trust

In light of the estate tax implications, it is frequently best that a party other than the insured own the life insurance policy in order to remove the proceeds from the estate of the insured. An effective alternative to ownership of a policy on one's own life is to have the life insurance acquired by or transferred to an irrevocable life insurance trust (ILIT). If certain provisions, known as Crummey powers, are included in the ILIT document, premiums paid by the insured may qualify for the annual gift tax exclusion (currently $14,000 per year, per beneficiary).

1. An investor who would like to increase current income from investments and, at the same time, pay taxes on that income at less than his marginal tax rate, would probably find which of the following to be most suitable?

    A. U.S. Treasury bonds
    B. Public utility stock
    C. Growth stock
    D. Money market mutual fund

2. Which of the following are possible sources of taxable income to an individual?

    I. Owning a sole proprietorship
    II. Being a shareholder in a subchapter S corporation
    III. Owning stocks and bonds
    IV. Proceeds paid on a life insurance policy

    A. I and II
    B. I, II and III
    C. I, II, III and IV
    D. II and III

3. Most new businesses operate at a loss for a period of time. If several of your clients were forming a group to fund a start-up enterprise but wished to limit their liability and, at the same time, be able to receive favorable tax treatment for the expected losses, you would suggest forming which of the following?

    A. C corporation
    B. General partnership
    C. LLC
    D. Sole proprietorship

Quick Quiz answers can be found at the end of the unit.

17. 2   CAPITAL GAINS AND LOSSES

The sale of a security can result in a **capital gain** or a **capital loss**. A **capital gain** occurs when a security is sold for a price higher than its cost basis; if the selling price is lower than the cost basis, a **capital loss** occurs.

17. 2. 1   ADJUSTING COST BASIS

An investment's **cost basis** (total cost of the investment) is used to determine whether a capital gain or a capital loss occurs when an asset is sold. Because many factors affect an asset's cost basis, the IRS requires the cost basis to be adjusted for such occurrences as stock splits and stock dividends.

EXAMPLE

An investor buys 100 shares of RST at $55. Later, the company declares a stock dividend and the investor receives 10 more shares. His total investment remains $5,500, but he now owns 110 shares of RST. The investor's adjusted cost basis per share is now $50 ($5,500 ÷ 110). When the securities are sold, the holding period is based upon the original purchase date; the date(s) of the acquisition of the shares through the stock dividend(s) or stock split(s) are of no consequence.

17. 2. 2   CAPITAL GAINS

A **capital gain** occurs when capital assets (securities, real estate, and tangible property) are sold at prices that exceed the adjusted cost basis. Usually, computing the capital gain or loss on an asset is a matter of comparing the purchase price with the selling price less commissions.

TAKE NOTE

A lower cost basis results in a larger capital gain. The gain is determined by comparing the sales proceeds with the cost basis.

EXAMPLE

If the investor's cost basis in stock is $50 per share and shares are sold for $60, the investor has a capital gain of $10. However, if the investor's cost basis is $55 and the shares are sold for $60, the investor's capital gain is only $5.

17. 2. 2. 1   Effects of Reinvesting on Cost Basis for Computing Capital Gains/Losses

A few pages ago, we discussed the fact that any distributions received, whether taken in cash or reinvested, were reported on the Form 1099 as taxable for that year. In the case of reinvestments, because they have already been taxed, when a sale takes place, they are not taxed again—the amount reinvested adds to the investor's tax basis (or cost).

EXAMPLE

An investor purchases 100 shares of XYZ common stock for $100 per share. Total cost is $10,000. After enrolling in the DRIP offered by XYZ, the investor receives dividends for three years in the total amount of $1,200. Let's say that these reinvested dividends have purchased 10 shares. The investor now sells the all of the XYZ for $125 per share. For tax purposes, there is a capital gain of $2,550. This is computed by subtracting the cost ($10,000 + $1,200 = $11,200) from the proceeds (110 shares × $125 = $13,750).

17. 2. 3 CAPITAL LOSSES

A **capital loss** occurs when capital assets are sold at prices that are lower than the adjusted cost basis.

17. 2. 4 NET CAPITAL GAINS AND LOSSES

To calculate tax liability, a taxpayer must first add all short-term capital gains and losses for the year. (Short-term gains are investments held 12 months or less and are taxed at the investor's ordinary income tax rate.) Then all long-term capital gains and losses are added. (A long-term capital gain or loss only occurs after the investor has held the investment at risk for a period exceeding one year.) Finally, the taxpayer offsets the totals to determine his net capital gain or loss for the year. If the result is a net long-term capital gain, it is taxed at the capital gains rate, currently at 15% for most taxpayers.

Capital losses that exceed capital gains are deductible against earned income up to a maximum of $3,000 per year. Any capital losses not deducted in a taxable year may be carried forward indefinitely as a deduction to offset capital gains in future years.

17. 2. 5 DETERMINING WHICH SHARES TO SELL

An investor holding identical securities, each with a different acquisition date and cost basis, may determine which shares to sell by electing one of three accounting methods: first in, first out (FIFO); share identification; or average cost basis. If the investor fails to choose, the IRS assumes the investor liquidates shares on a FIFO basis.

When FIFO shares are sold, the cost of the shares held the longest is used to calculate the gain or loss. In a rising market, this method normally creates adverse tax consequences.

When using the **share identification** accounting method, the investor keeps track of the cost of each share purchased and uses this information to liquidate the shares that would provide the lowest capital gain. Share identification is used to identify the specific per-share cost basis when shares are sold. The investor keeps track of the cost of each share purchased and specifies which shares to sell on the basis of his tax needs.

A shareholder may elect to use an **average cost basis** when redeeming mutual fund shares (but not shares of specific stocks). The investor would calculate average basis by dividing the total cost of all shares owned by the total number of shares. The shareholder may not change the decision to use the average basis method without IRS permission.

TAKE NOTE

Share identification may result in more advantageous tax treatment, but most accountants prefer the convenience of the averaging method for mutual fund shares. Share identification is most commonly used with stock sales.

17. 2. 6 WASH SALE

An investor may not use capital losses to offset gains or income if the taxpayer sells a security at a loss and purchases the same or a substantially identical security within 30 days before or after the trade date establishing the loss. The sale at a loss and the repurchase within this period is a **wash sale**. The loss that was disallowed, however, is added to the repurchased shares' cost basis.

EXAMPLE
An investor buys 100 shares for $50. One year later, the investor sells the shares for $40. Fifteen days after the sale, he repurchases 100 shares of the same stock for $42. His new cost basis is $52 because the $10 loss that was disallowed is added to the repurchase price of $42.

Wash Sale

Substantially identical securities include stock rights, call options, warrants, and convertible securities of the same issue.

The IRS compares three qualities of debt securities in determining whether they are substantially identical: the maturity, coupon, and issuer. A bond is substantially identical if all three qualities of the bond sold at a loss and the newly purchased bond are the same.

After selling a bond, an investor can buy another bond with either a different maturity, coupon, or issuer without violating the wash sale rule.

EXAMPLE
An investor could sell an ABC 8% bond that matures in 2030 at a loss and buy back an ABC 8% bond that matures in 2031 and claim the loss. This is commonly called tax-swapping.

TAKE NOTE
The wash sale rule applies only to realized losses—not to realized gains.

17. 2. 7 DONATED (GIFTED) AND INHERITED SECURITIES

Gifts. When a donor makes a gift of securities or virtually any asset, the cost basis to the recipient (the donee) is the donor's cost basis. This describes **carryover basis**.

In 1995, Joe Smith bought 1,000 shares of COD at $24 per share, for a total cost of $24,000. In 2002, when COD was trading at $32.50, Joe gave those 1,000 shares to his daughter, Sally. When Sally sells the shares, her cost basis is Joe's cost basis on the date of his original purchase—$24 per share, seven years ago—not the market value on the date of the gift. So, if Sally were to sell those shares for $33 per share one month after receiving the gift, she would be realizing a long-term capital gain of $9,000.

It gets more complicated if the securities are worth less than the donor's cost at the time of the gift and we don't expect the exam to deal with that situation.

If a charitable gift of securities held for more than one year is made, the tax treatment is more favorable. Under these circumstances, Joe's deduction is based on the fair market value on the date of the gift, not his cost basis. He would have received a $32,500 tax deduction and avoided capital gains taxes on the $8,500 profit.

Inherited Securities. When a person dies and leaves securities to heirs, the cost basis to the recipients is usually the **fair market value** on the date of the owner's death. In other words, the cost basis steps up to the date of death value.

In 1995, Joe Smith bought 1,000 shares of COD at $24 per share for a total cost of $24,000. In 2003, when COD was trading at $32.50, Joe died. His daughter, Sally, is Joe's sole heir and inherits the 1,000 shares upon his death. When Sally sells the shares, her cost basis is the fair market value on the date of Joe's death—$32.50 per share—not Joe's original purchase cost.

The step up provision does not apply when inheriting an annuity.

17. 2. 8 SALE OF A PRIMARY RESIDENCE

There are special tax benefits available to those selling their primary residence as long as it has been lived in as the primary residence for at least two of the past five years. For a couple, the first $500,000 in profit is excluded from capital gains taxation; for a single person, it is the first $250,000.

EXAMPLE   Chloe and Edgar bought their home 30 years ago for $50,000. Now that the children are all on their own, they decide to downsize and move to a retirement village. If they sell their home for $600,000, what is the tax consequence?

Chloe and Edgar are selling their home for a profit of $550,000. However, the first $500,000 for a couple is excluded from taxation. Therefore, they will only have to report the remaining $50,000 as a long-term capital gain.

17. 3 BUSINESS TAXATION

17. 3. 1 SOLE PROPRIETORSHIPS

Sole proprietorships are the simplest business form but offer no liability protection to the owner. In fact, this is the only form of business where the potential loss is unlimited because the personal assets of the owner are at risk in addition to any assets owned by the business. The owner computes the earnings of the business on the Schedule C of her Form 1040 so anything made (or lost) by the business is reflected directly on her tax return.

17. 3. 2 PARTNERSHIPS

Partnerships are relatively easy to form and dissolve and come in two types. Both offer flow-through of income and losses, the difference being in the degree of liability. General partnerships provide no liability protection to the partners. In other words, if the business goes under, they, collectively and separately, are liable for any losses. In a limited partnership, as the name implies, something is limited. In this case, it is the liability. A limited partner's maximum loss is what has already been invested plus any funds committed for but not yet contributed. That is why so many DPPs are organized as LPs.

Partnerships do not pay taxes. They file an information return, a Form 1065, and attach to that (and send a copy to each partner) a Schedule K-1 indicating the amount of income (or loss) to be inserted on the investor's personal Form 1040.

17. 3. 3 LIMITED LIABILITY COMPANY (LLC)

The LLC is somewhat of a hybrid between the partnership and the corporation. The federal government does not recognize an LLC as a classification for federal tax purposes. An LLC business entity must file as a corporation, a partnership, or sole proprietorship. Generally, a one-member LLC will use the Schedule C, just as if it were a sole proprietorship. Those with two or more members invariably file as partnerships using the Form 1065 to provide the IRS with the information and the Schedule K-1 for each member's share of income or loss. If filing as a corporation, they generally file as an S corporation, but it is unlikely, for test purposes, that you will have to know anything about an LLC filing as a corporation.

17. 3. 4   CORPORATIONS

As with partnerships, we have two types here as well—the C corporation and the S corporation. Of all the business entities we've discussed, the only one that actually files a tax return on which it must pay income tax is the C corporation. It files on Form 1120 and pays taxes at a rate that generally does not exceed 35%, although there are brackets where it can be as high as 39% (and that will not be tested). The key fact about the C corporation is that its dividends are paid out after paying income taxes and then that dividend is taxable to the shareholder, hence the term *double taxation*.

The S corporation (sometime referred to by its ancient name, Subchapter S corporation, on the exam), is treated for tax purposes the same as a partnership except that the return filed is the Form 1120S. Shareholders receive a Schedule K-1 indicating their share of income or loss. Just as with the LLC and the partnership, the business entity is not taxed; everything flows through to the owners.

Corporations are major investors in securities. Some **Internal Revenue Code (IRC)** provisions affecting corporations as investors include the following.

■ **Dividend exclusion rule:** Dividends paid from one corporation to another are 70% exempt from taxation. A corporation that receives dividends on stocks of other domestic (and certain qualifying foreign) corporations, therefore, pays taxes on only 30% of the dividends received. This avoids triple taxation to investors.

■ **Municipal securities:** Like individual taxpayers, corporations do not pay federal taxes on interest received from municipal bonds.

17. 3. 5   FILING DATES FOR BUSINESS TAX RETURNS

17. 3. 5. 1   Sole Proprietorship

A business organized as a sole proprietorship is an extension of the individual running the business, so its year-end is December 31, and the tax return due date is the same as the individual's—April 15 of the following year.

17. 3. 5. 2   Single Member LLC

If the business is an LLC with only one member, it is taxed like a sole proprietorship, using Schedule C with a year-end of December 31. The tax returns are due and taxes payable on April 15 of the following year.

17. 3. 5. 3   Partnership and Multiple Member LLCs

The tax filing requirements for a partnership and an LLC with more than one member are the same. An information return is filed on Form 1065, with a Schedule K-1 sent to the partners/members indicating the amount of income or loss attributable to each of them. Remember, the business entity pays no income tax—all income/loss flows through to the partners/members. Form 1065 is due on March 15 of the following year. The year-end for these businesses is typically December 31, and taxes are due on April 15, when the individual partners/members file their Form 1040s showing their share of the business's income or loss that was reported on the Schedule K-1.

17. 3. 5. 4 Corporations

A regular (C) corporation may choose any convenient date as their year-end (usually a quarter end date). Corporation tax returns are due and taxes are payable on the 15th day of the third month after the end of the company's fiscal (financial) year. So, a corporation with a year-end date of December 31 must file and pay taxes by March 15; a corporation with a year-end date of June 30 must file and pay taxes by September 15.

In the case of an S corporation, income/loss is taxed on individual income tax returns. Therefore, an S corporation must usually take a calendar year-end date (December 31) unless the corporation can establish a reasonable business purpose for a different date. The filing date and tax return due date is the same as for other corporations (March 15 for a December 31 year-end). As with the other flow-through entities, the Schedule K-1 is sent to shareholders and is used in the preparation of their Form 1040 return.

TEST TOPIC ALERT You may be asked about tax documents for each of these different forms of business organizations. Sole proprietors file their business information on a Schedule C. Members of LLCs and shareholders in S corporations receive a Schedule K-1 and C corporations report their income on a Form 1120.

17. 4 TAXATION OF TRUSTS

Trusts are considered legal persons and may be subject to taxation. In fact, if not handled properly, the taxes can be quite onerous.

17. 4. 1 TRUST TAX RATES

Taxation of trusts and estates is based on what is distributed and what is retained. In the case of non-distributed income, the tax consequences can be quite severe. For example, although a joint return filed for 2015 would have to report income in excess of $464,850 to be subject to the highest tax bracket of 39.6%, that rate is reached once a trust or estate has non-distributed income in excess of $12.300. Obviously, this can have a major impact on investment planning.

TEST TOPIC ALERT If the trust or estate has income, it must be reported on IRS Form 1041.

17. 4. 1. 1 Distributable Net Income (DNI)

Because of the onerous tax implications described above, most trusts and estates distribute their income. In the context of a trust or an estate, the taxable income is known as distributable net income (DNI). DNI determines the amount of income that may be taxable to beneficiaries (or the grantor in the case of a living trust), whereas the balance may be taxed to the trust as indicated above. Commissions and other fees charged for buying and selling securities held in a trust are subtracted from the trust's DNI. Realized capital gains that are reinvested in the corpus (Latin for "body") of the trust are not considered part of DNI.

EXAMPLE   The Gordon Clark Trust had dividend income of $10,000 and interest income of $7,000. In addition, the trust realized capital gains of $3,000, half of which were reinvested in the corpus of the trust. Transaction costs for the year were $2,000. The Gordon Clark Trust has DNI for the year of $16,500 ($10,000 + $7,000 + $1,500 − $2,000). The $1,500 of realized gains reinvested is not part of DNI.

Tax-exempt interest from municipal bonds remains tax exempt to trust beneficiaries.

Regardless of whether trust income is actually distributed to beneficiaries, each beneficiary is considered to be in receipt of taxable income, even if the beneficiary does not actually receive the income.

17. 4. 2 BYPASS TRUST

A bypass trust is an estate planning tool used to take advantage of the lifetime estate tax exclusion. It is commonly used between spouses when both are U.S. citizens. Even though the amount one spouse may leave another without incurring estate tax is unlimited, upon the death of the survivor, all that remains is that person's lifetime exclusion, currently $5.43 million and indexed for inflation.

Prior to the passage of the American Tax Relief Act of 2012 (ATRA), unless proper estate planning was done, such as creating a bypass trust, it was possible to lose the benefit of the full estate tax exemption of the first spouse to die. However, starting in 2013, other than in unusual circumstances, the necessity for using a bypass trust has been eliminated. ATRA allows the surviving spouse to utilize the first spouse's unused estate tax exemption amount without the need to use a bypass trust. What ATRA did was make permanent the "portability" provisions first set out in the Tax Relief Act (TRA 2010).

17. 4. 2. 1 Portability of Unused Estate Tax Exemption Under ATRA

As previously mentioned, TRA 2010 contained the concept of portability, which permits the surviving spouse to take the unused portion of the first deceased spouse's federal exemption and aggregate it with the surviving spouse's unused portion. Now, with ATRA 2012, that feature has become permanent.

To use an example, for 2015, each living spouse has a lifetime exemption from estate tax of $5.43 million. The husband dies in 2015, leaving his entire estate of $7 million to his wife. There would be no estate tax because of the unlimited marital deduction. Let's assume that the husband has not used any of his $5.43 million exemption by making taxable gifts in previous years. If the wife dies later with an estate of up to $10.86 million, the executor of her estate can use all of her exemption of $5.43 million as well as the husband's unused portion (up to $5.43 million) needed to reduce the federal estate tax to zero.

The problem is that we don't know how NASAA will treat this. When this was part of TRA 2010, it was only expected to be effective for 2011 and 2012, and normally the regulators do not write questions dealing with a temporary rule. However, now that this has become a permanent part of estate tax law, we expect questions will start to appear, first as inclusions in the 10 pretest questions, and, once properly vetted, into the actual test bank itself. Check the Exam-tips and Content Updates for any further information.

17. 4. 3 GENERATION SKIPPING TRUST (GST)

Just as the name implies, a generation skipping trust is used to pass money from family members to other members more than one generation removed (grandchildren and/or great-grandchildren). Therefore, instead of the assets being taxed upon the death of the parents and then again when their children pass them to the grandchildren, one level of estate taxation is eliminated.

Similar to the Bypass trust (a term sometimes also used here as well) because the unified credit may be used, sheltering in 2015 up to $5.43 million, it enables couples with this kind of wealth to leave up to $10.86 million without any estate tax liability. One enormous benefit of the GST is when the trust is funded with appreciating assets. For example, the grantor works for a start-up company involved in new technology and, because of the patents he turns over to them, he receives 10 million shares of untraded stock that is valued at 50 cents per share ($5 million). All of that stock is placed into the trust and, because the value does not exceed the $5.43 million limit for 2015, there is no estate tax. Several years later, after the grantor's death, the company goes public at $2.00 per share, and the stock is worth $20 million. The grandkids get to enjoy all of that without any estate tax. The portability concept mentioned previously with estate taxation under TRA 2010 and ATRA 2012 does not apply to the unused GST tax exemption of a predeceased spouse.

17. 4. 3. 1 Direct Skip

When the assets, either directly, through an estate, or through a trust, are left to a beneficiary at least two generations below the transferor, it is known as a direct skip—the assets are directly skipping a generation. With a direct skip, where the estate is left directly to the grandchildren or other younger recipients, the donor or the donor's estate via the executor pays the generation-skipping transfer tax (GSTT).

17. 4. 3. 2 Taxable Termination

Taxable termination applies when a trust is terminated and pays out the remainder of its funds. Under taxable termination, the trustee is responsible for paying the GSTT. A taxable termination is a distribution of principal and, if applicable, accumulated income to a trust beneficiary who is a skip person. The most common case of this is when the skip person is the contingent beneficiary for someone in the generation above who has now passed away, typically, that person's parent.

17. 4. 3. 3 Taxable Distribution

Taxable distribution means any distribution from a trust to a skip person (other than a taxable termination or a direct skip). With a taxable distribution, the recipient is required to pay the GSTT.

17. 5   ESTATE AND GIFT TAXES

The federal government imposes a tax on a decedent's estate based on the value of the estate, as well as on gifts conveyed to heirs, before a person dies.

17. 5. 1   ESTATE TAX

Estate tax is imposed on the transfer of substantial amounts of property at death. An individual may transfer an unlimited amount to a spouse who is a U.S. citizen without the imposition of federal estate tax. This is known as the marital deduction. In addition, an individual may transfer unlimited amounts of money and other property to an eligible charity with no federal estate tax. For heirs other than spouses, an estate tax credit will offset estate tax on transfers of up to $5.43 million in 2015, indexed for inflation of property. We have discussed some ways to reduce or eliminate estate taxes earlier in this unit.

17. 5. 1. 1   The Gross Estate vs. the Taxable Estate

Federal estate tax is calculated using a formula that begins with the **gross estate**. The **gross estate** includes all interests in property held by an individual at the time of death. Although amounts of property transferred to a spouse or a charity will generally not be subject to federal estate tax, such amounts are includable in calculating the gross estate.

Certain expenses are then deducted from the gross estate to arrive at the **adjusted gross estate (AGE)**. Examples of deductions for the AGE include funeral expenses, charitable contributions, and debts of the decedent.

Once the amount of the AGE is determined, the unlimited marital and charitable deductions are subtracted to arrive at the **taxable estate**.

EXAMPLE   Caroline, who is unmarried, dies in 2015, owning various property. The amount of her gross estate is $7 million. However, her estate incurred $20,000 in funeral expenses, she had made charitable gifts of $1,000,000, and she owed mortgages of $200,000 and $30,000 in credit card balances. Thus, her AGE is $5,750,000. In 2015, because of an estate tax credit that exempts the first $5.43 million property transferred after death, Caroline's estate will be taxed on the remaining $410,000 in transferred property.

17. 5. 1. 2   Alternative Valuation Date

The Internal Revenue Code provides that the executor of an estate may choose to value the assets in the estate as of date of death or, alternatively, six months later. This is particularly beneficial if the estate consists of assets that have dropped substantially in value following the date of death of the deceased. What value is used if an asset that is appraised at the date of death is subsequently sold for a different price? The executor will use that sale price as long as it represents the fair market value.

Fair Market Value is defined as: "The fair market value is the price at which the property would change hands between a willing buyer and a willing seller, neither being under any compulsion to buy or to sell and both having reasonable knowledge of relevant facts. The fair market value of a particular item of property includible in the decedent's gross estate is not to be determined by a forced sale price. Nor is the fair market value of an item of property to be determined by the sale price of the item in a market other than that in which such item is most commonly sold to the public, taking into account the location of the item wherever appropriate." In the case of mutual funds, FMV is the NAV, not the POP.

TEST TOPIC ALERT

If an asset is sold after death at a greatly reduced price from its appraised value in a transaction that does not meet the definition required under fair market value, the IRS will use the higher value.

17. 5. 1. 3 Payment Date of Estate Taxes

Regardless of whether the date of death or alternative valuation date is used, estate taxes are due no later than nine months after death. Just as with personal income taxes, it is possible to get an extension to *file* the return, but the taxes are due at the nine months' time and interest will be charged on any amount owed that is not paid at that time.

TEST TOPIC ALERT

The computation of the estate tax is done on IRS Form 706. From the gross assets, certain expenses (such as the costs of administration of the estate, funeral expenses, payments of outstanding debts, and charitable bequests) are deducted and the tax is levied on the remaining taxable estate.

17. 5. 2 TAXATION OF ESTATE INCOME

During the period of time before the estate is liquidated (and estates that are contested can drag on for years), it is likely that the executor will manage the assets in such a fashion that the estate receives income and possibly capital gains. If this is the case, the taxation to the estate is at the same rates mentioned earlier regarding trusts and, as with trusts, Form 1041 is used to report the income. Furthermore, the income is taxed at the same rates as trust income (39.6% for everything in excess of $12,300).

TEST TOPIC ALERT

Just as you may have to know that the estate tax computation is done on Form 706, you may also have to know that the estate income tax computation is done on Form 1041.

17. 6   TAXATION OF GIFTS

Gift tax is a federal tax imposed on the transfer of property during the lifetime of the donor; up to $5.43 million (2015) in lifetime gifts may be made without incurring gift tax. Additionally, an individual may give up to $14,000 per year (indexed for inflation in $1,000 increments) to any number of individuals without generating the federal gift tax. If a married couple join in the gift, the allowable amount is doubled to $28,000 per person per year. Gifts of securities are valued as of the current market price on the date of the gift. Please don't confuse this with cost basis of a gift discussed earlier in this session.

When a gift is made between spouses, the rule is somewhat different. Generally, there is an unlimited exclusion for these gifts. However, there are limits if your spouse is not a citizen of the United States. In 2015, a spouse may gift up to $147,000 to a noncitizen spouse. The number won't be tested because it changes each year, but the concept might be on your exam.

TEST TOPIC ALERT

Generally, a gift tax return must be filed whenever a gift in excess of $14,000 (or whatever the annual exclusion is at the time of the gift) is made to any individual (other than a spouse). The return is filed on *Form 709* and is due at the same time as the donor's income tax return, generally April 15.

TAKE NOTE

If a gift tax is due, it is the responsibility of the giver of the gift (donor), not the receiver of the gift (donee).

TEST TOPIC ALERT

This concept is pretty simple: you have some stock worth $22,000 and give it to a child or grandchild; you've exceed the $14,000 annual gift exclusion, so a gift tax return would have to be filed. However, it might look like this on your exam: "A grandfather received stock as a result of demutualization that is currently worth $22,000 and wishes to give it to his grandchild." Most students would waste their time trying to figure out what demutualization means and not realize how simple the question really is. It makes no difference how the stock was acquired, for gift tax purposes, the only thing that counts is the fair market value on the date of the gift.

TAKE NOTE

Taxation of estates and gifts are very similar. Both have a lifetime exclusion (2015) of $5,430,000 and both have a maximum tax rate (2015) of 40%. There are two significant differences:

1. the annual gift tax exclusion ($14,000 in 2015), and

2. gift taxes are due at the same time as the individual tax return (April 15) while estate taxes are due nine months after death.

17. 7   TAXATION OF FOREIGN SECURITIES

Dividend and interest income received from foreign securities, including ADRs, is normally subject to withholding tax, typically about 15%, by the issuer's country of domicile. Current U.S. tax law allows many investors to reclaim the withheld tax as a credit against taxes owed on their tax returns. For example, if you purchased some Matilda (also called kangaroo) bonds (remember them from Session 5), they are issued in the Australian marketplace by non-Australian entities. The Australian government requires that a withholding tax be placed on the interest, but U.S. taxpayers can take that tax withheld as a credit against U.S. income tax due on the interest. In almost all cases, income from foreign securities is taxed in the U.S. at all levels (federal and state).

17. 8   GIVING TAX OR LEGAL ADVICE

The topic of taxation and estate planning is extremely complicated and is best left to professionals. Although you may discuss these matters in a general way, any detailed recommendation should be referred to the client's tax and/or legal adviser.

QUICK QUIZ 17.B

True or False?

_____ 1. Straight line depreciation is considered a tax preference item for the AMT computation.

_____ 2. Dividend income from stock ownership is considered passive income by the IRS.

_____ 3. If an investor does not choose an acceptable basis when shares are sold, the IRS will assign LIFO.

_____ 4. Investors are not subject to capital gains tax when they receive stock dividends. Instead, the cost basis of shares is adjusted downward.

_____ 5. If an investor sells stock at a loss and within 20 days purchases a call option on that stock, the investor's loss on the stock is disallowed.

_____ 6. The cost basis of inherited securities is the original purchase price of the securities.

_____ 7. Although interest income on municipal bonds is exempt from federal taxation to individual investors, corporate investors are taxed.

_____ 8. A corporation is required to pay taxes on 70% of its dividend income.

_____ 9. The limit on the marital deduction is currently $5.43 million.

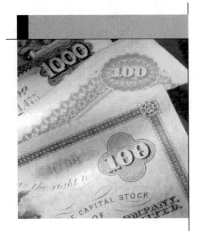

18

Trading Securities

By this time in the course, you're probably itching to go out and try some of these great strategies and techniques and get active in the market. In this session, we'll cover the first thing you have to do—decide what type of account you're going to open. Then, we'll discuss where the securities you wish to purchase or sell are traded. It isn't like you can visit your local Walmart and pick up a few hundred shares of stock. Nor can you go online to Amazon and, even if you have Prime®, order some bonds and have them delivered in two business days.

The Series 65 exam will include approximately five questions on the material presented in this session. ∎

When you have completed this session, you should be able to:

- **summarize** the features of cash and margin accounts;

- **compute** the equity in a margin account;

- **compare** and contrast the exchanges and the over-the-counter market;

- **explain** the difference between functioning as a broker and acting as a dealer;

- **identify** the features and uses of market, stop, and limit orders; and

- **state** the mechanics and risks of a short sale.

18. 1   CASH AND MARGIN ACCOUNTS

Customers can open either cash accounts or margin accounts, depending on how they choose to pay for securities. In cash accounts, customers pay the full purchase price of securities by the transaction settlement date, whereas in margin accounts, customers may borrow part of a security's purchase price from the broker-dealer.

18. 1. 1   CASH ACCOUNTS

A **cash account** is the basic investment account, and anyone eligible to open an investment account can open one. In a cash account, a customer must pay in full for any securities purchased. Certain accounts may *only* be opened as cash accounts, including:

- personal retirement accounts, such as IRAs, Keoghs, and TSAs;
- corporate retirement accounts; and
- custodial accounts, such as Uniform Transfer to Minors Act accounts (UTMAs).

18. 1. 2   MARGIN ACCOUNTS

Margin accounts allow customers to control investments for less money than they would need if they were to buy the securities outright because a margin account allows a customer to borrow money for investing. The term *margin* refers to the minimum amount of cash or marginable securities a customer must deposit to buy securities.

Margin also is a potential source of cash. If a customer has fully paid securities in an account and needs cash, a broker-dealer is permitted to lend money against those securities up to the margin limit that the Federal Reserve Board (FRB) has set.

Customers who open margin accounts must meet certain minimal suitability requirements. The customer may then buy securities on margin and pay interest on the borrowed funds. The securities purchased are held in street name as collateral for the margin loan.

When buying on margin, investors are using financial leverage. That is, they are increasing the potential for gain (and for loss as well) by using borrowed funds. Leveraging can be beneficial when the security is moving up, but it can result in a loss greater than the original investment if the security goes against the investor.

18. 1. 2. 1   Documenting a Margin Account

Opening a margin account requires more documentation than opening a regular cash account. The customer signs a margin agreement, which includes the required credit agreement, hypothecation agreement, and an optional loan consent. Under NASAA policies, it is an unethical business practice to execute any transaction in a margin account without securing from the customer a properly executed written margin agreement promptly *after* the initial transaction in the account.

Margin Account Agreements	
Credit Agreement	Discloses the terms under which credit is extended. SEC Rule 10b-16 requires firms to disclose the method of computing interest and the conditions under which interest rates and charges will be changed. Firms must send customers an assurance that statements accounting for interest charges will be sent with the same frequency that interest is charged (monthly or quarterly).
Hypothecation Agreement	Gives the firm permission to pledge (hypothecate) securities held on margin; a mandatory part of a margin agreement.
Loan Consent (optional)	Gives the firm permission to lend securities held in the margin account to other brokers, usually for short sales. It is not mandatory for customers to sign the loan consent agreement.

18. 1. 2. 2 Margin Call

The term *margin call* is properly defined as the initial call for funds when making a margin transaction. For example, with the margin requirements of Regulation T at 50% (as they have been since 1974), a purchase of $12,000 of stock will result in a margin call of $6,000. The broker-dealer lends the client the other $6,000 creating a debit balance in the account. The equity in the account is 50%, and the client's debt is the other 50%.

18. 1. 2. 3 Maintenance

The Self-Regulatory Organizations (SROs) (e.g., FINRA and the NYSE), rather than Regulation T, have established minimum levels of equity in a margin account below which a call will go out for additional funds. This is properly referred to as margin maintenance or a maintenance call. Current SRO levels are 25% for long margin accounts. For example, if, in the above purchase, the stock's price were to drop to $8,000, there would only be $2,000 of equity in the account (market value of $8,000 minus debit balance of $6,000 equals $2,000). At this point, the equity represents 25% of the current market value ($2,000 / $8,000). If the stock should drop any further, a maintenance margin call would be sent with a request for immediate funds. You will not have to do any of these computations, but you will need to know the term. If the maintenance call is not met, the broker-dealer will liquidate enough securities in the account to bring the equity back to the maintenance level. If there is more than one security in the account, the firm can select which to sell— it does not have to be one whose decline triggered the call.

18. 1. 2. 4 House Maintenance

This is the term used to describe stricter limits imposed by the broker-dealers themselves. Typically, instead of relying on the SRO maintenance level of 25%, the individual firm may require a minimum of 35% or even higher.

TAKE NOTE

This should help you remember the three terms we've just discussed:

Margin Call – Set by the Federal Reserve Board under Regulation T. This is the initial deposit required when purchase securities on margin (the broker-dealer lends the balance of the purchase price). For most equity securities, the initial margin requirement is 50% of the purchase price.

Minimum Maintenance – Set by the SROs. This is the minimum equity that must be maintained in a margin account. Should the equity fall below the minimum required, a maintenance call (sometimes called maintenance margin) will go out demanding an immediate deposit of enough equity to bring the account above the required level. Currently, the minimum maintenance level for long positions is 25%.

House Maintenance – Set by the individual broker-dealer firm. As a cushion, and to reduce the possible sellout caused by failure to meet a maintenance call, most firms set a minimum equity level above the SRO minimum. A common house requirement is 35%.

None of these numbers will be tested, only the concepts.

18. 1. 2. 5 Mixed Margin Account

A couple of pages ago, we described the short sale. Short sales must take place in a margin account. When the margin account contains both long and short positions, it is said to be a mixed margin account. Computing the equity, sometimes called net equity, in one of these accounts is done by calculating the equity for both the longs and shorts and then combining them.

In a long account, the equity is what you own, minus what you owe. That would be the current market value of the long stock minus the debit balance. In the case of the short position, it is basically the same, except the terms are different. What you owe in a short position is the cost to buy back the stock you've borrowed. What you own is the credit balance representing what you received when you sold the stock in the first place. So, the equity in a short account is the credit balance minus the current market value of the short stock. Perhaps the following will make it a bit easier:

CMV long – Debit balance = Long equity

Credit balance – CMV short = Short equity

We have two positive numbers: the stock we own, and the credit balance (you know that when you get a bill and there is a credit balance, it means they owe you money—that's yours). On the other side, we have two negative numbers: the cost to buy back the stock we're short and the debit balance. If we add the two positives and then subtract the two negatives, we've got our net equity.

EXAMPLE

A client's mixed margin account shows the following. Current market value of the long positions is $50,000, while the current market value of the short positions is $25,000. There is a debit balance of $20,000 and a credit balance of $40,000. What is the combined, or net equity in the account?

Either find the equity in each account, Long: $50,000 – $20,000 = $30,000 and short: $40,000 – $25,000 = $15,000, so the total is $45,000. Or, take the two positive numbers, $50,000 + $40,000, which equal $90,000 and subtract to the two negative numbers, $20,000 + $25,000, which equal $45,000 and you get the same $45,000.

18. 1. 2. 6 Positive (Negative) Margin

The term *positive margin* simply means that your returns are higher than the cost of the borrowed money to carry the positions in a margin account.

For example, if you buy $10,000 of stock on 50% margin, you will be borrowing $5,000 of that purchase price from the broker-dealer. If, over the holding period, you pay $400 in interest and sell the stock for $11,000, you've made a profit of $1,000 against the cost of $400 for net "winnings" of $600. That would be considered *positive margin*.

If, however, you sold the stock for $10,300, your interest cost would have exceeded the profit by $100, and that would be considered *negative margin*.

QUICK QUIZ 18.A

1. If a customer opens a margin account with ABC Discount Securities and signs a loan consent agreement, the firm is permitted to
   A. hypothecate securities in the customer's account
   B. loan out the customer's margin securities
   C. commingle the customer's securities with securities owned by the firm
   D. lend the customer money and charge interest

2. An investment adviser representative is reviewing the investments of a potential advisory client. The representative notices that the investor has a mixed margin account at a large, well-known broker-dealer. It would be expected that this account would contain
   A. stocks and bonds
   B. stocks and options
   C. long and short positions
   D. cash and securities

3. A client has a margin account with a broker-dealer. When making a purchase, the request for funds is known as a
   A. house call
   B. maintenance margin call
   C. margin call
   D. call rate

Quick Quiz answers can be found at the end of the unit.

18. 2   MARKETS AND MARKET PARTICIPANTS

After the initial offering, many stocks and bonds are bought and sold on exchanges in a two-way auction process. The major exchanges include the New York Stock Exchange (NYSE), the Chicago Stock Exchange (CHX), and Nasdaq. Other trades take place in the nationwide network of broker-dealers known as the over-the-counter (OTC) market.

18. 2. 1   SECURITIES MARKETS

There are two terms used to describe the market for securities. The **primary market** is the market in which the proceeds of sales go to the issuer of the securities sold. The **secondary market** is where previously issued securities are bought and sold. This session will focus on secondary market trading.

18. 2. 1. 1   Exchange Market

The **exchange market** is composed of the NYSE and other exchanges on which **listed** securities are traded. *Listed security* refers to any security listed for trading on an exchange. Each stock exchange requires corporations to meet certain criteria before it will allow their stock to be listed for trading on the exchange.

Location. Most stock exchanges, such as the NYSE and CHX, maintain central marketplaces and trading floors. Some, such as the Nasdaq Stock Market are strictly electronic markets. As of the date of this printing, there are 18 exchanges registered as national stock exchanges with the SEC. At one time, there were a number of regional stock exchanges, but they have either been closed or merged into the national ones.

Pricing System. Historically, listed markets operated as **auction markets**. Floor brokers competed to execute trades at the most favorable prices. That process still exists on some exchanges

Specialist. The **specialist** maintains an orderly market and provides price continuity. He fills limit and market orders for the public and trades for his own account to either stabilize or facilitate trading when imbalances in supply and demand occur.

The specialist's chief function is to maintain a fair and orderly market in the stocks for which he is responsible. An additional function is to minimize price disparities that may occur at the opening of daily trading. He does this by buying or selling, as a dealer, stock from his own inventory only when a need for such intervention exists. Otherwise, the specialist lets public supply and demand set the stock's price.

TAKE NOTE

The term *specialist* has been replaced with designated market maker (DMM), but you should expect to still see specialist on your exam.

18. 2. 1. 2   Over-the-Counter (OTC) Market.

The OTC market functions as an interdealer market in which **unlisted** securities—that is, securities not listed on any exchange—trade.

In the OTC market, securities dealers across the country are connected by computer and telephone. Thousands of securities are traded OTC, including stocks, corporate bonds, and all municipal and U.S. government securities.

Location. No central marketplace facilitates OTC trading. Trading takes place over the phone, over computer networks, and in trading rooms across the country.

Pricing System. The OTC market is an **interdealer network**. Registered market makers compete to post the best bid and ask prices. The OTC market is a negotiated market.

Market Makers. Market makers are broker-dealers who stand ready to buy and sell at least the minimum trading unit, usually 100 shares (or any larger amount they have indicated), in each stock in which they have published bid and ask quotes. Market makers, acting in a dealer (principal) capacity, sell from their inventory at their asking price and buy for their inventory at the bid price.

TAKE NOTE

The differences between the OTC and NYSE markets are summarized below.

OTC	NYSE
Securities prices determined through negotiation	Securities prices determined through auction bidding
Regulated by FINRA	Regulated by the NYSE
Traded at many locations across the country	Traded on the NYSE floor on Wall Street

Exchange = Listed securities = prices determined by auction

OTC = Unlisted securities = prices determined by negotiation

Government and municipal bonds and unlisted corporate stocks and bonds trade in the OTC market.

18. 2. 2   THE ROLE OF BROKER-DEALERS

Most securities firms act as both brokers and dealers but never in the same transaction. Let's examine the differences between these two terms.

18. 2. 2. 1   Brokers

When a broker-dealer acts in the capacity of a *broker*, it is said to be acting in an agency capacity. That is, the firm represents clients who wish to buy a security by finding a seller, or finding a buyer for those clients with a security to sell. For this service, they charge a commission.

Brokers do not buy shares for inventory but facilitate trades between buyers and sellers.

18. 2. 2. 2 Dealers

When a broker-dealer acts in the capacity of a dealer, it is said to be acting as a principal in the trade. Just as with any transaction, there are always two principals; the buyer and the seller. Dealers, acting as principals, buy and sell securities for their own account. When they receive a customer order to buy a security, they sell that security out of their inventory in the same manner as an automobile dealer sells you a car off the lot. When they receive a customer order to sell, dealers buy that security for their inventory, once again, similar to an automobile dealer who buys your old clunker from you.

When selling from their inventories, dealers charge the buying customers a markup rather than a commission. When buying for their inventory, dealers charge the selling customers a markdown (they buy for less than they can sell it for— think about what happens when the auto dealer buys your used car from you and what it sells for on the lot a week later after they've cleaned it up).

TAKE NOTE

The term *principal* has several meanings in the securities industry. A broker-dealer acts as a principal in a dealer transaction. A principal of a firm is a person who acts in a supervisory capacity. *Principal* can also mean the face value of a bond or asset in a trust.

A firm cannot act as both a broker and a dealer in the same transaction.

EXAMPLE

A firm cannot make a market in a stock, mark up that stock, and then add an agency commission. If the firm acts as a broker, it may charge a commission. If it acts as a dealer, it may charge a markup or markdown. Violation of this practice is called **making a hidden profit**.

Broker	Dealer
Acts as an agent, transacting orders on the client's behalf	Acts as a principal, dealing in securities for its own account and at its own risk
Charges a commission	Charges a markup or markdown
Is not a market maker	Makes markets and/or takes positions (long or short) in securities
Must disclose its role and the amount of its commission to the client	Must disclose its role to the client, but not necessarily the amount or source of the markup or markdown

An easy way to remember these relationships is to memorize the following letters.

BAC/DPP—Brokers act as **A**gents for **C**ommissions/**D**ealers act as **P**rincipals for **P**rofits.

ABCD—Agents that are **B**rokers for **C**ommissions that must be **D**isclosed.

18. 2. 3 BIDS, OFFERS, AND QUOTES

A **firm quote** is a market maker's current bid and offer on a security. The **current bid** is the highest price at which the dealer will buy, and the **current offer** is the lowest price at which the dealer will sell. The difference between the bid and ask is known as the **spread**. Remember, when acting in a principal capacity, there are no commissions added.

If WXYZ is quoted as 43.25 to .50, it means that the bid price (the price that a customer would receive for his shares) is $43.25, and the ask price (the price that the customer would pay to buy shares) is $43.50. The $.25 difference is the dealer's spread.

If a client has U.S. Treasury bonds she wishes to sell and receives a quote of 104.22, which represents the bid price (don't select an answer choice that says "a premium"). It is a premium, but that is not as good an answer.

18. 2. 4 TYPES OF ORDERS

Many types of orders are available to customers.

18. 2. 4. 1 Price

Orders that restrict the price of the transaction include the following:

- **Market**—executed immediately at the market price with no restrictions
- **Limit**—limits the amount paid or received for securities
- **Stop**—becomes a market order if the stock reaches or goes through the stop price
- **Stop limit**—entered as a stop order and changed to a limit order if the stock hits or goes through the trigger price

18. 2. 4. 2 Time

Limit orders based on time considerations include the following:

■ **Day**—expires if not filled by the end of the day
■ **Good till canceled**—does not expire until filled or canceled

---

Matching

A. Broker
B. Dealer
C. Auction
D. Negotiated
E. Immediate execution

___ 1.   Exchange market

___ 2.   OTC market

___ 3.   Agency capacity

___ 4.   Principal capacity

___ 5.   Market order

6.   Which of the following is appropriate justification for selling a stock short?

A.   To cut losses on a long position
B.   To benefit from a decline in the price of the stock
C.   To benefit from a rise in the price of the stock
D.   To seek a modest potential reward with limited risk

7.   When viewing several of your client's trade confirmations, you notice that a recent purchase was made of ABC stock where there was no commission indicated while a sale took place of DEF stock in which the commission listed was $55. From this information you could determine that

I.   ABC was purchased in an agency transaction
II.   ABC was purchased in a principal transaction
III. DEF was sold in an agency transaction
IV.   DEF was sold in a principal transaction

A.   I and III
B.   I and IV
C.   II and III
D.   II and V

18. 2. 4. 3 Market Orders

A **market order** is sent immediately to the floor for execution without restrictions or limits. It is executed immediately at the current market price and has priority over all other types of orders. A market order to buy is executed at the lowest offering price available; a market order to sell is executed at the highest bid price available. Those prices are usually referred to as the *inside market* or *inside quote*. As long as the security is trading, a market order guarantees execution.

18. 2. 4. 4 Limit Orders

In a **limit order**, a customer limits the acceptable purchase or selling price. A limit order can be executed only at the specified price or better. *Better* means lower in a buy order and higher in a sell order. If the order cannot be executed at the market, the order is left with the specialist (now called the DMM), who records the trade in the order book and executes the order if and when the market price meets the limit order price.

18. 2. 4. 4. 1 Risks and Disadvantages of Limit Orders

A customer who enters a limit order risks missing the chance to buy or sell, especially if the market moves away from the limit price. The market price may never go as low as the buy limit price or as high as the sell limit price.

TEST TOPIC ALERT   If any part of an order can be filled at the limit price, it is done. For example, if a day limit order to buy 400 shares at $22.45 is turned in and all that can be executed at that price or better is 200 shares before the market closes, that sale is confirmed and the order for the balance is cancelled.

18. 2. 4. 5 Short Sales

Selling short is a technique to profit from the decline in a stock's price. The short seller initially borrows stock from a broker-dealer to sell at the market. The investor expects the stock price to decline enough to allow him to buy shares at a lower price and replace the borrowed stock at a later date. Unless the stock price declines to zero, the short seller is obligated to buy the stock and replace the borrowed shares to close the short position.

Short sales are risky because if the stock price rises instead of falls, an investor still must buy the shares to replace the borrowed stock—and a stock's price can rise without limit. Therefore, the position has unlimited risk.

18. 2. 4. 6 Stop Orders

A **stop order**, also known as a *stop loss order*, may be entered to protect a profit or prevent a loss if the stock begins to move in the wrong direction.

The stop order becomes a market order once the stock trades at or moves through a certain price, known as the **stop price**. Stop orders for listed stocks are usually left with and executed by the specialist.

A trade at or through (lower in the case of a sell stop; higher in the case of a buy stop) the stop price *triggers* the order, which then becomes a market order. As a market order, there is no assurance of any specific price. The order may wind up being executed at, above, or below the stop price.

A stop order takes two trades to execute:

- **Trigger**—the trigger transaction at or through the stop price activates the trade
- **Execution**—the stop order becomes a market order and is executed at the market price, completing the trade

18. 2. 4. 6. 1 Stop Limit Order

A stop limit order is a stop order that, once triggered, becomes a limit order instead of a market order.

EXAMPLE

An order that reads "sell 100 COD at 52 stop, 51.50 limit" means that the stop will be activated at or below 52. Because a 51.50 limit applies, the order to sell cannot be executed below 51.50.

TAKE NOTE

The uses of buy and sell stop orders are summarized below.

Buy Stop Orders (might be called stop-buy on the exam)

- Protect against loss in a short stock position

- Protect a gain from a short stock position

- Establish a long position when a breakout occurs above the line of resistance (i.e., stock prices rise above historic high levels)

Sell Stop Orders (might be called stop-sell on the exam)

- Protect against loss in a long stock position

- Protect a gain from a long stock position

- Establish a short position when a breakout occurs below the line of support (i.e., stock prices decline below low level)

18. 2. 4. 6. 2 Mechanics of a Stop Order

As stated above, it takes more than one trade for a stop order to be executed. The first of those, the trigger, occurs whenever the subject security trades at or through the stop price. In the case of a buy stop order, *through* means *at a higher price.* In the case of a sell stop order, *through* means *at a lower price.*

Then, once the order has been triggered, unless it is a stop limit order, the next price in the market is the one at which the trade is executed. It will probably be easier to follow if we display an example.

EXAMPLE

A client enters a buy stop order for 100 shares of XYZ at 40. Trades then occur at 38, 39, 39.90, 40.05, 40.10, and 39.78. What price did the client pay for the stock? The order will be triggered as soon as the price gets to 40 or higher. That would be the trade at 40.05. At that time, a market order is entered and the client pays the next price (which could be more or less than 40). In this case, the next price is 40.10 and that is the price per share paid by the client (we're ignoring any commissions).

How is this different for a stop limit order? If we change the above example to make the order, buy stop at 40, limit 40, then the client is stating that once the order has been triggered, enter a limit order and do not pay any more than 40 for the stock. Once again, the order is triggered with the trade at 40.05, but now, because a limit order has been placed, we can't buy on the next trade—40.10 is too high. However, the following trade at 39.78 allows us to meet the client's limit of paying no more than 40 for the stock.

TEST TOPIC ALERT

There is a danger in using stop orders in that once they are triggered, the marketplace receives an increase of sell orders in a falling market and buy orders in a rising market. This can have the tendency to accelerate the direction of the market; sell stops in a bearish market, buy stops in a bullish one.

18. 2. 4. 7 Block Trade

NYSE Rule 72 defines a "block" as at least 10,000 shares or $200,000 USD, whichever is less. Thus, for stocks priced at less than $20, a 10,000-share trade can be a block, but in higher-priced stocks even a 1,000-share trade could constitute a block.

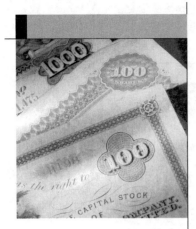

19

Performance Measures

U ltimately, the judge of the value of an investment adviser is the
performance of the client's account. There are a number of different ways to measure the performance and one must always keep
in mind that it is how well the account meets the investor's objectives that
counts. For example, an account that appreciated 10% in one year while distributing an income return of 1% is not meeting the goals of a client needing
current income.

The Series 65 exam will include three questions on the material presented in this session.

When you have completed this session, you should be able to:

- **compute** the investment return measurements most commonly found on the exam;

- **define** the difference between current yield and yield to maturity; and

- **select** the appropriate benchmarks for various portfolios.

19. 1   YIELD MEASURES

Referring to the short example given in the introduction to this session, for income oriented investors, probably the most important performance measurement is yield. In Unit 2, Session 5, we discussed the various types of yield on debt securities so we'll just mention a few highlights here.

19. 1. 1   CURRENT YIELD

The current yield on any investment, debt or equity, is simply the annual income stream (interest or dividends) divided by the current market price. In the case of a debt security, the annual interest is always fixed as a percentage of the par value and doesn't fluctuate when the market price of the security changes. That means that a bond with a 5% coupon (interest) rate, will always be paying $50 per year, divided into two semi-annual payments of $25. If the market price of that bond is currently 80 ($800), the current yield (also called current return) is 6.25% (50 divided by 800). If the current market price of the bond is 125 ($1,250), the current yield is 4% (50 divided by 1,250). The arithmetic is the same when computing the current yield on a stock.

TEST TOPIC ALERT

When asking for the current yield on a stock, the question will usually give you the quarterly dividend rate. Be sure to multiply that by 4 to arrive at the annual dividend payment. For example: ABC common stock's most recently quarterly dividend was $.36 per share. ABC expects to keep the dividend payments at that level. If ABC common stock has a current market value of $32 per share, the current return is? The first choice will probably be 1.1% which is incorrect because that is based on a single dividend. You must multiply the $.36 by 4 to arrive at the annual dividend of $1.44. Then, divide that by the current market price of $32 and the correct answer is 4.5%

19. 1. 2   YIELD TO MATURITY

Yield to maturity would only apply to a debt security because they have a loan principal that is to be paid back at some future date (the maturity date). It is often referred to as the true yield because it is the most accurate reflection of the actual return to be received by the investor. Unlike our work in a previous session, here you need merely understand the concept.

TEST TOPIC ALERT

The yield to maturity (YTM) of a bond is actually the bond's internal rate of return (IRR) because it represents the discount rate that equates to the discounted value of the bond's future cash flows to its current price.

19. 2   RETURN MEASURES

There will probably be two computations on your exam dealing with different types of returns. We'll cover all of them and indicate which are the most (and least)likely to appear on your test.

19. 2. 1   TOTAL RETURN

Total return includes the income from dividends or interest plus any capital appreciation (or less any capital depreciation) over a given time period, usually one year. As such, total return is considered to be the best measure of how a security has performed for an investor.

EXAMPLE

A common stock purchased for $20 with an annual dividend of $1 is sold after one year for $24. The total return on the investment is $5: $1 in dividends plus $4 in capital appreciation. The total return, then, is 25% ($5 ÷ $20 = 25%).

TEST TOPIC ALERT

The exam will require you to know how to calculate total return. Keep in mind that the total annual return on an investment includes income and capital appreciation. In the case of bonds held to maturity, this is the YTM. Otherwise, it is the coupon income plus any appreciation or less any price depreciation. In the case of stocks, one would use the dividend income plus or minus the appreciation or depreciation.

19. 2. 2   HOLDING PERIOD RETURN

The length of time an investor owns an investment is called the **holding period.** The return for that period is called the **holding period return (HPR).** HPR is the total return, income plus capital appreciation, of an investment over a specified period, the holding period. It is essentially the same as total return, but, whereas total return is usually computed on an annual basis, holding period return can be for any period.

EXAMPLE

An investment purchased for $100 and sold three years later for $120 ($20 capital appreciation) after paying a total of $30 ($10 per year) in dividends has a holding period return of 50% ($120 + $30 = $150). The total gain is $150 − $100 = $50. A $50 return on a $100 investment is 50% ($50 ÷ $100 = 50%).

TAKE NOTE

Holding period return is not an annualized return. It is the percentage return over a defined period.

We tend to focus on looking at the total return and holding period return for equities, but it is also a valid measurement for bond returns. In this case, we combine the interest received and any appreciation or depreciation. However, there is one other factor that is sometimes considered: the rate at which the coupons are reinvested. If we assume the bondholder will keep the bond until maturity date, in a period of rising interest rates, the bondholder should be able to reinvest the coupons at a higher rate than the coupon, thus causing the holding period return to exceed the yield to maturity. If, on the other hand, interest rates are falling, the coupons will only be able to be reinvested at a lower rate causing a holding period return that is less than the bond's YTM.

19. 2. 3 ANNUALIZED RETURN

Annualized return is the return an investor would have received had he held an investment for one year. Annualized return is determined by multiplying the actual return by an **annualization factor**. The **annualization factor** is the number of months in the year divided by the number of months an investment is held.

TAKE NOTE

An investor receives $5 on a $100 investment held for 6 months. The annualized return is determined by multiplying the 5% return by the annualization factor of 2 (12 months ÷ 6 months = 2) for an annualized return of 10%. Another investor has a capital gain of 30% from an investment held for 18 months. The annualized return is 20%, calculated as follows: 30 × (12 ÷ 18) = 20.

TAKE NOTE

The formula we've shown you is only approximate (the computation has never been asked on the exam). In reality, because of compounding, the annualized return would actually be a bit different. In the first example shown, it would be about 10.2% instead of 10%. In the second example (the 18-month holding period), it would be about 19.1% instead of 20%.

19. 2. 4 INFLATION-ADJUSTED RETURN (REAL RETURN)

Because inflation reduces the buying power of a dollar, investment performance measurements are often adjusted to provide a measure of the buying power earned from a given investment. Returns that have been adjusted for inflation are called **real rates of return**. This is a frequently required computation on the exam.

To determine the inflation-adjusted rate of return of debt security, reduce its nominal return by the inflation rate as reflected in the consumer price index (CPI).

To determine the inflation-adjusted rate of return of an equity security, reduce the total return (as taught above), by the inflation rate as reflected in the consumer price index (CPI).

TAKE NOTE

A bond with an 8% coupon has a nominal return of 8%. If inflation (as measured by the CPI) is 3%, then the inflation-adjusted return of the bond investment is 8% – 3%, or 5%.

TAKE NOTE

Let's revisit the total return example from a couple of pages ago:

A common stock purchased for $20 with an annual dividend of $1 is sold after one year for $24. The total return on the investment is $5: $1 in dividends plus $4 in capital appreciation. The total return, then, is 25% ($5 ÷ $20 = 25%). If the question asked for the "real rate of return" and told you that the CPI increase for the period was 6%, you would subtract that from the 25% total return to arrive at an inflation-adjusted return of 19%.

TAKE NOTE

For fixed income investors, inflation and taxes reduce the buying power of their dollars. For an investor in the 25% tax bracket in a 2.5% inflationary environment, an investment that yields 10% before taxes provides the investor with a 5% inflation-adjusted, after-tax return. To calculate the 5% after-tax inflation adjusted return, first determine the after-tax return. In this case, 10% less 25% for taxes results in a 7.5% after-tax return. The formal mathematical way to calculate inflation adjusted returns is to divide (1 + the return) by (1 + the inflation rate) – 1. In this case, divide 1.075 by 1.025 and then subtract 1, or 1.049 – 1 = 4.9%.

A shorthand way to approximate the real rate of return is to reduce the return by the amount of inflation during the period. In this case, 7.5% less 2.5% inflation results in a 5% after-tax inflation adjusted return. Even though a calculation of this type will not be on your exam, you need to understand the concept that your final returns are reduced by both taxes and inflation.

TEST TOPIC ALERT

The exam will require you to know how to calculate the approximate inflation-adjusted return by merely subtracting the CPI from the total return.

19. 2. 5   AFTER-TAX RETURN/YIELD

Capital gains and income are generally taxable; thus, taxes reduce the return of an investment. The **after-tax return, also known as the adjusted return,** is determined by reducing the investment's return by the client's tax rate.

The after-tax return of an investment that yields 10% for an investor in the 25% tax bracket is calculated by multiplying the return by (1 − .25), or .75. The investor retains 75% of the 10% yield, for a 7.5% after-tax return. Likewise, an investment that returns 45% over three years provides an after-tax return of 33.75% (.75 x 45%).

The importance of after-tax return is realizing that any investor's return is going to be reduced by the effects of taxation whether it is the favorable capital gains tax or the higher ordinary income rate. That is the beauty of programs such as the Roth IRA or Section 529 Plan where it is possible to have totally tax-free returns. Remember, even though the interest on a municipal bond may be tax-free, any capital gains are not.

19. 2. 6   PROBABLE

Unlike historical or actual rates of returns, **probable returns** are estimates of the likely returns an investment may yield. To determine the probable return of an investment, the adviser assigns a probability to each return that the investment is likely to earn and then multiplies that return by the probability of it occurring. The sum of those probable returns is the expected return for that investment. The formula is as follows: expected or probable return = (probability of return #1 × possible return #1) + (probability of return #2 × possible return #2).

EXAMPLE

The probable (expected) return of an investment with a 30% probability of returning 15% and a 70% chance of returning 10% has a total expected return of 11.5%, calculated as follows: (.30 × 15% = 4.5%) + (.70 × 10% = 7.0%), or 4.5% + 7.0% = 11.5%.

In effect, this return reflects the arithmetic (mean) return of the portfolio.. When one constructs a portfolio, there are usually securities with different grades of risk and, hence, different expectations of reward. Investors view the portfolio as a whole, looking to maximize for return for each level of risk. This overall view, or mean, of the entire portfolio is the expected or probable return of the portfolio.

TEST TOPIC ALERT

Don't be surprised to get a question similar to our example above, but, with one of the possibilities being a negative. Suppose our example had said there was a 30% probability of returning 15%, a 40% chance of returning 10%, and a 30% chance of losing 8%. The expected return would be (.30 × 15% = 4.5%) + (.40 × 10% = 4.0%) + (.30 × –8% = –2.4%) for a total of 6.1% expected return.

19. 2. 7 RISK-ADJUSTED RETURN (SHARPE RATIO)

Securities practitioners have developed many measures to quantify the risk characteristics of a portfolio. One such measure that may show up on the exam is called the **Sharpe ratio**. The ratio is calculated by subtracting the risk-free rate (e.g., the 90-day Treasury bill rate) from the overall return of the portfolio. This result, which is the portfolio's risk premium, is then divided by the standard deviation of the portfolio. This ratio measures the amount of return per unit of risk taken. The higher the ratio, the better or more return per unit of risk taken.

TEST TOPIC ALERT

The Sharpe Ratio measures risk-adjusted return.

TEST TOPIC ALERT

You must know that the three components of the Sharpe Ratio are:

- the actual return minus;

- the risk-free rate (the 90-day T bill rate) divided by; and

- the standard deviation.

Beta is not a part of this ratio.

19. 2. 7. 1 Risk Premium

It should be clear that in order to have a positive Sharpe Ratio, our actual return on an investment must exceed the risk-free return. Therefore, any investor would surely expect to achieve that higher return or the investment would not be made. This return is known as the risk premium. Specifically, the risk premium is a premium demanded for internal and external risk factors.

Internal risk factors are diversifiable and include business risk, credit risk, liquidity risk, currency risk, and country risk. *External risk factors*, such as market risk and interest rate risk, are macroeconomic in nature and are non-diversifiable.

The required rate of return on *any* investment is a combination of the risk-free rate plus a risk premium. For equity investments, the risk premium can be determined by reference to a risk premium curve or by using the capital asset pricing model (CAPM).

19. 2. 8 INTERNAL RATE OF RETURN (IRR)

IRR has been discussed previously in Session 12. We're just going to list a couple of the points that are important for the exam:

- IRR is the preferred method of measuring the return on a DPP;
- IRR takes into consideration the time value of money; and
- IRR is the way the yield to maturity of a bond is computed.

19. 2. 8. 1   Time-Weighted Returns

This is a method of determining an internal rate of return by evaluating the performance of portfolio managers without the influence of additional investor deposits or withdrawals to or from the portfolio.

19. 2. 8. 2   Dollar-Weighted Returns

This is a method of determining the internal rate of return that an individual investor earned on the basis of the investor's particular cash flow into and out of the portfolio.

19. 2. 8. 3   Time-Weighted vs. Dollar-Weighted Returns

Although time-weighted returns and dollar-weighted returns are both methods of determining an internal rate of return, they have very different purposes. **Time-weighted returns** are used to evaluate the performance of portfolio managers separate from the influence of additional investor deposits or withdrawals. **Dollar-weighted returns** are used to determine the rate of return an individual investor earned on the basis of the investor's particular cash flows into and out of a portfolio. The example comparing Portfolios A and B illustrates the difference between dollar-weighted returns and time-weighted returns.

Assume we are comparing two portfolios, A and B. Over a four-year period, they each earn exactly the same return per period. However, each portfolio has a different set of investor deposits and withdrawals.

Portfolio A				
Period	Investor Deposits or Withdrawals	Beginning of Period Value	End of Period Value	Periodic Rate of Return
0	$1,000	$1,000	$1,200	20.00%
1	($400)	$800	$700	−12.50%
2	$300	$1,000	$1,400	40.00%
3	($200)	$1,200	$1,000	−16.67%
4	($1,000)	—	—	—
DWR =	8.2311%		TWR =	5.2034%

Portfolio B				
Period	Investor Deposits or Withdrawals	Beginning of Period Value	End of Period Value	Periodic Rate of Return
0	$1,000	$1,000	$1,200	20.00%
1	$400	$1,600	$1,400	−12.50%
2	($400)	$1,000	$1,400	40.00%
3	$400	$1,800	$1,500	−16.67%
4	($1,500)	—	—	—
DWR =	2.0245%		TWR =	5.2034%

Using the uneven cash flow keys of a financial calculator (something you will *never* have to do on the exam), we have calculated the dollar-weighted return (DWR) for Portfolio A to be 8.23% and the DWR for Portfolio B to be 2.02%. Is it reasonable to use a methodology that results in drastically different returns when each portfolio produced the same periodic rates of return? The answer depends on our goal. To evaluate the overall return for the portfolio, we want to use DWR. This provides the investor with his actual return. For portfolio managers, we generally do not use DWR. This is because managers do not control the timing of additional investments into the portfolio or the timing of withdrawals from the portfolio. A more accurate measure of the portfolio manager's ability is the time-weighted return.

19. 3 BENCHMARK PORTFOLIOS

Tens of thousands of stocks trade in the stock markets. Stock indexes, such as the S&P 500 or the Utility Index, are smaller groups of stocks that serve as a benchmark for measuring the performance of the overall market or sectors of the market.

Indexes are generally weighted for the capitalization (number of outstanding shares) of the companies included. Therefore, a large company's stock price changes will have a greater effect on the index. Indexes are often used as benchmark portfolios against which managed portfolios are measured in order to gauge the performance, or added value, of the fund manager. In addition, index mutual funds and ETFs will invest in the securities that compose an index to specifically mirror the index's performance. Following is a listing of indexes or averages that may appear on the exam.

TEST TOPIC ALERT

The exam will want you to know which index serves as the benchmark for which type of portfolio:

- Large Cap—S&P 500

- Mid Cap—S&P 400

- Small Cap—Russell 2000

- International Stocks—EAFE

19. 3. 1 DOW JONES INDUSTRIAL AVERAGE

The best known of all of the market indexes are those published by Dow Jones & Company. There are probably two reasons why the Dow Jones Industrial Average (DJIA) is so well known: first, because the 30 industrial stocks are among the 30 best-known corporations in the world and second (and some would say more important), the Dow Jones & Company also publishes *The Wall Street Journal*, the nation's leading financial newspaper. Because it is price weighted, the Dow Jones is truly an average. Originally it was computed by adding together the prices of one share for each of the 30 different companies and then dividing by 30. That had to be changed as soon as the first one of those 30 companies had a 2:1 stock split. Because a stock split will cause the market price of the stock to drop—that is, the average would be distorted by continuing to divide the 30 current market prices by 30—an adjustment had to be made to the 30 (called the divisor). Over the years, stock splits and other distributions have caused that original divisor of 30 to be adjusted. There are three other Dow Jones Averages: the 20 transportations, the 15 utilities, and the composite of all 65. On November 1, 1999, history was made when non-NYSE stocks were included in the DJIA for the first time. Added to the average were Microsoft and Intel, which are both listed on Nasdaq. The most recent addition (as of the date of this writing) was Apple Computer, by market capitalization, the most valuable company in the world.

19. 3. 2   STANDARD & POOR'S 500

The composition of the Standard & Poor's 500 (S&P 500) Composite Index includes four main groups of securities: 400 industrials, 20 transportation companies, 40 public utilities, and 40 financial institutions. The S&P 500 is a cap-weighted index using a base period of 1941–1943 equal to 10. Although most of the stocks in the S&P 500 are listed on the NYSE, many of the highest priced issues—Google, Apple, and Priceline—are traded on the Nasdaq Stock Market.

19. 3. 3   NEW YORK STOCK EXCHANGE (NYSE) INDEX

The NYSE publishes a composite index that covers all of the common stocks listed on the NYSE, more than 3,000 different companies. This index provides the most comprehensive measure of market activity on the NYSE. The NYSE index is cap weighted, similar to the S&P 500, but the base is December 31, 1965, and the index for the base is 50.

19. 3. 4   NASDAQ COMPOSITE INDEX

The over-the-counter market is represented by the Nasdaq Composite Index, which covers more than 3,000 over-the-counter companies. The Nasdaq Composite Index is calculated in a manner similar to those used for the S&P and NYSE indexes, with a base period of February 5, 1971, and an index number of 100. These indexes, their subgroups, and several other popular indexes are quoted daily in *The Wall Street Journal*. As with the others (except for the Dow Jones), this is also a cap-weighted index.

19. 3. 5   RUSSELL 2000 INDEX

The Russell 2000 index measures the performance of the small-cap segment of the U.S. equity universe. It includes approximately 2,000 of the smallest securities based upon their market capitalization (minimum market cap of $300 million). Like most of the others, it is market-cap weighted with the median market cap being something approximating $600 million.

19. 3. 6 EAFE

The EAFE, sometimes referred to as the MSCI EAFE (it was developed by Morgan Stanley Capital International), is an index of foreign stocks. The index is market capitalization weighted. The EAFE acronym stands for Europe, Australasia, and Far East.

The index includes a selection of stocks from 21 developed countries outside of the U.S. and Canada. The index has been calculated since the end of 1969 making it the oldest truly international stock index. It is probably the most common benchmark for foreign stock funds.

19. 3. 7 THE WILSHIRE 500

This is another market or cap-weighted index, but what makes it different is that it consists of virtually every U.S.-based company listed on the stock exchanges including the Nasdaq Stock Market but not the OTC Bulletin Board. When it was initially created in 1974, it did contain close to 5,000 issues, but now it has about 3,700.

TEST TOPIC ALERT   If you are asked to identify the index that reflects the broadest coverage of the U.S. stock markets, it is the Wilshire 5000.

QUICK QUIZ 19.A

1. Which of the following is a price-weighted average?
   A. Dow Jones Industrial Average
   B. MSCI EAFE
   C. Russell 2000
   D. S&P 500

2. An investor following foreign securities would be most interested in the performance of the
   A. Dow Jones Industrial Average
   B. MSCI EAFE
   C. Russell 2000
   D. S&P 500

3. An investor purchases 100 shares of GHI common stock at a price of $50 per share. Six months later, the stock is sold for $52 per share. In the interim, the investor has received 2 quarterly dividends of $0.50 and the CPI has risen by 2%. Expressed as a percentage, which of the following statements is TRUE?
   I. The investor's total return is 6%.
   II. The investor's annualized return is approximately 12%.
   III. The investor's real rate of return is 4%.
   IV. The investor's holding period return is 6%.
   A. I and III
   B. II and III
   C. I and IV
   D. I, II, III, and IV

Quick Quiz answers can be found at the end of the unit.

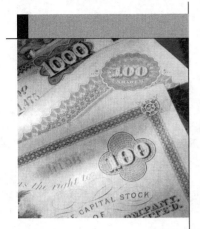

20

Retirement Plans and Educational Funding Programs

Retirement plans allow investors to accumulate resources to fund their retirement. Individuals accomplish this through business-sponsored retirement plans, personal plans, or individual and corporate retirement plans. To encourage Americans to save for retirement, Congress has passed legislation that allows investors to invest in certain retirement plans on a tax-deductible and/or tax-deferred basis.

Throughout this session, we give you the contribution limits for all plans described that are current for those filing 2015 tax returns. It is highly unlikely that any of those numbers, other than perhaps the IRA contribution limit, will be asked on the exam. Therefore, you should consider these as included for reference purposes, not for testing. The Series 65 exam will include approximately 9 questions on the material presented in this session.

When you have completed this session, you should be able to:

■ **describe** the unique features of traditional, Roth, and simplified employee pension plan individual retirement accounts;

■ **explain** the purpose of the Employee Retirement Income Security Act of 1974 and its primary features including the fiduciary obligations under the Uniform Prudent Investor Act;

■ **define** and differentiate between individual retirement accounts, Keogh plans, 403(b) plans, qualified corporate retirement plans, and nonqualified corporate retirement plans;

■ **understand** distributions from qualified plans and individual retirement accounts;

■ **recognize** the differences between the two major types of education funding programs; and

■ **compare** and **contrast** UGMA and UTMA accounts.

20. 1   INDIVIDUAL RETIREMENT ARRANGEMENTS (IRAs)

TAKE NOTE

Although *individual retirement arrangements* is the technical IRS term, (not tested), because everyone refers to these as individual retirement accounts (IRAs), we're going to use the common phrase to avoid confusion.

Individual retirement accounts (IRAs) were created to encourage people to save for their retirement. Most individuals with earned income may open and contribute to an IRA. Three types of IRAs are available, with different contribution, tax, and distribution characteristics: traditional IRAs, Roth IRAs, and simplified employee pension plan (SEP) IRAs.

IRAs are not to be confused with qualified plans or nonqualified plans used by businesses. Later in this unit we will cover topics such as pension plans, 401(k) plans, and deferred compensation plans. At this point, keep in mind that a qualified plan means that it meets the IRS requirements for the contributions to the plan to be tax deductible and the earnings to grow tax deferred. Nonqualified plans do not enjoy most of the tax benefits of qualified plans.

TAKE NOTE

Although we may include some actual contribution limits, it is unlikely that you will have to know any other than the IRA and Coverdell numbers.

20. 1. 1   TRADITIONAL IRAS

A **traditional IRA** allows a maximum *tax-deductible* annual contribution of the lesser of $5,500 per individual or $11,000 per couple, or 100% of earned income for the taxable year 2015. The income and capital gains earned in the account are tax deferred until the funds are withdrawn. For those covered by qualified employer plans, the tax deductibility of contributions to traditional IRAs is phased out as income increases over a specified level. It is unlikely to be tested, but when both spouses are covered by employer plans, the phase out begins at a lower level than when only one is.

TEST TOPIC ALERT

It is important to understand that anyone, as long as they received eligible compensation during the year and were not age 70½ by the end of the year, is eligible to open a traditional IRA. It makes no difference how much they earned or if they are covered by an employer plan—they can open a traditional IRA. Of course, earnings and plan coverage will have an impact on the deductibility of contributions, but the plan may still be opened, contributions made, and all earnings are tax deferred.

20. 1. 1. 1 Compensation for IRA Purposes

For purposes of contributing to an IRA, the IRS considers the following to be compensation:

- Wages, salaries, and tips
- Commissions and bonuses
- Self-employment income
- Alimony
- Nontaxable combat pay

20. 1. 1. 2 Not Compensation for IRA Purposes

For purposes of contributing to an IRA, the IRS does not consider the following to be compensation:

- Capital gains
- Interest and dividend income
- Pension or annuity income
- Child support
- Passive income from DPPs

TAKE NOTE

The contribution limit for IRAs is subject to increase based on the inflation rate. It is unlikely that the exact number will be tested, but it would make sense to verify the current contribution limits. These limits will also apply to the total combined contribution that might be made to a traditional IRA and a Roth IRA.

20. 1. 1. 3 Catch-Up Contributions for Older IRA Owners

The **Economic Growth and Tax Relief Reconciliation Act of 2001, (EGTRRA),** was the source of the legislation permitting certain individuals to make additional contributions to their IRAs. Individuals aged 50 and older are allowed to make **catch-up contributions** to their IRAs above the scheduled maximum annual contribution limit, which will enable them to save more for retirement. These catch-up payments can go either to a traditional IRA or to a Roth IRA.

Year	Additional Catch-Up Amount Allowed
2006+	$1,000

TEST TOPIC ALERT

The exam will want you to know that EGTRRA is responsible for the catch-up provisions.

20. 1. 2 ROTH IRAS

The Taxpayer Relief Act of 1997 created the Roth IRA. Contributions to Roth IRAs, unlike those of traditional IRAs, are not tax deductible. Regular contributions may always be withdrawn tax free because they are made with nondeductible contributions.

Earnings accumulated, however, may be withdrawn tax free, five years following the initial deposit, provided the:

■ account holder is 59½ or older;

■ money withdrawn is used for the first-time purchase of a principal residence (up to $10,000); or

■ account holder has died or become disabled.

20. 1. 2. 1 Contribution Limits

Contribution limits to Roth IRAs are the same as those for traditional IRAs. For an individual filing a 2015 tax return, the contribution limit is the lesser of $5,500 or 100% of earned income. In addition, a married employee may contribute an additional $5,500 to a nonworking or low-income spouse's Roth IRA. Unlike a traditional IRA, contributions may be made past age 70½ as long as the taxpayer has earned income.

An individual may contribute to both a traditional and a Roth IRA. However, the maximum combined contribution is $5,500 (or $6,500, if 50 or older).

20. 1. 2. 2 Eligibility Requirements

Anyone with earned income is eligible to open a Roth IRA provided the person's AGI falls below specified income levels. The following numbers are effective for those filing a tax return for 2015. A single person with an AGI of $116,000 or less may contribute the full amount to a Roth IRA. The ability to contribute to a Roth IRA is gradually phased out if the taxpayer's AGI is between $116,000 and $131,000.

For married taxpayers who file joint tax returns, the AGI limit is $183,000, with the contribution phased out for couples whose income is between $183,000 and $193,000.

20. 1. 2. 2. 1 Adjusted gross income (AGI)

Adjusted gross income, generally referred to as AGI, is computed on the bottom of the first page of your Form 1040. It might help you to take a look at yours. When you do your taxes, you begin by listing all of your earned income (salary, wages, bonuses) plus other income such as interest and dividends, capital gains, alimony received, and profits from a business you may own. From that total, you deduct certain items to arrive at the AGI. Among the more testable items that are deductible are:

■ traditional IRA contribution;

■ alimony paid;

■ self-employment tax; and

■ penalties paid on early withdrawal from a savings account.

20. 1. 2. 3 Roth Conversions

Anyone with a traditional IRA is permitted to convert it to a Roth IRA. However, there are income tax consequences. Basically, the entire amount converted is added to the investor's ordinary income. However, as long as the funds are transferred trustee to trustee, or, if distributed to the owner, are rolled over within 60 days, there will be no 10% early distribution tax penalty for those under age 59½. If some portion of the contributions to the traditional IRA were made with after-tax money, the IRS uses a proportionate system to determine how much is non-taxable, but that type of computation will not be tested. Conversions may also be done from any qualified employer plan such as 401(k) and 403(b) plans as well as Simple and SEP-IRAs.

20. 1. 2. 4 Key Points to Remember about the Roth IRA

- Maximum (current) contribution is $5,500 per year per individual.
- Contributions are not tax deductible.
- Distributions are tax free if taken after age 59½ and a Roth account has been open for at least five years.
- Distributions are not required to begin at age 70½.
- No 10% early distribution penalty for death, disability, and first-time home purchase.
- A minor can be named as beneficiary.

20. 1. 2. 5 myRA (my Retirement Account)

Please note: As of the date of printing, there has been no mention of this new program on the exam. We do not know when it will become a testable topic, but we've included it here not only so you will become familiar with it, but to ensure that when it does appear, our students will have the necessary information to answer the questions correctly.

In 2014, the U.S. Department of the Treasury developed myRA (my Retirement Account), a retirement savings account with a new type of Roth IRA investment that makes saving for retirement simple, safe, and affordable. Individuals can open a myRA account with no start-up cost and there are no fees for the maintenance of the account. myRA has no minimum contribution requirement, so savers can contribute the amount that best fits their budget. myRA is designed for people without access to employer-sponsored retirement savings plans. The investment in a myRA is backed by the United States Treasury and the account carries no risk of losing money.

Contributions to myRA accounts are invested in a new United States Treasury security, which safely earns interest at the same variable rate as investments in the government securities fund for federal employees. This fund has had an average annual return of 3.19% over the 10-year period ending December 2014.

The maximum annual contribution and income limits are the same as for any other Roth IRA.

Once the account value reaches $15,000 or the account has been opened 30 years (whichever comes first), savings will have to be transferred or rolled over into a private-sector Roth IRA. Savers can choose to transfer or roll over their account balance into a private-sector Roth IRA at any time prior to that if desired.

20. 1. 3   SIMPLIFIED EMPLOYEE PENSIONS (SEP IRAs)

Simplified employee pension plans (SEPs) offer self-employed persons and small businesses easy-to-administer pension plans. A SEP is a qualified plan that allows an employer to contribute money directly to an individual retirement account (IRA) set up for each employee, hence the name SEP IRA. Following is a list of the key points of which to be aware.

Eligibility. To be eligible, an employee must be at least 21 years of age, have performed services for the employer during at least three of the last five years, and have received at least $600 (for 2015) in compensation from the employer in the current year (the annual compensation figure is indexed for inflation).

Participation. SEP rules require the employer allow *all eligible employees* to participate.

Funding. A SEP allows the employer to contribute up to 25% of an employee's salary to the employee's SEP IRA each year, up to a maximum of $53,000 per employee per year in 2015. The employer determines the level of contributions each year and must contribute the same percentage for each employee, as well as the employer.

Vesting. Participants in a SEP IRA are **fully vested** immediately, meaning that once the money is deposited in an employee's SEP IRA, it belongs to the employee.

Taxation. Employer contributions are tax deductible to the employer. Contributions are not taxable to an employee until withdrawn, and earnings in the account accumulate tax deferred.

20. 1. 4   WITHDRAWALS FROM TRADITIONAL IRAS AND SEP IRAS

Distributions without penalty may begin after age 59½ and must begin by April 1 of the year following the year an individual turns 70½. Distributions before age 59½ may be subject to a tax penalty and withdrawals less than the required minimum distributions (RMDs), after age 70½ may also incur tax penalties.

TAKE NOTE

When is the deadline for receiving a RMD from an IRA? An account owner must take the first RMD for the year in which the account owner turns 70½. However, the first RMD payment can be delayed until April 1 of the year following the year in which the account owner turns 70½. For all subsequent years, including the year in which the first RMD was paid by April 1, the account owner must take the RMD by December 31 of the year.

Withdrawals may be made in lump sums, in varying amounts, or in regular installments and, to the extent withdrawals are from tax-deductible contributions, are taxable as ordinary income. When there are both deductible and nondeductible contributions, a formula is used whereby a portion of the withdrawal represents a nontaxable return of principal. Withdrawals before age 59½ are also subject to a 10% early withdrawal penalty unless they are due to death, disability, first-time purchase of a primary residence ($10,000 lifetime maximum), qualified higher education expenses for immediate family members, (including grandchildren, but not nieces or nephews), or certain medical expenses in excess of 10% of adjusted gross income (AGI). These exceptions also apply in the case of a nonqualified (taxable) distribution from a Roth IRA.

Withdrawals must begin by April 1 of the year following the year in which the account owner reaches age 70½, and they must meet minimum **Internal Revenue Code (IRC)** distribution requirements or incur a 50% penalty on the amounts falling short of the minimum.

One respect in which the Roth IRA differs from other retirement plans is that the age 70½ is irrelevant. There are no required minimum distributions and, as long as the individual has earned income, contributions may be made at any age.

There is one other way to tap your IRA before age 59½ without penalty—through the substantially equal periodic (SEPP) exception. The **substantially equal periodic payment exception** under IRS rule 72t states that if you receive IRA payments at least annually based on your life expectancy (or the joint life expectancies of you and your beneficiary), the withdrawals are not subject to the 10% penalty. The IRS has tables for determining the appropriate amount of each payment at any given age.

TAKE NOTE

For exam purposes, you can postpone beginning distributions until the later of:

- April 1 of the calendar year after you turn age 70½, or

- April 1 of the calendar year following your retirement (but only for qualified plans, not an IRA).

EXAMPLE

An IRA owner who reaches age 70½ on January 1, 2014, must begin withdrawals by April 1, 2015. However, if this individual is covered by an employer-sponsored plan, there are no RMDs from that plan (but there are from any traditional IRAs) until after retirement.

All distributions are treated as taxable income in the year in which received. Annuitized IRA distributions can be made to the account owner or jointly to the owner and spouse. If the account owner dies, payments are made to a designated beneficiary.

20. 1. 4. 1 Nondeductible Capital Withdrawals

IRA investors who contribute after-tax dollars to an IRA are not taxed on those funds when they are withdrawn from the account, but taxpayers are taxed at the ordinary income tax rate when they withdraw funds resulting from investment gains or income.

EXAMPLE

A client has invested $25,000 in after-tax dollars in an IRA currently worth $75,000. If the client were to withdraw $75,000, only $50,000 would be taxable.

TAKE NOTE

The early withdrawal penalties for all IRAs are waived in the event of death or disability.

TEST TOPIC ALERT

Assume questions are about traditional IRAs unless they specifically state *otherwise*.

20. 1. 5 CHARACTERISTICS OF IRAS

20. 1. 5. 1 Participation in an IRA

Any taxpayer younger than age 70½ who reports earned income for a given tax year may contribute to a traditional IRA, while there is no age limit on contributing to a Roth IRA. If one spouse has little or no earned income and a joint tax return is filed, a spousal IRA may be opened for that person and the contribution limits are the same as for any other IRA. Passive income from investments is not earned income.

20. 1. 5. 2 IRA Custodians

Taxpayers can appoint IRA custodians of their choice, selecting from securities broker-dealers, banks and savings institutions, insurance carriers, credit unions, and mutual fund distributors.

20. 1. 5. 3 IRA Contributions

For those filing a 2015 tax return, the maximum annual IRA contribution is $5,500 or 100% of earned income, whichever is less, for an employed individual and $5,500 for a spousal IRA, whether or not the spouse is employed.

The deductibility of an individual's contribution is reduced or eliminated if he participates in an employer-sponsored retirement plan and earns more than a specified amount.

Two persons who are part of a married couple, each of whom is ineligible to participate in a qualified plan and whose combined income is $200,000, may contribute and deduct a total of $11,000 ($13,000 if both persons are 50 or older). No deduction is allowed for a married couple who is eligible to participate in a qualified plan and whose combined income is $118,000 (for 2015) or more. Nevertheless, their contributions are permitted and all earnings are tax deferred.

IRA contributions for a specific taxable year may be made anytime from January 1st of that year through the required filing date of that year's return, (generally April 15 of the next year, unless the 15th falls on a holiday or weekend). If the individual obtains a filing extension, the deadline is still April 15.

IRA owners may withdraw any or all funds in their accounts at any time, although the funds attributable to earnings and deductible contributions are subject to income tax and may be subject to early withdrawal penalties.

TEST TOPIC ALERT

The exam may try to trick you into thinking that you can make a contribution later than April 15 if you have received an extension to file your taxes. You can't! You should know that an extension does not give you more time to **pay** your taxes, it only extends the time that you have to **file** your return.

20. 1. 5. 3. 1 Excess Contributions

Annual IRA contributions exceeding the maximum allowed are subject to a 6% penalty tax if the excess is not removed by the time the taxpayer files a tax return, but no later than April 15th.

20. 1. 5. 4 IRA Investments

Funds in an IRA account may be used to buy stocks, bonds, mutual funds, UITs, limited partnerships, REITS, U.S. government securities, gold or silver coins minted by the U.S. Treasury Department (American Eagles) as well as certain platinum coins and certain gold, silver, palladium, and platinum bullion, annuities, and many other investments.

IRA investments should be relatively conservative and should reflect the investor's age and risk tolerance profile. Because an IRA serves as a source of retirement funds, it is important that the account be managed for adequate long-term growth.

20. 1. 5. 4. 1 Ineligible and Inappropriate Investments

Collectibles, including antiques, gems, rare coins, works of art, and stamps, are not acceptable IRA investments. Life insurance contracts (such as whole life and term) may not be purchased in an IRA. Tax-free municipal bonds, municipal bond funds, and municipal bond UITs are also generally inappropriate for an IRA (or any tax-qualified plan) because their yields are typically lower than those of other similar investments, and the income generated is taxable on withdrawal from the IRA.

20. 1. 5. 4. 2 Ineligible Investment Practices

No short sales of stock, speculative option strategies, or margin account trading is permitted in an IRA or any other retirement plan. Covered call writing is allowed.

Ineligible Investments	Ineligible Investment Practices
Collectibles	Short sales of stock
Whole life insurance	Speculative option strategies
Term life Insurance	Margin account trading

20. 1. 5. 4. 3 Real Estate in an IRA (or Qualified Plan)

Legally, you may invest in real estate in your IRA or as a participant in a 401(k) or other qualified plan. It is not commonly something that is written into the documents, but it could be. Probably the biggest reason why the provision is rarely found is because of the extra care that must be taken when making a real estate investment. If done improperly, serious problems with the IRS can result. If it is done as a truly hands-off investment, it is unlikely that there will be an issue. However, the moment the participant derives any personal benefit from the property—such as staying in a condo purchased in resort area that is rented out most of the year, or allowing prohibited persons to use the property—look out.

TEST TOPIC ALERT

The IRS defines prohibited persons (people who can't benefit from real estate held in an IRA or qualified plan) as any "member of the family." Who are they? A member of the family includes a spouse, ancestors (parents and grandparents), children, grandchildren, great grandchildren, and spouses of children, grandchildren, and great grandchildren. Believe it or not, a brother or sister of an individual is not a member of the family for this purpose, but a legally adopted child of an individual is treated as a child by blood.

20. 1. 5. 5 Moving IRAs

Individuals may move their funds and investments from one IRA to another IRA through a rollover or transfer.

20. 1. 5. 5. 1 Rollovers

An IRA account owner may take temporary possession of the account funds to move the retirement account to another custodian. The account owner may do so only once per 12-month period, and the rollover must be completed within 60 calendar days of the funds' withdrawal from the original plan. However, 100% of the withdrawn amount must be rolled into the new account, or the unrolled balance will be subject to income tax and, if applicable, early withdrawal penalty.

A participant in a business-sponsored qualified plan may move his plan assets to a rollover IRA if he leaves the company and elects to take a lump sum distribution. If the transfer is made directly from the qualified plan to an IRA (direct transfer), the participant never takes possession of the funds. If the participant does take possession of the funds, he must complete the rollover within *60 calendar days* of withdrawing the funds from the qualified plan.

When the participant takes possession of the funds from a qualified plan to make a rollover, the payor of the distribution must, by law, withhold 20% of the distribution as a withholding tax. The participant must, nonetheless, roll over 100% of the plan distribution, including the funds withheld, or be subject to income tax and, if applicable, early withdrawal penalty.

EXAMPLE

A 50-year-old individual with $100,000 in his company retirement plan changes employers. His pension plan may be distributed to him as a rollover in a lump-sum payment, minus the mandatory 20% withholding of $20,000. He must then deposit $100,000 in an IRA rollover account within 60 days. Any portion not rolled over, including the $20,000 withheld, is considered a distribution subject to ordinary income tax and early withdrawal penalty. If he deposits the entire $100,000 into the IRA, he must apply on his next income tax return for a refund of the $20,000 withheld.

TAKE NOTE

Rollovers by nonspouse beneficiaries of certain retirement plan distributions. Effective January 1, 2007, the Pension Protection Act of 2006 amended the Internal Revenue Code of 1986 to allow nonspouse beneficiaries to roll over qualified retirement plan distributions to an inherited traditional IRA. Using the term *rollover* may be confusing because these distributions must be made via direct trustee-to-trustee transfer, and any checks made out to the beneficiary are not eligible for rollover. The IRA must be set up as an inherited IRA, with minimum distributions taken under the rules that apply to beneficiaries. It is possible that this will be tested on your exam.

20. 1. 5. 5. 2 Direct Rollovers from Retirement Plans to Roth IRAs

Effective January 1, 2008, the Pension Protection Act of 2006 amended the Internal Revenue Code of 1986 to allow rollovers from qualified retirement plans directly to Roth IRAs, providing the client meets the requirements for converting a traditional IRA to a Roth IRA. The main requirement is that the client must report the entire amount converted into the Roth as ordinary income in the year of conversion (or rollover).

20. 1. 5. 5. 3 Transfers

In a direct transfer of an IRA or a qualified retirement plan, account assets are sent directly from one IRA custodian to another, and the account owner never takes possession of the funds. The number of IRA transfers an account owner may make per year is unlimited. Transfers from qualified plans to IRAs generally make better sense than rollovers because the 20% federal tax withholding does not apply to direct transfers of portfolios and, since there is no specified time limit, you don't have to rush to meet the 60-day requirement.

20. 1. 5. 6 Earnings Limitations for Tax Benefits

Traditional and certain SEP IRA participants may deduct contributions to their IRAs from their taxable income. The deductibility limits are lowered for individuals who are eligible for other qualified plans.

These AGI limits increase every year and will NOT be tested. Individuals who are ineligible to participate in qualified plans may deduct IRA contributions regardless of income level.

For those filing 2015 tax returns, the IRA deductibility phaseout range is expressed in the table below.

Year	Phaseout Range: Single Filers	Phaseout Range: Joint Filers
2015	$61,000–$71,000	$98,000–$118,000

Income and capital gains earned from investments in any IRA account are not taxed until the funds are withdrawn and, if a qualified withdrawal, are not taxed at all in the case of a Roth.

20. 1. 5. 7 Inheriting an IRA

The rules on the treatment of an inherited IRA depend on whether the beneficiary is the spouse or is some other relative (or nonrelative) of the deceased. Another factor is if the deceased had already begun taking RMDs. This issue is very technical, and we will only cover points that might be tested.

20. 1. 5. 7. 1 Spousal Beneficiary

When the beneficiary is the spouse, there are two choices that can be made:

- Do a spousal rollover, meaning the amount of the inheritance is rolled over into the spouse's own IRA
- Continue to own the IRA as the beneficiary

When doing a spousal rollover, this is treated, logically, as your own with all of the normal rules applying (withdrawal ages, RMDs, and so forth). That means that if the spouse is younger than 59½, any distributions prior to then will be subject to the 10% penalty (unless meeting the exceptions).

If, however, the spouse elects to continue the account as the beneficiary, then there is no 10% penalty for withdrawals prior to age 59½. That's the good news. The bad news is that RMDs (from a traditional IRA or SEP IRA) must begin when the deceased would have had to take them, a disappointment if the survivor is the younger partner. However, the RMDs will be computed based on the beneficiary's age, not that of the deceased. Also, if it is a Roth IRA and the account hasn't been open for at least five years, any withdrawal of earnings will be subject to income tax but not the 10% penalty.

20. 1. 5. 7. 2 Nonspouse Beneficiary

Things are different when the person inheriting a traditional IRA is not the spouse of the deceased. For one thing, unlike the spouse, the beneficiary will not be allowed to rollover the inherited IRA into their own IRA, this is simply *not* an option. In general, there are four primary options available, the fourth of which probably won't be tested.

■ **Take the cash now:** the non-spouse IRA beneficiary can withdraw 100% of the IRA account immediately. If this option is chosen, then 100% of the amount withdrawn (assuming the IRA was funded completely with pre-tax contributions) will be included in taxable income during the year of withdrawal;

■ **Cash out the IRA in 5 years**: the non-spouse IRA beneficiary is allowed to withdraw all of the funds from the IRA by December 31 of the fifth year following the IRA account owner's death. If this option is selected, then each withdrawal will be included in taxable income (once again, assuming all contributions were pre-tax) during the year the funds are withdrawn. Interestingly, the IRS does not require the payments to be made with any designated frequency. That is, you can take a portion the first year because you can use some cash, nothing for the next three years, and the balance no later than December 31 of the fifth year;

■ **Take out required minimum distributions over the beneficiary's own life expec-tancy**: non-spouse IRA beneficiaries, may be able to take RMDs over their life expec-tancy, leaving the bulk of the account to continue to grow in the tax deferred account. Each distribution taken will be included in taxable income during the year the funds are withdrawn. In order to choose this option, a separate inherited IRA account in the deceased account owner's name for the benefit (FBO) of the beneficiary must be established and the first required minimum distribution must be taken by December 31 of the year following the year of the account owner's death. For example, the inherited IRA account would be titled "Sammy Jones, IRA (deceased 5/5/15), FBO Monique Gaillaird, beneficiary"; and

■ **Take RMDs based on the life expectancy of the oldest beneficiary:** If there are mul-tiple beneficiaries and the decision is to stretch out the withdrawals, the IRS requires that the life expectancy of the oldest beneficiary be used. Obviously, this will result in a higher payout (and more tax revenue) than if the life expectancy of the youngest was an option. This can be avoided if separate inherited IRA accounts are set up for each beneficiary. In that case, RMDs are figured for each account.

If the beneficiary does nothing by December 31 of the year following the year of death, the default option used by the IRA is the five-year withdrawal option.

EXAMPLE

Grandma Abigail died at age 82 with a traditional IRA valued at $100,000. Her daughter Betsy, 53 years old, was the sole beneficiary. Betsy's choices would include

   A.   rolling over this IRA to her own IRA

   B.   taking distributions spread out over a 5-year period

   C.   taking the cash by December 31st and paying the 10% tax penalty because she is under 59 ½

   D.   leave the IRA in the name of the deceased and continue with the RMDs

Answer: B. Among the options available to a non-spouse beneficiary is spreading the payout over 5 years. Betsy, being a daughter and not a spouse, could not rollover into her own IRA. Even though she is under 59½, inheritors of IRAs do not incur the 10% penalty tax on withdrawals.

TAKE NOTE

Just as with the spouse continuing the IRA as beneficiary, if the account were a Roth IRA and it had not been opened for the five-year minimum, any earnings distributed will be subject to ordinary income tax but not the 10% penalty.

20. 1. 5. 7. 3 Disclaiming an IRA

Believe it or not, there are actually people who inherit IRAs who don't want the money. There are any number of reasons why (none of which will be tested), but what will be tested is what happens when the beneficiary **disclaims** the proceeds.

A disclaimer is a refusal to accept a gift or inheritance. Perhaps it is easier to understand like this: If you accept an item left to you by someone who has died, you are claiming that asset; if you refuse it, you are disclaiming it. In order for the disclaimer to be effective, it must be done within nine months of death, it must be in writing, and, of course, you cannot have taken any of the money.

If the named beneficiary of an IRA disclaims all or part of the inherited IRA, the disclaimer has the effect of changing the beneficiary of the retirement plan. In general, the assets pass to the contingent beneficiary(s). What if no contingent beneficiary has been named? Unless the IRA adoption document provides for it, the person disclaiming cannot decide where the money goes—it will follow the provisions of the deceased's will.

When the proceeds pass to a single beneficiary, that person must begin RMDs, but they are based on his life expectancy. If there are multiple beneficiaries, the RMDs will either be based on the age of the oldest, or, if done properly, each of them can use their own life expectancy. This is a highly technical process and requires the use of qualified professionals to ensure that maximum benefit is achieved.

EXAMPLE

Joseph Miller passes away at the age of 72 and leaves his wife, Josephine, his traditional IRA with a value of $1,800,000. There are many other assets in the estate, and Mrs. Miller decides to disclaim the entire IRA. She would like to pass on the assets to her three grandchildren in equal shares with another share going to her favorite charity. Assuming the IRA adoption document permits the beneficiary to designate in this matter, the charity will receive $450,000 with no tax liability at all, and the three grandchildren will each receive $450,000 on which distributions may be stretched out over their life expectancy.

QUICK QUIZ 20.A

1. An individual younger than age 70½ may contribute to a traditional IRA
   A. only if he has earned income
   B. only if he is not covered by a pension plan through an employer
   C. only if he does not own a Keogh plan
   D. only if his adjusted gross income is between $91,000 and $118,000 if married, and $61,000 and $71,000 if single

2. If a 50-year-old individual wants to withdraw funds from her IRA, the withdrawal will be taxed as
   A. ordinary income
   B. ordinary income plus a 10% penalty
   C. capital gains
   D. capital gains plus a 10% penalty

3. Premature distribution from an IRA is generally subject to a
   A. 5% penalty plus tax
   B. 6% penalty plus tax
   C. 10% penalty plus tax
   D. 50% penalty plus tax

4. Who of the following will NOT incur a penalty on an IRA withdrawal?
   A. Man who has just become totally disabled
   B. Woman who turned 59 a month before the withdrawal
   C. Woman, age 50, who decides on early retirement
   D. Man in his early 40s who uses the money to buy a second home

5. Which of the following statements regarding IRAs is NOT true?
   A. IRA rollovers must be completed within 60 days of receipt of the distribution.
   B. Cash value life insurance is a permissible IRA investment, but term insurance is not.
   C. The investor must be younger than age 70½ to open and contribute to an IRA.
   D. Distributions may begin at age 59½ and must begin by April 1 after the year in which the investor turns 70½.

6. SEP IRAs
   A. are used primarily by large corporations
   B. are used primarily by small businesses
   C. are set up by nonemployees
   D. cannot be set up by self-employed persons

7. Which of the following statements regarding both traditional IRAs and Roth IRAs is TRUE?
   A. Contributions are deductible.
   B. Withdrawals at retirement are tax free.
   C. Contribution limits are identical.
   D. To avoid penalty, distributions must begin April 1 after the year the owner reaches age 70½.

Quick Quiz answers can be found at the end of the unit.

20. 2   KEOGH (HR-10) PLANS

Keogh plans are Employee Retirement Income Security Act (ERISA)-qualified plans intended for self-employed individuals and owner-employees of unincorporated business concerns or professional practices. Included in the self-employed category are independent contractors, consultants, freelancers, and anyone else who files and pays self-employment Social Security taxes. The term *owner-employee* refers to sole proprietors.

TAKE NOTE

Whenever the term *qualified plan* is used, it refers specifically to an employer-sponsored plan, not an IRA.

20. 2. 1   CONTRIBUTIONS

Contribution limits for a Keogh Plan are significantly higher than those for an IRA. For those filing tax returns in 2015, as much as $53,000 may be contributed on behalf of a plan participant. Those who are eligible for a Keogh Plan may also maintain an IRA. If the business has employees, they must be covered at the same contribution percentage as the owner in order for the plan to be nondiscriminatory.

TEST TOPIC ALERT

Only earnings from self-employment count towards determining the maximum that may be contributed. For example, if a corporate employee had a part time consulting job, only that income, not the corporate salary, could be included in the computation.

20. 2. 1. 1   Non-Tax-Deductible Contributions

In addition to tax-deductible contributions, a Keogh plan participant may make non-deductible contributions. The income and capital gains accumulate tax free until the owner withdraws them. However, if the voluntary contribution results in a total contribution that exceeds the annual maximum, the excess may be subject to a penalty tax.

20. 2. 1. 2   Eligibility

Employee participation in a Keogh plan is subject to these eligibility rules.

- **Full-time employees** are employees who receive compensation for at least 1,000 hours of work per year.
- **Tenured employees** are employees who have completed one or more years of continuous employment.
- **Adult employees** are employees 21 years and older and, just as with traditional IRAs, not in excess of 70½.

20. 2. 2 COMPARISON OF IRAS AND KEOGH PLANS

Keogh plans and IRAs are designed to encourage individuals to set aside funds for retirement income. Although both IRAs and Keoghs are tax advantaged, an IRA does not involve employer contributions and, thus, is not a plan qualified by **ERISA**. The principal similarities between Keoghs and IRAs are listed in the following.

- **Tax deferral of contributions to plans**. Taxes are deferred on contributions until the individual receives distributions.

- **Tax sheltered**. Investment income and capital gains are not taxed until withdrawn at which time they are subject to taxation at ordinary income rates.

- **Contributions**. Only cash may be contributed to a plan. In the event of a rollover or transfer, cash and securities from the transferring account can be deposited.

- **Distributions**. Distributions without penalty can begin as early as age 59½.

- **Penalties for early withdrawal**. The individual pays income tax on the total amount withdrawn, plus a 10% penalty. Early withdrawals without penalty are permitted in the event of death or disability.

- **Payout options**. Distributions may be in a lump sum or periodic payments.

- **Beneficiary**. Upon the planholder's death, payments are made to a designated beneficiary (or beneficiaries).

QUICK QUIZ 20.B

1. Which of the following may participate in a Keogh plan?

    I.   Self-employed doctor
    II. Analyst who makes money giving speeches outside regular working hours
    III. Individual with a full-time job who also has income from freelancing
    IV. Corporate executive who receives $5,000 in stock options from his corporation

    A. I only
    B. I and II
    C. I, II and III
    D. I, II, III and IV

2. Which of the following are characteristics of a Keogh plan?

    I.   Dividends, interest, and capital gains are tax deferred.
    II. Distributions after age 70½ are tax free.
    III. Contributions are allowed for a nonworking spouse.
    IV. Lump-sum distributions are allowed.

    A. I and II
    B. I and III
    C. I and IV
    D. II and III

3. Which would disqualify a person from participation in a Keogh plan?

    A. She turned 70 eight months ago.
    B. She has a salaried position in addition to her self-employment.
    C. Her spouse has company sponsored retirement benefits.
    D. She has an IRA.

20. 3   403(B) PLANS (TAX-EXEMPT ORGANIZATIONS)

403(b) plans are qualified tax-deferred retirement plans for employees of public school systems, (403(b) employees), and tax-exempt, nonprofit organizations such as churches and charitable institutions, (501(c)(3) employees). Qualified employees may exclude contributions from their taxable incomes provided they do not exceed limits.

Qualified annuity plans offered under Section 403(b) of the IRC, sometimes referred to as **tax-sheltered annuities (TSAs)**, are intended to encourage retirement savings. To ensure this objective, 403(b)s (like IRAs and other retirement plans) are subject to tax penalties if savings are withdrawn before a participant retires.

20. 3. 1   TAX ADVANTAGES

The following tax advantages apply to 403(b)s.

■ Contributions (which generally come from salary reduction) are excluded from a participant's gross income.

■ Participant's earnings accumulate tax free until distribution.

20. 3. 1. 1   Income Exclusion

If an eligible employee elects to make annual contributions to a 403(b), those contributions are excluded from the employee's gross income for that year. The amount of the contribution is not reported as income, resulting in lower current income taxes.

20. 3. 1. 2   Tax-Deferred Accumulation

Earnings in a 403(b) accumulate with no current taxation of earnings or gains and do not increase the participant's taxable income until the dollars are withdrawn at retirement, usually when that person is in a lower tax bracket.

20. 3. 1. 3   Investments

Although, historically, annuities have been the investment vehicle of choice, 403(b) plans offer mutual funds, stocks, bonds, and CDs (but not life insurance policies) as investment vehicles. Specific money market instruments, like commercial paper, are not allowable investments (although a money market mutual fund would be). Because of the range of investments, banks, brokerage houses, savings and loans, and credit unions may offer these plans.

20. 3. 1. 3. 1   Guaranteed Investment Contracts (GICs)

Another popular option for 403(b) plans (as well as 401(k) plans), is the Guaranteed Investment Contract, almost always referred to by its initials, GIC. These are contracts issued by insurance companies that offer a guaranteed return of principal at a certain date in the future and come with a fixed rate of return that is generally a bit higher than that offered by comparable bank CDs.

20. 3. 2 ELIGIBILITY REQUIREMENTS

To be eligible to establish a 403(b), an employer must qualify as a:

- public educational 403(b) institution;
- tax-exempt 501(c)3 organization; or
- church organization.

20. 3. 2. 1 Tax-Exempt 501(c)3

As stated earlier, 501(c)3 organizations are tax-exempt entities specifically cited in the IRC as eligible to establish 403(b)s for their employees. Typical 501(c)3 organizations include:

- private colleges and universities;
- trade schools;
- parochial schools;
- zoos and museums;
- research and scientific foundations;
- religious and charitable institutions; and
- private hospitals and medical schools.

20. 3. 2. 2 Public Educational 403(b)

To qualify as a public educational institution, an organization must be state supported, a political subdivision, or an agency of a state. Private school systems have a separate set of qualifying rules. State-run educational systems include:

- elementary schools;
- secondary schools;
- colleges and universities; and
- medical schools.

Individuals employed by the above school systems in the following job classifications may enroll in a 403(b) plan. These include:

- teachers and other faculty members;
- administrators, managers, principals, supervisors, and other members of the administrative staff;
- counselors;
- clerical staff and maintenance workers; and
- individuals who perform services for the institution, such as doctors or nurses.

20. 3. 2. 3 Definition of an Employee

Only employees of qualified employers are eligible to participate in a 403(b) plan. Independent contractors are not eligible. It is the employer's responsibility to determine an individual's status or definition.

Eligibility. Similar to other qualified plans, all 403(b)s (whether employer contribution or employee elective deferral) must be made available to each full-time employee who has both reached age 21 and completed one year of service.

20. 3. 3 PLAN REQUIREMENTS

A 403(b) plan must meet two requirements.

- The plan must be in writing and must be made through a plan instrument, a trust agreement, or both.
- The employer must remit plan contributions to an annuity contract, a mutual fund, or another approved investment.

20. 3. 4 CONTRIBUTION LIMITS

An employer can make contributions to a 403(b) solely on behalf of the covered employee or in conjunction with an employee deferral.

20. 3. 4. 1 Salary Reduction

403(b) Contributions are made by having the employee take a salary reduction. As such, the money is withdrawn prior to taxation. For 2015, the maximum is $18,000 with a $6,000 catch-up provision.

20. 3. 4. 2 Employer Contributions

Employer contributions to a 403(b) are generally subject to the same maximums that apply to all defined contribution plans: the lesser of 100% of the participant's compensation or $53,000 per year.

20. 3. 5 TAXATION OF DISTRIBUTIONS FROM A 403(B)

Distributions from a 403(b) must follow the same rules as distributions from all qualified plans. Because the employee's 403(b) contributions are made with pretax dollars and all earnings were tax deferred, any distribution is subject to ordinary income tax rates in the year it is received. A normal distribution can start at age 59½. Premature distribution is subject to a 10% penalty tax unless the distribution is made for waiver of the penalty.

Distributions must start by April 1 of the year following the year in which the participant reaches age 70½, or they will be subject to the excess accumulation tax. Once distributions begin, they must be paid annually by December 31 of each tax year following the initial distribution.

1. A customer works as a nurse in a public school and wants to know more about participating in the school's TSA plan. Which of the following statements is(are) TRUE?

    I.   Contributions are made with before-tax dollars.
    II. He is not eligible to participate.
    III. Distributions before age 59½ are normally subject to penalty tax.
    IV. Mutual funds and CDs are available investment vehicles.

    A. I, II and III
    B. I and III
    C. I, III and IV
    D. II only

2. A retirement plan that allows the employee to make pre-tax contributions (within certain limits), provides for tax deferral of earnings, and is available for employees of public school systems and certain tax-exempt organizations is

    A. a 403(b) plan
    B. a 401(k) plan
    C. an SEP IRA
    D. a payroll deduction plan

3. Minimum distributions from a TSA are required when a retired participant is age

    A. 59½
    B. 70½
    C. 85
    D. There is no minimum distribution rule applicable to TSAs.

4. The risk level of a typical guaranteed investment contract (GIC) with an insurance company is best described as

    A. conservative
    B. moderately risky
    C. extremely risky
    D. impossible to determine

20. 4   CORPORATE-SPONSORED RETIREMENT PLANS

In this section, we will be discussing qualified plans sponsored by corporations. These include pension plans, profit-sharing plans, and the highly popular 401(k) plans.

The **Employee Retirement Income Security Act of 1974 (ERISA)** is federal legislation that regulates the establishment and management of corporate pension or retirement plans, also known as **private sector plans**.

All qualified corporate plans must be established under a trust agreement. A trustee is appointed for each plan and has a fiduciary responsibility for the plan and the beneficial owners (the plan holders).

20. 4. 1 EMPLOYEE RETIREMENT INCOME SECURITY ACT OF (ERISA)

ERISA guidelines for the regulation of retirement plans include the following.

■ **Eligibility.** If a company offers a retirement plan, all employees must be covered if they are 21 years old or older, have one year of service, and work 1,000 hours per year.

■ **Funding.** Funds contributed to the plan must be segregated from other corporate assets. The plan's trustees have a fiduciary responsibility to invest prudently and manage funds in a way that represents the best interests of all participants.

■ **Vesting.** Employees must be entitled to their entire retirement benefit amounts within a certain time, even if they no longer work for the employer.

■ **Communication.** The retirement plan must be in writing, and employees must be kept informed of plan benefits, availability, account status, and vesting procedure no less frequently than annually.

■ **Nondiscrimination.** A uniformly applied formula determines employee benefits and contributions. Such a method ensures equitable and impartial treatment.

TAKE NOTE
ERISA is often referred to as the **Pension Reform Act**, but it regulates almost all types of employee benefit plans and personal retirement plans.

ERISA regulations apply to *private sector* (corporate) plans only. Plans for federal or state government workers (*public sector* plans) are not subject to ERISA.

20. 4. 1. 1 Fiduciary Responsibility Under ERISA

Because most retirement plans were set up under trust agreements, when it came for ERISA to address fiduciary responsibilities of plan trustees, there was a long history of trust law to fall back on.

It all began with the Prudent Man Rule. That legal standard was established in 1830 by a Massachusetts Court decision (*Harvard College v. Amory*, 9 Pick. [26 Mass.] 446, 461 [1830]):

All that is required of a trustee to invest is, that he shall conduct himself faithfully and exercise sound discretion. He is to observe how men of prudence, discretion and intelligence manage their own affairs, not in regard to speculation, but in regard to the permanent disposition of their funds, considering the probable income, as well as the probable safety of the capital to be invested.

Although it was possible to place common stock in a trust portfolio, the emphasis seemed to be on taking defensive positions that while preserving capital, did expose the portfolio to inflation risk. It was clear that some updating was necessary.

Beginning with the dynamic growth of the stock markets in the late 1960s, the investment practices of fiduciaries experienced significant change. As a result, the Uniform Prudent Investor Act (UPIA) was passed in 1994 as an attempt to update trust investment laws in recognition of those many changes. One of the major influences on this legislation was the growing acceptance of modern portfolio theory. The UPIA (now used in almost every state) makes five fundamental alterations in the former criteria for prudent investing. Those changes are as follows.

■ The standard of prudence is applied to any investment as part of the total portfolio, rather than to individual investments. In this context, the term *portfolio* means all of the trust's or estate's assets.

■ The trade-off in all investments between risk and return is identified as the fiduciary's primary consideration.

■ All categorical restrictions on types of investments have been removed; the trustee can invest in anything that plays an appropriate role in achieving the risk/return objectives of the trust and that meets the other requirements of prudent investing.

■ The well-accepted requirement that fiduciaries diversify their investments has been integrated into the definition of prudent investing.

■ The much-criticized former rule forbidding the trustee to delegate investment functions has been reversed. Delegation is now permitted, subject to safeguards.

With greater numbers of trustees delegating investment decisions to investment advisers, NASAA has determined that you must know how the UPIA affects your role. Here are some thoughts that will help you on the exam.

■ A trustee must invest and manage trust assets as a prudent investor would, by considering the purposes, terms, distribution requirements, and other circumstances of the trust. In satisfying this standard, the trustee must exercise reasonable care, skill, and caution.

■ A trustee's investment and management decisions about individual assets must be evaluated not in isolation but in the context of the total portfolio and as a part of an overall investment strategy with risk and return objectives that are reasonably suited to the trust.

■ Among circumstances that a trustee must consider in investing and managing trust assets are any of the following that are relevant to the trust or its beneficiaries:

— General economic conditions

— The possible effect of inflation or deflation

— The expected tax consequences of investment decisions or strategies

— The role that each asset plays within the total portfolio, including financial assets, tangible and intangible personal property, and real property

— The expected total return from income and the appreciation of capital

— Other resources of the beneficiaries

— Needs for liquidity, regularity of income, and preservation or appreciation of capital

— An asset's special relationship or special value, if any, to the purposes of the trust or to one or more of the beneficiaries

- A trustee who has special skills or expertise, or who is named trustee in reliance upon the trustee's representation that the trustee has special skills or expertise, has a duty to use those special skills or expertise. This particular item led to the most stringent standard, that of the **prudent expert** for one acting as a professional money manager.

- For those without special skills or expertise, a trustee may delegate investment and management functions as long as the trustee exercises reasonable care, skill, and caution in:

  — selecting the adviser,

  — establishing the scope and terms of the delegation, consistent with the purposes and terms of the trust, and

  — periodically reviewing the adviser's actions, to monitor the adviser's performance and compliance with the terms of the delegation. (However, something that cannot be delegated is the amount and timing of distributions. If it is for a trust, the trust document usually spells out those provisions and, in the case of a qualified retirement plan, the plan document accomplishes the same purpose.)

- A trustee who complies with all of the above is not liable to the beneficiaries or the trust for the decisions or actions of the adviser to whom the function was delegated.

- In performing a delegated function, the adviser owes a duty to the trust to exercise reasonable care to comply with the terms of the delegation.

20. 4. 1. 1. 1 Section of ERISA

Specifically, there are a number of regulations that apply directly to retirement plan fiduciaries. The details are spelled out in ERISA Section 404.

Under Section 404 of ERISA, every person who acts as a fiduciary for an employee benefit plan must perform his responsibilities in accordance with the plan document specifications. Under ERISA, trustees cannot delegate fiduciary duties, but they can delegate investment management responsibilities to a qualified investment manager.

TEST TOPIC ALERT   Although the UPIA permits the delegation of portfolio management decisions, trustees cannot delegate certain fiduciary duties, such as determining the amount and timing of distributions.

Fiduciary responsibilities to the plan are explicit. With respect to the plan, fiduciaries must act:

- solely in the interest of plan participants and beneficiaries;

- for the exclusive purpose of providing benefits to participants and their beneficiaries and defraying reasonable plan expenses;

- with the care, skill, prudence, and diligence under the circumstances then prevailing that a prudent professional would use (known as the **prudent expert rule**);

- to diversify investments to minimize the risk of large losses, unless doing so is clearly not prudent under the circumstances; and

- in accordance with the governing plan documents unless they are not consistent with ERISA.

Under ERISA provisions, the fiduciary must be as prudent as the average expert, not the average person. To act with care, skill, prudence, and caution, the fiduciary must also:

- diversify plan assets;
- make investment decisions under the prudent expert standard;
- monitor investment performance;
- control investment expenses; and
- not engage in prohibited transactions.

TAKE NOTE

A plan participant or beneficiary who controls his specific plan account is not a fiduciary.

TEST TOPIC ALERT

You may be required to know that transaction cost is not a determining factor in security selection. That is, when the fiduciary is deciding what security will fit the needs of the portfolio, the amount of commission involved in the purchase is not considered when determining if that security is an appropriate addition.

20. 4. 1. 2 Investment Policy Statement

Although it is not specifically mandated under ERISA, it is strongly suggested that each employee benefit plan have an investment policy statement, preferably in writing, which serves as a guideline for the plan's fiduciary regarding funding and investment management decisions. Investment policy statements address the specific needs of the plan.

For employee benefit plans that use outside investment managers (such as mutual funds), the fiduciary must ensure that the investment alternatives available to plan members are consistent with the policy statement.

A typical investment policy statement (IPS) will include:

- investment objectives for the plan;
- determination for meeting future cash flow needs;
- investment philosophy including asset allocation style;
- investment selection criteria (but *not* the specific securities themselves); and
- methods for monitoring procedures and performance.

TEST TOPIC ALERT

The IPS will NOT include specific security selection

20. 4. 1. 3   Prohibited Transactions by the Plan Fiduciary

ERISA allows for a wide range of investments and investment practices, but a plan fiduciary is strictly prohibited from any conflicts of interest, such as:

- self-dealing, dealing with plan assets in his own interest, or for his own account;
- acting in a transaction involving the plan on behalf of a party with interests adverse to the plan; and
- receiving any compensation for his personal account from any party dealing with the plan in connection with plan transactions.

TEST TOPIC ALERT
Under Section 407 of ERISA, a plan may not acquire any security or real (or personal) property of the employer, if immediately after such acquisition the aggregate fair market value of employer securities and employer real property held by the plan exceeds 10% of the fair market value of the assets of the plan.

20. 4. 1. 3. 1   Party in Interest

ERISA has a rather broad definition of the term *party in interest*, but it basically includes anyone who can have an impact on an employee benefit plan, including those who render advice to the plan. It is not an overstatement to say that all transactions involving parties in interest to an ERISA-covered plan are prohibited, unless there is an exemption for them.

TEST TOPIC ALERT
Anyone in the position of trustee over the assets of a qualified plan may not use the plan assets to make loans to the employer, even if failure to do so could lead to the company suffering a financial failure.

20. 4. 1. 4   Safe Harbor Provisions of Section 404(c)

Several times, we have mentioned the requirement for the plan fiduciary to diversify the plan's investments. There is a particular part of ERISA, Section 404(c) dealing with 401(k) plans that provides a safe harbor from liability for the trustee if certain conditions are met. Under ERISA Section 404(c), a fiduciary is not liable for losses to the plan resulting from the participant's selection of investment in his own account, provided the participant exercised control over the investment and the plan met the detailed requirements of a Department of Labor regulation—that is, the 404(c) regulation.

There are three basic conditions of this regulation:

- Investment selection
- Investment control
- Communicating required information

Let's look at these individually.

1. Investment selection—A 404(c) plan participant must be able to:

— materially affect portfolio return potential and risk level;

— choose between at least three investment alternatives; and

— diversify his investment to minimize the risk of large losses.

The practical effect of this is that it would be highly unlikely for the plan to meet the requirements by limiting the available choices to highly speculative funds, such as junk bond funds and highly aggressive growth funds.

TEST TOPIC ALERT   The trustee of a 401(k) would be able to reduce his ERISA fiduciary exposure and meet the safe harbor provisions of 404(c) if the plan offered a broad index fund, a medium term government bond fund, and a cash equivalent fund. It isn't the number of funds that counts, it is the different asset classes available. For example, if the plan offered 10 investment options, instead of 3, but they were all of the same asset class, such as 10 equity funds, or 10 bond funds, that would not comply with 404(c).

2. Investment control—control is defined as:

— allowing employees the opportunity to exercise independent control over the assets in their account by letting them make their own choices among the investment options companies have selected (at least three);

— informing employees that they can change their investment allocations at least quarterly (a growing number of plans allow employees to make plan changes daily); and

— even though the employees maintain investment control, the plan fiduciary is not relieved of the responsibility to monitor the performance of the investment alternatives being offered and replace them when necessary.

3. Communicating required information means:

— making certain information available upon request, such as prospectuses and financial statements or reports relating to the investment options (included must be information such as annual operating expenses and portfolio composition);

— a statement that the plan is intended to constitute an ERISA Section 404(c) plan and that plan fiduciaries may be relieved of liability for investment losses;

— a description of the risk and return characteristics of each of the investment alternatives available under the plan;

— an explanation of how to give investment instructions; and

— allowing real-time access to employee accounts either by telephone or the internet.

20. 4. 1. 5 Summary Plan Description (SPD)

Sometimes referred to as the summary plan document, one of the most important documents participants are entitled to receive automatically when becoming a participant of an ERISA-covered retirement plan or a beneficiary receiving benefits under such a plan is a summary of the plan, called the summary plan description (SPD). Under regulations of the U.S. Department of Labor (DOL), the plan administrator is legally obligated to provide to participants, free of charge, the SPD. The summary plan description is an important document that tells participants what the plan provides and how it operates. It provides information on when an employee can begin to participate in the plan, how service and benefits are calculated, when benefits become vested, when and in what form benefits are paid, and how to file a claim for benefits. Unlike the investment policy statement, it does not deal with the investment characteristics of the plan.

20. 4. 2 DEFINED CONTRIBUTION AND DEFINED BENEFIT PLANS

All qualified retirement plans fall into one of two categories. Those that offer no specific end result, but, instead focus on current, tax-deductible contributions, are **defined contribution plans**. Those that promise a specific retirement benefit but do not specify the level of current contributions are **defined benefit plans**. It is important to distinguish between these two approaches.

Defined Contribution Plans. Defined contribution plans include money-purchase pension plans as well as profit-sharing plans and 401(k) plans. As with other business plans (as compared to an IRA), the maximum employer contribution is currently $53,000.

Defined contribution plan participants' funds accumulate until a future event, generally retirement, when the funds may be withdrawn. The ultimate account value depends on the total amount contributed, along with interest and capital gains from the plan investments. In this type of plan, the plan participant assumes the investment risk. The deduction for contributions to a defined contribution plan, such as a profit sharing plan, (including 401(k)), or money purchase pension plan, cannot be more than 25% of the total payroll for the year to the eligible employees participating in the plan.

Defined Benefit Plans. Defined benefit plans are designed to provide specific retirement benefits for participants, such as fixed monthly income. Regardless of investment performance, the promised benefit is paid under the contract terms. A defined benefit plan sponsor assumes the investment risk. The benefit is usually determined by a formula that takes into account years of service and average salary for the last five years prior to retirement. Older, highly compensated employees are likely to have the largest annual contributions on their behalf. Because of the expenses and complexities involved (the Plan's annual return must be signed by an actuary), 3% of workers had defined benefit plans in 2011, whereas in 1979, that number was 28%.

✓ **TAKE NOTE**

Because of the actuarial assumptions and computations, the maximum has to be figured by an actuary.

Contributory versus noncontributory plans. In a contributory plan, both the employer and employee make contributions to the account. In a noncontributory plan, only the employer makes the contributions. Although it is more common (not tested) for defined contribution plans to be contributory, the term can apply to defined benefit plans as well.

Employer Deductions. The employer can usually deduct, subject to limits, contributions made to a qualified plan. The deduction limit for those contributions to a qualified plan depends on the kind of plan in place.

TEST TOPIC ALERT

Unlike an annuity payout or life insurance premium, contributions to a defined benefit plan are not affected by the participant's sex.

TEST TOPIC ALERT

Employer contributions to defined benefit or defined contribution, (money purchase), pension plans are mandatory. Although profit sharing plans and 401(k) plans are technically defined contribution plans, they are not pension plans, and employer contributions are not mandatory. In all cases, employer contributions are 100% deductible to the corporation. There is no tax obligation to the employee until withdrawal.

20. 4. 3 TAXATION

If all of the funds were contributed by the employer, (known as a noncontributory plan), the employee's tax basis (cost) is zero. Everything above the cost is taxed at the employee's ordinary income rate at the time of distribution.

20. 4. 4 PROFIT-SHARING PLANS

A **profit-sharing plan** established by an employer allows employees to participate in the business's profits. The benefits may be paid directly to the employee or deferred into an account for future payment, such as retirement, or a combination of both. This discussion concerns profit-sharing plans that defer benefits toward retirement.

Profit-sharing plans need not have a predetermined contribution formula. Plans that do include such a formula generally express contributions as a fixed percentage of profits. In either event, to be qualified, a profit-sharing plan must have substantial and recurring contributions, according to the Internal Revenue Code.

Profit-sharing plans are popular because they offer employers the greatest amount of contribution flexibility. The ability to skip contributions during years of low profits appeals to corporations with unpredictable cash flows. They are also relatively easy to install, administer, and communicate to employees.

20. 4. 5   401(K) PLANS

In a **401(k) plan**, an employee directs an employer to deduct a percentage of the employee's salary which will be a contribution to a retirement account. 401(k) plans permit an employer to make matching contributions up to a set percentage of the employee-directed contributions, making this a type of defined contribution plan. All contributions are made with pretax dollars. In effect, the employee is reducing his salary by the amount of his contribution and, therefore, his W2 will show the actual salary less the 401(k) contribution. However, even though income taxes are based on this lower amount, FICA (Social Security) taxes are levied against gross salary, not this reduced amount. In 2015, the maximum employee elective deferral is set at $18,000 with an additional "catch-up" contribution limit of $6,000.

TEST TOPIC ALERT

An employer sponsored 401(k) plan may be established with no required employer or employee contributions. As we will shortly learn, there is one case where employer contributions would be mandatory, but for exam purposes, unless that case is specified, it is up to the employer to determine if it will incorporate matching contributions into the plan.

TAKE NOTE

When one includes the catch-up amount, the maximum combined employer and employee contribution in a defined contribution plan increases from $53,000 to $59,000 per year.

TEST TOPIC ALERT

One of the benefits of investing through a 401(k) plan is that it takes advantage of dollar cost averaging, the technique described in Session 16, which always results in a lower cost per share in a fluctuating market.

20. 4. 5. 1   Hardship Withdrawals

401(k) plans are permitted to make hardship withdrawals available to participants facing serious and immediate financial difficulty. There are maximum limits; the amount withdrawn is not eligible for a rollover and, therefore, is taxable as ordinary income and possibly the 10% penalty. It differs from a 401(k) loan which is not taxable as long as the repayment requirements of the IRS are met.

20. 4. 5. 2 401(k) Plan Loans

Somewhat different from the hardship withdrawal is the ability to borrow from the 401(k). This has the advantage of not being treated as a distribution so there is no tax. However, if certain IRS rules are not followed, it will be considered a premature distribution and taxed as such. The IRS maximum loan amount is 50% of the participant's vested share or $50,000, whichever is the smaller. All loans must carry what the IRS considers to be a "reasonable rate of interest." Other than if used for a home mortgage, the loan must be paid back on a regular schedule (usually through payroll deduction) in a period not to exceed 60 months.

20. 4. 5. 3 Roth 401(k) Plans

Roth 401(k) plans combine features of Roth IRAs and 401(k) retirement plans. Just as with a Roth IRA, these plans require after-tax contributions but allow tax-free withdrawals, provided the retiring person is at least 59½ years old at the time of the withdrawal. Once again, paralleling the Roth IRA, the account must be at least five years old to take tax-free withdrawals.

Like a regular 401(k) plan, it has employer-matching contributions; however, the employer's match must be deposited into a regular 401(k) plan and be fully taxable upon withdrawal. Thus, the employee must have two accounts: a regular 401(k) and a Roth 401(k). Employees may contribute to either account but may not transfer money between accounts once the money has been contributed.

Unlike Roth IRAs, Roth 401(k) plans have no income limit restriction on who may participate. One may have both a Roth 401(k) plan and a Roth IRA, but the income limits would still apply to the Roth IRA. Unlike Roth IRAs, Roth 401(k) plans require withdrawals to begin no later than age 70½, following the same rules that apply to all RMDs.

20. 4. 5. 4 Self-Employed 401(k) Plans

Self-Employed 401(k) plans, also known as Individual 401(k) or Solo 401(k) plans, are a form of retirement plan brought about by the EGTRRA of 2001. The purpose of these plans is to allow sole proprietorships to set up and contribute to a 401(k) plan. The administrator of the plan may be the businessowner or spouse. To contribute to this plan, there can be no other full-time employees other than the businessowner and spouse.

Because the Self-Employed 401(k) plan allows for tax-deferred contributions, the rules surrounding withdrawals are the same as those for other tax-deferred retirement plans. For example, withdrawals made before age 59½ receive a 10% penalty, and withdrawals must commence by age 70½ and are fully taxable as income. Because the covered individual is both the owner and an employee, this plan generally offers the highest possible contribution level of any defined contribution plan.

20. 4. 5. 5 Top-Heavy Plan

Because all qualified plans must be nondiscriminatory, the IRS has defined a **top-heavy 401(k) plan** as one in which a disproportionate amount of the benefit goes to key employees. The plan must be tested on an annual basis to ensure that it complies with the regulations. On the exam, you may be asked to define a top-heavy plan and will have to choose between key employees and highly compensated employees. The easiest way to remember is to match the (k) in 401(k) with the word *key*.

20. 4. 5. 6 Safe Harbor 401(k) Plan

Several years after the top-heavy rules were written, relief was offered in the form of the safe harbor 401(k). A plan does not have to undergo annual top-heavy testing if set up properly.

There are two basic choices for setting up a safe harbor plan. The employer will either match employee contributions or use a nonelective formula (the employees don't have to contribute) of eligible employee compensation to satisfy IRS requirements. If a matching formula is elected:

■ the base formula is 100% of elective deferrals up to 3% of compensation and then 50% of elective deferrals on the next 2% of compensation. This means the maximum match is 4% (100% × 3% + 50% × 2% = 3% + 1%); or

■ the employer may elect the nonelective formula (minimum of 3%) of all eligible participants' compensation. Under this formula, all eligible employees would receive this nonelective contribution whether making salary reduction contributions or not.

In either case, all employer contributions are **immediately** vested.

20. 4. 6 SECTION 457 PLANS

A **Section 457(b) plan** is a deferred compensation plan set up under Section 457 of the tax code that may be used by employees of a state, political subdivision of a state, and any agency or instrumentality of a state. This plan may also be offered to employees of certain tax-exempt organizations (hospitals, charitable organizations, unions, and so forth, but NOT churches).

In a 457 plan, employees can defer compensation, and the amount deferred is not reportable for tax purposes. Therefore, the employee receives a deduction each year for the amount deferred.

There are several important facts to know about 457 plans.

■ These plans are exempt from ERISA—nongovernmental plans must be un-funded to qualify for tax benefits while government plans must be funded.

■ These plans are generally not required to follow the nondiscrimination rules of other retirement plans.

■ Plans for tax-exempt organizations are limited to covering only highly compensated employees, while any employee (or even independent contractor) of a governmental entity may participate.

■ Distributions from 457(b) plans of nongovernmental tax-exempt employees may not be rolled over into an IRA, but there is no 10% penalty for early withdrawal.

■ It is possible to maintain both a 457 and 403(b) and make maximum contributions to both ($36,000 in 2015).As a result, those 50 or older, using the "catch-up" provision in each plan, could actually contribute as much as $48,000.

■ Unlike 401(k) plans, loans from a 457(b) plan are available in governmental plans only, and only if the entity decides to include that feature in the plan. Furthermore, the requirements for "unforeseen emergency" withdrawals are much stricter than for hardship withdrawals under a 401(k) plan.

20. 4. 7 SIMPLE PLANS

Savings Incentive Match Plans for Employees (SIMPLEs) are retirement plans for a business with 100 or fewer employees who earned $5,000 or more during the preceding calendar year. In addition, the business cannot currently have another retirement plan in place.

The plans are easy to set up and inexpensive to administer. The employee's contribution, up to $12,500 with a $3,000 catch-up provision (2015), is pretax and may be matched by the employer using either of the following two options.

■ A 2% nonelective employer contribution, where employees eligible to participate receive an employer contribution equal to 2% of their compensation (limited to $265,000 per year for 2015 and subject to cost-of-living adjustments for later years), regardless of whether they make their own contributions.

■ A dollar-for-dollar match up to 3% of compensation, where only the participating employees who have elected to make contributions will receive an employer contribution (i.e., the matching contribution).

For small business looking for a way to have an inexpensive retirement plan for their employees, the SIMPLE is the way to go.

QUICK QUIZ 20.D

1. Regulations regarding how contributions are made to tax-qualified plans relate to which of the following ERISA requirements?

   A. Vesting
   B. Funding
   C. Nondiscrimination
   D. Reporting and disclosure

2. Which of the following determines the amount paid into a defined contribution plan?

   A. ERISA-defined contribution requirements
   B. Trust agreement
   C. Employer's age
   D. Employee's retirement age

3. Which of the following would best describe a prudent investor?

   A. A person in a fiduciary capacity who invests in a prudent manner
   B. A trustee who invests with reasonable care, skill, and caution
   C. An investment adviser representative handling a discretionary account
   D. The custodian for a minor under the Uniform Transfers to Minors Act

4. To comply with the safe harbor requirements of Section 404(c) of ERISA, the trustee of a 401(k) plan must

    I.   offer plan participants at least 10 different investment alternatives
    II. allow plan participants to exercise control over their investments
    III. allow plan participants to change their investment options no less frequently than monthly
    IV. provide plan participants with information relating to the risks and performance of each investment alternative offered

    A. I and III
    B. I and IV
    C. II and III
    D. II and IV

5. Susan participates in a Section 401(k) plan at work that includes loan provisions. Susan has recently enrolled in college and has inquired about the possible consequences of borrowing from the plan to help pay for her education. As her financial planner, what is your advice to her?

    A. The loan will statutorily be treated as a taxable distribution from the plan.
    B. The loan must be repayable within 5 years at a reasonable rate of interest.
    C. The 401(k) plan needs to be rewritten as loans are only available from qualified plans.
    D. The loan is not being made for reasons of an unforeseeable emergency and therefore is not possible.

20. 5 SUMMARY OF DISTRIBUTION RULES FROM BOTH QUALIFIED PLANS AND IRAS

Distributions from traditional IRAs must generally begin no later than April 1 of the year following the year in which the taxpayer attains age 70½.

In applying distribution rules, all traditional IRAs and SEPs are treated as a single account and must be liquidated at least to the extent of percentages specified on IRS tables. Qualified plans, however, are not aggregated; distributions from one qualified plan are not affected by distributions from another.

20. 5. 1 LIFETIME DISTRIBUTIONS

20. 5. 1. 1 Early Withdrawal Penalties

In general, withdrawals from both IRAs and qualified plans are taxed as ordinary income. However, withdrawals from such arrangements occurring before owners turn age 59½ are subject to an additional 10% premature withdrawal penalty. Withdrawals from both escape the penalty when they are made on account of death or total disability, correcting excess contributions, or as a series of substantially equal payments over the life of the plan participant and beneficiary, if applicable. Only in the case of a *qualified plan* is the penalty avoided in the case of a divorce [under a qualified domestic relations order (QDRO)].

TEST TOPIC ALERT

Although pre-59½ withdrawals from IRAs for education and first-time home purchase escape the early withdrawal penalty, withdrawals from qualified plans for those purposes do not.

The 10% tax will not apply on withdrawals from either of these before age 59½, however, if:

■ the distribution is made to a beneficiary on or after the death of the employee/individual;

■ the distribution is made because the employee/individual acquires a qualifying disability; or

■ the distribution is made as a part of a series of substantially equal periodic payments under IRS Rule 72t, beginning after separation from service with the employer maintaining the plan before the payments begin,

■ and made at least annually for the life or life expectancy of the employee/individual or the joint lives or life expectancies of the employee/individual and his designated beneficiary. (Excepting in the case of death or disability, the payments under this exception must continue for at least five years or until the employee/individual reaches age 59½, whichever is the longer period.)

TAKE NOTE

After a person begins taking distributions from an IRA under Rule 72t, contributions , asset transfers, or rollovers are not permitted while receiving payments.

20. 5. 1. 2   Penalty Tax on Failure to Make Required Minimum Distributions

As with IRAs, other than a Roth IRA, failure to distribute the required amount from qualified plans generates a 50% penalty tax on the shortfall in addition to ordinary income taxation. However, as mentioned earlier, and of particular importance as employees are working to much later ages than in previous generations, there are no RMDs from a qualified plan while still employed by the sponsor of that plan, regardless of your age.

20. 5. 1. 3 Withholding on Eligible Rollover Distributions from Qualified Plans

Distributions paid to an employee are subjected to a mandatory federal withholding of 20% if the distribution exceeds $200 for the year and is an eligible rollover distribution. Distributions that are not eligible rollover distributions are not subjected to the mandatory 20% withholding.

TAKE NOTE

An employee may avoid the 20% withholding by having the distribution processed as a direct rollover (also referred to as a *transfer*) to an eligible retirement plan. In a direct rollover the distribution check is made payable to the trustee or custodian of the receiving retirement plan.

10% Early Distribution Penalty Exceptions by Plan Types

	Qualified Pension, Profit-Sharing, and TSAs (403(b) Plans)	401(k) and SIMPLE Plans	Traditional, Roth, and SEP IRAs
Death	X	X	X
Disability	X	X	X
Separation from service after age 55	X	X	
Certain medical expenses	X	X	X
QDROs	X	X	
To reduce excess contributions or deferrals	X	X	X
As substantially equal payments over life	X	X	X
First-time home purchase			X
Higher education expenses			X
Health insurance premiums while unemployed			X

TAKE NOTE

In an example of IRS logic, they have this statement regarding avoiding the 10% tax penalty if withdrawals are made prior to age 59 ½:

"Even if you receive a distribution before you are age 59 1/2, you may not have to pay the 10% additional tax if you are in one of the following situations." The first situation they list is:

"You have unreimbursed medical expenses that are more than 10% (or 7.5% if you or your spouse was born before January 2, 1950) of your adjusted gross income." This is in the 2015 Edition of the IRS rules. So tell me, if you were born before 1950, aren't you over 59 ½ today? That means there wouldn't be a premature distribution penalty in any case.

QUICK QUIZ 20.E   True or False?

_____ 1. A defined contribution pension plan is a qualified plan that specifies an employer's annual funding.

_____ 2. The movement of funds from one retirement plan to another, generally within a specified period, is called a rollover.

_____ 3. In a defined benefit plan, all employees receive the same benefits at retirement.

_____ 4. In a safe harbor 401(k) plan, all employees are immediately vested.

_____ 5. In a defined benefit plan, high income employees near retirement may receive much larger contributions than younger employees with the same salary.

_____ 6. In a top-heavy 401(k) plan, a disproportionate benefit accrues to eligible highly compensated employees.

20. 5. 2 SUMMARY OF ROLLOVER AND TRANSFER RULES

Following is a summary of the rules applying to moving money from one tax-deferred account to another. Included is a Test Topic Alert which refers to a recent IRS change that will probably begin appearing on the exam before the end of 2015. Once we are aware of that, we'll post it to the Exam-tips and Content Updates and our questions will reflect the change. Here are the three key points:

1. **Direct rollover** – In the event the plan calls for a distribution upon separation from service, a request can be made to the plan administrator to send the payment directly to another retirement plan or to an IRA. In some cases, the administrator may pay the distribution directly to the employee in the form of a check made out to the new account. In either case, there are no taxes withheld from the amount transferred and no income is reported for tax purposes.

2. **Trustee-to-trustee transfer** – An investor who wishes to change trustees for an IRA, such as moving the account to another firm or mutual fund group, upon request, the trustee or custodian for the "old" IRA will make the payment directly to the trustee of the "new" IRA. In some cases, the IRA distribution may be made to the trustees of an employer sponsored plan in the fashion. In either case, there are no taxes withheld from the amount transferred and no income is reported for tax purposes.

3. **60-day rollover** – In the event the distribution from an IRA or qualified employer plan is paid directly to the participant, there is the option to deposit all or any part of it to another IRA or qualified plan within 60 calendar days. However, there will be a 20% withholding tax on this distribution. That means, in order to avoid any tax, the individual will have to find other funds to deposit to cover the withheld amount. Any portion of the distribution that is not rolled over will be subject to tax and, if under age 59½, will be subject to the 10% (unless qualifying for one of the exemptions from the penalty tax).

TEST TOPIC ALERT

Effective January 1, 2015, the IRS has tightened the "once per year" rule a bit. You can make only one rollover from an IRA to another (or the same) IRA in any 365 day period (not per calendar year), regardless of the number of IRAs you own. The limit will apply by aggregating all of an individual's IRAs, including SEP and SIMPLE IRAs as well as traditional and Roth IRAs, effectively treating them as one IRA for purposes of the limit. However:

■ Trustee-to-trustee transfers between IRAs are not limited

■ Conversions from traditional to Roth IRAs are not limited

20. 6   NONQUALIFIED CORPORATE RETIREMENT PLANS

A **nonqualified plan** does not allow the employer a current tax deduction for contributions. Instead, the employer receives the tax deduction when the money is actually paid out to the employee. However, depending on how the plan is structured, earnings may accumulate on a tax-deferred basis. A nonqualified plan need not comply with nondiscrimination rules that apply to qualified plans. The employer can make nonqualified benefits available to key employees and exclude others.

Nonqualified plans are not subject to the same reporting and disclosure requirements as qualified plans. However, nonqualified plans still must be in writing and communicated to the plan participants. Sponsors of nonqualified plans are fiduciaries.

20. 6. 1   TAXATION

The corporation cannot deduct nonqualified plan contributions made on behalf of participants until paid to the participant. However, if the nonqualified plan is properly designed, contributions are not taxable to the employee until the benefit is received.

Contributions to nonqualified plans that have already been taxed make up the investor's cost base. When the investor withdraws money from the nonqualified plan, the cost base is not taxed. However, earnings are taxed when withdrawn.

20. 6. 2 TYPES OF PLANS

Two types of nonqualified plans are payroll deduction plans and deferred compensation plans.

20. 6. 2. 1 Payroll Deduction Plans

A payroll deduction plan involves a deduction from an employee's check on a weekly, monthly, or quarterly basis as authorized by the employee. The money is deducted after taxes are paid and may be invested in investment vehicles at the employee's option.

20. 6. 2. 2 Deferred Compensation Plans

A **nonqualified deferred compensation (NQDC) plan** is a contractual agreement between a firm and an employee in which the employee agrees to defer receipt of current compensation in favor of a payout at retirement. The agreement underlying a deferred compensation plan usually includes the following:

- Conditions and circumstances under which some or all of the benefits may be forfeited, such as if the employee moves to a competing firm
- A statement to the effect that the employee is not entitled to any claim against the employer's assets until retirement, death, or disability
- A disclaimer that the agreement may be void if the firm suffers a business failure or bankruptcy

Company directors are not considered employees for the purpose of establishing eligibility for a deferred compensation plan, and as a result, may not participate in the plan.

TEST TOPIC ALERT   Because the employer can discriminate, one of the most common uses of deferred compensation plans is to provide benefits to retain key employees.

20. 6. 2. 2. 1 Business Failure

Generally, an employee enjoys no benefits from a deferred compensation plan until retirement. If the business fails, the employee is a general creditor of the business with no guarantee that he will receive the deferred payment.

20. 6. 2. 2. 2 *Funding*

Deferred compensation plans may be unfunded, in which case the deferred compensation is paid from the firm's operating assets. If the plan is funded, the advantages of tax deferral are lost. Many NQDC plans are informally funded through life insurance or trust arrangements.

Qualified Plans vs. Nonqualified Plans

Qualified Plans	Nonqualified Plans
Contributions tax deductible	Contributions not tax deductible
Plan approved by the IRS	Plan does not need IRS approval
Plan cannot discriminate	Plan can discriminate
Subject to ERISA	Not subject to ERISA
Tax on accumulation is deferred	Tax on accumulation may be deferred
All withdrawals taxed	Excess over cost base taxed
Plan is a trust	Plan is not a trust

QUICK QUIZ 20.F

Matching

A. Defined benefit plan
B. Keogh plan
C. Spousal IRA contributions
D. Payroll deduction plan

_____ 1. Nonqualified plan in which an employee authorizes regular reductions from his salary

_____ 2. Specifies the monthly amount an employee will receive at retirement

_____ 3. Qualified retirement plan for self-employed individuals and unincorporated businesses

_____ 4. IRA contributions made for a nonworking spouse

20. 7   EDUCATIONAL SAVINGS PROGRAMS

The examination will deal with two different types of programs designed to offer tax benefits when saving for education. We will begin with the Coverdell ESA and then move on to the Section 529 Plan.

20. 7. 1 COVERDELL EDUCATION SAVINGS ACCOUNTS

The Taxpayer Relief Act of 1997 also created **Education IRAs** with a $500 annual contribution limit. In 2002, these were renamed **Coverdell ESAs.** ESAs allow after-tax contributions for student beneficiaries. Contributions must be made in cash and must be made on or before the date on which the beneficiary attains age 18 unless the beneficiary is a **special needs beneficiary**—an individual who because of a physical, mental, or emotional condition requires additional time to complete their education. Coverdell ESAs fund educational expenses of a designated beneficiary by allowing after-tax (nondeductible) contributions to accumulate on a tax-deferred basis.

When distributions are made from a Coverdell ESA, the earnings portion of the distribution is excluded from income when it is used to pay qualified education expenses. Withdrawn earnings are taxed and subject to a 10% tax penalty when they are not used to pay qualified education expenses.

TAKE NOTE

If the money is not used by a beneficiary's 30th birthday (except for a special needs beneficiary), it must be distributed and the earnings are subject to ordinary income taxes and a 10% penalty.

Under EGTRRA, the maximum annual contribution limit to a Coverdell ESA was increased to $2,000 per beneficiary with a "sunset" provision in 2011 whereby the level would be reduced to the original $500 level. In 2013, Congress made the $2,000 limit "permanent". In addition to qualified higher education expenses (postsecondary education), the account can also be used for elementary and secondary education expenses and for public, private, or religious schools.

The contribution to a Coverdell ESA may be limited depending on the amount of AGI and filing status.

Allowable Contribution	Single Filers	Joint Filers
Full contribution of $2,000 at AGI of and below	$ 95,000	$190,000
Partial phaseout begins at	$ 95,001	$190,001
No contributions may be made at AGI of and above	$110,000	$220,000

TAKE NOTE

There is nothing to prevent more than one individual from contributing to a Coverdell ESA; the annual limit applies to each beneficiary. Parents and grandparents can contribute to a single account, as long as the $2,000 limit per child is not exceeded in any given year.

Other changes made by the EGTRRA of 2001 include:

■ provisions that allow contributions to continue past age 18 for beneficiaries with special needs;

■ extending the period during which corrective withdrawals can be made to avoid the early distribution and excess contribution penalties; and

■ allowing Coverdell ESA contributions, for any year, to be made up to April 15 of the following year (just like contributions to your IRA).

TEST TOPIC ALERT

Here are some key test points about Coverdell ESAs:

■ Contributions can be made by parents and other adults; the total for one child is still $2,000.

■ Contribution limit is $2,000 per year per child until the child's 18th birthday.

■ Contributions are not tax deductible, but all earnings are tax deferred.

■ Distributions are tax free if they are taken before age 30 and used for eligible education expenses.

■ If the accumulated value in the account is not used by age 30, the funds must be distributed and subject to income tax and a 10% penalty on the earnings or rolled over into a different Coverdell ESA for another family member. Their definition of family is extremely broad and, in addition to the obvious, includes cousins, aunts and uncles, and even in-laws.

20. 7. 2 SECTION 529 PLANS

Section 529 plans, legally known as qualified tuition programs (QTPs), are state-operated investment plans that give families a way to save money for college with substantial tax benefits. There are two basic types of 529 plans: prepaid tuition plans and college savings plans.

20. 7. 2. 1 Prepaid Tuition Plans

Prepaid tuition plans generally allow college savers to prepay for tuition at participating colleges and universities, and in some cases, room and board can be prepaid as well. Most prepaid tuition plans are sponsored by state governments and have residency requirements. The basic concept is that if you pay for the tuition at today's rates, the child will be able to attend in the future, regardless of how much higher the tuition is.

20. 7. 2. 2 College Savings Plans

College savings plans generally permit the contributor, known as the account holder, to establish an account for a student (the beneficiary) for the purpose of paying the beneficiary's qualified college expenses. The typical plan offers a number of investment options including stock mutual funds, bond mutual funds, and money market funds. A very popular option is the age-based portfolio that automatically shifts toward more conservative investments as the beneficiary gets closer to college age. Withdrawals from college savings plans can generally be used at any college or university regardless of the state carrying the plan or the state of residence.

20. 7. 2. 3 Differences Between the Two QTPs

The following chart outlines some of the major differences between pre-paid tuition plans and college savings plans.

Prepaid Tuition Plan	College Savings Plan
Locks in tuition prices at eligible public and private colleges and universities.	No lock on college costs.
All plans cover tuition and mandatory fees only. Some plans allow families to purchase a room and board option or use excess tuition credits for other qualified expenses.	Covers all qualified higher education expenses, including the following: ■ Tuition ■ Room and board ■ Mandatory fees ■ Books, computers (if required)
Most plans set lump sum and installment payments prior to purchase based on age of beneficiary and number of years of college tuition purchased.	Many plans have contribution limits in excess of $250,000.
Many state plans guaranteed or backed by state.	No state guarantee. Most investment options are subject to market risk. Your investment may make no profit or even decline in value.
Most plans have age/grade limit for beneficiary.	No age limits. Open to adults and children.
Most state plans require either owner or beneficiary of plan to be a state resident.	No residency requirement. However, nonresidents may only be able to purchase some plans through financial advisers or brokers.
Most plans have limited enrollment period.	Enrollment open all year.

Source: Smart Saving for College, FINRA®

20. 7. 2. 4 Tax Treatment of 529 Plans

A major factor in investing in a 529 plan is tax benefits. Although contributions are made with after-tax money, earnings in 529 plans are not subject to federal tax and, in most cases, state tax, so long as withdrawals are for eligible college expenses, such as tuition and room and board and even a computer.

However, money representing earnings that is withdrawn from a 529 plan for ineligible expenses will be subject to income tax and an additional 10% federal tax penalty. Unlike the IRS, many states offer deductions or credits against state income tax for investing in a 529 plan. But eligibility for these benefits is generally limited to participants in a 529 plan sponsored by your state of residence.

20. 7. 2. 5 Withdrawal Restrictions

Both plans place restrictions on withdrawals. With limited exceptions, you can only withdraw money that you invest in a 529 plan for eligible college expenses without incurring taxes and penalties. However, you can rollover any unused funds to a member of the beneficiary's family without incurring any tax liability as long as the rollover is completed within 60 days of the distribution. Immediate family includes the following:

■ Son, daughter, stepchild, foster child, adopted child, or a descendant of any of them

■ Brother, sister, stepbrother, or stepsister

■ Father or mother or ancestor of either

■ Stepfather or stepmother

■ Son or daughter of a brother or sister

■ Brother or sister of father or mother

■ Son-in-law, daughter-in-law, father-in-law, mother-in-law, brother-in-law, or sister-in-law

■ The spouse of any individual listed above

■ First cousin

TEST TOPIC ALERT

The earnings portion of a nonqualified distribution is taxable to the individual who receives the payment, either the account owner or the designated beneficiary. If the payment is not made to the designated beneficiary or to an eligible educational institution for the benefit of the designated beneficiary, it will be deemed to have been made to the account owner.

TEST TOPIC ALERT

What if you don't like the 529 plan you are invested in, can you make a change? Federal tax law allows a tax-free rollover of any or all of a 529 account from the current 529 plan to a different 529 plan, but only once in any 12-month period unless there is a change in beneficiary. Just as with an IRA, if the proceeds are distributed, they must be reinvested in the new plan within 60 days. Therefore, assets in the QTP may be moved from the plan of one state to the plan of another no more frequently than once per 12 months.

20. 7. 2. 6 Impact on Financial Eligibility

Investing in a 529 plan will generally impact a student's eligibility to participate in need-based financial aid. Both types of plans are treated as parental assets in the calculation of the expected family contribution toward college costs regardless of whether the owner is the parent or the student. This is a better deal than if they were non-529 assets of the student because parental assets are assessed at a maximum 5.64% rate in determining the student's Expected Family Contribution (EFC) rather than the 20% rate on non-529 assets owned by the student. These rates will not be tested, but the concept may.

20. 7. 2. 7 Contributions to a 529 Plan

Any adult can open a 529 plan for a future college student. The donor does not have to be related to the student.

With a 529 plan, the donor can invest a small or substantial lump sum or make periodic payments. When the student is ready for college, the donor withdraws the amount needed to pay for qualified education expenses (e.g., tuition, room and board, and books). Contributions are made with after-tax dollars, but qualified withdrawals are exempt from federal taxation. As stated above, taxation varies from state to state. If any tax is due on withdrawal, it is the responsibility of the student, not the donor.

A donor (typically a parent or grandparent) may contribute a maximum of $70,000 ($140,000 if married) in a single year for each Section 529 plan beneficiary without gift tax consequences. This represents a five-year advance on the (2015) $14,000 per recipient annual gift tax exclusion.

The donor of the 529 plan assets retains control of most 529 accounts and may take the money back at any time (although a 10% penalty tax may apply).

TAKE NOTE

Although it probably won't be tested, for those who bunch the annual gift exclusion allowing five years worth at one time, this is not limited to one time per beneficiary. If started with a one-year-old grandchild, the grandparents can do this again when the child is six (five years have elapsed) and then again at 11, and so forth as long as the total contribution does not exceed the state's limit. Sure would be nice to have grandparents like that, wouldn't it?

20. 7. 2. 8 Offering Circular

These plans are considered "municipal fund securities" and, under the rules of the MSRB, require delivery of an official statement, sometimes called an offering circular, but never referred to as a prospectus.

20. 7. 2. 9 Investment Options for 529 Plans

In general, these plans offer several different portfolio options ranging from aggressive (for those with a longer time horizon) to guaranteed (for those in college using the funds). In most cases, these portfolios are registered mutual funds, in others, they are separately managed accounts containing stocks and/or bonds. Some portfolios include insured bank CDs and some of the states offer managed fixed income pools.

TEST TOPIC ALERT

However, U.S. Savings Bonds are not available as investment options in Section 529 Plans.

TAKE NOTE

Key points to remember about Section 529 Plans include the following.

- The dollar amount of allowable contribution varies from state to state and may be as high as $300,000.

- Assets in the account remain under the donor's control even after the student is of legal age.

- There are no income limitations on donors making contributions to a 529 plan.

- Unlike Coverdell ESAs, these cannot be used for educational expenses incurred below the post-secondary level (post-high school).

- There are no age restrictions. That is, if at any age, an individual desires to go back to school, a 529 Plan may be used.

- Earnings are exempt from federal taxes (as are withdrawals) if they go toward qualified postsecondary educational expenses.

- Most states hire experienced investment management companies to manage their accounts.

- In almost all cases, residents do not pay state income tax on qualified withdrawals from home-state plans.

- In a majority of the states with an income tax, residents are afforded an income tax deduction or credit for a portion of their contribution.

- If funds are withdrawn for purposes other than education, earnings are subject to a 10% penalty as well as federal income tax. States may assess their own penalties. The tax is the obligation of the distributee (student/beneficiary).

- Because of their legal status as municipal fund securities, it is required to deliver an official statement or offering circular when opening a 529 Plan account.

1. The maximum amount that may be invested in a Coverdell ESA in one year is
   A. $500 per parent
   B. $2,000 per child
   C. $500 per couple
   D. $2,000 per couple

2. One of your clients is a successful professional couple with earnings in excess of $500,000 per year. They are interested in providing a funding source for post-secondary education for their grandchildren. Which would be appropriate to discuss with them?
   A. The Coverdell ESA
   B. The Section 529 plan
   C. Both the Coverdell ESA and the Section 529 plan
   D. Neither the Coverdell ESA nor the Section 529 Plan

20. 8 CUSTODIAL ACCOUNTS

Long before there were Education IRAs and Section 529 plans, a favored way of saving for a child's education (or anything else for that matter, was by the use of a custodial account under the Uniform Gift to Minors Act. In a **custodial account**, the custodian for the beneficial owner enters all trades. UGMA and UTMA accounts require an adult or a trustee to act as custodian for a minor (the beneficial owner). Any kind of security or cash may be gifted to the account without limitation.

The Uniform Law Commissioners adopted the Uniform Gift to Minors Act (UGMA) in 1956 (the same year as the Uniform Securities Act). The primary focus then was to provide a convenient way to make gifts of money and securities to minors. Later, it became clear that a more flexible law was desirable. The Uniform Law Commissioners adopted the Uniform Transfers to Minors Act (UTMA) in 1986. UTMA expands the types of property you can transfer to a minor and provides that you can make other types of transfers besides gifts.

Nearly all states have adopted UTMA, but people still tend to refer to UGMA out of habit. For exam purposes, it doesn't matter which law is in effect in your state because the essential principles of both acts are the same.

20. 8. 1 CUSTODIAN

Securities in an UGMA/UTMA account are managed by a custodian until the minor reaches the age of majority. The custodian has full control over the minor's account and can:

■ buy or sell securities;

■ exercise rights or warrants; and

■ liquidate, trade, or hold securities.

The custodian also may use the property in the account in any way the custodian deems proper for the minor's support, education, maintenance, general use, or benefit. However, the account is not normally used to pay expenses associated with raising a child.

20. 8. 2   OPENING AN UGMA/UTMA ACCOUNT

UGMA/UTMA account applications must contain the custodian's name, minor's name and Social Security number, and the state in which the UGMA/UTMA is registered.

TEST TOPIC ALERT   The minor's Social Security number is used on the account.

20. 8. 2. 1   Fiduciary Responsibility

An UGMA/UTMA custodian assumes fiduciary responsibilities in managing a minor's account. Restrictions are placed on improper handling of investments in an UGMA/UTMA. The most important limitations follow.

- UGMAs/UTMAs may be opened and managed as cash accounts only.
- A custodian may never purchase securities on margin or pledge them as collateral for a loan.
- A custodian must reinvest all cash proceeds, dividends, and interest within a reasonable period of time. Cash proceeds may be held in an interest-bearing custodial account for a reasonable period.
- Investment decisions must consider a minor's age and the custodial relationship; examples of inappropriate investments are commodity futures, naked options, and high-risk securities.
- Options may not be bought in a custodial account because no evidence of ownership is issued to an options buyer.
- Covered call writing is normally allowed.
- Stock subscription rights or warrants must be either exercised or sold.

A custodian may be reimbursed for any reasonable expenses incurred in managing the account. Compensation may be paid to the custodian unless the custodian is also the donor.

20. 8. 2. 2   Donating Securities

When a person makes a gift of securities to a minor under the UGMA/UTMA laws, that person is the securities' **donor**. A gift under UGMA/UTMA conveys an **indefeasible title**—that is, the donor may not take back the gift, nor may the minor return the gift until the minor has reached the age of majority. Once a gift is donated, the donor gives up all rights to the property. When the minor reaches the specified age, the property in the account is transferred into the minor's name.

20. 8. 2. 3 UGMA/UTMA Rules

Registered investment advisers should know the following UGMA/UTMA custodial account rules.

- All gifts are irrevocable. Gifts may be in the form of cash or fully paid securities.
- An account may have only one custodian and one minor or beneficial owner.
- A donor of securities can act as custodian or appoint someone to do so.
- Unless they are acting as custodians, parents have no legal control over an UGMA/UTMA account or the securities in it.
- A minor can be the beneficiary of more than one account, and a person may serve as custodian for more than one UGMA/UTMA, provided each account benefits only one minor.
- The minor has the right to sue the custodian for improper actions.

TAKE NOTE

Although an investment adviser representative is not responsible for determining whether an appointment is valid or a custodian's activities are appropriate, he should always be sensitive to the appearance of unethical behavior.

20. 8. 2. 4 Registration of UGMA/UTMA Securities

Any securities in an UGMA/UTMA account are generally registered in the custodian's name for the benefit of the minor and *cannot be solely in the minor's name* .

So that transfers may be accomplished more expeditiously, securities may be held by custodians in street name.

EXAMPLE

In an account where Marilyn Johns, the donor, has appointed her daughter's aunt, Barbara Wood, as custodian for the account of her minor daughter, Alexis, the account and the certificates would read "Barbara Wood as custodian for Alexis Johns" (or a variation of this form).

When the minor reaches the age of majority, all of the securities in the account are registered in her name. However, that change in registration is not automatic— the new adult must initiate the transfer.

20. 8. 2. 5 Death of the Minor or Custodian

If the beneficiary of an UGMA/UTMA dies, the securities in the account pass to the minor's estate, not to the parents or the custodian. If the custodian dies or resigns, either a court of law or the donor must appoint a new custodian.

20. 8. 2. 6 Uniform Transfers to Minors (UTMA)

Although UTMA and UGMA share many characteristics, there are a few important differences. First, although UGMA accounts may not hold real estate (real property), certain partnership interests, and other types of intangible property, UTMA accounts may. Thus, UTMA accounts offer greater investment choice.

In many states, UTMA account assets are not required to be transferred upon the age of majority of the beneficial owner (the child). In many UTMA states, the custodian may delay transferring the UTMA assets to the beneficial owner until he becomes age 21 or 25 (depending on the particular state statute).

TAKE NOTE

A potential estate tax trap is present with custodial accounts such as UGMAs and UTMAs. Under certain circumstances, the assets in the minor's custodial account may be includable, for federal estate tax purposes, in the estate of the custodian when the custodian dies. This could be a problem for the parent or grandparent who incorrectly assumes that the gift made to the minor is no longer in his estate.

20. 8. 2. 7 Taxation

The minor's Social Security number appears on an UGMA/UTMA account, and the minor must file an annual income tax return and pay taxes on any income exceeding $2,100 (2015) produced by the UGMA/UTMA at the parent's top marginal tax rate, regardless of the source of the gift, until the minor reaches age 19, unless the individual is a full-time student, in which case, under 24 (commonly referred to as the **kiddie tax**). Lower amounts of annual unearned income are not subject to the kiddie tax.

When the minor is no longer covered by the kiddie tax, the account will be taxed at the minor's tax rate. Although the minor is the account's beneficiary and is responsible for any and all taxes on the account, in most states it is the custodian's responsibility to see that the taxes are paid.

QUICK QUIZ 20.H

1. If a customer would like to open a custodial UGMA or UTMA account for his nephew, a minor, the uncle can

   A. open the account provided the proper trust arrangements are filed first
   B. open the account and name himself custodian
   C. open the account, but he needs a legal document evidencing the nephew's parents' prior approval of the account
   D. be custodian for the account only if he is also the minor's legal guardian

2. An investor wants to provide for his 3 nephews after his brother dies. Under the UTMA, the investor may open

   A. 1 account for all 3 nephews
   B. 3 separate accounts and deposit cash and securities
   C. 3 separate accounts and deposit insurance policies
   D. 3 separate accounts and deposit fixed annuities

UNIT TEST

1. John purchased securities in the yacht-building business. Two years ago, his securities had lost most of their value as a result of a congressionally imposed luxury tax on purchases of more than $30,000. John's purchase of an investment in the yacht-building business suffered

    A. interest rate risk
    B. business risk
    C. legislative risk
    D. volatility

2. Use the following chart to answer this question

Equity	100%	35%	20%	0%
Fixed income	0%	65%	80%	100%
High return	45.4%	34.2%	31.3%	28.7%
Low return	−7.4%	5.5%	8.2%	6.5%
Avg. return	18.8%	19.2%	16.5%	14.2%
Std. dev.	12.25	10.95	10.02	10.46

    Which of these portfolio allocations would you expect to show the least volatility over the next year?

    A. 100%/0%
    B. 35%/65%
    C. 20%/80%
    D. 0%/100%

3. Risk-adjusted return is calculated by

    A. multiplying the return of an investment by its standard deviation
    B. dividing the price of the stock by its standard deviation
    C. dividing the remainder of the risk-free rate subtracted from the security's actual return by its standard deviation
    D. dividing the security's price by its beta

4. What is the total return on a 1-year, newly issued (365 days to maturity) zero-coupon debt obligation priced at 95?

    A. The return cannot be determined without knowing current interest rates.
    B. 5%
    C. 5.26% plus the implied coupon rate
    D. 5.26%

5. Duration is

    A. equivalent to the yield to maturity
    B. a measure of a bond's volatility with respect to a change in interest rates
    C. the deviation of a bond's returns from its average returns
    D. identical to a bond's maturity

6. The yield to maturity is

    A. set at issuance and printed on the face of the bond
    B. determined by dividing the coupon rate by the current market price of the bond
    C. the annualized return of a bond if it is held to maturity
    D. the annualized return of a bond if it is held to call date

7. "Stock prices adjust rapidly to the release of all new public information." This statement is an expression of which of the following ideas?

    A. Arbitrage pricing theory
    B. Efficient market hypothesis
    C. Odd-lot theory
    D. Tactical allocation

8. Expected return is

    A. the difference between an investment's present value and its cost
    B. the current worth of future income discounted to reflect what that income is worth today
    C. an estimate of probable returns an investment may yield
    D. the one discount rate that equates the future value of an investment with its net present value

9. Dan is the owner of a mutual fund that returned him a before-tax return of 15% last year. Inflation is running at an annual rate of 3%, and Dan is in a 27% marginal income tax bracket. What has been Dan's approximate inflation-adjusted after-tax return on the fund over the course of the last year (rounded to the nearest 2 decimal points)?

   A. 7.95%
   B. 8.76%
   C. 10.95%
   D. 12.00%

10. Which two of the following statements are CORRECT?

   I. Time-weighted returns are generally of more use than dollar-weighted returns to evaluate portfolio manager performance.
   II. Time-weighted returns are generally of more use than dollar-weighted returns to evaluate individual investor performance.
   III. Dollar-weighted returns are generally of more use than time-weighted returns to evaluate portfolio manager performance.
   IV. Dollar-weighted returns are generally of more use than time-weighted returns to evaluate individual investor performance.

   A. I and II
   B. I and IV
   C. II and III
   D. III and IV

11. A portfolio manager who routinely shifts portfolio assets to take advantage of the business cycle is said to be engaging in

   A. asset allocation
   B. correlation
   C. rebalancing
   D. sector rotation

12. An investor has $50,000 to invest in bonds. Currently, 10-year bonds are offering very attractive yields, but the client is concerned that in a few years, rates will be even higher. What would you suggest?

   A. Barbell bonds
   B. Bullet bonds
   C. Diversifying
   D. Laddering

13. An investor invests $1,000 into the shares of the Stratford Growth and Income Fund, an open-end investment company registered under the Investment Company Act of 1940. On the purchase application, the investor checked the boxes signifying that dividends were to be paid out in cash and capital gains were to be reinvested. During year, the fund pays dividends of $20 and distributes a $250 capital gain. At the end of the year, the fund's value is $1,300. The total return to this investor was

   A. 25%
   B. 27%
   C. 30%
   D. 32%

14. Which of the following bond strategies would be considered passive?

   A. Barbell
   B. Bullet
   C. Buy and hold
   D. Laddering

15. A new account is opened for joint tenants with rights of survivorship. All of the following statements are true EXCEPT

   A. orders may be given by either party
   B. mail can be sent to either party with the permission of the other party
   C. checks can be drawn in the name of either party
   D. in the event of death, the decedent's interest in the account goes to the other party

16. If 3 individuals have a tenants in common account with a firm and one individual dies, then

   A. the account must be liquidated and the proceeds split evenly among the 2 survivors and the decedent's estate
   B. the 2 survivors continue as cotenants with the decedent's estate
   C. trading is discontinued until the executor names a replacement for the deceased
   D. the account is converted to joint with rights of survivorship

17. Which of the following are fiduciaries?

    I. Executor of an estate
    II. Administrator of a trust
    III. Custodian of an UGMA account
    IV. Investment adviser representative granted
    with discretionary authority over the account

    A. I and II
    B. I, II and III
    C. II, III and IV
    D. I, II, III and IV

18. Under the UGMA, which of the following statements is NOT true?

    A. An UGMA account may have only one custodian for only one minor.
    B. Only an adult can make a gift to a minor.
    C. The maximum amount of money an adult can give to a minor in any one year is $14,000.
    D. Once a gift is given to a minor, it cannot be reclaimed.

19. Which of the following accounts could be opened with a TOD designation?

    I. Individual
    II. Joint tenants in common
    III. Joint tenants with rights of survivorship
    IV. UTMA

    A. I and II
    B. I and III
    C. I, III and IV
    D. II and IV

20. In making suitable investment recommendations, the least significant element would be the client's

    A. retirement needs
    B. death and disability needs
    C. educational level
    D. current income

21. An estate account with an investment adviser must be managed at the direction of the

    A. investment adviser
    B. estate creditors
    C. estate's executor or administrator
    D. attorney with guardianship over the surviving children

22. Since a trust account is managed for the beneficial interest of the beneficiary, the investment adviser representative can

    A. have funds withdrawn from the account at the direction of the beneficiary
    B. arrange to have the trust's funds pledged to support a loan for the trustee
    C. have a check drawn on the account, and payable to the trustee for trustee expenses
    D. place the securities in the trust fund in a non-custodial brokerage account

23. Which of the following is an example of a passive investment management style?

    A. Use of index funds in conjunction with selecting specific securities in the index to overweight certain sectors
    B. Investment in small capitalization technology securities
    C. Exclusive use of index funds
    D. Value investing

24. In determining an investor's risk tolerance, an investment adviser representative must consider

    I. level of tolerance toward market volatility
    II. investment time horizon, long term or short term
    III. liquidity requirements
    IV. investment temperament

    A. I only
    B. I and II
    C. I, II and III
    D. I, II, III and IV

25. With respect to taxation, the investment adviser representative should not

    A. draft tax and estate documents to ensure compliance with current law in order to provide substantial after-tax returns
    B. discuss the tax implications of investments
    C. explain the taxable status of particular investments
    D. consider tax implications as a way of improving a client's after-tax returns

26. Which of the following statements is an accurate description of dollar cost averaging?

   A. An investor buys the same number of shares each interval, averaging out his purchase prices over time.
   B. An investor sells shares when the market rises and buys shares when the market declines in order to average his costs.
   C. An investor invests a set amount of money each interval to buy more shares when the prices are low and fewer shares when prices are high.
   D. An investor averages the costs of his shares purchased and then enters limit orders to purchase additional shares at the average price.

27. Which of the following statements regarding taxation is NOT true?

   A. Earned income includes salary, bonus, and income as an owner of a limited partnership.
   B. Passive income is derived from rental property, limited partnerships, and enterprises in which an individual is not actively involved.
   C. Portfolio income includes dividends, interest, and net capital gains derived from the sale of securities.
   D. Items that must be added back into taxable income for calculation of the alternative minimum tax (AMT) include: accelerated depreciation on property placed in service after 1986; local taxes and interest on investments that do not generate income; and incentive stock options exceeding the fair market value of the employer's stock.

28. As part of its suitability determination, an IA firm requires that all potential nonbusiness clients complete a family balance sheet. Items that would be included are

   I. gold jewelry
   II. loan secured by the family automobile
   III. the amount paid thus far this year for Botox injections
   IV. the balance owed to the dentist for new crowns

   A. I, II and IV
   B. I and IV
   C. II and III
   D. I, II, III and IV

29. During the previous fiscal year, The Kaplan Family Trust received $24,000 in dividends and $35,000 in interest from corporate bonds. Securities transactions during the year resulted in long-term capital gains of $48,000, $20,000 of which were reinvested in the corpus. The DNI for the Kaplan Family Trust is

   A. $11,000
   B. $79,000
   C. $87,000
   D. $107,000

30. A taxpayer's marginal tax rate is

   A. the rate of tax paid on margin account interest
   B. generally lower than the effective tax rate
   C. the rate of taxation on any additional taxable income received
   D. the rate of tax paid on total taxable income

31. Your client owns a beach-front home that he has been renting out to others for the past 5 years. He plans to start taking things a bit easier and wishes to make personal use of the home part of the year. Under IRS regulations, if he wanted to continue to receive the same tax benefits he's enjoyed in the past, he would be permitted to enjoy the property no more than

   A. 1 month per taxable year
   B. 2 weeks per year
   C. 3 weeks per year
   D. the greater of 14 days or 10% of the total days rented to others at a fair rental price

32. A wealthy individual has set up a GRAT. Should she die during the time the trust is active, how are the remaining assets in the trust taxed?

    A. The original value plus any appreciation is taxed as part of the grantor's estate.
    B. The original value plus any appreciation passes to the beneficiaries but is subject to gift tax.
    C. The original value plus any appreciation passes to the beneficiaries and is taxed as ordinary income.
    D. No tax is due if the grantor should die during the term of the trust.

33. An individual is a participant in the 401(k) plan offered by her employer. If she were to invest $400 per month into a large-cap growth fund, she would be

    A. following a constant ratio plan
    B. dollar cost averaging
    C. matching her employer's contribution
    D. using a tactical asset allocation style

34. An investment adviser representative specializes in the senior market. A number of his clients have reached the age where they are contemplating selling their homes and moving into an assisted living facility. The profit made on the sale of their homes will be used to defray the costs of their new residence. Under current tax laws, which of the following are TRUE?

    I. A single person pays no tax on the first $250,000 of net profit realized on the sale of a primary residence that has been occupied for at least 2 of the past 5 years.
    II. A single person pays no tax on the first $500,000 of net profit realized on the sale of a primary residence that has been occupied for at least 2 of the past 5 years.
    III. A married couple pays no tax on the first $250,000 of net profit realized on the sale of a primary residence that has been occupied for at least 2 of the past 5 years.
    IV. A married couple pays no tax on the first $500,000 of net profit realized on the sale of a primary residence that has been occupied for at least 2 of the past 5 years.

    A. I and III
    B. I and IV
    C. II and III
    D. II and IV

35. An exchange specialist is

    A. a trader who makes a market in OTC stocks and ADRs
    B. a floor broker on the New York Stock Exchange who only executes trades for other brokers in return for commissions
    C. a member of the New York Stock Exchange who executes orders for other members and who also acts as a market maker charged with the responsibility of keeping an orderly market in designated stocks
    D. an electronic brokerage concern that executes trades online and through specialized trading order executing services

36. Which of the following types of orders does NOT restrict the price at which an order is executed?

    A. Limit
    B. Stop
    C. Market
    D. Stop limit

37. A broker-dealer acting as a principal in a trade would

    A. add a markup to the bid price when offering shares to a client
    B. add a markup to the offering price when selling shares to a client
    C. must always disclose the amount of markup on a client's confirmation statement
    D. must disclose to clients the amount of earnings he made on principal transactions in excess of the amount he would have made had he charged a commission

38. Which of the following orders would be most likely to add fuel to a bullish stock market?

    A. Buy limit
    B. Buy stop
    C. Sell limit
    D. Sell stop

39. An investor wishing to buy US Treasury bonds receives a quote from the dealer of 98.16. This represents

    A. the bid
    B. a discount
    C. the offer
    D. an indication of falling interest rates

40. A broker-dealer quotes a stock 42 to a half. The difference between these two numbers is known as
    A. the broker's commission
    B. the dealer's markup
    C. the profit margin
    D. the spread

41. It would be correct to state that
    I. the specialist stands ready to buy or sell stock on the floor of an exchange in an effort to keep an orderly market
    II. the specialist stands ready to buy or sell stock on the over-the-counter market in an effort to keep an orderly market
    III. the market maker stands ready to buy or sell stock on the floor of an exchange in an effort to keep an orderly market
    IV. the market maker stands ready to buy or sell stock on the over-the-counter market in an effort to keep an orderly market
    A. I and III
    B. I and IV
    C. II and III
    D. II and IV

42. A client of a brokerage firm purchases 100 shares of ABC common stock at a price of $50 per share. On settlement date, the firm journals $2,500 from the client's money market account to pay for the trade. No further call for money is made. This trade must have taken place in a
    A. cash account
    B. depository account
    C. margin account
    D. wrap fee account

43. You have a client with a margin account at your broker-dealer. If the market price of the securities in the account should fall to a point where you have to ask the client for additional funds, it is
    A. a Regulation T call
    B. a maintenance margin call
    C. a margin call
    D. a market call

44. The minimum size order that would be considered a block trade is
    A. 500 shares
    B. 1,000 shares
    C. 10,000 shares
    D. 100,000 shares

45. Under ERISA, a fiduciary must act in all of the following ways EXCEPT
    A. solely in the interest of plan participants and beneficiaries
    B. with care, skill, prudence, and caution under the circumstances then prevailing that a prudent person acting in like capacity and familiar with such matters would use in the conduct of an enterprise of a like character
    C. in accordance with the governing plan documents unless they are not consistent with ERISA
    D. confining investments to only those most likely to achieve growth

46. Which of the following statements regarding a traditional IRA for someone filing a 2015 tax return is TRUE?
    A. A traditional IRA allows a maximum tax-deductible annual contribution of $2,500 per individual or $4,000 per couple.
    B. The income and capital gains earned in the account are tax deferred until the funds are withdrawn.
    C. Distributions without penalty may begin after age 59½ and must begin by April 1 of the year preceding the year an individual turns 70½.
    D. Distributions before age 59½ are subject to a 10% penalty in lieu of income taxes.

47. IRAs and Keogh plans are similar in the following ways EXCEPT
    A. deferral of taxes
    B. distributions without penalty can begin as early as age 59½
    C. identical amounts of cash contributions are allowed
    D. there is a 50% tax penalty for insufficient distributions

48. All of the following investments are eligible for a traditional IRA EXCEPT
    A. covered call writing
    B. bank CDs
    C. works of art
    D. growth-oriented securities

49. Which of the following is an allowable early withdrawal from a traditional IRA without penalty?
    A. A wealthy individual withdraws $10,000 from his IRA to purchase his first principal residence.
    B. A single parent withdraws funds from her IRA to pay for the education of a nephew.
    C. A single parent supplements a home equity loan with funds from her IRA to pay for an additional home (a vacation home).
    D. A person withdraws funds from his IRA to buy a principal residence after he sold his first home as a result of medical expenses.

50. All of the following statements regarding qualified corporate retirement plans are true EXCEPT
    A. all corporate pension and profit-sharing plans must be established under a trust agreement
    B. all qualified retirement plans are either defined contribution or defined benefit plans
    C. they are covered under ERISA
    D. with defined benefit plans, the employee bears the investment risk

51. Qualified annuity plans offered under Section 403(b) of the Internal Revenue Code, referred to as tax-sheltered annuities (TSAs), are not available to
    A. a public school custodian
    B. a church minister
    C. a nurse at a nonprofit hospital
    D. a student at a nonprofit college

52. Which of the following would not constitute a conflict of interest between the plan and a fiduciary?
    A. A fiduciary sells a real estate investment to the plan at the current market rate.
    B. A fiduciary participates in a transaction on the plan's behalf that involves a party with interests adverse to those of the plan in order to ensure favorable terms for the plan.
    C. A fiduciary offers reduced commissions to the plan for transactions that are executed through his employing financial institution.
    D. The fiduciary receives fees for acting as a trustee to the plan.

53. All of the following are true about college funding plans EXCEPT
    A. proceeds in ESAs may be withdrawn income tax free even if the child is under age 18
    B. proceeds in 529s may be withdrawn income-tax free only if used at an accredited academic institution
    C. Section 529 plans allow a gift tax exclusion equal to five times the annual limit that may be repeated every 5 years
    D. a beneficiary of an ESA who withdraws the funds for nonqualified expenses will be taxed on the entire amount of the withdrawal plus a 10% penalty

54. Keogh Plans are qualified plans intended for those with self-employment income and owner-employees of unincorporated businesses or professional practices filing a Form 1040 Schedule C with the IRS. Which of the following statements relating to the Keogh Plan is NOT true?
    A. Owner-employee businesses and professional practices must show a gross profit in order to qualify for a tax-deductible contribution.
    B. A participant in a Keogh Plan may also maintain an IRA.
    C. The maximum allowable contribution to a Keogh Plan is substantially higher than that for an IRA.
    D. A former corporate employee who decides to become self-employed may not rollover any distributions from a qualified corporate plan into a rollover IRA if he has created a Keogh Plan.

55. An employer whose 401(k) plan complies with ERISA Section 404 is placing investment risk with the

    A. Internal Revenue Service
    B. plan fiduciary
    C. plan participant
    D. Securities and Exchange Commission

56. Which of the following individuals is clearly eligible to make a catch-up contribution?

    A. Roger, who has completed 1 year of service
    B. Emily, who is fully vested
    C. Sam, who has completed 15 years of service
    D. Hannah, who is 55 years old

57. Which of the following statements regarding Coverdell ESAs and QTPs is NOT correct?

    A. If a portion or all of the withdrawal (QTP) is spent on anything other than qualified higher education expenses, the distributee will be taxed at her own tax rate on the earnings portion of the withdrawal.
    B. Coverdell ESAs currently permit up to $5,000 in annual contributions, whereas QTPs allow large contributions reaching as high as $250,000 and above.
    C. QTPs are extremely useful tools that provide significant tax savings, allow for substantial investments for a child's education and provide a tool for avoidance of gift and estate taxes if used correctly.
    D. Coverdell ESAs are designed to offer tax benefits to those individuals who wish to save money for a child/grandchild's higher education expenses.

58. Under the minimum distribution rules, Jason is required to take a minimum distribution of $10,000 this year from his IRA. However, a distribution of only $8,000 has been made. What is the dollar amount of penalty that may be assessed in this situation?

    A. $200
    B. $1,000
    C. $2,000
    D. $4,000

59. A basic difference between a Section 457 plan established on behalf of a governmental entity and one established by a private tax-exempt organization is that

    A. a governmental plan must hold its assets in trust or custodial accounts for the benefit of individual participants
    B. a tax-exempt plan participant does not have to include plan distributions in his or her taxable income
    C. a governmental plan cannot make a distribution before the participant attains age 70½
    D. a tax exempt plan's distributions are not eligible for a favorable lump sum 10-year averaging treatment

60. Which of the following could reduce the amount that an individual may contribute to a Traditional IRA?

    I. Roth IRA contributions made for the year
    II. High income level
    III. Participation in an employer-sponsored plan
    IV. Marital status

    A. I only
    B. I and II
    C. I, II and III
    D. I, II, III and IV

61. A person providing which of the following services to an ERISA plan would be performing in a fiduciary capacity?

    A. Selecting and monitoring third-party service providers
    B. Determining the age at which benefits are to be provided
    C. Amending the plan
    D. Changing the level of employer contributions

62. While in your office, you see that your firm is going to be holding a training session on municipal fund securities. You wish to attend because you are interested in being able to speak intelligently to your clients about

    A. the difference between GO bonds and revenue bonds
    B. the difference between using mutual funds or UITs to invest in municipal bonds
    C. Section 529 Plans
    D. Section 457 Plans

63. All of these are true about a traditional 401(k) plan EXCEPT
    A. in service employees may be eligible for hardship withdrawals
    B. employees can choose from a variety of investment options
    C. employees may have a portion of their contribution matched by the employer
    D. the employer can contribute more than 25% of total payroll

64. Which of the following would you expect to see in the investment policy statement of a qualified plan?
    I. The information in the summary plan document specified by the Department of Labor
    II. The method to be used to measure the investment performance of the plan
    III. A listing of the portfolio assets as of the most recent quarter
    IV. Investment limitations placed on the portfolio managers
    A. I and III
    B. I and IV
    C. II and III
    D. II and IV

65. Which of the following persons are considered fiduciaries?
    I. Executor of an estate
    II. Administrator of a trust
    III. Custodian of an UGMA/UTMA account
    IV. Conservator for a legally incompetent person
    A. I and II
    B. I, II and III
    C. III and IV
    D. I, II, III and IV

66. If a customer would like to open a custodial UGMA or UTMA account for his nephew, a minor, the uncle can
    A. open the account provided the proper trust arrangements are filed first
    B. open the account and name himself custodian
    C. open the account, but he needs a legal document evidencing the nephew's parents' prior approval of the account
    D. be custodian for the account only if he is also the minor's legal guardian

67. Which of the following regarding customer accounts is NOT true?
    A. Stock held in a custodial account may not be registered in the name of the minor.
    B. In some cases, a TOD account is referred to as a POD account.
    C. Stock held under JTWROS goes to the survivor(s) in the event of the death of one of the tenants.
    D. Margin trading in a fiduciary account does not require any special documentation.

68. An investor wants to provide for his 3 nephews after his brother dies. Under the UGMA, the investor may open
    A. 1 account for all 3 nephews
    B. 3 separate accounts and deposit cash and securities
    C. 3 separate accounts and deposit insurance policies
    D. 3 separate accounts and deposit fixed annuities

69. Which of the following individuals may not open a joint account?
    A. 2 spouses
    B. 3 sisters
    C. 2 strangers
    D. Parent and a minor

70. One of your clients enters a sell stop order at 60, limit 59. Subsequent to the entry of the order, trades occur at 61, 61.10, 60, 58.95, 59, 60. The client's order was most likely filled at
    A. 58.95
    B. 59
    C. 60
    D. 61.10

71. In this industry, many words have similar meaning. Which of the following choices consists of a pair which are NOT properly considered synonyms?
    A. Inflation risk—purchasing power risk
    B. Interest rate risk—money rate risk
    C. Financial risk—market risk
    D. Liquidity risk—marketability risk

72. There are number of potential sources of income to a client that would have to reported on their Form 1040 tax return. Among them could be all of these EXCEPT
    A. death benefit received from a life insurance policy
    B. operation of a sole proprietorship
    C. ownership of stock in an S corporation
    D. interests in a DPP

73. A participant in an ERISA qualified retirement plan is studying the investment policy statement (IPS) prepared by the plan's fiduciary. The contents of the IPS would not include
    A. determination for meeting future cash flow needs
    B. specific security selection
    C. investment philosophy including asset allocation style
    D. methods for monitoring procedures and performance

74. Regarding the treatment of estates by the IRS, it would not be correct to state any of the following EXCEPT
    A. estates may be valued either at date of death or 9 months later using the alternative valuation option
    B. a deceased person may reduce the value of the estate by taking advantage of the annual gift tax exclusion
    C. income received by the estate is reported on Form 1040
    D. the maximum tax rate on estates is the same as that on gifts

75. While attending a seminar given by one of your firm's analysts, you hear the term, feasible set. That would mean the discussion was dealing with the topic of
    A. the efficient frontier
    B. convexity
    C. a range of returns
    D. opportunity cost

ANSWERS AND RATIONALES

1. **C.** John's investment in the yacht-building business suffered a loss as a result of legislative risk. In other words, the rules of the game (i.e., tax laws) changed after John purchased the security.

2. **C.** This imposing-looking question should take 10 seconds to do. When the question is dealing with volatility, look for the standard deviation. The portfolio with the lowest (choice C at 10.02) is the least volatile, the one with the highest (choice A at 12.25) is the most volatile.

3. **C.** The return from a security can be adjusted for the risk associated with it by subtracting the risk-free rate from the security's actual return and then dividing that by its standard deviation, the basic measure of unsystematic risk. This is commonly known as the Sharpe ratio.

4. **D.** To determine the total return on this zero-coupon debt obligation, the $50 capital appreciation is divided by the cost of the bond, in this case $950, for a total return of 5.26%. Total return of a zero-coupon security is made up entirely of the difference between the cost of the security and its sale or maturity price. The market price of the security, not current interest rates, is used in the calculation of total return. Five percent would be the return had the debt obligation cost 100, or par. There is no coupon rate to be added to the calculation.

5. **B.** Duration measures a bond's sensitivity to a change in interest rates. The longer the duration, the greater the change in a bond's price with respect to interest rate changes.

6. **C.** The yield to maturity reflects the annualized return of a bond if it is held to its maturity. The computation reflects internal rate of return and is frequently referred to as the market required rate of return for a debt security. The rate set at issuance and printed on the face of the bond is the nominal or coupon rate. Dividing the coupon rate by the current market price of the bond provides the current yield. The return of a bond if it is held to the call date is the yield to call.

7. **B.** In an efficient market, all participants have equal access to information and, therefore, stock prices reflect that equality almost immediately.

8. **C.** The expected return is the estimate of probable returns that an investment may yield when added up.

9. **A.** First, compute Dan's after-tax rate of return of 10.95% as follows: .15 × (1 − .27), or .73 = .1095. Then, compute Dan's inflation-adjusted, or real, rate of return by subtracting the 3% inflation rate from his 10.95% after-tax return.

10. 10. **B.** Because dollar-weighted returns reflect the individual investor's cash deposits and withdrawals from the investment account, it is the preferred measure of return for them. On the other hand, time-weighted returns are generally a more important tool to show portfolio manager performance.

11. **D.** Sector rotation is the practice of moving out of those industries that are heading for a decline and into those whose fortunes are likely to rise as the economy follows the business cycle.

12. **A.** With the barbell strategy, the investor would place $25,000 into bonds maturing in 10 years and the other half into bonds maturing in two years. This makes $25,000 available for reinvestment in two years enabling the investor to take advantage of the higher rates (if they materialize).

13. **D.** Total return is all distributions plus/minus appreciation/depreciation. In this question, the $1,300 includes the $250 capital gain so all we add is the $20 dividend. $320 divided by $1,000 equals 32% total return.

14. **C.** Regardless of the investment, buy and hold is always a passive strategy. All of the others involve some degree of continual activity on behalf of the investor.

15. **C.** Although either party may enter an order, any money or securities delivered out of the account must be in the names of both owners.

16. **B.** The decedent's estate becomes a tenant in common with the survivors.

17. **D.** Each of these persons is in a relationship of trust to the customer and is therefore a fiduciary.

18. **C.** Any adult can give a gift to a minor in a custodial account. There is no limitation on the size of the gift. However, any gift in excess of $14,000 (or such higher number as indexing provides for) will possibly subject the donor to a gift tax liability.

19. **B.** The only types of accounts that may have the Transfer on Death (TOD) designation are individual and JTWROS. Minors can not designate a beneficiary. Upon the death of a minor, any assets belong in the deceased's estate.

20. **C.** A client's educational level is not as important as retirement, death and disability, and current income. However, the adviser should take note of the client's educational level to ensure that the client fully understands the investments recommended. Also, a person with a professional educational background may have more employment opportunities and be able to take more risk as a result.

21. **C.** Only the estate administrator or executor can make investment management and distribution decisions. This does not mean that the executor must manage the account, only that decisions as to who will do the management are within his purview. A guardian with authority over the children does not necessarily have power over the estate unless the guardian is also the administrator or the executor of the estate.

22. **C.** The trustee can be reimbursed for trustee expenses that are reasonable. A trust account must be managed by the trustee and not by the beneficiary. Only the trustee can withdraw funds, provided the withdrawal is done in a manner consistent with the trust document. Trust funds must be placed in custodial accounts, not in noncustodial accounts.

23. **C.** A passive investment style uses index funds because the manager does not believe that returns above the averages can be sustained for any length of time because the market is efficiently priced. Use of index funds in conjunction with specific securities in order to overweight sectors is an active style. Investment in small capitalization technology securities involves actively selecting securities that the manager believes will perform well or better than the market. Value investing involves the active search for securities that are undervalued by the market.

24. **D.** The investment adviser representative must consider a client's volatility tolerance, investment time frame, liquidity needs, and comfort with different types of investments. These are all elements in the understanding of a customer's attitude toward risk.

25. **A.** An investment adviser representative must not draft estate documents. This should only be drafted by an attorney because it constitutes practicing law. An investment adviser representative should, however, discuss tax implications of investments as a way of improving a client's after-tax returns.

26. **C.** Dollar cost averaging involves investing a set amount of money each interval. If the market fluctuates, this will cause the client to buy more shares when the prices are low and fewer shares when prices are high. The result of this is a lower average cost per share than average price paid. An investor who sells shares when the market rises and buys shares when the market declines is not dollar cost averaging, but is attempting to time the market. An investor who averages the cost of the shares purchased and then enters limit orders to purchase additional shares at the average price is not engaged in a dollar cost averaging program. In dollar cost averaging, the same dollar amount is invested each interval.

27. **A.** Earned income includes salary and bonus but not income as an owner of a limited partnership. Passive income is derived from rental property, limited partnerships, and enterprises in which an individual is not actively involved.

28. **A.** The balance sheet contains assets and liabilities as of a specific point in time. Personal property currently owned, such as jewelry, is an asset. A loan still outstanding, such as the car loan and the debt to the dentist, are liabilities. The amount already paid for the Botox injections is no longer on the balance sheet.

29. **C.** Distributable Net Income (DNI) is dividends and interest plus capital gains that have not been reinvested back into the trust. In this case, $24,000 + $35,000 + $28,000 = $87,000.

30. **C.** Marginal tax rate is defined as the rate of taxation on any additional taxable income received. It is sometimes referred to as the tax on the "next" dollar or the "last" dollar of income. The effective tax rate is the overall rate paid on the total taxable income.

31. **D.** The IRS allows deductions for expenses relating to owning rental property if personal use does not exceed the greater of 14 days or 10% of the total days that the property is in rental use. For example, if the client had the property rented out for 200 days, he could make personal use of it for up to 20 days that year and still be able to treat the rental as a business.

32. **A.** One of the risks in setting up a GRAT is that if the grantor dies during the term of the trust (usually 3–10 years), the assets put in the GRAT, plus any appreciation, are included in her estate.

33. **B.** Dollar cost averaging (DCA) is a funding method that consists of investing the same amount of money at fixed intervals into the same investment. Almost all participants in 401(k) plans use DCA. It is possible that the portfolio managers of the large-cap fund use a tactical style, but the investor is not buying and selling to try to time the market.

34. **B.** When a primary residence that has been lived in for at least 2 of the 5 years is sold at a profit, the first $250,000 for an individual and the first $500,000 for a married couple is not subject to taxation. Everything in excess of that is taxed as capital gain on Schedule D of the Form 1040.

35. **C.** A specialist is a member of the NYSE who executes orders for other members and who also acts as a market maker charged with the responsibility of keeping an orderly market in designated stocks. A specialist must have sufficient capital to buy and sell from his own account in order to maintain a liquid and orderly market. A trader who makes a market in OTC stocks and ADRs is a market maker in the OTC market and not a specialist on an exchange. A specialist executes trades on an exchange.

36. **C.** A market order does not reflect or restrict the price at which a security is executed. A limit order limits the amount to be paid or received for securities. A stop order becomes a market order if the stock reaches or goes through the stop price. A stop limit order becomes a limit order if the stock hits or goes through the trigger price.

37. **B.** When selling a security to a public customer, the broker-dealer adds his markup to the ask/offer (not the bid) price. A broker does not add a markup to the bid price when offering shares to a client. The broker-dealer would mark down the bid price. A broker-dealer does not usually have to disclose to the client the amount of markup on a client's confirmation statement. If a commission were charged, however, it would have to be indicated on the confirmation statement.

38. **B.** Buy stop orders are placed above the current market price and are usually used by those with short positions. As prices increase, these stop orders are triggered, sending more buy orders to the trading floors.

39. **C.** A dealer's quotes consist of the bid and the offer. The bid price is what the dealer will pay a customer to purchase a security, and the offer is the dealer's selling price. In this case, the client wishes to purchase bonds, so the 98.16 represents the price the dealer is offering them for. Yes, the quote is a discount, but the better answer for this question is offer.

40. **D.** The dealer's quote represents the bid and the offer (ask) prices. This quote is 42 bid and 42.50 offered. The difference between these two is the spread.

41. **B.** The specialist performs his activities on the floor of an exchange, while the market maker performs a similar function in the OTC market.

42. **C.** When a purchase is made and only 50% of the cost of the transaction is required, the trade is being made on margin.

43. **B.** The original call for funds is the Regulation T or margin call. When the call is for additional money, it is known as maintenance margin.

44. **C.** The term *block trade* refers to a transaction involving a minimum of 10,000 shares.

45. **D.** Under ERISA, a fiduciary is not limited to confining investments to only those most likely to achieve growth. The fiduciary is required to diversify investments so as to minimize the risk of losses, unless doing so is clearly not prudent under the circumstances.

46. **B.** The income and capital gains earned in the account are tax deferred until the funds are withdrawn. A traditional IRA allows a maximum tax-deductible annual contribution of $5,500 per individual ($6,500 for those age 50 and older), not $2,500 per individual. Distributions without penalty may begin after age 59½ and must begin by April 1 of the year following the year an individual turns 70½. Distributions before age 59½ are subject to a 10% penalty and subject to taxes.

47. **C.** IRAs and Keogh plans do not have identical contribution amounts; IRAs allow a maximum of $5,500 per individual or $11,000 per couple per year, whereas Keogh plans allow substantially more. Both IRAs and Keoghs allow tax-deferred growth until the individual withdraws the funds. IRAs and Keoghs have premature distribution penalties before age 59½. Once the participant reaches 70½, required minimum distributions must be made or a 50% tax penalty will be assessed.

48. **C.** Gems, intangibles, and works of art are ineligible investments for an IRA. Covered call writing is allowed, but speculative options strategies are not. Bank CDs are permissible investments for an IRA. Growth-oriented securities and securities in general are appropriate investment vehicles for IRAs.

49. **A.** Any individual withdrawing $10,000 from his IRA to purchase his first principal residence would have the penalty waived. The wealth of the individual is not relevant. The purchase must be a first-time purchase as well as the primary residence. A single parent who withdraws funds from her IRA to pay for the education of a nephew will pay a 10% tax penalty. Educational withdrawals are limited to the taxpayer or a spouse, child, or grandchild. A single parent who supplements a home equity loan with funds from her IRA to pay for an additional home will pay a penalty because only a primary residence can be purchased with early withdrawal funds. A person who withdraws funds from his IRA to buy a principal residence after he sold his first home as a result of medical expenses will pay a penalty because the purchase is not for his first principal residence.

50. **D.** With defined benefit plans, the employer (not the employee) bears the investment risk. The employer must fund the defined benefits, regardless of the investment performance of funds set aside for this purpose. The retiree receives a defined benefit regardless of investment performance. All corporate pension and profit-sharing plans must be established under a trust agreement. All qualified retirement plans are either defined contribution or defined benefit plans.

51. **D.** 403(b) plans are available to employees of nonprofit 501(c)(3) schools, not students. 403(b) plans are also available to employees of public educational institutions such as schools. Church organization employees are allowed 403(b) plans. Employees of tax-exempt institutions such as private colleges, research and scientific foundations, private hospitals, and medical schools are allowed to establish 403(b) plans.

52. **D.** A fiduciary can receive compensation from the sponsor of the plan for acting as a trustee, if fees are reasonable and consistent with duties performed. A fiduciary may not sell a real estate investment to the plan at the going market rate. Such self-dealing presents a conflict of interest regardless of the terms of the transaction. A fiduciary may not participate in a transaction on the plan's behalf that involves a party with interests adverse to those of the plan in order to ensure favorable terms for the plan. The situation is self-dealing and presents a conflict of interest prohibited under ERISA. Offers of reduced commissions to the plan for transactions that are executed through his employing financial institution are prohibited and a conflict of interest.

53. **D.** The tax and 10% penalty is only levied against earnings since the contributions were made with after-tax dollars.

54. **D.** Rollovers are permitted into an IRA regardless of any plans maintained. Tax-deductible contributions are not allowed unless there is potentially taxable income against which to deduct. Anyone with earned income may have an IRA, regardless of participation in another qualified plan, and the Keogh Plan contribution limits are much higher than those for an IRA.

55. **C.** In a 401(k) plan, a plan sponsor can shift investment risk to the employee by complying with ERISA Section 404(c) rules.

56. **D.** Catch-up contributions are allowed to participants who are age 50 and over.

57. **B.** Coverdell ESAs currently permit up to $2,000 (2015) in annual contributions, whereas QTPs (Section 529 Plans) allow large contributions reaching as high as $250,000 and above. When nonqualifying distributions are taken, any taxes are the responsibility of the distributee, defined by the IRS as the beneficiary (student) of the plan.

58. **B.** The penalty for failure to make the correct amount of required minimum distribution is 50% of the difference between the minimum required amount and the actual distribution. In this case, this would be 50% of $2,000 ($10,000 − $8,000) or $1,000.

59. **A.** A governmental Section 457 plan must be funded, that is, it must hold plan assets in trusts or custodial accounts for the benefit of individual participants. Conversely, a tax-exempt (nongovernmental) Section 457 plan may not be funded.

60. **A.** The maximum annual contribution applies as a total among your Roth and your traditional IRA. So, if the maximum is $5,500 and you put $3,000 into your Roth, you could only put $2,500 into your traditional IRA. You could do a total of $6,500 if you were 50 or older. High income level and participation in an employer-sponsored plan will impact the amount you may deduct but not the amount you may contribute. Even though a married couple can have their own IRAs or set up a spousal IRA if one is nonworking, that doesn't reduce the amount that either spouse can contribute.

61. **A.** The issue here is the distinction between fiduciary functions and something called settlor functions. ERISA defines fiduciary not in terms of formal title but rather in functional terms of control and authority over the plan. ERISA provides that a person is a fiduciary with respect to an employee benefit plan to the extent that such a person does any of the following: exercises any discretionary authority or control over the management of a plan or over the management or disposition of plan assets; renders investment advice for a fee or other compensation, direct or indirect, with respect to any monies or other property of such plan; or has any discretionary authority or discretionary responsibility in the administration of such plan including appointing other plan fiduciaries or selecting and monitoring third-party service providers. The other choices given in the question are known as settlor functions. The most common settlor functions are design decisions involving: establishment of the plan, defining who are the covered employees and benefits to be provided, and amending or terminating the plan. Because the likelihood of an IAR ever performing settlor functions is quite remote (usually they are done by employees of the sponsoring employer), I cannot fathom why NASAA would ask something like this on the exam.

62. **C.** The Securities and Exchange Commission has stated that certain Section 529 College Savings Plans established by states or local governmental entities are municipal fund securities. Accordingly, the purchase and sale of state-sponsored Section 529 Plans are governed by the rules of the Municipal Securities Rulemaking Board (MSRB).

63. **D.** There are exceptions to this, but, in general (and on the exam), you will have to know that the employer share of the contributions to a traditional 401(k) plan (or any other DC plan) may not exceed 25% of total payroll. Some students get this correct through process of elimination. The plan may have provisions for hardship withdrawals; there are a number of investment options available, and the employer may elect to match employee contributions.

64. **D.** The IPS would include information on how the investment performance of the plan is measured as well as the investment parameters to be followed by the portfolio managers. It would not include the summary plan description (document), generally referred to by the initials SPD. That is for the employees' to learn about eligibility, vesting, matching contributions, etc. It has nothing to do with how the money is invested. The purpose of the IPS is to set "policy" for the portfolio, not to list its composition.

65. **D.** All of the persons listed have fiduciary responsibilities because of the authority with which they are entrusted.

66. **B.** The donor may name himself the custodian of an UGMA or UTMA account. No documentation of custodial status is required to open an UGMA account, and the custodian is not required to be the minor's legal guardian.

67. **D.** Trading on margin is prohibited in fiduciary accounts except under special circumstances and with the appropriate documentation.

68. **B.** UGMA rules require that any UGMA account have only one beneficial owner and one custodian. Cash and securities may be donated into the account, but insurance contracts and fixed annuities may not.

69. **D.** A minor may not be a party in a joint account because minors cannot legally exercise control over an account. A custodial account should be set up for the minor.

70. **A.** This is really two orders. The first is to "stop" at 60. That is, once the stock trades at 60 or lower, enter the order. The second order is a sell, but with a limit of 59. In this sequence, the first time the stock hits 60 (or less), is the 3rd trade, the one at 60. That triggers the sell limit. The next trade is at 58.95 and that is not acceptable to the limit order at 59. Why not? Because the limit order is saying, "get me 59 or higher"; that makes the following trade at 59 an acceptable price.

71. **C.** Financial risk is an unsystematic risk; generally, the concern that an issuer will be unable to meet its debt obligations as they come due. It could be paired with either credit risk or default risk. Market risk is a systematic risk.

72. **A.** An individual can generate income from running a sole proprietorship or being a shareholder in an S corporation (the exam will possibly use the obsolete term, Subchapter S). And, if units of a DPP throw off income, that would be reported as well. Of course, taxable income can be generated by investments in the form of dividends, interest, and capital gains from any source. The death benefit is from a life insurance policy and those, unlike the death benefit from an annuity, are not subject to income tax. Depending on how the ownership is structured, the death benefit could be subject to estate tax, but that would be reported on the Form 706 and is generally not considered income.

73. **B.** One thing that could never be in an IPS is a listing of the securities that will be purchased in the future. Types of securities, yes, but not the specific ones.

74. **D.** The maximum tax rate on estates and gifts is 40%. The alternative valuation date is 6 months after death; 9 months after death is when the tax is due. Dead people can't make gifts and any income received by the estate before it is liquidated is reported on Form 1041.

75. **A.** The feasible set of portfolios represents all portfolios that can be constructed from a given set of stocks. An efficient portfolio is a feasible portfolio that provides the greatest expected return for a given amount of risk, or equivalently, the least risk for a given amount of expected return. This is also called an optimal portfolio. The efficient frontier is the set of all efficient portfolios. Obviously, an investor should choose a portfolio along the efficient frontier.

Q U I C K   Q U I Z   A N S W E R S

Quick Quiz 14.A

1. **C**

2. **A**

3. **B**

4. **A.** Transfer on death requires no additional legal work and allows the account owner to designate beneficiaries in whatever percentages she wants. Furthermore, changes can be made at any time prior to death.

5. **B.** The only way to limit liability is through a corporation (or LLC or limited partnership—neither of which is offered here as a choice). The S corporation allows for the flow-through of operating losses to the shareholders while the C corp does not

6. **D.** When a joint account is opened, financial information should be obtained on all of the account owners.

7. **A.** A sole proprietorship only has 1 owner. Therefore, the account would focus on the needs of that individual. Partnerships have partners; corporations have stockholders; LLCs have members.

Quick Quiz 14.B

1. **C**

2. **B**

3. **A**

4. **A.** The person who funds the trust is the grantor or settlor. The bank has been appointed to be trustee, and the daughter is the beneficiary of the trust.

Quick Quiz 14.C

1. **C**

2. **D**

3. **B**

4. **A**

5. **D.** A trust that first goes into effect upon the death of the grantor (the individual who established the trust) is properly referred to as a testamentary trust. Yes, it is an irrevocable trust because the deceased cannot make any changes, but irrevocable trusts can refer to trusts that don't involve the death of the grantor; testamentary trusts cannot. On the exam, you will sometimes have to choose from the *best* of two possible answers.

Quick Quiz 15.A

1. **D.** Time horizon does not end at retirement age. The portfolio will have to last them throughout their retirement until their death. On the basis of current life expectancy tables, the money will have to last them at least 20 years.

2. **A.** An individual's net worth is the difference between the individual's assets and the individual's liabilities. It is determined from the personal balance sheet rather than from the personal income statement. Net worth is relevant in determining an individual's investment objectives. Someone with a negative net worth might find it preferable to reduce his debt level before beginning an investment program.

3. **C.** One can't adequately present any investment recommendations without having an understanding of the client's risk tolerance. Home address and Social Security number are legal requirements for opening the account, but they don't enter into the decision-making process for portfolio design. Yes, you will want to know the beneficiary of any IRAs or qualified plans, but that has little to do with the nature of your recommendations.

4. **B.** There are 2 answers for preservation of capital on this exam. The strongest is a bank insured CD, followed by a money market fund (you'll never have both in the same question).

Quick Quiz 16.A

1. **E.**

2. **C.**

3. **A.**

4. **B.**

5. **D.**

Quick Quiz 16.B

1. **D.** EMH is really just an extension of the Random Walk Theory, which states that throwing darts at the stock market page is as good as any way to select investments. If the market is truly efficient, no one has an edge.

2. **B.** One of the uses of Monte Carlo simulations is to run thousands of potential scenarios to determine what withdrawal rate will likely last as long as your client does.

3. **C.** We take the risk-free rate of 8% and add that to the product of the stock's beta and the (expected return minus the risk-free rate). Expressed in numbers, it is 8% + 1.2(15% − 8%) or 8% + 1.2 (7%) = 16.4%

Quick Quiz 17.A

1. **B.** The key to this question is that dividends paid on stock issued by American companies (and certain qualified foreign corporations) generally qualify for a reduced tax rate (maximum 15 to 20%). No such benefit accrues to money market funds (their dividends are generated from interest income) and government bond interest is always taxed as ordinary income (although state income tax free). The dividends on a growth stock would also qualify, but, since the question deals with increasing current income, public utility is a more sensible approach. This is an example of how the test might present you with two answer choices that could be correct, and you must choose the one that is *more* correct.

2. **B.** An individual can generate income from running a sole proprietorship or being a shareholder in an S corporation (the exam will probably use the obsolete term, Subchapter S). Of course, taxable income can be generated by investments in the form of dividends, interest, and capital gains. Death benefits paid to the beneficiary of a life insurance policy are *not* subject to income tax.

3. **C.** The only way to limit liability is through a corporation (C or S), LLC, or limited partnership. The LLC allows for the flow-through of operating losses to the shareholders while the C corporation does not.

Quick Quiz 17.B

1. **F.** Only accelerated depreciation is a tax preference item for computing AMT.

2. **F.** Dividend income is considered portfolio, or investment, income. Passive income results from limited partnerships and real estate.

3. **F.** The IRS assigns FIFO when an acceptable basis has not been selected. FIFO generally results in the largest capital gain.

4. **T.** The same is true with a stock split.

5. **T.**   The investor has run afoul of the wash sale rule because a call option on a stock is considered *substantially identical* to the stock.

6. **F.**   The cost basis of inherited securities is the market value of the securities on the date of the owner's death.

7. **F.**   Interest income from municipal bonds is exempt from taxation when paid to corporations or individuals.

8. **F.**   A corporation is taxed on 30% of its dividend income; 70% is excluded.

9. **F.**   Marital deduction on transfer of property between spouses is unlimited.

Quick Quiz 18.A

1. **B.**   A signed loan consent agreement permits the firm to lend the customer's margin securities. Firms must keep customer margin securities segregated from firm securities—commingling is prohibited.

2. **C.**   The definition of a mixed margin account is one that contains both long and short positions.

3. **C.**   The initial margin required when purchasing a security is known as a margin call. If the equity in the account falls below the broker-dealer's minimum requirement, there is a house call for additional funds. If the BD doesn't have a house requirement or the call is not met and the account continues to lose equity, there will be a maintenance margin call in accordance with the rules of the SROs. The call rate is what banks charge broker-dealer on money loaned against stock market collateral.

Quick Quiz 18.B

1. **C**

2. **D**

3. **A**

4. **B**

5. **E**

6. **B.**   Selling short does not reduce the risk of a long position—the investor is selling borrowed, not owned, stock. The appropriate time to sell short is when one anticipates that the stock price is about to drop. The investor wants to sell at a high price and buy later at a lower price. Both the reward and risk potential of selling short are high. If the stock price moves down dramatically, the investor can reap a large gain. If it moves up dramatically, the investor can lose a great deal of money.

7. **C.**   Whenever a trade is made without a commission indicated on the confirmation, it means that a markup or markdown was charged. That makes it a dealer or principal transaction. Commissions are always disclosed on agency transactions.

Quick Quiz 19.A

1. **A.**   The only major benchmark that is price-weighted is the Dow Jones.

2. **B.**   The Morgan Stanley Capital International EAFE (Europe, Australasia, Far East) index is the most popular one for benchmarking foreign portfolios.

3. **D.**   All of these are true. The investor has a capital gain of $2 per share and has received $1 per share in dividends. That is a total return of $3 on an investment of $50 or 6%. Because the holding period was 6 months, the annualized return is approximately double the 6% or 12%. With an inflation rate of 2%, the real rate of return was 4% and the holding period return is the same as the total return.

Quick Quiz 20.A

1. **A.** Any individual with earned income who is under age 70½ may contribute to a traditional IRA. The deductibility of those contributions will be determined by that person's coverage under qualified plans and by his level of income.

2. **B.** All withdrawals from IRAs are taxed at the individual's ordinary income tax rate at the time of withdrawal. Distributions made before age 59½ will incur an additional 10% tax penalty.

3. **C.** The penalty for premature withdrawals from an IRA or a Keogh account is 10% plus ordinary income tax. The excess contribution penalty is 6%, whereas the 50% penalty applies after age 70½.

4. **A.** Early withdrawals, without penalty, are permitted only in certain situations (such as death or qualifying disability).

5. **B.** Cash value life insurance, term insurance, and collectibles are not permissible investments in an IRA.

6. **B.** Small businesses and self-employed persons typically establish SEP IRAs because they are easier and less expensive than other plans for an employer to set up and administer.

7. **C.** The common factor for both traditional and Roth IRAs is that the amount that may be contributed is the same for both. Traditional IRAs offer tax-deductible contributions, but withdrawals are generally taxed. Roth IRAs do not offer tax-deductible contributions, but qualified withdrawals are tax free. Traditional IRAs require distributions to begin by April 1 after the year an owner reaches age 70½, but this is not true for Roth IRAs.

Quick Quiz 20.B

1. **C.** A person with self-employment income may deduct contributions to a Keogh plan. Keogh plans are not available to corporations or their employees.

2. **C.** All interest, dividends, and capital gains accumulated in a Keogh are tax deferred until their withdrawal (which must begin between age 59½ and by April 1 after the year in which the account owner turns 70½). The account owner may choose to take distributions in the form of lifetime income payments or as a single lump sum.

3. **A.** Keogh contributions can only be made before the date on which an individual turns 70½.

Quick Quiz 20.C

1. **C.** Because he is employed by a public school system, the customer is eligible to participate in the tax-sheltered annuity plan. Employee contributions to a TSA plan are excluded from gross income in the year in which they are made. As in other retirement plans, a penalty tax is assessed on distributions received before age 59½. Mutual funds, CDs, and annuity contracts are among the investment choices available for TSA plans.

2. **A.** The giveaway here is the public school employees—the 403(b) is their plan as well as being offered to employees of certain, but not all, tax-exempt organizations.

3. **B.** Minimum distributions from TSAs are required to start by April 1 of the year following the year in which the participant turns 70½.

4. **A.** A guaranteed investment contract (GIC) is regarded as a conservative investment.

Quick Quiz 20.D

1. **B.** Funding covers how an employer contributes to or funds a plan.

2. **B.** The retirement plan's trust agreement specifies the formula(s) used to determine the contributions to a defined contribution plan.

3. **B.** Although all of these may have a fiduciary responsibility, the definition, as expressed in the Uniform Prudent Investor Act of 1994, requires reasonable care, skill, and caution.

4. **D.** To comply with the safe harbor provisions of ERISA's Section 404(c), the plan trustee must allow each participant control over their investments and furnish them with full performance and risk information. The rule only mandates a minimum of 3 alternatives and quarterly changes.

5. **B.** For a loan not to be treated as a taxable distribution for tax purposes, it must be repayable within 5 years at a reasonable rate of interest. The unforeseeable emergency requirements are found in a Section 457 Plan.

Quick Quiz 20.E

1. **T.**

2. **T.** Why isn't this a transfer? The key is the phrase, "generally within a specified period." That refers to the 60 days one has to complete the rollover without penalty. In the case of a direct transfer, time limits are not a relevant factor—the investor never has access to the funds.

3. **F.**

4. **T.**

5. **T.** The maximum contributions for defined benefit plans allow a larger contribution in a shorter period for highly paid individuals nearing retirement.

6. **F.** Remember the (k) in 401(k) reminds us that top-heavy plans benefit key employees.

Quick Quiz 20.F

1. **D.**

2. **A.**

3. **B.**

4. **C.**

Quick Quiz 20.G

1. **B.** Only $2,000 may be invested in each child's ESA per year. If a couple has three children, they may contribute $6,000 in total, or $2,000 per child, per year.

2. **B.** Although both plans will help them with their objective, their earnings are above the Coverdell ESA limits.

Quick Quiz 20.H

1. **B.** The donor may name himself the custodian of an UGMA or UTMA account. No documentation of custodial status is required to open these accounts, and the custodian is not required to be the minor's legal guardian.

2. **B.** UTMA rules require that any UTMA account have only one beneficial owner and one custodian. Cash and securities may be donated into the account, but insurance contracts and fixed annuities may not.

Appendix A
Federal vs. State Comparison Chart

FEDERAL VERSUS STATE LAW

FEDERAL	STATE
Definition of Investment Adviser	
Any person who, for compensation, engages in the business of advising others as to the value of securities or the advisability of investing in securities or, as part of a regular business, issues analyses or reports concerning securities.	Same as federal.
Exclusions from Above Definition	
1. Banks 2. Lawyers, accountants, teachers, engineers 3. Broker-dealers 4. Publisher of any bona fide newspaper, news magazine, or other publication of general circulation 5. Any person whose advice relates solely to securities issued or guaranteed by the U.S. government	1. Banks 2. Lawyers, accountants, teachers, engineers 3. Broker-dealers 4. Publishers of any bona fide newspaper, news magazine, newsletter, or other publication that does not consist of the rendering of advice on the basis of the specific investment situation of each client 5. Investment adviser representatives
Exemptions	

1. The Private Fund adviser exemption is available for advisers with less than $150 million in assets under management for private equity funds.
 	
2. The only clients are insurance companies.
 	
3. Intrastate business only and does not furnish advice with respect to securities listed on any national securities exchange, and do not have any private funds as clients.
	1. Private Fund adviser exemption more restrictive than federal law.
	
	2. Adviser has no place of business within that state and
	
	  a. The only clients are institutions such as investment companies, banks and trust companies, insurance companies, broker-dealers and other investment advisers, $1 million or larger employee benefit plans, governmental agency, or instrumentalities; or
	
	  b. Does not direct communications to more than five clients in the state (other than those above) during the previous 12 months (de minimis).

Registration	
File Form ADV with the SEC and pay initial and renewal fees based on their fiscal year. Effective within 45 days. No net worth requirements. No surety bonds. Withdrawal of registration is on 60th day. Successor firm pays fee. No registration of investment adviser representatives.	File Form ADV with the Administrator and pay initial and renewal (12/31) fees. Effective at noon of the 30th day. There are net worth and/or surety bonds required (custody or discretion). Withdrawal of registration is on 30th day. Successor firm pays no fee until renewal. Registration automatically registers any adviser representative who is a partner, officer, director, or similar in status.
Recordkeeping	
Investment adviser records must be kept easily accessible for five years.	Generally three years for broker-dealers and five years for investment advisers.
Fines/Penalties	
$10,000 and five years in jail	$5,000 and three years in jail

Custody of Customer Funds/Securities	
Kept by Qualified Custodian. It is custody if securities and/or checks are not returned or forwarded within three days. Third-party checks are not custody. An audited balance sheet would be required if adviser takes advance fees of more than $1,200, six months or more in advance, but not when the adviser maintains custody.	If not prohibited, with written notice to the Administrator. Requires minimum net worth or surety bond of $35,000. It is custody if securities or checks are not returned and third-party checks forwarded within three business days. An audited balance sheet would be required if adviser takes fees of more than $500, six or more months in advance or the adviser maintains custody.
Performance Fees	
Prohibited unless: 1. contract with investment company 2. certain clients with at least $1 million under management or net worth in excess of $2 million.	Same as federal law, except must make risk incentive statement and other disclosures.
Statute of Limitations for Civil Action	
Sooner of three years after the sale or one year after discovery.	Sooner of three years after the sale or two years after discovery.
A "Person"	
A natural person or company (includes a corporation, a partnership, an association, a joint stock company, a trust, or any organized group of persons, whether incorporated or not).	An individual, a corporation, an association, a joint stock company, a trust where the interests of the beneficiaries are evidenced by a security, an unincorporated organization, a government, or a political subdivision of a government.
Filing of Advertisements	
No filing with the SEC ever.	No filing for exempt securities or exempt transactions, otherwise filed with the Administrator.
Private Placement Exemption	
Sold to up to 35 nonaccredited investors under Rule 506(b). Exclusively accredited investors under Rule 506(c).	Up to 10 offers within the state over a 12-month period. The term *accredited investor* is meaningless. Institutions are not counted nor restricted.
Miscellaneous	
No assignment of the advisory contract may be made without the client's consent.	Same as federal.
The adviser, if a partnership, must notify the client of any change in the membership of the partnership within a reasonable period of time.	Same as federal.
The Brochure and Brochure Supplement Rule—120-day annual delivery.	Same as federal except 48-hour in advance rule.
The term *investment counsel* may not be used unless: 1. principal business is investment advice; and 2. substantial portion of his service is providing investment supervisory services (the giving of continuous advice on the investment of funds on the basis of the individual needs of each client).	An investment adviser representative is an associated person of an adviser firm (not clerical) who: 1. makes recommendations or otherwise gives advice; 2. manages accounts of clients; 3. solicits or negotiates for the sale of advisory service; and 4. supervises any of the above.
May not use initials RIA or IAR on business card or letterhead. Professional or educational designations are okay.	Same as federal.
Insolvency is *not* a cause for revocation.	Insolvency is a cause for revocation.
$110 million or more under management registers with the SEC. $100–$110 million can do either.	Less than $100 million under management generally registers with the state.
Registration renewal for IAs within 90 days of fiscal year	Registration renewal for all securities professionals on December 31
Register as an IAR only if a place of business in the state; no de minimis	Register in the state if retail clients resident in the state; subject to five or fewer de minimis
Employee benefit plans $5 million—institution	Employee benefit plans $1 million—institution

Appendix B
NASAA Model Rule on Unethical Business Practices of Investment Advisers, Investment Adviser Representatives, and Federal Covered Advisers [with review annotation notes]

The North American Securities Administrators Association has adopted a Model Rule on unethical business practices of investment advisers and their representatives. This Model Rule is reproduced here, with review notes included.

An investment adviser is a fiduciary and has a duty to act primarily for the benefit of its clients. While the extent and nature of this duty varies according to the nature of the relationship between an investment adviser and its clients and the circumstances of each case, an investment adviser shall not engage in unethical business practices, including the following:

1. Recommending to a client to whom investment supervisory, management or consulting services are provided the purchase, sale or exchange of any security without reasonable grounds to believe that the recommendation is suitable for the client on the basis of information furnished by the client after reasonable inquiry concerning the client's investment objectives, financial situation and needs, and any other information known by the investment adviser.

    Review Note: *An investment adviser providing investment supervisory, management, or consulting services has a fundamental obligation to analyze a client's financial situation and needs before making any recommendation to the client. Recommendations made to a client must be reasonable in relation to the information that is obtained concerning the client's investment objective, financial situation and needs, and other information known by the investment adviser. By failing to make reasonable inquiry or by failing to make recommendations that are in line with the financial situation, investment objectives, and character of a client's account, an investment adviser has not met its primary responsibility.*

2. Exercising any discretionary power in placing an order for the purchase or sale of securities for a client without obtaining prior written discretionary authority from the client, unless the discretionary power relates solely to the price at which, or the time when, an order involving a definite amount of a specified security shall be executed, or both.

    Review Note: *This rule pertains only to investment advisers that place orders for client accounts. Before placing an order for an account, an investment adviser exercising discretion should have written discretionary authority from the client. In most cases, discretionary authority is granted in an advisory contract or in a separate document executed at the time the contract is executed. The rule permits oral discretionary authority to be used for the initial transactions in a customer's account within the first 10 business days after the date of the first transaction. An investment adviser is not precluded from exercising discretionary power that relates solely to the price or time at which an order involving a specific amount of a security is authorized by a customer because time and price do not constitute discretion.*

TEST TOPIC ALERT   Be aware of the calendar. The 10-business-day period is equal to two normal work weeks. If a client opens a discretionary account and gives the OK orally, but three weeks has passed by since the initial trade and the written authorization has not been received, the IA can't exercise discretion in the account, even if not taking action would cause disastrous results to the client's portfolio.

3. Inducing trading in a client's account that is excessive in size or frequency in view of the financial resources, investment objectives, and character of the account.

    Review Note: *This rule is intended to prevent an excessive number of securities transactions from being induced by an investment adviser. There are many situations where an investment adviser may receive commissions or be affiliated with a person that receives com-*

missions from the securities transactions that are placed by the investment adviser. Because an adviser in such situations can directly benefit from the number of securities transactions effected in a client's account, the rule appropriately forbids an excessive number of transaction orders to be induced by an adviser for a customer's account.

4. Placing an order to purchase or sell a security for the account of a client without authority to do so.

   Review Note: *This rule is not new to either the securities or investment advisory professions. An investment adviser must have authority to place any order for the account of a client. The authority may be obtained from a client orally or in an agreement executed by the client giving the adviser blanket authority.*

5. Placing an order to purchase or sell a security for the account of a client upon instruction of a third party without first having obtained a written third-party trading authorization from the client.

   Review Note: *It is sound business practice for an investment adviser not to place an order for the account of a customer at the instruction of a third party without first knowing that the third party has obtained authority from the client for the order. For example, it would be important for an investment adviser to know that an attorney had power-of-attorney over an estate whose securities the adviser was managing before placing any order at the instruction of the attorney. Placing orders under such circumstances could result in substantial civil liability, besides being an unethical practice.*

6. Borrowing money or securities from a client unless the client is a broker-dealer, an affiliate of the investment adviser, or financial institution engaged in the business of loaning funds.

   Review Note: *Unless a client of an investment adviser is engaged in the business of loaning money, is an affiliate of the investment adviser, or is an institution that would engage in this type of activity, an investment adviser must not take advantage of its advisory role by borrowing funds from a client. A client provides a substantial amount of confidential information to an investment adviser regarding the client's financial situation and needs. Using that information to an investment adviser's own advantage by borrowing funds is a breach of confidentiality and may create a material conflict of interest that could influence the advice rendered by the adviser to the client.*

7. Loaning money to a client unless the investment adviser is a financial institution engaged in the business of loaning funds or the client is an affiliate of the investment adviser.

   Review Note: *Like borrowing money from a client, loaning funds to a client by an investment adviser should not be an allowable practice unless the investment adviser is a financial institution normally engaged in the business of loaning funds or unless the client is affiliated with the adviser. Loaning funds may influence decisions made for a client's account and puts the investment adviser in a conflict of interest position because the client becomes a debtor of the adviser after a loan is made.*

8. To misrepresent to any advisory client, or prospective advisory client, the qualifications of the investment adviser or any employee of the investment adviser, or to misrepresent the nature of the advisory services being offered or fees to be charged

for such service, or to omit to state a material fact necessary to make the statements made regarding qualifications, services or fees, in light of the circumstances under which they are made, not misleading.

Review Note: *When an investment adviser offers its services to a prospective client or when it provides services to an existing client, the qualifications of the investment adviser or any employee of the investment adviser and the nature of the advisory services and the fees to be charged must be disclosed in such a way as to not mislead. Overstating the qualifications of the investment adviser or disclosing inaccurately the nature of the advisory services to be provided or fees to be charged are not ethical ways to either acquire or retain clients.*

9. Providing a report or recommendation to any advisory client prepared by someone other than the adviser without disclosing the fact. (This prohibition does not apply to a situation where the adviser uses published research reports or statistical analyses to render advice or where an adviser orders such a report in the normal course of providing service.)

    Review Note: *If an investment adviser provides a report to a client that is prepared by a third party, the adviser has a responsibility to disclose the fact to the client. By entering into an investment advisory agreement, the client relies on the expertise of the adviser to provide the advisory service. Thus, if the advice is provided by a third party, it is imperative that the adviser disclose this fact to the client so the client is not misled. The prohibition does not apply when an invest-ment adviser gathers and uses research materials before making its recommendation to a client.*

10. Charging a client an unreasonable advisory fee.

    Review Note: *This rule is intended to prohibit an investment adviser from charging an excessively high advisory fee. Unreasonable as used in this rule means unreasonable in relation to fees charged by other advisers for similar services. Although no two advisory services are exactly alike, comparisons can be drawn. In those instances where an advisory fee is out of line with fees charged by other advisers providing essentially the same services, an invest-ment adviser should justify the charge. It would be very difficult for a client to compare various advisory services to evaluate those services and the fees charged. This rule will allow state Administrators to research the competitiveness of an adviser's services and fees, and to determine whether the fees being charged are unreasonably high.*

11. Failing to disclose to clients in writing, before any advice is rendered, any material conflict of interest relating to the adviser or any of its employees which could reasonably be expected to impair the rendering of unbiased and objective advice including:

    a. Compensation arrangements connected with advisory services to clients which are in addition to compensation from such clients for such services, and

    b. Charging a client an advisory fee for rendering advice when a commission for executing securities transactions pursuant to such advice will be received by the adviser or its employees.

    Review Note: *This rule is designed to require disclosure of all material conflicts of interest relating to the adviser or any of its employees that could affect the advice that is rendered. The two examples cited in the rule pertain to compensation arrangements that benefit the adviser and that are connected with advisory services being provided. However, full disclosure of all other material conflicts of interest, such as affiliations between the investment adviser and product suppliers, are also required to be made under the rule.*

12. Guaranteeing a client that a specific result will be achieved (gain or no loss) with advice which will be rendered.

    Review Note: *An investment adviser should not guarantee any gain or against loss in connection with advice that is rendered. By doing so, the adviser fails to maintain an arms-length relationship with a client and puts himself in a conflict of interest position by having a direct interest in the outcome of the advice rendered by the adviser.*

13. Publishing, circulating, or distributing any advertisement which does not comply with the Investment Advisers Act of 1940.

    Review Note: *An investment adviser should not publish, circulate, or distribute any advertisement that is inconsistent with federal rules governing the use of advertisements. Rule 206(4)-1 of the Investment Advisers Act of 1940 contains prohibitions against advertisements that contain untrue statements of material fact, that refer directly or indirectly to any testimonial of any kind, that refer to past specific recommendations of the investment adviser unless certain conditions are met, that represent that a chart or formula or other device being offered can, by itself, be used to determine which securities are to be bought or sold, or that contain a statement indicating that any analysis, report, or service will be furnished free when such is not the case. Third-party use of the "like" feature on an investment adviser's social media site could be deemed to be a testimonial if it is an explicit or implicit statement of a client's or clients' experience with an investment adviser or IAR. If, for example, the public is invited to "like" an IAR's biography posted on a social media site, that election could be viewed as a type of testimonial prohibited by the rule. These prohibitions are fundamental and sound standards that all investment advisers should follow.*

14. Disclosing the identity, affairs, or investments of any client unless required by law to do so, or unless consented to by the client.

    Review Note: *An investment advisory firm has a responsibility to ensure that all information collected from a client be kept confidential. The only exception to the rule should be in those instances where the client authorized the release of such information, or when the investment advisory firm is required by law to disclose such information.*

15. Taking any action, directly or indirectly, with respect to those securities or funds in which any client has any beneficial interest, where the investment adviser has custody or possession of such securities or funds when the adviser's action is subject to and does not comply with the requirements of the Investment Advisers Act of 1940.

    Review Note: *In instances where an investment adviser has custody or possession of client's funds or securities, it should comply with the regulations under the Investment Advisers Act of 1940 designed to ensure the safekeeping of those securities and funds. The rules under the act specifically provide that securities of clients be segregated and properly marked, that the funds of the clients be deposited in separate bank accounts, that the investment adviser notify each client as to the place and manner in which such funds and securities are being maintained, that an itemized list of all securities and funds in the adviser's possession be sent to the client not less frequently than every three months, and that all such funds and securities be verified annually by actual examination by an independent CPA on a surprise basis. The rule establishes very conservative measures to safeguard each client's funds and securities held by an investment adviser.*

16. Entering into, extending or renewing any investment advisory contract unless such contract is in **_writing_** and discloses, in substance, the services to be provided, the term of the contract, the advisory fee, the formula for computing the fee, the amount of prepaid fee to be returned in the event of contract termination or non-performance, whether the contract grants discretionary power to the adviser and that no assignment of such contract shall be made by the investment adviser without the consent of the other party to the contract.

> **Review Note:** *The purpose of this rule is to ensure that clients have a document to refer to that describes the basic terms of the agreement the client has entered into with an adviser.*

The conduct set forth above is not inclusive. Engaging in other conduct such as non-disclosure, incomplete disclosure, or deceptive practices shall be deemed an unethical business practice.

Appendix C
Abbreviations, Dates, and Calculations for the Series 65 Exam

Common Abbreviations

ADR/ADS American depositary receipt (share)
AIR assumed interest rate
APO additional public offering
AUM assets under management
BA banker's acceptance
BD broker-dealer
CD certificate of deposit
CEO chief executive officer
CMO collateralized mortgage obligation
CMV current market value
COGS cost of goods sold
CPI Consumer Price Index
CY current yield
DCF discounted cash flow
DJIA Dow Jones Industrial Average
DMM Designated Market Maker
DPP direct participation program
EE Series EE savings bonds
EIA equity index annuity
EPS earnings per share
ERA exempt reporting adviser
ERISA Employee Retirement Income Security Act of 1974
ETF exchange traded fund
FAC face-amount certificate
Fed Federal Reserve System
FDIC Federal Deposit Insurance Corporation
FIFO first in, first out
FINRA Financial Industry Regulatory Authority
FMV fair market value
FNMA Federal National Mortgage Association
FOMC Federal Open Market Committee
FRB Federal Reserve Board
GNMA Government National Mortgage Association
GDP gross domestic product
GO general obligation bond
IA investment adviser
IAR investment adviser representative
IARD Investment Adviser Registration Depository
IPO initial public offering
IRA individual retirement account

IRC Internal Revenue Code
IRS Internal Revenue Service
JTIC joint tenants in common
JTWROS joint tenants with right of survivorship
LIFO last in, first out
LOI letter of intent
MSRB Municipal Securities Rulemaking Board
NASAA North American Securities Administrators Association
Nasdaq National Association of Securities Dealers Automated Quotation system
NAV net asset value
NL no load
NYSE New York Stock Exchange
OTC over the counter
PE price-to-earnings ratio
POA power of attorney
POD pay on death
POP public offering price
REIT real estate investment trust
RF risk-free rate
SEC Securities and Exchange Commission
SEP simplified employee pension plan
SIPC Securities Investor Protection Corporation
SPO subsequent public offering
SRO self-regulatory organization
STRIPS Separate Trading of Registered Interest and Principal of Securities
TIC tenants in common
TOD transfer on death
TSA tax-sheltered annuity
TVA Tennessee Valley Authority
UGMA/UTMA Uniform Gift (Transfers) to Minors Act
UIT unit investment trust
UVL universal variable life insurance
VLI variable life insurance
YLD yield
YTC yield to call
YTM yield to maturity
ZR zero-coupon

Calculations

To Calculate...	Use Formula...
Current yield (stock)	$\dfrac{\text{Annual dividend}}{\text{Current market price}}$
Current yield (debt security)	$\dfrac{\text{Annual interest}}{\text{Current market price}}$
Number of shares for conversion	$\dfrac{\text{Par value}}{\text{Conversion price}}$
Parity	$\dfrac{\text{Bond market value}}{\text{Number of shares}}$
Tax-free equivalent yield	Corporate rate × (100% − tax bracket)
Tax-equivalent yield	$\dfrac{\text{Municipal rate}}{(100\% - \text{tax bracket})}$
NAV of mutual fund share	$\dfrac{\text{Fund NAV}}{\text{Number of shares outstanding}}$
Dollar cost average	$\dfrac{\text{Total dollars invested}}{\text{Number of shares purchased}}$
Average market price	$\dfrac{\text{Share price total}}{\text{Number of investments}}$
Shareholders' equity	Assets − liabilities
Total return	income (dividends or interest) + gain or loss /original investment
Annualized return	Total return on an annualized basis
Inflation-adjusted (real) return	Total return minus the CPI

After-tax return	Total return minus the marginal tax bracket
Rule of 72	Divide 72 by known interest rate = number of years to double investment; or, divide 72 by known number of years = interest rate required to double investment
Arithmetic mean	Simple average of the numbers
Median	In a group of numbers, the one with an equal above and below, i.e., the number in the middle
Mode	In a group of numbers, the one appearing most frequently
Range	In a group of numbers the difference between the highest and the lowest one
Alpha (RF not given)	Actual return − (beta × market return)
Alpha (RF given)	(Actual return − RF) − (beta × [market return − RF]}
Sharpe ratio	$\dfrac{\text{actual return} - \text{RF}}{\text{standard deviation}}$

Dates

48 hours prior to contract	State IAs deliver initial brochure, or 5-day withdrawal without penalty
Entering advisory contract	Latest time to delivery IA brochure
Same day	Time limit for execution of a day limit order. Also, time and/or price discretion only good that day
Next business day	Notification to Administrator that IA's net worth is insufficient (send details the following business day)
2 business days	Maximum and minimum offering prices and underwriting discounts on file for coordination
3 business days	Securities or funds received by non-custody IA must be returned to client
3 business days	3rd party checks received by non-custody IA must be forwarded to the 3rd party (USA only)
4 business days	Filing Form 8-K
5 business days	Penalty-free cancellation of IA contract if brochure not delivered at least 48 hours in advance (USA only)
7 days	Time limit for open-end investment company (mutual fund) to redeem shares
10 days	Schedule 13D filing
10 days	SEC can summarily suspend trading in a security
10 business days after first trade	Investment advisers may use oral discretion
15 days after written request	Hearing must be granted - Summary order
15 days after first sale	File Form D (private placement Rule 506)
18th birthday	Latest date for a Coverdell ESA contribution
20 days	Cooling off period under Securities Act of 1933. Also minimum time Administrator must have documents for coordination
30th day	State registration or withdrawal of securities professionals effective
30 days	Maximum residency under snowbird exemption.
30 days	Time limit within which rescission offer must be accepted or rejected
30 days	Mandatory waiting time to retest (first 2 failures)
30 days	Wash sale rule
30 days	New issues eligible for margin once owned this long
35 days	Full purchase price received by underwriters for any IPO
40 days	Days after end of each quarter to file Form 10-Q
45th day	Federal registration of BDs and IAs effective
45 days	Days after end of each quarter to file Form 13F
60th day	Withdrawal of federal covered adviser on ADV-W
60 days	Time limit to appeal an order under both state and federal law
60 days	Maximum time for tax-free rollover
60 days	Maximum termination clause with mutual fund adviser
90 days	After end of fiscal year, IA must file annual updating amendment

90 days	State IA with AUM at $110 million or above, must register with SEC
90 days	Maturity of T-Bill most commonly used as "risk-free" rate
90 days	Application for registered stock exchange effective or rejected
90 days	Maximum time a letter of intent (LOI) backdated
90 days	SEC, with notice to U.S. President, can suspend all trading on an exchange
120 days	Annual delivery of adviser brochure to clients (if material changes)
120 days	Time limit for an IA who expects to reach the required AUM to register with the SEC
180 days	SEC IA with AUM below $90 million must register with state(s)
180 days	Mandatory waiting time to retest (3rd and subsequent failures)
6 months	Alternative valuation date for estate taxes
9 months (270 days)	Maximum maturity of exempt commercial paper
9 months after death	Payment of estate taxes is due
13 months	Maximum time to complete a letter of intent
397 days	Maximum maturity of any holding in money market mutual fund
2 years	Records must be kept easily accessible
3 years	Time period for most records kept by broker-dealers
5 years	Time period for investment adviser recordkeeping

Glossary

A

accredited investor As defined in Rule 501 of Regulation D, any institution or individual meeting minimum net worth requirements for the purchase of securities qualifying under the Regulation D registration exemption. An individual accredited investor is generally accepted to be one who, individually or with spouse, has a net worth, excluding the net equity in the primary residence, of $1 million or more, or has had an annual income of $200,000 or more in each of the two most recent years (or $300,000 jointly with a spouse), and who has a reasonable expectation of reaching the same income level in the current year.

accumulation stage The period during which contributions are made to an annuity account. *See* accumulation unit; distribution stage.

accumulation unit An accounting measure used to determine an annuitant's proportionate interest in the insurer's separate account during an annuity's accumulation (deposit) stage. *See* accumulation stage; separate account.

acid test *Syn.* acid test ratio. *See* quick asset ratio.

active management style Unlike the passive style, analysts believe they can identify industries that are undervalued or overvalued in order to weight them appropriately and achieve returns in excess of the market. Some managers engage in sector rotation, which is overweighting or underweighting industries based on the current phase of the business cycle. *See* passive management style; sector rotation.

Act of 1933 *See* Securities Act of 1933.

Act of 1934 *See* Securities Exchange Act of 1934.

adjusted basis The value attributed to an asset or security that reflects any deductions taken on, or capital improvements to, the asset or security. Adjusted basis is used to compute the gain or loss on the sale or other disposition of the asset or security.

adjusted gross income (AGI) Gross income from all sources minus certain adjustments to income, such as deductible contributions to an IRA and net capital losses. It is basically the amount of income that will be subject to tax. *See* tax liability.

Administrator An official or agency that administers a state's securities laws.

ADR *See* American depositary receipt.

ADS *See* American depositary receipt.

advertisement Any notice, circular, letter, or other written communication addressed to more than one person, or any notice or other announcement in any publication or by radio or television, that offers (1) any analysis, report, or publication concerning securities, or that is to be used in making any determination as to when to buy or sell any security, or which security to buy or sell; or (2) any graph, chart, formula, or other device to be used in making any determination as to when to buy or sell any security, or which security to buy or sell; or (3) any other investment advisory service with regard to securities.

agency basis *See* agency transaction.

agency cross transaction For an advisory client, a transaction in which a person acts as an investment adviser in relation to a transaction in which that investment adviser, or any person controlling, controlled by, or under common control with that investment adviser, acts as broker for both an advisory client and for another person on the other side of the transaction.

agency issue A debt security issued by an authorized agency of the federal government. Such an issue is backed by the issuing agency itself, not by the full faith and credit of the U.S. government (except GNMA issues). *See* government security.

agency transaction A transaction in which a broker-dealer acts for the accounts of others by buying or selling securities on behalf of customers. *Syn.* agency basis. *See* agent; broker; principal transaction.

agent (1) An individual who effects securities transactions for the accounts of others. (2) Under state law, a securities salesperson who represents a broker-dealer or an issuer when selling or trying to sell securities to the investing public; this individual is considered an agent whether he actually receives or simply solicits orders. *See* broker; broker-dealer; dealer; principal.

aggressive investment strategy A method of portfolio allocation and management aimed at achieving maximum return. Aggressive investors place a high percentage of their investable assets in equity securities and a far lower percentage in safer debt securities and cash equivalents, and they pursue aggressive policies including margin trading, arbitrage, and option trading. *See* balanced investment strategy; defensive investment strategy.

AGI *See* adjusted gross income.

all or none order (AON) An order that instructs the floor broker to execute the entire order in one transaction; if the order cannot be executed in its entirety, it is allowed to expire.

alpha The risk-adjusted returns that a portfolio manager generates in excess of the risk-adjusted returns expected by the capital asset pricing model (CAPM). Suppose an index return is 10%; the risk-free rate is 3%, the portfolio beta is 1.5, and the actual return is 25%. According to the CAPM, the portfolio should be expected to return 1.5 times the index after netting out the risk-free rate. This is because the portfolio is 1.5 times riskier than the market. If we take the index return after subtracting the 3% risk-free rate, we get 7%. Multiply that times 1.5 and the measured portfolio should have returned 10.5% for taking extra risk. It actually returned 22% over the risk-free rate giving us an alpha of 10.5.

alternative minimum tax (AMT) An alternative tax computation that adds certain tax preference items back into adjusted gross income. If the AMT is higher than the regular tax liability for the year, the regular tax and the amount by which the AMT exceeds the regular tax are paid. *See* tax preference item.

American depositary receipt (ADR) A negotiable certificate representing a given number of shares in a foreign corporation. It is issued by a domestic bank. ADRs are bought and sold in the American securities markets, and are traded in English and U.S. dollars. *Syn.* American depositary share (ADS).

anti-dilutive covenant A protective clause found in most convertible issues (preferred stock or debentures) that adjusts the conversion rate for stock splits and/or stock dividends. This ensures that the holder of the convertible will not suffer a dilution in value.

appreciation The increase in an asset's value.

arbitrage A legal strategy that generates a guaranteed profit from a transaction. A common form of arbitrage is the simultaneous purchase and sale of the same security in different markets at different prices to lock in a profit. This is not considered market manipulation.

arithmetic mean The average of a set of numbers, such as annual returns on an investment.

ask An indication by a trader or a dealer of a willingness to sell a security or a commodity; the price at which an investor can buy from a broker-dealer. *Syn.* offer. *See* bid; public offering price; quotation.

assessable stock A stock that is issued below its par or stated value. The issuer and/or creditors have the right to assess the shareholder for the deficiency. All stock issued today is nonassessable.

asset (1) Anything that an individual or a corporation owns. (2) A balance sheet item expressing what a corporation owns.

asset class allocation Dividing an investment portfolio among different asset categories, such as stocks, bonds, cash, and tangible assets such as real estate and precious metals and other commodities. *Syn.* asset allocation.

auction market A market in which buyers enter competitive bids and sellers enter competitive offers simultaneously. The NYSE is an auction market. *Syn.* double auction market.

audited financial statement A financial statement of a program, a corporation, or an issuer (including the profit and loss statement, cash flow and source and application of revenues statement, and balance sheet) that has been examined and verified by an independent certified public accountant.

average basis An accounting method used when an investor has made multiple purchases at different prices of the same security; the method averages the purchase prices to calculate an investor's cost basis in shares being liquidated. The difference between the average cost basis and the selling price determines the investor's tax liability. *See* first in, first out; last in, first out.

B

balanced fund A mutual fund whose stated investment policy is to have at all times some portion of its investment assets in bonds and preferred stock, as well as in common stock, in an attempt to provide both growth and income. *See* mutual fund.

balanced investment strategy A method of portfolio allocation and management aimed at balancing risk and return. A balanced portfolio may combine stocks, bonds, packaged products such as investment companies, DPPs, or REITs, and cash equivalents.

balance of payments An international accounting record of all transactions made by one particular country with others during a certain period; it compares the amount of foreign currency the country has taken in with the amount of its own currency it has paid out. *See* balance of trade.

balance of trade The largest component of a country's balance of payments; it concerns the export and import of merchandise (not services). Debit items include imports, foreign aid, domestic spending abroad, and domestic investments abroad. Credit items include exports, foreign spending in the domestic economy, and foreign investments in the domestic economy. *See* balance of payments.

balance sheet A report of a corporation's financial condition at a specific time.

balance sheet equation A formula stating that a corporation's assets equal the sum of its liabilities plus shareholders' equity.

bank holding company A holding company whose primary asset is a commercial bank. *See* holding company.

basis Another term for yield to maturity (e.g., this bond is selling at a 5.78 basis).

basis point A measure of a bond's yield, equal to ¹⁄₁₀₀ of 1% of yield. A bond whose yield increases from 5.00% to 5.50% is said to increase by 50 basis points. *See* point.

bear An investor who acts on the belief that a security or the market is falling or will fall. *See* bull.

bear market A market in which prices of a certain group of securities are falling or are expected to fall. *See* bull market.

benchmark portfolio A model portfolio of a large number of assets, such as the S&P 500, against which the performance of a fund or portfolio is measured.

beta A means of measuring the co-movement of the return of a security or a portfolio of securities to the return on the overall market. A beta of 1 indicates that the security's returns will be expected to move in tandem with the market. A beta greater than 1 indicates that the security's returns will be expected to exceed those of the market. A beta less than 1 means returns will be expected to be lower than those of the market. *Syn.* beta coefficient.

bid An indication by an investor, a trader, or a dealer of a willingness to buy a security; the price at which an investor can sell to a broker-dealer. *See* offer; public offering price; quotation.

Black-Scholes One of the most popular options pricing models. Appears frequently on the exam as an incorrect choice.

block trade A large trading order, defined as an order that consists of 10,000 or more shares of a given stock or at a total market value of $200,000 or more. *Syn.* block sale.

blue-sky laws The nickname for state regulations governing the securities industry. The term was coined in 1911 by a Kansas Supreme Court justice who wanted regulation to protect against "speculative schemes that have no more basis than so many feet of blue sky."

board of directors Individuals elected by stockholders to establish corporate management policies. A board of directors decides, among other issues, if and when dividends will be paid to stockholders.

bona fide From the Latin "good faith," something that is bona fide is genuine, authentic, and real. An example would be a bona fide quote.

bond An issuing company's or government's legal obligation to repay the principal of a loan to bond investors at a specified future date. Bonds are usually issued with par or face values of $1,000, representing the amount of money borrowed. The issuer promises to pay a percentage of the par value as interest on the borrowed funds. The interest payment is stated on the face of the bond at issue.

bond fund A mutual fund whose investment objective is to provide stable income with minimal capital risk. It invests in income-producing instruments, which may include corporate, government, or municipal bonds. *See* mutual fund.

bond quote One of a number of quotations listed in the financial press and most daily newspapers that provide representative bid prices from the previous day's bond market. Quotes for corporate and government bonds are percentages of the bonds' face values (usually $1,000). Corporate bonds are quoted in increments of ⅛. Government bonds are quoted in increments of ¹⁄₃₂. Municipal bonds may be quoted on a dollar basis or on a yield-to-maturity basis. *See* quotation; stock quote.

bond rating An evaluation of the possibility of a bond issuer's default, based on an analysis of the issuer's financial condition and profit potential. Standard & Poor's, Moody's Investors Service, and Fitch Investors Service, among others, provide bond rating services.

bond ratio One of several tools used by bond analysts to assess the degree of safety offered by a corporation's bonds. It measures the percentage of the corporation's capitalization that is provided by long-term debt financing, calculated by dividing the total face value of the outstanding bonds by the total capitalization. *Syn.* debt ratio.

bond yield The annual rate of return on a bond investment. Types of yield include nominal yield, current yield, yield to maturity, and yield to call. Their relationships vary according to whether the bond in question is at a discount, at a premium, or at par. *See* current yield; nominal yield.

book-entry security A security sold without delivery of a certificate. Evidence of ownership is maintained on records kept by a central agency; for example, the Treasury keeps records of Treasury bill purchasers. Transfer of ownership is recorded by entering the change on the books or electronic files. *See* coupon bond.

book value per share A measure of the net worth of each share of common stock is calculated by subtracting intangible assets and preferred stock from total net worth, then dividing the result by the number of shares of common outstanding. *Syn.* net tangible assets per share.

Brady bonds Debt instruments, generally from third world countries, that may have a U.S. Treasury bond as collateral.

breadth-of-market theory A technical analysis theory that predicts the strength of the market according to the number of issues that advance or decline in a particular trading day.

BRIC An acronym referring to investments in Brazil, Russia, India, and China

bridge loan A short-term loan made to bridge the gap until permanent financing is arranged.

brochure A written disclosure statement that investment advisers must provide to most clients and prospective clients. The Form ADV Part 2A may be used for this purpose.

brochure supplement A written disclosure statement containing information about certain of an investment adviser's supervised persons. This disclosure is usually accomplished by the delivery of Form ADV Part 2B to most clients and prospective clients.

broker (1) An individual or a firm that charges a fee or commission for executing buy and sell orders submitted by another individual or firm. (2) The role of a firm when it acts as an agent for a customer and charges the customer a commission for its services. *See* agent; broker-dealer; dealer.

broker-dealer (BD) A person in the business of buying and selling securities. A firm may act as both broker (agency) and dealer (principal), but not in the same transaction. Broker-dealers normally must register with the SEC, the appropriate SROs, and any state in which they do business. *See* agent; broker; dealer; principal.

bull An investor who acts on the belief that a security or the market is rising or will rise. *See* bear.

bulletin board *See* OTC Bulletin Board.

bull market A market in which prices of a certain group of securities are rising or will rise. *See* bear market.

business cycle A predictable long-term pattern of alternating periods of economic growth and decline. The cycle passes through four stages: expansion, peak, contraction, and trough.

business risk The risk inherent in equity securities that poor management decisions will have a negative impact on the stock's performance. Can be reduced through diversification. *Syn.* unsystematic risk.

buy stop order An order to buy a security that is entered at a price above the current offering price and that is triggered when the market price touches or goes through the buy stop price.

bypass trust A trust that is funded with property in an amount equal to the exemption equivalent of the transfer tax credit amount applicable to the decedent ($5.43 million in 2015); thus, the property is not subject to federal estate tax. *See* generation skipping trust.

C

calendar year For accounting purposes, a year that ends on December 31. When an accounting year ends any other time, it is called a fiscal year. *See* fiscal year.

call (1) An option contract giving the owner the right to buy a specified amount of an underlying security at a specified price within a specified time. (2) The act of exercising a call option. *See* put.

callable bond A type of bond issued with a provision allowing the issuer to redeem the bond before maturity at a predetermined price.

callable preferred stock A type of preferred stock issued with a provision allowing the corporation to call in the stock at a certain price and retire it. *See* call price; preferred stock.

call buyer An investor who pays a premium for an option contract and receives, for a specified time, the right to buy the underlying security at a specified price. *See* call writer; put.

call date The date, specified in the prospectus of every callable security, after which the security's issuer has the option to redeem the issue at par or at par plus a premium.

call feature *See* call provision.

call protection A provision in a bond indenture stating that the issue is noncallable for a certain period (e.g., 5 years or 10 years) after the original issue date. *See* call provision.

call provision The written agreement between an issuer and its bondholders or preferred stockholders giving the issuer the option to redeem its senior securities at a specified price before maturity and under certain conditions. *Syn.* call feature.

call risk The potential for a bond to be called before maturity, leaving the investor without the bond's current income. Because this is more likely to occur during times of falling interest rates, the investor may not be able to reinvest his principal at a comparable rate of return.

call writer An investor who receives a premium and takes on, for a specified time, the obligation to sell the underlying security at a specified price at the call buyer's discretion. *See* call buyer; put.

capital appreciation An increase in an asset's market price.

capital asset All tangible property, including securities, real estate, and other property, held for the long term.

capital asset pricing model (CAPM) A securities market investment theory that attempts to derive the expected return on an asset on the basis of the asset's systematic risk.

capital gain The profit realized when a capital asset is sold for a higher price than the purchase price. *See* capital loss; long-term gain.

capitalization The sum of a corporation's long-term debt, stock, and surpluses. *Syn.* invested capital. *See* capital structure.

capitalization ratio A measure of an issuer's financial status that calculates the value of its bonds, preferred stock, or common stock as a percentage of its total capitalization.

capital loss The loss incurred when a capital asset is sold for a price lower than the purchase price. *See* capital gain; long-term loss.

capital market The segment of the securities market that deals in instruments with more than one year to maturity—that is, long-term debt and equity securities. In contrast, the money market is the raising of short-term capital such as Treasury bills and commercial paper.

capital stock All of a corporation's outstanding preferred stock and common stock, listed at par value.

capital structure The composition of long-term funds (equity and debt) a corporation has as a source for financing. *See* capitalization.

capital surplus The money a corporation receives in excess of the stated value of stock at the time of first sale. *Syn.* paid-in capital; paid-in surplus. *See* par.

capping An illegal form of market manipulation that attempts to keep the price of a subject security from rising. It is used by those with a short position. *See* pegging.

cash account An account in which the customer is required by the SEC's Regulation T to pay in full for securities purchased not later than two days after the standard payment period set by industry practice codes. *Syn.* special cash account.

cash dividend Money paid to a corporation's stockholders out of the corporation's current earnings or accumulated profits. The board of directors must declare all dividends.

cash equivalent A security that can be readily converted into cash. Examples include Treasury bills, certificates of deposit, and money market instruments and funds.

cash flow The money received by a business minus the money paid out. Cash flow is also equal to net income plus depreciation or depletion.

CBOE *See* Chicago Board Options Exchange.

CD *See* negotiable certificate of deposit.

cease and desist order Used by the Administrator when it appears that a registered person has or is about to commit a violation. May be issued with or without a prior hearing.

certificate of deposit (CD) A traditional CD pays a fixed interest rate over a specific period of time. When that term ends, you can withdraw your money or roll it into another CD. These are insured up to $250,000 by the FDIC and are considered the best method of preservation of capital. *See* negotiable certificate of deposit.

chartist A securities analyst who uses charts and graphs of the past price movements of a security to predict its future movements. *Syn.* technician. *See* technical analysis.

Chicago Board Options Exchange (CBOE) The self-regulatory organization with jurisdiction over all writing and trading of standardized options and related contracts listed on that exchange. Also, the first national securities exchange for the trading of listed options.

Chicago Stock Exchange Registered stock exchange located in Chicago's downtown "loop." Referred to with the initials CHX.

Chinese Wall A descriptive name for the division within a brokerage firm that prevents insider information from passing from corporate advisers to investment traders, who could make use of the information to reap illicit profits. The preferred term today is *information barriers*. *See* Insider Trading and Securities Fraud Enforcement Act of 1988.

churning Excessive trading in a customer's account by an agent who ignores the customer's interests and *seeks* only to increase commissions; violates NASAA's policies on unethical business practices. *Syn.* overtrading.

CHX *See* Chicago Stock Exchange.

closed-end investment company An investment company that issues a fixed number of shares in an actively managed portfolio of securities. The shares may be of several classes; they are traded in the secondary marketplace, either on a stock exchange or over the counter. The market price of the shares is determined by supply and demand and not by net asset value. *Syn.* publicly traded fund; closed-end management company. *See* mutual fund.

closing purchase An options transaction in which the seller buys back an option in the same series; the two transactions effectively cancel each other out and the position is liquidated. *See* opening purchase.

CMO *See* collateralized mortgage obligation.

coincident indicator A measurable economic factor that varies directly and simultaneously with the business cycle, thus indicating the current state of the economy. Examples include nonagricultural employment, personal income, and industrial production. *See* lagging indicator; leading indicator.

collateral Certain assets set aside and pledged to a lender for the duration of a loan. If the borrower fails to meet obligations to pay principal or interest, the lender has claim to the assets.

collateralized mortgage obligation (CMO) A mortgage-backed corporate security. These issues attempt to return interest and principal at a predetermined rate.

collateral trust bond A secured bond backed by stocks or bonds of another issuer. The collateral is held by a trustee for safekeeping. *Syn.* collateral trust certificate.

collateral trust certificate *See* collateral trust bond.

combination privilege A benefit offered by a mutual fund whereby the investor may qualify for a sales charge breakpoint by combining separate investments in two or more mutual funds under the same management.

commercial paper An unsecured, short-term promissory note issued by a corporation for financing accounts receivable and inventories. It is usually issued at a discount reflecting prevailing market interest rates. Maturities range up to nine months.

commingling The combining by a brokerage firm of one customer's securities with another customer's securities and pledging them as joint collateral for a bank loan; unless authorized by the customers, this violates SEC Rule 15c2-1.

commission A service charge an agent assesses in return for arranging a security's purchase or sale. A commission must be fair and reasonable, considering all the relevant factors of the transaction. *Syn.* sales charge. *See* markup.

common stock A security that represents ownership in a corporation. Holders of common stock exercise control by electing a board of directors and voting on corporate policy. *See* equity; preferred stock.

complex trust A trust that accumulates income over time and is not required to make scheduled distributions to its beneficiaries.

conduit theory A means for an investment company to avoid taxation on net investment income distributed to shareholders. If a mutual fund acts as a conduit for the distribution of net investment income, it may qualify as a regulated investment company and be taxed only on the income the fund retains. *Syn.* pipeline theory.

confirmation A printed document that states the trade date, settlement date, and money due from or owed to a customer. It is sent or given to the customer on or before the settlement date.

constant dollar plan A formula method of investing that attempts to maintain a fixed dollar, rather than ratio, amount in a specific asset class. Periodically, the account is reviewed and the specified asset class is either sold or purchased in order to get to the fixed dollar level.

constant ratio plan A formula method of investing that contemplates maintaining a fixed ratio, rather than dollar amount, between specific asset classes in the portfolio. Periodically, the account is reviewed and the specified asset class is either sold or purchased in order to get to the fixed ratio level.

Consumer Price Index (CPI) A measure of price changes in a "market basket" of consumer goods and services used to identify periods of inflation or deflation.

consumption A term used by economists to refer to the purchase by household units of newly produced goods and services.

contraction A period of general economic decline, one of the business cycle's four stages. *See* business cycle.

contributory plan A retirement plan to which both the employee and the employer make contributions. *See* noncontributory plan.

control person (1) A director or an officer of an issuer. (2) A stockholder who owns more than 10% of any class of a corporation's outstanding securities. (3) Spouse or other immediate family of any of the previous. Under the Investment Company Act of 1940, a control person owns more than 25% of the voting securities and, under the Investment Advisers Act of 1940, it is 25% or more. *See* insider.

control security Any security owned by a director or an officer of the issuer or by a stockholder who owns more than 10% of any class of a corporation's outstanding securities. Who owns a security, not the security itself, determines whether it is a control security.

conversion parity Two securities, one of which can be converted into the other, of equal dollar value. A convertible security holder can calculate parity to help decide whether converting would lead to gain or loss.

conversion price The dollar amount of a convertible security's par value that is exchangeable for one share of common stock.

conversion privilege A feature the issuer adds to a security that allows the holder to change the security into shares of common stock. This makes the security attractive to investors and, therefore, more marketable. *See* convertible bond; convertible preferred stock.

conversion rate *See* conversion ratio.

conversion ratio The number of shares of common stock per par value amount that the holder would receive for converting a convertible bond or preferred share. *Syn.* conversion rate.

convertible bond A debt security, usually in the form of a debenture, that can be exchanged for equity securities of the issuing corporation at specified prices or rates. *See* debenture.

convertible preferred stock An equity security that can be exchanged for common stock at specified prices or rates. Dividends may be cumulative or noncumulative. *See* cumulative preferred stock; noncumulative preferred stock; preferred stock.

convexity The most accurate way of indicating a debt security's sensitivity to changes in interest rates.

cooling-off period The period (a minimum of 20 days) between a registration statement's filing date with the SEC and the registration's effective date. In practice, the period varies in length.

corporate account An account held in a corporation's name. The corporate agreement, signed when the account is opened, specifies which officers are authorized to trade in the account. In addition to standard margin account documents, a corporation must provide a copy of its charter and bylaws authorizing a margin account.

corporate bond A debt security issued by a corporation. A corporate bond typically has a par value of $1,000, its interest is taxable, and it has a term maturity.

corporation The most common form of business organization, in which the organization's total worth is divided into shares of stock, each share representing a unit of ownership. A corporation is characterized by a continuous life span and its owners' limited liability.

correlation The extent to which two or more securities or portfolios move together. The correlation coefficient is a number that ranges from −1 to +1. A perfect correlation would have a coefficient of +1, whereas two securities that move in total opposite directions would have a −1. A coefficient of 0 would reflect a totally random correlation between the two securities.

cost basis The price paid for an asset, including any commissions or fees, used to calculate capital gains or losses when the asset is sold.

coupon yield *See* nominal yield.

covered call writer An investor who sells a call option while owning the underlying security or some other asset that guarantees the ability to deliver if the call is exercised.

covered security *See* federal covered security.

CPI *See* Consumer Price Index.

credit risk The degree of probability that the issuer of a debt security will default in the payment of either principal or interest. Securities issued by the U.S. government are considered to have virtually no credit risk. Note: credit risk only refers to debt securities—common stock has no credit risk because there is no debt obligation to the owner. *Syn.* default risk; financial risk.

cumulative preferred stock An equity security that offers the holder any unpaid dividends in arrears. These dividends accumulate and must be paid to the cumulative preferred stockholder before any dividends can be paid to the common stockholders. *See* noncumulative preferred stock; preferred stock.

current assets Cash and other assets that are expected to be converted into cash within the next 12 months. Examples include such liquid items as cash and equivalents, accounts receivable, inventory, and prepaid expenses.

current liabilities A corporation's debt obligations due for payment within the next 12 months. Examples include accounts payable, accrued wages payable, and current long-term debt.

current market value (CMV) The worth of the securities in an account. The market value of listed securities is based on the closing prices on the previous business day. *Syn.* long market value. *See* market value.

current ratio A measure of a corporation's liquidity; that is, its ability to transfer assets into cash to meet current short-term obligations. It is calculated by dividing total current assets by total current liabilities. *Syn.* working capital ratio.

current yield The annual rate of return on a security, calculated by dividing the interest or dividends paid by the security's current market price. *See* bond yield.

custodial account An account in which a custodian enters trades on behalf of the beneficial owner, often a minor. *See* custodian.

custodian An institution or a person responsible for making all investment, management, and distribution decisions in an account maintained in the best interests of another. Mutual funds have custodian banks responsible for safeguarding certificates and performing clerical duties.

customer Any person who opens a trading account with a broker-dealer. A customer may be classified in terms of account ownership, trading authorization, payment method, or types of securities traded.

customer statement A document showing a customer's trading activity, positions, and account balance. The SEC requires that customer statements be sent quarterly, but customers generally receive them monthly.

cyclical industry A fundamental analysis term for an industry that is sensitive to the business cycle and price changes. Most cyclical industries produce durable goods, raw materials, and heavy equipment.

D

day order An order that is valid only until the close of trading on the day it is entered; if it is not executed by the close of trading, it is canceled.

dealer (1) An individual or a firm engaged in the business of buying and selling securities for its own account, either directly or through a broker. (2) The role of a firm when it acts as a principal and charges the customer a markup or markdown. *Syn.* principal. *See* broker; broker-dealer.

debenture A debt obligation backed by the issuing corporation's general credit. *Syn.* unsecured bond.

debt security A security representing an investor's loan to an issuer, such as a corporation, a municipality, the federal government, or a federal agency. In return for the loan, the issuer promises to repay the debt on a specified date and to pay interest. *See* equity security.

debt-to-equity ratio The ratio of total long-term debt to total stockholders' equity; it is used to measure leverage.

decumulation Disposal of something accumulated. Investors spend much of their working years accumulating for retirement; taking the funds out is decumulation.

default The failure to pay interest or principal promptly when due.

default risk *See* credit risk.

defensive industry A fundamental analysis term for an industry that is relatively unaffected by the business cycle. Most defensive industries produce nondurable goods for which demand remains steady throughout the business cycle; examples include the food industry and utilities.

defensive investment strategy A method of portfolio allocation and management aimed at minimizing the risk of losing principal. Defensive investors place a high percentage of their investable assets in bonds, cash equivalents, and stocks that are less volatile than average.

deferred annuity An annuity contract that delays payment of income, installments, or a lump sum until the investor elects to receive it.

deferred compensation plan A nonqualified retirement plan whereby the employee defers receiving current compensation in favor of a larger payout at retirement (or in the case of disability or death).

deficiency letter The SEC's notification of additions or corrections that a prospective issuer must make to a registration statement before the SEC will clear the offering for distribution.

defined benefit plan A qualified retirement plan that specifies the total amount of money that the employee will receive at retirement.

defined contribution plan A qualified retirement plan that specifies the amount of money that the employer will contribute annually to the plan.

deflation A persistent and measurable fall in the general level of prices. *See* inflation.

delta One of the 4 Greeks used by options analysts. An option's delta is the rate of change of the price of the option with respect to its underlying security's price. The delta of an option ranges in value from 0 to 1 for calls (0 to -1 for puts) and reflects the increase or decrease in the price of the option in response to a 1 point movement of the underlying asset price.

demand A consumer's desire and willingness to pay for a good or service. *See* supply.

demand deposit Demand deposit (DDA) refers to a type of account held at banks and financial institutions that may be withdrawn at any time by the customer. The majority of such demand deposit accounts are checking accounts, although many now include savings accounts in the definition as well.

demutualization Demutualization is the process through which a member-owned company becomes shareholder-owned. Historically, this has usually been done by mutual life insurance companies (think MetLife and Prudential), but, in recent years has been done by other member-owned entities such as the New York Stock Exchange.

depreciation (1) A tax deduction that compensates a business for the cost of certain tangible assets. (2) A decrease in the value of a particular currency relative to other currencies.

depreciation expense A bookkeeping entry of a noncash expense charged against earnings to recover the cost of an asset over its useful life.

depression A prolonged period of general economic decline.

derivative An investment vehicle, the value of which is based on another security's value. Futures contracts, forward contracts, and options are among the most common types of derivatives. Institutional investors generally use derivatives to increase overall portfolio return or to hedge portfolio risk.

designated market maker (DMM) *See* specialist.

dilution A reduction in earnings per share of common stock. Dilution occurs through the issuance of additional shares of common stock and the conversion of convertible securities. *See* anti-dilutive covenant.

directed brokerage The ability of an investment adviser or a client to determine broker-dealers to be used in the execution of transactions in their advisory accounts. *See* soft-dollar compensation.

direct participation program (DPP) A business organized so as to pass all income, gains, losses, and tax benefits to its owners, the investors; the business is usually structured as a limited partnership. Examples include oil and gas programs, real estate programs, agricultural programs, cattle programs, condominium securities, and S corporation offerings.

discount The difference between the lower price paid for a security and the security's face amount at issue.

discount bond A bond that sells at a lower price than its face value. *See* par.

discount rate The interest rate charged by the 12 Federal Reserve Banks for short-term loans made to member banks.

discretion The authority given to someone other than an account's beneficial owner to make investment decisions for the account concerning the security, the number of shares or units, and whether to buy or sell. The authority to decide only timing or price does not constitute discretion. *See* limited power of attorney.

discretionary account An account in which the customer has given the agent authority to enter transactions at the representative's discretion.

disgorge(ment) In legal usage, the forced giving up of profits made through illegal activity, most commonly insider trading.

disposable income (DI) The sum that people divide between spending and personal savings. *See* personal income.

distributable net income (DNI) Taxable income from a trust that determines the amount of income that may be taxable to beneficiaries.

diversification A risk management technique that mixes a wide variety of investments within a portfolio, thus minimizing the impact of any one security on overall portfolio performance.

diversified common stock fund A mutual fund that invests its assets in a wide range of common stocks. The fund's objectives may be growth, income, or a combination of both. *See* growth fund; mutual fund.

dividend A distribution of a corporation's earnings. Dividends may be in the form of cash, stock, or property. The board of directors must declare all dividends. *Syn.* stock dividend. *See* cash dividend; dividend yield; property dividend.

dividend discount model The simplest model for valuing equity is the dividend discount model—the value of a stock is the present value of expected dividends on it. *Syn,* DDM.

dividend exclusion rule An IRS provision that permits a corporation to exclude from its taxable income 70% of dividends received from domestic preferred and common stocks. The Tax Reform Act of 1986 repealed the dividend exclusion for individual investors.

dividend growth model A valuation method which takes into consideration dividend per share and its expected growth. This model assumes that dividends grow at the same rate forever. Therefore, it is most commonly used to value companies belonging to for mature and stable industries, having steady dividend growth. It will show a higher valuation than the DDM. *Syn.* DGM.

dividend payout ratio A measure of a corporation's policy of paying cash dividends, calculated by dividing the dividends paid on common stock by the net income available for common stockholders. The ratio is the complement of the retained earnings ratio.

dividends per share The dollar amount of cash dividends paid on each common share during one year.

dividend reinvestment plan Frequently referred to as a DRIP, the plan allows shareholders the option of having cash dividends automatically reinvested in shares of the issuer's stock, frequently at a discounted price and/or without commissions. In most plans, additional investments are permitted.

dividend yield The annual rate of return on a common or preferred stock investment. The yield is calculated by dividing the annual dividend by the stock's purchase price. *See* current yield; dividend.

DNI *See* distributable net income.

Dodd-Frank Bill The general term by which the Wall Street Reform and Consumer Protection Act of 2010 is known. Considered to be the most significant legislation impacting the securities industry since the 1930s.

dollar cost averaging A system of buying mutual fund shares in fixed dollar amounts at regular fixed intervals, regardless of the share's price. The investor purchases more shares when prices are low and fewer shares when prices are high, thus lowering the average cost per share over time.

donor A person who makes a gift of money or securities to another. Once the gift is donated, the donor gives up all rights to it. Gifts of securities to minors under the Uniform Gift to Minors Act provide tax advantages to the donor. *See* Uniform Gift to Minors Act.

Dow Jones averages The most widely quoted and oldest measures of change in stock prices. Each of the four averages is based on the prices of a limited number of stocks in a particular category. *See* average; Dow Jones Industrial Average.

Dow Jones Composite Average (DJCA) A market indicator composed of the 65 stocks that make up the Dow Jones Industrial, Transportation, and Utilities Averages. *See* average; Dow Jones Industrial Average; Dow Jones Transportation Average; Dow Jones Utilities Average.

Dow Jones Industrial Average (DJIA) The most widely used market indicator, composed of 30 large, actively traded issues of industrial stocks.

Dow Jones Transportation Average (DJTA) A market indicator composed of 20 transportation stocks. *See* average; Dow Jones Composite Average; Dow Jones Industrial Average; Dow Jones Utilities Average.

Dow Jones Utilities Average (DJUA) A market indicator composed of 15 utilities stocks. *See* average; Dow Jones Composite Average; Dow Jones Industrial Average; Dow Jones Transportation Average.

DRIP *See* dividend reinvestment plan.

durable power of attorney A document giving either full or limited authority to a third party that survives the mental or physical incompetence (but not death) of the grantor. *See* full power of attorney; limited power of attorney.

duration Duration is an approximate measure of a bond's price sensitivity to changes in interest rates. Duration can be used to compare bonds with different issue and maturity dates, coupon rates, and yields to maturity. The duration of a bond is expressed as a number of years from its purchase date.

E

earned income Income derived from active participation in a trade or business, including wages, salary, tips, commissions, and bonuses. Also included is alimony received. One must have earned income in order to make contributions to an IRA. *See* portfolio income; unearned income.

earned surplus *See* retained earnings.

earnings momentum A term used to describe that earnings are growing at an increasing rate. That is, if they grew at a rate of 10% in the first quarter, 11% in the second quarter and 14% in the most recent quarter, this shows earnings increasing at an accelerating rate. That is positive earnings momentum. Used by those following a growth style of portfolio management.

earnings multiplier Another term for the *price-to-earning (PE) ratio*. The earnings multiplier is the price of the stock divided by its earnings per share.

earnings per share (EPS) A corporation's net income available for common stock divided by its number of shares of common stock outstanding.

effective date The date the registration of an issue of securities becomes effective, allowing the underwriters to sell the newly issued securities to the public and confirm sales to investors who have given indications of interest.

effective tax rate The overall rate paid on a taxpayer's total taxable income. It will always be less than the marginal tax rate. *See* marginal tax rate.

efficient market theory A theory based on the premise that the stock market processes information efficiently. The theory postulates that, as new information becomes known, it is reflected immediately in the price of a stock and therefore stock prices represent fair prices. There are three forms of this theory: weak, semi-strong, and strong, depending upon the amount of information available. *Syn.* Efficient market hypothesis.

employee stock options A form of employee compensation where the employing corporation makes available the opportunity for employees to acquire the issuer's stock. There are two forms: nonqualified (NSOs) and incentive (ISOs).

enjoined This term includes being subject to a mandatory injunction, prohibitory injunction, preliminary injunction, or a temporary restraining order issued by a court of competent jurisdiction.

equity Common and preferred stockholders' ownership interests in a corporation. *See* common stock; preferred stock.

equity financing Raising money for working capital or for capital expenditures by selling common or preferred stock to individual or institutional investors. In return for the money paid, the investors receive ownership interests in the corporation. *See* debt financing.

equity security A security representing ownership in a corporation or another enterprise. Examples of equity securities include:
- common and preferred stock;
- interests in a limited partnership or joint venture;
- securities that carry the right to be traded for equity securities, such as convertible bonds, rights, and warrants; and
- put and call options on equity securities.

eurobond A long-term debt instrument of a government or corporation that is denominated in the currency of the issuer's country but is issued and sold in a different country.

Eurodollar U.S. currency held in banks outside the United States.

exchange-listed security A security that has met certain requirements and has been admitted to full trading privileges on a stock exchange. The NYSE and regional exchanges set listing requirements for volume of shares outstanding, corporate earnings, and other characteristics.

exchange privilege A feature offered by a mutual fund allowing an individual to transfer an investment in one fund to another fund under the same sponsor without incurring an additional sales charge. *Syn.* conversion privilege.

exchange traded fund An investment company originally designed to track a specific index that is traded on a stock exchange. Rather than basing the price on NAV, the ETF's market price is constantly changing as does the price of any other listed stock. ETFs may be purchased on margin and sold short. Although most ETFs still track indexes, there are a number of ETFs that are actively managed. *Syn.* ETF.

executor A person given fiduciary authorization to manage the affairs of a decedent's estate. An executor's authority is established by the decedent's last will.

exempt security A security exempt from the registration requirements (although not from the antifraud requirements) of the Securities Act of 1933 or the Uniform Securities Act. Examples include U.S. government securities and municipal securities.

exempt transaction A transaction that does not trigger a state's registration and advertising requirements under the Uniform Securities Act. Examples of exempt transactions include:
- nonissuer transactions in outstanding securities (normal market trading);
- transactions with financial institutions;
- unsolicited transactions; and
- private placement transactions.

No transaction is exempt from the Uniform Securities Act's antifraud provisions.

exercise price The cost per share at which an option or a warrant holder may buy or sell the underlying security. *Syn.* strike price.

expansion A period of increased business activity throughout an economy; one of the four stages of the business cycle. *Syn.* recovery. *See* business cycle.

expansionary policy A monetary policy that increases the money supply, usually with the intention of lowering interest rates and combating deflation.

expense ratio A ratio for comparing a mutual fund's efficiency by dividing the fund's expenses by its net assets.

F

face value *See* par.

Fannie Mae *See* Federal National Mortgage Association.

Farm Credit Administration (FCA) The government agency that coordinates the activities of the banks in the Farm Credit System. *See* Farm Credit System.

Farm Credit System (FCS) An organization of 37 privately owned banks that provide credit services to farmers and mortgages on farm property. Included in the system are the Federal Land Banks, Federal Intermediate Credit Banks, and Banks for Cooperatives. *See* Federal Intermediate Credit Bank.

federal covered adviser As defined by the NSMIA of 1996, either an investment adviser registered with the SEC or excluded from the definition of investment adviser by the Investment Advisers Act of 1940. Under Dodd-Frank, these advisers registering with the SEC must generally meet a threshold of $100 million or more in assets under management.

Federal covered security Under the NSMIA of 1996, a new definition was created: covered security, generally referred to as federal covered security on the exam. State securities registration requirements were preempted with respect to covered securities, other than the ability to require notice filing, particularly in the case of registered investment companies. The most tested federal covered securities include those listed on the major U.S. exchanges and Nasdaq as well as investment companies registered with the SEC and securities offered pursuant to the provisions of Rule 506 of Regulation D under the Securities Act of 1933 (private placements).

Federal Deposit Insurance Corporation (FDIC) The government agency that provides deposit insurance for member banks and prevents bank and thrift failures.

federal funds The reserves of banks and certain other institutions greater than the reserve requirements or excess reserves. These funds are available immediately.

federal funds rate The interest rate charged by one institution lending federal funds to another.

Federal Home Loan Bank (FHLB) A government-regulated organization that operates a credit reserve system for the nation's savings and loan institutions.

Federal Home Loan Mortgage Corporation (FHLMC) A publicly traded corporation that promotes the nationwide secondary market in mortgages by issuing mortgage-backed pass-through debt certificates. *Syn.* Freddie Mac.

Federal Intermediate Credit Bank (FICB) One of 12 banks that provide short-term financing to farmers as part of the Farm Credit System.

Federal National Mortgage Association (FNMA) A publicly held corporation that purchases conventional mortgages and mortgages from government agencies, including the Federal Housing Administration, Department of Veterans Affairs, and Farmers Home Administration. *Syn.* Fannie Mae.

Federal Open Market Committee (FOMC) A committee that makes decisions concerning the Fed's operations to control the money supply.

Federal Reserve Board (FRB) A seven-member group that directs the operations of the Federal Reserve System. The President appoints board members, subject to Congressional approval.

Federal Reserve System The central bank system of the United States. Its primary responsibility is to regulate the flow of money and credit. The system includes 12 regional banks, 24 branch banks, and hundreds of national and state banks. *Syn.* Fed.

fiduciary A person legally appointed and authorized to hold assets in trust for another person and manage those assets for that person's benefit.

filing date The day on which an issuer submits to the SEC the registration statement for a new securities issue.

fill-or-kill order (FOK) An order that instructs the floor broker to fill the entire order immediately; if the entire order cannot be executed immediately, it is canceled.

final prospectus The legal document that states a new issue security's price, delivery date, and underwriting spread, as well as other material information. It must be given to every investor who purchases a new issue of registered securities. *Syn.* prospectus.

final order A term used in both state and federal law to refer to a decision rendered by a regulatory body. The final order may result in a suspension, revocation, or denial of registration. It is analogous to the judge passing sentence in a trial.

Financial Industry Regulatory Authority (FINRA) Organized in July 2007 as a joint effort of NASD and the NYSE to harmonize regulation in the securities industry.

financial risk *See* credit risk.

FINRA The acronym for the Financial Industry Regulatory Authority, the result of the cooperative effort of NASD and the NYSE to harmonize regulation in the securities industry.

firm quote The actual price at which a trading unit of a security (such as 100 shares of stock or five bonds) may be bought or sold. All quotes are firm quotes unless otherwise indicated.

first in, first out (FIFO) An accounting method used to assess a company's inventory, in which it is assumed that the first goods acquired are the first to be sold. The same method is used by the IRS to determine cost basis for tax purposes. *See* average basis; last in, first out.

fiscal policy The federal tax and spending policies set by Congress or the President. These policies affect tax rates, interest rates, and government spending in an effort to control the economy. *See* monetary policy.

fiscal year The term used to describe an accounting year that ends other than December 31st (calendar year accounting). *See* calendar year.

fixed annuity An insurance contract in which the insurance company makes fixed dollar payments to the annuitant for the term of the contract, usually until the annuitant dies. The insurance company guarantees both earnings and principal. *Syn.* fixed dollar annuity; guaranteed dollar annuity.

fixed asset A tangible, physical property used in the course of a corporation's everyday operations, including buildings, equipment, and land.

flat yield curve A chart showing the yields of bonds with short maturities as equal to the yields of bonds with long maturities. *Syn.* even yield curve. *See* inverted yield curve; normal yield curve; yield curve.

flow-through A term that describes the way income, deductions, and credits resulting from the activities of a business are applied to individual taxes and expenses as though each incurred the income and deductions directly. *See* limited partnership.

FNMA *See* Federal National Mortgage Association.

FOK *See* fill-or-kill order.

FOMC *See* Federal Open Market Committee.

foreign currency Money issued by a country other than the one in which the investor resides. Options and futures contracts on numerous foreign currencies are traded on U.S. exchanges.

foreign exchange rate The price of one country's currency in terms of another currency. *Syn.* exchange rate.

Form 706 The IRS form used for the computation of estate tax. It must be filed within nine months of death unless an extension has been obtained.

Form 709 The United States Gift (and Generation-Skipping Transfer) Tax Return is filed on Form 709.

Form 1040 The IRS form used to file individual income tax. Schedule C of the Form 1040 is used to report business income for sole proprietorships.

Form 1041 The IRS form used by estates and trusts to report their income for tax purposes.

Form 1065 The information return filed by a partnership or LLC. Because income and losses flow through to owners, the entity pays no tax.

Form 1120 and 1120S The tax returns filed by corporations. The "S" is for an S corporation.

Form D The SEC form required to be filed when engaging in a Regulation D private placement.

forward contract A forward contract is a direct commitment between one buyer and one seller for a specific commodity. Because forward contracts are direct obligations between a specific buyer and seller (unlike futures and options, they are not standardized), they are not easily transferred and are considered illiquid.

forward pricing The valuation process for mutual fund shares, whereby an order to purchase or redeem shares is executed at the price determined by the portfolio valuation calculated after the order is received. Portfolio valuations occur at least once per business day.

fractional share A portion of a whole share of stock. Mutual fund shares are frequently issued in fractional amounts. Fractional shares used to be generated when corporations declared stock dividends, merged, or voted to split stock, but today it is more common for corporations to issue the cash equivalent of fractional shares.

fraud The deliberate concealment, misrepresentation, or omission of material information or the truth, so as to deceive or manipulate another party for unlawful or unfair gain.

FRB *See* Federal Reserve Board.

Freddie Mac *See* Federal Home Loan Mortgage Corporation.

front-end load A mutual fund commission or sales fee that is charged at the time shares are purchased. The load is added to the share's net asset value when calculating the public offering price.

front running The prohibited practice of entering an order for the benefit of a firm or a securities professional before entering customer orders.

Full Disclosure Act *See* Securities Act of 1933.

full power of attorney A written authorization for someone other than an account's beneficial owner to make deposits and withdrawals and to execute trades in the account. *See* limited power of attorney; durable power of attorney.

full trading authorization An authorization, usually provided by a full power of attorney, for someone other than the customer to have full trading privileges in an account. *See* limited trading authorization.

fundamental analysis A method of evaluating securities by attempting to measure the intrinsic value of a particular stock. Fundamental analysts study the overall economy, industry conditions, and the financial condition and management of particular companies. *See* technical analysis.

futures Futures contracts are exchange-traded obligations for a specific commodity. A buyer goes long, or establishes a long position, and is obligated to take delivery of the commodity on the future date specified. A seller goes short, or establishes a short position, and is obligated to deliver the commodity on the specified future date. If the seller does not own the commodity, his potential loss is unlimited because he has promised delivery and must pay any price to acquire the commodity to deliver. Futures may be highly leveraged.

G

GAAP The acronym for generally accepted accounting principles, the standard method used in the United States by professional accountants.

gamma One of the 4 Greeks used by options analysts. An option's gamma is a measure of the rate of change of its delta. The gamma of an option is expressed as a percentage and reflects the change in the delta in response to a 1 point movement of the underlying stock price.

GDP *See* gross domestic product.

general obligation bond (GO) A municipal debt issue backed by the full faith, credit, and taxing power of the issuer for payment of interest and principal. *Syn.* full faith and credit bond. *See* revenue bond.

general partnership (GP) An association of two or more entities formed to conduct a business jointly. The partnership does not require documents for formation, and the general partners are jointly and severally liable for the partnership's liabilities. *See* limited partnership.

generation skipping trust A form of bypass trust that is designed to have assets pass to grandchildren (or great-grandchildren) in order to "skip" a generation of estate tax.

geometric mean A type of average that indicates the central tendency of a set of numbers that, instead of finding the sum as with the arithmetic mean, takes the product of the numbers and divides that by the nth root (where n is the count of numbers). It will always be lower than the arithmetic mean [unless all of the numbers are the same (e.g., 6, 6, and 6)].

good-til-canceled order (GTC) An order that is left on the specialist's book until it is either executed or canceled. *Syn.* open order.

goodwill An intangible asset that represents the value that a firm's business reputation adds to its perceived value. It is not included in net worth for purposes of computing book value per share.

Government National Mortgage Association (GNMA) A wholly government-owned corporation that issues pass-through mortgage debt certificates backed by the full faith and credit of the U.S. government. *Syn.* Ginnie Mae.

grantor An individual or organization that gives assets to a beneficiary by transferring fiduciary duty to a third-party trustee that will maintain the assets for the benefit of the beneficiaries. *Syn.* settlor, trustor.

grantor trust A trust that requires that the grantor be taxed on income produced by trust property if trust income is distributed to the grantor or to the grantor's spouse; trust income discharges a legal obligation of the grantor or grantor's family; and the grantor retains power to revoke or amend the trust.

gross domestic product (GDP) The market value of all final goods and services produced within a country in a given period of time. GDP = consumption + investment + government spending + (exports – imports) investment. To account for inflation, GDP is based on a constant dollar, currently the value in 2005.

gross income All income of a taxpayer, from whatever source derived.

gross margin Gross margin is the operating profit of a business prior to interest and taxes. It is computed by subtracting the cost of goods sold (COGS) from the company's sales (or revenues). Gross margin is frequently expressed as a percentage, called the margin of profit. The calculation is the gross margin divided by the sales (revenues). For example, a company has sales of $5 million and COGS of $3.5 million resulting in a gross margin of $1.5 million and a margin of profit of 30% ($1.5 million / $5 million).

gross revenues All money received by a business from its operations. The term typically does not include interest income or income from the sale, refinancing, or other disposition of properties.

growth fund A diversified common stock fund that has capital appreciation as its primary goal. It invests in companies that reinvest most of their earnings for expansion, research, or development. *See* diversified common stock fund; mutual fund.

growth industry An industry that is growing faster than the economy as a whole as a result of technological changes, new products, or changing consumer tastes.

growth stock A common stock that is believed to offer significant potential for capital gains. It often pays low dividends and sells at a high price-earnings ratio.

growth style investing A management style that attempts to find stocks with positive earnings momentum. These stocks typically sell at the upper end of their 52-week price range, have high P/E ratios and lower than average dividend payout ratios. *See* value style investing.

guaranteed security Under the Uniform Securities Act, the term guaranteed means guaranteed by a third party as to payment of principal, interest, or dividends, but not capital gains.

guardian A court-appointed fiduciary who manages the assets of a minor or an incompetent for that person's benefit. *See* fiduciary.

H

head and shoulders On a technical analyst's trading chart, a pattern that has three peaks resembling a head and two shoulders. The stock price moves up to its first peak (the left shoulder), drops back, then moves to a higher peak (the top of the head), drops again but recovers to another, lower peak (the right shoulder). A head and shoulders top typically forms after a substantial rise and indicates a market reversal. A head and shoulders bottom (an inverted head and shoulders) indicates a market advance.

hedge An investment made to reduce the risk of adverse price movements in a security. Normally, a hedge consists of a protecting position in a related security. *See* long hedge; selling a hedge; short hedge.

hedge clause Any legend, clause, or other provision that is likely to lead an investor to believe that he has in any way waived any right of action he may have.

hedge fund A fund that can use one or more alternative investment strategies, including hedging against market downturns, investing in asset classes such as currencies or distressed securities, and utilizing return-enhancing tools such as leverage, derivatives, and arbitrage. These funds tend to have very high minimum investment requirements.

high net worth individual An individual with at least $1 million managed by the IA or whose net worth the firm reasonably believes exceeds $2 million. The net worth of an individual may include assets held jointly with that individual's spouse. Performance-based fees may be charged to these clients.

high yield bond A bond with a less than investment grade rating, characterized by a return commensurate with the higher risk. *Syn.* junk bond

holder The owner of a security. *See* long.

holding company A company organized to invest in and manage other corporations. Control can occur through the ownership of 50% or more of the voting rights or through the exercise of a dominant influence. It is sometimes referred to as the parent organization.

holding period A time period signifying how long the owner possesses a security. It starts the day after a purchase and ends on the day of the sale.

home state If an investment adviser is registered with a state Administrator (state registered adviser), the firm's home state is the state where it maintains its principal office and place of business.

HR-10 plan *See* Keogh plan.

hypothecation Pledging to a broker-dealer securities bought on margin as collateral for the margin loan. *See* rehypothecation.

I

immediate annuity An annuity contract that provides for monthly payments to begin immediately after deposit of the invested funds. Payments usually commence within 30 to 60 days. *See* deferred annuity.

immediate-or-cancel order (IRC) An order that instructs the floor broker to execute it immediately, in full or in part. Any portion of the order that remains unexecuted is canceled.

impersonal investment advice Investment advisory services that do not purport to meet the objectives or needs of specific individuals or accounts.

incentive stock option A type of employee stock option. As long as stock purchased through exercise of an ISO is held at least two years after the date of grant and one year after the date of exercise, any profits are reported as long-term capital gains. If these time limits are broached, the ISO is taxed like an NSO. *See* nonqualified stock option.

income fund A mutual fund that *seeks* to provide stable current income by investing in securities that pay interest or dividends. *See* mutual fund.

income statement The summary of a corporation's revenues and expenses for a specific fiscal period.

indenture The agreement between a lender and a borrower that details specific terms of the bond issuance. The indenture specifies the legal obligations of the bond issuer and rights of the bondholders. It is sometimes called the deed of trust.

index *See* security market index.

index fund Investors who wish to invest passively can invest in an index fund, which *seeks* to replicate the performance of a security market index. There are index mutual funds and index exchange-traded funds. *See* security market index.

indication of interest An investor's expression of conditional interest in buying an upcoming securities issue after the investor has reviewed a preliminary prospectus. An indication of interest is not a commitment to buy.

individual retirement account (IRA) A retirement investing tool for employed individuals that allows an annual contribution of 100% of earned income up to a maximum of $5,500 ($6,500 for those 50 and older).

industrial development bond (IDB) A debt security issued by a municipal authority, which uses the proceeds to finance the construction or purchase of facilities to be leased or purchased by a private company. The bonds are backed by the credit of the private company, which is ultimately responsible for principal and interest payments. *Syn.* industrial revenue bond.

industrial revenue bond (IRB) *See* industrial development bond.

industry fund *See* sector fund.

inelasticity A lack of responsiveness on the part of consumers and producers to a change in prices. *See* elasticity.

inflation A persistent and measurable increase in the general level of prices. *See* deflation.

inflation risk *See* purchasing power risk.

initial public offering (IPO) A corporation's first sale of common stock to the public. *See* new issue market; public offering.

information barriers policies and procedures created to prevent misuse of material non-public information (MNPI) are commonly referred to as information barriers. Formerly referred to as Chinese Walls.

inside information Material information that has not been disseminated to or is not readily available to the general public.

inside market When viewing the quotes of all of the market makers in a security, the inside market, or inside quote, is the best (highest) bid and the best (lowest) offer (or ask).

insider Any person who possesses or has access to material nonpublic information about a corporation. Insiders include directors, officers, and stockholders who own more than 10% of any class of equity security of a corporation.

Insider Trading Act *See* Insider Trading and Securities Fraud Enforcement Act of 1988.

Insider Trading and Securities Fraud Enforcement Act of 1988 Legislation that defines what constitutes the illicit use of nonpublic information in making securities trades and the liabilities and penalties that apply. *Syn.* Insider Trading Act. *See* Chinese Wall; insider.

institutional account An account held for the benefit of others. Examples of institutional accounts include banks, trusts, pension and profit-sharing plans, mutual funds, and insurance companies.

institutional investor A person or an organization that trades securities in large enough share quantities or dollar amounts that it qualifies for preferential treatment and lower commissions. An institutional order can be of any size. Institutional investors are covered by fewer protective regulations because it is assumed that they are more knowledgeable and better able to protect themselves.

intangible asset A property owned that is not physical, such as a formula, a copyright, or goodwill. *See* goodwill.

interest The charge for the privilege of borrowing money, usually expressed as an annual percentage rate.

interest rate risk The risk associated with investments relating to the sensitivity of price or value to fluctuation in the current level of interest rates; also, the risk that involves the competitive cost of money. This term is generally associated with bond prices, but it applies to all investments. In bonds, prices carry interest risk because if bond prices rise, outstanding bonds will not remain competitive unless their yields and prices adjust to reflect the current market.

Internal Revenue Code (IRC) The legislation that defines tax liabilities and deductions for U.S. taxpayers.

Internal Revenue Service (IRS) The U.S. government agency responsible for collecting most federal taxes and for administering tax rules and regulations.

interstate offering An issue of securities registered with the SEC sold to residents of states other than the state in which the issuer does business.

intestate Dying without a legal will. Usually the probate court will appoint an administrator to handle the deceased's estate. For purposes of the Uniform Securities Act, transactions by this administrator (a fiduciary) are considered exempt transactions.

in-the-money The term used to describe an option that has intrinsic value, such as a call option when the stock is selling above the exercise price or a put option when the stock is selling below the exercise price. *See* at-the-money; intrinsic value; out-of-the-money.

intrastate offering An issue of securities exempt from SEC registration, available to companies that do business in one state and sell their securities only to residents of that same state. *See* Rule 147.

intrinsic value The potential profit to be made from exercising an option. A call option is said to have intrinsic value when the underlying stock is trading above the exercise price. *See* time value.

inverted yield curve A chart showing long-term debt instruments that have lower yields than short-term debt instruments. *Syn.* negative yield curve. *See* flat yield curve; normal yield curve.

investment adviser (1) Any person who makes investment recommendations in return for a flat fee or a percentage of assets managed. (2) For an investment company, the individual who bears the day-to-day responsibility of investing the cash and securities held in the fund's portfolio in accordance with objectives stated in the fund's prospectus.

investment adviser representative (IAR) Any partner, officer, director, or other individual employed by or associated with an investment adviser whose job function involves the rendering of advice, solicitation for clients, or supervision of those who do.

Investment Advisers Act of 1940 Legislation governing who must register with the SEC as an investment adviser. *See* investment adviser.

investment banker An institution in the business of raising capital for corporations and municipalities. An investment banker may not accept deposits or make commercial loans. *Syn.* investment bank.

investment banking business A broker, dealer, or municipal or government securities dealer that underwrites or distributes new issues of securities as a dealer or that buys and sells securities for the accounts of others as a broker. *Syn.* investment securities business.

investment company A company engaged in the business of pooling investors' money and trading in securities for them. Examples include face-amount certificate companies, unit investment trusts, and management companies.

Investment Company Act Amendments of 1970 Amendments to the Investment Company Act of 1940 requiring, in particular, that sales charges relate to the services a fund provides its shareholders. *See* Investment Company Act of 1940.

Investment Company Act of 1940 Congressional legislation regulating companies that invest and reinvest in securities. The act requires an investment company engaged in interstate commerce to register with the SEC.

investment constraints Limitations or restrictions that are specific to the adviser's client. Investment constraints include, among others, liquidity needs, time horizon, and personal ethical choices (no tobacco or alcohol stocks).

investment-grade security A security to which the rating services (e.g., Standard & Poor's and Moody's) have assigned a rating of BBB/Baa or above.

investment objective Any goal a client hopes to achieve through investing. Examples include current income, capital growth, and preservation of capital.

investment policy statement Used by those administering employee benefit plans to set out the objectives, policies, investment selections, and monitoring procedures for the plan. May also be used by investment advisers to determine policies to be followed with their clients.

investor The purchaser of an asset or security with the intent of profiting from the transaction.

IPO *See* initial public offering.

IRA rollover The reinvestment of assets that an individual receives as a distribution from a qualified tax-deferred retirement plan into an individual retirement account within 60 days of receiving the distribution. The individual may reinvest either the entire sum or a portion of the sum, although any portion not reinvested is taxed as ordinary income. *See also* individual retirement account; IRA transfer.

IRA transfer The direct reinvestment of retirement assets from one qualified tax-deferred retirement plan to an individual retirement account. The account owner never takes possession of the assets but directs that they be transferred directly from the existing plan custodian to the new plan custodian. *See also* individual retirement account; IRA rollover.

irrevocable trust A trust that cannot be altered or canceled by the grantor at any time.

issuer The entity, such as a corporation or municipality, that offers or proposes to offer its securities for sale.

J

joint account An account in which two or more individuals possess some form of control over the account and may transact business in the account. The account must be designated as either joint tenants in common or joint tenants with right of survivorship. *See* tenants in common; joint tenants with right of survivorship.

joint life with last survivor An annuity payout option that covers two or more people, with annuity payments continuing as long as one of the annuitants remains alive.

joint tenants with right of survivorship (JTWROS) A form of joint ownership of an account whereby a deceased tenant's fractional interest in the account passes to the surviving tenant(s). Used almost exclusively by husbands and wives. *See* tenants in common.

junk bond *See* high yield bond.

K

Keogh plan A qualified tax-deferred retirement plan for persons who are self-employed and unincorporated or who earn extra income through personal services aside from their regular employment. *Syn.* HR-10 plan. *See* individual retirement account.

Keynesian economics The theory that active government intervention in the marketplace is the best method of ensuring economic growth and stability.

L

lagging indicator A measurable economic factor that changes after the economy has started to follow a particular pattern or trend. Lagging indicators are believed to confirm long-term trends. Examples include average duration of unemployment, corporate profits, and labor cost per unit of output. *See* coincident indicator; leading indicator.

last in, first out (LIFO) An accounting method used to assess a corporation's inventory in which it is assumed that the last goods acquired are the first to be sold. The method is used to determine cost basis for tax purposes; the IRS designates last in, first out as the order in which sales or withdrawals from an investment are made. It is the system used for random withdrawals from a non-qualified annuity where the earnings are taxed first before receiving back a return of original principal. *See* average basis; first in, first out.

leading indicator A measurable economic factor that changes before the economy starts to follow a particular pattern or trend. Leading indicators are believed to predict changes in the economy. Examples include new orders for durable goods, slowdowns in deliveries by vendors, and numbers of building permits issued. *See* coincident indicator; lagging indicator.

legal list The selection of securities a state agency (usually a state banking or insurance commission) determines to be appropriate investments for fiduciary accounts such as mutual savings banks, pension funds, and insurance companies. This is used in states that do not have the prudent investor rule.

legislative risk The potential for an investor to be adversely affected by changes in investment or tax laws.

letter of intent (LOI) A signed agreement allowing an investor to buy mutual fund shares at a lower overall sales charge based on the total dollar amount of the intended investment. A letter of intent is valid only if the investor completes the terms of the agreement within 13 months of signing the agreement. A letter of intent may be backdated 90 days. *Syn.* statement of intention.

level load A mutual fund sales fee charged annually and based on the net asset value of a share. *See* back-end load; Class C share; front-end load.

leverage Using borrowed capital to increase investment return. *Syn.* trading on the equity.

liability A legal obligation to pay a debt owed. Current liabilities are debts payable within 12 months. Long-term liabilities are debts payable over a period of more than 12 months.

LIBOR LIBOR is a benchmark interest rate based on the rates at which banks lend unsecured funds to each other on the London interbank market. Published daily, the rate was previously administered by the British Bankers' Association (BBA). But in the aftermath of a scandal in 2012, Britain's primary financial regulator, the Financial Conduct Authority (FCA), shifted supervision of LIBOR to a new entity, the ICE Benchmark Administration, an independent subsidiary of the private exchange operator Intercontinental Exchange, or ICE.

limited liability An investor's right to limit potential losses to no more than the amount invested. Equity shareholders, such as corporate stockholders and limited partners, have limited liability.

limited liability company (LLC) A hybrid between a partnership and a corporation in that it combines the pass-through treatment of a partnership with the limited liability accorded to corporate shareholders.

limited partnership (LP) An association of two or more partners formed to conduct a business jointly and in which one or more of the partners is liable only to the extent of the amount of money they have invested. Limited partners do not receive dividends but enjoy direct flow-through of income and expenses. *See* flow-through; general partnership.

limited power of attorney A written authorization for someone other than an account's beneficial owner to make certain investment decisions regarding transactions in the account. *See* discretion; full power of attorney; durable power of attorney.

limited trading authorization An authorization, usually provided by a limited power of attorney, for someone other than the customer to have trading privileges in an account. These privileges are limited to purchases and sales; withdrawal of assets is not authorized. *See* full trading authorization.

limit order An order that instructs the broker-dealer to buy a specified security below a certain price or to sell a specified security above a certain price. These orders are entered either for the day or good-til-canceled (GTC). *See* stop limit order; stop order.

liquidation priority In the case of a corporation's liquidation, the order that is strictly followed for paying off creditors and stockholders: 1, unpaid wages; 2, taxes; 3, secured claims like mortgage bonds, equipment trust certificates, and collateral trust bonds; 4, unsecured liabilities (debentures) and general creditors; 5, subordinated debt; 6, preferred stockholders; and 7, common stockholders.

liquidity The ease with which an asset can be converted to cash in the marketplace. A large number of buyers and sellers and a high volume of trading activity provide high liquidity.

liquidity risk The potential that an investor might not be able to sell an investment when desired without adverse price disruption. *Syn.* marketability risk.

listed option An option contract that can be bought and sold on a national securities exchange in a continuous secondary market. Listed options carry standardized strike prices and expiration dates. *Syn.* standardized option.

listed security A stock, a bond, or another security that satisfies certain minimum requirements and is traded on a regional or national securities exchange such as the New York Stock Exchange. *See* over the counter.

living trust A trust created during the lifetime of the grantor; also known as an inter vivos trust.

LLC *See* limited liability company.

long The term used to describe the owning of a security, contract, or commodity. For example, a common stock owner is said to have a long position in the stock. *See* short.

longevity annuity A deferred income annuity that generally does not begin payout until the age of 85. If a QLAC (qualified longevity annuity contract), exempt from RMDs for up to 15 years in a qualified retirement plans.

long-term gain The profit earned on the sale of a capital asset that has been owned for more than 12 months. *See* capital gain; capital loss; long-term loss.

long-term loss The loss realized on the sale of a capital asset that has been owned for more than 12 months. *See* capital gain; capital loss; long-term gain.

loss carryover A capital loss incurred in one tax year that is carried over to the next year or later years for use as a capital loss deduction. *See* capital loss.

M

make a market To stand ready to buy or sell a particular security as a dealer for its own account. A market maker accepts the risk of holding the position in the security. *See* market maker.

Maloney Act An amendment enacted in 1938 to broaden Section 15 of the Securities Exchange Act of 1934. Named for its sponsor, the late Sen. Francis Maloney of Connecticut, the amendment provided for the creation of a self-regulatory organization for the specific purpose of supervising the over-the-counter securities market. *See* National Association of Securities Dealers, Inc.

management company An investment company that trades various types of securities in a portfolio in accordance with specific objectives stated in the prospectus. *See* closed-end management company; diversified management company; mutual fund; nondiversified management company.

margin The amount of equity contributed by a customer as a percentage of the current market value of the securities held in a margin account. *See* equity; initial margin requirement; Regulation T.

marginal tax rate The rate of taxation on any additional taxable income received. It is sometimes referred to as the tax on the "next" dollar or the "last" dollar of income. *See* effective tax rate.

margin of profit ratio A measure of a corporation's relative profitability. It is calculated by dividing the operating profit by the net sales. *Syn.* operating profit ratio; profit margin.

marital trust A trust that seeks to pass property to a survivor spouse while taking advantage of the marital deduction; also known as an A trust.

market capitalization The number of outstanding shares multiplied by the current market price. Classed as large-cap, mid-cap, small-cap and micro-cap.

market maker A dealer willing to accept the risk of holding a particular security in its own account to facilitate trading in that security. *See* make a market.

market order An order to be executed immediately at the best available price. A market order is the only order that guarantees execution. *Syn.* unrestricted order.

market risk The potential for an investor to experience losses owing to day-to-day fluctuations in the prices at which securities can be bought or sold. *See* systematic risk.

market value The price at which investors buy or sell a share of common stock or a bond at a given time. Market value is determined by buyers' and sellers' interaction. *See* current market value.

markup The difference between the lowest current offering price among dealers and the higher price a dealer charges a customer.

matched orders Simultaneously entering identical (or nearly identical) buy and sell orders for a security to create the appearance of active trading in that security. This violates the antifraud provisions of the Securities Exchange Act of 1934 and the USA.

material information Any fact that could affect an investor's decision to trade a security.

maturity date The date on which a bond's principal is repaid to the investor and interest payments cease. *See* par; principal.

mean When referring to a series of values, such as portfolio returns, the average. A measure of central tendency known as the arithmetic mean. Could also refer to the geometric mean.

median When viewing a series of values, such as portfolio returns, the number that has as many occurrences above as below. A measure of central tendency.

mode When viewing a series of values, the one that occurs the most frequently. A measure of central tendency.

modern portfolio theory (MPT) A method of choosing investments that focuses on the importance of the relationships among all of the investments in a portfolio rather than the individual merits of each investment. The method allows investors to quantify and control the amount of risk they accept and return they achieve.

monetarist theory An economic theory holding that the money supply is the major determinant of price levels and that therefore a well-controlled money supply will have the most beneficial impact on the economy.

monetary policy The Federal Reserve Board's actions that determine the size and rate of the money supply's growth, which in turn affect interest rates. *See* fiscal policy.

money market The securities market that deals in high quality, short-term debt. Money market instruments are very liquid forms of debt that mature in one year or less. Treasury bills, commercial paper, and jumbo CDs are examples of money market instruments.

money market fund A mutual fund that invests in short-term debt instruments. The fund's objective is to earn interest while maintaining a stable net asset value of $1 per share. Always sold with no load, the fund may also offer check-writing privileges and a low initial minimum investment. *See* mutual fund.

Monte Carlo simulation A statistical method to determine the return profile of a security or portfolio that recreates potential outcomes by generating random values on the basis of the risk and return characteristics of the securities themselves.

Moody's Investors Service One of the best known investment rating agencies in the United States. A subsidiary of Dun & Bradstreet, Moody's rates bonds, commercial paper, preferred and common stocks, and municipal short-term issues. *See* bond rating; Standard & Poor's Corporation.

mortgage bond A debt obligation secured by a property pledge. It represents a lien or mortgage against the issuing corporation's properties and real estate assets.

moving average chart A tool used by technical analysts to track the price movements of a commodity. It plots average daily settlement prices over a defined period of time (for example, over three days for a three-day moving average).

municipal bond A debt security issued by a state, a municipality, or another subdivision (such as a school, a park, a sanitation, or another local taxing district) to finance its capital expenditures. Such expenditures might include the construction of highways, public works, or school buildings. *Syn.* municipal security.

municipal bond fund A mutual fund that invests in municipal bonds and operates either as a unit investment trust or as an open-end fund. The fund's objective is to maximize federally tax-exempt income. *See* mutual fund; unit investment trust.

municipal note A short-term municipal security issued in anticipation of funds from another source.

Municipal Securities Rulemaking Board (MSRB) A self-regulatory organization that regulates the issuance and trading of municipal securities. The Board functions under the Securities and Exchange Commission's supervision; it has no enforcement powers. *See* Securities Amendments Act of 1975.

mutual fund An investment company that continuously offers new equity shares in an actively managed portfolio of securities. All shareholders participate in the fund's gains or losses. The shares are redeemable on any business day at the net asset value. Each mutual fund's portfolio is invested to match the objective stated in the prospectus. *Syn.* open-end investment company; open-end management company. *See* balanced fund; contractual plan; net asset value.

N

NASAA *See* North American Securities Administrators Association.

NASD *See* National Association of Securities Dealers, Inc.

Nasdaq *See* National Association of Securities Dealers Automated Quotation System.

NASD 5% markup policy A guideline for reasonable markups, markdowns, and commissions for secondary over-the-counter transactions. According to the policy, all commissions on broker transactions and all markups or markdowns on principal transactions should equal 5% or should be fair and reasonable for a particular transaction. *Syn.* markup policy.

National Association of Securities Dealers, Inc. (NASD) The self-regulatory organization for the over-the-counter market. NASD was organized under the provisions of the 1938 Maloney Act. *See* Maloney Act, FINRA.

National Association of Securities Dealers Automated Quotation System (Nasdaq) The nationwide electronic quotation system for up-to-the-second on approximately 3,500 over-the-counter stocks trade information. Sometimes referred to as the Nasdaq Stock Market. All securities traded here are federal covered as defined in the NSMIA of 1996.

NAV per share The value of a mutual fund share, calculated by dividing the fund's total net asset value by the number of shares outstanding.

negotiability A characteristic of a security that permits the owner to assign, give, transfer, or sell it to another person without a third party's permission.

negotiable certificate of deposit (CD) An unsecured promissory note issued with a minimum face value of $100,000. It evidences a time deposit of funds with the issuing bank and is guaranteed by the bank.

net asset value (NAV) A mutual fund share's value, as calculated once a day on the basis of the closing market price for each security in the fund's portfolio. It is computed by deducting the fund's liabilities from the portfolio's total assets and dividing this amount by the number of shares outstanding. *See* mutual fund.

net investment income The source of an investment company's dividend payments. It is calculated by subtracting the company's operating expenses from the total dividends and interest the company receives from the securities in its portfolio.

net worth The amount by which assets exceed liabilities.

new account form The form that must be filled out for each new account opened with a brokerage firm. The form specifies, at a minimum, the account owner, trading authorization, payment method, and types of securities appropriate for the customer.

new issue market The securities market for shares in privately owned businesses that are raising capital by selling common stock to the public for the first time. *Syn.* primary market. *See* initial public offering; secondary market.

no-load fund A mutual fund whose shares are sold without a commission or sales charge. The investment company distributes the shares directly. *See* mutual fund; net asset value; sales load.

nominal yield The interest rate stated on the face of a bond that represents the percentage of interest the issuer pays on the bond's face value. *Syn.* coupon rate; stated yield. *See* bond yield.

nominee A person or company whose name is given as having title to a stock, real estate, and so forth, but who is not the actual owner. *See* street name.

nonaccredited investor An investor not meeting the net worth requirements of Regulation D. Nonaccredited investors are counted for purposes of the 35-investor limitation for Rule 506(b) Regulation D private placements. *See* accredited investor; private placement; Regulation D.

noncontributory plan A retirement plan to which only the employer makes contributions. *See* contributory plan.

noncumulative preferred stock An equity security that does not have to pay any dividends in arrears to the holder. *See* cumulative preferred stock; preferred stock.

nondiversification A portfolio management strategy that *seeks* to concentrate investments in a particular industry or geographic area in hopes of achieving higher returns. *See* diversification.

nonqualified retirement plan A corporate retirement plan that does not meet the standards set by the Employee Retirement Income Security Act of 1974. Contributions to a nonqualified plan are not tax deductible. *See also* qualified retirement plan.

nonqualified stock option A type of employee stock option. When NSOs are exercised, the difference between the current market price at the time of exercise and the strike price is reported as wages on the tax returns of the employer and the employee. *See* incentive stock option.

nonrecourse financing Debt incurred for the purchase of an asset that pledges the asset as security for the debt but that does not hold the borrower personally liable.

nonsystematic risk The potential for an unforeseen event to affect the value of a specific investment. Examples of such events include strikes, natural disasters, poor management decisions, introductions of new product lines, and attempted takeovers. This risk is diversifiable. *Syn.* unsystematic risk. *See* systematic risk.

no-par stock An equity security issued without a stated value.

normal yield curve A chart showing long-term debt instruments having higher yields than short-term debt instruments. *Syn.* positive yield curve. *See* flat yield curve; inverted yield curve; yield curve.

North American Securities Administrators Association Organized in 1919, the North American Securities Administrators Association (NASAA) is the oldest international organization devoted to investor protection. NASAA is a voluntary association whose membership consists of 67 state, provincial, and territorial securities administrators in the 50 states, the District of Columbia, Puerto Rico, the U.S. Virgin Islands, Canada, and Mexico.

note A short-term debt security, usually maturing in five years or less. *See* Treasury note.

notice filing (1) Method by which a registered investment company and certain other federal covered securities file records with state securities Administrators. (2) SEC-registered advisers (federal covered) may have to provide state securities authorities (the Administrator) with copies of documents that are filed with the SEC and pay a filing fee.

O

offer (1) Under the Uniform Securities Act, any attempt to solicit a purchase or sale in a security for value. (2) An indication by an investor, a trader, or a dealer of a willingness to sell a security; the price at which an investor can buy from a broker-dealer. *See* bid.

open-end investment company *See* mutual fund.

opening purchase Entering the options market by buying calls or puts. *See* opening sale.

opening sale Entering the options market by selling calls or puts. *See* closing purchase; opening purchase.

open-market operations The buying and selling of securities (primarily government or agency debt) by the Federal Open Market Committee to effect control of the money supply. These transactions increase or decrease the level of bank reserves available for lending.

operating income The profit realized from one year of operation of a business.

operating ratio The ratio of operating expenses to net sales; the complement to the margin of profit ratio.

optimal portfolio The optimal portfolio under modern portfolio theory assumes that investors *seek* a portfolio of assets that minimizes risks while offering the highest possible return.

ordinary income Earnings other than capital gain.

OTC Bulletin Board (OTCBB) An electronic quotation system for equity securities that are not listed on a national exchange or included in the Nasdaq system. These are not federal covered securities and generally require registration with both the SEC and the states.

OTC Link An electronic inter-dealer quotation system that displays quotes from broker-dealers for many over-the-counter securities. Formerly known as the Pink Sheets, OTC Link does not require companies whose securities are quoted on its systems to meet any listing requirements.

OTC market The security trading system in which broker-dealers negotiate directly with one another rather than through an auction on an exchange floor. The trading takes place over computer and telephone networks that link brokers and dealers around the world. Both listed and OTC securities, as well as municipal and U.S. government securities, trade in the OTC market.

out-of-the-money The term used to describe an option that has no intrinsic value, such as a call option when the stock is selling below the exercise price or a put option when the stock is above the exercise price.

over the counter (OTC) The term used to describe a security traded through the telephone-linked and computer-connected OTC market rather than through a stock exchange. *See* OTC market.

oversubscribed The term used to describe a new security issue where the demand for the shares greatly exceeds the available supply. The issues usually appreciate rapidly on the first day of trading and failure to properly allocate them is a prohibited practice.

P

par The dollar amount the issuer assigns to a security. For an equity security, par is usually a small dollar amount that bears no relationship to the security's market price. For a debt security, par is the amount repaid to the investor when the bond matures, usually $1,000. *Syn.* face value; principal; stated value. *See* capital surplus; maturity date.

parity price of common The dollar amount at which a common stock is equal in value to its corresponding convertible security. It is calculated by dividing the convertible security's market value by its conversion ratio.

parity price of convertible The dollar amount at which a convertible security is equal in value to its corresponding common stock. It is calculated by multiplying the market price of the common stock by its conversion ratio.

participation The provision of the Employee Retirement Income Security Act of 1974 requiring that all employees in a qualified retirement plan be covered within a reasonable time of their dates of hire.

partnership A form of business organization in which two or more individuals manage the business and are equally and personally liable for its debts.

partnership account An account that empowers the individual members of a partnership to act on the behalf of the partnership as a whole.

partnership management fee The amount payable to the general partners of a limited partnership, or to other persons, for managing the day-to-day partnership operations. *Syn.* program management fee; property management fee.

par value The dollar amount assigned to a security by the issuer. For an equity security, par value is usually a small dollar amount that bears no relationship to the security's market price. For a debt security, par value is the amount repaid to the investor when the bond matures, usually $1,000. *Syn.* face value; principal; stated value. *See* capital surplus; discount bond; premium bond.

passive income Earnings derived from a rental property, limited partnership, or other enterprise in which the individual is not actively involved. Passive income therefore does not include earnings from wages or active business participation, nor does it include income from dividends, interest, and capital gains. *See* passive loss; unearned income.

passive loss A loss incurred through a rental property, limited partnership, or other enterprise in which the individual is not actively involved. Passive losses can be used to offset passive income only, not wage or portfolio income. *See* passive income.

passive management style In a perfectly efficient market, investors should use a passive investment strategy (i.e., buying a broad market index of stocks and holding it) because active investment strategies will underperform due to transactions costs and management fees. However, to the extent that market prices are inefficient, active investment strategies can generate positive risk-adjusted returns. *See* active management style.

pass-through certificate A security representing an interest in a pool of conventional, Veterans Administration, Farmers Home Administration, or other agency mortgages. The pool receives the principal and interest payments, which it passes through to each certificate holder. Payments may or may not be guaranteed. *See* Federal National Mortgage Association; Government National Mortgage Association.

pattern A repetitive series of price movements on a chart used by a technical analyst to predict future movements of the market.

payment date The day on which a declared dividend is paid to all stockholders owning shares on the record date.

PE *See* price-earnings ratio.

peak The end of a period of increasing business activity throughout the economy, one of the four stages of the business cycle. *Syn.* prosperity. *See* business cycle.

pecuniary Of or relating to money, such as operating for pecuniary profit.

pegging An illegal form of market manipulation that attempts to keep the price of a subject security from falling. It is used by those with a long position. *See* capping.

pension plan A contract between an individual and an employer, a labor union, a government entity, or another institution that provides for the distribution of pension benefits at retirement.

Pension Reform Act *See* Employee Retirement Income Security Act of 1974.

PE ratio *See* price-earnings ratio.

performance-based fee An investment advisory fee based on a share of capital gains on, or capital appreciation of, client assets. A fee that is based upon a percentage of assets that the IA manages is not a performance-based fee. This fee may only be charged to certain high net worth clients.

person As defined in securities law, an individual, corporation, partnership, association, fund, joint stock company, unincorporated organization, trust, government, or political subdivision of a government.

personal income (PI) An individual's total earnings derived from wages, passive business enterprises, and investments. *See* disposable income.

Pink Sheets *See* OTC Link.

point A measure of a bond's price; $10 or 1% of the par value of $1,000. *See* basis point.

political risk The risk that an investment's returns could suffer as a result of political changes or instability in a country such as from a change in government, orderly or not, nationalization of industries, or military control.

portfolio income Earnings from interest, dividends, and all nonbusiness investments. *See* earned income; passive income; unearned income.

portfolio manager The entity responsible for investing a mutual fund's assets, implementing its investment strategy, and managing day-to-day portfolio trading. *Syn.* fund manager.

position The amount of a security either owned (a long position) or owed (a short position) by an individual or a dealer. Dealers take long positions in specific securities to maintain inventories and thereby facilitate trading.

preferred stock An equity security that represents ownership in a corporation. It is issued with a stated dividend, which must be paid before dividends are paid to common stockholders. It generally carries no voting rights. *See* callable preferred stock; cumulative preferred stock.

preferred stock fund A mutual fund whose investment objective is to provide stable income with minimal capital risk. It invests in income-producing instruments such as preferred stock. *See* bond fund.

preliminary prospectus An abbreviated prospectus that is distributed while the SEC is reviewing an issuer's registration statement. It contains all of the essential facts about the forthcoming offering except the underwriting spread, final public offering price, and date on which the shares will be delivered. *Syn.* red herring.

premium (1) The amount of cash that an option buyer pays to an option seller. (2) The difference between the higher price paid for a security and the security's face amount at issue. *See* discount.

premium bond A bond that sells at a higher price than its face value. *See* discount bond; par value.

price-earnings ratio (PE) A tool for comparing the prices of different common stocks by assessing how much the market is willing to pay for a share of each corporation's earnings. It is calculated by dividing the current market price of a stock by the earnings per share. *Syn.* earnings multiplier.

primary offering An offering in which the proceeds of the underwriting go to the issuing corporation, agency, or municipality. The issuer *seeks* to increase its capitalization either by selling shares of stock, representing ownership, or by selling bonds, representing loans to the issuer. *Syn.* primary distribution.

prime rate The interest rate that commercial banks charge their prime or most creditworthy customers, generally large corporations.

principal (1) Every business transaction has two principals—the buyer and the seller. When a broker-dealer trades for its own account, it is acting in the capacity of a principal. (2) *See* dealer. (3) *See* par.

principal office and place of business The firm's executive office from which the firm's officers, partners, or managers direct, control, and coordinate the activities of the firm.

principal transaction A transaction in which a broker-dealer either buys securities from customers and takes them into its own inventory or sells securities to customers from its inventory. *See* agency transaction; agent; broker; dealer; principal.

private placement An offering of new issue securities that complies with Regulation D of the Securities Act of 1933. According to Regulation D, a security generally is not required to be registered with the SEC if it is offered to no more than 35 nonaccredited investors or to an unlimited number of accredited investors. *See* Regulation D.

profitability The ability to generate a level of income and gain in excess of expenses.

profitability ratio One of several measures of a corporation's relative profit or income in relation to its sales. *See* margin of profit ratio; return on equity.

profit-sharing plan An employee benefit plan established and maintained by an employer whereby the employees receive a share of the business's profits. The money may be paid directly to the employees or deferred until retirement. A combination of both approaches is also possible.

progressive tax A tax that takes a larger percentage of the income of high-income earners than that of low-income earners. An example is the graduated income tax. *See* regressive tax.

proscribed A term commonly used in legal situations to describe a prohibited action.

proxy A limited power of attorney from a stockholder authorizing another person to vote on stockholder issues according to the first stockholder's instructions. To vote on corporate matters, a stockholder must either attend the annual meeting or vote by proxy.

prudent expert rule A modern application of the prudent man rule to those with a fiduciary responsibility over qualified plans coming under the jurisdiction of ERISA.

prudent investor rule Legally known as the Uniform Prudent Investors Act of 1994 (UPIA). A modern adaptation of the prudent man rule, which, as a result of the development of modern portfolio theory, applies the standard of prudence to the entire portfolio rather than to individual investments. It requires the fiduciary to measure risk with respect to return.

publicly traded fund *See* closed-end investment company.

public offering The sale of an issue of common stock, either by a corporation going public or by an offering of additional shares. *See* initial public offering.

public offering price (POP) (1) The price of new shares that is established in the issuing corporation's prospectus. (2) The price to investors for mutual fund shares, equal to the net asset value plus the sales charge. *See* ask; bid; mutual fund; net asset value.

purchasing power risk The potential that, because of inflation, a certain amount of money will not purchase as much in the future as it does today. *Syn.* inflation risk.

put (1) An option contract giving the owner the right to sell a certain amount of an underlying security at a specified price within a specified time. (2) The act of exercising a put option. *See* call.

Q

QLAC A qualified longevity annuity contract. If certain limits prescribed by the IRS are met, RMDs do not have to include the value of these contracts until age 85.

QTIP trust A trust that is funded with qualified terminable interest property, meaning that the spouse's interest in the property terminates upon his death; also known as a Q trust, C trust, or current income trust.

QTP *See* qualified tuition program.

Q trust *See* QTIP trust.

Qualified Domestic Relations Orders (QDROs) Premature distributions that are taken pursuant to a qualified domestic relations order, or QDRO, are exempt from the 10% penalty. A QDRO is a court-issued order that gives someone the right to an individual's qualified plan assets, typically an ex- (or soon-to-be-ex-) spouse, and the QDRO is usually issued in the course of divorce proceedings or to satisfy child support obligations. A QDRO applies only to assets in a qualified employer plan; it would not be applicable to an IRA or a SEP.

qualified person Under both state and federal law, a client for whom an investment adviser may charge performance-based fees. Currently, the requirements are a minimum net worth of $2 million or at least $1 million in AUM with that adviser.

qualified retirement plan A corporate retirement plan that meets the standards set by the Employee Retirement Income Security Act of 1974. Contributions to a qualified plan are tax deductible. *Syn.* approved plan. *See also* individual retirement account; Keogh plan; nonqualified retirement plan.

qualified tuition program The technical name for Section 529 Plans. *Syn.* QTP.

quick asset ratio A more stringent test of liquidity than the current ratio. It is computed by taking the current assets, less the inventory, and dividing by the current liabilities. *Syn.* acid test ratio.

quick ratio *Syn.* acid test ratio, quick ratio.

quotation The price or bid a market maker or broker-dealer offers for a particular security. *Syn.* quote. *See* ask; bid; bond quote; stock quote.

quote machine A computer that provides representatives and market makers with the information that appears on the Consolidated Tape. The information on the screen is condensed into symbols and numbers.

R

rating An evaluation of a corporate or municipal bond's relative safety, according to the issuer's ability to repay principal and make interest payments. Bonds are rated by various organizations, such as Standard & Poor's and Moody's. Ratings range from AAA or Aaa (the highest) to C or D, which represents a company in default.

rating service A company, such as Moody's or Standard & Poor's, that rates various debt and preferred stock issues for safety of payment of principal, interest, or dividends. The issuing company or municipality pays a fee for the rating. *See* bond rating; rating.

real estate investment trust (REIT) A corporation or trust that uses the pooled capital of many investors to invest in direct ownership of either income property or mortgage loans. These investments offer tax benefits in addition to interest and capital gains distributions. However, unlike DPPs, these are not "flow-through" vehicles.

realized gain The amount a taxpayer earns when he sells an asset. *See* unrealized gain.

recession A general economic decline lasting from six to 18 months (at least two consecutive quarters of declining or negative DGP growth).

redeemable security A security that the issuer redeems upon the holder's request. Examples include shares in an open-end investment company and Treasury notes.

redemption The return of an investor's principal in a security, such as a bond, preferred stock, or mutual fund shares. By law, redemption of mutual fund shares must occur within seven days of receiving the investor's request for redemption.

refunding Retiring an outstanding bond issue before maturity by using money from the sale of a new debt offering.

regional exchange A stock exchange that serves the financial community in a particular region of the country. These exchanges tend to focus on securities issued within their regions, but also offer trading in NYSE and Nasdaq-listed securities.

registration by coordination A process that allows a security to be sold in a state. It is available to an issuer that files for the security's registration under the Securities Act of 1933 and files duplicates of the registration documents with the state Administrator. The state registration becomes effective at the same time the federal registration statement becomes effective as long as paperwork is on file with the Administrator for the required period, which ranges from 10 to 20 days depending on the state.

registration by qualification A process that allows a security to be sold in a state. It is available to an issuer who files for the security's registration with the state Administrator, meets minimum net worth, disclosure, and other requirements, and files appropriate registration fees. The state registration becomes effective when the Administrator so orders.

registration statement The legal document that discloses all pertinent information concerning an offering of a security and its issuer. It is submitted to the SEC (and/or the Administrator) in accordance with the requirements of the Securities Act of 1933 and/or the Uniform Securities Act, and it forms the basis of the final prospectus distributed to investors.

regressive tax A tax that takes a larger percentage of the income of low-income earners than that of high-income earners. Examples include gasoline tax and cigarette tax. *See* progressive tax.

regulated investment company An investment company to which Subchapter M of the Internal Revenue Code grants special status that allows the flow-through of tax consequences on a distribution to shareholders. If 90% of its income is passed through to the shareholders, the company is not subject to tax on this income.

Regulation D The provision of the Securities Act of 1933 that exempts from registration offerings sold in private placements. Rule 506(b) limits the sale to a maximum of 35 nonaccredited investors during a 12-month period with no advertising permitted, while Rule 506(c) permits advertising but requires that all purchasers be accredited investors. *See* private placement.

Regulation T The Federal Reserve Board regulation that governs customer cash accounts and the amount of credit that brokerage firms and dealers may extend to customers for the purchase of securities. Regulation T currently sets the loan value of marginable securities at 50% and the payment deadline at two days beyond regular way settlement. *Syn.* Reg. T.

regulatory risk The risk that changes in regulations may negatively affect the operations of a company.

reinstatement privilege A benefit offered by some mutual funds, allowing an investor to withdraw money from a fund account and then redeposit the money without paying a second sales charge.

remainderman A remainderman is the person who inherits or is entitled under the law to inherit property upon termination of the estate of the former owner. Usually, this occurs due to the death or termination of the former owner's life estate.

remuneration Money paid for work performed or a service provided.

repurchase agreement Sometimes just referred to as a REPO, this is widely used in the money market where the seller of a security agrees to buy it back (repurchase it) at a higher price (the imputed interest rate).

required minimum distribution (RMD) The amount that traditional and SEP IRA owners and qualified plan participants must begin withdrawing from their retirement accounts by April 1 following the year they reach age 70½. Exceptions apply to those covered under a qualified plan who are still employed. RMD amounts must then be distributed by December 31 that year and each subsequent year.

reserve requirement The percentage of depositors' money that the Federal Reserve Board requires a commercial bank to keep on deposit in the form of cash or in its vault. *Syn.* reserves.

residual claim The right of a common stockholder to corporate assets in the event that the corporation ceases to exist. A common stockholder may claim assets only after the claims of all creditors and other security holders have been satisfied.

resistance level A technical analysis term describing the top of a stock's historical trading range. *See* support level.

restricted security An unregistered, nonexempt security acquired either directly or indirectly from the issuer, or an affiliate of the issuer, in a transaction that does not involve a public offering. *See* holding period; Rule 144.

retained earnings The amount of a corporation's net income that remains after all dividends have been paid to preferred and common stockholders. *Syn.* earned surplus; reinvested earnings.

retiring bonds Ending an issuer's debt obligation by calling the outstanding bonds, by purchasing bonds in the open market, or by repaying bondholders the principal amount at maturity.

return on common equity A measure of a corporation's profitability, calculated by dividing after-tax income by common shareholders' equity.

return on equity A measure of a corporation's profitability, specifically its return on assets, calculated by dividing after-tax income by tangible assets.

return on investment (ROI) The profit or loss resulting from a security transaction, often expressed as an annual percentage rate.

revenue bond A municipal debt issue whose interest and principal are payable only from the specific earnings of an income-producing public project.

reverse churning The prohibited practice of parking assets that will only be traded infrequently in a fee-based advisory account.

reverse split A reduction in the number of a corporation's shares outstanding that increases the par value of its stock or its earnings per share. The market value of the total number of shares remains the same. *See* stock split.

revocable trust A trust that can be altered or canceled by the grantor. During the life of the trust, income earned is distributed to the grantor, and only after death does property transfer to the beneficiaries.

right A security representing a stockholder's entitlement to the first opportunity to purchase new shares issued by the corporation at a predetermined price (normally less than the current market price) in proportion to the number of shares already owned. Rights are issued for a short time only, after which they expire. *Syn.* subscription right; subscription right certificate.

right of accumulation A benefit offered by a mutual fund that allows the investor to qualify or reduced sales loads on additional purchases according to the fund account's total dollar value.

risk-adjusted return Return from a security adjusted for the market risk associated with it. Usually measured by the Sharpe Ratio.

risk-free rate Generally refers to the interest rate of 90-day U.S. Treasury bills.

risk premium The amount in excess of the risk-free rate demanded by investors to compensate for the additional risks inherent in the specific security being described.

risk tolerance Risk tolerance is an investor's ability and willingness to lose some or all of the original investment in exchange for greater potential returns. An aggressive investor, or one with a high risk tolerance, is more likely to risk losing money in order to get better results. A conservative investor, or one with a low-risk tolerance, tends to favor investments that will preserve the original investment.

RMD *See* required minimum distribution.

Roth 401(k) As with a Roth IRA, contributions are not tax deductible, but qualified withdrawals are free from income tax. There are no earnings limits in order to participate, but it is required that distributions begin no later than age 70½.

Roth IRA Funded with after-tax contributions, but, if qualified, withdrawals are tax-free. There are earnings limits but no required distributions at age 70½.

Rule 144 SEC rule requiring that persons who hold control or restricted securities may sell them only in limited quantities, and that all sales of restricted stock by control persons must be reported to the SEC by filing a Form 144, Notice of Proposed Sale of Securities. *See* control security; restricted security.

Rule 147 SEC rule that provides exemption from the registration statement and prospectus requirements of the 1933 Act for securities offered and sold exclusively intrastate.

S

safe harbor A provision in a regulatory scheme that provides protection against legal action if stated procedures are followed. In this exam, it may apply in three different cases: (1) Section 28(e) of the Securities Exchange Act of 1934 describes those research and brokerage activities that may be received by an investment adviser in exchange for directed brokerage transactions; (2) Section 404c of ERISA describes what a fiduciary of a qualified plan must do to minimize personal responsibility; and (3) top-heavy 401(k) concerns are minimized if the employer covers all employees with immediate vesting. *See* soft-dollar compensation; top heavy.

sales load The amount added to a mutual fund share's net asset value to arrive at the offering price. *See* mutual fund; net asset value; no-load fund.

Savings Incentive Match Plan for Employees A form of employer sponsored IRA for businesses that have 100 or fewer employees who earned $5,000 or more during the preceding calendar year. In addition, the employer cannot currently have another retirement plan.

S corporation A small business corporation that meets certain requirements and is taxed as a partnership while retaining limited liability. *Syn.* Subchapter S corporation.

Schedule K-1 The form supplied by a partnership, LLC, or S corporation to owners indicating their proportionate share of income/loss to be reported on their Form 1040 tax returns.

secondary distribution A distribution, with a prospectus, that involves securities owned by major stockholders (typically founders or principal owners of a corporation). The sale proceeds go to the sellers of the stock, not to the issuer.

secondary market The market in which securities are bought and sold subsequent to their being sold to the public for the first time. *See* new issue market.

secondary offering A sale of securities in which one or more major stockholders in a company sell all or a large portion of their holdings; the underwriting proceeds are paid to the stockholders rather than to the corporation. Typically, such an offering occurs when the founder of a business (and perhaps some of the original financial backers) determine that there is more to be gained by going public than by staying private. The offering does not increase the number of shares of stock outstanding. *See* secondary distribution.

Section 457 Plan A deferred compensation plan set up under Section 457 of the tax code that may be used by employees of a state, political subdivision of a state, and any agency or instrumentality of a state. This plan may also be offered to employees of certain tax-exempt organizations (hospitals, charitable organizations, unions, and so forth), but NOT churches. Even independent contractors may be covered under these plans.

Section 28(e) A code section of the Securities Exchange Act of 1934 hat deals with soft-dollar compensation. *See* soft-dollar compensation; state harbor.

sector fund A mutual fund whose investment objective is to capitalize on the return potential provided by investing primarily in a particular industry or sector of the economy. *Syn.* industry fund; specialized fund.

sector rotation An active portfolio management technique that attempts to take advantage of the fact that different sectors of the economy rise and fall in the business cycle at different times. Rotating from one to the other at the right times can lead to investment success. *Syn.* Sector rotating. *See* active management style.

secured bond A debt security backed by identifiable assets set aside as collateral. In the event that the issuer defaults on payment, the bondholders may lay claim to the collateral. *See* debenture.

Securities Act of 1933 Federal legislation requiring the full and fair disclosure of all material information about the issuance of new securities. *Syn.* Act of 1933; Full Disclosure Act; New Issues Act; Prospectus Act; Trust in Securities Act; Truth in Securities Act.

Securities Amendments Act of 1975 Federal legislation that established the Municipal Securities Rulemaking Board.

Securities and Exchange Commission (SEC) Commission created by Congress to regulate the securities markets and protect investors. It is composed of five commissioners appointed by the President of the United States with the advice and consent of the Senate. The SEC enforces, among other acts, the Securities Act of 1933, the Securities Exchange Act of 1934, the Trust Indenture Act of 1939, the Investment Company Act of 1940, and the Investment Advisers Act of 1940.

Securities Exchange Act of 1934 Federal legislation that established the Securities and Exchange Commission. The act aims to protect investors by regulating the exchanges, the OTC market, the extension of credit by the Federal Reserve Board, broker-dealers, insider transactions, trading activities, client accounts, and net capital. *Syn.* Act of 1934; Exchange Act.

Securities Investor Protection Corporation (SIPC) A nonprofit membership corporation created by an act of Congress to protect clients of brokerage firms that are forced into bankruptcy. Membership is composed of all brokers and dealers registered under the Securities Exchange Act of 1934, all members of national securities exchanges, and most FINRA members. SIPC provides brokerage firm customers up to $500,000 coverage for cash and securities held by the firms (although cash coverage is limited to $250,000).

security Other than an insurance policy or a fixed annuity, any piece of securitized paper that can be traded for value. Under the Act of 1934, this includes any note, stock, bond, investment contract, debenture, certificate of interest in a profit-sharing or partnership agreement, certificate of deposit, collateral trust certificate, preorganization certificate, option on a security, or other instrument of investment commonly known as a security.

security market index A security market index is used to represent the performance of an asset class, security market, or segment of a market. They are usually created as portfolios of individual securities, which are referred to as the constituent securities of the index. An index has a numerical value that is calculated from the market prices (actual when available, or estimated) of its constituent securities at a point in time. An index return is the percentage change in the index's value over a period of time. Popular examples are the S&P 500 and the Russell 2000.

self-regulatory organization (SRO) One of eight organizations accountable to the SEC for the enforcement of federal securities laws and the supervision of securities practices within an assigned field of jurisdiction. For example, the National Association of Securities Dealers regulates the over-the-counter market; the Municipal Securities Rulemaking Board supervises state and municipal securities; and certain stock exchanges, such as the New York Stock Exchange and the Chicago Board Options Exchange, act as self-regulatory bodies to promote ethical conduct and standard trading practices.

sell To convey ownership of a security or another asset for money or value. This includes giving or delivering a security with or as a bonus for a purchase of securities, a gift of assessable stock, and selling or offering a warrant or right to purchase or subscribe to another security. Not included in the definition is a bona fide pledge or loan or a stock dividend if nothing of value is given by the stockholders for the dividend. *Syn.* sale.

selling away An associated person engaging in private securities transactions without the employing broker-dealer's knowledge and consent. This violates the NASAA Policy on prohibited practices.

selling dividends Inducing customers to buy mutual fund shares by implying that an upcoming distribution will benefit them. This practice is illegal.

sell stop order An order to sell a security that is entered at a price below the current market price and that is triggered when the market price touches or goes through the sell stop price.

senior security A security that grants its holder a prior claim to the issuer's assets over the claims of another security's holders. For example, a bond is a senior security over common stock.

separate account The account that holds funds paid by variable annuity contract holders. The funds are kept separate from the insurer's general account and are invested in a portfolio of securities that match the contract holders' objectives. *See* accumulation unit; annuity.

settlor An individual or organization that gifts assets to a beneficiary by transferring fiduciary duty to a third-party trustee that will maintain the assets for the benefit of the beneficiaries. *Syn.* grantor, trustor.

Sharpe ratio The Sharpe ratio measures the risk adjusted return of an investment. It is calculated by dividing the excess return of an asset over the 90-day Treasury bill rate by its standard deviation. It measures the reward per unit of risk so the higher the ratio, the better.

short The term used to describe the selling of a security, contract, or commodity that the seller does not own. For example, an investor who borrows shares of stock from a broker-dealer and sells them on the open market is said to have a short position in the stock. *See* long.

short sale The sale of a security that the seller does not own, or any sale consummated by the delivery of a security borrowed by or for the account of the seller.

short-term capital gain The profit realized on the sale of an asset that has been owned for 12 months or less. *See* capital gain; capital loss; short-term capital loss.

short-term capital loss The loss incurred on the sale of a capital asset that has been owned for 12 months or less. *See* capital gain; capital loss; short-term capital gain.

S.I.M.P.L.E. Plan *See* Savings Incentive Match Plan for Employees.

simple trust A trust that accumulates income and distributes it to its beneficiaries on an annual basis.

soft-dollar compensation Noncash compensation received by an investment adviser from a broker-dealer, generally in exchange for directed brokerage transactions. Must always be disclosed and should come under the safe harbor provisions of Section 28(e). *See* safe harbor.

solicitor A person either contracted or employed by an investment adviser for the purpose of bringing in advisory business. If an employee, registration as an IAR is required. If contracted, the person must not be statutorily disqualified from registration and is subject to the terms of a written agreement between the IA and the solicitor.

solvency The ability of a corporation both to meet its long-term fixed expenses and to have adequate money for long-term expansion and growth.

specialist Stock exchange member who stands ready to quote and trade certain securities either for his own account or for customer accounts. The specialist's role is to maintain a fair and orderly market in the stocks for which he is responsible. *Syn.* designated market maker, DMM.

special situation fund A mutual fund whose objective is to capitalize on the profit potential of corporations in nonrecurring circumstances, such as those undergoing reorganizations or being considered as takeover candidates.

speculation Trading a security with a higher than average risk in return for a higher than average profit potential. The trade is effected solely for the purpose of profiting from it and not as a means of hedging or protecting other positions.

spousal IRA A separate individual retirement account established for a spouse with little or no earned income. Contributions to the account made by the working spouse grow tax deferred until withdrawal.

spread In a quotation, the difference between a security's bid and ask prices.

Standard & Poor's Composite Index of 500 Stocks (S&P 500) A value-weighted index that offers broad coverage of the securities market. It is composed of 400 industrial stocks, 40 financial stocks, 40 public utility stocks, and 20 transportation stocks. The index is owned and compiled by Standard & Poor's Corporation. *See* index; Standard & Poor's Corporation; Standard & Poor's 100 Stock Index.

Standard & Poor's Corporation (S&P) A company that rates stocks and corporate and municipal bonds according to risk profiles and that produces and tracks the S&P indexes. The company also publishes a variety of financial and investment reports. *See* bond rating; Moody's Investors Service; rating; Standard & Poor's 100 Stock Index; Standard & Poor's Composite Index of 500 Stocks.

standard deviation A measurement of a security's or a portfolio's total risk. The greater the standard deviation, the more the security's returns deviate from its average return, hence indicating greater volatility. *See* total risk.

standardized contract A futures contract in which all the contract terms are set by the exchange except for price.

stock certificate Printed evidence of ownership in a corporation.

stock exchange Any organization, association, or group of persons that maintains or provides a marketplace in which securities can be bought and sold. Examples include the New York Stock Exchange (NYSE), the London Stock Exchange (LSE), and the Tokyo Stock Exchange (TSE).

stock split An increase in the number of a corporation's outstanding shares, which decreases its stock's par value. The market value of the total number of shares remains the same. The proportional reductions in orders held on the books for a split stock are calculated by dividing the stock's market price by the fraction that represents the split.

stop limit order A customer order that becomes a limit order when the market price of the security reaches or passes a specific price. *See* limit order; stop order.

stop order (1) A directive from the SEC or the Administrator that suspends the sale of new issue securities to the public when fraud is suspected or filing materials are deficient. (2) A customer order that becomes a market order when the market price of the security reaches or passes a specific price. *See* limit order; market order; stop limit order.

street name Term used in the industry to refer to customer securities held in the name of the broker-dealer as nominee.

subordinated debenture A debt obligation, backed by the general credit of the issuing corporation, that has claims to interest and principal subordinated to ordinary debentures and all other liabilities. *See* debenture.

suitability A determination made by an agent as to whether a particular security matches a customer's objectives and financial capability. The agent must have enough information about the customer to make this judgment.

supply The total amount of a good or service available for purchase by consumers. *See* demand.

supply-side theory An economic theory holding that bolstering an economy's ability to supply more goods is the most effective way to stimulate economic growth. Supply-side theorists advocate income tax reduction insofar as this increases private investment in corporations, facilities, and equipment.

support level A technical analysis term describing the bottom of a stock's historical trading range. *See* resistance level.

systematic risk The potential for a security to decrease in value owing to its inherent tendency to move together with all securities of the same type. Neither diversification nor any other investment strategy can eliminate this risk. Systematic risks are sometimes referred to as external risk factors because they take place outside of the company being analized *See* market risk, systematic risk.

T

taxable gain The portion of a sale or distribution of mutual fund shares subject to taxation.

tax credit An amount that can be subtracted from a tax liability, often in connection with real estate development, energy conservation, and research and development programs. Every dollar of tax credit reduces the amount of tax due, dollar for dollar. *See* deduction.

tax-equivalent yield The rate of return a taxable bond must earn before taxes in order to equal the tax-exempt earnings on a municipal bond. This number varies with the investor's tax bracket.

tax-exempt bond fund A mutual fund whose investment objective is to provide maximum tax-free income. It invests primarily in municipal bonds and short-term debt. *Syn.* tax-free bond fund.

tax liability The amount of tax payable on earnings, usually calculated by subtracting standard and itemized deductions and personal exemptions from adjusted gross income, then multiplying by the tax rate. *See* adjusted gross income.

tax preference item An element of income that receives favorable tax treatment. The item must be added to taxable income when computing alternative minimum tax. Tax preference items include accelerated depreciation on property, research and development costs, intangible drilling costs, tax-exempt interest on municipal private purpose bonds, and certain incentive stock options. *See* alternative minimum tax.

tax-sheltered annuity (TSA) An annuity contract that entitles the holder to exclude all contributions from gross income in the year they are made. Taxes payable on the earnings are deferred until the holder withdraws funds at retirement. TSAs are available primarily through a 403(b) plan to employees of public schools, church organizations, and other tax-exempt organizations. *Syn.* tax-deferred annuity.

technical analysis A method of evaluating securities by analyzing statistics generated by market activity, such as past prices and volume. Technical analysts do not attempt to measure a security's intrinsic value. *See* chartist; fundamental analysis.

Telephone Consumer Protection Act of 1991 (TCPA) Federal legislation restricting the use of telephone lines for solicitation purposes. A company soliciting sales via telephone, facsimile, or email must disclose its name and address to the called party and must not call any person who has requested not to be called.

tenants in common (TIC) A form of joint ownership of an account whereby a deceased tenant's fractional interest in the account is retained by his estate. *Syn.* tenants in common. *See* joint tenants with right of survivorship.

tergiversation The practice of continually changing one's mind, attitude, or opinion.

testamentary trust A trust created as a result of instructions from a deceased's last will and testament.

testimonial An endorsement of an investment or service by a celebrity or public opinion influencer. The use of testimonials by investment advisers is prohibited.

theta One of the 4 Greeks used by options analysts. An option's theta is a measurement of the option's time decay. The theta measures the rate at which options lose their value, specifically the time value, as the expiration date draws nearer. Generally expressed as a negative number, the theta of an option reflects the amount by which the option's value will decrease every day.

time horizon Time horizon is the expected number of months, years, or decades over which the investments will be made to achieve a particular financial goal. An investor with a longer time horizon may feel more comfortable taking on a riskier, or more volatile, investment because that investor can wait out slow economic cycles and the inevitable ups and downs of our markets. By contrast, an investor saving up for a teenager's college education would likely take on less risk because of the shorter time horizon.

time value The amount an investor pays for an option above its intrinsic value; it reflects the amount of time left until expiration. The amount is calculated by subtracting the intrinsic value from the premium paid. *See* intrinsic value.

tombstone advertisement A printed advertisement that is used to generate interest in a securities offering. The text is limited to basic information about the offering, such as the name of the issuer, type of security, names of the underwriters, and where a prospectus is available. A tombstone ad is not considered to be an offering of the subject security.

top heavy The term used to describe a 401(k) plan that offers a disproportionate benefit to **key** employees. Top-heavy testing must be done on an annual basis unless the plan qualifies as a safe harbor 401(k). *See* safe harbor.

total capitalization The sum of a corporation's long-term debt, stock accounts, and capital in excess of par.

total risk (As measured by standard deviation) can be broken down into its component parts: unsystematic risk and systematic risk. That is, total risk = systematic risk + unsystematic risk.

toxic debt Debt whose quality has dropped and is now indicating a high likelihood of default. This can be toxic for the investor's portfolio.

trading authorization *See* full trading authorization; limited trading authorization.

transfer agent A person or corporation responsible for recording the names and holdings of registered security owners, *seeing* that certificates are signed by the appropriate corporate officers, affixing the corporate seal, and delivering securities to the new owners.

Treasury bill A marketable U.S. government debt security with a maturity of less than one year. Treasury bills are issued through a competitive bidding process at a discount from par; they have no fixed interest rate. *Syn.* T-bill.

Treasury bond A marketable, fixed-interest U.S. government debt security with a maturity of more than 10 years. *Syn.* T-bond.

Treasury note A marketable, fixed-interest U.S. government debt security with a maturity of between 2 and 10 years. *Syn.* T-note.

trendline A tool used by technical analysts to trace a security's movement by connecting the reaction lows in an upward trend or the rally highs in a downward trend.

trough The end of a period of declining business activity throughout the economy, one of the four stages of the business cycle. *See* business cycle.

trustee A person legally appointed to act on a beneficiary's behalf.

trustor An individual or organization that gifts assets to a beneficiary by transferring fiduciary duty to a third-party trustee that will maintain the assets for the benefit of the beneficiaries. *Syn.* settlor, grantor.

12b-1 asset-based fees Investment Company Act of 1940 provision that allows a mutual fund to collect a fee for the promotion or sale of or another activity connected with the distribution of its shares. This fee will not exceed .75%.

U

underlying securities The securities that are bought or sold when an option, right, or warrant is exercised.

underwriter An investment banker that works with an issuer to help bring a security to the market and sell it to the public.

underwriting The procedure by which investment bankers channel investment capital from investors to corporations and municipalities that are issuing securities.

unearned income Income derived from investments and other sources not related to employment services. Examples of unearned income include interest from a savings account, bond interest, and dividends from stock. *See* earned income; passive income; portfolio income.

Uniform Gift to Minors Act (UGMA) Legislation that permits a gift of money or securities to be given to a minor and held in a custodial account that an adult manages for the minor's benefit. Income and capital gains transferred to a minor's name are usually taxed at the minor's rate. However, if the child is under a specified age and has unearned income above a certain level, those earnings are taxed at the parent's rate. *See* Uniform Transfers to Minors Act.

Uniform Securities Act (USA) Model legislation for securities industry regulation at the state level. Each state may adopt the legislation in its entirety or it may adapt it (within limits) to suit its needs.

Uniform Transfers to Minors Act (UTMA) Legislation adopted in most states that permits a gift of money or securities to be given to a minor and held in a custodial account that an adult manages for the minor's benefit until the minor reaches a certain age (not necessarily the age of majority). Income and capital gains transferred to a minor's name are usually taxed at the minor's rate. However, just as with UGMA, if the child is under a specified age and has unearned income above a certain level, those earnings are taxed at the parent's rate. *See* Uniform Gift to Minors Act.

unit A share in the ownership of a direct participation program that entitles the investor to an interest in the program's net income, net loss, and distributions.

unit investment trust (UIT) An investment company that sells redeemable shares in a professionally selected portfolio of securities. It is organized under a trust indenture, not a corporate charter.

unit of beneficial interest A redeemable share in a unit investment trust, representing ownership of an undivided interest in the underlying portfolio. *Syn.* share of beneficial interest. *See* unit investment trust.

unrealized gain The amount by which a security appreciates in value before it is sold. Until it is sold, the investor does not actually possess the sale proceeds. *See* realized gain.

unsystematic risk The potential for an unforeseen event to affect the value of a specific investment. Examples of such events include strikes, natural disasters, poor management decisions, introductions of new product lines, and attempted takeovers. This risk is diversifiable. Unsystematic risks are sometimes referred to as internal risk factors because they deal with risk arising from the events taking place within the company *Syn.* nonsystematic risk. *See* systematic risk.

U.S. government and agency bond fund A mutual fund whose investment objective is to provide current income while preserving safety of capital through investing in securities backed by the U.S. Treasury or issued by a government agency.

V

value style investing A management style that looks for stocks currently selling at distressed prices that have solid underlying fundamentals. These stocks typically sell at the lower end of their 52-week price range and have low P/E ratios and higher than average dividend payout ratios. *See* growth style investing.

vega One of the 4 Greeks used by options analysts. An option's vega is a measure of the impact of changes in the underlying volatility on the option price. Specifically, the vega of an option expresses the change in the price of the option for every 1% change in underlying volatility.

vesting (1) An ERISA guideline stipulating that employees must be entitled to their entire retirement benefits within a certain period of time even if no longer employed. (2) The amount of time that an employee must work before retirement or before benefit plan contributions made by the employer become the employee's property without penalty. The IRS and the Employee Retirement Income Security Act of 1974 set minimum requirements for vesting in a qualified plan.

volatility The magnitude and frequency of changes in the price of a security or commodity within a given period.

volume of trading theory A technical analysis theory holding that the ratio of the number of shares traded to total outstanding shares indicates whether a market is strong or weak.

W

warrant A security that gives the holder the right to purchase securities from the warrant issuer at a stipulated subscription price. Warrants are usually long-term instruments, with expiration dates years in the future.

wash sale Selling a security at a loss for tax purposes and, within 30 days before or after, purchasing the same or a substantially identical security. The IRS disallows the claimed loss. wash trade A wash trade occurs when a customer enters a purchase order and a sale order for the same security at the same time. It is done to create a false appearance of activity in a security. This is a prohibited practice.

Wells notice A Wells notice indicates that the regulator intends to bring an enforcement action against an individual or a business. If the notice is against a publicly traded company, it usually has the effect of depressing the current market price.

Wilshire 5000 The Wilshire 5000 Total Market Index represents the broadest index for the U.S. equity market, measuring the performance of all U.S. equity securities with readily available price data. As of the date of printing, it includes some 3,700 issues.

withdrawal plan A benefit offered by a mutual fund whereby a customer receives the proceeds of periodic systematic liquidation of shares in the account. The amounts received may be based on a fixed dollar amount, a fixed number of shares, a fixed percentage, or a fixed period.

working capital A measure of a corporation's liquidity—that is, its ability to transfer assets into cash to meet current short-term obligations. It is calculated by subtracting total current liabilities from total current assets.

wrap fee program Any advisory program under which a specified fee or fees not based directly upon transactions in a client's account is charged for investment advisory services (which may include portfolio management or advice concerning the selection of other investment advisers) and the execution of client transactions. The exclusion from the definition of investment adviser available under both state and federal law to broker-dealers is not in effect for those offering wrap fee programs.

Y

yield The rate of return on an investment, usually expressed as an annual percentage rate. *See* current yield; dividend yield; nominal yield.

yield curve A graphic representation of the actual or projected yields of fixed-income securities in relation to their maturities. In most cases, the securities of a single issuer are plotted over varying maturities. *See* flat yield curve; inverted yield curve.

yield to call (YTC) The rate of return on a bond that accounts for the difference between the bond's acquisition cost and its proceeds, including interest income, calculated to the earliest date that the bond may be called by the issuing corporation. *See* bond yield.

yield to maturity (YTM) The rate of return on a bond that accounts for the difference between the bond's acquisition cost and its maturity proceeds, including interest income. *See* bond yield.

Z

zero-coupon bond A debt security usually issued at a deep discount from face value. The bond pays no interest; rather, it may be surrendered at maturity for its full face value. The duration of a zero-coupon bond is equal to its maturity.

Index